My Blue Heaven

HISTORICAL STUDIES OF URBAN AMERICA

My Blue Heaven

Life and Politics in the Working-Class Suburbs
of Los Angeles, 1920–1965

BECKY M. NICOLAIDES

The University of Chicago Press
Chicago and London

BECKY M. NICOLAIDES is associate professor of history and urban studies and planning at the University of California, San Diego.

The University of Chicago Press, Chicago 60637
The University of Chicago Press, Ltd., London
© 2002 by The University of Chicago
All rights reserved. Published 2002
Printed in the United States of America

11 10 09 08 07 06 05 04 03 02   1 2 3 4 5

ISBN: 0-226-58300-7 (cloth)
ISBN: 0-226-58301-5 (paper)

Library of Congress Cataloging-in-Publication Data

Nicolaides, Becky M.
  My blue heaven : life and politics in the working-class suburbs of Los Angeles, 1920–1965 / Becky M. Nicolaides.
      p. cm. — (Historical studies of urban America)
  Includes bibliographical references and index.
    ISBN 0-226-58300-7 (cloth : alk. paper) — ISBN 0-226-58301-5 (pbk. : alk. paper)
  1. Working class—California—South Gate.   2. South Gate
(Calif.)—Social conditions.   3.   South Gate (Calif.)—Economic conditions.   4.   South Gate (Calif.)—Politics and government.   I. Title.
II. Series.
  HD8083.C2 N53 2002
  307.76'09794'93—dc21

                                                                                    2001004911

For my mother and David

My Blue Heaven

Day is ending,
Birds are wending
Back to the shelter of
Each little nest they love.
Night shades falling,
Love birds calling,
What makes the world go 'round?
Nothing but love!

When whippoorwills call and ev'ning is nigh
I hurry to my blue heaven.
A turn to the right, a little white light
Will lead you to my blue heaven.
You'll see a smiling face, a fireplace, a cozy room,
A little nest that's nestled where the roses bloom.
Just Mollie and me
And baby makes three.
We're happy in my blue heaven.

Words by George Whiting
Music by Walter Donaldson

Contents

Illustrations

Following page 332

Robbert Flick, "South Gate Weave" (photo essay)

Tables

Acknowledgments

During the years it took to complete this project, I have been humbled by the generosity of numerous people and institutions. Their encouragement, insights, interest, and financial support made this book possible. While I'd love to thank each and every one of them in my favorite way—with a platter of homemade baklava—the sheer number of people to thank would keep me baking for years. Instead, I offer my heartfelt appreciation on these pages.

Several institutions supported this project with financial assistance, and I am grateful for the time and resources this bought me. At the dissertation stage, this project was supported by the Columbia University Center for the Social Sciences, the Phi Alpha Theta History Honor Society, the Hellenic University Club of New York, the Walter P. Reuther Library, and the Columbia University Graduate School of Arts and Sciences. While revising the dissertation into a book, I received generous assistance from Arizona State University, Arizona State University West, the Getty Research Institute, the U.C. San Diego Department of History, and the Hellman Family's Fellowship Program.

Top-notch librarians from South Gate to Detroit helped me in numerous ways, guiding me to invaluable sources and sometimes bending rules to accommodate my needs. Special thanks to Victor Zazueta and Eileen Tokar at Weaver Library in South Gate, Glen Creason at the Los Angeles Public Library, Dace Taube of USC's Regional History Center, Jeff Rankin at UCLA's Special Collections, Robert Marshall at CSUN's Urban Archives Center, Alan Jutze at the Huntington Library, Nancy Zimmelman of the California State Archives, Elliot Kanter of U.C. San Diego's Social Sciences and Humanities Library, and Denis Isbel of Arizona State University West. Thanks as well to the staffs of the Walter P. Reuther Library at Wayne State University and the Seaver Center of the L.A. County Museum of Natural History.

At South Gate City Hall, I received generous help from Nina Banuelos of the City Clerk's office and Elizabeth Lefson of the Planning Department. Thanks to Sharon Ramos of the First Baptist Church of South Gate and the staff of the South Gate Community Presbyterian Church for allowing me access to church records. Special thanks to Larry Winans for eleventh-hour assistance. I also extend appreciation to Donaldson Publishing Co. and George Whiting Publishing for granting permission to reprint the lyrics to "My Blue Heaven."

This book has been enriched by the able research assistance of Gina Anzivino, Stacy Berger, Linda Brunk, Pak Couch, Cecily Feltham, Richard Lester, Elizabeth Lopez, Matt McNeill, Lisa Orr, Heather Parker, and Laura Schiesl. David Deis composed the excellent maps. And thanks to Vicki O'Riordan and Christine Stuart for their assistance with several figures.

Because this book began as a doctoral dissertation, I owe a special debt to my mentors at Columbia University who guided this study in its genesis. My adviser, Ken Jackson, was a generous critic, editor, and coach from the get-go. His consistent encouragement and support—during graduate school and beyond—are deeply appreciated. Betsy Blackmar, mentor extraordinaire, offered priceless intellectual guidance and the warmest friendship. I am grateful for her generosity of mind and spirit. The other members of my doctoral committee, Alan Brinkley, Herbert Gans, and Marc Weiss, offered excellent advice and feedback as I embarked on the revision process. At this early stage, I also benefited immensely from the scholarship and generosity of geographer Richard Harris. At a crucial juncture in my work, his studies of working-class suburbs reassured me that South Gate was no quirky anomaly.

I am especially grateful to the Getty Research Institute for offering me the opportunity to participate as a postdoctoral fellow in the "Perspectives on Los Angeles" scholars year. This near-utopian experience provided a setting that was unimaginably comfortable, free of interruptions, mind-opening, and intensely collegial. My understanding of Los Angeles was deepened by the work of my fellow scholars. For their intellectual and personal support, I especially thank Brenda Bright, Dana Cuff, Robert Dawidoff, Bill Deverell, Phil Ethington, Doug Flamming, Roger Friedland, Tom Hines, David James, Susan Phillips (hoedown buddy), Michael Roth, Sabine Schlosser, and Harold Zellman. I extend special thanks to Robbert Flick, a true artist whose creative approach to visualizing Los Angeles photographically opened my eyes to new ways of looking at historical evidence. Our "drive by" photographic shoot of South Gate resulted in the color plate that closes this book. I thank Robbert for so generously allowing me to reproduce his work. And Harold Zellman, I do owe you a plate of baklava for suggesting the book's title.

A number of friends and colleagues read all or parts of the manuscript; others generously shared their own work with me. While I fell far short of incorporating their many excellent suggestions and addressing their criticisms, I hope they will realize what rich contributions they have made to this book. I especially thank Eric Avila, Amy Bridges, Clark Davis, Mike Davis, Susan Davis, Shank Gilkeson, Jim Gregory, Greg Hise, Cat Nilan, Paula Petrik, Matt Roth, Robert Self, Josh Sides, Denise Spooner, and Andrew Wiese. Several students—perhaps the most important readers of all—offered invaluable perspective on the manuscript: Marghi Merzenich, Andy Strathman, and the members of my "History of Los Angeles" colloquium at UCSD in spring 1999. I extend a special thanks to the Los Angeles History Research Group at the Huntington Library, whose members read parts of the manuscript; I'm particularly grateful to Allison Baker, Michael Engh, Lisa Orr, and Mike Willard. Thanks to my history colleagues at U.C. San Diego for their encouragement of this project, especially Michael Bernstein, David Gutierrez, Rachel Klein, Stephanie Smallwood, and Danny Vickers.

I owe a particular debt to the people who shared their life stories with me through oral histories. Their patience at my endless questions, their honesty, and their cooperation breathed real life into this story. I especially thank Virgil Collins, Edward Greenspan, Pamela James, Ruth Lampmann, Ray Markle, Mary North, Grace Sheehy, Floyd Wakefield, and Dorothea Weaver. Three of the most important persons I interviewed—Juanita Hammon, Glenn Seaborg, and John Sheehy—passed away during the preparation of this manuscript. Their contributions were immense.

My editors at the University of Chicago Press enriched this book enormously, through their perceptive criticism and enthusiasm. I particularly thank Jim Grossman, Tim Gilfoyle, and Doug Mitchell. Thanks also to Jennifer Moorhouse and Robert Devens for their contributions.

My family has been my bedrock, the source of sustenance and perspective. For their ongoing encouragement and love, thanks to Alex, Louie, and Leslie Nicolaides, and Barbara Weisenberg. My father passed away just when I began this study. As a biochemist, he dedicated his life to understanding the dynamics of the life process. I would like to think that we share that goal. My sweet boy, Desmond, kept me company in my belly during the final stages of writing this book. In our house, the running joke was which "baby" would be birthed first, Desmond or the book. It was a tight race but Desmond won. The first several months of his life were inextricably tied to the completion of this book, and I thank Des for putting up with his mom's many hours rat-a-tatting at the computer. My final and deepest thanks go to two vital people in my life. My husband David, beloved partner, has been a model of generosity. His steady, unwavering support and love gave me much-needed strength for the final push on this book. Thank you, David, for *everything*. My mother, Elizabeth, has been behind this project since "day one," when it was germinating as a doctoral dissertation. For her boundless love, encouragement, and faith in me, I offer my deepest gratitude and love.

Introduction

On a warm August night in 1965, the white residents of South Gate stood guard over their beloved homes. Yards away across the railroad tracks in Watts, African-American anger was raging in one of the worst urban riots of the decade. Fires were searing, store windows were shattering, and unsuspecting whites found themselves the targets of violence. In South Gate, residents puzzled over this outburst. Why, they wondered, such an uncontrolled display of anger? In their minds, nothing warranted such behavior. As the violence crept ever closer to home, residents raised physical barriers around their community, giving material form to the policies and practices they had followed for decades. The South Gate police hauled shotguns and tear gas out to blockades they'd set up at streets passing from Watts into South Gate. And residents stood guard over their homes, some on rooftops, others on porches, some brandishing weapons, many fearing that the riot would spill over into their own domestic space. Their homes, their families, their lives, it seemed, were under siege.

The image of these white residents urgently guarding their homes is teeming with symbolism. Homes represent the heart of this picture. For residents of South Gate, a suburb in southern Los Angeles, the home was key to their status, their history, and their very identity. As members of the twentieth-century working class, these residents found the center of gravity in their lives had shifted away from the workplace to life outside of work. It was a shift that shaped not only their social existence but also their economic strategies and political commitments. The home lay at the core of life, both literally and figuratively, as working people made their way through the challenges facing them in a maturing industrial economy. By the time the riots broke out in 1965, South Gaters had been defining their homes and neighborhoods in racialized ways that had everything to do with black discontent, although white South Gate would never see it this way.

This book tells the story of how South Gate residents ended up in this place. It begins in 1920, following the lives of a first generation of migrants to Los Angeles seeking family security in a hostile capitalist economy. These working-class families made their way to new suburbs like South Gate, places that offered rich opportunities for creating an economic safety net for themselves. In the process of creating this buffer, residents cultivated a political sensibility that revered self-help and reviled threats to those efforts. The seeds of working-class conservatism were sown in this early period. The second part of the book follows South Gate into the post–World War II era, when the town's blue-collar residents were thriving in the context of postwar prosperity. In their quest for the postwar suburban dream, they shifted their focus toward defending their new standard of living against outside threats—the most ominous and dramatic of these being the civil rights movement. When South Gate residents displayed a sense of ingenuous disbelief at the 1965 rioting, their reaction represented a neglect of their own history and place in it.

At the broadest level, this book is an exploration of the changing mentalities, concerns, and political outlooks of American workers in the twentieth century. I began with a simple—but large—question: how did the social, community, and economic setting of modern workers influence their political beliefs and behaviors? Taking my cues from the rich field of nineteenth-century working-class histories—particularly the many studies of northeastern communities, which focus on workers undergoing the process of industrialization—I sought to conduct a parallel study for the twentieth century, of workers already adjusted to industrial capitalism. I chose Los Angeles because it represents an archetypal twentieth-century metropolis. Rabidly open shop, suburban in form, brimming with class and racial volatility, Los Angeles presents a setting with rich potential for understanding the experiences and mentalities of twentieth-century workers. I selected South Gate as my case-study community, which lay central among Los Angeles's southern suburbs. As early as the 1920s, this area became an important locus of industrial activity and working-class settlement. It was a sub-urban industrial "belt" devoted to the mass-production of durable goods, such as automobiles, tires, and steel, representing Los Angeles's own De-troit.[1] South Gate is located about seven miles south of downtown, along major thoroughfares leading to the port. Neighboring suburbs like Hunt-ington Park, Bell Gardens, Lynwood, Walnut Park, and Maywood shared South Gate's profile, and as such appear throughout this story.

As a working-class suburb, South Gate represents an important yet little understood type of community in twentieth-century America. To many, the term "working-class suburb" is something of an oxymoron. Tra-ditionally, a suburb has been defined as the exclusive preserve of upper- and middle-class whites seeking to nurture family life away from the corrup-tion of the city. Class and racial specificity shapes the definition: a suburb is a suburb only when it is inhabited by privileged whites. This interpretation has guided a number of important histories of suburbanization.[2] Some scholars have argued further that class concerns precipitated suburbaniza-tion: the upper strata fled to the periphery to escape proximity to workers and minorities in the inner cities. Suburbanization expressed "the basic pattern of escapism from capitalist reality." In this model, the bourgeoisie sought refuge from the odious consequences of capitalist production— poverty, exploited workers, and the misery of their lives. Class, itself, de-fined the process of suburbanization. Accordingly, the assumption is that workers were largely excluded from suburbia until the post–World War II era, when federal housing programs and mass-produced suburbs like Levit-town and Lakewood opened the door to workers for the first time.[3]

In reality, however, American suburbs have displayed marked class and racial diversity over time, calling into question these interpretations. While sociologists since the early twentieth century have known this,[4] historians have been slower to recognize this fact, leading them "to end up writing clichés," as one critic has put it.[5] Only recently have historians turned their attention to suburbs of the working class and people of color, revealing a much more variegated picture of suburban life. Richard Harris, Andrew Wiese, Robert Bruegmann, and James Borchert, among others, have begun to outline the nature of these communities, which stand in contrast to elite suburbs.[6] One primary difference lies in the meaning and use of property. In many working-class suburbs, residents turned their domestic property into sites of production, growing fruits and vegetables and raising small livestock in backyards as a means of family sustenance. These suburbs ex-isted all over North America, from Toronto to Cleveland, Chicago to Pitts-burgh. And they varied in size, landscape, social nature, economic function, and even culture. Within Los Angeles alone, I have identified four distinct types of working-class suburbs that existed before 1940.[7] South Gate, clearly, was hardly alone.

The nature of homes, especially, highlighted the difference between working-class and upper-class suburbs of the early 1900s. Homeownership was critical to the advantage that working-class residents found in suburban living, and ultimately shaped important aspects of their identity. Seeking to minimize their dependence on cash, many residents built homes for themselves. These dwellings fall under the category of informal housing that emerged during the Gilded Age. This class of housing was most often shaped by and for working people, particularly the unskilled and semi-skilled workers whose ranks were swelling with industrialization. Informal housing was frequently self-produced, small in scale, modest, and often jerry-built. Three broad classes of informal housing emerged, in different contexts. First, in dense metropolitan areas, alley housing and shantytowns in the midst of the city represented an informal response to severely constricted housing options. These homes represented a grassroots adaptation to existing urban conditions. Second, in smaller industrial cities, alley housing and later garage housing were responses to similar constraints. Restrictions on peripheral land development created densities and housing shortages in these areas, forcing workers to invent their own housing solutions. Again, these were largely unplanned, improvised solutions operating within the existing housing market. Third, self-built housing in working-class suburbs appeared in cities that were expanding horizontally. Unlike alley housing, which was a response and adaptation to existing urban structures, the owner-built suburban home began from ground zero. Owner-builders weren't squeezing into alleys, coping with density, and tucking their homes among other structures. Instead, they were the first home producers in their community, building in the unfettered space of suburbia. All these housing forms represented ways that working people pursued individualized solutions to the pressures of industrial capitalism.[8]

And in working-class suburbs like South Gate, the productive ways that residents used their property is yet further evidence that the urbanization process, as experienced by individuals, was an incremental one. The move to a city did not signify the end of self-sufficiency, of insulation from the wage economy, or even of ruralism. In the most literal sense, these early working-class suburbs stood midway between farm and city, as transitional communities where rural practices were adapted to metropolitan conditions. Louis Wirth captured this idea in his classic 1938 essay, "Urbanism as a Way of Life": "Because the city is the product of growth rather than of instantaneous creation, it is to be expected that the influences which it exerts upon the modes of life should not be able to wipe out completely the previously

dominant modes of human association. To a greater or lesser degree, therefore, our social life bares the imprint of an earlier folk society, the characteristic modes of settlement of which were the farm, the manor, and the
village." The working-class suburbs of twentieth-century Los Angeles displayed this transitive quality, embodying in microcosm the urbanization
process itself.[9]

The South Gate story also reveals a slice of labor and working-class history. My approach to exploring the issue of class follows on the broad body
of working-class scholarship that takes community and culture as the
prime areas of analysis. In this view, class does not signify simply an economic category—defined by occupation or wealth and expressed mainly in
the workplace—but it refers to broader experiences expressed in all realms
of life: political, social, cultural. Class represents a relationship "best dis-
cernible over time and evident in all the areas in which people within the
system of productive relations confronted each other."[10] The scholarship
has shown that a *coherent* working-class identity has been lacking in American history. Instead, apart from key moments like the rise of the Congress
of Industrial Organizations (CIO) in the 1930s, American workers have
been a fragmentary lot, defined by sources of identity such as gender, race,
ethnicity, and skill. As Paul Faler summarizes, "it was precisely in the non-
economic areas that a common cultural identity or class consciousness was
lacking."[11] The South Gate story bears this out in several ways. As the routines of everyday life pulled working-class families in many directions in the
metropolis—for work, leisure, consumption, and other pursuits—their experiences became highly individualized. And the strategies these families
used to survive in a maturing capitalist economy—through homeownership and self-provisioning in backyards—further promoted fragmentation.
These characteristics, combined with certain ideological inclinations, contributed to a working-class mentality that embraced self-reliance, independence, Americanism, familism, and racial separatism. Loyalty to labor
unions was not a central preoccupation and was often more a utilitarian
move than a deeply ideological one. If any identity cohered South Gate's
working class, it was their status as white homeowners. Indeed, this aspect
of their identity most emphatically shaped their political behavior and
commitments.[12]

Historians emphasize a critical turning point for American labor in the
late 1930s and 1940s, with the rise of a bureaucratized and institutionalized
system of relations among labor, management, and government. The center
of gravity shifted away from the shop floor to the headquarters of powerful
national unions, particularly the CIO, which assumed a "top-down" system
of control. Because of this structural transformation, the importance of lo-

calism (in terms of both unions and community) is usually deemed less important by chroniclers of labor struggles for power—the big decisions were made at national headquarters and Washington, D.C. This explains much of labor history's de-emphasis on community in the postwar period. The irony is that these historians often end up attributing changes in postwar working-class mentalities to factors *outside* the workplace—such as the consumer culture and the Democratic Party—without actually showing how these forces affected workers' lives.[13]

Indeed, much is lost by abandoning the community perspective in the postwar era, given the forces that began unsettling many working-class neighborhoods in profound ways. Race was critical here.[14] As the civil rights movement gained momentum in the 1940s and 1950s, it imposed new pressures and challenges on the white working class. To a greater degree than ever, property relations became the primary mediator of class and racial power, in conflicts over neighborhood control and the disposition of urban and suburban space.[15] In northern and western cities, the sharpest, fiercest conflicts often erupted in working-class neighborhoods, where lines of segregation were the starkest.[16] Los Angeles was no exception, and South Gate uncomfortably found itself front and center in such a clash. While local white positions on race were neither unified nor consistent, they did reveal a working-class attempt to come to terms with personal identity, status, and values. This process of white working-class politicization ultimately manifested as Democrats voting Republican in the late 1960s, tax revolts in the 1970s, and total white flight by the 1980s.

The political values forged in the struggles of the 1960s reflected not only the immediate circumstances of that moment, but the deeper roots of the South Gate community. It began with the survival challenges of the early era, the centrality of homeownership, and the social and cultural experience of life in Los Angeles. The first generation of South Gate began collecting the kindling that would ignite forty-five years later in Watts.

PART   I

THE QUEST FOR INDEPENDENCE, 1920–1940

1   Building Independence in Suburbia

"Southgate Twilight" (1918)

Southgate Gardens is an ideal place,
Where "Home Sweet Home" rings true;
Where the sun at last drops the day that is past
From a cloudland of azure and blue . . .
The hands that are weary from labor and toil,
Contentedly "rest on their oars."
One listens in peace as night's murmurs increase
Borne in from the ocean-washed shores.
'Tis a dear spot of land where one meets the glad hand
Of friendship from friends who are true,
While the moon and the stars, greet the sunset bars,
I want to live there, don't you?[1]

The story of working-class Los Angeles necessarily begins somewhere else. Throngs of Americans from points east— seeking opportunity, a fresh start, a gentler climate, a living wage—left behind people and roots to find the good life at the physical edge of the American frontier. More than a million newcomers arrived in L.A. County in the 1920s; about half as many came the following decade, even as they coped with the deprivations of the Great Depression.[2]

For working-class migrants, both decades posed daunting challenges. As laboring people, they struggled to survive in a maturing capitalist world, in an industrial economy increasingly hostile to organized labor, and in a society with no mature welfare structure. With economic precariousness a fact of life, these workers focused on the overarching goal of finding ways to keep the family ship afloat. In the early twentieth century, the young city of Los Angeles emerged as an excellent place to work out these strategies, a city where the natural elements were kinder and opportunities promising. So working people packed up their belongings and headed west. They came from small towns, cities, rural hamlets, suburbs, and farms. Places like Memphis, Marion, Shawnee, Utica. And Pond Switch, Tennessee.

Juanita Smith was one of these migrants.[3] Born in 1912, Juanita grew up in Pond Switch, a small rural railroad junction about forty miles west of Nashville. One blink and the passing traveler missed the hamlet, whose modest town center contained a hotel, two houses, a small depot, and a grocery store. The Smith family, including Juanita, her parents, and three older sisters, owned and ran the single hotel in town. Her father, Daniel, also worked as a carpenter. In the surrounding countryside, twenty farmhouses dotted the landscape.

Community was real and tangible in Pond Switch. Although the local economy was connected to the national marketplace, physical isolation compelled residents to rely upon one another. Food supplies came out of family gardens that produced the staples of an informal barter network, where neighbors exchanged homegrown vegetables and fruit. Sporadic medical care, in the form of an aging itinerant doctor who showed up every six months, compelled families to care for one another. When a neighbor was sick, Juanita's mother, Jessie, hiked over dirt roads to the house and asked, "What shall I do first?"

In hard times, neighbors acted as human social security. One afternoon, young Juanita and her sisters visited newcomers to the community and discovered their only food was cornmeal simmering on the stove. When the girls told their mother, she promptly collected a stash of groceries from the hotel's supply and delivered it to the new neighbors. Although families pursued the goal of independence, material realities made self-sufficiency difficult. In isolated rural Tennessee before the advent of the welfare state, a commitment to the community was essential for collective survival. There was no other safety net to catch people on the edge of poverty or trouble. And if the community was not enough, the only alternative was to leave.

On a cold day in January 1922, disaster struck the Smiths. A little boy boarding in the hotel sneaked a box of matches into an upstairs closet and began playing with them. Sparks flew, setting off a fire that ravaged the hotel. The fire destroyed the livelihood—and economic bedrock—of the Smiths. When the insurance company took a year to pay the meager settlement, the family grew desperate and made the tough decision to leave Pond Switch. They moved to suburban Nashville to begin anew. Daniel Smith, now employed as a carpenter, immediately built the family a small home. It wasn't long before misfortune struck again. Within a year of their arrival, doctors diagnosed Daniel with tuberculosis and warned him that the cold Tennessee winters were only worsening his condition. The Smith family, sliding down the socioeconomic ladder, grew desperate for a solution.[4]

As if to answer the family's prayers, Juanita's Uncle Walter appeared on the scene. A career soldier and world traveler, Uncle Walter had recently visited Southern California and was so impressed by the region's salubrious and auspicious climate that he bought multiple lots in a new suburban tract called Home Gardens,[5] about seven miles south of downtown Los Angeles. He immediately urged the Smiths to move west for the sake of Daniel's health. And he offered his relatives the gift of land, along with the promise of a better life. Realtors sent the Smiths picture postcards of the new development, showing a beautiful lake surrounded by palm trees and flowers. It was enough to convince the family to pull up their Tennessee roots and settle in California. The year was 1925.

After selling the Nashville home and their larger furniture, the Smiths packed up their belongings in two Ford Model Ts—a sedan and a truck purchased by Uncle Walter—and headed west. They beat a path for families of the dust bowl exodus, who would follow a decade later. Like the fictional Joads, the Smiths pitched a tent along the way. Campgrounds with showers and cooking facilities were few and far between, so Jessie cooked resourcefully wherever she could. And Daniel insisted that they rest on the Sabbath, telling his family: "Sunday is the Lord's day, and we're not going to drive."

When they finally reached their destination after a long, tiring month on the road, Juanita's heart dropped at the sight of Home Gardens. She looked in vain for the lake, flowers, and palm trees, but all she saw were vacant lots overgrown with weeds, dirt roads, curbs, and sidewalks—the skeleton of a suburb. A few tiny homes—call them shacks—were scattered here and there in the distance, but mostly there was empty space.

As the Smiths began to unpack their belongings, it was their ideological baggage they brought out first: independence, resourcefulness, frugality. Drawing on both their entrepreneurial impulse from the Pond Switch days and their economic desperation as members of the working class, they displayed a powerful streak of resourceful self-reliance. Rather than rent a place downtown while their house was constructed, the Smiths pitched a tent right on their vacant lot. Then they began the long, exhausting process of securing permanent shelter. They did this not by opening savings accounts and visiting mortgage lenders, but rather by spending their spare cash on lumber, nails, and other building materials, then rolling up their sleeves and becoming home builders. Daniel built the house with the aid of Jessie and the children. The garage was the first to go up, a small structure barely big enough to accommodate two cars. The family of six immediately moved into this meager space. Daniel installed a gas main so Jessie could cook, then he hung mattresses from the ceiling to serve as beds. They lived in that garage for several months as they continued to build the house. When the family finally moved in, the house was still unfinished—lacking a roof—and Daniel carried on construction even as they occupied it. In this way, the Smiths became suburban homeowners.

It soon became clear that their home represented a financial anchor, a source of sustenance in dire times, especially as other resources disappeared. Just months after they arrived in Los Angeles, Uncle Walter died suddenly, sadly scuttling his dream of retiring in Home Gardens alongside his relatives. No longer could the Smiths rely on this generous relative for help. And with Daniel's health weakening, his prospects for handling full-time work began to dim. He took a job as a night watchman downtown; although the pay was small, he was permitted to lie down and rest during his shift.

With cash sources weak and unpredictable, the suburban home became the Smiths' most reliable financial resource, providing much more than mere shelter. Jessie tapped the full potential of the property, raising vegetables, poultry, rabbits, and even a goat that ate its way through the vacant lots of Home Gardens. She sold chickens to a small poultry business on Central Avenue. She bartered vegetables with neighbors, saving money for her family when they couldn't spare the extra penny for produce from the grocer. If Daniel was out of work, Jessie bartered her homegrown goods to keep the family afloat. By turning their property into a veritable suburban homestead, the Smiths devised a strategy for coping with the pressures of industrial capitalism.

The Smiths lived in an era of increased market dependency, an economic life of wage work, market fluctuations, and layoffs, all looming above a deep chasm of poverty without the safety net of state-based welfare. In the face of these forces, the family's key goal was to maintain some semblance of economic security by minimizing their dependence on cash assets and wages. This followed a long historic tradition in America that valued family security over profit maximization.[6] For the Smiths, like many work-ing-class Americans, the last rope to grasp before falling from autonomy was the home. And as it became a critical source of family security, the sub-urban home also came to shape the experience, identity, and political loyal-ties of working-class whites.

These broad functions of homeownership realized their fullest fruition in the blue-collar suburbs of North America during the first half of the twentieth century. These suburbs offered families like the Smiths an ex-cellent opportunity to pursue their goals of economic security and in-dependence from cash assets and wages, by enabling them to draw upon sweat—rather than cash—equity to gain entry into the community and homeownership. In so doing, working-class suburbs, by their very nature, came to represent a domain of life outside the factory that workers could shape to meet their needs.

Nestled in the borderland between rural and urban life, working-class suburbs fused elements from both to fulfill the particular needs of their in-habitants. In contrast to upper-class suburbs that melded rural and urban elements to create an aesthetic of romantic pastoralism, the working-class suburb combined these milieus for the more prosaic purpose of economic survival in the modern industrial metropolis. These suburbs enabled fami-lies to secure the basic necessities of shelter and food cheaply and effi-ciently. Especially in Los Angeles of the early twentieth century, where land was cheap, abundant, and often vacant, such suburbs fulfilled these func-tions effectively and often.[7]

South Gate was one of these suburbs. Located about seven miles south of downtown Los Angeles in the heart of the metropolitan industrial hub, South Gate shared many of the characteristics typical of the blue-collar suburbs that proliferated across North America before World War II.[8] The story of its early development richly conveys the tenor of life in working-class suburbia. In the community building process, both developers *and* residents shaped the suburb. The early developers made pivotal choices that determined the demographic, economic, and housing profile of the commu-nity. Local realtors, the occupational descendants of the developers, contin-ued to exert these influences in subsequent years. Even more important, however, were the residents. Particularly in Home Gardens, the poorer part of town, minimal planning and provisioning threw the initiative for devel-opment into the hands of residents. Far from a planned, garden community of ready-built homes and shady streets, South Gate offered its citizens only the bare bones of suburbia. From the barren raw materials of vacant lots and dirt roads, residents had to build the rest. South Gate was a product of

the sweat, labor, and vision of its inhabitants. If the developers laid a scaffolding, it was up to residents to build—often literally—the structure. In
the process, they became critical agents in the process of suburbanization.

"SOUTHGATE GARDENS — GATEWAY TO THE SEA"

The early developers of South Gate accelerated the process that was transforming southern Los Angeles into the industrial and working-class hub of
the metropolis. Their actions represented a shaping influence on working-
class suburbia in Los Angeles, by making available certain living options,
pitching the land to a particular population segment, opening the suburb to
industry, imposing certain types of restrictions on the community, and *not*
imposing others. The vision and actions of South Gate's developers indicated how forces "from above" helped mold the community. They envisioned a double identity for the suburb: residential and industrial. While
certain internal contradictions inhered in this vision, by the late 1920s the
community had resolved them to settle on an identity that shed all pre-
tenses of suburban romanticism and embraced working-class reality.

South of downtown Los Angeles on the plain that swept to the Pacific,
lush farmlands gradually gave way to factories and subdivisions during the
1910s and 1920s. This rich land had been used for sheep grazing, dairying,
and farming of lucrative cash crops like cauliflower, beets, barley, corn,
apples and walnuts. Most of the farms were large-scale operations that relied upon wage labor, although some small farmers operated as well, like the
Chinese cauliflower growers who leased the land and sold their produce to
local agents. As late as 1920, 25 percent of L.A. County's entire agricultural
output was produced in this southern section. Although land ownership in
the area would change radically during the 1920s, diffusing from a few
large to many small owners, agricultural production continued to define
this part of Los Angeles even as it became "suburban."

Among the large landholders of southern Los Angeles was Michael
Cudahy, who made his fortune in the meatpacking industries of Chicago.
Cudahy dreamed of retiring on his sprawling 2,777-acre ranch to raise
pedigree cattle and thoroughbred horses. But when his death—and the designs of acquisitive Los Angeles developers—scuttled that dream, Cudahy's land was converted into the industrial belt of L.A., almost as if to
mock his pastoral fantasy. In 1917, the year the United States entered
World War I, the Cudahy Ranch Company sold its property to the Southern Extension Company (SEC), which immediately began subdividing it
for suburban developments. One of these suburbs was dubbed "Southgate

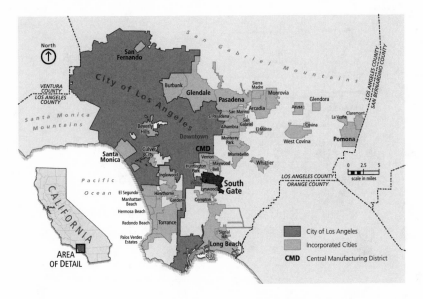

Figure 1-1 The communities of the L.A. metropolis, 1940

Gardens—Gateway to the Sea," as it rested midway between downtown Los Angeles and the port of San Pedro (see fig. 1-1). The SEC divided this 140-acre tract into 268 lots, mostly half-acre parcels 120-feet wide by 150-feet deep, platted according to the grid pattern to maximize land efficiency. This area became the original northwest section of the suburb. Although it did build some homes, the SEC mostly sold empty lots to residents who would build their own homes or hire builders. Although inflation and material shortages during World War I stymied the development of planned communities in Los Angeles, working-class suburbs like South Gate still went forward, most likely because individual property buyers were expected to build and provision on their own.[9] The word "Gardens" fell from the name by 1919 and the suburb became South Gate. By the summer of 1920, it encompassed $1^{1}/3$ square miles and realtors had sold nearly all of the lots.[10]

In addition to the SEC, other developers subdivided adjacent tracts that became part of South Gate by 1930. Each tract varied in the extent of development, ranging from some mass-building of homes with utilities provided, to the mere dividing up of empty land. The nature of development helped direct the class settlement patterns in South Gate, representing in microcosm the suburbanization process occurring at broader metropolitan levels elsewhere.[11] To the west, for example, the Magnolia Park section was developed by a small local residential developer and the Mason Case Com-

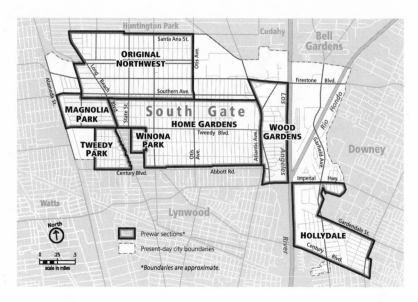

Figure 1-2   The major sections of South Gate, 1920s

pany, an industrial real estate firm. They divided the area into 591 lots—
some with finished homes—abutting on property designated for industry.
To the south, the Home Gardens section was subdivided in 1922 by Sam
Dudlext. Comprising about five square miles by 1925, this area was the
poorest section of South Gate, offering mainly empty lots with very little
infrastructure. In the southeast part of town, the Hollydale section remained underdeveloped through most of the 1920s and 1930s. Though
sixty-nine families and seven factories inhabited the area in 1926, in the
1930s most of the land was turned over to gardens and dairies. The Tweedy
section, a 175-acre tract opened in 1924, was pegged as a higher-grade area
where the Tweedy Homesite Company planned to build uniform housing.
In most sections of South Gate, however, families could purchase vacant
lots on which to construct their own houses. This was not meant as a community of finished homes for cash-toting buyers. Instead, South Gate's future lay in the sweat equity of its individual working-class residents.[12]

How did these developers envision this community? One clue emerges
in their early sales pitches for South Gate property, which expressed the developers' conceptions about the meaning and benefits of suburban life. The
sales push began in 1917. Typical of L.A. real estate promotions of the era,
the SEC rented twelve buses, picked up prospective buyers downtown, and
drove them out to the open fields of Southgate Gardens. While homeseek-

ers ate a free hot supper in a large carnival tent, a "lecturer" extolled the virtues of Southgate Gardens in a scene part religious revival, part advertising scam.[13] In these exhortations, three themes emerged: civic fulfillment, economic advantage, and the "rural ideal." In essence, the developers professed that suburban living in Southgate Gardens would fulfill the political, economic, and aesthetic needs of American workers.

The political pitch centered around the idea that suburbia and homeownership would foster civic participation because citizen-residents would feel a genuine stake in their community. The suburbs, they contended, placed people back into small-scale communities where the civic spirit could once again take root. Such neighborhoods would be composed of responsible, independent citizens whose property gave them a firm stake in the community's welfare. The citizen's status as homeowner was essential to his civic identity: the home was the key to his independence, and in turn the cornerstone of full civic participation. As one promoter proclaimed in 1920: "[The homeowner] owns something. The town is his town because he owns a piece of it. The community is his community because he is a part of it. Whatever threatens the community threatens his property. . . . Homeowners as a class are universally considered to be thrifty, law abiding, religious, public spirited, good workmen, desirable citizens." Another contended in 1919, "It elevates a man to own a home. It gives a certain independence, a force of character that is obtained in no other way. . . . Homes make patriots." This idea aligned with widespread concerns during this period about working-class radicalism, a response to both the Bolshevik Revolution and working-class activism in Los Angeles. Voicing these worries, the sellers of South Gate identified the capacity of homeownership to diffuse radical discontent and to cultivate a responsible citizenry. "Home owners do not go about with torch and bomb, bent upon destruction," wrote one realtor. "Men who have roofs of their own do not go about scattering firebrands. Of the forty percent of Americans who do own their own homes, not one has yet been classed with the malcontents." This pitch gave civic legitimacy to the low-density residential form. Far from being an abandonment of the city, suburbs were presented as a place where Americans could contribute to the commonweal and become better citizens. These appeals echoed ideas being articulated at the national level by housing reformers and national leaders, who believed that suburban homeownership promoted democracy among the middle and working classes alike.[14]

The second pitch emphasized the economic advantages of South Gate, aimed at both factory and office workers. Not only was land affordable in South Gate, but ownership assured economic security in two ways: through land use and through property equity. Early ads highlighted the productive capacities of a South Gate lot, which could support bountiful home gardens to supply food and extra cash for families seeking a buffer against the vicissitudes of the free market economy. "Marvelous crops are being produced by home owners in Southgate," wrote a promoter in 1918, "without the aid of fertilizers, *Potatoes* in a number of instances, *maturing in four to five weeks* after planting. . . . All of the fruit, vegetables, rabbits, poultry, etc., which can be consumed by the average family of six people, can be produced on a Southgate Unit [lot size 120′ × 150′] and with a little added effort along some specialized line, a Southgate Unit may be made to produce a profit besides." This pitch underscored the economic advantages of suburban homesteading, the notion that the land itself could provide some economic security. This idea, too, was being articulated at the national level by housing reformers like William Smythe. The second part of the economic appeal emphasized the investment potentials of a South Gate lot. Either through purchasing a property large enough to be split later and sold (typically, a half-acre lot) or simply by benefiting from climbing real estate values in the region, the prospective buyer was bound to profit.[15]

The third pitch evoked the rural ideal, a theme widely emphasized in suburbs of all classes. The sellers of South Gate promised peace, quiet, beauty, and expansive space away from the unpleasant city, more often portrayed as some distant eastern entity rather than Los Angeles itself.[16] As one booster intoned in 1919: "I can imagine no sweeter way to end one's life than in the quiet of the country, out of the mad race for money, place and power—away from the congested noisy homeless centers where fools struggle for the hollow praise of other fools. Surrounded by pleasant fields and faithful friends, by those I have loved, I hope to end my days. And this I hope may be the lot of all. I hope that you in the country, in houses covered with vines and clothed with flowers, looking from the open window upon rustling fields, over which will run the sunshine and the shadows, surrounded by those whose lives you have filled with joy, will pass away as serenely as the Autumn dies."[17] Promising pristine air, a warm hearth, true friends, and the murmurs of nature, South Gate offered a haven of wholesome living. To those who toiled with their hands at physically arduous jobs, the image was particularly compelling. In this way, the rural ideal resonated uniquely for the working class.

When rosy rhetoric gave way to concrete reality, the developers ended up acting on only some of these ideals. Their greatest emphasis, by far, was on catering to the economic concerns of prospective homeseekers, by making it affordable to buy in and stay in. This approach had two repercussions: it shifted the initiative for community building onto the residents themselves, and it created a rough-and-tumble suburban environment, yielding a gritty rural reality more than a dreamy rural ideal. The developers shaped the town in other ways as well, by imposing race restrictions, allowing laxness in building and land-use regulations, and erecting the scaffolding of an economically diverse community. Above all, they made it eminently affordable for white workers to grab their piece of the American suburban dream.

The early developers imposed certain regulations that shaped the suburb's social makeup. Through housing options and race restrictions, they ensured that only white families would be allowed into the community. The vast majority of residential lots were subdivided for single-family dwellings, meaning the town would be dominated by families. There were some exceptions. Scattered throughout the suburb were duplexes, triplexes, and bungalow courts (typically six to ten units), often on double- or triple-sized lots nestled on residential streets. And along Long Beach and Firestone Boulevards, the latter a major state highway feeding into Los Angeles, several auto courts and motor hotels sprang up by the late 1930s. In all, however, these structures were vastly outnumbered by single-family homes, which constituted 98.9 percent of total dwellings in 1930. This not only reinforced the centrality of homeownership, but it privileged the family as the dominant social unit.[18]

Various racial restrictions, in turn, ensured an all-white population. One historian claimed that the original deeds to the land, presumably those controlled by the SEC, stipulated that only whites could own or rent property. In subsequent years, this exclusion was sustained by race-restrictive covenants on individual property deeds, a practice lasting through the late 1940s. Noted one resident in 1919, "We have the assurance that only good residences can be built here, and our neighbors must be white." More emphatically, the South Gate Property Owners' Protective Association, formed before the war, assured in a handbook, "South Gate . . . is one of the comparatively new communities of Southern California . . . to benefit from the mistakes of other districts where the subdividers did not foresee the danger of allowing race restrictions to lapse too soon. . . . Practically all of this city's residential tracts have perpetual restrictions against occupancy by non-Caucasians." Even local government supported the racial exclusion by inserting a clause into the city charter that limited the local population to Caucasians. South Gate's racial preoccupations were typical of Los Angeles's white suburbs in this period, a time of heightened concerns about maintaining racial boundaries in the metropolis.[19]

Although South Gate was exclusive regarding race, it was highly inclusive in terms of class. Virtually no restrictions operated to control the local class character, which enabled the poorest of homeseekers to enter into the community. The process was accelerated by the annexation of poorer subdivisions, especially Home Gardens in 1927 and Hollydale in 1928. Prospective working-class residents were enticed by cheap lots, the opportunity for homebuilding, few construction or land-use restrictions, and minimal improvements, keeping living costs low. In this way, local developers made available the "unplanned suburb" that appealed so strongly to workers and their families in early twentieth-century America. This openness was so pronounced that it could make nearby middle-class suburbs, such as Downey, nervous about the invasion of the poor.[20]

The nature, price, and terms of property sales were a boon to prospective residents seeking to economize. The sale of empty lots opened the subdivision to diligent homeseekers—short on cash but long on energy—who intended to self-build. In 1918, lot sizes began at 40' × 130' with prices starting at $490, a sum less than half the average annual income of a wage earner in manufacturing or construction for that year—or roughly the value of a good car. Lots in Home Gardens sold for as low as $295. A local ad offered to trade oil acreage in New Mexico for "lots in Home Gardens or good automobile." Also common was the half-acre parcel, particularly attractive to residents seeking to raise home gardens. (The names Southgate Gardens and Home Gardens called attention to this feature.) These larger parcels promised the buyer "partial economic independence" through gardening on the "rich, fertile soil" or through selling off portions of these multiple "Three Lots at the Price of One." In Southgate Gardens, a typical half-acre lot (120' × 130') sold for about $780 in 1917. By 1919, prices ranged from $1,200 to $1,500 depending on the location, and jumped to $2,000 by 1924. The terms of sales also made property affordable. Home Gardens developer Sam Dudlext sold thirty-foot frontage lots in 1921 for $35 down and $5 per month, at 7 percent interest. In 1924, he offered lots for $20 down and $10 per month, which was cheaper than rent in many areas of Los Angeles. In 1920, typical rents ranged from $20 to $37.50 per month for "moderately priced houses" in Los Angeles. Classified ads showed comparably priced lots in Home Gardens on similar terms.[21]

For buyers with cash, cheap homes could be had. The SEC, Tweedy Homesites, and small local builders were available to construct dwellings for a modest price. One seller offered to exchange a house and lot for either a "small auto" or $950. In 1924, a two-room house and garage on a 60' × 130' lot was listed for $1,200 ($300 down and $25 per month). Dudlext listed these "bargains" in 1925: a four-room house on Virginia Avenue for

$1,400 ($400 down and $30 per month), and a two-room house on San Carlos for $725 ($378 down and $10 per month). Such housing affordability, in fact, was widespread in Greater Los Angeles after World War I.[22]

The developers imposed few building regulations, which facilitated the process of owner-building. Although the SEC originally imposed "moderate" restrictions to ensure a "high grade residence place," this quickly gave way to flexibility about the kinds of homes allowed in the community. Apart from meeting minimal safety and sanitary requirements and having foundations at least twenty inches below the ground, homes could be built as the owner pleased. A local rule required homes worth less than $1,500 to sit at the back of the lot. Although the intention was to ensure a uniform appearance in the neighborhood, this provision was a sheepish admission that cheap homes were allowable as long as they were not too conspicuous. This laxity in regulation represented an open invitation to the owner-builder, making it viable to produce a home on one's own terms.[23]

The importance of lax building regulations to working-class homeseekers is illustrated by the early failure of one working-class suburb, Torrance. Located in southwest Los Angeles in the heart of oil country, Torrance was incorporated in 1921. It diverged from unplanned blue-collar suburbs—like Home Gardens—in being highly planned and regulated. It was envisioned as a "model industrial suburb" for the working class, designed by John C. and Frederick Law Olmsted Jr. to incorporate elements of City Beautiful into the suburban landscape. Part of this involved imposing restrictions on housing style and quality. Their strict requirements shut out many prospective homebuilders, who instead headed to hospitable working-class suburbs like Home Gardens, where laxity was the watchword. As a result, Torrance languished and grew at a snail's pace during this period.[24]

In South Gate, another frugal measure taken by the developers was to refrain from extensive infrastructure development, a key attraction to working-class homeseekers because it minimized local taxes. Northwest South Gate boasted the most improvements, although even here one resident complained in 1924 about the "wild grass growing in the streets." Conditions were even cruder in the rest of the suburb, where kerosene lamps, electric torches, cesspools, and dusty roads prevailed. In Home Gardens, the streets were unimproved except for sidewalks and curbs installed three years after the first properties were sold. Streetlights did not reach the southern part of town until the late 1920s, and only then in the face of public resistance. The lack of improvements, which ensured lower property tax rates, was the very thing that attracted many residents to South Gate and would eventually galvanize them politically.[25]

INVENTING THE "DETROIT OF THE COAST"

The SEC originally pictured Southgate Gardens as a self-sufficient community of wage-earning residents, small shopkeepers, and factories. To minimize the suburb's dependence on the broader metropolis, the developers ambitiously planned a business district just east of the original homesites. They hoped to sell nearly as many business lots as residences, making for a self-contained village where people lived, shopped, and worked. This plan faltered early, however, as buyers purchased lots and built homes in the planned business district despite early zoning laws.[26]

More striking was the developers' vision of industry in South Gate. Belying any pretense of rural romanticism, South Gate's boosters embraced manufacturing as an integral part of the suburb by the 1920s. They opened wide the door to industry, encouraging factories to sink roots in and around the community. Indeed, they envisioned South Gate at the heart of brisk industrial growth in southern Los Angeles. By the 1920s, they had jettisoned any concern for maintaining a rural ideal far from the industrial smokestacks—they were luring those very smokestacks into their own backyard.

As early as 1924, city promoters spoke enthusiastically of a $4 million "industrial program" of plant construction for South Gate, destined to make it "one of the most important [communities] in Southern California." In fact, they held grandiose visions for the industrial future of all the southern suburbs: "The entire strip from Huntington Park to the Harbor is so wonderfully situated for industrial purposes that it will be a matter of only a few years until it will be filled to overflowing with industry." And South Gate, they beamed, lay smack in the middle. "Southgate is in an ideal location between the city of Los Angeles and Long Beach harbor," intoned the L.A. Chamber of Commerce, "directly in the path of Southern California's industrial development. Power is cheap; living conditions for workers excellent; in all, it is 'The Complete City' where 90% of the residents own their own homes."[27] (See fig. 1-3.)

Several local promoters emerged as critical agents in attracting industry to South Gate. R. C. Mason, a prominent industrial realtor, was credited with helping to bring nineteen factories to the suburb, including General Motors (GM), Firestone, Rheem Manufacturing, and Purex. Another key leader was Hugh Pomeroy, a South Gate resident who served as secretary of the L.A. County Regional Planning Commission and as a member of the Harbor District Chamber of Commerce. His dual role in industrial boosterism and regional planning—with zoning and planning power for the entire county—surely influenced the industrial development of southern L.A.

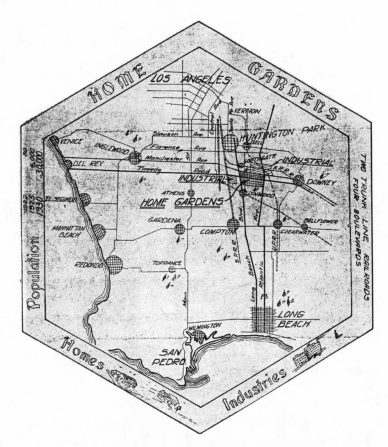

Figure 1-3   This 1926 publicity map produced by the Home Gardens Business Men's Association
emphasized the locational advantages of Home Gardens, a working-class industrial suburb.
Huntington Park City School District files, Los Angeles County Board of Education
collection, Los Angeles County Board of Supervisors Archives.

and his own hometown. In 1930, for example, Pomeroy was instrumental
in bringing a steel manufacturer to South Gate.[28]

To sell their suburb to industries, local promoters emphasized four
main advantages. First, convenient access to freight transportation made
the transport of goods cheap and convenient. South Gate boasted four
"team tracks" (public loading and unloading spurs) of the Southern Pacific
and Union Pacific railroads, with cheaper railroad rates than in L.A. city.
Second, they highlighted the proximity of a dependable labor force. The
blue-collar residents of Home Gardens and South Gate, they asserted, were
"accessible," "plentiful," "of the better class," and "100 per cent Ameri-

can"—all referring to their status as white homeowners with few ties to organized labor. Third, they emphasized the low cost of water, electricity, and
gas in South Gate, which compared favorably to eastern cities as well as Los
Angeles itself. Fourth, developers underscored the area's cheap land and tax
rates, particularly in areas that lay just beyond municipal boundaries in unincorporated territory. Boosters of Home Gardens, still unincorporated in
the mid-1920s, repeatedly stressed this point. Developers like Mason Case
subdivided factory sites on land just outside the borders of South Gate and
neighboring towns. This geographic arrangement gave industries the best
of both worlds: access to municipal services without the steep costs of establishing them. These plants purchased water services and fire protection
from South Gate for nominal fees, and paid only a *county* property tax that
was substantially lower than rates in incorporated cities.[29] The efforts of
South Gate's industrial promoters were typical of industrial community
developers operating in Los Angeles during this period.[30]

South Gate city hall did its part to attract prospective industries, often
with little concern for preserving the local residential aura. It zoned for industry as early as 1924, including a strip of land that ran right through the
heart of the suburb (see fig. 1-4). During the 1920s, it granted numerous
zoning variances to benefit manufacturers. In 1925, for example, the city
council amended local zoning laws "without hesitating" to allow a factory
to locate in a business district; similar rulings followed over the next several
years.[31] By 1929, while manufacturing zones were confined more carefully
to the northeast and far western parts of town, two light manufacturing
districts remained in the heart of the civic center. In some cases, city hall
made direct pitches to industries considering a South Gate site. As well, the
city offered concessions to plants located just beyond South Gate's borders,
such as providing transportation for workers from South Gate to the Firestone plant (outside city limits in the 1920s), pressing for the improvement
of local municipal services, and contracting with industries for water and
fire protection.[32]

Industries quickly responded to the call. In 1922, Bell Foundry became
the first plant to locate in South Gate, followed two years later by the A.R.
Maas Chemical Company, which produced chemicals for the film industry.
In 1928, South Gate scored a major coupe with the arrival of Firestone Tire
and Rubber, which employed about fifteen hundred people by 1940. By the
late 1920s, fifteen major industries had established plants in and adjacent to
South Gate; the value of manufactured products in South Gate topped $24
million in 1928, with $4.7 million paid in wages. Remarkably, twenty-two
more major industries arrived during the Depression decade, including
a large GM auto assembly plant in 1936. The majority of South Gate's fac-

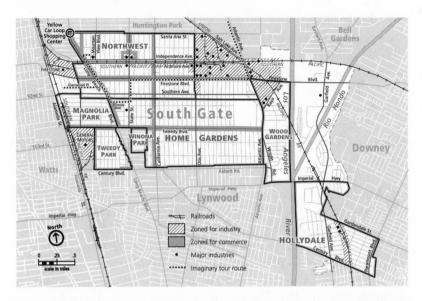

Figure 1-4   Industrial and commercial zones, railroads, and major industries in South Gate, 1920s
to 1930s. Map based on information in *South Gate Tribune*, January 24, 1924 and September
24, 1929; South Gate City Council minutes, February 4, 1924; Tom Thienes, "Contributions
Toward the History of the City of South Gate, California" (unpublished manuscript, 1942,
SGHWL), 123–140; South Gate Book field notes, FWP.

tories produced durable goods, such as iron products, concrete pipe, machinery, automobiles, tires, and products used in manufacturing. As the un-
derbelly of glamorous Hollywood, South Gate supplied 70 percent of the
chemicals used by motion picture processing plants. About half of the suburb's plants were local start-ups, while the others had relocated from other
parts of Los Angeles or were national branch plants. Local industrial expansion was so impressive that by the late 1930s, South Gate had earned the
appellation "Detroit of the Coast." Indeed, the suburb sat squarely within
Los Angeles's industrial heartland: by 1940, there were nine hundred factories within a two-mile radius of South Gate.[33]

By the late 1920s, South Gate had solidified its identity as a community
of white working-class families. As boosters vigorously targeted industries
and their workforces, they squarely identified the suburb as a prime destination for working-class homeseekers. Home Gardens, which annexed to
South Gate in 1927, did this most strikingly. From the days of its earliest
subdivision in 1922, Home Gardens touted itself as "the workingman's
ideal home town" that was "situated conveniently to scores of factories in
different industrial centers, and with property values and terms within the

reach of every honest workingman." In 1925, the local booster-editor asserted, "Home Gardens is a town of, by and for workingmen—and we want
hundreds more of them. The only restrictions are racial—the white race only
may own property here." By 1927, Home Gardens called itself the place
"where the working man is welcomed and given an even break." While
parts of northwest South Gate tried to bill itself as "middle-class," such
words resonated with only a certain sector of the population. As far as most
residents were concerned, South Gate was the "ideal residence for people of
moderate means." And they would work to keep it that way.[34]

HOMESEEKERS AND OWNER-BUILDERS: SHAPING THE SUBURB

If the developers erected a scaffolding for the suburb, the residents built the
structure themselves—often literally. In the process, they imprinted their
own vision of suburbia upon South Gate. Theirs was an image shaped by
class needs, motivated by the desire for family security, and driven by an intensive need to economize. As relatively poor people, many living on the
brink of ruin, they turned to the suburb to fulfill their class-specific needs.
Molded by these concerns and pressures, South Gate became a rough-hewn
suburb where homes were humble, yards were productive, streets were
dusty, and families made do. The "quiet of the country" extolled so roman-
tically by South Gate's poet-boosters gave way to the squawks of chickens,
the shaky wails of goats, and the sharp crack of hammers driving nails into
solid wood.

It is no coincidence that migrants to California in the early twentieth
century were labeled "homeseekers." The quest for homes reflected several
important impulses, motivations that extended beyond the ideology and
controlling influences of the developers and builders. It is true that land
developers controlled the housing options of many, yet we need to look beyond these forces "from above" to understand how and why these Americans embraced homeownership so fervently. Their perspective is critical for
understanding not only the development of working-class suburbia specifically, but also the phenomenal growth of homeownership nationally in the
twentieth century. To workers in 1920s Los Angeles, a home represented
independence, a goal highly valued in both American and immigrant traditions.[35]

For workers living on the edge of poverty, particularly in the period before the New Deal ushered in the welfare state, family security and autonomy were the pressing goals. They pursued these goals in many ways: some
through workplace actions like unionization and demands for job security,

others in realms outside of work such as neighborhoods, popular culture, and public space. As workplace autonomy became more elusive for the laboring class with the maturing of industrial capitalism in the late nineteenth century, life beyond the factory gates took on greater significance. As Ira Katznelson has written, "Paradoxically, just at the moment when the development of industrial capitalism undercut the skill levels and control over work that artisans had exercised, the working class became capable of developing and controlling the institutions of daily neighborhood life."[36]

Housing represented a crucial aspect of this quest for independence. To working-class residents of suburbs like South Gate, individual housing production and ownership were perceived as a viable route to family security. A solid piece of land and shelter became tangible forms of stability within the context of an unpredictable job market, where sources of cash income were often fleeting. Longtime South Gate resident John Sheehy explained that homeownership "meant nobody could evict you. Security for your family, when you're raising five kids you pretty much think you need to own a place. . . . It was tragic if you couldn't buy a house. You really were at the bottom . . . floundering around, trying to survive. There was no such thing in those years as real stability in employment that we came to have later."[37] Economic stability, via homeownership, was the key aspiration of South Gate's citizenry. With homeownership such a central goal, it followed that their status as "homeowner" would profoundly shape their identity.

The meaning of homeownership for working-class suburbanites takes on added significance if seen in light of the movement toward welfare capitalism during the 1920s. In the wake of Progressivism, it was widely acknowledged that industrial capitalism required a safety net for working Americans living on the edge, those most vulnerable to unpredictable swings of the economy. In the era before state-based welfare, sickness, old age, or simply bad luck could spell doom and poverty for an otherwise hardworking family. Large industrialists proposed one solution in the form of welfare capitalism. By offering new forms of security to labor, business hoped both to chill simmering radical tendencies spreading during that era and to circumvent new state intrusions into corporate autonomy. Yet welfare capitalism received a lukewarm reception from many working Americans, who embraced the concept yet resented the failure of business to deliver on its promises.[38]

Another solution was suburbanization and single-family homeownership, for the middle and working classes alike. Both capital and labor supported this approach. Some scholars have stressed the manipulative role of capital in supporting homeownership, claiming it was a means of co-opting worker interests by tying them down to property and making them "slaves

to the bungalow." This, ultimately, worked against labor militancy and autonomy since the working-class homeowner had a stake in the status quo.
To Marxist scholars, this "lawns for pawns" scenario enervated an assertive
working class.[39] Yet this perspective does not tell the whole story, because it
leaves out the voice of workers themselves. To many working Americans,
homeownership promised family autonomy and a palpable sense of security in the soil they could call their own. The historically higher rates of
working-class homeownership—compared to the middle class—attests to
this belief. Moreover, they considered homeownership far superior to welfare capitalism, under which workers paid the price of flagrant dependency
on their employers in exchange for "security." As suburban dwellers and
homeowners, they perceived themselves as more independent and insulated from an unpredictable marketplace. This was a more viable solution to
the problems of industrial capitalism, and it acted as a surrogate to Los Angeles workers who lacked an alternative in a strong labor movement because of the city's rabidly open-shop climate.[40]

Yet the inclination toward working-class homeownership was hardly
unique to Los Angeles. Evidence from Toronto, Detroit, Milwaukee, Chicago,
Cleveland, and other cities suggests that the same impulse for family security drove working-class homeownership in those cities, nurturing an inclination among residents to resist infrastructure development as a means of
keeping taxes low.[41] What stands out in Los Angeles is the timing, for the
process began later there than in the older eastern cities. While Los Angeles
was developing as a cutting-edge, decentralized metropolis, a paradigm of
the new twentieth-century city, the persistence of working-class suburbs
and the political mentalities they fostered resembled a holdover of working-class communities from an earlier time and place—transplanted into a
thoroughly modern (some might say postmodern) urban setting.

In the ways they used homeownership, South Gate's residents showed
certain traits of "semiproletarianism," a class deriving part of its livelihood
from wage work and the other through labor on its own land and property.[42] It was a status peculiar to workers in rural areas, in working-class
suburban areas of abundant vacant land, and in cities of earlier centuries.[43]
As urban land resources shrank in the twentieth century, this semiprole-
tariat class moved to the suburbs. In many ways, working-class families in
suburbia had more options for achieving family security than their urban
counterparts. In older cities, for example, wage reductions or price increases
forced families to seek solutions within the market economy, such as sending children to work or organizing protests. In New York City, housewives
responded to rising food costs by protesting politically since they had few
alternatives for producing their own food.[44] In suburbs like South Gate,

however, residents responded to similar crises by self-provisioning on their own land. It was a more individualized solution, but it was an equally viable one. Suburban settlement represented a way that workers coping with severe strains on cash assets could survive in a maturing industrial economy.[45]

For workers who turned their suburban plots into productive property, the use value—as opposed to commodity value—of homeownership was paramount. The relative importance of use versus commodity value of housing depends largely on the broader geographic, economic, and social context of that housing. In 1920s Los Angeles, an abundance of peripheral vacant land promoted the use value (i.e., purely functional value for the dwellers) of self-built housing, since land prices were cheap enough for even struggling workers to afford. The urban labor market had a more complex impact. While unemployment could promote the "commodification" of housing by forcing owners to liquidate their homes for cash, it could also foster higher use value. Particularly in suburbs with few regulations and low taxes, owner-builders could rely more heavily on self-provisioning in times of joblessness, providing some insulation from market fluctuations.[46]

Semiproletarian practices in South Gate derived not only from the context of suburban Los Angeles but also from the traditions and cultural orientations of the town's new residents. The propensity for cheap self-building, for example, may have reflected a deep-seeded fear of debt, particularly among recent migrants from the Upper South where tenancy had a long, notorious history. As one L.A. owner-builder remarked, "I'm not going to borrow a lot of money and get out on a limb. A fellow at the bank wanted me to borrow money to fix this place up, but I'm not going to do it." Many of these migrants also embraced the tenets of "plain-folk Americanism," a worldview that prized self-reliance, toughness, and independence. The arduous process of owner-building required all of these traits. In their self-reliance, South Gate's suburbanites also displayed aspects of entrepreneurialism. Through selling backyard produce, taking in boarders, running a small business out of the home, or selling off an extra parcel of land, residents used their property to generate income—all means for coping in a maturing cash-based economy. South Gate's residents tried all strategies, some that insulated them from the wage-driven market, others that sought to profit within that marketplace. With one foot in and the other out, the overriding goal remained family security.[47]

The critical functions of homeownership were evident in South Gate during the early years, particularly in the processes of settlement, home production, and domestic property use. These processes reflected not only how workers used suburbia but also how they shaped it. The first requirement for entrance into South Gate was the resources to move there, particularly since many residents migrated from other states. Having the means or connections to come west set them slightly apart from the truly down-and-out worker. Some families, like the Smiths, relied on kin for assistance. Such networks were common among newcomers to the suburb.[48]

Once they arrived, the initial settlement process could be an arduous ordeal. Mirroring the experience of the Smiths, many families purchased a vacant lot then immediately erected temporary shelter to house the family during the self-building process. This could be a tent, a shack made of old boxes or tar paper, a trailer, or a garage. In 1920, thirty-six South Gate families were living in garages while building their homes. Later in the decade, the South Gate City Council passed several rulings that allowed residents to live in tents and garages on their property while their homes were under construction. Other families opted for auto camps, such as the Parker Auto Camp on the suburb's outskirts, which rented one-room cottages with car shelters for five dollars per week. These camps, often shoddy and run down, were waystations on the road to homeownership.[49]

The next step was to build the home. Self-builders needed at least some cash to purchase building materials such as lumber and nails. Some families like the Smiths arrived with modest cash reserves, raised by selling off property back home or by borrowing from generous relatives. Some families managed the expenses by extending the building process over a long period of time or by purchasing secondhand lumber. As a self-builder in nearby Bell Gardens remarked, "You can almost always scrape together ten dollars a month as long as you can have a place to live. We've built our house a little at a time as we could pay for it." By the late 1920s, seven lumber supply houses were operating in South Gate, catering to these homebuilders.[50]

While the precise frequency of owner-building is difficult to determine, several sources indicate the practice was fairly widespread in South Gate. Sanborn Fire Insurance Maps are one clue. Especially for Home Gardens, they suggest frequent self-building by revealing an erratic pattern of dwelling placement on the lots: some at the front, some in the middle, some at the back. By contrast, homes constructed by the same builder tended to have uniform setbacks (see fig. 1-5).[51] Oral histories and building permits also disclose the prevalence of owner-building during the 1920s. Similarly suggestive is a sociological study conducted in the early 1930s of neighboring Bell Gardens, close to South Gate in terms of class and physical appearance. It revealed that 73 percent of the homes there were self-built; 5 percent were purchased partially completed, meaning the buyer had to finish the job; and 17 percent were purchased as finished homes.[52]

The task of self-building—and the conditions it created—were wrought

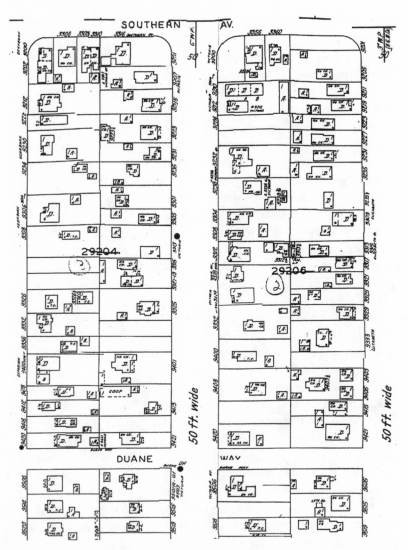

Figure 1-5 Sanborn Company fire insurance maps show that the shape and position of homes on their lots varied considerably in Home Gardens. Some homes lay at the front of the property, others in the middle, and others at the back. This evidence strongly suggests the presence of owner building in the area. (*D*, dwelling; *A*, auto garage; *coop*, chicken coop.) Sanborn Map Company, "Insurance Maps of Los Angeles, California," volume 29 (New York: Sanborn Map Company, 1929–1940). Copyright © 1940 Sanborn Map Company, The Sanborn Library, LLC. All Rights Reserved. This Sanborn Map® has been reproduced with written permission from The Sanborn Library, LLC. All further reproductions are prohibited without prior written permission from The Sanborn Library, LLC.

with difficulty. The job itself consumed the spare hours of wage earners who worked by day, then returned at night to put in an hour or two on the house, and more on weekends. As the wife of one owner-builder remarked, "[I]f you think it easy to start from raw land with weeds as high as my head, just you try it. . . . A lot of these folks in grand houses couldn't do this." The building process could drag on for years, forcing families to live with the discomfort and inconvenience of unsealed walls, exposed pipes, bare studs, and strewn materials. One housewife noted, "The back rooms have never been finished although we've lived here for three years. My husband works six days a week and his health hasn't been very well." And the Smith family, as we saw, moved into their house before it had a roof. As the sociologist studying Bell Gardens observed: "We stop to visit a family in a tent. Here's the usual procedure. $20. down, then $10. a month. (1-3 acre.) They move 'on.' They start with anything over their head. Everyone of them full of ambition. They buy a little second-hand lumber. They start to build. Piece by piece. Week by week. They make progress. Their expense is nil. With a little left over they buy more lumber. They add to. They improve. They sow a lawn. Plant a garden. They 'connect the lights.' They install a piece of plumbing. They paint, etc., etc. Some are complete to the last detail. (Old timers.) Others are just starting. You can tell how long they've been there by the progress they've made."[53]

The process of self-building typically involved the entire family. Juanita (Smith) Hammon recalled, "My dad was a good builder, and he had help. My mother was just as good a carpenter as he was. She laid hardwood floors and kept up with him. They used the narrow oak floors, and that living room was 21 feet long. . . . She helped nail those floors in. . . . And all us kids helped. We'd hold a board while my dad was sawing, or we would climb up to take supplies to him, or help hold something. I know I climbed up that ladder many times to take him some more nails or a certain piece of wood he wanted. We all helped build that house." For the more specialized work, Juanita's father hired out a plasterer, electrician, and plumber.[54]

These "jackknife carpenters" built as cheaply as possible, sometimes erecting nothing more than shacks. As longtime resident John Sheehy reminisced, "More than half built them themselves [laughs]. But what did they build? 600 square feet, maybe. Little tiny places. They lived in tents a lot of people. . . . It was as common as dirt. . . . They'd build a little garage that they slept in and cooked out of doors. That was common. We were delivering milk here, and got stiffed for a few milk bills here, I'll tell you that. They were really poor. . . . But [out here] you had a chance, even the working people had a chance because land was cheap, they could scrounge around and buy a lot. . . . [A]nd they'd buy a little bit of lumber every month and put in a foundation, mix it by hand. I saw hundreds of them do that." The "shack" was particularly common in Home Gardens. As Juanita (Smith) Hammon remembered, many residents built their own homes, "and a lot of them did it badly, because there was no inspection."[55]

The typical South Gate home was a modest bungalow consisting of one bedroom, a living room, a kitchen, and a bathroom. On the smaller thirty-foot frontage lots, offset requirements meant a home could measure only eighteen feet across. The Bell Gardens sociologist described such a structure:"[A]ny layman may see that this strange box-like affair is much too tall and long for its depth and that the one next to it looks for all the world like a stucco shoe box with a hole gouged in the side. Here is a perfectly cubical building about half the size of a one-car garage and covered with tar paper. It is not a chicken coop or a rabbit pen but the home of a family. There is a *little* bungalow which with the addition of a porch and the application of paint might prove to be attractive; but no, it is left porchless and eaveless, and the combinations of oranges and yellows used in the painting are enough to make even the soul of a toughened social worker writhe in agony." To make matters worse, some of these homes were constructed of poor materials. During the 1920s, magnesite stucco was a popular type of construction material across Southern California. When the magnesite got wet, it dissolved and the walls literally crumbled. This spelled inconvenience at the least and disaster at the worst. The presence of the South Gate House Wrecking Company in a community just over a decade old was poetic testimony to the quality of local housing.[56]

The ways residents used their homes reflected their aspiration for economic security. While property in South Gate won no prizes for appearance, it was highly valued for its function as a site of domestic production. In backyards, residents raised vegetables, fruits, and small animals for home consumption and sale. A rabbit hutch or chicken pen were common sights, as was the occasional milk goat. Even the local doctor's family raised rabbits and a home garden, critical during lean years when cash was scarce and patients couldn't pay their bills. As these practices flourished, they created a distinctly rural veneer in South Gate. "Chickens and other poultry . . . entering my Home Gardens properties," warned one resident in 1924, "will provide excellent short-range practice for me with my new Winchester repeating shot gun."[57]

South Gate and neighboring suburbs supported the raising of small livestock and home gardens in several ways. In South Gate, city ordinances allowed residents to raise chickens, ducks, geese, fowl, and rabbits in a backyard, as long as they were kept at least twenty feet from the closest neighbor. Up to fifty chickens were permissible. Local shops supported these practices as well. Several feed stores supplied scratch feed for chickens and barley for rabbits, and local builders advertised to construct chicken houses and other small livestock shelters. In 1928, local rabbit growers formed the South East Rabbit Club in nearby Compton. They held several large "Rabbit Shows" in the late 1920s, attracting thousands of growers and interested onlookers. South Gate hosted the show in 1929. Finally, the local papers lent advice to self-provisioners. "If you have poultry troubles," urged the *Southgate Gardener* in 1919, "write them to the 'Poultry Department,' 611 S. Hill St., and real advice will be supplied." Other articles offered detailed advice on planting and cultivating backyard gardens, a practice begun with the victory garden movement during World War I and sustained after the war.[58]

Food produced in backyard gardens was consumed at home, sold, and bartered. Home consumption made good economic sense for working-class residents. Food represented 35.7 percent of the consumer spending of a typical industrial wage earner in 1929, amounting to roughly $551. (This was significantly more than the 27.8 percent spent on housing.) If a family raised fruits, vegetables, chickens, and rabbits on their property, a substantial portion of that bill could be saved. John Sheehy remembered that residents grew produce for their own use since "pennies counted in those days."[59]

Selling homegrown produce and poultry was also common in South Gate and Los Angeles as a whole. As early as 1913, thirty-two hundred small growers peddled their produce at several thriving municipal markets. Many owners of suburban land, even as small as quarter-acre lots, raised produce expressly to sell. J. C. McGrayne, Southgate Gardens resident and realtor, grew a mixed crop of potatoes, corn, cantaloupe, and lettuce in his first year. He earned $198 from this harvest, claiming, "I have been able to accomplish the above results while actively engaged each day in business." Backyard chicken growers could sell excess livestock to the many poultry farms that lined Atlantic Avenue, just north of South Gate.[60]

As well, many neighbors participated in a local, informal barter network. Juanita (Smith) Hammon recalled the importance of this exchange for working families: "Sometimes residents would trade vegetables, they would exchange produce if someone had a big crop of this or that. Instead of money, like bartering. There was all that land around. I remember one lady saying, 'Why do they bother growing produce when it's so cheap anyway?' Well they were cheap according to her. She was buying vegetables for a penny a bunch. But when they're a penny a bunch and you don't have the penny, they're expensive."[61]

The appearance and function of property in South Gate show how working-class aspirations for security defined the meaning of suburban living for these residents. In most cases, they favored the use value over the commodity value of their homes. While some early speculative buying occurred in South Gate mainly in the northwest section, the practice subsided by 1924, when an overwhelming majority of building permits were issued to individual homeowners.[62] In their quest for independence, residents launched the community in a direction to best meet their needs. Ironically, South Gate's working-class residents had more control over their environment than middle-class inhabitants of the typical garden suburb. Since they couldn't afford a well-developed community, it was up to them to create one.

SOME "TRAJECTORIES" OF EARLY SOUTH GATE

The social meaning of a suburb like South Gate unfolds most vividly in the physical landscape. Drawing on scattered sources that give clues about this landscape, it becomes possible to imagine our way into this scene, to visualize the physical textures, to feel the balances between built and open spaces, to sense the presence of ruralism within suburbia. By reading land use and fire insurance maps, we can take an imaginary drive through South Gate of the late 1920s and 1930s, observing the landscapes that pass us by.[63]

We begin in northwest South Gate, the original town site (see fig. 1-4 for the route of the "tour"). Driving along a residential street like Poplar, we notice immediately how built up this section is, with hardly a vacant lot in sight. The modest homes vary in shape and style, mostly tidy bungalows. Nearly all have small, almost identically sized front yards. These homes consistently sit near the front of their lot, a detached garage hidden in the back. At the end of the block, we reach an open, wide boulevard, with lots of vacant lots and scattered stores in each direction. This is Long Beach Boulevard, a major commercial thoroughfare that still awaits development. Turning south down Long Beach, we pass by Herb's Liquor Store on the corner, with a small home tucked behind it. Attached to the liquor store is Penn's Lawnmower Exchange. After passing an empty lot, we come upon a cluster of six adjoining storefronts, including the South Gate Ornamental Iron Works, Mac's Furniture, and the Firestone Social Club, followed by another expanse of empty lots. A few more stores and homes are visible in the distance. On the next block, a lone store and small, adjoining house are the only occupants, standing out in an expanse of vacant land. A few yards down we pass the railroad tracks of the Southern Pacific. We follow the railroad tracks westward, pass another neat row of homes, a multifamily bun-

Figure 1-6   This 1930 view of the Firestone Tire and Rubber plant, just outside of South Gate, shows that factories were an integral part of the landscape in working-class suburbia. The abundance of cheap land attracted many branch plants like Firestone to Los Angeles. From the *Los Angeles Examiner,* Hearst Collection. Photo courtesy of University of Southern California, on behalf of the USC Library Department of Special Collections.

galow court on the corner, then come suddenly upon the backside of the sprawling Firestone Tire and Rubber plant. We travel south along the plant's edge, until we reach the elegant facade that houses its managers and clerks. The sprawling factory looms massively against the small homes that surround it.

To the south of the plant are open fields, with only eight residences scattered on them. Continuing south, residences become increasingly sparse. Turning east on Glenwood Place, we enter a more random collection of homes. Looking to our right, we pass three vacant lots, then three homes that sit side by side with a similar design. But behind the second home we catch glimpse of a duplex tucked in the backyard, probably an owner-built dwelling. Across the street sits another modest structure, tucked modestly at the back of its lot. We come upon a bungalow court for eight families, tiny adjoining structures surrounding a small courtyard. Then four more vacant lots, followed by a tiny cottage sitting at the back of its lot, surely a jerry-built affair. Next, we see a few more homes of varying shapes and sizes, undoubtedly individually built, with vacant lots between them. The sense of open space becomes more and more palpable the farther south we go.

Deep into Home Gardens, the poorer part of town, the homes become even more sparse, more varied in shape. From the desolation of Long Beach Boulevard, we turn east on Illinois Avenue, and notice a few duplexes to our left, then a crooked row of self-built homes sitting here and there, along the back edges of their lots. Fertile gardens are everywhere. And at the end of the block, we come upon a sprawling expanse of row crops, perhaps community gardens for neighbors in the area. Looking southward, we notice more of these large gardens at the end of each block, right in the heart of the suburb. Moving farther south, settlement in Home Gardens becomes thinner yet. Mostly we see empty lots overgrown with weeds. Only a few homes appear in the distance, overshadowed by the enormous GM plant stretching over forty-three acres of land, just beyond South Gate's borders.

We turn around and speed up to the northeast part of town, where we reach Firestone Boulevard, another major thoroughfare. Starting at Alexander, we head east on Firestone. Again, buildings are few and far between. Along the south side of Firestone, an expanse of empty lots stretches out for four blocks—no merchants have settled here yet. To the north, we see industries looming about a hundred yards away: in the distance is the Industrial Lubricants Oil Refinery. A little farther down is the smaller Composition Roofing Manufacturers. Behind the roofers sits the huge Emsco Refractories, the industrial furnace refractory with its cluster of facilities—brick storage sheds, the molding department, the kiln, and clay bins. Down the road sits a lone brick building, housing an office equipment store. We continue driving, passing more empty lots. A block later, we come upon a modest carpentry shop and a building contractor. In the distance to the south, a few houses, with detached garages behind them, dot the landscape in a mostly empty expanse of land. Some of the homes are small, ramshackle affairs, sitting at the rear of their lots. Looking to the left, northward, we see the American Concrete and Steel Pipe factory stretching over its vast property. We pass a long block of empty lots, then finally reach Atlantic Avenue. We turn left, and head north.

A couple of oddly shaped homes stand at the corner, along with a tiny restaurant. Then we come upon a pair of machine shops, one across the street from the other. Wandering up the road, we leave South Gate, crossing into unincorporated territory. Here, we begin to feel like we're in farm country, yet with small factories dotting this rural landscape. Surrounding us on all sides are small homes sitting at the front of long, narrow lots. Behind the homes are profuse gardens, with some chickens and goats. The land feels more rural than ever in this section. A little farther up Atlantic, we come upon the first of several small chicken farms, one lined up against the next. Swarms of chickens are everywhere. A home and garage sit at the front of the large chicken ranches, as cars pass up and down Atlantic—reminding us that we are still in the suburbs, that this is still the heart of the Los Angeles metropolis. In this spot, suburban, industrial, and rural blur into a common landscape.

The sociologist of Bell Gardens recorded a description of that community in the mid-1930s, conveying an even more visceral sense of place. "As one visits Bell Gardens for the first time, he is impressed by the large number of open spaces. The tiny houses set on large lots seem scattered about with little attempt at order, and tall weeds grow in between. Some streets are relatively free from this unkempt appearance, but for the most part an impression of disorder is predominant. If one invades Bell Gardens by automobile, he must travel along a narrow oiled road without curbs or sidewalks and bordered, in clear weather, by fine dust. The land is flat and seems even more so because of the scarcity of trees which are present only in a thin line of eucalyptus which runs along Florence Avenue."

As his narrative tour continued, he began to record his impressions of the people, offering a glimpse into the rhythms of life in the working-class suburb."If one should alight from his automobile and wander around the streets some bright afternoon he would experience contact with a type of social life which the great city seldom offers. For when houses are small, and the whole family works at house building (along with a dozen other families on the same streets), when money is scarce, employment irregular, and problems common, people cannot avoid contacts with at least their immediate neighbors. Should one walk onto a side street in a relatively new area he would feel almost as if he had walked accidentally into the bosom of some one's family. . . . Children play in the streets, on lawns, and in dusty dooryards. Women dig industrously [sic], sit in a spot of shade, or perhaps wash clothes in the open. Men work in gardens, on houses, or on automobiles. On a sunny afternoon people are to be seen everywhere, and the stranger is necessarily in the midst of a dozen households. As the areas grow older, hedges and houses begin to shield the populace, and the more urgent construction jobs have been done; but even in the oldest sections, the streets are social gathering places of no mean importance."[64]

In the interwar years, the working-class suburb was, thus, far from the sleepy bedroom community of the postwar period. It was a bustling, coarse neighborhood where domestic property was a locus of ongoing productive labor, where rural and urban rhythms blurred, where working people struggled to make ends meet, and where space and structures often enabled them to succeed in this struggle.

2   Peopling the Suburb

The year is 1926, the place is South Gate. Again imagining our way into this time and place, we take a walk down Garden View Avenue, past the homes and people of the neighborhood. Starting at the northern end of the street, we work our way south and begin to see the faces of the suburb. In the first house lives a pump fitter and his wife. Next door to them is a bookkeeper and his family, whose neighbor is a manager. In the next houses are a clerk, and then an oil worker, a conductor, and an electrician. Then follows the Treptow residence, home of Officer Frederick Treptow, his wife Martha, and their daughter Winnifred, who works as a cashier. Their next-door neighbors are Mr. and Mrs. Suesmilch, a retired couple. In the next homes live a bookkeeper and his wife, followed by a cement contractor, and finally a laborer. We cross the street to head back north. The first house is owned by an auto mechanic and his family. A vacant lot sits next to them, providing a bit of open space; the Wagners, owners of a bakery, live on the other side. In the next houses are another auto mechanic, followed by a brakeman, a painter, and an electrician who works for the city. Next to him is Andrew Schoby, who owns a service station and serves as mayor of South Gate. A house is under construction on the next lot, followed by the homes of a glass worker, a cabinetmaker, and a bookbinder. Finally, in the last house on the block, a watchman lives with his family. On Garden View Avenue, blue- and white-collar workers live side by side. At the same time, every head of household is married and owns his home—and everyone is white.[1]

In prewar South Gate, the admission ticket into the suburb was the color of your skin and the ability to get a home. If you were white, you were welcome. If you could procure or build your own home, you were welcome. These were the most important filters sifting newcomers to the community, the requirements for becoming a suburbanite, and as such the most important defining features of the local populace. Class was a much less significant factor. As a result, people who spanned the occupational spectrum —from professionals to domestics, from business owners to unskilled laborers—could find their way into South Gate, as long as they had the right skin color, a house, and the inclination for such a lifestyle.

The socioeconomic landscape of South Gate, thus, suggests that homeownership and race were more important in determining inclusion in the community than occupation. Indeed in Los Angeles as a whole, suburban living often blurred the line between job strata, allowing residents of various occupations to coexist as neighbors. A surprising number of L.A. suburbs—large and small—had such occupational diversity, suggesting this was the normative profile there (see table 2-1).[2]

In South Gate, class diversity, perhaps minor at the surface, set the stage for local politics. Certain class divisions eventually translated into important political schisms. While most residents coexisted peacefully, South Gate's small elite of businessmen and boosters distanced—and sometimes alienated—themselves from the rest by exerting their local power in unpopular ways. The contestations between the suburb's petite bourgeoisie and wage earners showed that despite their common status as property owners, divergent class interests overshadowed this shared identity. Yet property ownership continued to exert its influence, even in the thick of these conflicts. Indeed, it became the linchpin of workers' class interests as defined in the community. In this way, working-class interests and identity, divorced from workplace concerns, were forged in the neighborhood. It was an identity that hinged on the workers' status as suburbanites. And this status, as we bring it full circle, hinged on race and housing.

A DEMOGRAPHIC PROFILE

From 1920 to 1940, South Gate's population grew at a rapid pace, transforming the suburb from a skeletal subdivision into a bona fide community. Even in the face of this major human influx, the suburb's social restrictions

Table 2-1 Percentage of Residents in Working-Class Jobs, in Suburbs of the L.A.
Metropolitan Area, 1940 (shown as percentage of employed residents)

Suburbs with population less than 15,000			
La Verne (3,092)	71.8	Huntington Beach (3,738)	57.9
El Segundo (3,738)	71.1	El Monte (4,746)	55.3
Azusa (5,209)	69.9	Fullerton (10,442)	55.1
Maywood (10,731)	68.8	Montebello (8,016)	54.9
Signal Hill (3,184)	67.5	Monterey Park (8,531)	54.3
Hawthorne (8,263)	67.4	Anaheim (11,031)	53.1
Glendora (2,822)	66.4	Covina (3,049)	53.1
Torrance (9,950)	65.6	Monrovia (12,807)	51.0
Chino (4,204)	65.5	Sierra Madre (4,581)	45.6
Brea (2,567)	65.4	Hermosa Beach (7,197)	44.6
Bell (11,264)	64.9	Claremont (3,057)	44.2
Lynwood (10,982)	63.6	San Gabriel (11,867)	43.4
San Fernando (9,094)	62.8	Arcadia (9,122)	42.0
Culver City (8,976)	61.9	Manhattan Beach (6,398)	40.0
Gardena (5,909)	61.7	S Pasadena (14,356)	32.0
Redondo Beach (13,092)	58.9	San Marino (8,175)	31.5

Suburbs with population greater than 15,000			
Belvedere (37,192)	70.5	Inglewood (30,114)	52.5
South Gate (26,945)	63.8	Whittier (16,115)	52.0
Compton (16,198)	57.3	Pasadena (81,864)	50.6
Huntington Park (28,648)	55.2	Santa Ana (31,921)	46.2
Burbank (34,337)	54.1	Alhambra (38,935)	41.7
Pomona (23,539)	53.7	Glendale (82,582)	40.7
Santa Monica (53,500)	53.2	Beverly Hills (26,823)	33.5
Total LA metro area (1.2 million)	51.9		

Notes: Individual populations of suburbs are given in parentheses. "Working-class jobs" include the census categories of craftsmen and foremen, operatives, laborers, service workers, and farmworkers. Because the suburbs of Avalon, Palos Verdes, Vernon, and West Covina had populations below 2,500, they were not enumerated for occupations by the census.

Source: U.S. Bureau of the Census, *Sixteenth Census of the United States, 1940. Population.* vol. 2, *Characteristics of the Population. Part 1* (Washington, D.C.: GPO, 1943), 558, 592-598, 614-620, 668. Data compiled by Laura Schiesl.

ensured that these newcomers conformed to certain demographic characteristics. As a result, South Gate's demography remained fairly static during these years in terms of race, ethnicity, family structure, age, and education. Put simply, early South Gate was a community of modestly educated, native-born whites in nuclear families.

Table 2-2   South Gate Population Increases, 1920–1970

	Population	Rate of change from previous decade (in %)
1920	500	—
1930	19,632	3,826
1940	26,945	37
1950	51,116	90
1960	53,831	5
1970	56,909	6

Sources: Bicentennial Heritage Committee, *South Gate, 1776–1976* (South Gate: South Gate Press, 1976), 9; U.S. Bureau of the Census, *Fifteenth Census of United States: 1930, Population,* vol. 3, *Composition and Characteristics, Part 1* (Washington, D.C., GPO, 1932) 262; idem, *Sixteenth Census of the United States, 1940: Population,* vol. 2, *Characteristics of the Population, Part 1* (GPO, 1943), 620; idem, *Seventeenth Census of the United States, Census of Population: 1950,* vol. 2, *Characteristics of the Population, Part 5, California* (GPO, 1952), 5-104; idem, *U.S. Census of Population: 1960,* vol. 1, *Characteristics of the Population, Part 6, California* (GPO, 1963), 6–55; idem, *Nineteenth Census of the United States, Census of Population: 1970,* vol. 1, *Characteristics of the Population, Part 6, California* (GPO, 1971), 6–14.

While South Gate's population climbed ever since it first became a suburb in 1917, certain periods saw explosive growth. The 1920s experienced the highest rate of all, jumping from 500 to 19,632. This increase reflected three factors: the quick expansion of a young community that started from nothing, a steady influx of migrants, and the annexation to South Gate of neighboring subdivisions, such as Home Gardens, Magnolia Park, and Hollydale. Home Gardens, for example, was substantially populated when it became part of South Gate in 1927. Even the Great Depression did not halt the trend; the population increased 37 percent during the 1930s (see table 2-2).

The racial and ethnic makeup of South Gate remained fairly constant in the midst of this expansion. Racially, the suburb remained lily-white throughout the prewar period, proof that local race restrictions were working. Only two blacks—both adult males—showed up on the census rolls in 1930 and 1940. Their numbers stayed this low, never exceeding ten people, up to the mid-1960s. Ethnically, South Gate—like many Southern California communities—appeared to be re-creating the demography of the early nineteenth-century Northeast. In the interwar years, nearly 90 percent of residents were native-born whites, with the remainder "old immigrants."[3] While the origins of these natives are difficult to determine, it is possible to infer certain patterns from general Los Angeles data.[4] The largest group of native-born Los Angelenos came from the Midwest (nearly 40 percent), followed by Pacific states, the South, and the mid-Atlantic states. Fully 23 percent came from Oklahoma, Texas, Arkansas, and Missouri in the 1930s.

Most migrants hailed from either very urban or very rural areas; the majority relocated from cities whose populaces exceeded 50,000 both in 1920 and 1930. Many newcomers thus had some experience with urban living and brought with them urban cultural and political sensibilities.[5]

Scattered sources suggest that South Gate shared these demographics, with one exception: a sizable number hailed from the Great Plains. Longtime residents recalled that many newcomers, particularly in Home Gardens, came from Arkansas, Oklahoma, Tennessee, and Texas. They settled not only in South Gate but also in neighboring Bell, Bell Gardens, Maywood, and Lynwood. Although these communities would not become true "Little Oklahomas"—the diversity of origins was too wide—they did contain sizable populations from the Great Plains and the South. In the 1920s, these residents represented the precursors to the "Okie" and "Arkie" migrations of the Depression decade. In the 1930s, they came as part of this important migrant stream. Los Angeles, in fact, was the prime destination of the dust bowl exodus, taking in more refugees than any other region of California. Nearly 100,000 Oklahomans, Texans, Arkansans, and Missourians settled in Los Angeles from 1935 to 1940. Most of them hailed from urban areas, while rural migrants tended to settle in the agricultural regions of the state.[6] These migrants embraced a sociopolitical culture that James Gregory has characterized as plain-folk Americanism, rooted in the long-lived political and cultural traditions of southwestern agrarianism. This ideological persuasion valued "hard work and plain living and promised deliverance from the forces of power, privilege, and moral pollution, near and far." It adapted old traditions to new circumstances and challenges. Elements of this persuasion, such as a neopopulism that glorified producers, independence, and nativism, predisposed these newcomers to certain strains of political thought that found a fertile seedbed in Los Angeles's working-class suburbs.[7]

Many of South Gate's newcomers came as part of chain migrations, where family or friends spurred others to migrate. This process reinforced social ties and common beliefs after their arrival. Ruth Barrett's family moved west because a former neighbor in Ohio had recently settled in Huntington Park, an adjacent suburb, and encouraged them to come out. Juanita Smith and her family came to Home Gardens at the behest of her uncle Walter. Virgil Collins and his aunt, who raised him, migrated from Marion, Ohio, because his aunt's younger brother urged them to join him in Southern California. Wallace McFadden's family of eleven came from a Philadelphia suburb to Los Angeles after frequent letters from his father's close friend urged them to relocate.[8]

The remaining foreign-born population constituted a minor presence in South Gate. From 1930 through the 1960s, their numbers never exceeded 10 percent of the total population, and even declined slightly over these years. They constituted 9.4 percent in 1930 and 7.1 percent in 1940. Furthermore, the composition of this foreign element helped mitigate against ethnic tension in the community. Up to 1940, the largest immigrant groups were from Canada, England, and Germany, in descending order. Mostly English-speakers with long immigrant traditions in America, these newcomers adjusted rather easily to their new environs. One clue of this was that they did not cluster in residential enclaves but instead were dispersed throughout the suburb. "New immigrants" from eastern and southern Europe were a minuscule presence in South Gate, making up only about 1 percent of the population up to 1940. Even less conspicuous were Latinos. Up to 1940, all Latinos—first- and second-generation immigrants from Mexico and Central and South America—were a mere 0.3 percent of the population, numbering only fifty-nine in 1940. This paralleled the disproportionately low representation of Latinos in many white suburbs of L.A. during this period, a result of exclusionary practices. The Asian population actually declined in South Gate before World War II: from 1930 to 1940, the number of Japanese dropped from fifty-three to eleven, while the five Chinese enumerated in 1930 disappeared altogether by 1940.[9] Thus, in its first two decades, South Gate constituted itself as a suburb of white, English-speaking Americans. Apart from the plain-folk Americanism of native-born whites, there was a notable absence of ethnic traditions to shape the beliefs and behaviors of the local populace.

In terms of social composition, South Gate was a suburb of nuclear families in the early stages of family formation. In 1930, the median family size was 3.11 persons, and a whopping 44 percent of these families had children under ten years of age, a rate substantially higher than in many areas, including the county and state. The result was a relatively young population. Youth under twenty years old made up about one-third of the population during the interwar years. The working-age population (twenty to fifty-nine years old) constituted about 60 percent, while people over sixty represented only 4 percent of residents. This age distribution was unsurprising. Like many suburban communities, South Gate drew people seeking a family-friendly environment of single-family homes, yards, and open spaces. The fact that South Gate's age distribution held fairly steady to 1940 suggests that the community was successfully fulfilling a particular phase in the life cycle of its families. The nuclear family was the primary social unit in South Gate. In 1930, about three-quarters of all adults (age fifteen and older) in the suburb were married, while 17 percent were single, 6 percent widowed, and 2 percent divorced. Yet even many of these singles were attached to nuclear families. In 1930, only 6 percent of households comprised one person, while 90 percent of families contained from two to five members, suggesting that single adults too lived with nuclear family or relatives.[10]

The frequency of young, working adults living with parents attested to the importance of the nuclear family and its economic centrality to the lives of residents. In 1926, 18 percent of homeowning families had wage-earning offspring living with them.[11] Through such a living arrangement, these young adults both lent and received support from families. At the Darsey residence on Dearborn Avenue, for example, three working sons—an auto mechanic, a lineman, and a salesman—lived with the parents. The Smith family's adult daughter and her husband lived with them for a few years after their wedding. The couple eventually saved enough money to purchase a small "shack" one block away for $500 (at the back of the lot, of course), which they later rebuilt. In the Collins family, three brothers lived with their aunt after their mother died and until each were married. All three brothers worked and contributed their earnings to family expenses, like food and bills. At one point during the Depression, Virgil, nine years younger than the next oldest brother, was the only family member working, earning 12 cents an hour at a factory that made wooden milk boxes. Family cohesion was reinforced by the challenges of working-class life, demanding the pooling of resources and labor to keep the household ship afloat.[12]

School attendance figures reveal the working-class nature of the suburb before World War II. In 1930, while nearly all youngsters under sixteen attended school, the figure dropped off slightly for sixteen- to seventeen-year olds (83.9 percent), then fell dramatically at the college level. Only about 24 percent of South Gate's young adults attended college, a figure markedly lower than in other L.A. neighborhoods and the state (in California, nearly 40 percent of college-aged people attended school). A similar pattern prevailed in 1940, with very high attendance through high school, then a sharp drop at the college level. Even so, the suburb's youth were better educated than their elders. Of adults over twenty-five in 1940, fully 64 percent had not completed high school (the median school years completed was 10.4), compared to roughly 90 percent of students in 1940. Yet overall, South Gate's population possessed the basics of educational competency, illustrated by the fact that the local literacy rate was over 99 percent.[13]

All in all, South Gate was relatively homogeneous in its social makeup. The vast majority of residents were native-born whites from the Midwest and Great Plains, modestly educated, and clustered in nuclear families. Lots of children filled the suburb's dirt roads and vacant lots. The minuscule immigrant and minority populations were barely noticeable, either because of their small numbers or the "acculturated" nature of their ethnicity. The suburb sustained this profile for the first two decades after its founding, even as waves of newcomers arrived. Thus, even under the pressures of explosive growth, it appeared that the early social restrictions were working.

AN ECONOMIC PROFILE

The suburb's homogeneity ended, however, when it came to class. Although wage earners in blue-collar jobs predominated, they lived beside professionals, proprietors, and white-collar employees. The coexistence of blue- and white-collar residents set the stage for conflict at the local level, which often arranged itself by class. Hence, the economic profile of the community offers a critical setting to this story, two key aspects of which are occupations and housing.

The occupational character of South Gate revealed a subtle but notable change in the 1920s and 1930s. The suburb began with a significant white-collar presence in the mid-1920s, then emerged as a wage earners' town by 1940. Reflecting changes in the metropolitan economy, South Gate's labor force evolved in tandem with the growth of industry in Los Angeles.

In the mid-1920s, South Gate showed marked class diversity (see table 2-3). Fully one-fifth of the population held high-level white-collar positions, as professionals, managers, and proprietors. About 19 percent were low-level white-collar workers in clerical and sales positions. Blue-collar workers made up the largest group, constituting 55 percent of the labor force, while service workers were about 4 percent. Most manual workers were skilled craftsmen, followed in descending order by operatives, unskilled laborers, and service workers. More specifically, in 1926 the largest occupational groups (in descending order) were carpenters, laborers, clerks, salespersons, and auto mechanics. The relatively high proportion of white-collar workers reflected the fact that industry had not yet fully arrived, although the region stood on the cusp of an industrial boom. Instead, occupations were more oriented to downtown stores and offices, and suburban expansion. A good number of jobs related to the production and sale of homes: carpenters, construction bosses, and realtors were all well represented. This occupational distribution was also a result of the suburb's early borders, which encompassed only the original northwest area in 1926. Adjacent tracts like poorer Home Gardens had not yet joined South Gate. Even despite these class variations, South Gate in the 1920s was overwhelmingly comprised of wage earners: 77 percent of locals held low-level white-collar or manual labor jobs, while about 22 percent were professionals or proprietors.

Table 2-3 Occupational Distribution of South Gate Residents, 1926–1970
(Percentage of Total Workforce)

	1926	1930	1940	1950	1960	1970
High-level white-collar						
Professionals	7.8	5.4	5.7	7.9	7.1	7.9
Managers, officials	9.9	6.6	8.8[a]	11.3[a]	6.8	6.2[a]
Proprietors	4.1	5.7			1.1	
Low-level white-collar						
Clerical, kindred	10.5	9.1	21.0[b]	17.3	21.8	25.1
Sales	8.3	8.0		8.3	7.2	5.9
Blue-collar						
Craftsmen, foremen	29.8	22.0	21.9	21.2	19.2	18.3
Operatives, kindred	16.2	34.9	27.4	23.6	23.6	24.1
Laborers	8.9	2.6	5.3	3.1	2.8	3.6
Service						
Domestics	0	0.3	1.7	0.8	0.7	0.7
Service (except domestic)	3.7	5.4	7.1	5.8	6.4	8.0
Farm						
Farmers	0.8		0.3	0.1	0.1	0.1
Farmworkers	0		0.4	0.2	—	0.2
Not reported			0.7	0.5	3.3	
Total[c]	100	100	100	100	100	100

[a]Figure combines managers, officials, and proprietors.
[b]Figure combines clerical, sales, and kindred workers.
[c]Total figures are rounded off

Notes: 1926 figures determined from a 50% sample of city directory; 1930 figures from a 5% sample. 1926 figures also excluded Home Gardens and other areas annexed to South Gate by 1929.

Sources: Arthur Newton, *City and Telephone Directory of South Gate, 1926* (South Gate: Tribune News Publishing Co., 1926); idem, *City and Telephone Directory of Greater South Gate, 1930*; U.S. Bureau of the Census, *Sixteenth Census of the United States, 1940: Population,* vol. 2, *Characteristics of the Population* (Washington D.C.: GPO, 1943), 620; idem, *Seventeenth Census of the United States, Census of Population: 1950,* vol. 2, *Characteristics of the Population, Part 5, California* (GPO, 1952), 5-124; idem, *Eighteenth Census of the United States, Census of Population: 1960,* vol. 1, *Characteristics of the Population, Part 6, California* (GPO, 1963), 6-322; idem, *Nineteenth Census of the United States, Census of Population: 1970,* vol. 1, *Characteristics of the Population, Part 6, California* (GPO, 1971), 6-512.

During the Depression, the suburb became more decisively working class. The proportion of professionals, managers, and proprietors fell from 18 to 15 percent in the 1930s; these were concentrated in finance, insurance, real estate, and government. In turn, the wage-earning populace swelled to more than 80 percent of the workforce. While workers in clerical and sales jobs represented nearly one-fifth of the total, the majority of wage earners

held blue-collar jobs. By 1930, an important shift among this group surfaced: semiskilled operatives now ranked as the largest group, followed by
skilled craftsmen and foremen, then unskilled laborers. The predominance
of semiskilled workers—consistently the largest occupational group in
South Gate from the 1930s to the 1960s—in part reflected the emergent industrial labor market of Los Angeles.

From 1910 to 1940, Los Angeles evolved from a regional backwater to
an industrial powerhouse, ranking eighth nationally in manufacturing by
1924 and fifth by 1935. Up to 1920, the metropolitan economy was centered
around trade, the professions, and service, it was regionally oriented, and it
lacked a substantial manufacturing base. This changed in the 1920s. The
transformation was propelled by massive population growth: the metropolitan population jumped from 936,000 to 2.2 million, making it the
largest western city by far.[14] This boom—driven by real estate, oil, and the
film industry—stimulated the industrialization of Los Angeles. As one
economist noted in 1939, "Los Angeles is sharply differentiated from other
metropolitan centers, in that the industrial activity of the community
largely developed in response to the needs of a growing population,
whereas in most metropolitan areas, the employment needs of increasing
industrial activity led to the immigration of population."[15] In the 1920s,
Los Angeles's rate of industrial growth exceeded all major American cities.
Led by the fast-growing petroleum, motion-picture, meatpacking, and
printing industries, Los Angeles outranked all Pacific coast cities in manufacturing output by 1929.[16]

Branch plants of eastern industries helped drive this early growth. Attracted by thriving markets, an abundance of cheap land, easy access to raw
materials, low-cost utilities, and good transportation, eastern firms considered Southern California an auspicious region in which to expand. Furthermore, the city's open-shop reputation and low wages boded well to eastern
industrialists hoping to minimize labor costs.[17] By the end of the 1930s,
nearly two hundred branch plants were operating in Los Angeles. One
economist noted that the influx of "eastern factories" had caused "an industrial community to spring up in Los Angeles almost over night. Instead
of a long period of slow and painful growth, these industries suddenly came
into being."[18]

Even during the Depression the industrial sector continued to grow and
diversify, after a decline in the early 1930s. Although by 1933 industrial activity fell in Los Angeles to 60 percent of its 1929 level, it took a smaller hit
than in most eastern industrial cities. And the region recovered relatively
quickly.[19] From 1930 to 1939, 3,350 plants were established or expanded,
generating 76,000 new jobs.[20] By 1937, the value of Los Angeles's industrial

output exceeded the pre-Depression level of 1929, and thirty-six different industries each generated an annual output exceeding $5 million, showing impressive diversification. By 1939, the top L.A. industrial employers were, in descending order, motion pictures, food processing, apparel, aircraft, furniture, oil refining, rubber, auto assembly, and oil-well equipment. These industries employed 71 percent of the city's industrial workforce in 1939. The revival of the construction industry, bolstered by federal relief programs, also propelled Los Angeles's economic recovery. By the late 1930s, the city had emerged as an industrial center of national stature. It ranked first nationally in employment in motion pictures, aircraft, and oil-well equipment, while the city's auto industry ranked second only to Detroit, and its rubber industry second to Akron. By 1935, L.A. County was considered the largest industrial area west of Chicago.[21]

Mike Davis and Greg Hise have analyzed the diversity of Los Angeles's industrial landscape. The metropolis possessed a highly distinctive industrial geography during the interwar years, marked both by clustering at the urban core and dispersal to the suburbs. Industrial zones, Davis writes, "correlated with surprising fidelity to firm size, market orientation, capitalization, and dominant labor process." The East Side Industrial District was the city's old industrial center, concentrated east of Alameda Street between Broadway and Ninth Streets. These factories were typically locally owned, labor-intensive operations like apparel and food processing, and they produced mainly for home markets. A second industrial zone was dominated by branch plants for automobiles, tires, and steel. They produced for home markets at first, expanded into western regional markets, then achieved national ranking by the late 1930s. These factories clustered southeast of downtown in the Central Manufacturing District (CMD), the industrial suburb of Vernon, the Union Pacific Industrial District, and suburbs in southern Los Angeles. GM and Firestone, located in the South Gate area, were prime examples of such branch plants. Farther afield, scattered in the agricultural periphery, were industries producing for national markets, including motion pictures, oil, and, after 1940, aircraft; these constituted a third industrial zone. "[T]he suburban enclaves," Davis notes, "were favored locations for the extraordinarily large assemblages of craft labor— 'flexible manufacturing'—intrinsic to motion pictures and airframe manufacture."[22]

Southern Los Angeles, in fact, became an important center of industry, a result of several factors. On one level, the dispersal of industry southward reflected trends of industrial deconcentration occurring nationally. This diffusion was influenced by the emergence of auto and truck transportation, which freed manufacturers from a dependence on downtown

transportation nodes; Fordist production processes, which encouraged hor-
izontal expansion and hence locations on the urban periphery where land
was cheap and plentiful; and business pressure to physically disperse workers as a means of thwarting labor organization.[23] Certain characteristics
specific to Los Angeles promoted industrialization in the southern suburbs.
The development of major truck highways and a consolidated harbor railroad system made it cheap and easy to move goods from the southern suburbs to the port of San Pedro. The natural geography of oil reserves, which
swept across southern Los Angeles, further promoted working-class residential and industrial suburbanization. A final factor was zoning. In 1908,
Los Angeles passed the first major land-use zoning law in the United States,
eight years before the more famous New York City measure. This legislation created seven industrial districts—mainly along the L.A. River and the
railroad lines that traversed the central, eastern, and southern suburbs—
and reserved the west side for "higher class residential areas." City leaders
believed such a plan would allow Los Angeles to avoid the urban congestion
typical of older industrial cities and to maximize accessibility for workers.
Despite numerous zoning variances granted by the city in the western residential section, this plan established a general schema that guaranteed an
industrial future for southern Los Angeles.[24]

A great many L.A. plants required semiskilled labor, and they drew on
workers from suburbs like South Gate. For male workers in South Gate, the
largest employer was construction; this was true in the mid-1920s and
again in 1940. The local plethora of construction workers undoubtedly
facilitated the owner-building of homes. By 1930, a more diversified industrial base supplied jobs to locals. Among semiskilled operatives—the
biggest occupational group in the suburb—the largest number worked in
rubber (most likely at nearby Firestone Tire & Rubber), followed by oil refineries, trucking, and welding. Skilled craftsmen worked as machinists, auto
mechanics, foremen, painters, and electricians. Among low-level white-
collar workers, salespeople and clerks had the highest representation. By
1940, industrial employment continued to diversify for local male workers.
While construction continued to hold the lead, this was followed closely by
iron and steel, machinery, automobiles, food, transportation equipment
(except auto), and oil, in descending order. South Gate's residents found
jobs in places like Bethlehem Steel and Hercules Foundries in nearby Vernon, the GM plant next to South Gate, Willys Overland and Chrysler near
Bell Gardens, and the oil refineries that spread southward. Because of the
aggressively open-shop climate in Los Angeles, most workers in these industries lacked unions until the late 1930s, when conditions for organized
labor improved.[25]

In South Gate, women gradually entered the paid workforce in the years before World War II. Although representing only 5 percent of the workforce in 1926, by 1940 they constituted one-fifth of all workers. Seen another way, 22 percent of adult women (fifteen and older) in South Gate then worked for wages. Most women found work in clerical and sales positions—the "pink-collar" sector. Fully 65 percent of women earning a paycheck were employed in such jobs in 1926. By 1940, women found a much broader range of jobs. Although most still worked in pink-collar positions, many found work as semiskilled operatives, while some were employed as service workers, professionals, domestics, and proprietors (see table 5-1). Factory women found jobs in apparel, food processing, glass, iron and steel, and paper plants. Overall, while women concentrated in pink- and blue-collar semiskilled jobs, there was a notable range of occupations among them.[26]

Despite their small numbers, the merchant class was critical to the history of South Gate. They were a highly self-conscious class—perhaps the most self-conscious of all—who frequently voiced their hopes and concerns. They consistently held positions of local political power, exerting influence over the community and shaping it to serve their interests. Because they played such a central role in the South Gate story, they deserve careful attention.

Merchants composed only between 4 and 6 percent of the local workforce in the interwar years. The predominant businesses were real estate, grocery stores, service stations, restaurants, barbershops, and beauty salons, with a scattering of stores selling building supplies, feed and fertilizer, hardware, and meat. Most proprietors owned and operated their own establishments, while providing few jobs to the suburb's residents. In 1929, for example, they employed only 2.9 percent of local workers.[27] To the merchants, South Gate residents were customers, not employees.

Roughly 75 percent of South Gate's operations had a building devoted specifically to the business, suggesting they were fairly well capitalized. The remainder were home-based enterprises, meaning the home sat on the same property as the business. The latter ranged from substantial business structures with separate housing, to modest affairs amounting to little more than a business sign hung on the home's front porch. Mirroring local self-provisioning practices, these home-based entrepreneurs maximized the economic use of their suburban property. Grocery stores, real estate agencies, restaurants, beauty shops, and mortuaries were the most common home-based businesses. Several residents along Firestone Boulevard, like Alex Bokor and Hugh Friedley, sold groceries on their home lots, while Theodore Arnold and J.C. Hutton ran restaurants. On Tweedy Boulevard, the Hewitt residence served triple duty as a home, a grocery store run by the wife, and a real estate office run by the husband. Typically, the store sat at the front of the lot, with the home in the back.[28]

Some of these operations hardly qualified as businesses. Families that sold rabbits or chickens, a seamstress who sewed or mended for her neighbors for a small price—these entrepreneurs barely crossed the line between domestic and business life. The sociologist of Bell Gardens observed such practices: "The people in Bell Gardens use every possible device to secure an income. Here is a sign nailed to a fence which reads in large gold letter, 'Tattooing' and notes in smaller letter below, 'Social Security Numbers 50c.' Dressmaking signs are relatively frequent, and plumbers and carpenters advertise their services by signs in their door yards. . . . Is this fellow sitting on a corner lot with a few barrels of oil and a rude hut operating a 'business' or not?"[29]

In the interwar years, more and more women joined the ranks of South Gate's proprietors. Although they owned only 5.5 percent of local businesses in 1930, by 1940 they ran 22 percent of them. Women were much more likely than men to run home-based operations. In 1930, nearly half of their shops were home-based, compared to 23 percent for the whole suburb. For women who had fewer opportunities for wage work, operating a home-based business made economic sense. A small grocery, cafe, beauty parlor, or clothing shop—the most common female-run operations—required little capital and could be managed on a small scale. Evelyn Peterson set up "The Cozy Frock Shoppe" in her home, while Ethyl Sobinski and Evelyn Craig transformed living rooms into beauty parlors. Ina Gabriel opened the Chic-Chic Cafe, and Minnie Havener ran the Minnie Mouse Cafe. Their businesses signified a strategy for bypassing the closed door to wage work and generating income from their residential property. By 1940, the simultaneous decline in home-based operations and rise in female-run stores suggest women were increasing their access to capital to open larger shops.[30]

Moderately sized businesses thus dominated the commercial life of South Gate. These proprietors had such a strong hold on local power that they successfully fended off the encroachment of large-scale retailers, like chain stores. From 1926 to 1940, chains as a proportion of total retail establishments dropped from 7.7 percent to 1.3 percent. This occurred even as Los Angeles's larger concerns, like department stores, were rebounding from the Depression. The successful resistance of South Gate's merchants set their community apart from many working-class neighborhoods, where chains frequently gained a foothold during the Depression.[31]

Despite their local political clout, South Gate's businesses trailed behind the retail sectors of neighboring suburbs. In 1929, the annual per capita sales of South Gate's stores was $176, substantially smaller than comparable suburbs. In nearby Compton, Huntington Park, and Inglewood, per capita retail sales ranged from $451 to $487. These communities were relatively similar to South Gate in terms of socioeconomic status and size, although they were older. But even the suburb of Bell, five years younger than South Gate, had per capita retail sales of $393, far ahead of South Gate.[32] The size and type of South Gate's stores were a particular problem. In a period when aggressive advertising was galvanizing a new consumer ethos and inventing demands for extensive variety and brand names, South Gate's shops were sorely out of touch. They were "small businesses, damn small businesses," as one local resident recalled. "A barber, a grocer, a mechanic, garageman—one-man operations." For South Gate's size, it had exceedingly limited retail choices, with no department stores and only two apparel stores. By contrast, nearly all comparably sized neighborhoods had at least one department store and usually two; nearby Huntington Park had four. Compton had seventeen clothing stores, Huntington Park had thirty-seven, and Inglewood had twenty-seven. Even Bell, with 7,800 residents in 1930 compared to South Gate's 19,600, had seven apparel stores. The inferiority of South Gate's retail base impelled many residents to shop elsewhere, which sparked a round of local political conflict. Yet the character of South Gate's retail sector, small in scale and stubbornly protectionist, also attested to the power being consolidated by the suburb's petite bourgeoisie.[33]

An even more important social marker than occupations in South Gate, however, was homeownership, which became so central to the identity of the community's citizenry. The type, value, and tenure of housing were all important indicators. From 1920 to 1940, the vast bulk of local dwellings were single-family homes; in 1930, they constituted 99 percent, and in 1940, 88 percent of total dwellings. This was much higher than in most areas of Los Angeles County. By 1940, duplexes and triplexes gained minor popularity in South Gate, representing about 8 percent of all dwellings. Only a minuscule 1 percent of dwellings were apartments, motor courts, and other facilities accommodating more than five families. Among these were a row of motor hotels that sprang up along Firestone Boulevard, which connected to a major state highway feeding into Los Angeles. Overall, the suburb privileged single-family dwellings while discouraging drifters, singles, and other unattached folk.[34]

The value of South Gate's homes started out comparatively low, then rose by 1940. In 1930, the U.S. Census Bureau registered the median value of South Gate's homes at $4,264, which placed it well behind other working-class neighborhoods, such as Lynwood, Maywood, Torrance, and Compton (see table 2-4). By 1940, South Gate home values fell to $3,260 reflecting the effects of the Depression, but pulled ahead of these same communities, partly because a problem with local tax assessments had been resolved. But building permits in South Gate reflected lower housing values than the U.S. Census figures. These records showed that in 1923, the average home value was $1,470; it rose to $2,695 in 1930, and by 1940 declined to $2,242. In 1935, 95 percent of building permits issued for single-family dwellings in South Gate were for an estimated cost under $4,000.[35]

Homeownership was perhaps the most important indicator of the economic status of residents. Particularly for those who built their homes, the ownership of a house was the raison d'être of suburbia. It also came to represent a critical source of identity for residents, who placed increasing emphasis on this neighborhood-based status. Homeownership rates, thus, tell an important part of the story. Throughout the 1920s, the rate of homeownership was very high in South Gate, compared to national and Los Angeles figures. In 1926, 77 percent of South Gate's adult residents owned their own homes (see table 2-5). If adults living in a home owned by a family member are excluded from the total, the figure jumps to 89 percent—and stayed there until 1929.[36] By 1930 the figure fell to 57 percent, still high compared to L.A. County (42 percent) and the nation (46 percent), then dropped again to 53 percent by 1940. Among South Gate's tiny foreign-born population, the homeownership rate was highest, mirroring national trends. In 1930, about 64 percent of first- and second-generation ethnics owned their own homes, compared to 52 percent of native-born whites. South Gate's one black family rented, a fitting symbol of their exclusion from the true community. Because of the home's critical meaning in working-class suburbia, the changes in homeownership rates had both economic and political repercussions. The notable drop did not happen quietly; rather, it stimulated the most heated political altercations in the suburb's history.[37]

The social geography of South Gate subtly reflected some of the economic variations in occupation and housing status. As with most communities, there were "good" and "bad" parts of town. The northwest section, the original town site of South Gate, was the more prosperous area. In 1940, the labor force there was split equally between blue- and white-collar workers, with the largest occupation group comprising clerks and salespeople. In the rest of South Gate, blue-collar outnumbered white-collar workers almost two to one. Unsurprisingly, the median home value was highest in the northwest section, reaching $3,607 in 1940. By contrast, poorer Home Gardens was dominated by manual laborers from its founding in 1922. In 1930,

Table 2-4 Median Values of Owner-Occupied Homes in Selected L.A. Communities, 1930–1960 (In Dollars, in Descending Order)

1930		1940		1950		1960	
South Pasadena	$9,538	South Pasadena	$5,453	Santa Monica	$13,024	Santa Monica	$22,700
Santa Monica	7,561	Santa Monica	4,511	Pasadena	11,870	South Pasadena	19,400
Pasadena	7,131	Pasadena	4,159	Whittier	11,294	Culver City	19,100
Whittier	6,366	Whittier	3,966	Inglewood	11,277	Inglewood	18,800
Huntington Park	6,302	Inglewood	3,745	Culver City	11,024	Gardena	18,700
Culver City	5,807	Huntington Park	3,681	South Pasadena	10,383	Torrance	17,800
Inglewood	5,161	Culver City	3,603	Huntington Park	9,526	Pasadena	17,500
Bell	4,888	South Gate	3,260	South Gate	9,198	Whittier	16,100
Lynwood	4,871	Lynwood	3,199	Lynwood	9,189	Lynwood	14,200
Torrance	4,805	Bell	3,147	Bell	8,956	Huntington Park	14,000
Gardena Township	4,647	Compton	3,006	Compton	8,920	Bell	13,900
Maywood	4,503	Torrance	2,939	San Fernando	8,806	Redondo Bch	13,800
Compton	4,471	Maywood	2,937	Torrance	8,558	South Gate	13,600
Redondo Beach	4,350	San Fernando	2,677	Gardena	8,442	San Fernando	13,400
South Gate	4,264	Gardena	2,592	Azusa	7,989	Compton	12,800
San Fernando	3,964	Redondo Beach	2,335	Maywood	7,846	Maywood	12,000
Azusa	3,589	Azusa	2,218	Redondo Beach	7,120	Azusa	11,700

Sources: U.S. Bureau of the Census, *Fifteenth Census of the United States, Census of Population: 1930, Population*, vol. 6, *Families* (Washington, D.C.: GPO, 1933), 181–188; idem, *Sixteenth Census of the United States: 1940, Housing*, vol. 2, *General Characteristics, Part 2* (GPO, 1943), 291–293; idem, *Seventeenth Census of the United States, Census of Housing: 1950*, vol. 1, *General Characteristics, Part 2* (GPO, 1953), 5-3 to 5-4; idem, *Eighteenth Census of the United States, Census of Housing: 1960*, vol. 1, *States and Small Areas, Part 2* (GPO, 1963), 6-4 to 6-6; U.S. Home Owners Loan Corporation, City Survey files for Los Angeles, RG 195, NA.

Table 2-5   Homeownership Rates in South Gate
              and the United States, 1920–1970
              (% of total dwelling units)

	South Gate	U.S.[a]
1920	—	40.9%
1926	76.9[b]	—
1929	78.2[b]	—
1930	57.0	46.0
1940	52.5	41.1
1950	69.3	53.4
1960	57.4	61.0
1970	46.9	62.0

[a]U.S. figures for nonfarm areas.
[b]Excluding family lodgers, the South Gate owner-occupied rates
   for 1926 and 1929 rise to 89.1 and 89.7%, respectively.

Sources: Arthur Newton, *City and Telephone Directory of South
   Gate, 1926* (South Gate: Tribune News Publishing Co., 1926);
   idem, *City and Telephone Directory of South Gate, 1929;* U.S.
   Bureau of Census, *Fifteenth Census of the United States, Census of Population: 1930, Population,* vol. 6, *Families* (Washington, D.C.: GPO, 1933), 183; idem, *Sixteenth Census of the U.S.:
   1940, Population,* vol. 2, *Characteristics of the Population*
   (GPO, 1943), 142; idem, *Census of Housing: 1950,* vol. 1, *General Characteristics, Part 2* (GPO, 1953), 5-4; idem, *Eighteenth
   Census of the United States, Census of Housing: 1960,* vol. 1,
   States and Small Areas, Part 2 (GPO, 1963), 6-6; idem, *Nineteenth Census of the United States, U.S. Census of Population
   and Housing: 1970, Census Tracts, Los Angeles—Long Beach,
   California* (GPO, 1972), H-5; idem, *Historical Statistics of the
   United States, Colonial Times to 1970* (GPO, 1975), 646.

71 percent of the labor force there was blue-collar, and median home values
only reached $2,948 in 1940. Even the retail sector reflected these patterns.
Home Gardens had a greater proportion of home-based businesses (38 percent) than the northwest section (30 percent). All in all, Home Gardens was
the workingman's part of town, while the northwest was the province of
professionals, proprietors, and the suburb's putative middle class.[38]

Other nearby working-class suburbs showed a similar class schism. As
in South Gate, the older north side of Bell Gardens was the better part of
town. Residents there worked in nearby factories, paid more for their property, and kept their homes and yards tidy. The south end was poor, dominated by people on work relief, many recently arrived from Oklahoma and
Arkansas. Compared to the north side, southern Bell Gardens had more
tents and shacks, the weeds were taller, the fences made of chicken wire
rather than pickets, and the homes small "box-like affairs." The residents

most cognizant of the neighborhood cleavage were the north-siders, who looked down on their poorer neighbors. "The people down in the corner next to the river and down next to the refinery [south section] are the poorest class," noted one north-ender. "They won't get anywhere. But then most every town has its slums."[39]

South Gate was thus a town of blue-collar and low-level white-collar workers, composing an amalgamation of the lower-middle and working class. Indeed, this combination worked to blur the qualitative conception of just what kind of community South Gate was in the minds of its residents. For example, consider how two South Gate residents responded when asked whether they felt South Gate was "middle-class" or "working-class" in the interwar period. A realtor replied it was middle-class. An autoworker responded it was working-class.[40] The key point here is that both felt comfortable in this suburb, and both felt a sense of belonging to this place. To these residents, South Gate was fulfilling their needs regardless of their class.

The Great Depression in South Gate

As in most communities across the country, the Great Depression had profound impact on the economic character of South Gate's populace. The very worst damage was sustained in the domestic sphere, in the ownership of homes. Employment conditions were less devastated, partly because of the continued expansion of local industry throughout the 1930s. Even so, the suburb underwent an important shift during the decade under the weight of this global crisis.

The steady influx of industries into South Gate and neighboring suburbs insulated the community somewhat from massive unemployment, although joblessness was still a problem. In the early 1930s, unemployment in South Gate hovered at 16 percent, mild compared to Los Angeles (near 30 percent in early 1933) and the nation (25 to 30 percent in 1932).[41] The hardships of reduced income through unemployment were exacerbated by bank failures in South Gate. In the dreary winter of 1932, when the national banking system was faltering, the suburb's two major banks closed their doors. In Los Angeles, economic conditions began improving in 1933 until a downturn in late 1936, then continued upward again. By 1938, unemployment had dropped to 4.8 percent in South Gate, with 220 residents employed on public works projects, though it climbed to 8.7 percent in 1940.[42]

Since the 1920s, South Gate residents had grown accustomed to frequent layoffs and unsteady work, but they continued to turn to homeown-ership as a reliable source of family security. When this faltered, their entire strategy crumbled. With cash income either cut off or curtailed, it became difficult to meet certain household expenses. It was true that self-building eliminated mortgage payments for many, yet they still had to pay special assessments and property taxes. And thanks to an overambitious program to develop South Gate's infrastructure in the 1920s, tax rates escalated pre-cipitously. Families were now forced to raise substantial amounts of cash merely to keep the home they owned. And the bill came due just as the Depression kicked in. Exorbitant property taxes subverted working-class strategies of minimizing cash dependency through owner-building.

The tax crisis had both political and economic repercussions. The inter-twined issues of development and taxation spurred intensive political conflict in South Gate between working-class residents struggling to stay afloat and merchants concerned with infrastructure development. As tax delinquencies mounted, residents faced the prospect of losing their prop-erty and slipping from their cherished status as homeowners. This fear be-came a reality in the early 1930s. The tax delinquency rate hit 28 percent in 1932–33, then peaked at 32 percent in 1934–35. One WPA researcher esti-mated that several thousand lots in South Gate reverted to the state. The southern suburbs were hit harder than most, with the highest delinquency rates in working-class communities like Bell, Compton, Gardena, Haw-thorne, Lynwood, and South Gate. As a result, homeownership crumbled swiftly, dropping from 89 percent in 1929 to 55 percent by 1935. Moreover, there was substantial turnover in the community, likely spurred by the staggering tax burdens. From 1926 to 1930, nearly half of local residents moved away, while 9.6 percent moved within South Gate. A number of the homes of emigrants were purchased by speculators, then rented to new-comers. With the rise in tenancy, the very purpose of working-class subur-ban life began to transform—for the worse, in the eyes of many.[43]

Even more threatening was an influx of the desperately poor. In the early 1930s, squatter camps, known derisively as Hoovervilles, began ap-pearing around the area. Just west of South Gate's original town site in the Graham neighborhood, one Hoover Town was home to forty-five families, who lived in tents, shacks, and other makeshift shelters (see fig. 2-1). An-other squatter colony formed in the L.A. River bed within the borders of South Gate. While the "riverbed district" was tolerated early on, even re-ceiving police services, by late decade local police were more intent on evict-ing the squatters rather than serving and protecting them. Yet the colony persisted. In 1938 about fifteen families, many Mexican, lived in "rickety river bottom shacks" made of wood scraps, metal, and "other junked mate-

Figure 2-1 A Hooverville in the Graham section of Los Angeles, adjacent to South Gate, March 1932. The physical proximity of the desperately poor, in squatter camps such as this, symbolized the economic instability wrought by the Great Depression. Los Angeles County Department of Health Services Collection, 396 vol. 1 (30), Huntington Library, San Marino, California. Reproduced by permission of the Huntington Library, San Marino, California.

rial." They lacked water, sanitation, and covered floors. One Mexican woman gave birth to twins who both died from exposure. Despite their acute need, the squatters were largely shunned by local residents. The city council voted to condemn the dwellings as the best means "by which the moneyless individuals and families may be permanently kept out of the city." Their race was surely a factor in this policy, since poverty was widespread among South Gate whites as well. Eventually, the squatters were aided by county welfare agencies. Yet their temporary presence in the community suggested how the Depression had changed the face of South Gate.[44]

In the midst of these hardships, nature struck its own devastating blow. On March 10, 1933, an earthquake rumbled through southern Los Angeles, leaving a trail of physical damage in its wake. Property damage mounted to $40 million, the death toll topped 100, and nearly 5,000 people were seriously injured. While the worst damage hit Long Beach and Compton, nearby South Gate, Lynwood, and Huntington Park also sustained significant property loss. Few buildings collapsed completely, but many brick fronts crumbled and plate-glass windows shattered. South Gate alone had about $600,000 in damage to public buildings and private homes. Public schools relocated to temporary tents, which ended up serving as classrooms for the next two years.[45] The earthquake, coming when it did, put even more strain upon a community already buckling under the pressures of the Great Depression.

Class and Community in Comparative Perspective

The 1933 earthquake, like the jarring jolt it was, stunningly reminds us of our broader setting, Los Angeles. South Gate's conditions of working-class life took place in the context of a distinctive, modern, suburban metropolis. To appreciate the significance of the setting, it helps to compare South Gate with other working-class neighborhoods and other suburban areas. Likewise, contextualizing South Gate's social composition affords us similar perspective. How did South Gates people stack up against other working-class communities in Los Angeles and beyond?

In one critical respect, South Gate was representative of other working-class suburbs of Los Angeles in comprising both blue- and white-collar residents. In many suburbs predominated by manual workers, white-collar employees constituted a substantial portion of the population. Table 2-1, for example, lists the proportion of residents for each community that labored in "working-class" jobs; the remaining proportion for each suburb was white-collar. These data show not only the high proportion of L.A. suburbs that contained a working-class majority, but also the pervasiveness of class diversity in these communities. Every suburb was represented by every type of occupation. In working-class towns like Hawthorne, Signal Hill, Bell, Lynwood, Maywood—and South Gate—about a third of local workers were white-collar. Even Azusa, a farmworkers' suburb, was 28 percent white-collar. This finding belies the image of Los Angeles as a metropolis of middle-class midwesterners seeking to segregate themselves into homogeneous suburbs.[46]

This class diversity was not unusual among North American suburbs. As Kenneth Jackson has shown, the elite, railroad suburbs of the nineteenth century were notable for their class heterogeneity. The posh homes of these "main line" suburbs were serviced by gardeners, domestics, and other laborers, who made their own modest homes in the community. This pattern continued into the twentieth century in the "domestic service suburbs," which housed blacks, immigrants, and others who worked in the homes of wealthy residents. In the few blue-collar suburbs that we know about, class variances were likewise common. The best data is available for Toronto, where blue- and white-collar residents coexisted in certain working-class suburbs, especially after 1930.[47]

The willingness of blue- and white-collar residents to share residential space can be explained by several factors. First, by the early twentieth century, neighborhood and community—as opposed to the workplace—had become important centers of identity for many Americans, particularly the working class. As laborers lost power in the workplace with the maturing of industrial capitalism, they gained some control over "the institutions of daily neighborhood life."[48] Community, public space, and popular culture became arenas where they could assert their own interests and exercise autonomy. Meanwhile, occupations became less important in representing social standing.

Second, homeownership introduced important new dimensions to the ways that suburban dwellers identified themselves and were identified by others. Among blue- and white-collar workers alike, homeownership provided a common status apart from class. If a person accomplished homeownership—by whatever means—he achieved a particular identity derived from this possession. This is not to say that homeownership automatically made a person "middle class." To the contrary, many residents of towns like South Gate continued to see themselves as working class; their mentality, culture, and political behavior all reflected this orientation. Their class interests, indeed, led them to create, use, and ultimately protect their homes in ways reflecting the pressures of class. Yet their status as homeowners conferred on them an additional source of identity, derived in the neighborhood, based on the nature of one's property instead of one's form of labor.

Third, the line between blue- and white-collar in early twentieth-century Los Angeles was itself quite fluid. For example, the status and experience of a low-level white-collar worker were often closer to a factory worker than a professional. Indeed, the class identity of a clerk or salesperson might go either way—working or middle class—depending on variables like age and prospects for upward mobility. In his study of corporate cultures in prewar Los Angeles, Clark Davis found this variability had an impact on residential patterns. It was not unusual for low-level white-collar employees to live in mixed-class neighborhoods. This was especially true for "men on the make," those young, lower-wage white-collar employees who frequently jumped from job to job. They tended to associate more with their working-class brethren, living in the same neighborhoods and sharing the same concerns about layoffs and poor wages.[49] So it came as little surprise that on a street in South Gate like Garden View, an oil worker lived next door to a clerk; or that on San Miguel, a salesman lived across the street from a driver. The shared experiences of low-level white-collar and manual workers—the clerks, salesmen, and factory workers—made the color of one's occupational "collar" seem less important.

Finally, the heritage of American suburbs promoted interclass communities. Since the nineteenth century, upper- and middle-class Americans had embraced suburbia as a peaceful haven of domestic privatism, away from the clamor of the city. Many early suburbs embodied this pastoral, romantic ideal. The better-off classes, thus, had a tradition that revered the suburban lifestyle, an inclination that carried forward into the twentieth century. So strong was their propensity that even a suburb like South Gate could capture some of this upper class, simply by emphasizing the rural, pastoral nature of the community. As a result, South Gate attracted some higher-class folks into its midst. The professionals, managers, and proprietors who moved to the suburb followed comfortably on a long-lived tradition, making this residential choice a logical one. In the 1920s, South Gate seemed pristine and young enough to rival any of the other thousands of subdivisions springing up in Los Angeles.

In its lack of immigrants, South Gate differed significantly from many working-class districts in America. The ethnic diversity in industrial cities of the Northeast and Midwest has been well documented, and it is likewise well established that most "new immigrants" concentrated in the blue-collar sector of the labor market. In Chicago of 1920, for example, immigrants constituted 43 percent of total workers, and a whopping 54 percent of the industrial labor force. Chicago was a city of Poles, Italians, Czechs, Greeks, and Jews, among others, who filled the factories and inhabited the working-class neighborhoods. This contrasts with Los Angeles's overwhelmingly native-born white population. In the small size of its immigrant population, Los Angeles as a whole lagged behind cities like New York, Detroit, Chicago, San Francisco, and Seattle. The major exception in Los Angeles, of course, was the presence of Mexican immigrants. Yet because they often inhabited relatively segregated neighborhoods, their ethnic presence did not touch most communities of working-class whites. Los Angeles was thus distinguished by a preponderance of working-class communities composed overwhelmingly of native-born whites.[50]

In cities across the United States, many working-class neighborhoods were thus characterized by strong ethnic cultures, which residents drew upon in adapting to their new environs. Again taking Chicago as the example, immigrants pulled together to create welfare programs, mutual benefit societies, financial institutions, and churches, among other things. Shared ethnic cultures shaped their experiences in neighborhoods, factories, and the political arena, and significantly mitigated class differences within their communities. Ethnic business owners—the "faithful neighborhood merchants"—were perceived positively by their ethnic, working-class neighbors for supplying the material goods of the Old World and thus strengthening traditional cultural mores. In the 1920s, the cultural ties that united ethnic merchant and worker were much stronger than the class differences that separated them.[51] By contrast, the lack of strong ethnic identities among South Gate's residents left them open to new cultural and political orientations, and it cleared the way for class discord to arise.

Los Angeles compares more closely to a city like Flint, Michigan, characterized by a predominance of native-born working people, suburban communities for workers, and respectable homeownership rates (around 50 percent). The age and economy of Flint, however, set it apart: Flint was a virtual one-industry city devoted to automobile manufacturing. Out of this milieu, a labor aristocracy emerged by the 1920s. Their long experience of social connections with the city's business elite created a different kind of class configuration, one that united an important stratum of laborers with the local bourgeoisie.[52] We don't know enough about the *community*-based dynamics of this class configuration in Flint to make true comparisons with Los Angeles, but it appears that certain differences were at work in terms of class relations.

A comparison with Bobigny, a working-class suburb outside of Paris, presents perhaps the most provocative insights of all. In terms of demographics during the interwar years, Bobigny and South Gate were similar in significant respects: a high population growth rate, the predominantly urban origins of newcomers, a low proportion of foreign-born immigrants, a child-heavy age distribution, and a predominance of nuclear families. In many cases, the demographic proportions were almost identical. In both communities, the lack of strong ethnic or regional subcultures opened residents to new customs, and the predominant cultural pattern was an urban one. Yet in two respects, the suburbs deviated radically. In terms of housing tenure, homeownership prevailed in South Gate, while tenancy was the norm in Bobigny. This difference ultimately fed into contrasting expectations about suburban standards of living. Class-wise, South Gate was much more diverse; blue- and white-collar commingled, and the small business class constituted itself as a powerful local elite. In Bobigny, professionals and other white-collar workers were virtually nonexistent. The rigid residential segregation of the Parisian periphery turned suburbs like Bobigny into "great working-class ghettos" and eradicated class conflict from local communities. As Tyler Stovall has written of Bobigny's residents, "Their limited contact with local elites did reduce the workers' conflict in everyday life." These configurations had corresponding political repercussions. In Bobigny, where class conflict was absent at the local level, workers focused their energies instead on the broader canvass of metropolitan politics and embraced radical solutions to the problems they faced as working-class suburbanites.[53] In South Gate, by contrast, conflicts erupted at the local level between workers and businessmen. Rather than targeting the broader metropolitan power structure as Bobigny residents did, South Gate's working families aimed their wrath against the suburb's political leaders and pursued more conservative solutions.

Suburban South Gate, thus, was a town united most tenaciously around the shared identities of race, homeownership, family status, and nativity. These characteristics bound neighbors together, defining who was in and who was out. Definitions blurred, however, when it came to class. Like the realtor and autoworker who couldn't agree on the kind of town South Gate was, internal class differences ultimately created tensions in the community that erupted when it came to defining the future of the suburb.

These differences were reinforced by the tenor of social life in South Gate. Indeed, the nuances of South Gate's demographic and socioeconomic landscape become animated when we turn to the social existence of the suburb's residents. South Gate's people lived, worked, played, and consumed by certain spatial and temporal rhythms. Because they were white, their mobility was unfettered. Some of these rhythms bound residents to their suburb. Others propelled them into the larger city. In certain surprising ways, class influenced how South Gate residents interfaced with the larger metropolis. As merchants bound themselves tightly to the local community, workers ventured out beyond their suburb's borders into the sprawling, strange, secular world of Los Angeles—the place, in the words of Louis Adamic, that was "endlessly entertaining and absorbing."[54]

3   The Texture of Everyday Life

To a working-class teenager like Juanita Smith, Los Angeles was a vast but familiar place. Juanita ventured outside of South Gate to play, shop, and eventually work. She and a girlfriend frequented movie houses downtown, like the Paramount. "They'd always have vaudeville shows. They'd have one movie, a newsreel, and a comedy, and then a live show." They preferred the Saturday matinees because tickets were cheaper, but attended evening shows once they started dating. Juanita's family also shopped downtown, "because there was nothing out here [in South Gate], very few stores." They took the bus for a nickel to Huntington Park, then for another nickel the Yellow Car straight to the heart of downtown. "Everybody got off at 7th and Broadway and hotfooted it down to Walker's on 5th Street, because they were a real good department store, a good place to shop." Soon after graduating from high school, Juanita landed a job as a secretary for Bayly-Underhill in Long Beach, a branch plant that produced overalls. For a year, Juanita lived in South Gate and commuted to work by Red Car, bus, or hitchhiking the thirty-minute ride along Long Beach Boulevard. In the summertime, she and her coworkers closed shop around 4:30 and headed to the beach almost daily. Juanita began dating a man whose parents were charter members of the affluent Pacific

Coast Club in Long Beach. The couple attended dinner dances and swam at the club where, Juanita recalled, "I could go swimming out there, take my wet bathing suit off, drop it down sand and all, and leave it in the shower. When I went back it would be washed and in my locker." Such luxury was a new experience for the young woman. Juanita Smith had an easy familiarity with Los Angeles, navigating its thoroughfares and the many opportunities for work and leisure the metropolis had to offer. The constant mobility around Los Angeles that defined her life opened up new vistas both spatial and social, even allowing her access to enclaves of affluence. For Juanita geographic and social mobility were mutually reinforcing.[1]

Virgil Collins was an autoworker and union activist for most of his adult life. During the 1930s, he worked at the Wilys-Overland automobile plant, several furniture factories, and briefly at GM South Gate. In 1936, he married Aretta Tullis, who worked at a meatpacking plant in Vernon preparing spices and who was also active in her union. After serving as a merchant marine during World War II, Virgil landed another job at GM South Gate, where he stayed for the next thirty-one years. The Collinses lived in the Florence district until 1952, a working-class suburb next to South Gate, then bought a house in South Gate in 1955.

In his labor union, Collins found the strongest sense of community. "My social life was involved with group activities that involved the union. Trade union members. We'd go to parties and picnics and so forth. It would be with no particular person, but in groups," he recalled. It was mainly a small group of union leaders—about 10 percent of all workers—who participated in this social life. In the 1930s and early 1940s, the years of arduous union organizing, Collins also socialized extensively with his family. Every Saturday night, Virgil and his wife played poker with his aunt, brothers, and their wives. For Collins, union and family carried about equal weight as centers of sociability. Neighborhood played only a marginal role.[2]

Leland Weaver, a businessman, lay at the other extreme. A descendant of Southern California natives, Weaver grew up in southern Los Angeles and moved to South Gate in the late 1920s. In the 1930s, he owned and operated a drugstore in Home Gardens. Following the war, he opened an insurance business in South Gate and soon added a credit and collection bureau. In 1959, he started a travel agency. With his business life rooted firmly in South Gate, Weaver experienced his richest social interaction in the suburb. He was a member of the South Gate and Lynwood Chambers of Commerce, the Masons, the Al Malaikah Shrine, the South Gate Kiwanis Club (where he served as president), the Los Nietos Valley Shrine Club, and the Coordinating Council of South Gate; he also volunteered with the Boy Scouts and the YMCA. Leland and his wife Dorothea were active in the

Grace Bible Church, which they helped found and where they formed some of their closest social ties. For the Weavers, running a business in South Gate solidified an economic and social commitment to the suburb. As for many merchants, this loyalty transformed into power. Weaver served as mayor of South Gate for three terms and on the city council for more than twenty years.[3]

These personal histories illustrate a pervasive social fact in South Gate: the symbiosis of social and economic life. For residents, social experience often depended upon one's occupation and place of work. While a merchant like Weaver, a secretary like Smith, and an autoworker like Collins shared an identity as homeowners, conferring on them the status of suburbanites, class distinctions emerged in the texture of their everyday lives. In particular, class tended to dictate the locus of community experience, be it inside or outside of South Gate.

This chapter explores patterns in the everyday lives of South Gate's residents as they traveled to work, play, shop, socialize, and worship. South Gate was founded in a time and place when local attachments were weakening from the compelling pull of an enticing and sprawling metropolis.[4] While American cities in general were fragmenting spatially, the trend was especially true in Los Angeles. This contrasted to older industrial cities where working-class neighborhoods were places of rich sociability, with long histories of working-class culture forged in that context. In such communities, workers shared memories of the industrialization process and their eroding place within that system. By contrast, South Gate was tabula rasa, a new town in a relatively new city that emerged when industrialization had matured. Community would be built from ground zero, among disparate newcomers of various backgrounds and worldviews. And they would forge social experiences in the context of a thoroughly modern city.

On the cutting edge of twentieth-century urban life, Los Angeles particularly encouraged a mobile, cosmopolitan, recreational existence among residents. Los Angeles in the 1920s and 1930s was a vastly sprawling yet highly accessible metropolis, thanks to an extensive streetcar system that linked suburbs to downtown, the beaches, and inland areas. Even when the automobile entered, an open culture of hitchhiking promoted mobility. Furthermore, Los Angeles extolled itself as a city of leisure, where opportunities for natural and commercial amusements abounded. Among all American cities, Los Angeles was at the vanguard of embracing the broad twentieth-century shift from "work ethic" to "leisure ethic," expressing this in a new urban ethos. Urban ideologues sang the praises of recreation, of gaining fulfillment not merely through toil but through outdoor recreation, commercial amusements like the cinema, and even gardening.

Charles Lummis, editor of *Land of Sunshine*, preached this gospel early on. With the help of its perfect climate, Los Angeles would become a "community whose units shall live easier, live better, live longer; shall be more alive, and more glad to be alive, and more fit to be alive, than the units of any other population." Los Angeles would teach the rest of the nation how to shed its Yankee neurosis of overwork and learn to enjoy life. As Lummis wrote in 1897:"Surely there is no federal law forbidding Americans to have a good time. . . . And yet it is a fact, notorious to travelers, that the people of the United States know less about the art of recreation than any other people now extant. They haven't time to live. . . . But the Southwest is appointed schoolmaster—and the lesson is going to be learned. . . . We shall probably continue to 'get as much done' as the Saxon has ever done anywhere; and we shall unquestionably get very much more out of it. Indeed, by force of our environment rather than by our deliberate wit, we are destined to show an astonished world the spectacle of Americans having a good time."[5] The city's natural beauties and recreational offerings became a booster theme for decades; the rise of Hollywood only intensified Southern California's identity as a place of enjoyment and pleasure. Los Angeles, thus, seasoned residents quickly—even working-class residents—in the ways of play and fun.[6]

As residents ventured into Los Angeles to fulfill various social and economic needs, the nature of community experience took shape. The concept of community is a slippery one, often loosely applied to a range of social forms, meanings, and even prescriptions. The key to studying community, Thomas Bender reminds us, is to look for varied forms of social interaction —not simply geographically fixed spaces containing people in highly specified ways. For the twentieth century, this approach is essential. With the advent of cheap, convenient transportation and new communication technology, physical proximity became less important to social and economic relations. For many Americans by the early twentieth century, the residential neighborhood was spatially separate from wage work, leisure, consumption, and socializing. Suburbanization often reinforced this schism. In working-class suburbia, however, the line between work and home was never so clear. Not only did "production" occur in the domestic sphere, it also occurred in local factories. The multiplicity of functions served by the working-class suburb suggests the potential for a diverse range of community experiences.[7]

This chapter starts by identifying the patterns of life of South Gate residents. Where did they work, play, consume, and socialize? Where—if at all—did they experience a sense of "we-ness," a sense of belonging to a community? Where did they find themselves interacting with the broader metropolitan (cosmopolitan) society?[8] From here, we can begin to comprehend the community experience of residents. And from this, we might explore questions of identity. Where and how did residents define their identities—as part of which communities and experiences? Because the experiences of blue-collar residents sharply contrasted with those of local merchants, who made up a small but politically important group in the suburb, this chapter considers them separately. Workers and merchants had distinctly different experiences in their suburb and city. In the day-to-day rhythms of their lives, workers experienced a more cosmopolitan existence, moving easily and frequently outside of South Gate and into their metropolis. Merchants, by contrast, were firmly rooted to the locality—socially, economically, and ultimately politically. This divergent social reality pointed to coexisting communities of interest in South Gate, which eventually combusted in the political arena.

THE WORKING PEOPLE OF SOUTH GATE

The lived reality of South Gate's residents began inside the home itself. In South Gate, families were at the heart of social life. Family cohesion was reinforced by the challenges of working-class life, which demanded the pooling of resources and labor to keep the household ship afloat. The self-building and self-provisioning practices common in many households were carried out by entire families. When the Smiths built their house, for example, the mother and four daughters provided critical assistance to the father, the main homebuilder. The sociologist observing Bell Gardens noticed similar patterns in that suburb. "Families perform useful and significant functions for most of the residents of this community," he wrote. The daily routines of life brought "various members of the family into relative frequent contact with each other. The majority of the people seem to spend most of their free time at home. As one travels up and down the streets one sees many men and women working in the yards and gardens and the children probably playing nearby. The man goes to work, if he has a job. He returns between 4:30 and 6:00 in the afternoon and works in the garden or on the house. The woman's life is a round of housework, made more difficult by inadequate housing and the prevalence of dust. She goes away from home relatively little, for lack of money, poor transportation, and few outside interests restrict her activities."[9] The poverty and economic instability of working-class life, together with the productive potentials of suburban

homeownership, promoted family cohesion and domesticity. The centri-
petal pull of family and the home was especially strong for women, who experienced the domestic sphere as a center of both production and sociability.

Families commonly interacted as a unit with outside groups. For example, church membership was often a family affair. Of the earliest members of the First Baptist Church and the Community Presbyterian Church,
more than two-thirds joined as part of a family group.[10] Families frequently socialized together as well. "The whole family is likely to make an
occasional visit to some relative or friend," wrote the sociologist studying
Bell Gardens. Several South Gate residents recalled the importance of the
family in social outings. Juanita Smith frequently accompanied her sisters
on visits to a neighbor's house. When her sisters began dating, their entire
families would have square dances at the young men's homes just a few
blocks away. "We'd go to their houses, and of course the whole family was
there. We'd move all the furniture back and dance. I loved it, we had a ball,"
she recalled. Almost every Sunday, the DeVries family paid a visit to friends
in other parts of Los Angeles, from Long Beach to El Monte to West L.A.
Virgil Collins maintained very close relationships with his older brothers
throughout his youth and adulthood. When they lived together as young,
single adults, they spent much time with one another socially. After they
had all married and moved out, the three brothers, along with their wives
and the aunt who had raised them, met every week to play penny-ante
poker—three-cent limit—during the Depression years. "Every Saturday
night, that was a ritual with us. We'd take turns going to each others'
house. . . . Whose ever house it was at, they'd maybe have chili or sandwiches for us. We'd get started at about 7 and then stop at 10 and have a bite
to eat, then play until midnight." This continued for seven years.[11]

Family-centeredness likewise characterized the experience of the
Seaborgs. The Seaborg family settled in Home Gardens in 1922. In 1927,
fifteen-year-old Glenn Seaborg, the oldest of two children, began keeping a
daily diary.[12] This extraordinary document provides a rare glimpse into
daily routines during the 1920s and 1930s. By taking one year—1928—
and analyzing it closely, it is possible to discern patterns of social life in
Home Gardens. While Glenn was involved in a variety of organized youth
activities, including Boy Scouts, band, and sandlot football (but not church),
much of his social life revolved around his family. Over a four-month
period in 1928, the Seaborgs entertained their friends—mostly fellow
Swedish migrants from Ishpeming, Michigan—on nine occasions. These
convivial get-togethers lasted well into the night and involved all members
of both families. On one evening, the Velins brought over a Victrola and
they played records until a very late hour; another time, the families were

together for an entire day. Glenn also spent many hours with his cousins who lived across the street, where he listened to their phonograph, helped the youngsters with homework, and just hung around. And nearly every weekend, he cleaned the family's chicken pen, yard, or home, tying him closely to the domestic fold. The hours he devoted to this family-oriented activity surpassed the time he spent with friends. Similarly, John Sheehy recalled that his most common activity as a youth was "just hanging around" at home.[13]

While many family activities kept residents at home, even stronger forces drew them into the broader metropolis. For many blue-collar workers, much of life occurred in places beyond the suburb's borders. Indeed, their patterns of social life strongly suggest that the working-class people of South Gate were mobile and cosmopolitan. Social ties, work, leisure, and shopping drew them out of South Gate. To them, Los Angeles was a safe, welcome, familiar place. They experienced an easy openness and permeability between their hometown and the larger city.

GETTING AROUND

The multiplicity of transportation options in Los Angeles facilitated such mobility. Commuting for work or leisure was feasible for a range of people, from the poor to the affluent. In Los Angeles during the interwar years, residents could choose from public streetcars, automobiles, or even hitchhiking.

By 1910, Los Angeles had an impressive two-pronged public transportation system that traversed much of the metropolis. It consisted of the Pacific Electric, a high-speed interurban system known as the "Red Cars," and the Los Angeles Railway (LARY), an urban streetcar system known as the "Yellow Cars." While the Red Cars traveled over 1,164 miles of track in four counties at its peak (the largest electric railway system in the world at the time), the Yellow Cars in fact handled nearly 90 percent of the city's rail traffic. A 1911 survey found that L.A. city residents averaged one ride per day on the LARY. LARY cars charged a five-cent fare, typical of streetcar systems nationwide.[14] The interurban Red Cars charged higher fares, which varied according to distance. The rate established in 1918 was 3 cents per mile for one-way trips, and 2.5 cents per mile for round-trips. During the Depression, a round-trip ticket from downtown to Long Beach was 80 cents for adults, 40 cents for children.[15]

A few problems with these systems surely diminished their use by South Gate residents. First, they barely reached the edges of South Gate, making them usable only to residents willing and able to walk to the stations. A Yellow Car loop, signifying the end of the line, sat at the suburb's northwestern corner. While this was convenient for residents of northwest South Gate, it was an average two-mile (or forty-five-minute) walk from Home Gardens or the eastern end of town. For many, it was simply too far. In 1924, the Home Gardens Improvement League pleaded with the LARY for an extension of the Yellow Car line into Home Gardens, claiming that residents were "leaving our community because of the poor service." The plea was to no avail. The absence of convenient public transportation, in fact, may help explain the sparser settlement in Home Gardens in the 1920s. The closest Red Car station was in Watts, about a mile and a half from Home Gardens and two miles from the heart of northwest South Gate. Regardless, the high cost of the Red Car was probably an even bigger deterrent than distance. For example, a Red Car trip from Watts to downtown was about 22 cents one-way, 37 cents round-trip, according to the 1918 schedule. At these prices, it made better sense for residents to hop the five-cent Yellow Car when they could. Another drawback was the slow service of these systems. On average, it took forty to fifty minutes to travel from South Gate to downtown by public transportation, even though the distance was only about six miles. In Los Angeles overall, ridership on both the Red and Yellow Cars started a long-term decline in the 1920s, due to the poor service of these systems and to the rise of alternative transportation modes.[16]

The most important of these was the automobile. The car came into general usage in Los Angeles after 1910, and it did so at a rate unmatched in other cities.[17] From 1918 to 1923, auto registration in L.A. County nearly quadrupled, from 110,000 to 430,000, far outdistancing the per capita national average. In 1920, Los Angeles had one car for every 3.6 residents, compared to one per thirteen nationally, and one per thirty in Chicago. By 1925, one out of two L.A. residents owned a car, compared to one out of six in the nation and one out of eleven in Chicago. Los Angeles's high rates continued even into the Depression. While auto owners in the 1910s used their vehicles mostly for recreation, like weekend drives, by the 1920s daily commuting to work and shopping became commonplace. By 1924, nearly as many people traveled to downtown by automobile as by streetcar. And on Long Beach Boulevard, which cut through South Gate, traffic quadrupled from 1918 to 1923.[18]

By the 1930s, auto ownership spanned class lines. In 1934–35, the automobile was the main means of transportation for about 80 percent of wage earners in Los Angeles. In 1940, a WPA survey of industrial workers reported that 71.7 percent used autos, 20 percent used public transportation, and 7 percent walked. In southeastern Los Angeles, which included South Gate and other working-class suburbs, the proportion of auto users was slightly higher: 75.7 percent used autos, 19.3 percent public transportation, and 5 percent other means. While some carpooling occurred in other areas of the metropolis, the southeast district had the lowest persons-per-vehicle rate. By this time, the configuration of streets and highways superceded the routes of streetcars in importance. The automobile had become the norm.[19]

While auto ownership made travel easier, it certainly was no prerequisite for physical mobility around Los Angeles. Even people of limited means found ways to get around for next to nothing. Hitchhiking became a favored mode. Indeed, it became a critical ticket to mobility for many working-class people, particularly the younger set. In the 1920s and 1930s, hitchhiking was considered safe and socially acceptable. Sociologist Emory Bogardus observed that boys were "begging rides to everywhere" in the mid-1920s: to the beach, jobs, the movie studios. South Gate residents Juanita Smith and John Sheehy regularly hitchhiked to play and work. As Smith recalled, "Anybody driving by the boulevard would pick you up if you were walking . . . nothing ever happened, we weren't a bit afraid to ride." While auto transportation is often considered atomizing, hitchhiking in fact promoted social interaction and mutual aid among strangers, symbolizing a sort of "mobile community" experience in Los Angeles. As Julia Sloane wrote, "One late afternoon a friend of ours was driving alone and offered a lift to two young men who were swinging along on foot. 'Your price?' they asked. 'A smile and a song,' was the reply. So in they got, and those last fifty miles were gay." Women were frequent hitchhikers as well. One driver remarked in 1923, "Neat looking dames nail me all the time around L.A. . . . On the road to the beach, most of them. They go back and forth just for the fun of riding in nifty cars. I picked up one gal who wasn't more'n eighteen and a good looker too. I asked her if she didn't get in a jam, sometimes, grabbing rides with strangers. 'Oh no,' she answers, chipper as can be, 'you'd be surprised to know how many nice fellows there are.'"[20] The universal "open door" policy of auto owners represented a sort of informal system of mass transportation in Los Angeles.

The Journey to Work

From South Gate's inception, local boosters promoted it as "The Complete City," where home and work would coexist. "South Gate is a community of fine homes, businesses and diversified industries enjoying ideal climate and advantageous location," wrote the Chamber of Commerce in 1931. In contrast to upper- and middle-class suburbs seeking distance from the industrial city, South Gate purposely emphasized the connection between residence and workplace. The town's economic base, in fact, rested on two main foundations: industry and retail. Though not wholly self-sufficient, South Gate was much more than an economically static bedroom suburb.[21]

The presence of industry in the suburb did not mean, however, that residents necessarily found jobs in those factories. In fact, the journey-to-work patterns of South Gate's blue-collar residents suggest quite the opposite. Most residents commuted to jobs outside of their hometown. For residents employed in industrial jobs, a profile of journey-to-work patterns in the 1920s and 1930s emerges in surveys of employment, traffic patterns, and industrial location. While this evidence is neither comprehensive nor methodologically coherent in some cases, it is suggestive about where South Gate's blue-collar residents found employment.

A good way to begin is to clarify the economic landscape of South Gate, to identify where potential jobs existed locally. Industry began arriving in South Gate in the 1920s. Since no sources indicate where workers in these factories lived, we can make inferences comparing data on the number of local jobs versus the number of blue-collar workers living in South Gate. In 1926, the number of manufacturing jobs was approximately 390, while the number of blue-collar workers was 922. If we assume that every blue-collar position was filled by a South Gate resident, then about 42 percent of blue-collar residents worked locally, while 58 percent commuted to jobs outside of the suburb. The number of commuters was probably much higher, since it was unlikely that local factories employed only South Gate residents. For most of the 1920s, thus, a majority of working-class residents commuted to jobs outside of their home community.[22]

Traffic surveys confirm the likelihood of commuting during the mid-1920s. In 1924, Kelker, De Leuw & Co. conducted an extensive study of traffic and employment patterns in Los Angeles. One part of this study drew on a survey conducted by the LARY, which traced the residential location of 80,000 employees working in 650 industrial and commercial establishments in and around downtown Los Angeles, a primary center of industry at this time.[23] Although it surveyed workers at the point of employment rather than point of residence (thus excluding workers who might have worked near their suburban homes), it still offers useful data considering that few industries were operating in the southern suburbs this early. That is, few "points of employment" would have existed in South Gate when the survey was taken. The survey found that among workers living in north South Gate and Huntington Park, about 40 percent worked in the central business district, 30 percent in Vernon, and 28 percent in east side industries. For workers living in Home Gardens, Watts, and Lynwood, 49 percent worked in the central business district, 29 percent in eastside industries, and 19 percent in Vernon. A scattering worked in industries north of downtown. The largest group, thus, worked in establishments in and around downtown and the Central Manufacturing District (CMD), roughly six miles from South Gate. Another part of the same study traced passenger movement on public transportation in L.A. County.[24] Although the study was problematic on a few levels, it did reveal predominant patterns.[25] The survey found that—on a given weekday—about 50 percent of passengers from northern South Gate and Huntington Park traveled to the Central Business district, while 28 percent went to the industrial districts of the eastside, south side, and Vernon.[26] Again, this suggests the importance of downtown and the CMD for local commuters.

By the 1930s, the local job base increased dramatically as industry expanded in southern Los Angeles. In 1930, there were fifteen major plants in and adjacent to South Gate, the largest of these Firestone Tire & Rubber and National Paper, each of which employed from 500 to 1,000 people in the late 1920s. By 1930, an estimated 2,000 jobs existed in South Gate's factories.[27] In the same year, about 4,200 residents were classified as blue-collar workers. This suggests that even if all local factory jobs were filled by South Gate residents, then 48 percent of local blue-collar workers found work in the suburb while 52 percent commuted to jobs elsewhere. Again, the number of commuters was probably much higher since factories did not hire locals in such great numbers. If we make the same estimate for 1940 based on data for available jobs and employment, then potential employment of local residents rises to 64 percent of the blue-collar workforce. But the number of residents finding work locally was never this high in the prewar period, and most of South Gate's blue-collar residents commuted to their jobs.

The best journey-to-work data was collected around 1940 by Federal Writers Project workers, in a detailed survey of local factories and their employees' places of residence. This data, along with union membership lists from the local GM plant, offer a comprehensive portrait of commuting patterns. This evidence suggests that about 29 percent of persons employed in South Gate factories also lived in South Gate (see table 3-1). Correlating this figure with South Gate occupational data indicates that approximately 32 percent of all blue-collar residents of South Gate found jobs in local factories. This represented 17.7 percent of the *total* workforce in South Gate. Thus, despite a strong industrial presence in the suburb, two-thirds of South Gate's blue-collar workers commuted to jobs outside the community.[28] Given the steady growth of industry in the southern suburbs up to

Table 3-1 Major Industries Locating in South Gate, 1920–1939

| | | | | Employee data[a] | |
Company	Date Est. in South Gate	Product	Total workers	No. living in South Gate	% living in South Gate
Bell Foundry	1922	Iron products	40	10	25%
E.E. Brown Cabinet	1923	Cabinets, fixtures	11	6	50
Bent Concrete Pipe	1924	Concrete pipes	—		
A.R. Maas Chemical	1924 LA	Photo chemicals	55	(15)[b]	—
Service Equipment	1924	Gas stations, aircraft mnfg products	27	19	70
Royal Rubber	1924	Rubber products	10[c]	(3)	—
Fibreboard Products	1926 b	Paper boxes	200	50	25
Western Concrete Pipe	1926 LA	Concrete pipes	—		50
Am. Concrete & Steel Pipe[d]	1926 LA	Concrete pipes	225	113	50
Weiser Manufacturing	1926 LA	Locks, hardware	58	23	40
National Paper	1927	Paper products	1,000[e]	(276)	—
Dayton Foundry	1927 LA	Iron castings	100	(28)	—
Electric Heating Co.	1927	Electric products	5	5	100
Emsco Refractories	1928	Ind. furnace refractories	100	25	25
Firestone Tire & Rubber	1928 b	Tires	1,525	(421)	—
Los Angeles Chemical	1929 LA	Insecticides, ind. chem.	60	6	10
Philadelphia Quartz	1931 b	Sodium silicate	20	10	50
Rheem Manufacturing	1931 b	Steel products	300	195	65
L.C. Flewelling	1933	Typewriter desks	4	2	50
Balian Ice Cream	1934 LA	Ice cream	14	1	10
Brown–Saltman	1934 LA	Home furniture	130	13	10
Pioneer Textile Dyers	1934	Textile dying	4	2	50
United States Gypsum	1934b	Roofing material	—	—	
Davenport Mnfg.	1935 LA	Road/farm machinery	18	9	50

Company	Year	Product			
Hollydale Pottery	1935	Dinnerware, pottery prods	80	72	90
Keeno Packing	1935	Pet food	11	10	90
General Motors	1936 b	Auto assembly	1,487[f]	202	13.6
Pacific Cast Iron Pipe	1936 LA	Iron products	250	(69)	—
Harbor Furniture	1937 LA	Home furniture	75	60	80
Industrial Lubricants	1937	Lubricants	5	3	50
Lunday-Thagard Oil	1937	Asphalt products	15	8	50
Purex Corp.	1937	Cleansers	60	18	30
South Gate Casket	1937	Caskets	15	11	75
Amstrong Cork	1938 b	Asphalt tile	46	9	20
Halsivent	1938	Gas appliance vent pipes	11	11	100
De Long Engineering	1938	Oil equip overhauling, aircraft parts	25	3	10
Benson Cabinet Works	1939	House cabinets	10	5	50
Schumacher Wall Board	1939 LA	Wall board, lath	122	26	21
		Average			29.2%

Key:

b   Branch plant of national company

LA   Moved from other site in Los Angeles metropolitan area to South Gate

—   Data not reported

[a]Most of this data is from 1940, with a few exceptions.

[b]Numbers in parentheses are estimates based on the average of 29.2% of employees living locally, calculated from employees' places of residence that were actually reported in the surveys.

[c]For this company, 2 employees were reported in 1924, and 80 in 1963. I've estimated 10 in 1930.

[d]In 1926, American Concrete and Steel Pipe was formed out of a merger of two existing South Gate plants, Bent Concrete Pipe and Western Concrete Pipe. As such, employment figures are given only for American Concrete, and have been omitted for Bent Concrete and Western Concrete.

[e]*Home Gardens Press*, October 29, 1926, estimated the plant would employ 1,000.

[f]This number is taken from UAW Local 216 membership lists for 1940. The local newspaper reported that GM employed about 900 in 1936 (*South Gate Press*, June 20, 1963).

Sources: Tom Thienes, "Contributions Toward the History of the City of South Gate, California" (unpublished manuscript, 1942, SGHWL), 123–140; South Gate Book field notes, FWP; *South Gate Tribune*, January 24, 1924; UAW Local 216 "Membership List" 1940, UAW216, ALUA.

this point, it is probable that these figures reflected journey-to-work patterns for most of the prewar period.

A final survey taken by the Works Progress Administration in 1939, which queried factories within ten miles of downtown about the residences of their workers, found that 30 percent of workers living in the southeast (including Vernon, Huntington Park, South Gate, and Maywood) were also employed in that district. For these residents, the most common places of employment were, in descending order, the southeast, South Central, and East L.A. districts. (Significantly, the central business district was excluded from this portion of the study.) Among streetcar users, the survey found that residents of southeast Los Angeles traveled most frequently to downtown and Hollywood. Southeast residents often worked in Hollywood, and "rather large numbers of persons" employed in the southeast resided in the Hollywood district. "These districts showed the greatest concentration and crossing of traffic of any so analyzed," the survey concluded.[29]

One final pattern is worth noting. In South Gate, the smaller factories of local origin tended to hire residents from the area more than larger plants with distant roots. Industries that hired at least half of their workers locally had an average of 38 employees, compared to an average of 195 employees for plants with less than half of their workers as residents. And plants with hiring policies friendly to locals tended to originate in South Gate—they were not branch plants or industries relocated from other sites. Of plants employing a majority of South Gate residents, 75 percent were local start-ups; of those hiring under half of their workers locally, only 33 percent originated in South Gate. Plants of local origins, thus, appeared to be the most loyal to South Gate residents.[30] At the same time, these patterns meant that the vast majority of local jobs—mainly in branch plants—went to residents of outside communities. The largest plants were least friendly to locals in their hiring practices.

Taken together, the journey-to-work evidence suggests that the vast majority of South Gate's blue-collar residents commuted to work outside their hometown, typically less than ten miles away. The result was a milieu different from the communities of many American workers. In contrast to many eastern mill towns or even industrial cities like Chicago, South Gate was not a tight-knit, physically compact community where residents traveled a short distance to the factory then returned to a common area of neighborhood and leisure, creating a seamless sociospatial existence in which a working-class culture could be forged.[31] In southern Los Angeles, commuting to work had become a way of life.[32] The duties of breadwinning turned wage earners into a mobile people, familiar with the larger metropolis beyond their borders.

Work Life

In the 1920s and 1930s, the work life of most industrial laborers who lived in South Gate was marked by social disconnection. Few forged meaningful social ties in the workplace, a result of several key influences. The first was the daily reality of commuting to work. While most traveled to factories within ten miles of South Gate, commuting still denoted a separation between hometown and workplace and a substantial amount of time in transit. This experience was shared by a steelworker who lived in Maywood and worked in Vernon, who recalled, "In Maywood you had a more isolated life. Your social life wasn't connected with the mill. . . . Half of the workers here lived 30 to 40 miles away."[33] While work pulled residents out of their suburb, it did not always pull them into a meaningful community experience at work.[34]

Contributing to this social disconnection was job instability. Periodic layoffs were common for workers in both large and small factories around southern Los Angeles. Virgil Collins, an autoworker, union leader, and South Gate resident, recalled the period he worked for Wilys-Overland in Maywood during the mid-1930s: "In those days when you had a model change over, you'd be down 2 or 3 or 4 months, and you had to get out and scrounge because you didn't have unemployment insurance until 1937." During plant shutdowns, Collins did "springing up" at a furniture factory, which involved tying down the springs in furniture cushions, a task that resembled auto upholstery assembly.[35] The Great Depression exacerbated job insecurity. A typical casualty was Herman Seaborg, who moved his family from Ishpeming, Michigan, to Home Gardens in 1922. Once a foreman of a machine shop in Ishpeming, Seaborg was unable to find steady work after arriving in Los Angeles. In the 1920s, he took occasional jobs in the factories of Vernon and downtown, then worked for the Cyanide Company spraying fruit trees. In 1930, his eighteen-year-old son Glenn recorded in his diary, "Dad came home from work at noon, having lost his job due to the layoffs caused by the Depression sweeping through our country." At this time, Glenn himself was seeking work at local tire and rubber factories, "but with no success." Three weeks later, Glenn wrote, "Dad still out of work, which raises problems with paying the bills, buying our food, etc." After three years of joblessness, Herman moved with his wife, suffering from bronchitis, to a small cabin in the San Gabriel Mountains, which they purchased for $25. They left their two children, ages twenty-one and nineteen, behind in South Gate. Herman finally landed a job with the WPA in the mountains.[36]

Finally, an ambivalence toward labor unions reinforced social fragmen-

tation at work. The unions, representing perhaps the best potential framework for camaraderie and social bonding among industrial workers,[37] got a
mixed reception from local workers for a number of reasons. The story of
labor organizing at GM South Gate suggests why.

There is little irony in the fact that GM opened its South Gate plant in
1936, the year of the most militant action by workers at the company's
Michigan plants. It was the year autoworkers organized the great sit-down
strike at Flint, founded the United Auto Workers (UAW), and aligned with
the more radical, newly formed Congress of Industrial Organizations
(CIO). In this volatile climate, open-shop Los Angeles appeared ever more
attractive to GM management. GM's arrival in South Gate, in fact, was part
of a small regional boom in automobile manufacturing. In 1926, L.A.
County had two auto assembly plants, and by the mid-1930s three more
had arrived. They were attracted not only by the city's open-shop reputation but also by thriving western markets. In the mid-1930s, the eleven
counties of Southern California purchased about 40 to 45 percent of new
cars sold on the entire West Coast. Los Angeles was a booming auto town.[38]

GM built its first L.A. plant on a forty-three-acre bean field in unincorporated territory, just west of South Gate. The plant sat beside the railroad
tracks that separated South Gate from Watts. It was GM's second-largest
assembly plant in the nation and headquarters of the company's West
Coast Division. As a "BOP" facility producing Buicks, Oldsmobiles, and
Pontiacs, it was the first in the nation to manufacture more than one type of
automobile on a single assembly line. The two-story, fifteen-acre plant had
body and paint shops above, body and chassis sections below, and a large
employee cafeteria.[39]

When the assembly line started rolling in 1936, GM South Gate had
1,000 workers on its payroll; the number rose to 1,400 a year later. The
plant favored workers who hailed from the southern states. "G.M. in 1936
had three classes of people they hired. One was Arkansas, one was Texas,
and one was Oklahoma," recalled Virgil Collins, who worked at GM in the
late 1930s. When the plant opened each day, about 150 to 200 people waited
in line for jobs. "The personnel guy would come out, maybe talk to them
and see which ones he liked. . . . He'd walk up to 'em, 'Where you from?'
and he'd come back, 'You, you, you, and you, come on in' . . . They zeroed in
on the southwestern states." It was a deliberate action on the part of GM,
according to Collins, because management believed these migrants were
hostile to unions. Collins estimated that 70 percent of the plant's early
workforce hailed from those three states. This hiring preference spurred
more migration from that region, as recent arrivals urged family members
left behind to come work at GM South Gate. One resident remembered his

neighbors, the Dunnes: "When the word got out that they were going to build the GM plant, every cousin the Dunnes had came out here from Texas to get a job in the GM plant. . . . They moved heaven and earth, you know mutually supportive. Hell there wasn't a Dunne left in Texas." The majority of the time, the hiring process was quite arbitrary, which made employment prospects hard to predict.[40]

A campaign to unionize local autoworkers began as soon as the plant opened. It was spurred by national events, including passage of the labor-friendly Wagner Act; GM's recognition of the UAW in February 1936, which applied to factories nationwide; and the economic pressures of the Depression. And in Los Angeles, the dismal state of unionization left ample room for growth. By mid-1936, the UAW began a spirited organizing drive at the South Gate plant. But organizers soon met stubborn resistance, both from outside foes and from workers themselves, many of whom were ambivalent about unionism. This ambivalence had both cultural and economic roots. Culturally, a good number of workers subscribed to the tenets of plain-folk Americanism, a belief system of migrants from the Upper South and Great Plains states. Part of this worldview included a distrust of unions, stemming from notions of individualism, personal salvation, and anticommunism. Plain-folk Americanism revered independence and toughness, qualities that seemed antithetical to the collective strategy of unions. Collins described it as "the John Wayne syndrome . . . 'Let me do it myself, Uncle Sam,' that sort of thing. 'I don't need any help, I can work hard.'" Many workers viewed unions as unnecessary, telling organizers, "Why should I pay union dues to have somebody tell me what I can do? Why should I let you negotiate for me with the company? I'll do it myself." Another dimension was the concept of salvation espoused by the evangelical Protestant churches, to which some of these workers belonged. These churches discouraged outside loyalties—such as unions—because they distracted members from the pursuit of individual salvation. Finally, plain-folk Americanism harbored a deep antipathy to communism, which was easily associated with the labor movement. A number of local workers shared this hostility, especially evident after World War II. In addition to cultural influences, economic concerns fueled skepticism about organized labor. According to Collins, who was active in early organizing efforts, economic fears were the most powerful deterrent to joining a union. The fear of being fired was powerful, particularly before the Wagner Act of 1935. "There was a great deal of uncertainty in the plants," he recalled. "There was an inherent fear in the blue-collar workers because they was always able to fire them. They would just come down and, 'C'mon you're out of here.' There was no recourse, none whatsoever for a person."[41]

Despite these formidable barriers, a militant, persistent core of organizers made rapid progress. Though the first formal meeting drew only 20 of about 1,400 workers, the UAW chartered Local 216 a month later in February 1937, making GM South Gate the second automobile plant to unionize in Los Angeles (Wilys-Overland had organized a few weeks earlier). Thirty-seven ardent unionists spearheaded the drive, and within four months they had signed up all but 93 workers in the GM plant.[42] The pragmatic benefits offered by the union, appreciated acutely during the Depression, helped break down older misgivings. The UAW vowed to fight for better work conditions, job security, and wage parity with eastern plants (the starting wage was 50 cents per hour at GM South Gate, compared to 75 cents in Detroit). Job security was especially compelling, coming at a time when the other economic cushion for local working-class families—the home—was under siege by economic and political forces. The local practice of self-provisioning, moreover, may have encouraged some workers to risk unionization since they had food sources in the event of a strike.[43]

While the union succeeded in its functional capacity of protecting the interests of autoworkers, it faltered in promoting social cohesion. Autoworkers in South Gate lacked the "culture of unity" that characterized workers elsewhere in the 1930s, undergirding the CIO's success.[44] The UAW tried to achieve such social unity at GM South Gate through regular meetings, basketball and softball teams, parties, excursions, free movies, and a women's auxiliary whose purpose was largely social. But the rank-and-file response was lukewarm at best. Collins woefully recalled the paltry attendance at meetings: "Most of the time, if you got 10 percent, that would be a big meeting." Another 20 percent, he estimated, were partially involved, while 70 percent took no interest whatsoever. They preferred to have their union leaders do their business for them. Collins remembered pleading with fellow workers to show up at meetings, to which they responded, "Well, that's why I elected you. I don't want to come to the meeting." Instead of attending meetings after work, they opted for drinks at the Keg or the Backdoor, two popular watering holes near the factory, or more likely they went home. "The majority would walk across the street, get in their cars, and go home—right by the union hall," said Collins. For the vast majority of workers who were commuters, this was not surprising. After a long day on the assembly line and the prospect of a tiring drive after work, home was the most compelling destination. This was especially true for the GM workers from the east San Gabriel Valley, who faced commutes ranging from forty-five to ninety minutes each way. Some arose very early in the morning, drove to work in a camper to beat the traffic, slept for an hour or so, then went in to start the day's work. Where commuting was commonplace, the unions suffered. Labor organizers at Bethlehem Steel in Vernon faced a similar problem. With social life unconnected to the plant, "it was harder to organize," one labor leader conceded. An organizer in the aircraft industry concurred: "The problem was how to reach these fellows . . . [it] was quite enormous because the plants were widely scattered."[45]

For the majority of workers, the union commanded a minimal commitment. The geographic disjunction of work and home life played some role in this, as did certain cultural beliefs of the autoworkers. Although the union served as the focal point of social and political commitment for a small group of union leaders, for most it served a more utilitarian function.[46] This was perhaps best illustrated in the huge turnouts at company picnics sponsored by GM management. As Collins ruefully reminisced, "They'd have a picnic once a year for all the employees. Old man Clark [the plant manager] would stand out on the back of a truck . . . looking down on the masses. And he would throw coins out and let the kids scramble for them. I would never go. I said, 'I'm not no goddamn slave, nobody is gonna do that to me or even when I'm around.' But some didn't look upon it as being that way. To me, that was real significant as to what his mentality was. No way was I going to their damned picnic. *Did a lot of workers go?* Yeah, sorry to say that. I wished that no one had gone."[47]

PLAYING IN LOS ANGELES

As working-class suburbanites, South Gate residents might spend their leisure hours contributing to the family's sustenance through gardening, raising small livestock, or building a home. Or they might have fun. As for workers across the country, leisure was an important dimension of life that helped define one's experience and identity. It was a sphere that individuals could control to meet their own needs, to best achieve social fulfillment. All was not toil and hardship for the working-class people of South Gate. They found ways to enjoy the good life they had made for themselves, even if it was done cheaply or simply.[48]

Residents of South Gate lacked the sort of ethnic ties that united immigrant communities in older industrial cities, with their fierce loyalties to ethnic merchants, newspapers, and churches. As acculturated, native-born whites, they had mostly dissolved their ties to the old country. The cultural proclivities that did exist revolved loosely around whiteness and southernness. Remnants of southern culture appeared locally, inclining those from that region toward certain religious and social practices. For the most part, however, South Gate residents were ripe targets of a different kind of culture—the culture of consumption and recreation. Indeed, they proved to be voracious consumers of popular culture and the recreational opportunities that Los Angeles offered.

Even as it defined them culturally, leisure also shaped their spatial existence and relationship with the city. Like work, leisure pulled South Gate's blue-collar residents out of their suburb and into the broader metropolis. The scale tipped outward, quite simply, because the paltry choices for amusements in South Gate paled in comparison to the cornucopia of entertainments in Los Angeles. While this was not a static situation—patterns shifted under the influence of political and economic conditions—for the most part South Gate residents were a cosmopolitan people when it came to having fun. In their easy mobility and frequent interfaces with Los Angeles, working-class families contrasted with the more firmly rooted merchants of South Gate.

On the local scene, a few commercial venues, organized activities, and informal diversions offered some opportunity for play. In the 1920s and 1930s, commercial leisure in South Gate was typical of most working-class communities, dominated by dance halls, vaudeville, baseball, boxing, and movies. In fact, such recreation became confined to working-class suburbia as a result of successful efforts by Progressives in the first two decades of the twentieth century to abolish working-class amusements from L.A. city. By 1910, Los Angeles had considerably fewer saloons, dance halls, and boxing rings than San Francisco, despite Los Angeles's larger population.[49] What few commercial venues remained were pushed into small working-class districts around the metropolis. Just before World War I, the industrial suburb of Vernon was renowned as "a carnival of vice day and night," with saloons, liquor-serving dance halls, baseball, and boxing venues. Prohibition only pushed such establishments underground and deeper into the suburbs. As one historian put it, "Roadhouses and clubs fell like roaches on Watts, Vernon, and other working-class suburbs with every noisy, politically expedient housecleaning in Los Angeles." Thus while Progressives and Prohibitionists thought they had cleansed Los Angeles of cheap amusements, in truth they had merely pushed them to the suburbs.[50]

While cheap commercial amusements were condemned by reformers, they were embraced by many working people. In South Gate, the main offerings were dance halls, movies, vaudeville, live theater, and sports. There was not, however, a large selection within this range. In scanning the landscape of leisure in South Gate, the place to begin is at its physical locus: the auditorium. Typically owned and operated by community leaders, these multipurpose buildings served as vaudeville houses, dance halls, movie theaters, lecture halls, and boxing arenas, as well as venues for social events sponsored by civic groups. Occasionally, they served as makeshift churches. Between two and four such auditoriums operated in South Gate during the interwar years.[51]

Auditoriums frequently served as dance halls. In Home Gardens, Gibbo Hall hosted a five-piece jazz orchestra every Tuesday night, while Dudlext Auditorium sponsored dance contests with a "loving cup" awarded to the best couple. As a teenager, Juanita Smith learned to dance at a hall in Home Gardens. "The fireman and his wife that lived in back of us, they would take me with them up there," she recalled. "They would teach me how to dance, like waltzes, fox-trots, things like that. They had a real good turnout, and I never heard of a fight or any trouble in that dance hall." Often sponsored by local women's groups, these dances were well chaperoned but still good places for young people to socialize. By the 1930s, the Casino Ball Room had opened, serving as the town's sole venue devoted exclusively to dancing.[52]

South Gate also hosted a modest offering of motion pictures and vaudeville, some held in auditoriums. In 1924, Dudlext Auditorium featured a mixed program of movies, vaudeville, theater, and dancing every Saturday night. On Mondays, Thursdays, Fridays and Sundays, the auditorium screened motion pictures only. The Garden Theater was the lone movie house in South Gate, presenting a mix of film and vaudeville in the 1920s, and movies exclusively by the 1930s. Given the scarcity of local movie houses at a time when Hollywood was in its heyday, residents eagerly sought the cinema outside the suburb. A glittering movie palace downtown held greater allure than a plain auditorium at home.[53]

Live theater was more successful in South Gate and neighboring suburbs, routinely attracting large crowds. Several local and traveling theater troupes provided the talent, including the South Gate Community Players, the Shelley Dramatic Players, and the Murphey Comedians. The Shelley Players were the biggest draw. Formed in 1925, this troupe staged comedies and dramas, such as *Chicken Legs, Give and Take,* and *Twin Beds.* They offered a different show every week, making them a rival to motion pictures in terms of variety. To assure capacity crowds, they offered promos like admitting the first twenty-five adults free, and they kept ticket prices low, ranging from ten to fifty cents. When the Depression hit, they disbanded but then regrouped in 1931 as the Radio Players, and held performances in a tent in South Gate. One of the Shelley Players' most loyal enthusiasts was Glenn Seaborg of Home Gardens, who attended performances religiously as a teenager. "As usual we walked [three miles] to the tent site, southwest corner of State St. and Florence Ave.," he recorded in his diary in 1927. With few cash reserves, Glenn and his buddies devised a scheme for entering free. They waited until intermission, mingled with audience members as they stretched their legs, then shuffled in and found empty seats in general admission. They would watch act 2, then wait around for the next performance to see act 1. Their ploy worked so well that on the rare occasion when it failed, Glenn recorded, "had to pay."[54]

Another popular pastime in South Gate was amateur and semiprofessional sports. By 1930, South Gate had five pool halls, which had replaced the saloon as a center of working-class male sociability during Prohibition. Over a few racks of the game, men talked, socialized, and sometimes gambled. Some pool halls also served as informal job bureaus. Amateur boxing was another local favorite. Matches were held at Dudlext Auditorium and Dahlgren Hall, and often got regular front-page coverage in the local paper during the late 1920s.[55] But the most popular sport of all in South Gate was baseball. Like most Los Angeles suburbs, South Gate and Home Gardens hosted teams in a semipro league. Incorporated towns like South Gate and Watts sponsored teams, as did unincorporated communities like Graham, Florence, and Home Gardens, and industrial plants like Firestone, GM, and Nehi Bottling Works. More strikingly, the league also included ethnic and racial ball clubs, like the "L.A. Orientals" (Chinese), "Brown Buffaloes" (African Americans), and "Carta Blanca" (Latinos).[56]

Free admission to these games made them highly popular. The teams were financed by local merchants, by passing the hat at the games (a typical collection was $40), and by occasional appropriations from the city.[57] It comes as little surprise that the local team was dubbed the South Gate Merchants. In the summertime, the Merchants played almost every Sunday at the local baseball field, usually against traveling industrial teams that lacked home fields. A typical game drew 150 people in the stands, and more aside the cars parked along the outfield. For the majority of residents not involved in local civic groups, baseball provided one of few activities that promoted loyalty to their hometown. When a rivalry between South Gate and Home Gardens developed in the mid-1920s, opposing fans concocted the epithets "slop gate" and "home garbage." By the 1930s, the semipro leagues gave way to local amateur leagues, most likely brought on by economic woes. South Gate joined the amateur Southeast Commercial Softball League, composed of clubs sponsored by companies or civic groups, and it had a team in a small indoor baseball league.[58]

Besides these legitimate diversions, South Gate had its bawdier side as well. As in many working-class neighborhoods, drinking and gambling were perennial fixtures during the interwar years, Prohibition notwithstanding. In the 1920s, bootleg activity flourished. Homes, predictably, were the centers of operation. Police made numerous raids on these places, confiscating 300 gallons of "grape wine" at one home, and at another 400 gallons of mash, 48 boxes of capping equipment, and liquor labels saying "Made in Chihuahua, Mexico." These operations attracted customers near and far. On Glenn Seaborg's block in Home Gardens, one bootlegging home had autos constantly cluttering the driveway. Given the importance of homes in the suburb, South Gate undoubtedly had its share of "kitchen barrooms," although no direct evidence confirms this. Gambling often went hand in hand with imbibing. Several drinking places had slot machines, while a "Chinese game joint" operated in the 1920s on a large vacant lot southwest of the city—the future site of the GM plant.[59]

By decade's end, a local reform campaign had curbed gambling. The suburb passed a series of morality laws from 1926 to 1931, aimed particularly at gambling. By the mid-1930s, the laws were working. Over a fifteen-month period from 1933 to 1934, only 1 percent of local arrests were for gambling. The police chief noted in 1935 that "very little gambling" existed in South Gate. Drinking, however, was another story. The repeal of Prohibition in 1933 spawned a proliferation of local drinking places. By the mid-1930s, seventy-eight South Gate businesses were selling beer—fifteen of them connected to clubs or dance halls—and nineteen sold spirits. Arrest statistics confirmed the popularity of drinking. Over the same fifteen-month period, 347 persons were arrested for drunkenness, representing 28 percent of total arrests.[60]

Commercial leisure in South Gate thus consisted mainly of dancing, a movie theater, vaudeville, live theater, intermittent sports, and illicit amusements. Few sources specify exactly who patronized these venues. From scattered references, however, it appears that the most probable patrons were the young and "better off" residents. Most working-class parents, particularly women, devoted their spare time to their homes and gardens. The sociologist studying Bell Gardens noticed a similar pattern there: "The more expensive recreational activities are not entirely absent, but only less common than among more prosperous and less busy people."[61]

Besides commercial amusements, residents also engaged in informal leisure activities within South Gate, most of which occurred in the home. If leisure *time* is used as the definition, then working around the house and garden "on some 'small farm' project" consumed a good deal of it. The study of Bell Gardens found that residents devoted the greatest amount of their free time to such projects. Whether these tasks were considered work or play, the study noted, "many of the people regard such activities as pleasure as well as economic aids."[62] Like their middle-class suburban counterparts, working-class families found fulfillment in these domestic activities. But their actions were also highly motivated by the pressures of economic insecurity.[63]

Apart from household tasks, radio listening was a common home-centered leisure activity. Residents either purchased a set or assembled one, following instructions printed in local newspapers.[64] By 1930, 68.1 percent of families in South Gate owned a radio set, higher than the national average of about 50 percent.[65] Although radio was a home-based medium, it sometimes promoted neighborly sociability. Families who did not own sets frequently listened at the home of a neighbor. This was the case for Glenn Seaborg. Before his family mustered the means to buy a radio, Glenn spent numerous afternoons and evenings at his neighbor's house listening to his favorite shows, like the Tuesday evening program when Nick Harris would "tell a detective story over the radio." He averaged about one visit per week. Once his mother bought a radio, Glenn did most of his listening at home, occasionally in the company of a friend or neighbor. While the radio thus encouraged a modicum of neighborly contact, it was mostly a privatized domestic activity. Lizabeth Cohen argues that the content of radio helped forge a common culture for workers in Chicago. In Los Angeles, radio quite likely performed a similar function, although the act of listening itself could promote detachment.[66]

South Gate residents were mostly on their own when it came to free, informal leisure. Public space in the suburb, where people might gather to socialize and interact, was sorely lacking. Most notably, public parks and playgrounds were scarce, largely by choice of the residents themselves. South Gate's penurious citizenry repeatedly rejected a series of park proposals from 1925 to 1935, fearing the tax burden. Some local leaders saw the lack of public space as a detriment to the community and called on citizens for a more enlightened approach. As a local minister intoned, "An investment of a few thousand dollars in a city park and playground would be very worthwhile and would contribute to the moral welfare of the community. It would also be a great factor in establishing a community consciousness, without which no community can prosper." But residents ignored such pleas. Only in 1935 did South Gate finally get a park, when it purchased twenty-two acres of tax-delinquent land at a bargain price. Equally dismal was the availability of playgrounds for local children. In the late 1920s, the city sporadically financed supervised playgrounds in the summertime. By 1935, these funds had dried up, forcing children to play on the streets or in vacant lots turned into makeshift play spaces (see fig. 3-1). In its reluctance to subsidize play space and activities for children, South Gate

Figure 3-1   Ethel Johnson (left), Glenn Seaborg's cousin, with Alice Williams, Home Gardens,
1920s. Lacking playgrounds and parks, the children of South Gate used vacant lots and yards
as recreational spaces. Photo courtesy of Glenn T. Seaborg and Helen L. Seaborg.

contrasted with upper-class suburbs that generously provided community
resources for children.[67]

In relative terms, the recreational offerings in South Gate were meager
at best, paling in comparison to the abundance of amusements in Greater
Los Angeles. Both natural and commercial amusements lured the suburb's
working class, offering an impressive mélange of experiences and pleasures.
For the most part, local residents commuted to play. In the process, they
deepened their familiarity with the metropolis, strengthening a cosmopolitan sense of comfort with places beyond the borders of their neighborhood.

Already in the 1920s, Southern California was renowned for its scenic
mountains, beaches, and deserts. A map produced by the Junior Chamber of

Figure 3-2   This map, portraying L.A. County as a "Sport Land," conveyed the tremendous
recreational resources of the metropolis in the 1930s. Los Angeles Junior Chamber of
Commerce file, Haynes Collection, Department of Special Collections, University Research
Library, UCLA.

Commerce in 1930 depicts Los Angeles as a "Sport Land" with golf and tennis in Hollywood, fishing and swimming off the coast, and leisurely drives
in the mountains and deserts (see fig. 3-2). The possibilities abounded.
Many of the natural attractions—like the beaches and mountains—were
free to all comers. As a result, outdoor recreation came to represent a sort of
social leveler in Los Angeles, a place where people of different classes might
mix. Although the upper classes tried to change this by establishing elite
beach clubs, designed to keep away the "riffraff," most L.A. beaches remained open to a wide cross section of classes. The line, however, was drawn
when it came to race. Nearly all Southern California beaches were off-limits to blacks, more by de facto practice than written law. Although no
beaches explicitly prohibited blacks, public officials and public pressure encouraged blacks to use certain beaches set aside for them, such as a part of
Santa Monica known as "the Inkwell" and a section of Manhattan Beach.[68]

For South Gate residents, the beach was the most popular recreational
destination, partly because of its easy accessibility. The favored spot was
Long Beach, only twelve miles away down Long Beach Boulevard and
home of "The Pike," an amusement park on the shoreline in the tradition of
Coney Island and Atlantic City.[69] Hermosa and Redondo Beaches were also
popular, fifteen miles from South Gate and accessible by Red Car. Young
people resourcefully minimized the costs of these excursions. "We never
spent anything but the time of day when I was a teenager," recalled John
Sheehy. "We went out, but we didn't do anything that cost any money." Be-

ginning around age eleven, Sheehy went to the beach "everyday in the summertime." He and friends hitchhiked the twenty-five-minute ride to Long Beach, then spent the day swimming, roaming, and just hanging out. "You go to the beach all day, you go swimming about six times, you get a ravenous appetite, you never have a nickel in your pocket. Pretty soon, you get so hungry you just gotta go home. . . . We'd leave the house at 9 in the morning and we'd come home about 4—sunburned, weary, hungry." Typically, he went to the Pike with a small group of friends, then met up with other classmates, numbering from twenty-five to fifty on any given day. "Every kid that could get away without cutting the lawn or something would be out hitchhiking. . . . You'd know many, many kids." Sheehy frequented Long Beach in his youth, then Hermosa Beach during his high school years. Famous Venice Beach, farther up the coast, was rarely a destination: "We never went near Venice. It was too tony, it wasn't free." Glenn Seaborg showed the same beachgoing patterns as a youth. The beach was also popular with families. Ralph DeVries, a carpenter, took his family to Long Beach "quite often" in the summertime. His daughter recalled, "My dad had been in a band in Iowa, and they had a band concert every Sunday at Long Beach. . . . While he was listening, we'd walk around the Pike and maybe ride the merry-go-round." And Juanita Smith, who worked as a secretary in Long Beach, frequently went to the ocean after work in the summer with her coworkers.[70]

Another favored outdoor activity was the all-day drive. A family might hop in the car and head to the mountains, desert, or coastline. As a youngster, Wallace McFadden and his friends took all-day "truck rides" to the beaches or mountains. "We didn't have to go but twenty or thirty miles and we were right out in the country again." Mountain camping was less accessible to the people of South Gate, due partly to public policy. Los Angeles County developed several mountain camp areas targeted at "business and professional men," while L.A. city operated municipal camps only for city residents, thus excluding those who lived in outlying suburbs.[71]

In addition to natural recreation, the L.A. metropolis offered a dizzying array of commercial amusements. It was hardly surprising that the cinema was by far the most popular among South Gate residents. Not only was Hollywood a touchstone of metropolitan culture, but the movies had become a staple of working-class leisure nationally by the 1920s. As one observer of Los Angeles workers noted in 1927, "[W]eekly or biweekly visits to moving picture theatres, . . . is perhaps the most usual form of relaxation among families of low income groups." The study of Bell Gardens found that working-class families, often quite poor ones, "attend the movies once a week or oftener, and many children go to the special Saturday afternoon

matinees. A very few people there are who seldom attend the movies." The
study also noted that the cinema "probably takes people outside of Bell
Gardens more frequently than any other type of leisure-time activity." The
movies could act as a strong centrifugal force on the lives of working people
in Los Angeles.[72]

This was overwhelmingly true for South Gate residents. Most ventured
to theaters in neighboring suburbs like Huntington Park, Graham, Florence, Walnut Park, and Watts. South Gate's sole movie house, the Garden
Theater, was less popular because it was smaller and showed second-run
movies. The movie houses in neighboring suburbs ranged from modest
halls to elaborate movie palaces. On the low end was the Lyric Theater in
Walnut Park, little more than a storefront. A small step up was the Alcazar
Theater in Bell, nestled between shops in the commercial district. Despite
its modest size, the Alcazar was adorned with an elaborate exterior and a
plush interior with wood detailing along the walls. At the high end was the
Fox Florence Theater, a grand movie house. Occupying a generous plot of
land in a residential section, the Fox was designed in Spanish mission style,
complete with courtyard, archways, fountain, draping flowers, and a curv-
ing stairway. The interior was sprawling and plush, with high ceilings, deep
oriental carpets, candelabras, carved hardwood beams, stained-glass windows, and floral displays. Like all movie palaces of the period, such lavish
decor was meant to transport moviegoers to a fantasy world the moment
they entered. In working-class suburbia, the effect was even more pronounced, the palaces contrasting sharply with the gritty surroundings of
the area. The wide selection of theaters outside of South Gate was a compelling pull to residents seeking the full movie experience.

The experiences of several residents suggest common patterns of
moviegoing. Home Gardens residents Herman and Selma Seaborg went to
the cinema nearly every week during the 1920s. Their favorite theater was
the Nadeau in nearby Graham, with its ten-cent admission price. As a
teenager, Juanita Smith and a girlfriend took the Yellow Car downtown
to attend Saturday matinees. Mary DeVries, daughter of a carpenter, attended the movies almost weekly in the 1930s, mainly in Walnut Park,
Huntington Park, Florence, and occasionally in South Gate. On the other
hand, neither John Sheehy nor Virgil Collins attended the movies much at
all, preferring instead activities like beachgoing or playing poker at home—
both virtually free.[73]

A precise record of movie attendance can be found in Glenn Seaborg's
diary. As a preteen, he attended the Garden Theater in Home Gardens quite
regularly. An industrious lad, he found ways to avoid the admission charge
like distributing handbills for the theater on Saturdays in exchange for four

passes. By his teenage years, Glenn began frequenting theaters outside of South Gate. From ages fourteen to twenty-one (1927–34), Glenn attended the movies 300 times. Fully 96 percent of these outings were to theaters outside of South Gate, particularly in Huntington Park, Walnut Park, Graham, and Bell. His most frequent destination was the California Theater in Huntington Park. Glenn also ventured to theaters downtown on Broadway, Los Angeles's cinema counterpart to New York City's theater district. He also attended a few films in West L.A. after he became a student at UCLA, as well as in Alhambra, East L.A., and Belvedere. Most striking of all, given his love of the cinema, Glenn attended South Gate's Garden Theater only 13 of 300 times over the seven-year span. For Seaborg, the cinema was a compelling force that drew him out of South Gate and into the greater city. The decision of which theater to attend was based, not surprisingly, on where the best movie was playing. Glenn and his friends would drive around the various neighborhoods until they found a picture they liked.[74]

Sports was another attraction that pulled residents into the city. Before Los Angeles had a professional baseball team, the city hosted spring training for the Chicago Cubs. The Cubs played at Los Angeles's Wrigley Field, a smaller version of the Chicago stadium, located at 42nd Street and Avalon Boulevard in South Central, about four miles from South Gate. Penniless as ever, John Sheehy and his buddies loved to watch these big-leaguers as they prepared for opening day. The boys would hitchhike to the stadium, then watch the action from the street beyond the left field wall. "We'd stand in the street near an open gate. When one of the balls would be hit over the fence, we'd have a guy waiting on Avalon. We'd catch the ball and throw it to him and he was gone. That was how we'd get our balls." While Sheehy's mode of attendance was free, a modest admission price enabled many adults to attend the games. In addition to baseball, other professional sports lured residents to distant points around Los Angeles, such as boxing in Vernon and football games at the local universities.[75]

The Seaborg diary suggests that the geographic patterns of play could change under certain influences, such as the Great Depression or a change in the life cycle. For Glenn Seaborg, recreation was a powerful centrifugal force during the 1920s when he was a youngster, pulling him out of his hometown and into Los Angeles. During a single week in the summer of 1927, between Glenn's sophomore and junior year at Jordan High, Glenn took a Sunday drive with his family, attended the Shelley Players in Huntington Park, went to three movies (in Bell, Graham, and Walnut Park), went to Long Beach to swim and watch a vaudeville show, and went roller-skating at Dudlext Auditorium. Nearly all of these activities occurred outside of South Gate. As economic resources shrank during the Depression and his work routine intensified at UCLA, Glenn stayed closer to home during his leisure hours (he commuted to school from South Gate). For example, he continued to frequent the cinema in the early 1930s, but confined his outings to the southern suburbs. During the late 1920s and 1930s, radio also rooted him closer to home. Radio appeared to parallel, rather than replace, the movies for Glenn, since the frequency that he engaged in each increased and decreased simultaneously. Seaborg's diary suggests that he perceived radio, films, and live theater similarly. For all three, he faithfully noted the names of the programs. During a typical week in July 1933, Glenn ventured to a park in Wilmington, his friend Stanley Thompson's home in Watts, a concert at the Hollywood Bowl, and two "shows" (location unidentified), but he also spent evenings at home reading or listening to the radio. Although his activity had subsided and occurred closer to home, he still made an impressive number of trips outside of his hometown.[76]

In all, the scant resources of South Gate compelled working-class residents to venture outside of the town's borders in their quest for amusements. Even the limited resources of a working-class budget did not stop them in this pursuit. Youngsters especially found ways to play cheaply. To save on transportation costs, they hitchhiked. To avert admission costs, they went to the beach for free, they bartered labor for a free ticket, they attended local ballgames, or, more deviously, they sneaked into theaters at opportune moments. Adults also found ways to economize. While they ventured to commercial recreation less often than their children, they too frequented the beach, baseball games, dances, and the movies—activities that were either free or very cheap. Life was not so hard that they sacrificed leisure. Even working-class suburbanites enjoyed a slice of the good life that was coming to define the identity of Los Angeles.

COMMUTER CONSUMERS

One final activity that shaped the rhythm of working-class life was the consumption of goods. Although shopping generally was not an activity with significant social dimensions, it did constitute a regular, important part of day-to-day experience. Like work and leisure, consumption drew residents into the greater city. The prime reason for this was the weakness of the local retail base. "Although there are three business districts, they do not afford adequate opportunity for the citizens to do all their shopping in South Gate," noted a local pastor. "Splendid markets are operating which offer the very best opportunities in buying food, but there are no clothing stores of equal rating." This deficiency in local businesses, he concluded, contributed to a "lack of common community interest." There was truth in his comments. Aside from grocery shopping, residents made most of their purchases outside of South Gate, particularly in Huntington Park and downtown Los Angeles. In the era before decentralized shopping malls dominated Los Angeles, the very best shopping was found in the downtown cluster of popular department stores. The biggest draws—cheaper prices and better selection—were enough to turn residents into commuter consumers.[77]

John Sheehy recalled that his family shopped most frequently in Watts during the 1920s. "They had nice stores in Watts of all kinds—furniture, clothing, hardware. . . . There was grocery shopping closer to home. But the big market, what became known as the supermarket, was in Watts." For purchases like school clothes, Sheehy's mother took him downtown to department stores like May Company, Bullocks, Robinsons, and the Broadway. Shopping, in fact, was the main reason he ventured into downtown at all as a youth. Juanita Smith's family also shopped downtown for lack of good choices in South Gate. For groceries, the Smiths patronized stores around the Yellow Car loop in South Gate. Adam Krooke, one of few renters in South Gate, also conceded that "much of my wages are spent in Los Angeles where I work, for clothing and other supplies."[78]

Glenn Seaborg's shopping habits were similar. His family made its main local purchases at Dittman's grocery and meat market in South Gate. "This is where we usually buy our food," he wrote. "To go there we walk through the vacant lots (which serve as our baseball field) at the back of our house." Otherwise, consumption took them beyond the suburb's borders. As a teenager, Glenn made trips into Huntington Park to purchase school supplies, clothing, shoes, and Christmas gifts. When he began attending UCLA, he ventured more frequently into downtown, again for school clothes and supplies ("paper and other little things"). The downtown stores were also a lure to Glenn's younger sister, Jeanette. In 1929, fifteen-year-old Jeanette, passing for eighteen, landed a summer job sorting tiles at a local factory. She earned $2 per day, squirreling much of it away. In September, she quit her job, telling her boss she was planning to start business college. As Glenn recorded, "She earned a total of $75. Today she spent it all in Los Angeles on clothes, etc., buying a black coat with a red fox collar, costing $40, shoes, purse, and other clothing for school. Mom is angry at her for 'squandering' so much money."[79]

A similar pattern of consumption occurred in Bell Gardens. Most of the local stores sold staple items, such as food, gasoline, and packaged drugs. But clothing and specialty items in which "tastes and needs differ widely" and which require "relatively large capital" to sell were purchased outside the community. "A large number of [residents] spent large proportions of their income elsewhere," the sociological study noted. The most popular shopping area was Huntington Park. Some Bell Gardens residents even went elsewhere to purchase groceries, particularly at a "large Smith's market" across the L.A. River where prices were markedly lower—a key concern for families fastidiously economizing. One young housewife remarked, "We really do believe in patronizing home stores, but a housewife does have to save where she can. We buy here only in emergency. When we want to spend as much as four or five dollars we go where we can get it all under one roof and cheaper."[80]

Shopping was not only another force pulling residents into the city, but it had political repercussions as well. The choice to buy elsewhere antagonized local merchants who struggled to keep their own businesses afloat. They politicized the issue, defining local patronage as critical to the health and survival of the community. To residents, virtually oblivious to these pleas, shopping was yet another force expanding their horizons and deepening their familiarity with the broader metropolis. Furthermore, the act of consumption did not automatically signal a working-class absorption of "consumer culture" values, whereby one's identity was defined by one's possessions. Instead, consumption was part of the everyday routine, a necessary task to keep cupboards stocked and closets supplied. Working-class interests were protected—not co-opted—by this process, as families sought out the cheapest possible goods.[81] The persistence of a working-class consciousness in the act of shopping became even more apparent when it became a point of contention between working-class residents and the merchants of South Gate.

THE MERCHANTS OF SOUTH GATE

In contrast to South Gate's working-class residents, the merchants were a more provincial lot. The rhythms of their lives resonated much closer to home. Indeed, their economic and social lives were rooted firmly in the suburb, giving them a more palpable experience of localized community. In many ways, their lives were invested in South Gate. This group emerged to take local leadership in the community, since they felt the strongest sense of community proprietorship and had the greatest financial interest in local political decisions.

The most important force that anchored merchants to the suburb was their livelihood. For the vast majority of merchants, there was hardly a job commute to speak of—work and home were both in South Gate. From 1926 to 1940, the proportion of merchants who made their homes in South Gate hovered between 71 and 76 percent. Most lived in a home separate from the business, although they were often close enough to walk to work. A significant number of proprietors—about one-quarter of the total—had home-based businesses, especially in Home Gardens. For these people, their domestic and work life occupied the same spatial universe. Of the merchants who lived outside the suburb, most resided in nearby communities like Walnut Park and Huntington Park, although a few lived as far away as Glendale, Alhambra, Beverly Hills, and Hermosa Beach, all commutes of at least thirty minutes by automobile. But even these commuter merchants stayed active in local civic groups like the Chamber of Commerce.[82]

When it came to work, the locality was both an experiential and material reality for the merchants. Not only did they spend their working hours in the suburb, but their economic success depended upon the place. Most worked solo, or with only a handful of employees. In 1929, South Gate's stores averaged one employee each. Thus, the typical proprietor had to work long hours, performing most tasks alone (see fig. 3-3).

The diverse character of local businesses suggests a fracture among the town's merchants. Those with home-based operations catered to a small local clientele. These small merchants turned their homes into economically

Figure 3-3 An interior view of the W.O. Parks Hardware store in Home Gardens, 1920s. W.O. Parks stands behind the counter. Most business proprietors worked alone, lacking the capital to hire employees. Photo courtesy of Glenn T. Seaborg and Helen L. Seaborg.

productive property—like their neighbors who raised home gardens and small livestock—and sought mainly to "stay afloat." The larger businesses, whose operations were separate from the home, had more capital to begin with and were more concerned with growth, improvements, and profits in the community. These were the merchants who assumed political leadership in pursuit of this agenda.

Despite their fierce loyalty to the suburb, South Gate's merchants experienced high turnover rates. They found it difficult to stay in business, particularly as the Depression set in. From 1926 to 1930, only 40.2 percent of the suburb's merchants remained in the same business, while 18.2 percent changed occupations but stayed in South Gate, and 41.2 percent left the community altogether. During the Depression, the turnover rates intensified. From 1930 to 1940, only 22.5 percent of local businesses remained in operation, 11.7 percent of the proprietors had different occupations, and 65.8 percent had disappeared. The most stable businessmen were those with some specialization, such as jewelers, plumbers, and physicians. The one exception was owners of building materials stores, who survived due to persistent demand among local self-builders, even in the worst of times. Those businesses with the highest turnover rates during the Depression were bakeries, banks, cabinet shops, dry goods stores, mortuaries, pool halls, women's clothing retailers, furniture stores, and restaurants. Like everyone else, merchants struggled to survive during the Depression. But unlike the rest, for them the suburb constituted the source of their own personal survival—if residents patronized their stores, then they could stay in business and put food in their mouths.[83]

For many businessmen, social life was firmly rooted around civic clubs and organizations in South Gate. Merchants were the lifeblood of local secular institutions, and in return they enjoyed a social existence reminiscent of small-town life, where geographic community overlapped with meaningful social commitments. For the merchants, community shared social and spatial boundaries.

Although merchants dominated civic groups for most of the interwar period, it wasn't always this way. In the earliest years, these institutions welcomed a broad cross section of people into their ranks. Among the earliest civic groups in South Gate were "improvement" societies, which acted as surrogate political bodies before municipal incorporation. The South Gate Improvement Society was formed in 1919, soon after the first residents purchased lots, and met every two weeks "as a means of getting together in a social way, and to agree on ways and means of improving the community." Membership was open to South Gate property owners of all classes, proving the importance of homeownership to civic and social inclusion. In 1920, they established a Sunday School and helped launch a PTA. A similar group coalesced in Home Gardens in 1923. Believing social ties would fortify political ones, the group enlivened its meetings with live music, films, vaudeville, and dancing. At the beginning, it encouraged all residents to attend the bimonthly meetings, which many did. A typical meeting attracted 200 residents. The early inclusiveness of these improvement societies suggests that the community-building process, a stage in the suburb's life cycle, promoted a geographic sense of community among all residents. But this did not last.[84]

As South Gate grew, stabilized, and institutionalized its various municipal functions, these groups transformed into associations strictly for local businessmen. For example, the Chamber of Commerce grew out of the South Gate Improvement Society, while a Businessmen's League and Chamber of Commerce spawned from the Home Gardens Improvement League. In turn, membership narrowed to businessmen and professionals only. With municipal services now handled by a city government, the necessity for broad citizen involvement diminished. No longer was everyone urged to join. By the late 1920s, merchants dominated most of South Gate's civic and service clubs, such as the Kiwanis, Masons, and Rotary Club. Within these groups, businessmen formed networks, shared interests, and promoted their class interests. For merchants, local organizations were vibrant nodes of community life. Perhaps the best illustration of this was the Business Men's Church, formed in the 1930s, that united religion with business fraternization. Despite its name, it was described as "not a church, merely a businessman's breakfast club organized on religious lines for men only. They have breakfast and prayer and a speaker." This was the clearest example of the strong and deep social bonds forged among businessmen. These organizations also represented springboards to local power.[85]

The business orientation of local civic groups was evident in their formal missions. The Rotary Club, for example, was open only to business owners and professionals, or persons with "discretionary control" over their livelihood. Most wage earners and blue-collar workers failed on this count. The charter members of the Rotary Club included the vice principal of South Gate High, the owners of a laundry, a hardware store, a mortuary, a jewelry store, and a photo finishing company, as well as a doctor, a urologist, a dentist, an attorney, a newspaper publisher, a realtor, a grocer, two insurance men, and a dealer in industrial contracting equipment. The Kiwanis Club similarly targeted proprietors and professionals. Established in 1923 as a weekly "businessmen's luncheon club," its early leaders included a furniture store owner, an attorney, and the South Gate city clerk. Its stated purpose was "to render service to the community; give primacy to human and spiritual rather than to material effort and need; encourage daily living of the Golden Rule; promote higher social living and more aggressive serviceable citizenship; and form enduring friendships and better community." The Kiwanis Club was clearly dedicated to forging bonds among its members.[86]

The Chamber of Commerce was another key group in South Gate. Established in 1920, it carried out the work of boosting South Gate, promoting local business, and protecting merchants from outside competition. It also served as an important center for local proprietors, providing a forum for them to network, discuss and promote their mutual needs, and forge social bonds. When the Chamber of Commerce ran into political troubles and disbanded in the early 1930s, it was not long before the merchants regrouped. In December 1936, they founded the South Side Business Men's Association and within two years consolidated with the South Gate Booster Club to form the South Gate Business Men's Association. They made it a point to keep an organizational base alive in one form or another throughout these years.[87]

In addition to businesses, children were a strong social "glue" in local institutional life, providing the common denominator that brought people together into secular organizations. This mirrored patterns in other communities.[88] In South Gate, Parent-Teacher Associations were among the first civic groups to coalesce. The very first organization of the area was the Tweedy School PTA, established in 1911 (even before South Gate was subdivided). Two more PTAs were formed in 1920 and 1923, and more followed as new schools were built. Every school eventually boasted a vibrant PTA that sponsored a variety of activities, including child psychology classes, a library (at Liberty School), high school dances, and six scout troops. During the Depression, they were key providers of welfare assistance to needy families. The merchant-dominated civic groups also focused much of their philanthropic energies on children, although such endeavors were usually secondary to social and business networking. The Kiwanis Club, for example, devoted at least half of its community projects to "youth character building." They gave scholarships to high school students and sponsored Boy and Girl Scout troops, a youth band, and Key Club and Kiwanettes, junior versions of the organization. They also helped stage annual Halloween and Easter parties for local kids. The Fraternal Order of Eagles sponsored youth teams in the South Gate Junior Athletic Association, while the Masons participated in laying the cornerstone for South Gate High School.[89]

These youth projects were especially needed in a town like South Gate, where modest family resources limited public expenditures on children's activities. Yet even the best efforts of the merchant groups fell far short of need. Evidence from the mid-1930s suggests that not only were few children accommodated, but the civic groups' involvement had its limits. One observer noted that these sponsors showed only "spasmodic interest" in the progress of youth groups like the Boy Scouts and left the bulk of responsibility to a single troop leader.[90] Within their organizations, merchants devoted most of their energies to civic boosterism, business promotion, and socializing.

While merchants found strong social ties in local institutional life, some evidence suggests they too ventured into Los Angeles in pursuit of leisure. As a teenager, Ruth Barrett, daughter of a doctor in Huntington Park, shopped and attended movies both in Huntington Park and downtown. Her parents also took the family to swim and dance at the Belmont Beach Club in Long Beach, where they were members. In 1934, Ruth married the owner of a water company and the couple moved to South Gate. They continued to shop in Huntington Park and at downtown department stores like May Company and Bullocks. Wallace McFadden, who worked as an accountant before opening an upholstery business in 1937, would close up shop on hot afternoons, load up his wife and young children in the family car, and drive due south to an undeveloped beach at the mouth of the L.A. River. When developers started building up the area, they went to Huntington Beach, farther away but less crowded. The family would play, swim, and relax until dark. McFadden recalled taking these outings twice per week during the summers, for at least ten years.[91]

Like their working-class neighbors, some merchant families enjoyed the recreational offerings of Los Angeles. Yet at the same time, their inclination to join and participate in local organizational life rooted them firmly to South Gate and defined their primary community experience as a local one. Ruth (Barrett) Lampmann, for example, was active in the Chamber of Commerce, Women's Club, and PTA, groups that were meaningful to her sense of community and identity. The merchants were joiners. By contrast, working-class residents rarely belonged to such organizations. They participated marginally in unions and rarely in clubs or civic groups.

The merchants of South Gate were rooted socially and economically in the suburb, their livelihood and identity deeply intertwined with the locality. Shaped by this experience, they developed a parochial mentality, an ethos of local protectionism and a powerful sense of civic stewardship. Their focus was not only an outgrowth of this lived reality, but also a self-defense mechanism. It made economic sense for merchants to prize insularity as a means of excluding outside competition. Their economic survival required as much. The booster impulse among these merchants, thus, seems to beg explanation. Would not boosterism open up the suburb to competition?

Not necessarily. By boosting South Gate, the merchants sought merely to bring other businessmen into the fold, into their insular midst, thus strengthening their civic influence.

THE WOMEN OF SOUTH GATE

For the women of South Gate, domestic work bound them to the home and the locality. Unpaid housework and self-provisioning, the most important labors they performed, were integral elements in the subsistence of local families. Indeed, the "survival" function of the home made this form of labor critical. In some cases, domestic work outweighed in importance the unsteady wages brought in by males. Women typically carried out or supervised self-provisioning work, often with the aid of their children. Jessie Smith raised chickens, a milk goat, fruits, and vegetables on her family's suburban property, with the help of her daughters. The local doctor's wife raised rabbits as food for her family. Many women sewed as a means of economizing, particularly during the Depression. "That was one thing that saved us," remembered Ruth (Barrett) Lampmann, "we didn't have to buy our clothes. My mother sewed, we girls all sewed at an early age." Women also found ways to raise cash through home-based labor. Many sold the vegetables, chickens, and rabbits they raised. Jessie Smith earned a little extra money sewing for neighbors, and at one point she took in a boarder. And as noted earlier, some women converted their homes into actual businesses.[92]

In these practices, South Gate's women followed on a long-lived American tradition. Jeanne Boydston has described the "in-doors" work of women, across classes and regions, in antebellum America. Middle-class women in the city's outskirts kept kitchen gardens, chickens, and hogs and engaged in cash-generating activities like sewing, selling eggs, or taking in boarders. Working-class women led "an intricate battery of activities aimed at avoiding cash expenditures," such as scavenging in cities and forging networks of interdependence with other women. And farm women engaged most heavily in home-based production of food, clothing, and other necessities of life. In early twentieth-century South Gate, women performed an updated amalgam of these activities, reflecting both the possibilities attendant in their spatial environment as well as the ongoing hardship that defined working-class existence. The sociologist studying Bell Gardens observed that tending a home with fewer amenities increased the domestic workload. The rigorous demands of housework not only kept women rooted in the community, but it strengthened their ties with neighbors facing similar conditions.[93]

As they strove to fulfill the family's goal of economizing, women negotiated a careful balance between home-produced and purchased goods. For poor families, this meant diligence and care when it came to shopping. Finding the best deals was imperative. Shopping thus became an activity that drew women out of South Gate. While perishable goods like groceries were purchased from local merchants, other shopping took place in downtown Los Angeles. In the quest to economize, shopping became the most important activity that pulled women out of the suburb and into the broader metropolis.

For the most part, however, work and home were one and the same for women. Rooted to the suburb as they were, women of all classes forged social ties in the local community. They formed bartering networks to exchange homegrown produce and animals, they relied upon one another in times of need, and they shared in the day-to-day challenges of life. Because of these daily contacts, women were also more inclined to connect with one another through organizations. South Gate women resembled the merchants in that the geography of their work lives—situated primarily in the suburb—fostered local social ties. Women's clubs were one center of social interaction. The South Gate Women's Club, one of the earliest local organizations, began as a sewing circle of seven women. Its eventual mission was to promote "literary and philanthropic work among its members, and to develop an interest in civic, social and economic conditions of the community." Most of their early activities were social, but during the Depression they shifted to mutual aid and welfare work. This club was the most select of the women's groups; from 1920 to 1940, club presidents were the wives of white-collar employees and business proprietors. By contrast, the South Side Woman's Club attracted the wives of skilled laborers.[94] Formed out of the Home Gardens PTA, this organization was dedicated to promoting cultural development and helping needy children, mothers, and "stranded strangers." Other groups also attracted working-class women, such as the Woman's Christian Temperance Union, whose first head was the wife of a local "poultry man," and the Odd Fellows' Rebekah Lodge, whose early leaders were wives of skilled blue-collar workers. By 1939, at least ten women's groups had coalesced. Women also participated in PTAs, which were prolific, active, and class inclusive during the prewar years.[95]

Institutional life was thus experienced by women across socioeconomic lines, although their clubs tended to stratify by class. Women's clubs may not have promoted class inclusion, but they did reinforce local ties among

women. Because their energies were expended largely on service and philanthropic projects, often for youth, a different ethos developed among
women's groups in South Gate. They were less concerned with the economic success of the suburb—as was true for merchants' groups—than
with the well-being of children and families. It came as little surprise, thus,
that women took the lead in welfare work during the Depression. This was
a logical continuation of their earlier group concerns.

The Heart of Localism: Churches and Neighbors

Come to Southgate Gardens and dwell in the open air
Where the nights are cool, where the flowers bloom
And the skies and the earth are fair.
Come build a home 'neath our orange trees,
Come pluck our fruit of gold
Where the clime is fanned by the cool sea breeze,
And our people would fain grow old.

Come with a character staunch and true,
Come with receptive heart;
Bring your religion along with you
Ready to do your part.
Help build a moral atmosphere,
As pure as our balmy air.
Let your life be in tune with this sunkissed realm
Leave your sins and your shortcomings there.[96]

Thus far, our social survey of South Gate before World War II suggests
a distinct difference in the experiences of the suburb's merchants and working-class residents, especially among men. Particularly when it came to *local* social life, these groups circulated in different ways and among their
own kind. Two final realms held the possibility of cross-class interaction in
South Gate: the churches and the neighborhood. To what extent did residents find community and identity in these areas?

Churches constituted important nodes of community in South Gate,
following a deep tradition in American history. Just as churches had welcomed newcomers to the frontier, they likewise provided centers of sociability, fellowship, and faith in the new suburb.[97] Yet as promoters of
broad-based community interaction, the churches of South Gate were limited in two major respects. First, they catered to a minority of the total

population. And second, the ecumenical differences among South Gate's churches reinforced class divisions and ultimately promoted isolated religious experiences among different denominations. Churches may have failed to bridge social divides in South Gate, but they did provide important sources of identity for local congregants, particularly among the Evangelicals.

Although churches made up almost 50 percent of South Gate's institutions, they served a minority of local residents. The best existing data on prewar church membership was collected in 1934 by Clarence Miller, pastor of the First Methodist Episcopal Church in South Gate. He surveyed about 60 percent of local churches and found they had a combined membership of approximately 3,400. Extrapolating from Miller's survey, we can estimate the total membership of all South Gate churches to be 5,600, or 34 percent of South Gate's population age fifteen and older.[98]

What about those residents who attended church outside of South Gate? Impressionistic evidence suggests that a good number commuted to church in other areas of Los Angeles. Pastor Miller reported that a "large number" of South Gate residents worshiped in Los Angeles, Lynwood, Huntington Park, and Maywood. Juanita Smith's family commuted to church in Long Beach for two years, because South Gate lacked a Church of Christ when they first arrived. For these residents, religion represented yet another force pulling them out of the suburb. At the same time, South Gate's churches also attracted worshipers from suburbs like Watts, Lynwood, and Compton. All in all, there was much coming and going of congregants into and out of South Gate.

Within South Gate, a sizable proportion of residents shunned church altogether. For some, the tasks of working-class life consumed so much time and energy that little was left for church. Such was the case in nearby Bell Gardens. Characterizing that suburb as "a terrible place for desecrating the Sabbath," the Nazarene Church minister complained that attendance at morning services was low because people were working on their homes. At the Full Gospel Church, attendance rose as people finished building their homes, leaving them "time to remember God." In such cases, the pressing needs of individual families obstructed participation in religious communities.[99]

Despite their limited reach, South Gate's churches still acted as meaningful centers of community for a significant minority of residents. By the late 1930s, South Gate had twenty-five places of worship. Fully seventeen of these were in Home Gardens, five in the northwest section, one in Magnolia Park, and two in the eastern area (see table 3-2). South Gate's churches divided into two broad groups, Evangelical and non-Evangelical.

Table 3-2   Chronology of Churches Established in South Gate, by Geographic Area,
1919–1939

	Date of founding/official establishment	Number of members
Northwest		
Community Presbyterian	1919/1921	411
Redeemer Lutheran	1922/1923	216
St. Helens Catholic	/1931	850
Grace Fundamental Baptist Church	—	
Jehovah's Witnesses	—	
Home Gardens		
Home Gardens Community	1922/	
(1929 became Second Four Square Gospel)		
Church of Jesus Christ of Latter Day Saints	1923/1926	541
Christ Sanctified	/1924	
South Gate Four Square	/1924	251
First Methodist Episcopal	1922/1924	160
Interdenominational Evangelistic		
Association	/1924	35
First Central Baptist	/1925	
Friends Community	/1925	
Bible Assembly (Pentecostal)	1922/1926	257
South Gate Church of Christ	1927/1927	
Home Gardens Four Square	1922/1928	55
First Church of Christ Scientist	/1928	175
First Brethren	/1929	159
Church of Christ	1929/1929	
First Baptist	1930/1931	157
Pentecostal Mission	/1930	
Church of the Nazarene	/1936	
Magnolia Park		
First Christian Church	/1925	142
Hollydale & Eastern End		
Bethel Community Church		
(renamed Grace Bible in 1975)	/1927	
Hollydale Cumberland Presbyterian	/1929	

Note: Church dates refer to date when church began meeting (when that date was available), followed by the date of official establishment; "—" means no founding date was available. Membership numbers provided when available.

Sources: Clarence E. Miller, "A Study of Community Forces of South Gate, California, in Their Relation to Character Education" (Master of Theology thesis, University of Southern California, 1935), passim; *Home Gardens Press,* July 10 and August 21, 1925; Arthur Newton, *City and Telephone Directory of Greater South Gate, 1930* (South Gate: Tribune-News Publishing Co., 1930); McFadden interview; (Smith) Hammon interview; Bicentennial Heritage Committee, *South Gate, 1776–1976* (South Gate: South Gate Press, 1976), 47–48; South Gate Book Field Notes, Box 160, FWP.

The Evangelical churches vastly outnumbered the rest, constituting 77 percent of all Protestant denominations. These churches generally had small
congregations and were concentrated in Home Gardens. By contrast, the
non-Evangelical churches had larger memberships and were clustered in
the northwest section. In terms of the number of individual worshipers,
South Gate divided fairly evenly between Evangelicals and non-Evangelicals.[100]

The Evangelical churches bestowed a distinctive cast on religious and
social life in South Gate. This was a life of highly emotional worship, in-
wardly focused clans, and a rejection of worldly concerns. These churches
especially appealed to the suburb's southern migrants, mostly blue collar,
who adapted southern religious practices to new conditions in California.
This religious transformation, shaped by the migration process, was part of
a national, historical phenomenon. As Timothy Smith has pointed out, such
new churches were not simply transplanted communities of faith. The
dislocation of the migration experience, with its attendant insecurities,
doubts about breaking with the past, loneliness, and yearning for stasis and
fellowship, intensified the religious experience and united strangers into
"communities of commitment . . . shaped to meet pressing human need."
Believers thus were bound by both faith and the shared pressures of migration.[101]

In California, a unique set of events reaching back into the nineteenth
century gave rise to an intensely radical Evangelicalism of the sort that
flourished in South Gate. During the sectional crisis of the 1850s, American
Protestant churches split into Northern and Southern factions, a cleavage
that persisted into the twentieth century. Northern churches shifted from
Evangelical enthusiasm to religious and social liberalism, while the Southern churches clung to the Evangelical traditions of revivalism, biblical liter-
alism, piety, and individual salvation through faith. The fundamentalist
movement, one strain of Evangelical Protestantism, flourished in the
South. As Northern services became more restrained and intellectual,
Southern worship remained emotional, expressive, and vigorous. In California, a 1912 agreement prevented Baptist churches from affiliating with
the Southern Baptist Convention, leaving southern Evangelical migrants
without a church home. They soon gravitated toward fundamentalist denominations such as the Seventh-Day Adventists, Churches of Christ, and
the many churches belonging to the Holiness and Pentecostal movements,
such as the Assembly of God, Church of the Nazarene, Pentecostal Holiness, Church of God, and Full-Gospel Assemblies. James Gregory has
shown that these radical Evangelical sects grew disproportionately in California compared to the South, where the Baptists reigned. The Baptist

church agreement was finally rescinded in 1941, but by then a whole spate of Evangelical churches had blossomed in California—South Gate included.[102]

A good proportion of South Gate's churches fell into this category—more than three-quarters of the suburb's total. Of these, about 70 percent were "very conservative in theology and methods of religious education," according to Pastor Miller. "Only three approve of methods and doctrines with a modern emphasis as taught in major seminaries and universities today." By 1930 they included two Churches of Christ, two Four Square churches, a Bible Assembly (Pentecostal), a Christ Sanctified Church, an Interdenominational Evangelical Association, and a Pentecostal Mission. Even the local Redeemer Lutheran Church could be classified as fundamentalist.[103]

The Evangelical churches tended to draw residents of the working class. At the First Baptist Church in the early 1930s, members whose occupations could be identified came mostly from blue-collar families (about two-thirds of the total). Impressionistic evidence corroborates this pattern for the Evangelical churches. Poor residents felt free to worship at these sanctuaries without feeling inferior to more prosperous congregants, who gravitated to the non-Evangelical churches. As Wanda Shahan of nearby Compton recalled, "We were more or less poor white trash," and some neighbors resented their presence. An independent church not only allowed them to avoid being embarrassed by their lack of fine clothes, but endowed them with a deeper sense of mission.[104] The Pentecosts based their theology on the earliest Christians in the Book of Acts, a group also poor in worldly goods. The belief that true rewards would come in the next life assuaged any insecurities about their tiny churches and meager resources. Luke 12:32 reassured them: "Fear not, little flock; for it is your Father's good pleasure to give you the kingdom." As Gertrude Keene, a student of Pentecostal churches in 1930s Los Angeles, observed, "'Little Flock' is applied to the church to bring out the idea that this group may be small and weak in comparison to the other churches and political groups surrounding them but that it is rich in heavenly blessings."[105]

Most of these smaller, Evangelical churches were located in Home Gardens, where working-class families clustered. Both literally and figuratively, the churches blended into this home-centered environment. Spatially, many churches nestled into residential areas. Many were tiny structures, no larger than the owner-built homes surrounding them, plain in design and neighborly in character. Many were built by the congregants themselves, suggesting that self-building habits carried over to ecumenical life. Indeed, church-building in South Gate strongly resembled local practices of owner-building. Both relied on sweat equity and willing spirits. And in the church's case, the building process itself forged social bonds.

This process reflected the context of struggle in South Gate. Before a church building was constructed, worshipers congregated in temporary facilities, such as a member's home, a rented hall, a tent, or even a dance hall. Improvised facilities typically served for several years before members raised sufficient funds for a permanent structure. Once they accumulated enough money to buy land, church members often did the building themselves.[106] This culture of self-reliance was reinforced by the ecclesiastical structure of the Evangelical churches. In general, Evangelical congregations required little contact with larger church institutions. The Pentecostal and Holiness denominations did not require ordained preachers to begin a church but found leaders among the ranks of laymen. This meant congregants themselves could take the initiative and responsibility for establishing their own churches.[107]

The Bethel Community Church was typical. This church began as a Sunday school class, held in a local hall used for dancing on Saturday nights. On Sunday mornings, Leland Weaver, future mayor of South Gate, and his wife Dorothea arrived early to clear away liquor bottles, stack tables, and set up chairs for worship. When the congregants finally raised enough money for land, they purchased four lots and began building their church. As Dorothea Weaver recalled, "the people helped, all the people helped. Like a plumber would donate his time." The First Baptist Church in Home Gardens had similar roots. It began in January 1930 with worship in private homes, moved to Alexander Hall in South Gate, then relocated to a large tent erected on a lot "loaned" by a church member. During these formative months, fellow worshipers grew close. They met for Bible study three times a week, services on Sundays, and countless planning sessions for the building of their sanctuary. By late fall 1930, they had pooled sufficient resources to purchase two Home Gardens lots for $800. Members volunteered their labor to construct the church; they finished in three weeks. By the end of 1930, membership reached sixty-one; two-thirds of them lived in South Gate, the rest in Lynwood and neighboring suburbs.[108] For these members, the process of church building suggests that church was much more than a simple organizational affiliation. It represented an important personal commitment and a source of authentic community.

The decentralized structure of the Pentecostals sometimes caused splintering, resulting in small, tightly knit churches. The Home Gardens Community Church, for example, began as Methodist in 1922. After a group of Pentecostals took charge, the Methodists seceded and formed another church. Soon, a second Pentecostal faction arose in the original Home Gardens church and broke off in 1926 to form the Bible Assembly. Finally, the original church became the Home Gardens Four Square Church in 1928. While the local Methodist-Episcopal minister criticized such factionalism because it stretched already tight resources, many worshipers found solace in these close-knit groups. Indeed, the very profusion of churches allowed for small, intimate communities where members were mutually supportive in matters both spiritual and material. The experience of the Shahan family is illuminating. In the early 1930s, the Shahans left Oklahoma and settled in the working-class suburb of Compton, close to South Gate. For the Shahans, church was their initial, crucial source of community. "When we moved to California," Wanda Shahan recalled, "we found the people to be very unfriendly. . . . It took us quite awhile to get used to the fact that we lived on a block with people we didn't even know. . . . They didn't want to get acquainted. They had their own lives to live, and they weren't interested in being neighbors with you. When we started going to church in California, we met people who took us in and accepted us as part of the church family. . . . We had more in common with them than we did with the people that we lived by." The Shahans attended the Church of God, then the Church of the Nazarene.[109]

The theology of the Evangelicals further encouraged tight, inward-focused communities of faith. The Pentecostal and Holiness sects believed the Bible was the literal word of God, and that man achieved salvation only through conversion and regeneration. Worship services were highly expressive, emotional, and participatory. "The first thing to impress one in the service is the fact that there is a feeling of each worshipper being a part of the service," Keene wrote. Worship involved lively singing, shouting, praying audibly, raising hands, and, in some churches, speaking in tongues. Some churches held all-day services. Such sustained, participatory worship fostered intimate bonds among congregants.

These bonds were reinforced by the Evangelicals' aversion to secular activity, both social and political. They believed that a good Christian's energies should be focused on internal religious conversion, not worldly concerns. Change, they believed, came from within, not without. As Keene wrote, "They are not seeking to save the world, but to save individuals out of a world which is getting worse and worse." Most Evangelicals practiced austere piety, refraining from card-playing, dancing, theater-going, and similar leisure activity. As the deacon of a neighboring Four Square Church claimed, when club work and other social activities are introduced to a church, "God goes out." South Gate's Bethel Community Church had one social activity every six months, even that focusing on "spiritual" matters. The Four Square Church only sponsored socials that included devotions and prayer. The Bible Assembly held no recreational or social activities except "that which is spiritual." This insulated the Evangelicals in their own religious world, and in turn disconnected them from the broader community.[110]

Despite their asceticism, some Evangelicals found complete social fulfillment in the church. Their community needs were easily met by the friendship and understanding of fellow worshipers. This was true for Gerald Shahan. While the Nazarene Church he attended forbade dancing, shows, smoking, and gambling, it did not matter to him. "We have never had to worry about having friends. . . . You can get together and have just as good a time as if you were associating with the worldly people." And it is conceivable that their recreational needs were met during worship services and the occasional revival, with their lively music, emotional expression, and spectacle.[111]

Revivals, in fact, were common occurrences in South Gate as in much of Los Angeles during the 1920s and 1930s. They were usually held in churches or in tents for roving, itinerant preachers who would sweep through towns to save souls. In the late 1920s, the South Gate City Council received several requests by preachers to erect tents "to be used for Evangilistic purposes" on vacant lots in the city. Such requests were typically granted.[112] Revivals served multiple purposes. First, they focused attention on Christianity and allowed believers to make public professions of faith. Worship extended for long hours over several days, redirecting people from worldly pleasures and toward God. The typical revival included a call to "come forward" to show a desire for a deeper spiritual experience. The Friends Community Church in Home Gardens was thankful "for the many who wept their way thru to God" during a revival in 1925. Second, revivals stimulated broader religious interest—or at least curiosity—in the suburb. The spectacle of these services—big tents, lights, music, startling emotionalism, charismatic preachers—easily drew big crowds. The pentecostal Bible Assembly Church reported a turnout of 420 at their tent revival in 1928, with many more standing outside. About a quarter of them were young people. Many who answered the spiritual call followed through by becoming church members. The Baptists, for example, added a few dozen members at each revival. Revivals not only facilitated a personal spiritual experience, but they fostered community by uniting people through common experience and faith.[113]

All in all, the fundamentalist Evangelical churches of South Gate promoted meaningful communities for their members, centered mindfully on devotion to Christ. Yet their emphasis on strict piety over secular matters isolated them from social interaction outside the church community. And frequently their small size and inward focus promoted insularity. Evangelical churches with stringent guidelines for spiritual and social life felt the need to shield themselves from the corrupting influences of outside associations—other churches included, in some cases. Many small congregations were thus unwilling to break the narrow ecumenical barriers of their denominations, evident in the notable degree of splintering off and factionalism among churches. In South Gate, therefore, high levels of religious enthusiasm coexisted with religious isolation, reinforcing broader patterns of social disconnection in the suburb. Likewise, this same orientation discouraged participation in local politics and governance. Church life became a force that distanced Evangelicals—mostly working class—from the local seats of power, leaving leadership to those of other persuasions.

By contrast, the non-Evangelical churches reached into the broader community, more successfully bridging the gap between secular and religious life in South Gate. Less strict and doctrinal than the Evangelicals, they served both social and spiritual needs. Two of the most important churches were Community Presbyterian and St. Helen's Catholic, among the largest in South Gate and both located in the northwest section. Another was the First Methodist Episcopal Church in Home Gardens, also quite active in the community. All promoted a broad array of social activities to foster church community. This secular component set them apart from the Evangelicals, and it positioned members for broader participation in local political and civic life.

The secular connections were especially visible at South Gate's oldest church, Community Presbyterian. Even at its founding, this church sprang from secular roots. In 1919, two years after South Gate's initial subdivision, residents established the South Gate Improvement Society as a social and political body. Out of this group, members organized a nondenominational Sunday school class. In 1921, members of the class and the Improvement Society decided to establish a community church, of an indeterminate denomination. As charter member Lucia Mason recounted, "We began to talk of forming a church. Some of us spent many days walking the dusty streets and across vacant lots, with cards on which to get expressions from persons as to the denomination of church they preferred." Almost as a formality to give them a religious identity, they affiliated with the Presbyterians. The earliest members represented twelve different denominations, suggesting that religious creed was less important than a set of shared values about community and the place of a church within it.[114]

Community Presbyterian grew rapidly, from 25 charter members to 358 by 1930 and to nearly 700 by 1940. As part of its expressed mission, the church sought to connect with the broader community. As Pastor F. L. Ben-

netts put it, "Conscious of a world mission this church endeavors to maintain a co-operative relation with all other churches and all community and
social agencies and movements that are contributing factors to its own objective, vis., Christian character." The church sponsored numerous social
activities, including indoor and outdoor picnics, parties, athletics, a Boy
Scout troop, a women's league, and YMCA Christian citizen clubs. The
church also hosted basketball games for youth, supplying the basketball
court and equipment. For the DeVries family, this church became the center of social life. Ralph DeVries sang in the choir; his wife, Hazel, belonged
to a women's group; and their daughter, Mary, belonged to a few church
clubs. Ralph and Hazel formed their closest friendships with other church
members.[115]

Community Presbyterian attracted the upper stratum of South Gate's
populace. The vast majority of members lived in northwest South Gate and
came from white-collar families. Although church records are spotty, an
analysis of the membership roll from 1921 to 1922, the roll of church elders
from 1921to 1940, and the trustees from 1921 to 1940 reveals that white-
collar members outnumbered blue-collar members at least three to one,
and in the case of the trustees six to one.[116] The biggest groups were
professionals and managers, proprietors, and low-level white-collar workers. The roll of church elders, which provides the best data on members over
time, showed that 70 percent of congregants held white-collar positions:
30 percent were professionals or managers, 19 percent proprietors, and 19
percent salesmen or clerks. Even blue-collar church members mostly held
skilled jobs. The skewing toward the higher end of the job spectrum suggests that Community Presbyterian was the "elite" church of South Gate.
It followed, then, that several church members found their way into local
government. At least five city councilmen, the wife of a sixth, and the city
treasurer were all members of Community Presbyterian. As one resident
remembered it, "All those people belonged to the [Community] Presbyterian Church, they were the power. Upper-class area of South Gate 50 years
ago. They had a big congregation. They got behind candidates for the council, elected them, and peopled all the commissions and all, the Chamber of
Commerce, the bank, the lumberyard. The power house." Community Presbyterian represented a nexus where localized social ties were forged among
the suburb's white-collar professionals and merchants, ties that easily
translated into local power.[117]

Another important church was St. Helen's Catholic. Begun in the 1920s,
St. Helen's boasted the largest congregation in South Gate by the mid-
1930s, with 25 percent of the city's total church membership. The church's
parish boundaries encompassed northwest South Gate and extended east

to Atlantic Boulevard, but excluded Home Gardens. Church services began in a club room, moved to a school, then relocated to a permanent structure in 1931. The parish's first priest, born and educated in Ireland, estimated in 1934 that 700 people attended services every Sunday. The church offered both religious and social activities, including clubs, social societies, and athletics. The Sheehy family, devoutly Catholic, attended St. Aleuitious Church in neighboring Florence before St. Helen's was built. As a young-ster, John Sheehy's social life centered around the church, in youth clubs and socials. "They put on shows, minstrels, plays. There were clubs for young people. Your life was pretty much centered there, constant . . . You knew everybody." For St. Helen's parishioners, church could represent an important center of community life, linking members both spiritually and socially. The parish represented a source of neighborhood cohesion.[118]

The First Methodist Episcopal Church similarly fostered secular social-izing. Founded in 1924, First M.E. sponsored indoor and outdoor activities that included educational programs, youth sports, YMCA Christian citizen-ship clubs, and theater. "Drama," wrote the pastor, "has had a very impor-tant place in the cultural and spiritual activity of the church." Even the local Mormon church offered public speaking forums, storytelling, dances, dra-mas, music, social work, games, and various "character building" activities. The outward orientation of non-Evangelical congregations ultimately pro-moted deeper involvement in the secular life of South Gate.[119]

Overall, churches in South Gate provided meaningful community ex-periences for their members. In their respective oral histories, John Sheehy, Juanita (Smith) Hammon, Mary North, and Ruth Lampmann all identified church as their most important center of community, although they did not all attend church in South Gate. The Evangelicals found fellowship in small, tight congregations isolated from secular life. The non-Evangelicals experi-enced both spiritual and social life in their churches, which connected with the broader community. Church life, thus, represented perhaps the most compelling locus of local community experience for those who belonged.

At the same time, churches did little to bridge class lines and promote a common experience in South Gate. Instead, religious life fostered a variety of cultural modes and identities, some at odds with each other. Although they were all "localized" communities, the meaning of localism differed across congregations. The working-class Evangelicals were highly pious, close congregations, but they had few connections to the broader commu-nity. Their belief in personal salvation—an individualist approach—rein-forced their suspicions of organized secular groups, such as unions and civic clubs. They lived strict religious lives, shunning the leisure opportunities around them. Although their religious community and identity were local, it was a localism defined solely by the church. In a sense, Evangelicals were in, but not of, South Gate. By contrast, the non-Evangelicals found community in their churches, but they participated in the secular world as well. The churches themselves fostered this orientation, sponsoring a range of social activities and maintaining interest in the well-being of South Gate. White-collar members of Community Presbyterian served in local politics, while the minister of First Methodist Episcopal Church conducted a study of the town. To these congregants, the localism of church encouraged an interest in the suburb as a whole. Given their acceptance of secularism, the non-Evangelicals also embraced opportunities for leisure and recreation in Greater Los Angeles; they were not circumscribed by the strictness of fundamentalism. Non-Evangelicals found identity in church as well as in the broader metropolis. For the merchants who belonged to Community Presbyterian, the church constituted an excellent social, spiritual, even political center, where social ties were reinforced and community concerns expressed. Religion, thus, could promote both community cohesion and fragmentation. While congregants of various classes might find fellowship in some churches, the socioeconomic differences between Evangelicals and non-Evangelicals also accentuated the divide between blue- and white-collar families.

Neighborhood life, like that of the churches, provided an uneven experience of community for residents. Most residents did not have rich social interaction with neighbors. They might have known their neighbors, but they didn't necessarily count them as friends or social companions. Juanita (Smith) Hammon recalled, "We didn't have anybody within a block that we knew at all." Virgil Collins's experience was similar. Collins first recollected, with some nostalgia, that there was "much more community then, with neighbors. You'd speak. 'How are you doing, and what are you doing? How's it going at work?' We don't have that closeness now." But he finished his thought by stating, "There wasn't that much socialization within the neighborhood. We had friends, and neighbors and that. And families, the families was closer together." Collins' reminiscence suggests that neighbors knew one another superficially but were rarely close friends. In the 1920s, part of the problem was the sparseness of settlement, especially in Home Gardens. Neighborhood life was weak simply because there were so few neighbors around. "On the street in back of us," (Smith) Hammon recalled, "they built two little houses, awfully small . . . quite a long block from our house. But there wasn't anybody real close for quite a while. . . . We didn't really have neighbors until they started building about 1940." This social fragmentation was typical of many white suburbs in interwar Los Angeles.[120]

Where neighboring was vital and alive in South Gate, it grew out of the cohesiveness spawned by poverty and children. Both in the 1920s and the 1930s, the deprivations of working-class life forged local interdependence. Among women who supervised the work of self-provisioning, neighbors represented allies in a common pursuit. They relied on one another when they bartered or sold homegrown goods. They interacted out of economic need more than social frivolity. The sociologist studying Bell Gardens wrote, "[T]he average woman in Bell Gardens has a rather close informal association with her immediate neighbors, born not of formal calls and bridge parties but of common experiences in house-building and weed-pulling." As a Bell Gardens resident put it, "it is a borrow, lend, and trade neighborhood." Jessie Smith, Juanita's mother, epitomized this ethos. Carrying over practices from her Pond Switch days, Jessie housed people who were down on their luck. She took in a young unemployed man, telling him "he could pay when he got the money." When a young mother died in Home Gardens leaving an infant behind, she immediately stepped in to help. As Juanita recalled: "My mother walked right on down there, and she asked why this man was walking the floor. He said, 'What on earth am I going to do with this baby?' Mama said, 'I'll take him home with me.' He looked at her. But people did things like that then. And she took that baby home, and she kept him until he was about six years old. Never any board or anything. The father went back to Missouri and sent something when he could. He was trying to help his folks. My mama said, 'That baby was no trouble, he didn't eat much.' . . . [The father] came out here and took the boy, and about broke my mother's heart."

Such practices also occurred in Bell Gardens, where neighbors cooked for one another during times of sickness and sewed clothes for families in distress. The Great Depression accelerated this interdependence. In Bell Gardens, 15 percent of families boarded kin or unrelated persons "on a somewhat permanent basis" in the early 1930s. As one explained, "Oh yes, John lives here, but he's no relation to us. He came home from C.C.C. camp with my boy, and started to board here, but he was out of work all last winter. His mother doesn't want him. . . . He wrote her and wanted to borrow some money, but she didn't reply . . . of course, it was somewhat of a problem for us. . . . Now he's joined the Army."[121]

Children also bound neighbors together. As playmates, kids often forged the closest ties among neighbors. "There was no swimming pool, no organized activities. If you wanted activities, you organized them yourself," recalled John Sheehy. During the summers, John and his young neighbors played baseball everyday on a field behind his house, sometimes against the kids from Watts. Kids visited one another's homes to socialize, play games, hold "sings," and square-dance. As a teenager, Glenn Seaborg frequented his cousin's house across the street to play the phonograph and his neighbor's house to listen to the radio, while Mary DeVries played "kick the can" with boys and girls on her street. As a youngster, Mary was "always very close to the neighbors. We were playing back and forth, back and forth." Children, in turn, could unite parents. Ruth Lampmann described, "we all could run in and out of homes because our children were all in the same school." Children, thus, served as a source of social cohesion among some neighbors, a trend that accelerated after the war.[122]

In general, localized community was most meaningful for certain churchgoers, neighbors in need, children, women, and, of course, the merchants. For some working-class families, religious life fostered a disassociation from secular South Gate, as they shunned worldly concerns to focus full attention on God. For others, church provided one source of sociability and identity in their lives, alongside family, leisure, and work. For some merchants, church provided yet another social locus that rooted them deeper to the locality. In a community where neighborhood ties were weak, church could provide the most compelling ties to place. Yet for the majority of residents without a church affiliation and with superficial neighborhood ties, local life left much to be desired.

COMMUNITIES OF INTEREST

In 1934, Pastor C. E. Miller of the First Methodist Episcopal Church observed that for most of the 1920s, "there was very little community consciousness" in South Gate. He continued, "There was very little in the way of community centered activity. The people had most of their interests outside of the community. Thus there was a population of nearly 20,000 people with very little in the way of a common bond to tie them together."[123] Miller's observation was an astute, but incomplete, one. His description fit the experience of many male working-class residents, whose lives of work, leisure, and consumption drew them out of South Gate and into the L.A. metropolis. But it missed the mark when it came to South Gate's women and merchants. Both groups found their lives firmly rooted in the suburb, economically, socially, and, in the merchants' case, civically and politically. Evangelical Christians likewise found community with fellow worshipers in South Gate churches, as did some non-Evangelicals. A person's community experience depended upon whom—and when—you asked. For working-class families, neighborhood assumed greater importance as economic conditions worsened. Time also affected the character of local institutions.

Following an initial period of inclusiveness, civic groups came to represent the exclusive province of businessmen who ultimately dominated civic and political life in South Gate.

With their interests rooted locally as they were, merchants soon became the voice of local community. And as they witnessed their blue-collar neighbors seeking "interests outside of the community," to use Pastor Miller's words, they began expressing concern. Before long, they branded this trend a crisis. To them, community meant local institutions and local patronage, and the "crisis" was nonparticipation in local affairs, an emphasis on individual families over civic matters, clannish churches that discouraged civic involvement, and, worst of all, the inclination to shop outside the suburb. In sum, it was the failure of local residents to participate in the town's institutions and endeavors.

In truth, residents experienced community on their own terms, through informal associations, helping the disadvantaged, a staunch commitment to family integrity, and participation in church life. And they engaged in social activity and interaction beyond the suburb's borders, in leisure pursuits around the city. Because they were not contained geographically or institutionally in South Gate, these experiences existed beyond the purview of most local civic leaders.

In contrast to upper-class suburbs of the era, with their focus on neighborhood, children, and club life, South Gate was a looser, less organized environment for working-class families struggling to make ends meet. Their patterns of leisure, work, and consumption were mobile and far-reaching, taking them out of their hometown frequently and easily. While commercial amusements like the cinema, live theater, and sports may have helped forge a common cultural language among working people, their own individual jaunts in and around Los Angeles were also important aspects of their leisure experience—and these were less collective and more individualistic and family oriented. Historians have too often assumed that when cars and mass culture entered in, working-class culture dissipated and declined.[124] The South Gate story reveals a more complex reality; working-class identity persisted in the face of these forces, but it took on new forms within the context of modern metropolitan life.

The mobile pattern of working-class life reinforced the ethos of individualism and familism among South Gate residents. As they worked, shopped, and played at scattered destinations in Los Angeles, broadening their spatial horizons and comfort with the city, they often did it alone or in small social units like the family or a few friends. It was not a communal experience. So as they became a "cosmopolitan" people, they largely forfeited the sense of neighborhood-based community that defined the working-class experience in other regions. Church life was an exception, representing for some the last bastion of place-based community. For the Evangelicals, church was a defining aspect of their lives. For the non-Evangelicals, it was one of several sources of social identity and experience—one anchor to home, in a sea tossing them in many directions. The predominant pattern of life, however, was one of individualistic experience and an aversion to local institutional life. Yet individualism did not mean the end of working-class identity. Residents clung to working-class concerns, driven by the need to survive in a maturing capitalist world. Many sought out the cheapest ways to shop, to spend leisure time, and to travel around town, while some found churches that accepted and soothed them in their struggle. The reality of meager resources and day-to-day economic hardship was constant, the inescapable backdrop to the story of social life.

By contrast, South Gate's merchants lived out the suburban ideal of the era: a life rooted in the local neighborhood, expressed through local institutions. The difference between these orientations hinted at a bigger rift in the suburb, one that would find ultimate expression in the political arena.

4   The Politics of Independence

In the years before World War II, working-class families like the Smiths, Seaborgs, and DeVries made their way to South Gate in search of family security through insulation from the wage-driven marketplace. The way they got homes—often by the sweat of their brow—and the ways they used those homes testified to this aspiration. The story of local political life likewise reflected this goal. The political commitments of South Gate's residents were molded by the economic and social context of their suburban lives. Concerns of the neighborhood shaped political outlooks and mobilized residents to assert themselves in ways that would support their suburban strategies for survival in a maturing capitalist world.

In South Gate, political concerns grew out of local conditions and experiences. In the open-shop climate of Los Angeles, which hampered the ability of working people to agitate for security in the workplace, the neighborhood became a focal point for action. South Gate residents forged an identity as white, working-class homeowners within the local political arena. Although both class and race were foundational to this identity, class took center stage in the 1920s and 1930s. These were the years before a mature state-based welfare system was in place, when the vagaries of the free market subjected working people to lives of economic instability and unpredictability. If the family bread-winner got sick, laid off, or simply grew old, there were few institutional "safety nets" to catch a family on the way down. A fierce concern for family security thus shaped working-class politics before the war.

This chapter begins at the local level and ends on the broader canvas of state and national politics. In the neighborhood, residents formulated and expressed political sensibilities that revealed the importance of class-based concerns and the centrality of homeownership to political identities. These political experiences ultimately sowed the seeds that matured into blue-collar conservatism in the postwar era. In South Gate, the politics of neighborhood pitted wage earners against merchants, whose divergent goals translated into conflicting visions for the suburb's future. Merchants, concerned with local economic growth and development, promoted an expansive, market-centered vision for the suburb. They hoped to build South Gate economically, and in turn bolster their own chances for economic success. They saw themselves as the champions of local progress and the beneficiaries of the wealth they hoped to attract into their community. Wage earners pursued an opposite agenda. Fiercely concerned with their own financial well-being and family security, they sought to live as economically as possible and, as such, formed a mentality opposed to development, growth, and taxation. Their outlook was borne of the material realities of their lives. Working-class suburbs offered the opportunity to minimize dependence on cash and thus achieve some insulation from the marketplace, by enabling residents to build their own homes and provision on their property—and by promising a low tax rate. Residents would put up with rough-and-tumble conditions—the consequence of low taxes—in exchange for a cheap ticket into suburbia. Their vision for South Gate was to keep it true to its working-class roots, to make certain it fulfilled the needs of its laboring residents. These conflicting visions for the suburb combusted in local politics over the issues of consumption, development, and education. In each case, merchants and wage earners fought for their economic survival. Far from being a bastion of property-based consensus, the suburb became a site of contention among property holders, ordered around class.

The political sensibilities formed in the neighborhood ultimately found expression in state and national politics. As residents fought to preserve their way of life—drawing on notions of self-help, independence, and homeownership—they found outlets for these ideals in state and national political programs. Working-class suburbanites enthusiastically supported Upton Sinclair's EPIC (End Poverty in California) and Franklin Roosevelt's New Deal, programs that resonated within this local historical experience. The terrific challenges of the 1920s boom and the 1930s bust, which played out jarringly in South Gate, magnified the importance of homeownership to residents. Their identity as homeowners positioned them ideologically to embrace a federal agenda that would finally stabilize this hard-won status. By the end of the 1930s, South Gaters had become members of the New Deal coalition. Suburban life ultimately created a nuanced, complex political sensibility among working-class residents, in ways that were sometimes surprising, often volatile.

THE STRUCTURE OF LOCAL POLITICS

The civic structure of South Gate set the stage for this political story. In 1922, a dozen residents met in a garage to discuss the possibility of incorporating their community. Over the next few months, they circulated petitions, gaining enough support to incorporate South Gate in 1923 as a "sixth class" general law city. The original town encompassed what became the northwest section of the suburb, covering 1.3 square miles. The governing body consisted of a "board of trustees" (renamed city council in 1927), with a mayor and four representatives. Elections were held every two years, alternating between council members who were elected to four-year terms.[1] Neighboring subdivisions, like Home Gardens, Hollydale, and Magnolia Park, remained unincorporated until they were annexed to South Gate in the late 1920s. Before incorporation, civic groups like the South Gate Improvement Society and Home Gardens Improvement League substituted for city councils. These groups lobbied the county for a post office, gas lines, and even electric lights for certain parts of town, and they fought nuisances. In 1924, for example, one civic group called on Home Gardens residents to unite against an effort by neighboring Huntington Park to establish a sewage dump in the eastern part of town.[2] The importance of these improvement associations diminished once the suburb achieved political autonomy through incorporation. After this, local city government took over.

The composition of local leadership evolved from a broadly democratic pool in the early 1920s to a narrow, circumscribed group of merchants by 1930. During the "pioneer" stage of South Gate, when the challenges of city-building were most acute, crude conditions and profound need required widespread participation from residents.[3] In one sense, civic duty resembled local housing and provisioning practices. Residents gave their time and labor—rather than tax dollars—to keep the city functioning. In Home Gardens, residents formed a volunteer fire department in 1923, serving a critical function in a community where few building regulations and the widespread use of kerosene stoves and lamps posed fire hazards. The volunteer firefighters constituted a diverse group, including a musician, a driver, a laborer, a realtor, a farmer, a painter, a clay worker, a clerk, and a tailor. In some cases, residents performed work for the city and submitted a bill to cover their expenses for materials. The high attrition rates of officeholders suggested broader citizen participation in the early years; in the city's first year alone, ten out of thirteen officeholders resigned and were replaced. In these ways, a wide segment of the populace contributed to the early functioning of South Gate.[4]

Table 4-1 South Gate City Council Members (Including Mayors), 1920–1940

Council Member	Council Term	Occupation(s)
Baumgardner, George	1936–40	Proprietor: plumbing, gas appliances
Bryant, Knoles	1926–28	Manufacturer
Catland, Raymond	1928–30	Mechanical engineer
Fike, Earl	1934–42	Proprietor: barbershop
Foster, Agnes	1923–24	—
Hobart, Dewey	1938–42	Electrician
Hodgson, Roy	1930–32	Superintendent
Holden, Carle	1934–38	—
Lampmann, I.W.	1923–24	Proprietor: water company
Lannon, John	1930–32	Proprietor: service station
Martin, Louis	1928–30	Proprietor: service station, real estate
Middlemiss, Ralph	1930–38	Plasterer and contractor
Moore, Frank	1923–26	Salesman
Neville, Guy	1928–30	Proprietor: real estate
Nellar, Ernest	1938–42	—
Poteet, Archie	1926–34	Proprietor: real estate; laundryman
Pomeroy, Harold	1932–36	Secretary, Chamber of Commerce
Rempel, William	1932–38	Proprietor: lumber company
Rutherford, Robert	1926–30	Building contractor
Schmidt, Fred	1924–26	Building contractor
Shaw, C.A.	1923–24	Building contractor
Sines, Asa	1924–26	Foreman
Schoby, Andrew	1924–30	Proprietor: service station, real estate
Stirdivant, C.	1923–26	Manufacturer
Tweedy, Lorenzo	1930–34	Proprietor: real estate

Note: Occupations for Foster, Holden, and Nellar were unavailable.

Sources: South Gate Press, April 13, 1928, November 29, 1929, April 14, 1938, January 18, 1983; *South Gate Tribune,* April 17, 1924, April 15 and September 5, 1930, June 27, 1938; Bicentennial Heritage Committee, *South Gate 1776–1976* (South Gate: South Gate Press, 1976), 21; South Gate files, FWP; South Gate City Council minutes and resolutions, SGCH; Arthur Newton, *City and Telephone Directory of South Gate, 1926* (South Gate: Tribune News Publishing Co., 1926); idem, *City and Telephone Directory of Greater South Gate, 1930* (South Gate: Tribune-News Publishing Co., 1930); *South Gate and Walnut Park City Directory, June 1, 1940* (K.I. Strand, 1940).

After 1925, a local elite assumed leadership. This shift occurred after the early "community building" work was done, when the city began professionalizing its services and financing them through taxes. The group that came to dominate political life in South Gate was composed primarily of merchants, and secondarily of managers. Table 4-1 shows the occupations of city council members from 1920 to 1940. Of the twenty-two councilmen for whom occupations were available, eleven were proprietors (including the secretary of the Chamber of Commerce) and five were managers (three of them building contractors). The remaining councilmen were mainly white-collar workers and professionals. These men shared a vested interest in the development of the suburb and in the move toward contractor-built housing. South Gate's "merchant elite," with their lives and livelihoods rooted firmly in the suburb, used their institutional connections and political power to steer their town down a particular road—one that put them on a collision course with the suburb's working class.

The Politics of Consumption:
"Mr. and Mrs. South Gate Go a Shopping"

The sensibilities of South Gate's merchants—their interests and the way they acted to protect them politically—first surfaced in the politics of consumption. Merchants elevated the significance of consumerism by linking it to the very meaning of community and to their own self-identity. In a public discourse that connected consumer and civic loyalty, the merchants constructed a definition of community that glorified the local neighborhood, politicized shopping, and asserted an indispensable position for themselves in the body politic. As in many American towns during this period, consumption became contested terrain, an arena beyond the workplace where different classes asserted their self-interests.[5]

The politics of consumption, in fact, lay at the surface of a much deeper conflict over the meaning of community in twentieth-century America. Community—and all which that slippery term connotes—had undergone profound transformation by the twentieth century. As modern metropolitan life grew more complex, segmented, and geographically fragmented, community was signified less by place and more by other forces like ethnicity, race, work, and leisure.[6] In some cities, merchants often reinforced this transition. Immigrant and black merchants, for example, saw themselves as reinforcing ethnic and racial pride. "Shopping at a particular neighborhood store was a matter of cultural loyalty," Lizabeth Cohen observed. Consumers who patronized these stores were not merely buying goods, they were strengthening community in both the social and economic act of consumption. They gabbed with ethnic storekeepers and fellow shoppers in their native tongue, they forged ties of mutual obligation—which could translate into credit during hard times—and they helped subsidize a healthy immigrant economy. For blacks, similarly, patronage of "race businesses" was intertwined with aspirations of black nationalism.[7] By contrast, the native-born white merchants of South Gate had no such ties of identity to stake a claim for consumer loyalty. All they were left with was a purely place-based conception of community. The town itself—South Gate—was the community, and they assumed all residents would share an unflagging loyalty to it.

The merchants formulated their ideas about community when they became leaders of political and institutional life in South Gate. Of course as businessmen, they also had a vested interest in their own economic success. By incorporating their personal interests with the interests of the suburb, they blurred the line between public and private prosperity. They spoke of duty and loyalty to the community but very quickly redefined it as patronage of local stores. This was a class-specific precept. As the merchants perceived it, good citizenship for laboring-class residents meant consumer loyalty. For the business class, it meant participation and leadership in civic organizations. Ultimately, consumption emerged as a contentious issue that divided merchants and laborers. In their frequent, sometimes desperate public articulations, South Gate's merchants came to define community as commerce, the upright citizen as a loyal consumer, and civic duty as patronage of local shops.

This ideology put the merchants at direct odds with working-class residents. Concerned first and foremost with economizing, most South Gate families felt little loyalty to their town and hometown merchants if it meant paying a higher price for goods. This economic motivation, combined with the relatively weak retail base in South Gate, compelled many residents to shop outside the suburb, particularly in Huntington Park and downtown Los Angeles, where goods were cheaper and selections wider. Likewise, families distanced themselves from merchants through the practice of growing food in backyards. For workers, consumption choices and self-provisioning became a means of protecting their class-based interests and safeguarding family security. In the process, it afforded them a degree of autonomy from the suburb's merchants.

The Depression intensified the importance of self-provisioning—individual and collective—which further detached families from local business. Amid rising unemployment and poverty, families relied more heavily than before on homegrown produce and livestock. One sign of its value was a rash of thefts that hit these backyard operations in the 1930s, such as the abduction of eighty-seven rabbits from backyard hutches in 1935.[8] The Depression also encouraged the development of cooperative markets, a sort of collective extension of self-provisioning. Cooperatives especially caught on in Los Angeles County, which represented "the national center of the self-help movement," according to Carey McWilliams. "By December 1934, the county had nearly 45% of all the self-help units in the United States and about one-tenth of the entire national membership." About 50,000 people in Southern California participated in these organizations by March 1936.[9]

In South Gate, co-ops allowed participants to supply staples for one another and to barter labor for goods. Co-ops both centralized the informal bartering already practiced in the suburb and allowed unemployed workers to labor directly for food and services. At South Gate's two producers' co-ops, a person wholly or partially unemployed could work ten hours per week for the co-op, then draw a week's ration of food and small amounts of cash from the sale of excess products. At one of these operations, the twenty-seven members baked bread as their principal commodity and also performed blacksmith work, handled firewood, produced mayonnaise, and expanded into oil production by taking over a reclaimed oil refinery. They bartered these goods and services with 103 other co-ops around the county. One co-op even staged entertainment programs, like a theater and dance show that drew an audience of two hundred. These cooperatives represented not only independence from merchants but also competition, especially in the case of consumers' co-ops. Operating more on a cash—rather than labor—basis, these cooperatives used money from membership dues to purchase goods from wholesalers, then sold them at low prices to members. In contrast to producer co-ops, which drew mainly from the laboring class, members of consumer co-ops were mostly low-level white-collar workers, especially clerical and semiskilled professionals. South Gate's one consumer co-op, dubbed the Hermit's Club, claimed about forty members.[10]

In nearby Compton, which had its own thriving cooperative system, merchants and community leaders mostly opposed this movement. Their objections ranged from political condemnation to self-defensiveness. In their minds, the odious link between cooperatives and radical politics was a significant cause for alarm. As the secretary of the Compton Chamber of Commerce put it, "They are too Communistic, or perhaps it is better to say, too Socialistic, to gain any support from this bureau. . . . If they don't actually belong, they sympathize with all those schemes of anti-American tactics. . . . I hope they lose their support from the city, and have to close up." More pragmatically, he intoned, "I am opposed to them in principle . . .

they hurt business by their methods." Some businessmen were more ac-
cepting of the co-ops, at least paternalistically. As one explained, "The [co-
op] unit has done a good piece of work. Many of the businessmen were
interested in these men who were actually hungry. . . . we got together and
helped them a little. . . . We just kept a fatherly guidance over them so they
could get ahead in the best way possible." Yet this was not simply charity
for charity's sake. This businessman believed his "fatherly guidance" kept
the wrong elements from infiltrating the co-op. "I think we kept down any
possibility of Communism starting, by our attitude. It wouldn't have done
for us to just leave them to themselves. . . . It has helped them to help themselves and to save the taxpayer a lot of money, too. We have not had violence when these men could get something to eat."[11]

As this merchant's comments suggested, businessmen and residents did
not always turn their backs on one another. In some cases, grocers helped
carry families through the Depression by extending credit. The Seaborg
family ran up a huge bill with a grocer near their home, which they eventually paid back. Another grocer allowed the doctor's family to pay with services rather than cash.[12]

For the most part, however, loyalty to local merchants meant little to
residents struggling for economic survival. Among the families of autoworkers, oil workers, and factory operatives, necessity drove them to seek
out the cheapest possible goods, even if it meant shopping in other towns.
Class-based concerns dictated consumption decisions. Unlike ethnic neighborhoods where specialty stores catered to immigrants and fostered community ties, mutual aid, and loyalty to merchants, South Gate's wage
earners lacked common ethnic bonds that committed them to local shopkeepers.[13] They were mostly native-born whites whose common experience was rooted more strongly in poverty than in any shared ethnic
culture. As a result, residents let class-based concerns determine what sort
of consumers they would be. And for the most part they were bargain shoppers, willing to travel distances to find the cheapest goods. As working-class
residents displayed mobility and autonomy in their capacities as consumers, South Gate's merchants were left by the wayside. To the town's
shopkeepers this represented a crisis, not only for their own businesses but
for the community itself.

In the midst of this disturbing trend, South Gate merchants began articulating a distinct conception of community that reflected their anxieties
over this decline in hometown loyalty. In the face of strong countercur-
rents, they sought to create a community where citizens would, in the
mayor's words, "unite and cooperate in working for the common good in
building up the greater city." Paramount in this concept was loyalty to

place. In 1925, the editor of the *Home Gardens Press* wrote that communities prosper and citizens find ultimate contentment "by pulling together; by standing for home institutions; by supporting those enterprises that enlarge community life by enlarging wholesome activities. This is loyalty to home—loyalty to our merchants, to our schools, our churches, and our industries. These are the things that make life in every community worth while. Loyal people will support them." Three months later, he reiterated, "The acre of diamonds is at home and there are no greener pastures than your own. Loyalty to home, loyalty to the job you are doing and eternal perseverance are fixed rules of success." Reflecting the attitude of the suburb's merchant leaders, this editor articulated in local terms a concern manifesting at the national level. At least since Herbert Hoover, national leaders had emphasized the importance of a stable, homeowning citizenry, who belonged to organic communities. This, they believed, was indispensable to social and political order and an antidote to radicalism.[14]

It was not long before the merchants' definition of community constricted. When merchants assumed the reins of local power, they contended that the act of consumption—rather than political or social participation by all—was the true basis of one's civic duty. In their minds, the purchase of goods loomed as *the* central act that defined one's standing as a good citizen and one's loyalty to the town. "[H]ome trading is the most vital element in community welfare and progress," claimed an editorial in 1928. "Did you ever stop to think?" mused another, "THAT if you have pride in your home city, BUY AT HOME! THAT if you believe in your home city and want to see it grow, BUY AT HOME! ... THAT if you see your neighbors spending their money in some other city, don't get down-hearted but talk to them and show them the error of their ways. Some of them sometimes don't realize how they are harming the city they should love. BUY AT HOME!"[15]

South Gate's businessmen believed local consumption helped the community prosper in several ways. It strengthened the tax base, which in turn bolstered the local infrastructure. "If you live in town you want [good schools, churches, telephone service, mail delivery], good streets and sidewalks, wholesome amusements, those things that go to make a community worth living in. These advantages are the natural outcome of . . . the growth and condition of your locality, which in turn is dependent upon the extent of local trade activities." Hometown patronage strengthened the suburb's economic independence and viability, particularly during times of economic hardship. "In order to make financial conditions good in any community there must be a circulation of money equal to the needs of the community." The citizen's duty was to "spend what money you have to spend among your home merchants and thus keep the conditions as good as possible."[16]

Local patronage also lent indispensable support to community leaders, who were invariably merchants. "The businessmen of Home Gardens are the backbone of the community," ran an editorial in 1926. Not only did they take the lead in civic projects, but they contributed more than their fair share in taxes. Nevertheless, "Some do not give the home town merchant the credit he deserves. He is entitled to more than the retailer elsewhere, or the mail order house, because he is the backbone of the community, the central force that holds the community. . . . [I]t is cheaper to trade at home to say nothing of the spirit of reciprocity that should be shown by every loyal home town citizen." Because merchants did so much for the community, it followed that residents should support their endeavors. "South Gate business men have the interests of the community at heart," a local editor wrote in 1928. "Other things being equal, they are entitled to the undivided patronage of the people."[17]

When the appeal to community cohesion floundered, merchants turned to a third rationale, the economic benefits to property owners. "Buying At Home Raises Value of Your Property," ran a front-page headline in 1928. The article noted with alarm that "property values here [in South Gate] are lower than in other cities of like population" largely because "too many dollars are going out of town to help build up commercial establishments elsewhere." In every prosperous community, it was an "economic fact" that a flourishing commercial sector enhanced property values. "It is apparent, therefore, that every property owner, when purchasing of his home stores, is working directly for his own interest." If the spirit of reciprocity toward local merchant-leaders meant little, implored the editor, "your selfish interest demands that you do your utmost to build up prosperous business houses in South Gate." The fact that some of these statements were reprinted from other suburban newspapers around Los Angeles suggests the crisis of local merchants was widespread (see fig. 4-1).[18]

To spur cooperation, merchants launched a number of promotional campaigns and contests. The "Mr. and Mrs. South Gate Go a Shopping" contest, run by the *Tribune* in 1924, challenged readers to guess the mystery stores described in a hypothetical shopping spree taken in South Gate. A typical clue read, "'I like Shell gas best, don't you?' Mrs. South Gate asked her mate. 'Nope. I prefer Speedene.' 'We won't have to change our service station because of our preference since they carry them both . . . ' 'No, I don't think anything could make me change, since we're patronizing the home town boys—and since the place is so close to the post office that when we get the mail we can fill her up.'" The winners, who demonstrated close familiarity with the suburb's shops, won modest prizes of cash and merchandise. In 1928, the "Merchants Bargain Refund Contest" awarded

Where Do Your Dollars Go?

Mr. Model Citizen spends his dollars in South Gate, where they stand a chance of coming back
—Courtesy Long Beach Sun.

Figure 4-1   This cartoon, which appeared on the front page of the *South Gate Press* in 1928, encouraged residents to patronize neighborhood businesses. The merchants launched numerous publicity campaigns to get this message across. *South Gate Press,* November 23, 1928.

fifty dollars to the organization whose members shopped the most in South Gate's stores. Similar contests were held in 1931 and 1935.[19]

The most poignant and telling of these promotions was the "Home Gardens Dollar" stunt. It began when the *Home Gardens Press* launched a dollar into circulation in the hopes that it would stay within the suburb for a month. Attached to the back of the dollar was a note reading, "THIS IS THE HOME DOLLAR—Keep it in Home Gardens. Let's see how many accounts it will settle in 30 days if kept at home. Everybody into whose hands this dollar falls is requested to turn it over to someone else in Home Gardens within 24 hours. . . . Please cooperate and oblige." This plea, alas, was impertinently ignored. The following month, the dollar was missing. "The Home Gardens Dollar—Where Is It?" the editor asked. "Thus far this dollar has not 'shown up.' . . . It is feared someone went contrary to request and spent it out of town. This was, to say the least, not a very sportsmanlike thing to do. . . . It would seem . . . that a better spirit would have been shown had all been willing to cooperate in a matter involving so little inconvenience. The Home Gardens dollar is apparently lost—like many a good dollar is when it is spent outside of the community."[20]

The fugitive dollar symbolized the obstinate consumption choices of residents and, consequently, what merchants perceived as a crisis of community. In retaliation and frustration, Home Gardens shopkeepers refused to sponsor a hometown baseball team. Since the ballplayers themselves "didn't patronize them," the merchants saw little reason to return the favor.[21]

When civic appeals and promotional stunts failed, South Gate businesses turned to informal and political strategies to boost local patronage. In some cases, their efforts worked against the interests of working-class residents and exposed a growing rift between these groups. One tactic was to influence local bank practices. By the early 1930s, some South Gate shopkeepers provided informal banking services for workers by cashing their paychecks on Saturdays. The workers usually spent some of that money in the store cashing the check. In 1931, talk began of reopening banks on Saturday nights, thus reinstating a practice from earlier years. Many merchants vociferously objected, fearing that workers would spend their money elsewhere or for unnecessary "pleasure jaunts." "With the banks closed, as at present," noted one proprietor, "I cash scores of pay checks every Saturday afternoon and evening with the following result: Those I cash checks for invariably spend from $2 to $10 for food and other necessities of life in my store. . . . When the banks were open on Saturday evenings, many of these people would have the banks cash their checks and their first thought then . . . was the week-end pleasures, a trip out-of-town. . . . As matters now stand they buy their week's supplies first and use the money remaining for pleasure and other purposes. That is as it should be." This merchant estimated that his business was "at least 40 percent better" when the banks were closed than when they were open. Through such means, the merchants sought to steer not only where, but how, workers spent their money.[22]

Another approach was political. In these efforts, proprietors focused mainly on eradicating the competition. They initiated several measures to lock out merchants from outside South Gate, who ranged from small-fry traveling grocers to large-scale chain stores. The first incident occurred in 1924, when the city council refused to grant a license to a "travelling grocery store." This transient merchant, asserted councilman Fred Schmidt, presented a "grave injustice": in contrast to South Gate proprietors, he paid no local taxes to support the community. Yet this ruling worked against the interests of some working-class families, who relied on him for the convenient delivery of goods. Especially for housewives in remote areas of the suburb, the ruling meant long walks to markets at the center of town.[23]

In 1929, the city council stepped up its efforts by passing a "handbill ordinance" that prohibited out-of-town businesses from advertising in South Gate. Pushed through by councilman and business owner Archie Poteet and plumber Joe Capps, the measure was supported by 90 percent of local storekeepers. It penalized the circulators who had been aggressively saturating South Gate with handbills and other advertising sheets. The penalty was stiff: a fine of up to $300 or three months in county jail, or both. Over the next several months, a number of people were arrested for violating the new law, including a distributor for the "Los Angeles Down Town Shopping News," perceived as a particular threat. In 1931, eight more men were jailed for distributing Compton-based fliers. The "undesirable citizen" behind this violation, complained the local editor, was like the "tenant on the farm who takes everything possible from the soil and puts nothing back in the way of replacement." The South Gate handbill law became a model for other L.A.-area communities, suggesting the crisis for neighborhood merchants was widespread. Santa Monica adopted a similar measure in late 1930, while Los Angeles and several other cities made inquiries about the law.[24] Such legislation, however, could work against the interests of working-class residents, many of whom benefited from information about sales, bargains, and prices in stores outside the suburb's limited retail world. By squelching this news, merchants hampered the efforts of residents to economize through comparative bargain shopping.

The final campaign by merchants to compel consumer loyalty centered on the battle against chain stores. Following on national trends, chains multiplied locally during the 1920s. In Los Angeles, Chicago, New York, Boston, and other cities, consumers purchased more than half of all retail products in such outlets—even though they were vastly outnumbered by independent markets. Most chains were confined to upper- and middle-class communities in the 1920s. They only began penetrating working-class neighborhoods by decade's end, when the Depression drove many small merchants out of business and created openings for these standardized retailers.[25] By 1926 there were four chain groceries in South Gate, including two Safeways, a Vons, and a Daley's market. In this period, the chain and the independent store were not necessarily antagonists. When Vons opened in 1925, for example, a butcher and fruit seller opened stalls within the market and handled all meat and fruit sales. By 1929, the number of grocery chains jumped to fourteen, including eight Los Angeles-area chains and six markets connected to regional or national chains. They represented only about 8 percent of retail establishments, and their sales amounted to 10 percent of retail sales in South Gate, much less than the national average. For the time being, local merchants maintained a position of dominance.[26]

The Great Depression threatened this advantage. From 1930 to 1940, nearly 80 percent of local businesses went bust.[27] When the chains tried to take advantage of this opening afforded by weakened local competition, South Gate's merchants mobilized a counteroffensive. In 1931, they formed an organization to address the problems of the small merchant and to devise solutions. Four years later, they pressed for political action. State Assemblyman A. Franklin Glover, representing South Gate's district, was one of twelve lawmakers to propose legislation imposing a progressive tax on chain stores. Under this measure, the tax rate rose as the number of stores in the chain increased. When the measure died in committee, local merchants continued their campaign. In 1938, the local newspaper renewed the call for "community loyalty" through consumption, and chastised a Seville Avenue market for being taken over by a Los Angeles chain. Worse yet, charged the editor, some markets were aligning with retailers in Huntington Park, "the strongest rival to South Gate's future as a trading center."[28]

In their fervent opposition to outside competition, South Gate's merchants revealed a paradox in their thinking. At the same time they lobbied to exclude these businesses, they remained fervent boosters of South Gate, tirelessly singing the praises of the suburb to attract newcomers—businesses included. As a result, they attracted their own competition to town. The local press, the mouthpiece of South Gate's businessmen, exposed this tension between protectionism and boosterism most clearly. Throughout the 1920s and 1930s, they featured articles, editorials, and advertisements urging residents to be loyal hometown consumers. Yet simultaneously, they ran ads for the nemesis, out-of-town stores. In a 1924 issue of the *Tribune*, for example, more than half of the advertisements were for out-of-town stores. By the early 1930s, these ratios persisted. The newspapers also printed articles on chain store openings in South Gate and neighboring communities.[29]

Even against these powerful counterforces and their own contradictions, the merchants successfully maintained ascendancy in South Gate. The number of chain groceries actually decreased from nine to three during the 1930s, while independent groceries only fell from forty-nine to forty over the same period. Even the few local department stores resisted the incursion of the chains: in 1940, three were owner-run while only one was part of a chain.[30]

The competitive power of merchants aside, they still languished in their struggle for local patronage. From the start, South Gate's proprietors faced a tough challenge. They operated in the milieu of working-class suburbia, where frugality was the watchword. These were tough customers, constrained by limited resources and an intense concern with economizing. What the merchants soon discovered was that residents made their own consumption choices, regardless of impassioned pleas, advertisements, incentives, and policies. And these choices often pulled shoppers outside of the suburb. Many of the merchants' efforts, from the attempts to lock out small and large retailers to endeavoring to control where workers should cash and spend their paychecks, worked against the interests of wage earners, who were concerned chiefly with family economy. The merchants' actions could make life more difficult for working-class families by limiting their retail choices and ultimately forcing them to travel elsewhere for the cheapest goods. Yet it was by no means an insoluble problem. As consumption became politicized, working families simply voted with their feet—by leaving the suburb to shop. It was an inconvenient but cheap solution that ultimately put local merchants on the defensive.

The conflict over consumption exposed a rift between the town's merchants and residents. It also revealed the importance of class concerns among local groups. While South Gate's working-class families did not consciously politicize consumption as would occur after the war, their consumer behavior nonetheless reflected their fundamental concern with family security and autonomy. In the sphere of consumption, residents expressed a class identity based on a material concept—in their case, limited income and expenditures—rather than on their relationship to other class interests. The group that *did* politicize consumption with a clear awareness was the merchants. By articulating a position that cast consumerism in terms of community loyalty, they defined the meaning of good citizenship and civic duty, and in the process delineated their own class interests. The merchants incorporated a relational element—between themselves and working-class residents—in the formation of their own class identity.

The conflict over consumption revealed the limits of merchant authority and power in South Gate. This resulted not only from class tension but from the outmoded premise of certain merchant beliefs. To a startling degree, they were sorely behind the times. In the ways they articulated and disseminated their ideas—evoking a plaintive discourse of community boosterism in the pages of small local newspapers—these merchants struggled to establish themselves using the arguments of an earlier age. Indeed, they used the methods and language of an old-style elite, the boosters and businessmen of nineteenth-century American communities who truly *had* authority, to define themselves, their interests, and their ideology of community. This

approach was problematical on many levels. It ignored the realities of twentieth-century consumer culture, no small influence upon the American
landscape. As putative purveyors of consumerism, the merchants bumbled
badly on this count. More importantly, their approach ignored the larger
structural changes unfolding in modern metropolitan life, changes that
placed critical authority outside of the community. That authority resided
in the large companies that provided jobs, the firms that shaped consumer
demands and social values, the professional experts who designed products
and argued public policy, and agencies of federal, state, and county government. South Gate's merchants struggled to maintain influence in the face of
these structural monoliths, and faltered on the one issue that hit closest to
home—consumption.[31]

Failing this fight, merchants turned to the politics of development in
their struggle to maintain authority. Local politics would prove to be
ground much firmer than the slippery terrain of consumption, where obstinate residents made autonomous choices. But though the political terrain
was firm, it was rarely smooth. As the diametric interests of merchants and
residents collided head on, consensus in South Gate became as elusive as
the fugitive "Home Gardens Dollar."

The Politics of Development:
"Have Mercy Upon the Laboring Man and Woman"

The most significant political issue in South Gate during the interwar years
centered on development and the related issue of taxation. More than any
other controversy, the tax fight demarcated the profoundly different goals
of the merchants and the town's laboring-class residents. This was a conflict
between two types of property: business versus residential. Although both
were "productive" in a suburb like South Gate, the means toward enhanc-
ing that productivity differed significantly. Far from promoting consensus,
property ownership lay at the heart of local discord. The conflict emerged as
one between growth versus stability, boosterism versus family security, community advancement versus individual independence. It embodied clashing
visions for the community. Would that vision support the worker struggling to establish security through cheap homeownership? Or would it be
committed to growth, internal improvements, and industrial development?
These questions erupted in the politics of development, where the suburb
faced a choice between high taxes to finance improvements versus low taxes
to protect the fiscal integrity of individual families.[32] Throughout the 1920s
and 1930s, it was a consistent, enduring controversy.

Because the businessmen derived their livelihood and status through the local community, it was in their interest to promote growth. Following a long American tradition of the "businessman as city booster" who fused public and private prosperity, local merchants were the neighborhood standard-bearers of expansive, capitalist growth in the twentieth century, and they campaigned tirelessly to pull South Gate into the heart of America's industrial economy. Throughout the 1920s, these merchant leaders aggressively boosted South Gate to attract business, industry, and residents. Working through civic organizations such as the Chamber of Commerce and through the political channels of city hall, their strategy was to improve municipal services, build good roads, install ornamental lights, and beautify landscapes to enhance the suburb's appeal. The Chamber of Commerce's duty, noted the secretary, is to "envision the needs and advantages of the growing city and prepare the public mind to take the initiative in securing all needed improvements. . . . The Chamber is backing up to the limit every legitimate enterprise that makes for civic betterment and a greater city."[33] In the minds of the petite bourgeoisie, growth and prosperity represented South Gate's highest good.

As the most active participants in South Gate's civic and political affairs, the merchants saw themselves as the proper leaders of the community. Yet in a suburb of penurious residents, they also felt the need to legitimize their power and agenda. Echoing earlier arguments for consumer loyalty, they emphasized their selfless contributions to civic life. "Back of every movement for good, for development, for progress and advancement are the home-town merchants, and often they stand alone while the others fold their hands and look on complacently. . . . He does his share . . . [in] fostering every public spirited movement that is initiated." Realtors epitomized this role, particularly in their efforts to attract newcomers. Noted an editor in 1924, "Today there is undoubtedly no more valued asset in the community than the realty dealer—the man who legitimately boosts the town in which he is located by his sale of 'main street' property."[34]

In the 1920s, merchants and realtors backed an agenda of vigorous development, integral to their notion of "the perfect town." As one explained, the perfect town "forgets individual squabbles and unites for the common good of all. . . . The perfect town should have pure water and streets the taxpayers are proud of; . . . a town with a playground for children, so they won't have to be in the streets, and with public comfort stations for both women and men." The Chamber of Commerce played a critical role, advocating the twin tenets of boosterism and development. Such efforts attracted factories, pivotal in generating growth. "The movement to pave streets," the booster-editor noted, "can be traced to chamber of commerce activity in inviting industries to locate in this city. 'Are your streets paved and can we get material out to the plants if we locate there? Can we get spur tracks from the railroad?' are the questions asked." The chamber's efforts, he noted approvingly, was enabling South Gate to answer "yes." The local push for infrastructure development in the 1920s was part of a national trend in North American suburbs. As new suburban communities sprang up farther and farther away from the city, the need for new services in these virgin areas escalated, as did the costs. Swayed by the boom mentality of the decade, development went forward in many communities.[35]

To the laboring-class residents of South Gate, however, the perfect town was something different. The original attraction of South Gate and particularly Home Gardens was the low price of lots, the potential for self-building, and provisions for home gardens and small livestock on one's property—in short, all the necessities for family security through self-sufficiency. They preferred to depend more upon sweat equity than unpredictable cash income. To this end, these homeowning families adamantly opposed higher taxation and its causes, especially costly municipal improvements. Sam Dudlext, a land seller in Home Gardens, was one leader who understood this thinking. "What brought all these people here," he explained in 1925, "[was] the terms on which they could get their homes and be able to get a start without too much interference." By interference, he meant high taxes and assessments. The conflict over development thus pitted suburban boosters, who embodied "a deep American optimism about the effects of economic expansion," against workers suspicious of an unpredictable marketplace and seeking insulation from it. In its orientation, South Gate's working class became part of a lineage of American workers— at least since the nineteenth century—seeking economic security through homeownership and opposing taxes that threatened this security.[36]

Apart from its relation to development and taxes, boosterism elicited a range of responses from working-class families. Some perceived it as an attack on the interests of labor because it intensified competition for jobs by attracting new residents. This ensured a constant surplus of workers, creating a "self-generating and self-perpetuating" system that weakened the power of labor. H. J. Buhrmann, a painter, recognized this concern in a 1925 letter to his hometown newspaper in Wisconsin: "Our people here can't get no kind of a job even at low wages and half of the time they are idle. If you people in Wisconsin have money to spend for railroad fare, you had better stay home and buy coal and fruit rather than come out here and have to work for less than a living wage in order to make expenses, and even take the jobs away from our own poor workingmen who are trying hard to make a living." Organized labor suffered worse still from industrial booster campaigns that emphasized Los Angeles's open-shop status.[37]

Industrial boosterism in South Gate raised other objections as well. The rapid influx of industry could spoil the suburban landscape, forcing residents to cope with noxious odors, noise, and other nuisances.[38] Because of lax zoning regulations and enforcement, some factories were nestled among homes. In 1930, for example, three blocks of Otis Street (from Santa Ana to Firestone) housed Weiser Manufacturing, Long Beach Steel Foundry, the National Paper Products Company, and, a few years earlier, Western State Chemical. Along the same three blocks were thirty-two houses. In some cases, homes were virtually next door to the plants. On other streets, factories sat adjacent to backyards, separated only by a narrow alley. For the poorer homes set at the back of the lot, it was not uncommon for them to abut a factory (see fig. 4-2). Some residents objected to this configuration. In 1927, for example, Otis Street residents complained to city hall about the "parking of cars and litter thrown on the streets" by workers at the National Paper Products Company. The following year, forty-three householders on San Vicente Street signed a petition complaining about the noise at nearby Service Iron and Boiler Works. The council ordered the police chief to talk to the owner to work out an "amicable agreement."[39]

The very framework of an industrial suburb like South Gate, which mixed residences and industries, virtually assured such complaints. Yet these agitated residents seemed to object more to the uncontrolled effects of industrial boosterism rather than to boosterism per se. Their complaints put them in the odd position of opposing efforts to attract industries in a period when good jobs were hard to find. Many working-class residents in fact welcomed industries for providing jobs and bolstering the local economy. "Most people were tickled pink to have [the industries] come because of the money they spent here," recalled Juanita (Smith) Hammon. "My gosh, look at the taxes the plants paid. And of course the men working there spent a lot of money in South Gate even if they didn't live here. They'd stop and buy something on the way home." Ruth Lampmann concurred: "The revenue that goes into the city [from industry] helps to maintain our city. . . . They gave employment to many of our people."[40] The perception that industries were paying generously into South Gate's city coffers was not always borne out by reality; GM and Firestone, the two largest factories, paid no local tax whatsoever because they sat outside of South Gate's borders. Still, the big payrolls and spillover business generated by these plants were seen by many as a benefit to the suburb. In these cases, residents eagerly supported industrial boosterism. But they made a critical dis-

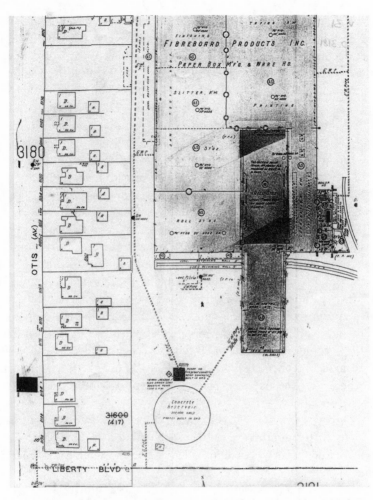

Figure 4-2   Sanborn fire insurance map showing an industrial section in northeast South Gate,
along Otis Avenue. Factories and homes, *D*, often abutted each other, raising the potential for
conflict over the uses of local space. Sanborn Map Company, "Insurance Maps of Los Angeles,
California," volume 31 (New York: Sanborn Map Company, 1929). Copyright © 1929
Sanborn Map Company, The Sanborn Library, LLC. All Rights Reserved. This Sanborn Map®
has been reproduced with written permission from The Sanborn Library, LLC. All further
reproductions are prohibited without prior written permission from The Sanborn Library,
LLC.

tinction between boosterism and development; they supported efforts to
attract factories as long as they did not entail costly development.

During the early years before the merchants came to dominate local
politics, residents and city leaders shared a moment of consensus around
the twin goals of municipal economizing and low taxes. After businessmen

achieved control of city hall in the mid-1920s, this consensus dissolved when they launched an ambitious campaign to develop the suburb's infrastructure, making South Gate one of countless suburbs nationwide caught in the 1920s development boom. In 1925, city leaders initiated programs to pave roads, install ornamental lights, and purchase a municipal water company. The costs escalated precipitously. From 1927 to 1930, $4 million worth of bonds were issued to finance various improvements, including sewers, water lines, curbs, lights, paving, and sidewalks. The city also purchased and began operating eight buses.[41] Besides the costs for infrastructure development, general public spending also rose substantially, from $11,870 to $156,230 between 1923 and 1931. From just 1924 to 1925, the general city tax rate jumped from $1 to $1.46 per $100 valuation.[42]

The political road to an improved South Gate was not nearly as smooth as its newly paved streets. The development push sparked heated conflicts between merchants and working families, revealing the nature of class structure and struggle in the blue-collar suburb. A close look at a few key episodes illustrates the schism. The discourse around these conflicts reflected not only the competing interests of these groups, but contentious ideas about the role of local government, the structure of taxation systems, and the very meaning of the public good. "Whenever local governments collect taxes," Stephen Diamond reminds us, "it may be asked who gains and who loses." Development politics in interwar South Gate hinged on this very question.[43]

The story begins in 1924, when citizens elected Andrew J. Schoby to office, along with four other councilmen. Schoby was typical of South Gate's merchant leaders. He was a realtor, a service station operator, and a member of the Chamber of Commerce, serving as vice president in 1928. His personal business interests were firmly linked to local growth and development. Schoby would serve as mayor during the next six years, the critical period of South Gate's frenzied improvement activity.[44]

The first major skirmish centered on something as seemingly innocuous as ornamental streetlights. Such adornment, in fact, was a part of City Beautiful, a national movement committed to using municipal power to promote the beautification of functional urban elements. City Beautiful peaked in Los Angeles during the 1920s. In 1925, South Gate leaders embraced the tenets of City Beautiful by proposing a system of decorative streetlights. "From the standpoint of protection alone," intoned the local editor, "a city should be properly lighted. But good lights make a far more attractive city. They furnish the best possible advertising. Their cost is little compared to their growth." The "little" cost was estimated at $100,000.[45]

City Beautiful meant little to working-class families in South Gate.

Alarmed by the fiscal burden of such a venture, a group of residents—led by a carpenter, a small grocer, and the wife of another carpenter—circulated petitions to recall three of the councilmen responsible for the project. The protesters thought the city leaders were "in defiance of the law and of the will" of South Gate's citizens, because the improvement was superfluous and fixed a large indebtedness on homeowners. Carpenter L. Clemens Baier articulated the objection in an open letter to the city council in 1925: "Before adding more financial burdens upon us such as the proposed street lighting improvements, wouldn't it be well to stop and consider these various improvement questions from several angles? . . . [F]or a great many it would mean deprivations and hardships over a long period. I think I am safe in stating that the majority of South Gate home-owners are in the wage-earning class. . . . With the ever-increasing taxes and the business depression and lack of employment during the past year, the average wage-earner has about all he can pay for now."

Certain improvements were acceptable, such as provisions for water supplies. Furthermore, Baier claimed, the city fathers could take cheaper, easier steps to beautify the city. "No disrespect is intended," he continued, "but may it be suggested that if the weeds and grass were removed from the . . . streets it would improve the appearance of our city just about as much as the proposed new lights." But the worst aspect of this improvement was the fiscal threat to residents. Imploring his councilmen, Baier concluded that South Gate "is financially burdening its property owners too fast. . . . Have mercy upon the laboring man and woman who is struggling hard to make and pay for a home within your borders."[46]

In the face of a recall threat, the city council began taking autocratic measures. It tabled recall petitions signed by 454 residents and assembled its own counterpetition with signatures of 376 residents who supported the streetlights. The two sides faced off in a council meeting, "the most largely attended and stormiest session ever held in the city of South Gate," according to the local press. Several hundred residents attended. The anti-light forces loudly objected to the project's fiscal burden, the council's neglect of their recall petitions, and the rushing of the proceedings. One resident was nearly thrown out for calling Mayor Schoby a "pussyfoot." Council members ignored these objections and ruled unanimously in favor of the lights. They argued that the pro-light petitioners prevailed because they owned more acreage than their opponents, sending a disturbing message that property carried more weight than citizenship in South Gate.[47]

Angered by this ruling, the recall forces intensified the fight. They obtained a summons for the council members to appear in Los Angeles Superior Court to show cause why the recall election was never held; they petitioned the court to force a recall election; and, striking at the heart of the matter, they requested a temporary restraining order to prevent the city council from launching more improvements until after the recall election. After hearing arguments during the next few months, the judge threw out the case on a minor technicality.[48] Undeterred by this setback, the protesters formed a new group called the South Gate Taxpayers' League to continue the fight. They distributed fliers in the community, rebuking the "city hall crowd" for ignoring the popular will and authorizing needless improvements. The flier noted angrily that South Gate's property tax rate had climbed to $1.46 per $100 valuation, higher even than neighboring (and more upscale) Huntington Park's rate of $1.33. Furthermore, the annual cost of simply *maintaining* the streetlights amounted to an additional $3.50 for each forty-foot lot. The city council lashed back, passing a resolution condemning the Taxpayers' League circulars as "scurrilous, un-American and thoroughly despicable." The city attorney demanded the flier be classified as "syndicalism" and turned over to the district attorney for appropriate action. He charged that it "slandered good government, good citizenship, and Americanism." The *Tribune* was equally contemptuous. "Who the Taxpayers' League is, no one seems to know," ran a page-one editorial. "[It] raps improvements in general and brands the people of the city as slaves because they are so progressive as to want South Gate to be modern. It is stated that such things are being FORCED upon the people as water bonds, city hall bonds, Metropolitan Sewer bonds, fancy lights and patented pavements. . . . The TAXPAYERS, themselves, are getting the improvements that they want and need, and, because there is a minority which will ALWAYS be against ALL improvements, is no indication in the world that the people are getting a lot of stuff that they don't want crammed down their throats. . . . Of course the taxes in South Gate are higher this year than they were last, but the people are getting more for their money." This diatribe prompted the Taxpayers' League to circulate petitions against the *Tribune*, claiming it was acting against the public interest. They were rightly convinced that the *Tribune* sided squarely with the town's boosters and businessmen.[49]

Shaken by this display of public resistance to development, South Gate's merchants moved to fortify their most important institutional base, the Chamber of Commerce. Immediately following the streetlight controversy, the newspapers ran a series of articles praising the chamber's work. "A city has few assets which are greater than its chamber of commerce," claimed an editorial. "[It] is working all the time to . . . make the community a more desirable place in which to live, and, consequently, to bring in more people." The merchants also attempted to bolster the chamber's finances with city funding, clearly a move to maintain political momentum behind development and growth. With help from the pro-development city council, the chamber won sporadic city funding from 1926 to 1928, then secured a $200-per-month municipal appropriation in 1928. One vocal opponent of this subsidy was Nathaniel Barragar, a sales-man from Home Gardens, who accused Mayor Schoby of pocketing the money—Schoby also served as chamber vice president. "[I]t will be the taxpayer who will pay dearly for these mistakes," Barragar warned. "Folks, you are just out-witted, that's all! Your votes, like your majority petitions, do not go very far with your City Council." In a final attempt to secure mu-nicipal funding, the chamber called for a tax of one mill on the dollar (10 cents per $100 valuation of property) to subsidize its work.[50] Despite strong backing from the mayor and newspapers, the "one mill tax" was de-feated at the polls, prompting Mayor Schoby to resign as chamber vice president to curb expenses. Another, more vigorous, "one mill tax" cam-paign five months later met a more decisive defeat, with Home Gardens showing the strongest opposition.[51]

Thus far, South Gate citizens had begun to articulate the local conflict over infrastructure development as between "bigger" property versus "smaller" property. To the alarm of working-class homeowners, those with the larger frontage seemed to have the louder voice in decision making. In so defining the conflict, South Gate citizens echoed debates over municipal financing that had raged at least since the nineteenth century. What ser-vices did residents expect a city government to provide? How would those services be paid for, and who would make those finance decisions?[52] South Gate's working-class homeowners were beginning to answer these ques-tions in a way that conferred equal power to every property owner, re-gardless of the value of that property. The status of homeowner, they believed, gave them a voice in decision making, even if that home was hum-ble, self-built, and worth little. Homeownership—period—conferred citi-zenship.

As South Gate residents clashed over answers to those larger questions about municipal financing, they joined a long line of urban citizens work-ing out answers to those very questions. It is a history too long and complex to detail here, but one thread of the story deserves mention—the mecha-nism of special assessments. In the broadest terms, cities moved from a "segmented system"—where only affected property owners would decide on and pay for services—to a more democratic system, where all citizens had input and financial responsibility. Under the segmented system, the prime policy-making tool was the special assessment, a one-time payment by a property owner to help finance a specific improvement project. Applied especially to street and sewer improvements, special assessments were meant to confine the cost and benefit of such improvements to those property owners abutting the project. Assessments were preferred over general taxes because it was believed the greatest benefit of street improvements came to the abutting landowners, and they should therefore bear the costs. This was considered a nonredistributive system of taxing and spending. In the nineteenth century, the special assessment was a radically localized mechanism, putting the initiative and decision-making power in the hands of property owners. The process began and ended at the local level. While older, eastern cities largely abandoned the special assessment system by the late nineteenth century, it survived—though often in "distorted" form— in newer cities into the twentieth century, particularly in the West.[53]

In 1920s Los Angeles, one such distorted version of special assessments was known as the Mattoon Act. This statewide acquisition and improvement law had particularly odious consequences for small property owners because it shifted decision-making powers away from them and onto central planners, while keeping the financial burden on the smaller homeowner. Ultimately, it became a means for prodevelopment forces to insulate themselves from popular resistance. The Mattoon Act brought the politics of development to a climax in South Gate. As in many communities across the state, the measure drove the engine of unbridled overdevelopment during the 1920s, creating the circumstances that not only brought disaster upon neighborhoods and homeowners, but bred political hostility to government spending.

The story of the Mattoon Act begins in the mid-1920s, when Everett W. Mattoon, chief deputy county counsel of Los Angeles, authored a state bill to consolidate the funding and execution of internal improvements. The Acquisition and Improvement Act of 1925 was quickly recognized as "the most important legislative act affecting public improvements" and was considered particularly useful for Los Angeles because of its rapid development during the decade. The Mattoon Act streamlined the process of municipal improvements by allowing assessment districts to acquire and improve land simultaneously and to transcend municipal boundaries, which promoted the idea of "metropolitan planning." Most significantly, the measure entitled city councils to spread assessments *without the consent* of property owners in a district. Whereas previous laws required a two-thirds vote of popular support before an improvement could commence, the Mattoon Act allowed proceedings to start "immediately regardless of protests, if the governing body so wishes." For pro-improvement city councils, this was a legalistic boon.[54] Finally, the Mattoon Act placed a collective lien on all real estate parcels when an improvement bond was issued. This element, buried deeply in convoluted language, had the potential for disaster. A person's property was subject to the bonded lien until *all* the property owners in the district had paid their obligation in full. When a neighbor defaulted, his assessment burden was distributed among the remaining residents. Delinquent amounts from previous years were added onto the assessment debt, which could create a pyramiding effect. In the worst-case scenario, foreclosures against an entire district (including those residents who had paid their own taxes) could be launched if there were partial defaults within that district. In essence, the Mattoon Act imposed a collective fate upon California property owners: they would sink or swim together. Given the law's complexity, few taxpayers understood it at the outset.[55]

The Mattoon Act sprang from Progressive roots.[56] It was originally proposed by backers of the Los Angeles Major Traffic Street Plan of 1924, an elaborate series of highways and roads that fostered residential and business decentralization. Designers of the plan believed the most orderly system called for a regional approach to planning. Following this logic, the Mattoon Act took a regional approach to infrastructure financing. By enabling assessment districts to traverse political entities, it allowed for large-scale planning without the stunting interference of local control. As one contemporary put it, the Mattoon Act "cut away much of what might be termed red tape." In this case, "red tape" became a euphemism for local resistance. The Mattoon Act, highly centralized in nature, thus differed from nineteenth-century special assessments that were "radically local." In Los Angeles, the impetus for improvements came from regional planners rather than individual property owners.[57]

The Mattoon Act received hearty endorsement from boosters and developers across Los Angeles. The *Los Angeles Times* called the measure "the greatest forward step in facilitating public improvements that ever has been taken in California . . . [and] of vital importance to Southern California." South Gate's leaders joined the chorus. Indeed, they considered the Mattoon Act the answer to the vexing problem of local opposition. Everett Mattoon himself visited the suburb and reassured residents that the law which bore his name would save time, money, waste, and misunderstandings in the implementation of public improvements.[58]

Once a friendly suit established the Mattoon Act's constitutionality in 1926, South Gate's leaders invoked the measure to fund infrastructure development. They used it to issue a $750,000 bond for water and sewer mains, street upgrades, a major-highway project, curbs, sidewalks, fire hydrants, and ornamental streetlights. By late 1928, the city had launched ten major improvements under the act, and by 1930 its bonded indebtedness was nearly $4 million. Nearly all of South Gate fell into Mattoon Act assessment districts. Part of this frenzied activity was spurred by the dramatic population jump in the suburb, from 500 to nearly 20,000 in the 1920s. A good part of this growth occurred in 1927 and 1928, when populated tracts like Home Gardens and Hollydale were annexed to South Gate. City leaders saw a particularly acute need for improvements in Home Gardens, where municipal services were lacking.[59]

Residents quickly felt the sting of mounting tax rates. The city's general fund tax was $1.17 per $100 valuation[60] in the original northwest section and $1.02 in the remaining areas, including Home Gardens. While these amounts were reasonable, the special assessments mounted quickly. In newly annexed Home Gardens and Magnolia Park, the acquisition of new water systems resulted in assessments averaging $4.56 (above the general fund tax). On top of this came taxes to finance Mattoon Act improvements. In Home Gardens, two acquisition and improvement districts were established to finance the installation of sewers, lights, sidewalks, and curbs, amounting to a tax rate averaging $5.18.[61] With all levies combined, the tax bill of a Home Gardens resident could run approximately $10.76 per $100 valuation. Presuming a "taxable" home value of about $2,200,[62] the average South Gate resident faced a tax bill of $236.72. For the typical wage earner, this represented a hefty 16 percent of one's income of $1,500.[63] This tax placed severe pressure on the town's families, who now had to raise substantial amounts of cash merely to *keep* the property they owned.

The excessive burdens wrought by the Mattoon Act, in fact, affected many areas of Los Angeles. As one report stated, the measure "was used by many promoters to stimulate unwarranted initiating of costly improvements, and became the object of deplorable abuse. . . . Shortly, the over-use and abuse of the Act became apparent." Some neighborhoods had as many as 12 "layers" of overlapping assessment districts. In Inglewood, low property assessment values, high public spending, and pyramiding tax debt resulted in tax rates up to 111 percent of the assessed valuation of homes. A property owner in the Westlake area, just northwest of downtown, claimed that property there "just died a natural death it seems from over taxation and assessments." A district in western Los Angeles near Beverly Glen had special assessment taxes that reached $13 per $100 valuation. The Anaheim Telegraph Road project created a bonded debt that amounted to over 91 percent of the total assessed value of the land in that district. And Lynwood, directly below South Gate, had a total of 20 assessment districts blanketing its small area. L.A. county had about 125 special assessment districts "staggering under ad valorem assessments," in the words of Supervisor John Anson Ford. For many neighborhoods, the tax problem was simply out of control.[64]

In the late 1920s, Mattoon Act overdevelopment spurred a political backlash in South Gate. Hamstrung by the political exclusion rendered by the law, antidevelopment residents found they had little leverage in fights against specific projects, evident in several futile protests. Their prime weapon, thus, became the ballot box. If they could not intervene in the acquisition and improvement process itself, at least they could elect councilmen less obsessed with development. As a result, local politics in the late 1920s became a series of recalls and elections focused on development. Most of this resistance was reactive, responses to deeds already done.

It wasn't until 1929 that residents against improvements finally organized an opposition movement. At the outset, they rallied under the leadership of Nathaniel Barragar, the salesman from Home Gardens who earlier spoke out against municipal funding for the Chamber of Commerce. Barragar organized a recall campaign against Mayor Schoby, a logical target since he had presided during the years of costly development. These residents collected 400 signatures on recall petitions, prompting several local institutions—including the city council, the *Tribune*, the Property Owners and Businessmen's Club of South Gate, and the Kiwanis Club—to rally behind the mayor. When the initial recall drive fell short, Barragar tried again, this time collecting 650 signatures, which barely missed the required minimum.[65]

A few months later, a new group took up the fight. Calling themselves the Citizens Cooperative League, they vowed to fight against exorbitant public spending and the men who supported it—an appeal that took on new urgency with the onset of the Depression. Attorney Stanley Moffatt, a Republican turned radical Democrat, headed the group. They quickly organized a campaign to recall Mayor Schoby and councilman Louis Martin, charging them with favoring "extravagant paving and lighting proceedings in the city of South Gate to the extent that taxes and assessments . . . have become very burdensome to the people." After a long, tiring petition drive resisted by the city council,[66] the Cooperative League finally succeeded in getting their recall election in June 1930. They won a resounding victory— both men were ousted by majorities exceeding 90 percent.[67]

The Cooperative League likewise turned the council election of April 1930 into a referendum on development. They ran a slate of candidates who pledged to cut municipal spending and alleviate, as much as possible, the damage done by the previous administration. In response, the pro-improvement forces formed their own "league"—dubbed the Progressive League— which openly endorsed improvements and a probusiness approach to governance. "Real business men are needed," they asserted, to lead the city properly. In a working-class suburb like South Gate, this approach was a serious miscalculation. A page-one endorsement by the *Tribune* exposed the flaw in thinking. The editor asked whether corporations choose their leaders by "going out on the highways and by-ways picking a truck driver here or a laborer there and placing them at the head of affairs." He answered, "No, you derned fool." South Gate had to elect "men with business knowledge and ability." The citizenry disagreed. The Cooperative League candidates won the election, despite much heavier advertising by their opponents, and two months later they took the two seats vacated by the recall of Schoby and Martin. The anti-improvement forces finally controlled city hall.[68]

For the first time in the suburb's history, the forces against improvements had achieved political success. Several factors explain their overdue ascendance in 1930. First, the Cooperative League provided an effective organizational base with savvy leadership. Attorney Stanley Moffatt, in particular, armed them with legal expertise to counteract the questionable tactics of the city council.[69] Second, by this time residents felt the acute financial sting of overdevelopment and the incipient effects of the Great Depression, inclining them toward a more active role in city policies. Out of self-defense alone, citizens realized they had to act. Finally, the antidevelopment forces at long last won the sympathy of one local paper, the *South Gate Press*. This Home Gardens–oriented newspaper issued its first forceful statement against improvements in August 1929, when it chastised city leaders for favoring the interests of large property owners over those of the people. The editor warned that excessive improvements overburdened the small property owner: "taxes become an impossible burden, and he finally passes out of the picture as a home owner. And the individual home owner is the bulwark of any community. To burden him unnecessarily is little short of a crime." A fundamental conflict was becoming clear. "Will it be property rule, or . . . 'the greatest good to the greatest number'?" The dire consequence, the editor predicted, was that South Gate would become a city of renters, the ultimate ruination of the community in his eyes.[70]

As the language of this struggle was suggesting, the politics of development delineated the conflicting interests of homeowners and business owners. While merchants sought profits through community investments that would make South Gate a more attractive marketplace, homeowning residents sought financial independence from the marketplace. Far from creating a property-based "suburban" consensus, homeownership represented a distinct basis of identity for laboring-class residents that set them apart from other suburban interest groups.[71] Residents sought to protect the security they had achieved through owning a home. High taxes threatened this autonomy, and posed the specter of default, forced sales, and tenancy.

Their opposition to improvements was testimony to their goal and expressed a popular resistance to the merchants' ideas about "progress."[72] While the anti-tax forces represented a broad base of the local population—including workers, salesmen, even some professionals—they were united in their status as homeowners and in their economic struggles. And since homeownership was a prerequisite for full membership in the community, they fought against taxes to protect their civic standing.

The exclusion of renters proved just how important this status could be. In the 1920s, renters constituted about 9 percent of the population in South Gate.[73] Because they did not own property, renters were not allowed to sign petitions on city affairs. "Being a resident and a voter," mused tenant Adam Krooke, "I am wondering if I have no rights as a citizen." Krooke was especially frustrated by his exclusion from the politics of development, which frequently utilized recall petitions. To him, the tightfisted position of homeowners worked *against* the public good. "Surely, every right-thinking person will grant that, for my $20 a month [rent] brought into town from outside, I should have not only a house to live in but well-paved streets, sidewalks, street lights, schools, playgrounds for my children, fire and police protection. . . . If this sort of money-pinching is persisted in and we renters who bring in the wealth that keeps up the landlord class are not supplied more liberally with the things we want, I hereby give notice that I for one will move away and leave the town to its own headlong destruction." The marginal position of this writer was precisely what homeowners sought to avoid. They were committed to protecting their dearly won position on the inside.[74]

Once the Cooperative League councilmen took charge, they immediately implemented a program of retrenchment, starting with a resolution opposing the Mattoon Act generally and patent paving projects specifically. They curbed the maintenance of streetlights, reduced bus service, trimmed the salaries of city employees, eliminated city jobs, and rationed appropriations to municipal departments. And during most of the Depression, South Gate's notorious streetlights remained dark. The city council also canceled a $350 monthly appropriation to the Chamber of Commerce, which helped bring on its demise in 1931. Altogether, these cuts amounted to a reduction of more than $3,000 per month in city expenses.[75]

It soon became clear that these cutbacks were too little too late, especially since the new council could do nothing to eliminate previous Mattoon Act debt. Special assessment taxes had ballooned enormously in South Gate. Conditions worsened to the point that by the 1930s, 40.2 percent of municipal spending went toward interest payments on bonded indebtedness, diverting funds from other basic services.[76] The tax burden on individuals also escalated, especially as the collective lien provision of Mattoon kicked in. As residents in Mattoon Act districts began defaulting, their debts were distributed among their neighbors, as were delinquency debts from previous years. Tax rates surged. Like the overlap of assessment districts that blanketed the suburb, South Gate was caught in the sticky web of overdevelopment.[77]

As a result, tax defaults and property losses mounted. Even for families who had cut corners to achieve homeownership by self-building and who had paid their own tax bills, the pyramiding tax debt could be devastating. The economic pressures of the Great Depression only worsened matters. The first sign was tax delinquency. For all of South Gate, the delinquency rate peaked at 32 percent in 1934–35, then gradually declined to 11 percent by 1938–39. Certain sections of town, especially those with overlapping tax districts, had higher rates. For example, the State Street Acquisition and Improvement District (which included 6,000 properties) had delinquency rates between 42 and 55 percent from 1936 to 1937. Delinquency did not automatically mean property confiscation, however. A property owner had to default on taxes for five years for this to happen. In South Gate, the first homes began reverting to the state around 1933, five years after the first Mattoon Act improvements were initiated. According to one estimate, several thousand lots in South Gate ultimately reverted to the state. In Los Angeles as a whole, mortgage foreclosures peaked in June 1933, at 205 per 100,000 families, a rate substantially higher than in most American cities. The southeastern suburbs of Los Angeles were hit especially hard.[78]

One result was a rapid increase in tenancy in South Gate. The homeownership rate dropped from nearly 90 percent in 1929 to 56.6 percent in 1930 and 54.6 percent in 1935.[79] Why the steep fall between 1929 and 1930, still a few years before Mattoon Act defaults would result in confiscation? Most likely homeowners simply could not bear the burden of mounting special assessments, so they left and were replaced by tenants. Indeed, nearly half of all residents moved out of the suburb from 1926 to 1930. Many homes of the outmigrants were purchased by speculators, then rented out to newcomers.[80] The city council acknowledged this shift in housing tenure when it proposed to change all R-1 property (single-family residences) to R-2, which would allow residents to build duplexes for renting. A vocal crowd successfully blocked the proposal, fearing it would bring more taxes upon their already overburdened property.[81] Although it was becoming ever more difficult to protect, single-family homeownership maintained its tenuous grip in South Gate even as the menace of overdevelopment began to change the essence of working-class suburban life.

The story of South Gate's escape from the mire of costly improvements played out in the context of state and national political developments. Efforts at the state level were crucial in bringing about relief of Mattoon Act damages. In the early 1930s, campaigns were launched all across California to repeal the Mattoon Act and secure relief from its effects. These initiatives sprang up at many levels, from small communities to the state legislature. At the grassroots level, communities formed "special assessment relief associations" and hired lawyers to formulate repeal measures. In 1931, for example, property owners in San Diego formed the Mattoon Act Relief Association and raised $40,000 to fund two legal suits against the act. A similar group coalesced in the Normandie section of Los Angeles, where in 1932 about 80 percent of property was delinquent on Mattoon Act assessments. The Tax Reduction Club of California formed in the early 1930s to "lower public expenditures and reduce taxes." It urged citizens to "vote against all measures you do not understand." In L.A. County, officials passed a tax moratorium in 1932, which froze property confiscation, and they allocated gasoline tax funds to help alleviate the assessment debt.[82] At the state level, the California legislature formed the Committee on Special Assessment Laws to tour the state and meet with local civic leaders on the matter. Even Everett Mattoon joined the crusade. Realizing the law's defects, he supported legislative measures in 1929 and 1931 to protect property owners against special assessments.[83]

Organized labor also weighed in against excessive taxation. The L.A. Central Labor Council (CLC), which represented the American Federation of Labor, accused the L.A. Realty Board of producing the boom and bust in the region and then calling for tax and wage cuts to solve the problem. The CLC singled out Mason Case, an industrial realtor active in South Gate, for "conducting a vile and traitorous campaign of misrepresentation" in his capacity as spokesman for the L.A. Realty Board's Taxpayers' Division. They charged Case and his fellow realtors with overdevelopment, inflating real estate values, and ballooning tax rates in the 1920s, then demanding a general wage cut as the solution for lowering the tax levy in the 1930s. As the Labor Council stated in a resolution,

Whereas, this clan of despoilers and the vested interests they represent brought about the high taxes of which they complain, and are now through subterfuge and vicious propaganda, attempting to escape the penalty of their own greed by heaping further hardships upon the common people already harassed beyond endurance, and

Whereas, this group has made, and continues to make, attacks upon wage earners who are the dominant purchasing power of the community by demanding a general wage cut. . . .

Resolved, that the Central Labor Council . . . does hereby register its
most earnest protest against such procedure.[84]

As this statement made clear, taxation and development had become a locus
of colliding class interests.

By the early 1930s, the problem had become a national one as tax delinquencies pushed many cities toward bankruptcy. It began in the 1920s as
municipalities went into debt to bring services to new suburbs, and escalated in the 1930s with the onset of the Depression. The crisis was compounded by decreases in assessed valuations of real property, which shrank
the tax base further. As David Beito has shown, the stock market crash unleashed unprecedented tax burdens on more Americans than ever. Across
the nation, local taxes more than doubled, from 5.4 percent of the national
income in 1929 to 11.7 percent in 1932. State taxes similarly jumped. The
fallout was surging tax delinquencies; for cities with populations exceeding
50,000, the median delinquency rate jumped from 10.1 percent in 1930 to
26.3 percent in 1933.[85] Most of these were real estate taxes, the primary
source of state and local revenue. While all large cities felt the pressure, Los
Angeles especially suffered from the boom and bust. Assessed valuations
fell 45.2 percent from 1929 to 1933 in Los Angeles, compared to 42.2 percent in Cleveland and 17.8 percent in Detroit. In the same period, unpaid
taxes rose from under 10 percent to almost 30 percent in all urban areas. In
response to the problem, cities could trim services but they could not law-
fully curtail interest payments on bonded debt. They ultimately turned to
Washington, D.C. for help. Congress in 1934 passed the Municipal Debt
Adjustment Act, which allowed cities and bondholders to negotiate debt
settlement under judicial supervision.[86] The measure gave creditors so
much power that it proved of little real use to cities, evident in the fact that
no city of over 30,000 population ever invoked it. Then in 1936, the conservative U.S. Supreme Court ruled the law unconstitutional because it in-
fringed on state responsibility. With judicial gridlock at the state and
federal levels, relief for homeowners appeared ever elusive.[87]

Not only was the problem a national one, but anti-tax resistance was
also a nationwide phenomenon. The rise in real estate taxes during the
Depression spurred a wave of anti-tax protests in a number of midwestern
and eastern cities, similar to the grassroots activity in California. Although
these protests were rarely well-organized or effective, they did achieve
some notable results: from 1932 to 1934, seven states enacted overall limitations on the general property tax (six through popular initiative); several
dozen localities enacted similar limitations; and taxpayers' and economy

leagues were formed in every state and hundreds of counties. All in all, this movement constituted a viable challenge to state authority.[88]

In California, the Mattoon Act was repealed in 1931 with the support of Everett Mattoon himself. But because the repeal did not nullify tax debts retroactively, the new challenge became relieving accumulated debts. In 1935, the state legislature passed a law allowing for the modification of assessment bond contracts if 50 percent of the property owners so consented. Federal measures bolstered this code. Congress passed another municipal bankruptcy law stipulating that a compromise settlement on bond issues would be binding with the approval of 75 percent of the bond holders. In 1938, it won judicial approval from a federal district court in Florida. The legal path toward relief was finally cleared.[89]

As these events unfolded in distant places, political life in South Gate focused obsessively on the tax problem, and for good reason. With delinquencies mounting, the suburb was fiscally hamstrung until a legal solution emerged. In the meantime, the damage wrought by overdevelopment was coming into stunning focus, as people continued to lose property and services came to a halt. At this point, everyone could agree that the Mattoon Act had been a bad thing for South Gate. This united realization caused an important shift in local political sensibilities. A new consensus emerged, united around staunch opposition to the Mattoon Act. While this position was no surprise for wage-earning residents, it was a big change for the erstwhile prodevelopment leaders of the suburb. Yet it was a change that made political sense. By scapegoating the Mattoon Act, merchants effectively deflected attention away from their earlier complicity in the debacle. This strategy worked well—they convinced the public as well as themselves. Judging by their words in the 1930s, it would be hard to detect that these leaders had *ever* supported development. The crisis they instigated ultimately changed their own political ideas about development, growth, and public spending. This change of heart, politically expedient and realistic by the early 1930s, nudged the merchants closer toward the interests of their working-class constituents. Thus began a process of political convergence.

The merchants' new posture was widely accepted while their earlier actions were conveniently forgotten, evident in public memory about overdevelopment and in the merchants' ultimate return to political power. In the minds of most residents, the villain was the Mattoon Act, not the suburb's leaders. As one recalled, the Mattoon Act "ended up costing a lot of people in South Gate their homes." Another recollected, "In South Gate, hell there wasn't anything on the tax rolls to speak of. There were thousands of lots that drifted into the city coffers because no tax had been paid on them. . . . [The Mattoon Act] was like all those cock-and-bull economic panaceas being thrust on California. . . . Whoever heard of the fact that if Norm Smith next door to me couldn't pay his taxes, everybody's gonna pay part of his taxes? What the hell kind of goofball thing was that?"[90] This characterization told only part of the story. It curiously neglected the complicity of the leaders who had invoked the measure in the first place.

By the early 1930s, nearly every local politician had jumped aboard the anti-Mattoon bandwagon. In the 1932 city council race, *all* candidates came out against the Mattoon Act, improvements, and spending—including Harold Pomeroy, a former chamber officer and proponent of improvements and the "one mill tax." With the factional lines thus blurred, the merchant candidates invented issues to set them apart from their opponents. They launched a mudslinging campaign by accusing the Cooperative League's reform councilmen of corruption. Although their charges had little basis in fact, the ploy worked and they won seats on the council.[91] Pomeroy assumed the office of mayor, and William Rempel, a lumberyard owner, became a city councilman. Their victory might be partially explained by the high residential turnover rate in South Gate and a newcomer population unaware of recent local history. When Stanley Moffatt launched a recall campaign against the two on the grounds that they were high spenders, Pomeroy invoked the corruption charges again, and the recall movement died.[92] The path was thus cleared for the leaders who had created the problem now to solve it.

In tandem with state and national efforts for tax relief, South Gate's leaders devised their own solutions. They appealed to the county for gasoline tax money to relieve local tax burdens, a solution advocated widely in Los Angeles. Councilman Rempel and City Attorney Clyde Woodworth also drafted several state assembly bills to provide Mattoon Act debt relief.[93] Rempel, in fact, emerged as the key figure in South Gate's fiscal rescue. Drawing upon his background in banking, he drafted a plan to abolish Mattoon Act debt, in which the city would purchase in cash the outstanding Mattoon bonds at a reduced rate. The city would raise the cash by issuing general obligation bonds, paid for by property owners who would vote on this in an election. To pay off these bonds, property would be assessed and taxed individually—no more blanket obligations—for a period of ten years. And to protect against tax delinquencies, the city would create a sinking fund for three years, until the situation stabilized.[94]

One month before the Rempel plan was put to a vote in 1938, a council election solidified the business leaders' hold on local power. In a contest that generated little press coverage, a merchant ticket ran against a "taxpayers" ticket. What little newspaper coverage did exist focused on the merchant candidates, including prominent articles, large ads, and several supportive letters to the editors. These endorsements emphasized the merchants' promise of clean, honest government, and most importantly their commitment to continuing Mattoon Act debt relief. The rival taxpayer's ticket, which included several working-class candidates, ran a lackluster campaign. Though endorsed by organized labor, they did little to publicize this fact. Their press coverage was brief and vague, and they ran no advertisements. Their platform—quite similar to the businessmen's—was buried in a letter to the editor. This was a contest devoid of class distinctions—neither side emphasized the candidates' occupational backgrounds. Given the stilted coverage, it was hardly surprising that the business ticket won handily. The merchants were now positioned to preside over the death of the Mattoon Act in South Gate, the most celebrated political event of the suburb's first two decades.[95]

The May 1938 election was the deciding moment, when citizens would vote on Rempel's refunding plan. The ensuing campaign to "Kill the Mattoon Act" bordered on public ritual. Through extensive public discourse, a massive publicity barrage, and the curious specter of a zealous campaign for a position with no opponents, this crusade enabled South Gate to display an unprecedented level of political unity. Spearheaded by the real estate board, the "Kill the Mattoon Act" campaign clarified Rempel's plan and assured residents that the new bond was the best means of finally ridding the city of debt. The merchants, their civic groups, the city council, and the press rallied hard behind the plan, splashing the motto "Kill the Mattoon Act" all over town: on leaflets, car windshields, correspondence via rubber stamps, and trucks. They gave speeches heartily supporting Rempel's plan. A week before the election, the South Side Business Men's Association sponsored a "Kill the Mattoon Act Dinner" for all residents, with lamb and "hundreds of pounds of other edibles" donated by local merchants. The South Gate Democratic Club endorsed the relief plan as well. The publicity barrage was an extraordinary success. The Rempel plan passed by a landslide of 5,361 to 158, and Rempel became something of a local hero. The city council praised his "outstanding service . . . far and above the ordinary measure of duty." At a victory picnic in his honor, he burned Mattoon Act bonds in effigy. When the city offered to name a new park after him, he modestly refused.[96]

The inglorious end of this story unfolded in the 1940s, when the suburb's leaders finally got the civic infrastructure they so fervently desired at a bargain price. From 1940 to 1950, more than $1 million in new buildings and recreational facilities were constructed for the city, largely financed by the proceeds from 4,000 tax-delinquent properties. This money helped build a new city hall, a civic auditorium, fire department facilities, a hall of justice, and a community swimming pool. The city celebrated its progress in a gala dedication ceremony.[97] In the midst of the joviality, merriment, and boosterism, most overlooked the fact that this indeed was a Pyrrhic victory.

THE POLITICS OF EDUCATION AND RACE: STRANGE BEDFELLOWS

The fierce concerns of South Gate's residents with family security, munici-pal economy, and insulation from a cash wage found their most dramatic expression in the politics of education. This issue revealed the primacy of class-based concerns by juxtaposing them against the ever-sensitive issue of race. For South Gate residents, the main "racial group" to contend with was African Americans, who were gradually moving into the suburbs di-rectly to the west. The politics of education posed difficult questions to res-idents: was their concern for low taxes and municipal economy strong enough to overshadow their preference for racial distance? Would they be willing to accept racially integrated schools, as a means of minimizing taxes? Did class concerns outweigh racial concerns? For the many ex-southerners living in South Gate, this was no small matter. As they began answering these questions, they engaged in a drastic reordering of their so-cial priorities in ways that felt foreign, unjust, and uncomfortable.

The significance of the race question lies in the strength of racial preoc-cupations among whites in interwar Los Angeles. Relations between blacks and whites—social and spatial—set an important backdrop to the story. The history of black-white relations in early Los Angeles was a story of de-terioration. The period from the 1890s to 1920, dubbed the "Golden Era" by one scholar, was one of relative prosperity for many blacks in Los Angeles. Constituting less than 3 percent of the total population, African Americans enjoyed a "considerable degree of acceptance," evident in their ready access to homeownership and, more strikingly, in their extensive residential dis-persal throughout the city. The California courts supported this pattern in early rulings against race-restrictive covenants. The situation changed by 1920. The black population rose dramatically in the 1920s to nearly 39,000, making them a more visible presence. They soon experienced intensified discrimination in public accommodations, employment, and residential choice. Backed by state court rulings starting in 1919 that upheld restrictive covenants, white Los Angeles began confining blacks to an area around Central Avenue, which became the heart of the city's black "ghetto." Central Avenue, in fact, became a vibrant center of black economic and cultural life, but discrimination also promoted its overpopulation.[98]

The crackdown against blacks in the 1920s was a symptom of a much broader effort by whites to Anglicize the city. A metropolis with an unusually high proportion of racial minorities for its time, Los Angeles was ferociously preoccupied with maintaining Anglo dominance during the 1920s to almost eugenic proportions. The city prided itself as a destination of "old immigrants"—from northern and western Europe—during a period when "new immigrants" were inundating eastern cities. Los Angeles would be the last frontier of the white Anglo-Saxon Protestant. Yet as Mexicans, Asians, and blacks also found a place in the city, Anglos felt impelled to assert white dominance in the metropolis. The 1920s thus became a decade when the labor force was explicitly racialized, when civic culture was Anglicized, and when segregation intensified.[99]

Close to South Gate, blacks had gained a foothold in Watts, a working-class suburb just across the railroad tracks along Alameda Street. Watts was a working-class suburb of startling racial and ethnic heterogeneity in the 1920s. It began as a labor camp of the Pacific Electric Railway, then evolved into a permanent settlement. Its swampy terrain and small-scale development made it possible for homeseekers to buy cheap land and self-build homes, much like their white neighbors to the east. Reflecting its labor camp roots, Watts emerged as a community of blacks, Mexicans, European immigrants, and native-born whites who populated distinct sections of the town. A thriving black community and Mexican "colonia" clustered in portions of southern Watts, while whites concentrated in the northern area. Watts incorporated as an independent municipality in 1907, then consolidated with L.A. city in 1926. Although blacks did not become a majority in Watts until the 1940s, their presence was keenly felt by their white neighbors across the tracks.[100]

In South Gate and other southern suburbs that sat beside the growing black community, residents displayed a tenacious concern with residential segregation. Beginning with the earliest subdivisions, race restrictions were a regular selling point of suburban property. They appeared in advertisements, homeowner handbooks, even billboards for residential tracts. Realtors played a pivotal role in implementing this policy. In 1938, for example, the Southeast Realty Board devoted several meetings to the issue of racial exclusion. At one of them, Don Huddleston, manager of an escrow company, claimed that several black families resided in the district and, if the practice continued, property values would drop. He was named head of a committee to investigate race restrictions, and four years later he was elected mayor of South Gate.[101] The concern with residential segregation intensified as the African-American community spread southward. Alameda Street soon became a racial dividing line. This thoroughfare, which ran from downtown to the harbor alongside several railroad lines, eventually became known as "the wall" and the "cotton curtain." It marked a rigid residential barrier, separating the suburbs of working-class blacks and whites.[102]

The race line, however, proved penetrable in other realms of life. Whites from suburbs like South Gate frequently shopped in Watts, while more affluent whites went "slumming" in the nightclubs along Central Avenue. Even blacks found occasion to cross the line, although it was more difficult for them. Certain white-owned suburban stores catered to black customers, evident in a 1931 study showing that about 98 percent of blacks in Los Angeles shopped in white-owned clothing and grocery stores. South Gate also wedged open a small space for blacks in the local labor market at Topsy's Southern Home, one of South Gate's better restaurants and dance clubs. Blacks were hired as cooks and waiters in an attempt to capture the "atmosphere of the old South." And a snippet of evidence shows that blacks were welcomed at the First Baptist Church in South Gate, at least on a one-time basis, as singers for morning services. The races intermingled more significantly in sports and recreation. The semipro baseball league, the most popular spectator sport in South Gate, included teams representing minority groups like the "Brown Buffaloes" (African Americans), the "L.A. Orientals" (Chinese), and the "Carta Blanca" (Latinos). They competed on an equal footing against whites and attracted mixed audiences. The South Gate newspapers reported on their games with no hint of prejudice or condescension. At public swimming pools in L.A. city, moreover, racial integration was mandated by the courts by summer 1932. Both blacks and whites were permitted to use the public pools at the same hour.[103]

Perhaps the most vivid evidence of racial coalescing was in politics, specifically the 1934 election of an African American to the California State Assembly. Augustus Hawkins represented the Sixty-second Assembly District, a mixed area of working-class whites and blacks directly south of downtown. He successfully garnered white working-class votes by emphasizing class issues and the needs of working people. Weakened by the economic conditions of the Great Depression, the color line was flexible enough to allow a prolabor black to win political office by the votes of whites.[104]

The line was also permeable when it came to education. During the interwar years, L.A. school leaders showed some commitment to racial equity in the schools. On numerous occasions, the L.A. school board refused the demands of white communities for racially segregated schools. Particularly when the requests were blunt and the targets were African American, the board remained firm.[105] South Gate was one community that experienced the consequences of this policy. Indeed, the most intensive contact that whites in South Gate had with blacks in Watts occurred in the schools. As a result, education eventually became a locus of political activity. At the outset Home Gardens was involved most deeply, but by the end of the 1920s the school controversy involved all of South Gate. Poverty prevented Home Gardens residents from attaining the degree of racial segregation they preferred. While they successfully excluded blacks from the housing market, a policy that cost them nothing, it was harder for them to regulate municipal services like schools, which involved tax outlays. Indeed, when money entered the picture, concerns like segregation dropped away.

Cost deterred South Gate from establishing its own independent school district in the 1920s. As a result, the various sections of South Gate piggybacked onto neighboring districts. The incorporated part of South Gate, which included the more prosperous northwest section, attached itself to the Huntington Park City School District (HPCSD), where the expenditure per student was $32 in 1924. Huntington Park was a suburb of middle- and working-class white Anglos, located directly north of South Gate.[106] In contrast stood poorer Home Gardens. As an unincorporated neighborhood that had not yet annexed to South Gate (that occurred in December 1927), Home Gardens was responsible for its own services. It opted to become part of the Watts School District as an economy measure, where the expenditure per student was only $8 and the tax rate was accordingly low. To Home Gardens parents, the affiliation with Watts had two odious implications. First, their teenage children were required to attend racially mixed Jordan High in Watts, where the black population was rising gradually in the 1920s. And second, school facilities in Home Gardens were squalid because of the meager outlays of public funds. These conditions provided the backdrop for political turmoil that refracted concerns about city services, taxes, and spending through the prism of race. Like earlier conflicts, the politics of education divided the community along the lines of class. Merchant leaders agitated to extricate Home Gardens from the Watts schools, while working-class residents fought against this move in the name of municipal economy.[107]

Home Gardens businessmen raised the school issue for the first time in 1924, when they proposed a plan to transfer their community into the Huntington Park district. Complaining that they had no representation on the Watts school board and that their schools got "second hand" resources while new material went to the Watts schools, they accused the Watts district of showing "discrimination against Home Gardens children." While nothing came of this plan, the issue resurfaced a few months later when the

Watts district proposed a bond issue of $128,000 for school improvement. Home Gardens residents vociferously opposed the bonds, claiming that little of this money would go to their schools but would all be funneled into Watts. Worse still was the racial inequity of the plan. As one Home Gardens resident pointed out, "[T]here is one thing certain, there are too many people from Oklahoma, Texas, Arkansas and other southern states to support an issue for schools in Watts where the Negro pupils outnumber the whites." Sounding like poor whites in the Piedmont South, Home Gardens residents were frustrated by an economic scenario that cast them as inferior to the blacks across the tracks. As resentments swelled against school leadership in Watts, a hastily formed Citizens Committee urged locals to vote "no" on the issue. The bond issue was defeated 652 to 490, with Home Gardens supplying the swing votes.[108]

Three months later in early 1925, the same bond issue was proposed with backing from L.A. County School Superintendent Mark Keppel, a staunch advocate of class equity in education.[109] This time, the bond was attached to a plan to annex the Watts School District to the Los Angeles Unified School District (LAUSD). The $128,000 bond would represent, in Keppel's words, the "wedding garments." Keppel supported the school annexation, believing it would effect economic parity for Watts, an area "rich in children but poor in money." The annexation, Keppel promised, would correct the disparity and even lower taxes for Watts district families. While some in Home Gardens were convinced by this argument, others continued to harbor suspicion of bonds in general and the Watts superintendent in particular, given his poor track record with the Home Gardens schools. Since he supported the measure, they reflexively opposed it. Though the bond measure passed by a four-to-one margin overall, the biggest resistance came from Home Gardens, where 59 percent of voters opposed it. The *Home Gardens Press* attributed the outcome to "lack of confidence in the present school management." Nonetheless, the Watts District became part of the LAUSD. Home Gardens residents welcomed the slight tax break (it apparently was not as much as Keppel had promised), but their leverage with the school board was even weaker within the much larger district. By late summer of 1925, they were still waiting for improvements to their school facilities while "scores of buildings were underway for Los Angeles." As would soon become clear, most Home Gardens residents could live with this disparity if it meant lower taxes.[110]

But not the merchants. A group of Home Gardens businessmen, led by barbershop-owner Earl Fike, initiated efforts to break away from the LAUSD and annex to the more costly Huntington Park district. They emphasized the powerlessness and inferiority of Home Gardens within the vast L.A. Unified School District. At this stage, they said little about race. The merchants' efforts faltered in the face of opposition on two fronts: in the repeated rejections by the L.A. County Board of Supervisors, the governing body on this matter; and in counterpetitions filed by tax-wary residents, who opposed the annexation plan because it promised tax increases.[111]

In January 1926, the merchants tried again, this time by openly racializing the issue. Spearheaded by the Chamber of Commerce, Business Men's Association, and Community Church, they recommenced the campaign to annex to the Huntington Park district by circulating petitions and pressing their case more vocally.[112] Admitting that earlier they hesitated in raising the race issue "for fear of being misunderstood," they now conceded that race indeed lay at "the very heart of the controversy." In an open letter to the L.A. County Board of Supervisors, they argued: "Home Gardens is distinctly a white man's town. None but Caucasians may own or lease real estate here. . . . A goodly percentage of our people were born south of the Mason and Dixon line. You know what this means as to racial feeling. More than ninety per cent own their own homes here [and] . . . one of the controlling factors in their choice of a location was the racial restrictions. It naturally never entered their heads that once having located here, their children would be dragged off to another community to attend school with a mixed population."

Then evoking images meant to startle Home Gardens parents, the editor concluded:

> The other day, this writer passed the Jordan school in Watts. The girl pupils were out for a "trot" doing the Charleston or something around school grounds for exercise. They were lined up in two long columns. At the head of one column was a beautiful, flaxen haired girl of twelve or fourteen years. By her side pranced a negro girl, black as coal, and the blacks were freely interspersed in the two lines.
>
> Now this writer is not prejudiced against the negro race. . . . We are not protesting giving the negro boy and girl an equal chance—they should have it; but there is no necessity for forcing Home Gardens pupils into these unwelcome associations. Doing so is positively killing the school ambitions of many of our young folks—and that's a situation to be deplored.[113]

In early February 1926, the Board of Supervisors ruled on the annexation request. After weighing the arguments, the board flatly denied the annexation on the grounds that it was motivated by "race prejudice," making it unconstitutional and "un-American." Disgruntled parents, suggested the supervisors, should move to another district "where they would be better pleased with the race of the school students." This ruling, in fact, was one of several early education decisions by L.A. leaders that revealed a surprisingly progressive position on race.[114]

Supporters of the Board of Supervisors' ruling made strange bedfellows. Tax-wary residents of Home Gardens applauded the decision because it thwarted a potential tax increase. At the same time, the black community of Los Angeles praised the decision because of its progressive racial stand. "It was indeed gratifying to know the stand that you took on the matter," wrote the chairman of the Los Angeles NAACP school committee to the supervisors, "not only on account of the races concerned, but for the common benefit of all, otherwise it would only have set a precedent which would have no doubt been the beginning of an arbitrary situation in our splendid public school system. Your precept will go far toward teaching true Americanism, and the meaning of a better citizenry." And a member of the Woman's City Club wrote, "your action in this matter, displayed much of the spirit of the Emancipator, Abraham Lincoln."[115]

Some Home Gardens residents were not as sanguine. "Parents of Home Gardens will show you that you cannot make their children attend schools with niggers and Mexicans," wrote resident Thomas Carter to the supervisors. The merchants were equally disgruntled. Their response was to try yet again, this time by pursuing a more radical strategy. Recognizing the political weakness of unincorporated Home Gardens in the vast county government system of Los Angeles, they proposed to annex Home Gardens completely to the city of Huntington Park, which would place them in that school district once and for all. The plan was spearheaded by James R. Tweedy, a prominent landowner, subdivider, and realtor in Home Gardens. At the outset, Huntington Park officials enthusiastically endorsed it. They promised Home Gardens residents superior municipal services, low property taxes, and, in the words of the city attorney, "not a child of African descent in any of the Huntington Park schools." But fatal flaws in the plan soon emerged. The geography of the proposed city was highly impractical (see fig. 4-3). It would be horseshoe-shaped, with Home Gardens and Huntington Park at opposite prongs, and South Gate lying awkwardly in the middle. Moreover, the annexation plan contained a dubious scheme involving Jordan High School. One of the largest and newest schools in the area, Jordan lay in an unincorporated strip of land between Home Gardens and Watts. The plan proposed to expropriate Jordan and bring it along to Huntington Park as a whites-only school, a scheme that obviously antagonized the black residents of Watts.[116]

A war of petitions broke out. The Home Gardens merchants collected

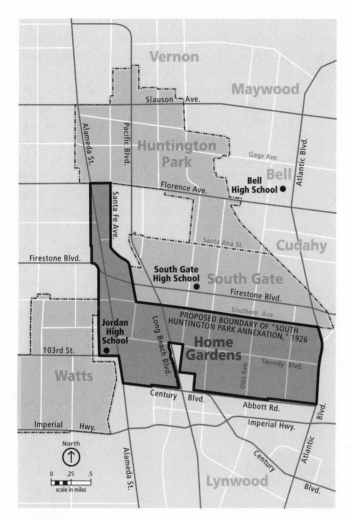

Figure 4-3   The proposed boundary of the South Huntington Park annexation, 1926. Boundary
approximated from descriptions in *Huntington Park Signal*, March 20 , March 22, and March
27, 1926.

nearly 1,000 signatures, over one-third of registered voters, in support of
the "low tax" annexation plan. As long as residents believed the plan involved no tax increases, they supported it. Watts quickly countered with its
own petition to annex the land under Jordan to its jurisdiction, and got all
twelve residents of the property around the school to sign. Significantly,
the following week Watts was slated to hold an election to decide whether
to consolidate with L.A. city. The school controversy surely accelerated
Watts' motivation to consolidate because it would protect Jordan.[117]

Within a week, the bubble burst for the pro-annexation forces. The first blow came from the Huntington Park city council, which suddenly realized the unfairness of the Jordan school scheme. The council passed a resolution refusing to accept Jordan as part of the annexation, claiming the plan was "manifestly unfair and grossly unjust, and would work irreparable hardship and damage" to Watts residents. Now that Home Gardens no longer held the trump card of Jordan, Huntington Park retreated from its generous offer of tax breaks and warned instead of a tax increase. Home Gardens residents quickly grew suspicious. One Home Gardens resident predicted the property tax rate would jump from $2.47 to about $3.80, while others claimed that few resources would be funneled from Huntington Park to Home Gardens. Residents would thus face the familiar problem of weak local control compounded by a heavier tax burden.[118]

Home Gardens merchants, along with the local press, strongly maintained their support for annexation. They formed the Huntington Park Annexation League, which answered the fear of higher taxes with the dictum, "you have to pay something for what you get." As the *Home Gardens Press* reasoned, "Say five hundred dollars is the average [valuation of a Home Gardens house]. Multiply that by 96 cents, the present municipal tax rate in Huntington Park, and you have $4.80 as the increased taxation. Who would begrudge that in order to get away from the Watts schools?" The issue thus boiled down to two competing fears: high taxes versus racial integration.[119]

A popular vote on the annexation plan dramatically settled the issue. Voters killed the plan 1,403 to 379. The fear of high taxes proved stronger than racial antipathy, pushing Home Gardens into a racial accommodation with Watts. While there were continued complaints over the school situation into the late 1920s, Home Gardens citizens were reluctant to make a change for fear of extra tax burdens. The school fight had become one element in the broader conflict over taxation.[120]

While this settlement did not exactly inaugurate an era of racial amity, it did force a grudging acceptance of interracial coexistence. Home Gardens residents simply could not afford the level of segregation they desired. But there was some inkling that the students themselves handled matters well. Home Gardens resident Glenn Seaborg, who attended Jordan High from 1925 to 1929, recalled a state of peaceful coexistence among the races at Jordan. Gerald Shahan, a migrant from Oklahoma, attended an integrated high school in nearby Compton during the mid-1930s. Although integration was a radical departure from his previous experience, he adjusted: "They had blacks, whites, yellows, Mexicans, and everybody going to the school. . . . [I]t didn't bother me any to go to school like that . . . but . . . I couldn't quite believe it for a while." School yearbooks in the early 1930s showed racial intermingling among students at Jordan High. Jordan's "merit board," for example, had five white, four black, four Asian, and two Latino students in 1932; minority students were likewise active in an array of extracurricular activities, mostly interracial.[121]

It was a different story among some adults. Frustrated by political defeat, some expressed heightened racism. A rash of stories in the local press demonized blacks. "Demented Negro Empties Shotgun at Auto Party," proclaimed a headline in the same issue that reported on the annexation's failure. About a month later, the paper printed a story about a "pocket edition race riot" at Jordan, in actuality a melee between a handful of black and white students. Ku Klux Klan activity was another outlet. In southern Los Angeles, Klan activity peaked with a series of open-air meetings in suburbs like South Gate, Maywood, and Lynwood in the mid-1920s, the same years when economically strapped parents in Home Gardens were sending their children to integrated schools. The local Klan met three nights per week in Dahlgren Auditorium, owned by the South Gate city marshal. While the KKK attracted ex-southerners, it also drew merchants who hailed from California and the Midwest. A number of businesses supported the Klan by placing publicity placards in their store windows, while the *South Gate Tribune* detailed their local doings. Like much Klan activity in the 1920s nationwide, the Klan in southern L.A. focused on xenophobia, morality, temperance, and racial purity. Typical was a 1924 gathering in Home Gardens, which drew a reported 3,500 people, featuring James Rush Bronson. In his lecture on "The Ideals of Pure Americanism," Bronson charged that lawbreakers and bootleggers were foreigners deserving deportation. The Klan burned crosses periodically on vacant lots around town, at one in honor of a Klansman "who died a martyr to the Klan in the Inglewood raid . . . upon an illicit liquor establishment two years ago." While evidence on local Klan racial attacks is hard to come by, one resident remembered being harassed by the children of Klansmen because he was Catholic. Finally, some evidence suggests the KKK was active in Watts, working to wrest political control of the town in the mid-1920s.[122]

In 1930, a final conflict erupted in the politics of education. In this round, the pressures of the Great Depression forced a settlement on the entire area, laying the groundwork for postwar racial segregation. A complicated web of shifting borders and jurisdictions set the stage. In December 1927, Home Gardens finally annexed to South Gate. This civic change, however, did not affect the school district boundaries, which remained as before: northwest South Gate was in the more expensive Huntington Park district, and Home Gardens remained in the L.A. district. Although Home Gardens children attended elementary schools locally, high school students had to attend either racially integrated Jordan High in Watts or all-white Bell High, about a mile and a half from Home Gardens and lacking in bus service (see fig. 4-3). The conflict began when the new South Gate High School opened in January 1930 and became part of the Huntington Park district. It served students living in north South Gate, but Home Gardens pupils were barred from attendance because they resided outside the Huntington Park district—even though they lived in South Gate.[123]

This configuration immediately spurred protest, led by the South Gate Chamber of Commerce. Not only was Home Gardens "socially and civically" part of South Gate, they argued, but forced attendance at Jordan caused "social problems." The chamber formed a school committee to devise alternative plans,[124] and they came up with three options: annex Home Gardens to the Huntington Park district, annex all South Gate schools to the L.A. district to bring parity to the suburb's schools, or issue temporary permits for Home Gardens students to attend South Gate High. They adopted the final option, a stopgap measure since the influx of students would eventually force a tax increase in the Huntington Park district.[125] They needed a more permanent solution that would balance the social and economic concerns of Home Gardens families.

At a meeting in August 1930, leaders explained why the situation had to change. H. S. Munro, an oil representative and chair of the chamber's school committee, emphasized the race issue, claiming it was "undesirable" to force Home Gardens children to attend school with black pupils at Jordan. Others stressed the political unfairness in excluding Home Gardens from South Gate's schools. A final argument framed the issue in metropolitan terms that reversed traditional conceptions of the core-periphery relationship. The school committee argued that cash-poor South Gate suffered from an imbalance of power and wealth with Los Angeles. As the committee put it, "The economic inequality . . . is readily understood when we stop to realize that the assessed value of property facing on Pershing Square in Los Angeles is probably . . . nearly twice that of South Gate. Our area . . . contributes to the wealth of downtown Los Angeles as the economic laws do not observe artificial boundary lines." It was unfair, then, that suburban school districts had to pay higher taxes for schools when their residents were poorer. This was a case of the urban core draining resources from the periphery. A persuasive case for municipal economy was taking shape.[126]

The proponents of change turned to the second solution, annexing the Huntington Park district to Los Angeles; but this effort failed under pressure from those who feared the "negro menace," as they put it. Seeking to maintain political autonomy and separation, others suggested consolidating the entire southeast district into one large city. This plan, designed by the Southeast Chamber of Commerce, would unify Huntington Park, Walnut Park, South Gate, Lynwood, Maywood, Bell, and Cudahy into one municipality called San Antonio City.[127] This configuration would guarantee racial homogeneity, political muscle, greater local control, and economies of scale regarding municipal services, thereby curbing property tax rates. Most importantly, the new city would have its own school system, preventing what appeared in 1930 as the inevitable annexation of South Gate to the L.A. district. Like previous schemes that portended tax increases, this proposal also failed.[128]

Just as they ultimately coalesced over the tax issue, the suburb's leaders and wage-earning residents finally converged on the school issue. Driven by desperate concerns for municipal economy exacerbated by the Depression, they decided to consolidate the entire Huntington Park district with the L.A. district, a move that would save taxpayers about $0.60 per $100 valuation in school taxes. This occurred in early 1932, during the Cooperative League administration. Even the conservative *Tribune* claimed the consolidation would "relieve a people staggering under a burden of oppressive taxation." What was once considered anathema—a plan placing blacks and whites in the same, enormous district—was now embraced by South Gate and Huntington Park alike, both suffering from the Depression.[129] Economic concerns overwhelmed all others. In January 1932, the L.A. Board of Supervisors approved a mammoth petition of 7,040 signatures, which represented one of the largest school annexations in the history of L.A. County.[130] The massive popular support for this move revealed how South Gate chose to balance its fears. The tax fear had won out, overpowering even concerns about race. This final settlement in the politics of education, a forceful request for inclusion into a racially diverse school district, was the most powerful testimony that the prime aspiration among South Gate's families was economic security.[131]

Local political struggles before World War II, thus, planted a seed in the political consciousness of residents. On one level, these experiences fostered a deep suspicion of public spending, taxation, and government, remnants that remained as the suburb moved into the postwar period. Groups like the Tax Reduction Club of California, in their commitment to lower public expenditures, held the ideological potential of opposing all public spending programs. And among working people in suburbs like South Gate, the difficult process of getting and then losing property was a stunning lesson. The anti-tax mentality fostered by this experience presaged later tax revolts in California. For some, the historical connection was direct. One tax revolt leader of the 1970s admitted that his ideas on taxes were formed during the Depression, "when he saw so much property sold for taxes."[132]

Political life also solidified residents' identity as white working-class homeowners. They had worked hard to achieve this status, and they engaged in politics when that status was threatened. In their minds, they held certain rights as upstanding homeowners, which neither free-spending councilmen nor progressive liberals were entitled to jeopardize. Local politics reflected a working-class sensibility that magnified the importance of class concerns, solidified a self-identity as homeowners, and forced an uncomfortable racial accommodation in the process. In the neighborhood, a distinct political orientation had emerged.

From South Gate to Sacramento to Washington, D.C.

The identity of residents as working-class homeowners galvanized them to act politically as a means of economic self-defense. When boom hit bust in the 1930s, their assumptions about the role of individuals and government began to shift. As both the politics of development and education revealed, residents began with the unspoken assumption that the burden of financing municipal services—from streets to schools—should fall on the backs of individual property owners, including the humble working-class home owner. Embracing an ethos of privatism, they believed property ownership conferred the responsibility of municipal stewardship. All property owners—regardless of wealth—became urban stewards. It was thus up to individuals, not government more broadly, to pay for services. In a poorer suburb like South Gate, residents simply chose to limit these services, to create a modest infrastructure that they could reasonably afford. There was no assumption that urban services were a right, and that they should be financed through a redistributive system of taxation. This reflected their deeply held ideals of individualism, self-help, hard work, plain-folk Americanism, and anticommunism, an outlook asserting that urban fiscal policy ought to be based on a private approach rather than a collective one.[133]

As shown in the politics of development and education, the anti-tax mentality that emerged in the 1920s was an attempt by residents to protect the original spirit of working-class suburbia, a place where families could achieve homeownership and, in the process, grasp a modicum of economic security. The sacrifice of public services became a part of this strategy. Their position, class-based in every respect, hinged on their peculiar status as working-class homeowners. They would behave politically to protect this hard-won status. If they laid a claim to any right, it was that of owning a home and ensuring that this ownership would be protected. This was a right based on the private, individually won status of property ownership rather than on a more abstract belief in social equity and justice for working people.[134]

The outlines of a political identity were, thus, coming into focus. South Gate residents embraced self-help, hard work, frugality, and individualism; they valued homeownership; they recognized their class-based needs; and they opposed profligate public spending that might threaten these values. Their ideals—forged in everyday life in the neighborhood—shaped both their local political commitments as well as their attraction to certain state and national programs. In South Gate, working-class homeowners supported Upton Sinclair's EPIC and Franklin Roosevelt's New Deal, which each tapped into these values in different ways. The ideological path leading to these positions showed how local experience shaped broader political commitments—and how these programs offered something for everyone. South Gate residents could embrace aspects of these policies that reflected their values, while refuting the more progressive elements. The seeming contradictions of their position, in fact, lay in the eclecticism of the programs themselves. Thus, South Gate's staunch individualists could support a socialist in Sinclair, and its anti-tax citizens could support a federal program predicated on massive public spending. Both EPIC and the New Deal contained enough concessions to white homeowners to win over voters in South Gate.

The broader political sensibilities of residents were also shaped by the palpable hardships in their lives. As residents struggled to cope with intensifying poverty and destitution during the Depression, the concerns of class began pointing them toward new types of solutions, including a tentative acceptance of an activist government. They arrived at this position much as the nation did; when private, localized relief efforts fell short of need, they turned to government as a social safety net. To the extent that they benefited from New Deal programs, they could accept this political solution. But in the minds of South Gate residents, such programs were meant for those who deserved them, for those who had earned such an entitlement. South Gate residents interpreted the New Deal to mean help for those who helped themselves—a hand up, not a handout. This allowed room for the values of individualism and hard work, even in the context of a budding welfare state. Their support for EPIC also brought home this point. The core values of working-class homeowner identity—self-help, frugality, a strong work ethic, individualism—thus found outlets in Sinclair's EPIC and Roosevelt's New Deal.

In the gubernatorial election of 1934, residents of Los Angeles's southeastern suburbs, including South Gate, voted overwhelmingly for radical democratic Upton Sinclair and his EPIC (End Poverty in California) program. South Gate's electorate, in fact, was typical of Sinclair's supporters. Sinclair secured his strongest backing from the urban working class, particularly in Los Angeles. Although he lost the election, due largely to an aggressive smear campaign by his opponents, Sinclair's campaign marked a critical moment in the state's political history.[135] And it ultimately helps explain the overall political sensibilities of South Gate's residents. The path that working-class suburban voters traveled to reach this position further illuminates how homeowner identities were transmuting into concrete political positions.

This political story unfolded against the backdrop of intensifying economic distress and relief efforts in South Gate. Hardship was nothing new to its residents. Throughout the 1920s and early 1930s, the burden of welfare and relief was left mainly to individuals, neighbors, and a few local organizations. When the safety net of the domicile was not enough, neighbors helped one another. In some cases, organizations stepped forward to lend sporadic assistance to the needy. In 1924, the South Gate Women's Club formed an "Emergency League," which held a clothing drive for poor children in the neighborhood, while realtor Sam Dudlext sponsored a benefit dance to raise funds for Christmas gifts for "the children of needy families." Even before the stock market crash in 1929, a Central Committee on Community Affairs was formed to "attend to cases of needy persons in South Gate."[136]

The Depression deepened the hardship. In 1933, approximately 3,500 families were in need of relief, representing well over half of local families. Some of their stories were poignant. One seven-year-old boy lived with his destitute grandparents who could barely feed and clothe him; his mother had deserted him and his father had gone to seek work in the Imperial Valley. A family of nine suffered from hunger, the father gravely ill and the mother "greatly weakened through long weeks of undernourishment and unable to find any employment." The family of an unemployed oil worker ate potatoes for ten straight days. When he was finally rehired, his coworkers spotted him eating potato peelings for lunch. The peelings, he said, made his children sick.[137]

In the face of this suffering, a few new organizations stepped forward to help. Most important was the South Gate Relief Center, formed in early 1931 as a central clearinghouse for assistance to the unemployed. It was wholly dependent on donations. Various civic groups and individuals contributed money, goods, and labor to the center, which then parceled out the aid. Donors included postal employees, teachers, the South Side Woman's Club, the police department, and a theater group. The center mainly provided goods that could not be easily self-provisioned, such as staple foods, clothing, and cash for payment of gas and water bills. By October 1931, the Relief Center had aided 330 families. Parent-Teacher Associations also became active in relief efforts, raising funds to supply clothing, hot lunches, and other aid to the children of impoverished families. By the end of the 1930s, the State Street PTA identified its primary purpose as that of welfare provider. The county provided assistance mainly to the unemployable; its aid to the able-bodied unemployed generally excluded owners of property over $250 in value if they were unwilling to accept a lien against their property. Many of South Gate's unemployed homeowners thus were excluded from county relief programs, evident in that in 1931, only 94 families were receiving county aid.[138]

It wasn't long before these local efforts fell severely short. A mere eight months after its inception, the Relief Center found itself on the brink of bankruptcy and begging for donations from a growingly poor populace. Desperate for solutions, the center looked inward and drew a lesson from its own community's past. It turned to self-provisioning and expanded it to a collective level by starting a community vegetable garden. The garden spanned seven acres—a full residential block—on the east side of the suburb. Two seed companies donated $75 worth of seeds for lima beans, beets, squash, tomatoes, lettuce, spinach, potatoes, and other vegetables, while unemployed residents planted and maintained the garden. These vegetables would supplement the food supply of relief-case families. The Relief Center envisioned this as the beginning of a large-scale community garden movement in South Gate, marking a key turning point in the evolution of local relief. The community garden inaugurated the cooperative approach, a strategy that gained widespread acceptance in South Gate because it represented an extension of the self-provisioning ethos, a core value among working-class suburbanites.[139]

As the Depression wore on, the cooperative movement gained momentum. As in other suburbs in southern Los Angeles, veterans' organizations spearheaded these efforts. In mid-1932, the Veterans Relief Association (VRA) replaced the South Gate Relief Center as the primary relief organization in the suburb. It adopted the co-op approach, patterning itself after the successful Compton operation. Occupying an auditorium across from city hall, the co-op supplied vegetables, baked goods, staple foods, and meats to the able-bodied unemployed, who worked about one day a week in exchange for a week's worth of food. Co-op members harvested vegetables on nearby farms; packinghouses donated lemons and oranges; some meats and groceries were also donated. Members established a bakery on the premises, and they baked bread using flour donated by the Red Cross. The VRA's cooperative approach quickly proved more effective than the Relief Center's charity approach. In two months in 1932, the co-op issued provisions to 4,400 families, over thirteen times more families than the Relief Center had reached. Not only was the co-op more efficient but its philosophy aligned more closely with the mores and practices of residents. Rather than create a dependence on charity, the co-ops allowed residents to rely on their own labor for the goods they needed, keeping their ethos of self-sufficiency and hard work intact. South Gate had several cooperative associations by the late 1930s, as did Huntington Park, Lynwood, Maywood, and Bell.[140]

As the founders and early leaders of cooperatives in southern Los Angeles, veterans—namely American Legion leaders—defined the movement in ways that aligned with local working-class values. They conceived of co-ops in terms of patriotic, American ideals, emphasizing the notions of self-help, fair compensation for hard work, and an aversion to charity. As a placard in one co-op warehouse reminded members, "NO WORK, NO EAT." At the same time, co-op leaders took pains to distance themselves from any association with radicalism, especially communism or socialism. They delivered public lectures on the "Red menace," they insisted that church services be held at the co-ops, and they quickly ousted all "agitators" from membership. These actions made the co-ops politically acceptable to South Gate residents, whose plain-folk Americanism embraced individualism and rebuked communism. In the hands of veterans, cooperatives became as American as the Model T.[141]

In nearby Compton, a suburb similar to South Gate, the co-op was equally successful. One operation, established by local veterans, had nearly 1,000 members by 1933. In exchange for labor, co-op members received staple foods, vegetables grown by members, meats, clothing, furniture, and services like haircuts. Some received cash for gas, water, and electric bills, while a few even received housing.[142] By 1933, a county welfare official acknowledged that the co-op was "far superior" to the county welfare department in administering relief. Because of its efficiency and success, the Compton co-op became a model for others in southern Los Angeles.[143]

Members of the Compton co-op shared the attitude that embraced self-help and rejected charity. As one woman explained, "Most of us just needed the help we got, we couldn't get help from the charities because we had property, or thought we did. It is much better than charity for most of us, though, because we felt we were supporting ourselves, and we were too." Another explained the dilemma of the destitute homeowner: "We had a small amount of property, but we got so we didn't have anything to eat. People brought us things in, but I couldn't stand that." So she turned to the co-op, claiming, "I wouldn't take anything like some of these women have, unless I worked for it. . . . We are proud, too proud to accept things for nothing, that is why I worked so hard down here [at the co-op]—someone had to do it." Many of those who joined had breadwinning family members who were too ill or old to work. "I have been a carpenter in my days, but I ain't much good any more," said one sixty-year-old member. "I can't keep going like these younger fellows do, and so they don't want me. . . . [S]o I just come down here to see what they were doing. They said I could work for my vegetables, and I don't take very much away from here, but I like to be busy and active." The same penchant for work emerged in other personal narratives. "I don't want to ask anybody for help if I can stop it," noted an aging, unemployed shipbuilder. "I am always glad to work where they want me to do something." Another explained, "We want something we can 'count on' that isn't charity. We can work like this for a long time to come." A sociologist studying the Compton co-op emphasized the importance of the self-help ethos: "The habits of work in many men are ends in themselves which must be exercised regardless of whether they are paid for working or not. They know how to work and just keep active, feeling that some good will come out of it all somewhere."[144]

The successful experience of residents with cooperatives explains why they easily embraced this as a political strategy for economic relief, evident most dramatically in their support for Upton Sinclair's EPIC program. Although Sinclair's agenda was radical at the surface, in fact it conformed to deeper principles of self-help and self-sufficiency familiar to residents. Cooperative principles lay at the center of Sinclair's 1934 gubernatorial campaign. A socialist who ran as a Democrat, Sinclair proposed a bold solution to the problem of poverty in California. His EPIC plan called for the establishment of a state-managed cooperative economy, oriented around a network of state-run, cooperative farms and factories. These collectives would operate on a "production for use" basis, instead of production for profit, streamlining the distribution of goods from producers to consumers and thereby eliminating the "parasitical" chain of middlemen, banks, and corporations. Sinclair's campaign was a grassroots affair, organized around a network of EPIC clubs that rapidly proliferated. By mid-1934, there were more than eight hundred of these clubs statewide.[145]

Invoking the language of plain-folk Americanism rather than radical socialism, Sinclair effectively couched his program in terms that resonated with residents in towns like South Gate. Most importantly, he associated the cooperative approach with the deepest American traditions. In a campaign tract that appeared two months before the election, he wrote, "I assert that these self-help and barter groups represent Americanism more truly than any other phenomenon of our time. They embody all our true pioneer virtues—self-reliance, initiative, frugality, equality, neighborliness." Such was the essence of working-class suburbia. While some of this ideological "softening" was undoubtedly a defense against his opponent's smear campaign, it was also a politically adroit message that rang true for many working-class Californians steeped in the self-help tradition. He made the connections direct by praising the cooperative efforts in Compton, Alhambra, and other L.A. neighborhoods.

Sinclair also proposed establishing cooperative urban gardens. The state would rent land and furnish seeds and tools, turning peripheral land into "thriving gardens surrounding our cities—a much pleasanter spectacle than the burned-over weeds we now gaze upon." This represented a large-scale extension of working-class suburban practices. And of particular concern to Los Angelenos, Sinclair confronted the issue of taxes. Sensitive to the hardships of good, honest taxpaying citizens, Sinclair proposed two tax plans—one emergency, one permanent—which had particular appeal to working-class homeowners. The emergency EPIC tax, a progressive taxation system vaguely reminiscent of Huey Long's Share Our Wealth plan, was an ad valorem tax upon property valued over $100,000. All property below this amount was exempt. If the state so chose, it could collect this tax "in goods and services instead of money." Sinclair proposed to target gas, electric, oil, railroad, timber, and cement companies, since they could contribute directly to the functioning of the state's cooperative economy. "This tax," he asserted, "would not make the taxation of big business proportionately any greater than now borne by farmers, home owners, and small taxpayers," who heretofore had carried "an unfair burden." The permanent EPIC tax entailed shifting from the existing regressive sales tax, to progressive taxes on income, inheritance, and unimproved property (mainly owned by speculators). Best of all, it promised to exempt "all homes occupied by the owners . . . which carry an assessed value of less that $3,000." Surely this was music to the ears of South Gate's tax-weary residents.[146]

This EPIC agenda, with its cooperative approach and concern for small, humble property owners, easily appealed to homeowners in blue-collar suburbs like South Gate. It spoke to the heart of working-class concerns, which focused especially on neighborhood issues. Carey McWilliams recognized this early on. "The mass political movements of the 'thirties," he wrote, "were not inspired by the trade union movement. They were popular, largely spontaneous, political movements, based upon the prior political experience of the community, the inevitable reaction to twenty-five years of irresponsible boosterism. . . . Unanchored to a strong trade-union movement, having few roots in the community, the dispossessed masses of Los Angeles were quick to invent new forms of action and new forms for the expression of social discontent."[147]

In South Gate, support for EPIC swelled in 1934 and continued for at least a year. In the 1934 gubernatorial election, fully 61 percent of South Gate residents voted for Sinclair, 27 percent for Republican Frank Merriam, and nearly 11 percent for Progressive Raymond Haight, a middle-ground candidate. The Communist and Socialist candidates each received less than 1 percent of local votes. Five months after Sinclair's defeat, enthusiasm for the movement remained strong enough in South Gate to prompt the formation of an EPIC club, which then forged links with local Democrats. The common leader of both the EPIC and Democratic clubs was Stanley Moffatt, who earlier had led efforts to oust the high-spending councilmen in South Gate. Moffatt vowed that the EPIC club would "be forced to take an active part in all matters of civic and political importance in South Gate." A months later, two more EPIC clubs were in the works. Over the following year, the clubs mustered support for EPIC candidates for the L.A. District Board of Education, who ultimately won several seats with strong backing from working-class suburbanites. And the clubs backed the efforts of State Assemblyman A. Franklin Glover, representing South Gate's district, to pass the Self-Help Cooperative Act, a measure designed to provide relief "by encouraging the sound development of producer and consumer cooperative organizations." The state would provide land, machinery, and other facilities—but no money—to launch these cooperatives. This measure passed in 1935.[148]

But South Gate's ideological support for Sinclair, EPIC, and cooperatives had its limits. South Gate residents could accept Sinclair's program as a solution to an emergency crisis, but they balked at waging a broader critique of "the system" that embraced socialism, communism, or other radical doctrines. Their political behavior reflected this distinction. In presidential elections, Socialist and Communist candidates consistently received less than 1 percent of votes in South Gate during the 1930s, with the minor exception of 4.1 percent for Socialist Norman Thomas in 1932. Similar patterns prevailed at the congressional and state levels.[149] The limits of local radicalism were confirmed by one observer of the cooperatives, a field representative of the Quakers. "The members lived on the unit because of necessity. There was a perennial desire of everyone to be freed from the necessity of co-operation. . . . To live on the surplus foodstuffs by trading labor, or by receiving quasi-donations in the form of communal charity, is the most rudimentary form of co-operation. It is artificial co-operation to cooperate only when one is hungry, or when one is starving. . . . All were anxious to escape from the co-operative as soon as they could, hoping from day to day to 'get a pay job.'" Then capturing the moderating effects of this mentality on politics, the Quaker explained, "Their character demoralized by the industrial system, they yet continued to hold to the outworn modes of thought and action ill befitting those of a new social order. Without moral indignation to develop into radicals, or moral courage to be liberal reformers, they languish in the stupor of relief."[150] South Gate citizens thus embraced co-ops as a survival strategy while clinging firmly to their core beliefs of self-help and hard work. This was a cooperative sensibility shaped by the desperation of the times and moderated by a fundamental faith in individual effort.

These values likewise survived into the New Deal era, as residents threw their support behind Franklin Roosevelt. South Gate voters generally followed national trends in the interwar period: they voted Republican in the 1920s, then joined the New Deal coalition in the 1930s. The majority of residents voted for Republicans at both the presidential and congressional levels during the 1920s, with the exception of Progressive Robert LaFollette in 1924. By the 1930s, South Gate swung Democratic like much of the nation. Franklin Roosevelt won hefty majorities in the suburb in 1932, 1936, and 1940 (see table 4-2). At the congressional level, Democrats also dominated. By contrast, left-leaning third parties won only negligible support from local voters in both presidential and congressional races. The third party that made the strongest showing was the Prohibition party. In the U.S. senate race of 1932, Prohibitionist Robert Shuler won one-third of local votes; Shuler, in fact, had been accused of ties with the Ku Klux Klan, and he had made public statements imploring blacks to stay out of public office. Trailing far behind were the Communists and Socialists, whose strongest showing was 4.1 percent for the Socialist candidate in the 1932 presidential election.[151]

South Gate's working-class electorate was ultimately moderate in its liberalism. Residents continued to prize the values of hard work, self-help, and individualism, even as they backed Roosevelt and the New Deal that gave birth to the welfare state. They supported the New Deal to the extent that it fostered their values and fulfilled their own needs. They were merely one constituency of many finding something to support in FDR's program. So while they entered the New Deal coalition, they did so clinging firmly to their core values as working-class homeowners. As Tom Sugrue, Liz Cohen, and others have shown, the New Deal was in fact contested ground in America, inviting various groups to lay claim to a new federal activism reshaping public policy. Underlying New Deal social policy were two

Table 4-2 South Gate Voting Returns (by Party) for Presidential Elections from 1924 to 1972 (Percentage of Total South Gate Vote)

	Democrat	Republican	Socialist	Communist	Prohibition	Independent/ Progressive	Liberty	Peace & Freedom
1924	6.1	56.3			2.9	34.8		
1928	29.4	69.5	0.8		0.4			
1932	69.1	25.3	4.1		0.9		0.6	
1934[a]	61.4	27.3		0.5		10.7		
1936	78.9	19.5	0.5	0.7	0.5			
1940	72.5	26.3		0.4	0.2	0.5[b]		
1944	65.4	34.2			0.4			
1948	56.9	39.2			0.5	3.5		
1952	47.2	52.0			0.4	0.4		
1956	46.9	52.9			0.2			
1960	50.6	48.9			0.5			
1964	56.6	43.4						
1968	40.7	48.0				11.0[c]		0.4
1972	33.9	61.6				4.0		0.5

[a]These returns are for the California gubernatorial election. Democrat was Upton Sinclair, Republican was Frank Merriam.
[b]Candidate was listed as "Progressive."
[c]Candidate was "American Independent" George Wallace.

Sources: All voting returns are taken from "General Election Returns, Los Angeles County," precinct-level returns, CSA, with the following exceptions. 1924: South Gate Tribune, November 7, 1924. The data was taken from the newspaper because it included Home Gardens, which was not yet part of South Gate (the state archive returns apparently did not include Home Gardens). Home Gardens voted most heavily for LaFollette. 1968 and 1972: Frank M. Jordan, Statement of Vote, State of California, General Election, November 5, 1968; Edmund G. Brown, Statement of Vote, State of California, General Election, November 7, 1972.

competing ideals: one that emphasized help for the disadvantaged and neglected, and another that demanded expanded opportunity for those with some resources. Adherents of each would ultimately attempt to "appropriate on their own terms" the New Deal state, as Sugrue has written. And they would draw on an invigorated sense of entitlement and rights, fostered by the New Deal and later World War II, to stake these political claims.[152] South Gate's working-class homeowners fell into the second category, those who sought to expand opportunity for people who already had some resources—in their case, they owned homes. Their own hard work to reach the status of homeowners, in their minds, especially entitled them to aid—and it set them apart from (and above) the propertyless poor merely seeking a handout.

Citizens of South Gate benefited from several New Deal programs. As noted earlier, many residents were excluded from county relief assistance because they were homeowners. Federal relief, however, was more liberal in its eligibility requirements. The Works Progress Administration, for example, extended benefits to small property owners. Some residents also found employment in Public Works Administration jobs, particularly the rebuilding of three schools damaged by the 1933 earthquake. By 1938, about 220 residents were employed on public works; by 1940, the number was 212 (about 2 percent of the labor force). Federal policy also assisted labor organizing efforts in the area after 1936, giving employed residents important leverage in the workplace.[153]

Beyond aiding individuals, New Deal programs benefited the suburb's infrastructure more broadly. The painful political struggles over development and taxation in the 1920s—predicated on the popular notion that it was up to individual property owners, not municipal government, to finance infrastructure—gently evaporated as the federal giant came into view. Money from Washington, D.C., in the form of public works projects helped finance local improvements, such as the construction of a new library, a post office, and a fire station.[154] This easy acceptance of government aid represented a fundamental shift in popular thinking about the role of government and individuals in financing public projects. By the 1940s, South Gate residents had come to expect a certain quality of infrastructure, something the federal government had finally made possible. The New Deal, thus, fostered a newfound sense of entitlement to adequate public services.

But perhaps the most meaningful New Deal programs to South Gate residents were those that assisted homeowners. Indeed, federal housing programs eventually played an important role in bringing white, working-class homeowners into the New Deal fold. For residents of suburbs in southern Los Angeles, this did not happen immediately. They were handicapped by the "tax blight" that plagued their communities, a residue of overdevelopment during the 1920s. Ironically, they were locked out of help even as their need intensified. The tax problem delayed the provision of federal assistance until the late 1930s and 1940s, when it was welcomed with open arms.

The first key housing program of the New Deal was the Home Owners Loan Corporation (HOLC), established in June 1933. This federal agency rescued homeowners from foreclosure by refinancing mortgages in danger of default and granting low-interest loans to recover homes lost through foreclosure. Its main charge was to protect existing homeowners. In its brief life span, the HOLC refinanced 1,021,587 loans. Beyond this emergency function, the HOLC was historically significant for introducing and implementing the long-term, self-amortized mortgage, and for developing a systemized appraisal policy that became the national standard. The HOLC appraisal standards favored neighborhoods that were suburban, Anglo, middle-class, racially and ethnically homogeneous, distant from industries, and economically sound. The opposite traits, in turn, were penalized. So for example, neighborhoods of minorities and the poor were given the lowest, or "red," rating, thus introducing the term "redlining" into the parlance of federal home financing. The Federal Housing Administration (FHA), established in 1934, largely took over for the HOLC. Instead of building homes or lending money directly, it insured mortgages granted by private lenders and assisted new home buyers and existing homeowners. And it followed the appraisal guidelines set by the HOLC. These appraisals became significant because they influenced the financial decisions of banks and other lenders, who often based their loan decisions upon them.[155]

The L.A. housing crisis crested during the first half of the 1930s. In Los Angeles as a whole, mortgage foreclosures peaked in June 1933, at 205 per 100,000 families, a rate substantially higher than in most American cities. Yet Los Angeles's recovery was also swifter than elsewhere. The foreclosure rate declined rapidly after 1933 as the HOLC and FHA bailed out faltering homeowners. The rate dropped to 50 per 100,000 families in late 1935, and 30 in 1937, indicating the "healthy state" of the L.A. real estate market, according to one FHA study.[156]

In areas where Mattoon Act assessments were heavy, however, sales of single-family homes were slower to rebound than elsewhere, partly a result of HOLC and FHA policy. In addition to the well-known practice of "redlining" minority and poor neighborhoods, these agencies penalized areas suffering from "tax blight," as they put it. Neighborhoods were flagged if they were burdened by excessive tax debt. At least one-third of the redlined communities in Los Angeles were so designated. Although the HOLC claimed that "no penalty was imposed . . . on areas affected by 'Mattoons' because of the rapidity with which the outstanding bonds against their districts are being refunded," there was some evidence to prove otherwise. At least a few neighborhoods were graded downward because of Mattoon debt, such as Inglewood and Alondro Village. Tax blight could impede state and county relief as well; even into the late 1930s, "direct lien" districts around Los Angeles were excluded from state and county relief.[157]

As a result, some white, working-class neighborhoods were denied federal housing relief until the late 1930s and 1940s. Because of tax blight, poverty, proximity to industry, or other social traits deemed odious by federal appraisers, these suburbs were redlined and thus locked out of home loans. Bell Gardens was one example. This white working-class suburb, distinguished by its prevalent owner-building, self-provisioning, outdoor toilets, and general poverty, was flagged by the FHA as a bad risk. As County Supervisor John Anson Ford noted, bankers "have refused to make small loans to these people under FHA," claiming reasons like "too great a risk, not enough assured income, and—perhaps—not big enough to bother with." South Gate was likewise flagged for its "tax blight," although it was not redlined.[158]

But the tax stigma on many of these neighborhoods, including South Gate, was a temporary one. Once the tax problem was solved, federal assistance poured in. After the bonds were redeemed in 1938 under Rempel's plan, building activity in South Gate rose under the stimulus of FHA Title II financing, which granted loans up to $6,000 on single-family owner-occupied dwellings.[159] Many took advantage of these programs. Their ultimate access to federal housing money distinguished white working-class suburbs from neighborhoods of African Americans, Mexicans, and other people of color, whose redlined status was immutable because of their race.

For white residents in South Gate, who became prime beneficiaries of federal homeowner programs, it was an easy leap into the Democratic column. Their identity as working-class homeowners, forged in the terrific challenges of the boom and bust of the interwar years, positioned them to embrace a federal agenda that stabilized their hard-won status. Federal housing programs for homeowners were a welcome solution. Ideologically, they were acceptable because they offered loans, not outright charity. They essentially undergirded the hard work of attaining a home—they did not simply give out housing. They integrated individual achievement into the process itself; FHA loan recipients, after all, were still responsible for a down payment and monthly installments. This was an optimal solution to South Gate residents, who prized self-help, independence, and work. The HOLC and FHA essentially made room for these values, and they contrasted sharply with the flip side of federal housing policy: public housing for the poor. Residents, thus, developed a sense of entitlement to programs like the HOLC and FHA, because they earned it through their own hard work. They had paid the price. Their own local history planted the hearty roots of a homeowner rights sensibility. The nuances of their position ultimately situated them tenuously within the New Deal coalition and presaged the tensions that fractured this alliance in the postwar era.[160]

After the war, South Gate became a bastion of blue-collar antiliberalism, a haven of the "silent majority." The roots of this political sensibility reached deeply into the landscape of local life, where experiences of the neighborhood in the 1920s and 1930s taught residents certain hard lessons. In conflicts with the community's merchant leaders, working-class residents fought tenaciously against spending, taxes, and unbridled development, all to maintain family security. These experiences forged a suspicion of excessive government spending and activism. Although the New Deal worked to soften their critique of a statist approach, they would support an activist government only to the extent that it helped people like themselves: white, working-class homeowners. Progressive policies beyond this to help the disadvantaged and neglected, as advanced by the Democratic Party after the war, crossed the line of acceptability. South Gate's support of the Democrats and New Deal, thus, had its limits. In this respect, residents found themselves uncomfortably situated within the labor-liberal alliance that sustained the New Deal after the war.

As the South Gate story reveals, political sensibilities among working-class suburbanites were fuzzier, more nuanced, and more complex than a simple "right wing–left wing" dichotomy. Their political loyalties were powerfully shaped by concerns of the neighborhood, by the economic pressures they experienced in residential life, and not by partisan agendas established elsewhere—even in the workplace. So working-class homeowners, struggling to secure a modicum of economic stability for themselves through residential strategies, asserted their political will locally in ways that appeared traditionally conservative—anti-tax, antigovernment, antidevelopment—while supporting a state program that appeared profoundly radical—Sinclair's EPIC. Yet this political orientation was no contradiction. It was a very logical response to the circumstances of their lives. Steeped in a tradition of self-help, frugality, hard work, and autonomy, and acting out their lives according to these dictates, residents interpreted their political choices in light of these values.[161]

In the interwar years, the outlines of a working-class identity and mentality emerged. As expressed in the neighborhood, it was tied to workers' status as homeowners and their desire to protect this hard-won status and the security it afforded them. They embraced the values of hard work, self-help, individualism, and family integrity. The fragmentary nature of their social life reinforced this, as they commuted to work and to play, and as they lived as neighbors with others from diverse occupational backgrounds. Spatially, their lives lacked a sense of working-class coherence; their neighborhoods were not bounded geographically into a working-class community, unified by factory, working-class neighbors, and common cultural outlets. Theirs was a more individual, family-oriented existence, where the ideal of self-help was embraced by necessity.

In the postwar era, South Gate residents clung to similar values but highlighted them differently in the political arena. In a new era of prosperity, the path was cleared for fresh political preoccupations to emerge. The postwar period saw residents develop a new agenda: to segregate, protect, and defend their suburb.

"A Beautiful Place"

As the Great Depression finally subsided, Juanita Smith found herself moving up in the world. She had been working as a "general office girl" at Bayly-Underhill in Long Beach, a branch plant that produced overalls for J.C. Penney stores in the west. While 132 female workers sewed the garments, Juanita kept the front office running, answering phones, doing payroll and billing. When the president of the firm came out from company headquarters in Denver to the Long Beach plant, Juanita became an executive secretary. She moved to an apartment near work, but came "home" to South Gate nearly every weekend to visit family and socialize with old friends. She began dating Ernie Hammon, a man she met through high school friends, and soon the two fell in love. In 1941, Juanita and Ernie were married.

Ernie Hammon was likewise moving up in his life. Pegging his future at Firestone Tire and Rubber in South Gate, Ernie got his first job there digging ditches for the plant's foundation during its construction in 1927. He enrolled in night school and correspondence courses to gain some technical training, and it soon paid off. When the factory opened, he was hired as an instrument technician "because he could use a slide ruler." His boss took him under his wing, training him on the job. Ernie worked his way up in the plant, moving into guided missiles during World War II, and finally landing a position as supervisor of the instrument shop. "He had a whole group of men working under him. For a guy who grew up without much education . . . he had a dandy job," Juanita recalled.

During the war, the couple bought their first home in South Gate. With the help of FHA financing, they purchased a home that had been built in 1941, with two bedrooms and a big two-car garage. They paid $6,500, part of it in cash, and assumed the $21 per month mortgage payments—which included insurance and property taxes. The couple raised two children in South Gate and built a life for themselves. In the early 1960s, Juanita embarked on a new career. Showing just how far the Smith family had come from their early days in Home Gardens, Juanita became a realtor.[1]

Juanita and Ernie Hammon moved up not only through their hard work but also through the changing context of their lives. Los Angeles's industrialization—a process that accelerated during World War II—provided them jobs with good paychecks and good possibilities for advancement. And the federal government helped underwrite their entry into homeownership. This new role of the federal government, in fact, represented a highly significant change in the lives of many white Americans. As state power expanded during the economic crisis of the 1930s, it came to have a profound impact on the ways working people strategized to survive and even prosper. If hard times hit, families could now turn to the federal government for help. For the people of blue-collar suburbs like South Gate, the welfare state superceded the home as the final safety net. At the same time that it enlarged its role as welfare provider, the federal government also demarcated exactly who would benefit from its programs. It began to draw lines between races and regions, renters and homeowners. As housing policy especially came to reveal, the government began to privilege white, homeowning Americans who lived in the suburbs—people like the residents of South Gate. They were well positioned to become the plump beneficiaries of federal largesse, a phenomenon with profound implications in the postwar years.

This new federal activism, combined with a robustly recovered economy, turned postwar South Gate into a different type of suburb. By the 1950s, South Gate began to resemble its postwar counterparts—the Levittowns and Lakewoods—more than its own prewar roots. No longer was it a rough-and-tumble community, bustling with home-centered productivity and families stretching every last resource. Now it had developer-built homes, tidy lawns, and smoothly paved streets. And residents, enjoying the fruits of postwar prosperity, shifted their priority from sheer survival to protecting their rising affluence and identity as white homeowners. The entire suburb had experienced upward mobility.[2]

Ultimately, a new concern with race emerged to dominate local political commitments. No longer did divergent class interests make antagonists of homeowners and proprietors. Now the threats loomed instead from the outside. The changed landscape of the suburb set the scene.

THE FEDERAL EFFECT

Postwar South Gate was profoundly shaped by two interrelated influences: the federal government and World War II. While the government began expanding its powers during the Depression, it accelerated the process during and after World War II in ways that had particular impact on the West. From federal subsidies for interstate highways that further opened up the West, to a social security system that allowed comfortable retirement in good-weather areas, to the defense-driven high-tech economy, federal spending speeded the pace of urban growth in the South and West. California was at the vanguard. During World War II, industry grew by 96 percent in California cities. The aircraft and shipbuilding industries were especially attracted to western cities for their topography, climate, abundant land, nonunion workforces, and proximity to supporting institutions such as research universities.[3]

Los Angeles was a prime beneficiary of federal spending. During the war, Southern California grew four times faster than the rest of the nation. Los Angeles had become "the leading city of the newly industrialized west," spurred by $11 billion in war contracts between 1939 and 1945, representing 10 percent of the nation's entire war production. The greatest growth occurred in the aircraft, shipbuilding, petroleum, steel, and electrical industries. Los Angeles's industrial expansion was illustrated by several critical shifts—from 1939 to 1945, the number of industrial workers increased 280 percent, industrial establishments climbed from 5,594 to 7,500, and the average number of employees per plant rose from 27 to 77. In 1941, fully 13,000 new industrial workers were hired *per month* in Los Angeles. By 1943, defense production occupied 80 percent of Los Angeles's manufacturing sector and supplied one-quarter of all jobs. At the same time, population surged; by 1944, one-quarter of L.A. residents had arrived since 1940.[4]

Industrial growth continued during the Cold War era. Federal subsidy remained hefty enough to make Los Angeles "epitomize the state-managed

industrial metropolis."[5] This was a moment when it was thriving as a destination of the plant relocations beginning to deplete older cities like Detroit,
already feeling the pressures of deindustrialization by the 1950s. By 1947,
Los Angeles ranked third in the total number of factories, behind only New
York and Chicago. In 1947, Los Angeles's top five industries were transportation equipment (including aircraft, automobiles, and ships), food, fab-
ricated metal products, machinery, and apparel. While the city's industrial
economy fell abruptly after August 1945 from the effects of military de-
mobilization, it rebounded sharply in 1950 with new spending for the Ko-
rean War and ultimately for the Cold War. Overall, the expansion of L.A.
industry, particularly the high-tech defense plants in an era of Cold War
fear, ensured postwar growth and good job prospects for the next two
decades.[6]

Some scholars have cautioned not to overestimate the impact of federal
policy on cities during this period. They point out that most federal spending privileged suburbs over cities, that little in the way of an explicit "urban
policy" existed, and that benefits to cities were mostly an unintended consequence. In this vein, Roger Lotchin argues that World War II was hardly
a watershed for California cities. Instead, it merely continued processes
already underway and the changes it did effect—if taken in national context—were smaller than generally assumed.[7] Even considering these
caveats, the "federal effect" in fact reverberated deeply in Los Angeles.[8] In
grappling with two successive "national emergencies"—the Depression
and World War II—the government intervened in the economy and housing market in unprecedented ways that reshaped the lives of working families.

Housing policy was especially influential, particularly in working-class
communities where homes held such vital meaning to residents. Beginning
in the 1930s, the federal government enacted housing policies to stimulate
employment, the economy, and homeownership by jump-starting the construction industry. As noted earlier, the Home Owners Loan Corporation
(HOLC) was established in 1933, designed to protect existing homeowners
by assuming defaulted mortgages. The following year, the Federal Housing
Administration (FHA) was formed; it ultimately proved to be the more important, long-lived agency. The FHA insured long-term, low-interest home
loans granted by private lenders, a policy that put home buying within the
grasp of workers of modest incomes. This represented a radical break with
the past. Prior to the FHA, home mortgages were a costly affair. Nationally
in the 1920s, the mortgage repayment period averaged five to ten years;
in Los Angeles, San Diego, and San Francisco, at least two-thirds of all
mortgages had repayment periods of less than six years. This meant high

monthly payments, well out of reach of most working-class people. The FHA changed this. It lengthened the amortization period of home mortgages, and it also insured them. By 1940, the average repayment period of an FHA home loan was twenty-three years, allowing for much lower monthly payments. The Veterans Administration's mortgage guarantee program, part of the GI Bill, made home acquisition even more affordable. Returning veterans could borrow the entire value of the home without a down payment.[9]

After working out the glitches caused by the Mattoon Act, the FHA began deeply impacting the L.A. housing market by the 1940s. Indeed, with the FHA's proclivity for suburban, single-family dwellings, it came as little surprise that Los Angeles—the suburban metropolis par excellence—led the nation in new FHA homes by 1940.[10] As early as 1937, FHA-insured loans accounted for 40 percent of total institutional lending activity for new homes in Los Angeles; it hit 47 percent in 1938 and 57 percent during the first five months of 1939. This well exceeded the national rates, suggesting L.A. residents took advantage of federal housing programs earlier than most areas, foreshadowing postwar trends. By 1950, U.S. Census data showed that of first mortgage loans among all homeowner properties in Los Angeles, 35.3 percent were underwritten by the FHA or VA, compared to 31.4 percent nationally. By 1960, the L.A. rate was 46.6 percent, the national rate 41.9 percent.[11] Working-class homes were well represented in this pool. Indeed, several FHA policies of the late 1930s targeted smaller homes, making FHA loans more accessible to blue-collar families. By 1940 over one-quarter of FHA-insured homes in Los Angeles were sold to workers whose incomes ranged from $1,500 to $1,999. And among all Class 3 applications (for loans with principals below $2,500) nationally, one-fifth were filed at the Southern California FHA office. Los Angeles had become a national leader in the provisioning of FHA benefits to working-class people.[12]

Before long, federal housing policy—coupled with a healthier job market—began to discourage owner-building. With home loans now more affordable, it became easier for working-class families to purchase a home rather than build it. By the 1940s, tighter FHA loan policies added to the pressures against owner-building. The FHA increasingly drew on appraisal standards of the HOLC, which tended to rank owner-built neighborhoods like Home Gardens as bad credit risks. And certain FHA construction regulations further hindered owner-building.[13] The impact in Los Angeles was immediate. As early as 1939, a federal report on Los Angeles noted that "'Jerry' building is at a minimum and confined to the cheaper areas built up in 3-4 room buildings." Furthermore, it warned that speculative building had grown "very active" in Los Angeles, because of the "plentitude of mortgage money available in the community" that resulted in "intensive competition to place this money."[14] These comments suggested the demise of owner-building and rise in speculative development. In South Gate, this pattern manifested as a shift in housing production from a "cottage industry" to large-scale production.[15]

World War II accelerated this process. The war created an intensive, immediate need for defense production and, in turn, housing for defense workers, particularly those recently arrived to the area. With in-migrants vastly outpacing housing supply and with wartime restrictions on building, it was not long before a massive housing shortage developed, as was true nationally. For Los Angeles County, the most dramatic proof of this was the sharp decline in vacancies, from 6 percent in 1940 to 0.4 percent in 1943. The housing shortage was especially acute in southern Los Angeles, where nearly half of all defense plants were located. Evidence of the shortage was rampant, even in South Gate. In 1942, local residents were urged to turn their idle property into rental housing, or to fix up or add onto their homes to rent rooms. They were offered refinancing help from the FHA's Defense Housing Program. A full-page ad run by local home improvement stores read: "It's the patriotic duty of every American who owns suitable old property to fix it up for rent—to turn idle buildings into modern apartments and put vacant houses in good repair so they can be rented." Building-supply stores offered to help residents fill out FHA applications. The local problem was still acute by 1945. The *South Gate Press* urged residents to rent rooms to the "homeless hundreds of persons in this area," while the YWCA reported that of fifty-four women seeking rentals in South Gate, only eight could be placed. "What will the others do?" asked a YWCA representative. "How can they be expected to do good work at their jobs? Sitting up in all night movies or waiting endlessly in hotel lobbies, only to be turned out to spend the night wandering the streets. . . . These girls are exhausted and depressed from walking the streets in a vain effort to get a decent roof over their heads."[16]

To overcome the severe housing shortage, the government intervened in the housing market once again. In March 1941, it passed Title VI of the Housing Act, which applied exclusively to 146 industrial areas facing critical housing shortages. To spur private construction of homes near defense plants, Title VI targeted large-scale builders, offering them direct, guaranteed loans of up to 90 percent of the project's value. This was a boon to "community builders," because it gave them money up front and placed nearly all risk on the federal government itself. These homes could be sold or leased only to defense workers making less than $3,000 annually. These policies encouraged mass production of homes in working-class areas. Among the tangible results were large-scale privately constructed suburban developments around key industrial nodes, such as Westside Village in Mar Vista, Toluca Wood in North Hollywood, and suburban Westchester, located near Douglas Aircraft, Lockheed, and North American Aviation, respectively. On the public side, joint federal-city public housing programs built 33,000 units in Los Angeles. By 1943, this included fifteen federally funded and owned housing projects, including the famous Channel Heights Project designed by Richard J. Neutra, adjacent to the San Pedro shipyards.[17]

Another effect of World War II with deep implications for South Gate was the influx of African Americans into Los Angeles. During World War II, jobs and good working conditions attracted more blacks to Los Angeles than any other West Coast city, making this the Great Migration era for L.A. blacks. From 1940 to 1944, the black population in L.A. city nearly doubled from 63,774 to 118,888, accounting for nearly one-third of *total* population growth in the city. The inflow continued after the war. By 1950, the black population in the L.A. metropolitan area rose to 170,880, and by 1960 to 334,916. Because of persistent race restrictions, most of these newcomers settled in established African-American communities, especially in the corridor south of downtown, Watts, and a few pockets west of Main Street. Blacks were disproportionately confined to the City of Los Angeles. By 1950, L.A. city housed 78 percent of all blacks in the county; by comparison, the city contained 47 percent of all residents in the county, meaning a majority resided in outlying communities. Yet most suburbs remained off-limits to blacks.[18] African Americans were segregated residentially to a greater degree than any other minority group. This practice of confinement coupled with the general wartime housing shortages meant that blacks felt the housing pinch acutely. Only a miniscule 3 percent of new private housing construction went to blacks in 1945, despite the fact that they constituted over 12 percent of in-migrants. They fared better in public housing, occupying 27.4 percent of the 11,170 units controlled by the L.A. City Housing Authority in 1946. Still, this fell well below need.[19]

Closer to South Gate, Watts was dramatically affected by the war. Previously a diverse community of blacks, Anglos, and Latinos, by 1947 an estimated 80 percent of residents were African American. Wartime housing shortages and intensified crowding contributed to a growing perception of Watts as a ghetto. In reality, the physical appearance of postwar Watts was not all that different from the typical prewar working-class suburb: tent churches, unpaved streets, homes that seemed "about to fall apart," and scattered vacant lots. Yet while white working-class suburbs advanced through government-subsidized development after the war, black suburbia

deteriorated under the dual pressures of race restrictions and discriminatory federal policy. When federally underwritten housing did arrive,
it often caused more social disruption than stability. From 1953 to 1955,
three public housing projects were erected in Watts (Jordan Downs, Nickerson Gardens, and Imperial Courts), accommodating 9,694 people. The influx of a large, poor population brought a host of social problems to the
community. Adding to the strain was increasing industrial land use near
residential areas, particularly along the Alameda corridor. Alameda Street,
the racial dividing line between black and white Los Angeles, soon grew
cluttered with salvage yards and industrial trash. The forces of segregation
were strong enough that by 1958, a survey found that four out of five members of minority groups in Los Angeles would move out of their present
neighborhood if they could.[20]

Federal housing policies worked to harden the lines of racial segregation
in Los Angeles. The very programs that promoted white homeownership
not only excluded people of color but flagged their communities as inferior
and thus solidified boundaries of segregation. At the crux of this policy
were the appraisal standards first developed by the HOLC. These standards
privileged white, middle-class suburban communities that were newer and
racially "stable," while penalizing neighborhoods of the poor, of people of
color, and containing "hazards" like industry. While a low (or red) rating
did not preclude a neighborhood from receiving HOLC aid, the real damage
of the HOLC system lay in its legacy. The HOLC appraisal standards were
adopted by the FHA and ultimately by private lending institutions. The
FHA intensified some of the worst qualities of these standards, openly recommending race restrictions to promote the sort of homogeneous neighborhoods it favored. With the FHA holding the purse strings of federal
housing money, these policies dictated who would—and who would not—
benefit from the postwar suburban housing boom.[21]

As it did for cities nationwide, the HOLC composed appraisal maps of
Los Angeles in the late 1930s, which demarcated the racial landscape of the
metropolis. Black, Mexican, Asian, and poor white areas invariable received
the worst ratings (red or yellow), while upper- and middle-class Anglo
neighborhoods got high ratings (green or blue). The African-American
neighborhoods along the Alameda corridor and directly southwest of
downtown showed up red, as did the Mexican-American communities of
East Los Angeles, Highland Park, Chavez Ravine, Elysian Park, and what
was known as "Dog town" near downtown. Scattered working-class pockets around Santa Monica and southwestern Los Angeles likewise got redlined, although not always for racial reasons.[22]

In their L.A. survey, the HOLC appraisers filled out worksheets for each

neighborhood. These documents shed light on the reasons behind the ratings. In most cases, race was key when it came to redlining. Of seventy-one
red-rated areas in Los Angeles, all but two had racial minorities living in
them. The most commonly noted "subversive" racial groups, in the HOLC's
parlance, were Mexicans, blacks, and Japanese. For example, the Lankershim
area, populated by Mexicans, blacks, and Japanese, was described as "utterly
blighted. . . . Population is made up 100% of subversive racial elements,
with very meager incomes." Of a black neighborhood in Pasadena, the ap-
praiser wrote, "This old unrestricted area has long been inhabited by the
servant class who were employed by wealthy families in the higher grade
areas to the west and south. This district was originally much smaller but
constant infiltration into other sections as deed restrictions expired has created a real menace." Showing the liability of race, another Pasadena neighborhood was branded red "solely on account of racial hazards" posed by a
small, encroaching black population. This, even after appraisers conceded
that these blacks were "of the better class." The Jefferson district, "considered the best Negro residential district in the city" of "well maintained"
bungalows with "evident pride of ownership," still got a red grade strictly
because of its racial makeup. Likewise, Mexican neighborhoods were automatically graded down, such as this San Gabriel neighborhood: "The vast
majority of the population, while American-born, are still 'peon' Mexicans,
and constitute a distinctly subversive racial influence." The most egregious
comment was recorded for the San Gabriel Wash area, populated by first-
and second-generation Mexicans: "Infiltration of goats, rabbits and dark
skinned babies indicated." Similar comments abounded in these records.[23]

One result of these policies was the confinement of African Americans
to the South-Central corridor, along a well-demarcated path. By designat-
ing this area a poor security risk for home loans, the HOLC and FHA gave
official sanction to existing racial patterns and assured the section a dismal
future by excluding it from homeowner programs. In its new activist role in
the housing market, the federal government both helped and hurt Americans—depending upon the color of one's skin.

THE PEOPLE OF POSTWAR SOUTH GATE

During and just after World War II, South Gate experienced a convulsive
population boom, which then leveled off during the next two decades. The
war and its aftermath brought thousands of newcomers to the suburb, who
arrived to take advantage of well-paying jobs in the area. The biggest population jump occurred during the 1940s, particularly during the war (see

table 2-2). By 1950, the population had nearly doubled to 51,116. After this point, growth was much slower as the suburb reached a comfortable saturation point.[24]

As the suburb grew, the characteristics of its residents remained static in terms of race and ethnicity but began showing signs of social diversification in other ways. South Gate, in effect, became more itself. Racially and ethnically, the suburb remained mostly native-born white. African Americans continued to be excluded from the community. Foreign-born residents remained a small minority during the postwar years, hovering near 7 percent of the total from 1940 to 1960. As in the earlier period, the largest immigrant groups were from England, Canada, and Germany; in 1960, the suburb had 1,900 English immigrants, and about 1,600 each from Canada and Germany. Asians constituted only 0.1 percent of the local population. The biggest change came among Latinos. By 1960, almost 1,000 Mexican-born immigrants lived in the suburb, representing nearly 2 percent of the population. The number of Mexican Americans was probably much higher; the U.S. Census did not enumerate them as a separate group from 1930 to 1960, instead lumping them together with "whites." By 1970, when the census began counting "Spanish language" persons separately, they totaled 17.3 percent in South Gate. This influx represented a precursor to a major demographic transition in the area after 1970, from white to Latino.[25] During the postwar years, South Gate's Latinos were moderately prosperous. In 1950, fully 72 percent owned their own homes, valued from $5,000 and up. Only five Latino families owned homes worth $3,000–$4,999, the low end of the local housing market. Clearly, only better-off Latinos could buy their way into the community. By 1960, the proportion of Latino homeowners declined to 47 percent; they continued to own homes in the midrange value.[26]

Overall in the postwar period, South Gate remained predominantly native born and Anglo. The origins of this native-born population are difficult to determine, since no data were systematically collected apart from scattered hints in U.S. Census records. In 1960, the census found that 38 percent of South Gate residents were California natives, the rest hailing from other states. For this same year, data from L.A. city is suggestive: the largest group was born in California (36.2 percent), followed by the north central states (22.7 percent), the South (16.7 percent), the Northeast (11.3 percent) and the West (7.2 percent). In 1970, 40.9 percent of South Gate residents were born in California. Suggestive evidence comes from nearby Lakewood, a suburb with a similar occupational profile as South Gate. As D. J. Waldie recalled of his boyhood there in the 1950s, "about a third of my neighbors came from the border South. That meant that they, or their parents, had come to California from Oklahoma, Texas, Missouri, Arkansas, or

Kansas." Given South Gate's proximity to Lakewood, about eight miles away, as well as its precedent of settlers from the Great Plains and border South, it is likely that migrants from this region also continued to settle in South Gate after the war.[27]

From 1940 to 1960, South Gate's population reached a more mature stage in the life cycle, with a greater proportion of older adults than ever before. No longer was this a suburb of young families, struggling to get off the ground. Like the rest of the country, South Gate experienced the surge of the postwar baby boom, but the proportion of young children tapered off by 1960, in contrast to city and state trends that continued upward. While South Gate's young population was declining, its elderly population was on the rise. The proportion of residents over 59 increased from 8 to 14 percent from 1940 to 1960, aligning South Gate with trends in metropolitan Los Angeles. In South Gate, an aging population was not offset by an influx of young, child-rearing families, to replicate its prewar demography. Instead, it had become a more settled suburb of aging families with relatively fewer and older children than in comparable areas.[28]

By contrast to the prewar years when nuclear families predominated, in postwar South Gate the number of singles was rising and their characteristics were changing. The number of widowed and divorced residents registered a steady rise in 1950 and 1960, revealing both the graying of the population and a notable increase in failed marriages. Widowed or divorced residents rose from 8 percent of the total population in 1930 to nearly 15 percent by 1960. Women were disproportionately represented in this group, with more of them widowed than divorced, according to 1960 data. Overall, the presence of nonmarried residents became more apparent during the postwar years, with important implications for local community life.[29]

School attendance remained steady after the war, except for a small but notable rise in college attendance. The number of students completing high school remained high, then dropped to around 32 percent for first-year college-age students. While this was still considerably lower than the L.A. average (44 percent), it represented an increase from South Gate's prewar level (24 percent). Among local adults, the median for school years completed rose slightly in 1950 and 1960, up to 11.5 years, although this too was lower than the metropolitan average. Still, this data showed a new interest in higher education among South Gate residents, a trend borne out by impressionistic evidence. It revealed, too, the makings of a shift from a working-class to a more middle-class orientation.[30]

In the postwar period, the suburb's population was highly mobile. Between 1949 and 1950, fully 22 percent of residents had changed addresses (this rate was actually low for California cities).[31] From 1955 to 1960, 47 percent of South Gate's residents were living at a new address in South Gate; most came from a different home in L.A. County, while some were newcomers from out of state. This indicates that while the population rate leveled off in the 1950s, internally it was in great flux. By 1960, only a small proportion of residents (8 percent) lived in the same home since before 1939, while 20 percent had arrived from 1940 to 1949; 25 percent from 1950 to 1956; and fully 47 percent since 1957. While movement *within* South Gate was not recorded, clearly local residents did not stay long in their homes.[32]

Overall, South Gate's social profile revealed the persistence of certain key strains—white, native-born residents in nuclear families—although certain changes were apparent. By 1960, a nascent Latino population had gained a foothold in the community, signifying the first signs of a tremendous demographic transformation about to unfold—but one that would happen after 1965. And the nuclear family, while dominant, was beginning to share space with single adults unattached to families. The gradually rising divorce rate was especially foreboding, portending a change in local life that simmered under the surface of outward appearances. And high mobility rates strongly suggest that residents of postwar South Gate represented a veritable second generation of the suburb. By 1960, few could call themselves longtime residents of the community.

The Economic Landscape

The war and its aftermath had an uplifting effect on the suburb's economic character, bleaching its collective occupational collar white and sprucing up its homes. South Gate shed its early roots as a gritty working-class suburb and began resembling the middle-class suburbs proliferating throughout the nation. While South Gate would never be a typical postwar planned suburb—it was simply too old and too developed for this—it did take on certain traits of these communities.

In terms of occupations, South Gate's populace experienced collective upward mobility. One cause of this was the recovery to full employment, thanks to wartime and postwar industrialization. The unemployment rate in South Gate dropped to 4.9 percent in 1950, and 4.8 percent by 1960. Another factor was the type of jobs South Gate residents were landing. The proportion of white-collar workers rose considerably, from 35.5 to 44 percent between 1940 and 1960 (see table 2-3). By the latter year, the number of white- and blue-collar workers was nearly even, for the first time in

South Gate's history. The socioeconomic characteristic that defined South Gate before the war—class diversity—had intensified by the 1960s. South Gate continued to be a suburb where factory and office workers lived side by side.

This occupational heterogeneity became a hallmark of many new, planned communities in postwar Los Angeles. As Greg Hise has shown, an important wave of suburban development, anchored around decentralized defense industries, was an engine of metropolitan growth during and after the war. The large-scale "operative builders" who developed these suburbs, such as Fritz Burns, Fred Marlow, and Henry Kaiser, intended these communities to contain a socially and occupationally diverse populace. Lakewood Village, for example, was touted as a $15 million "community of individualized homes for defense workers and executives," while Fritz Burns insisted on a range of home prices "to provide a varied community atmosphere and to prevent un-American economic and social stratification." D. J. Waldie recalled such interclass unity in suburban Lakewood in the 1950s. "One neighbor on my block ran a lathe. Another worked on the assembly line in a plastics plant. Another was an oil refinery worker until his death. My father was an engineer for the Gas Company. There was no obvious way to tell a factory worker from a business owner or a professional man when I grew up. Every house on my block looked much the same."[33] South Gate contained such diversity much earlier, and continued the trend after the war, now aligning with the larger, planned suburbs proliferating in the metropolis.

The apparent upward mobility of South Gate's workers, in fact, masked a gendered transformation of the local labor force. During the postwar years, an unprecedented number of women entered paid jobs, especially in clerical and sales positions. This influx expanded the ranks of white-collar employees. Yet while the quantity of white-collar workers was rising, their qualitative dimensions were declining. For the most part, women occupied less stable, lower paying positions. A closer look at the occupational differences by gender clarifies these distinctions.

In the postwar era, the majority of men in South Gate continued to labor in blue-collar jobs (see table 5-1). A slight decline of unskilled laborers from 1940 to 1960 suggests a small rise in skill level among blue-collar workers. Men also made modest gains in the white-collar sector. The proportion of male professionals and managers rose unevenly, ending up slightly ahead by 1960. Conversely, their representation in low-level white-collar jobs edged down, as women were taking over this sector. In 1940 and 1950, the top occupational groups for men were construction, iron and steel manufacturing, machine manufacturing, wholesale trade, auto

Table 5-1 South Gate Labor Force by Sex, 1940–1960 (Percentage of Gender Group)

	1940		1950		1960	
Occupational Group	Male (n = 7,866)	Female (n = 1,977)	Male (n = 14,954)	Female (n = 5,916)	Male (n = 16,144)	Female (n = 8,600)
Total white-collar	31.5	51.0	37.3	63.7	32.6	65.4
High-level white-collar						
Professional, semiprofessional	4.8	9.4	7.4	9.2	7.3	6.7
Managers, officials, proprietors	9.7	5.1	13.5	5.6	9.8	4.3
Low-level white-collar						
Clerical, kindred	17.0[a]	36.5[a]	8.3	40.2	8.6	46.5
Sales			8.1	8.7	6.9	7.9
Total blue-collar	62.3	24.3	57.9	22.0	59.1	19.8
Craftsmen, foremen	27.1	1.2	28.8	1.9	28.3	2.0
Operatives, kindred	28.8	22.0	24.9	20.1	26.9	17.4
Laborers (except farm)	6.4	1.1	4.2	—	3.9	0.5
Total service	4.9	23.6	4.2	12.8	4.9	11.2
Domestics	—	8.0	—	2.8	—	2.1
Service (except domestic)	4.9	15.6	4.1	10.0	4.9	9.1

[a]Figure combines clerical, sales, and kindred workers.

Sources: U.S. Bureau of the Census, *Sixteenth Census of the United States, 1940: Population*, vol. 2, *Characteristics of the Population* (Washington, D.C.: GPO, 1943), 620; idem, *Seventeenth Census of the United States, Census of Population: 1950*, vol. 2, *Characteristics of Population, Part 5, California* (GPO, 1953), 5–124; idem, *Eighteenth Census of the United States, Census of Population: 1960*, vol. 1, *Characteristics of the Population, Part 6* (GPO, 1963), 6–322.

manufacturing, and food processing. By 1960, they were iron and steel, machine manufacturing, construction, transportation equipment (excluding autos), the auto industry, and food processing. Overall, the changes in the male labor force were very slight from 1940 to 1960, showing a barely perceptible shift from blue-collar to white-collar.[34]

The continued strength of South Gate's blue-collar sector occurred in the context of Los Angeles's postwar industrial boom. South Gate too experienced this expansion, evident in the proliferation of local industry. Defense plants multiplied during and immediately after the war, while some existing factories converted to defense production. They increased output and expanded their labor forces, often by drawing on female workers. For example, in just two years Firestone bolstered its workforce from 1,671 to 4,000, one-third of them women. Factories like Hardman Aircraft Products, Aerco, Reisner Metals, A&M Casting, and Pacific Screw Products provided jobs to workers from South Gate and other southern suburbs. The one exception was GM, which shrank during the war. After retooling to produce tanks, GM slowed production because of delays in the delivery of materials, then shut down during the last two years of the war. But the main trend was industrial growth. The number of South Gate plants rose from 35 to 137, over the years 1935 to 1947, while the value added by manufacturing increased tenfold to $44.6 million. This surge continued through the 1950s. The number of factories reached 245 in 1954, making South Gate the sixth largest industrial suburb in Los Angeles. That year, local plants employed 9,119 people, with an average of 37 workers per plant. By the early 1960s, the number of factories topped 300, and it peaked at over 400 in 1970. The Chamber of Commerce sang the praises of South Gate's continued industrial expansion, touting the suburb as one "where industry, commerce, employment and family living harmonize side by side."[35]

For the women of South Gate, occupational trends showed dramatic change after 1940. The war period marked the beginning of a large, steady influx of women into the paid workforce, into fields previously closed to them.[36] In 1940, 22 percent of adult women in South Gate worked for a paycheck. By 1960, this jumped to 41 percent. Concomitantly, women as a percentage of South Gate's *total* workforce rose from 21 percent in 1940 to 35 percent by 1960, slightly higher than the national average (33 percent).[37] As table 5-1 shows, women were flooding into clerical and sales positions, particularly as typists and stenographers. The second-largest category comprised semiskilled operatives. Some women gained a foothold in manufacturing during World War II, although it slipped slightly over the next two decades. They worked mostly in machinery, iron and steel, and textiles, with only a scant few landing jobs in the large local auto and rubber

factories. Very few women found work as skilled operatives. The proportion
of women in service jobs declined in the postwar years, as did those in professional and managerial positions. Of the women who climbed the ranks
into the professions, most worked as teachers or nurses. For South Gate
women, the occupational door that opened the widest led into an office.

Despite their decisive entrance into the workforce, women clearly stood
on a lower rung of the economic ladder than men. The wage differential between South Gate men and women was striking: in 1950, females earned
only one-third the income of males. This had improved little by 1960, when
the median income for men was $5,427, compared to $2,104 for women.
The sex segregation of jobs contributed to the differential; clerical jobs—
dominated by women—paid less overall ($3,530 median), while skilled
blue-collar jobs—dominated by men—paid well ($6,262). Yet even when
women and men fell into the same job category, such as semiskilled operatives, women earned considerably less ($3,279 for women, compared to
$5,320 for men). Part of this can be explained by the difference between
full-time and part-time work. In 1950 and 1960, roughly half of South
Gate's working women earned less than $1,000 annually, suggesting they
were probably part-time workers. In 1960, 58 percent of working women
were married. Although this was considerably higher than the L.A. average
(48 percent), it was close to the rate in other working-class suburbs, like
Lynwood (60 percent) and Maywood (59 percent). In South Gate, the
largest group of working women were older, aged forty-five to sixty-four,
suggesting they were a more permanent part of the workforce, as opposed
to young single women merely biding their time until marriage. South
Gate's female workers were working to supplement the family budget.[38]

While the occupational trends of South Gate's women mirrored national ones, they also broke dramatically with conditions in many middle-
class suburbs. In these communities, only about 9 percent of women
worked for a paycheck. The image of the isolated, frustrated suburban
housewife did not describe reality in South Gate, where women were out of
the house at least part of the day, earning a paycheck in an office or factory.
This posed an entirely different context for women's experience and gender
relations in South Gate.[39]

Distinctions between blue- and white-collar, working and middle class,
became more hazy than ever in the postwar years. One factor obfuscating
the difference was the second-class status of working women. Judging by
pay and prestige, blue- and white-collar did not mean much if one compared the status of a unionized skilled male worker to a female secretary in
her forties. The blue-collar man surely commanded as much, if not more,
prestige as the secretary. Blue-collar workers, in fact, found their status

climbing during and after the war, due partly to an invigorated labor move-ment in Los Angeles, which further complicated the boundary between working and middle class. Income levels were excellent proof of this. A comparison of median family income levels in South Gate with sixteen other middle- and working-class suburbs of Los Angeles shows South Gate's climbing status (see table 5-2). In 1939, South Gate ranked on the lower end of the scale. By 1950, income levels rose considerably, lifting South Gate to a fifth rank. This was a year when nearly half the local work-force was blue-collar. By 1960, as more pink-collar women entered the workforce at lower pay rates, South Gate's rank fell once again to tenth. The

Table 5-2   Median Family Income Rates in Selected L.A. Communities, 1939–1960

1939[a]		1950		1960	
Neighborhood	Median income (families)	Neighborhood	Median income (families)	Neighborhood	Median income (families)
		L.A. SMSA	$3,650	L.A. SMSA	$7,066
		L.A. City	3,575	L.A. City	7,831
Pasadena	$3,715	So. Pasadena	4,612	So. Pasadena	8,245
So. Pasadena	3,175	Whittier	4,211	Torrance	8,050
Glendale	2,812	Inglewood	4,161	Inglewood	7,764
Santa Monica	2,667	Glendale	4,112	Burbank	7,757
Burbank	2,617	*South Gate*	*4,043*	Gardena	7,741
Torrance	2,017	Burbank	4,039	Whittier	7,740
Inglewood	2,006	Lynwood	3,949	Glendale	7,563
Bell	1,975	Torrance	3,870	Lynwood	7,182
Compton	1,900	Bell	3,835	Pasadena	6,922
South Gate	*1,775*	Maywood	3,814	*South Gate*	*6,892*
Huntington Park	1,700	Huntington Park	3,770	Santa Monica	6,845
Azusa	1,667	Compton	3,761	Azusa	6,501
Lynwood	1,425	Santa Monica	3,677	Bell	6,438
Gardena	1,350	Pasadena	3,676	Huntington Park	6,285
Maywood	1,250	Gardena	3,645	Compton	6,256
Whittier	1,100	Azusa	3,474	Maywood	5,951
				Lakewood	7,600

[a]The 1939 statistics are rough estimates at best. Because the U.S. Census did not provide income data for the commu-nities included in this table, I used income levels reported on the City Survey files of the HOLC, taken in 1939. For each suburban community, I took an average of the estimates provided on these forms.

Sources: Los Angeles City Survey Files, RG 195, NA; U.S. Bureau of the Census, Seventeenth Census of the United States, Census of Population: 1950, vol. 2, General Characteristics of the Population, Part 5, California (Washing-ton, D.C.: GPO, 1952), 5-128 to 5-131; idem, Eighteenth Census of Population: 1960, vol. 1, Characteristics of the Population, Part 6 (GPO, 1963), 6-222 to 6-224.

year 1950 represented a high point for South Gate's economic fortunes, as it basked in the glow of Los Angeles's postwar boom.[40]

The blurring between white- and blue-collar was evident in other ways. For example, the blue-collar sections of South Gate had the highest income levels. Hollydale and Atlantic City, dominated by skilled blue-collar workers, had the highest median income levels in 1950 (see table 5-3 and fig. 5-1). The northwest section, where white-collar workers predominated, trailed behind these sections in terms of income. The exception was Home Gardens, which remained the poorest and most blue-collar section of all. Nevertheless, the prosperity of manual workers, especially those at the large local plants, was evident everywhere. As John Sheehy recalled, the men working at Firestone or GM "had nicer homes because, hell, they made $30 a week and they worked about nine months of the year." Many of these workers settled in the Magnolia Park section between those plants, where better homes had been constructed. The murky distinction between blue- and white-collar was made eminently clear in a planning study of South Gate conducted by a group of USC graduate students in the mid-1960s. At the very moment South Gate's white-collar sector was *expanding,* this study noted the outflow of the "upper-social strata" from the suburb and emphasized the need to lure these types back.[41]

The wartime and postwar expansion of the suburb's economy helped not only local industry but the retail sector as well. From 1929 to 1954, the number of retail establishments nearly tripled, rising from 182 to 508, while total sales increased from $3.4 million to $67 million. At the same time, the average number of employees per establishment rose from 1.1 to 4. By 1954, South Gate stores provided 2,050 retail jobs. While it is difficult to determine how many of these positions were filled by residents, it is clear

Table 5-3   South Gate Resident Income and Property Values, by Neighborhood, 1950

South Gate Neighborhood	Median income	Median home values	% of homes built after 1940	% of workers blue-collar	% of workers white-collar
Atlantic City	$3,995	$9,704	73.1%	50%	44%
Hollydale	3,993	9,049	90.4	54	37
Magnolia Park	3,899	9,191	51.1	47	45
Northwest South Gate	3,543	9,107	23.4	40	53
Home Gardens	3,377	7,942	30.6	55	37

Sources: U.S. Bureau of the Census, *Seventeenth Census of the United States, Census of the Population: 1950, Census Tract Statistics, Los Angeles, California and Adjacent Areas* (Washington, D.C.: GPO, 1952), 49; idem, *Seventeenth Census of the United States, Census of Housing: 1950,* vol. 1, *General Characteristics, Part 2* (GPO, 1953), 5-48.

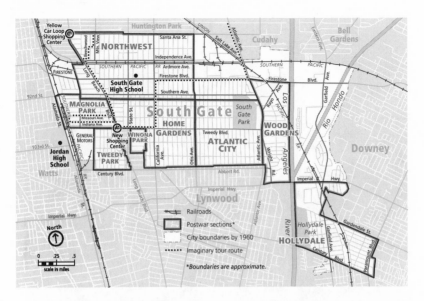

Figure 5-1   The suburb of South Gate, 1940–1960s

that local retail jobs finally outnumbered residents who worked in retail. In the late 1940s and 1950s, the most numerous types of local businesses were service stations, food stores, eating places, furniture and appliance stores, and automotive shops. By the mid-1950s, there were twenty-nine apparel stores in South Gate, suggesting that residents no longer *had* to shop elsewhere for clothing. And along Firestone Boulevard, new and used car lots abounded, giving South Gate a reputation as the auto center of Los Angeles.[42]

In this expansive context, new retail nodes emerged in South Gate. Three proprietors—including William Rempel, the local hero who rescued South Gate from Mattoon Act debt—invested in commercial development along Tweedy Boulevard, partly on formerly tax-delinquent land (fig. 5-2). The centerpiece was a $25 million shopping center at Tweedy and Long Beach Boulevards, launched in 1948. This investment shifted the city's commercial center from northwest South Gate—especially around the Yellow Car loop—to the Tweedy corridor in Home Gardens. The businesses around the loop survived on the patronage of Yellow Car passengers who disembarked at this point.[43]

The service sector grew slower than retail after the war. By the mid-1950s, South Gate had 281 service establishments, which employed only 640 persons. Total revenue in 1954 was $6.85 million. By 1954, the most numerous establishments were auto repair shops, business services, bar-

Figure 5-2 View of one of South Gate's business districts along Tweedy Boulevard, 1942. The
retail base of South Gate grew substantially in the 1940s, a result of economic expansion
during and after World War II. Federal Writers Project collection, Department of Special
Collections, University Research Library, UCLA.

bershops, beauty salons, and garment repair. While there were about half as
many service as retail operations in South Gate, service commanded only
one-tenth as much revenue. The service sector was the domain of small
proprietors, with less capital, fewer resources, and a guarded approach to local growth and expenditures.[44]

Despite overall growth in retail and service, South Gate still lagged behind comparable suburbs. Alhambra, similar in population size, had 94 more
stores than South Gate that earned $28.6 million more in 1954. Compton,
Inglewood, Huntington Park, and Whittier all had smaller populations than
South Gate, yet had significantly more stores and revenue. Whittier, half the
size of South Gate, had 33 more stores and nearly $16 million more in net
sales. South Gate also had a much lower per capita sales rate than comparable communities, lagging well behind Pasadena, Glendale, Santa Monica,
Alhambra, Compton, Inglewood, Huntington Park, and Bell. The merchants
of South Gate still lacked the economic strength of their counterparts in
other suburbs.[45]

In the midst of the rise in local economic fortunes, a few residents slipped through the cracks. One group was the elderly. A survey of the housing conditions of "Old Age Security" recipients in Los Angeles, taken in 1950, found that while the vast majority lived under suitable circumstances, a small percentage contended with substandard conditions. Among the elderly of South Gate, Bell Gardens, Compton, Downey, Vernon, Willowbrook, and Watts, about 2 percent were found to be "inadequately housed." The ramshackle conditions evoked images of prewar working-class suburbia. One senior was found "living in [a] converted chicken house—too small windows—no plumbing facilities inside or out." Another resident and spouse were "living in a garage—rent $20.00 per month —concrete floor covered with three inch layer of newspapers—damp and musty—couple eat and sleep in this one room." Yet another lived "in a room 6 feet by 8 feet, made from chicken coop—rent is $15 per month—no plumbing or cooking facilities." Others lived in a tool shed, a homemade trailer, and other makeshift shelters. These hardship cases suggested how the succession of owner-built housing and its accoutrements could promote destitution, especially as these structures aged, deteriorated, and became rental property.[46]

While representing a grim reminder of prewar South Gate, such conditions were the exception after 1945. For the most part, residents emerged into a more stable state of economic security, even as they became fully dependent upon cash wages. The importance of sweat equity declined in the postwar era, while the reliance on earned income increased. South Gate residents had become squarely situated in the wage-based economy.

The Housing Landscape

During and after the war, housing in South Gate took on a new, more affluent character. In one sense, the town's dwellings were a visual symbol of the community's prosperity, signifying the improved status of workers after 1940. No longer was South Gate a suburb of ratty, owner-built homes, unpaved roads, kerosene lamps, and yards overgrown with fruits, vegetables, and small livestock. Now it looked more like its middle-class counterpart: paved streets, orderly rows of matching homes, yards of lawns and flowers, and plenty of street lamps. By the looks of the landscape, the status of South Gate's residents had appreciated.

The housing shortage and federal housing policies had significant impact on housing in South Gate. The first effect was a local building boom. When Mattoon Act debts were cleared in 1938, this released a flurry of federally underwritten building. By 1939, 451 HOLC loans had been granted

Table 5-4   Years That Structures Were Built in South Gate (Among Those Still
             Standing in 1960)

Year Built	Number of Housing Units	% of All Housing Units
1929 and earlier	3,401	16.1
1930–39	4,167	19.7
1940–49	8,834	41.9
1950–59	4,708	22.3
Total in 1960	21,110	100

Source: U.S. Bureau of the Census, *Census of Housing: 1960*, vol. 1, *States and Small Areas, Part 2* (Washington, D.C.: GPO, 1963), 6-42.

in South Gate. A year later, FHA mortgage insurance for South Gate properties totaled $5 million. In the 1940s, the boom mushroomed. Table 5-4 shows that construction during the 1940s far outpaced that of any other decade in South Gate's history. During those ten years, 8,834 new housing units were constructed, more than the entire number built since the suburb's founding in 1917 (and still standing in 1960). The greatest activity occurred during the war; from 1940 to 1942 alone, 3,267 dwellings were built. And in the first six months of 1946, 399 homes went up.[47]

Second, federal incentives promoted the mass production of dwellings. Able to build quickly and profusely, large developers took the lead. In South Gate, the Capitol Company built up the Atlantic City section in the 1940s, around the new regional park. This firm profited from the rampant tax delinquencies of the 1930s by buying land at bargain prices and developing it with FHA assistance. In the southeast part of town, the Meadow Park and South Gate Manor subdivisions offered several floor plans and exteriors, with a choice of colors, fixtures, and interior amenities. Homeseekers could peruse several model homes, choose their favorite, then offer a down payment to start construction of the home (see fig. 5-3). The emergence of large-scale builders in working-class suburbia reflected a national trend during and after the war. With the expansion of jobs, federal housing programs, and mass production of homes, workers no longer were forced to rely on sweat equity to attain a house. The days of the self-reliant owner-builder were largely over. As a result, most of the housing starts after 1940 were the product of larger-scale builders rather than individual property owners.[48]

Third, the number of apartments and other multifamily dwellings in the suburb shot upward. In 1930, only 1 percent of dwellings in South Gate were multifamily; this increased to 9 percent in 1940, 21 percent by 1950,

Figure 5-3   The Meadow Park development in South Gate illustrated the importance of large-scale builders in the community after 1945. *South Gate Press,* May 8, 1947.

and 31 percent by 1960. South Gate was no longer a suburb exclusively of detached single-family homes. This critical transition was partly a by-product of the intense wartime housing shortage, when all manner of housing became acceptable and desperately welcomed. With so many people seeking shelter, especially recently arrived servicemen and defense workers, rentals became commonplace and even encouraged. During the war, homeowners were urged to fulfill their patriotic duty by renting out rooms to homeless families. The local disdain for tenancy dissipated, at least temporarily.[49]

Finally, the quality of new housing improved dramatically. This was apparent as early as 1939, when the HOLC surveyors came to town. They observed that South Gate's newer dwellings were a "much higher" caliber than the older homes. By 1940, the value of homes reflected this trend. Relative to other suburbs, median home values in South Gate rose considerably from 1930 to 1940, stayed strong in 1950, then began to taper by 1960 (see table 2-4). The 1940s and 1950s represented the apex period as new, quality construction invigorated the local housing market and enhanced real estate values. The continued housing shortage also contributed to the jump in home values, where demand far outpaced supply.[50]

All of these changes shaped a new kind of housing landscape in South Gate, one that contrasted with its prewar form. South Gate was now a better-built, sharper community. Residents mortgaged homes rather than made them. In 1950, fully 66.4 percent of owner-occupied homes were mortgaged, considerably higher than the rate for Los Angeles (56 percent) and the state (53 percent).[51] Building permits likewise reflected the trend. An analysis of building permits in South Gate, along several blocks in the northwest section of town, suggests a general decline in permits issued to owners and an increase in those issued to private and specialized contractors. The proportion of all permits issued to owners began at 26 percent in the 1920s, although this was probably an undercount since building often occurred without permits in the early years. This dropped to about 14 percent by the 1960s. The proportion of private contractors peaked in the 1940s during the local building boom; they received a quarter of all building permits in the 1960s. The largest group comprised specialized contractors, who received more than half of all permits in the 1930s, 1950s, and 1960s. Their importance was a likely result of the saturation of built homes in South Gate, the aging of properties, and the need to upgrade existing dwellings. Overall, these numbers indicate the demise of owner-building and rise of contractor-building in South Gate.[52]

Some evidence suggests, however, that owner-building habits did not disappear altogether. In South Gate, fewer residents may have built the *entire* home themselves, but they continued to expend sweat in upkeep and improvements. The prevalence of building supply stores attested to this. In 1951, South Gate had eight lumber companies, five building materials stores, two businesses that rented out concrete mixers, another that sold ready-mixed concrete, six wholesale plumbing supply outlets, and twenty-four paint dealers. One study of Los Angeles housing in the 1950s found that homeowners in suburbs like South Gate "often purchased their own tools and paint and refurbished their homes themselves." It is likely, however, that many residents also hired out small-scale contractors to do home maintenance, given their prevalence in the area. The local phone book listed at least fifty-four contractors, both general and specialized (including lathing, pipe line, plaster, electrical, and roofing).[53]

In nearby Bell Gardens, complete owner-building of homes persisted immediately after the war. The new Gage Acres tract established around 1946 was noted for its widespread owner-building. "Instead of hiring their homes built," wrote a sociologist in 1948, "most of the men in Gage Acres are building as much of their homes by themselves as is possible to do. The homes are small." To the chagrin of their neighbors, some of these owner-builders were dragging their feet, living "in tents for a long time without trying to build their homes." What set these postwar owner-builders apart, however, was their new penchant for infrastructure development and municipal incorporation. They formed the Gage Acres Improvement Association to lobby for fire hydrants, sewers, streetlights, sidewalks, curbs, and telephone lines. This suggests that even though self-building may have persisted in certain quarters, perhaps driven by the housing shortage, these homebuilders had shifted their outlook on spending.[54]

By 1950, home values—like income levels—reflected distinctions among the sections of South Gate (see table 5-3). The best part of town was Atlantic City, with its newer housing stock and preponderance of well-paid factory workers. The largest, costliest homes there surrounded the new county park. As John Sheehy recalled, "South Gate really looked very well in the new parts. On all the streets that ran around the park, there were all brand-new homes. . . . This was a beautiful place." Another newly developed area, Hollydale, likewise had respectable home values, as well as a majority of factory workers as residents. Northwest South Gate, the oldest part of town with the oldest housing stock, maintained relatively high home values, suggesting housing there had appreciated in value. Magnolia Park, where just over half of the structures were built after 1940, had similar home values. Meanwhile, Home Gardens remained the poor cousin. The bulk of housing there dated from the 1920s, vestiges of owner-built homes. The HOLC characterized these dwellings as "more or less substandard."[55]

Postwar prosperity was evident in South Gate's homeownership rates (see table 2-5). After dipping to 52.5 percent in 1940, it rebounded to nearly 70 percent by 1950, well above the national average (53.4 percent). This high level was especially noteworthy given the introduction of more rental units in South Gate. By 1960, the rise of multiple-family dwellings pulled the rate down to 57.4 percent, just below the national average.[56]

Overall, South Gate's housing recovered and expanded in the 1940s, leveled off in the 1950s, then began a gradual decline in the 1960s. Part of the decline was caused by rising density in the suburb. If the 1940s marked a period of intensive growth, in the 1950s South Gate reached its saturation point. A comprehensive city plan for South Gate prepared by Gordon Whitnall and Associates in 1959 recognized this fact: "[B]y 1950 most of the area of the city had become occupied. There were getting to be very few vacant lots. But, by 1958, a trend toward higher densities by adding one or more dwelling units had begun to evidence itself." Data on density told the same story: in 1930, population density per acre was 5.91; it rose to 15.40 by 1950 and remained there through the decade. Since opportunities to annex land to South Gate were closing off as adjacent land was developed, growth was possible only by intensifying the use of existing land. This created a need for alternatives to the detached, single-family home.[57]

It was in the context of this rise then gradual decline in the value of local housing that residents developed an intense concern with protecting property value in South Gate. As a purchased—rather than self-built— commodity, real estate came to represent a means of accumulation in the postwar suburb. As residents became increasingly enmeshed in the wage-driven economy, cash and real assets became the bedrock of family security and prosperity. As a result, property ownership took on a whole new meaning. It represented status and success more than mere safety net. And property value became the yardstick of that success.

Residents soon developed new concerns with warding off threats to that value. In the postwar years, the biggest perceived threat was the encroaching African-American community to the west. As it expanded into South Central Los Angeles, directly adjacent to white working-class suburbia, South Gate residents intensified their efforts to maintain racial barriers as a way of protecting property values. Their economic fears were not unfounded. As we have seen, no less than the federal government contributed to racializing property values, declaring that the color of one's skin dictated the worth of one's property. Housing in Black and Mexican neighborhoods, these policies contended, was worth eminently less than housing in white neighborhoods. Federal policy influenced banking practices, feeding into a system of structural discrimination. For South Gate residents, the impulse to maintain hard lines of segregation stemmed as much from this structural pressure as from their own personal prejudices.

As the economic security of South Gate residents rose, stringent segregation in all areas of life now became affordable. South Gate and its neighboring white communities worked to maintain racial barriers with increasing resolve. For example, in the 1940s when multiracial public housing projects approached the white neighborhood of Willowbrook, unincorporated territory just south of Watts, white residents threatened to burn the dwellings and attack any blacks who tried to move in. They warned the L.A. City Council that Willowbrook would "either stay lily-white or would run red with blood."[58] In South Gate, meanwhile, residents and realtors fortified the racial barriers around their suburb. Until the late 1940s, the favored method was race-restrictive covenants, a strategy carried out by individual homeowners but encouraged by the state. The HOLC, FHA, and California Supreme Court all supported the practice. The state finally rescinded its support in the U.S. Supreme Court case *Shelley v. Kraemer* (1948), which declared restrictive covenants unenforceable in the courts; by 1950, the FHA refused to grant loans on homes with racial covenants. Yet even this new legal mandate did not end the judicial story. The L.A. Realty Board and the California Real Estate Association brashly proposed a constitutional amendment to bypass the *Shelley* decision, while others tried to restore the status quo by encouraging signers of the old covenants to bring damage suits against those violating the covenants. A U.S. Supreme Court case that originated in California, *Barrows v. Jackson* (1953), finally outlawed these tactics, bringing an end to litigation over restrictive covenants.[59]

But law and everyday practice were very different things. Like many Americans across the country opposed to civil rights, South Gate residents found ways to circumvent the force of law on race. Local realtors were at the vanguard of resistance. They devised, codified, and strictly enforced a system for evading the *Shelley* decision. The South Gate Realty Board led the way for the entire southeast district. An incident in 1954 illustrates how it worked. The Stevens family, who lived one block below the South Gate border in Lynwood, decided to sell their home. They listed their property with realtor Henry Beddoe, a member of the South Gate Realty Board. Soon the Portugals, a Mexican family friendly with the Stevens, decided to buy it and commenced escrow negotiations. The Portugals and Stevens reached a verbal agreement sealing the transaction. When word got out that the Portugals were Mexican, neighbors sent a letter to the Realty Board demanding the sale be stopped. Immediately, other realtors brought customers around to see the property and the transaction was delayed. Merle Stevens, who insisted on his right to sell to the Portugals, was disgusted with the practice: "They were trying to substitute a buyer. . . . I thought they were stalling for time in hopes that the Portugals would get disgusted and not take the place."

Beddoe ultimately stood by the wishes of his client and sold the property to the Portugals. At this point, the South Gate Realty Board came down hard and fast. It fined both the buying and selling realtors $310.85 each, and denied Beddoe his commission. When Beddoe refused to pay the fine, he was expelled from the Realty Board. The board claimed he had violated Article 35 of the National Association of Real Estate Boards, which read: "A realtor should not be instrumental in introducing into a neighborhood a character of property or use which will clearly be detrimental to property values in a neighborhood."[60] The expulsion denied him access to the multiple listing service, an indispensable tool for realtors, and it tainted his professional reputation. A "whispering campaign" against him alleged that his true intention was to "open the gates to the Negroes." Through professional pressures like this, realtors maintained control over the local housing market and sustained the essence of racial covenants, long after their invalidation by the courts.[61]

The persistence of racial exclusion in South Gate's housing market, even after such practices were outlawed, was one sign of heightened racial concern after 1945. While this apprehension was not new, the *degree* of alarm was unprecedented. Housing, it turns out, was just one arena of white concern. It would reach full fruition in the white backlash against civil rights in Los Angeles.

LEVITTOWN WEST

The emergence of South Gate as a tidy, well-developed suburb aligned the community more closely with its postwar counterparts—the Levittowns and Lakewoods—than the gritty blue-collar suburbs of old. This was evident in the physical landscape, as well as the public's intensified aversion to industry in their midst. While there was some opposition to industry in the early years, the majority of residents seemed to welcome factories in the 1920s and 1930s, even if it meant turning their suburb into something quite less than a pastoral paradise. This changed by the 1950s. The heightened intolerance of mixed land use in the suburb, where homes and factories coexisted, strongly suggested that postwar residents desired a different kind of community. They preferred one that was clean, quiet, safe for children, and free of noxious industrial side effects. By the 1950s, their community standards had risen, and the meaning of suburban living had transformed in South Gate.

The physical landscape reflected this new priority. After the war, certain additions to the landscape signified the economic progress of the community and the shedding of earlier financial worries. South Gate established two municipal parks, one of them a 93-acre expanse of grassy fields and recreational facilities. It had lighted baseball diamonds, a lighted nine-hole golf course, an Olympic-sized swim stadium, a wading pool, tennis and badminton courts, a $100,000 girls' clubhouse, an auditorium, and plenty of shaded picnic tables. The suburb, which had grown to 7.5 square miles by 1961, also boasted a mature physical infrastructure: 125 miles of tree-lined streets, more than 3,700 streetlights, 115 miles of sewers, and 109 miles of water mains. Two hospitals sat within South Gate's borders. The local police force comprised eighty-five officers, while three fire stations housed sixty-five firefighters. The suburb now had the amenities of a well-developed community, comfortably distanced from the edge of poverty.[62]

Physically, South Gate was a much denser, more mature community. Using Sanborn fire insurance maps from 1955, we can take another imaginary tour of the suburb in the postwar years (see fig. 5-1 for the route of the "tour").[63] The differences are immediately striking. South Gate now looks developed and filled in, with few vacant lots in sight. Starting in the northwest section, we drive down Mountain View Avenue, a quiet residential street, and notice that homes sit on every lot, one after the other. The place is thoroughly built up. Mostly they are single-family homes, often with uniform setbacks, some looking very similar to others. A block west on Beechwood Avenue, we see multiple housing units on the larger lots: a bungalow court here, a duplex or triplex there. On the occasional deep, narrow lot, a cluster of three or four small units extends into the backyard, filling in the places where chicken coops and gardens once sat. As we near the Firestone plant, we notice the factory has expanded into a sprawling complex of buildings, with traffic coming and going. Along Long Beach Boulevard, new businesses line the roadway—restaurants, car sales lots, motels, "tourist courts," and "auto courts." Many of these cater to people passing through, or to people in town on business. In this section especially, we notice how the automobile permeates South Gate. The local factories produce them, the businesses sell them, the motels house their itinerant drivers. A few vacant lots remain along Long Beach Boulevard, reminding us of a time when open space defined this place.[64]

Moving south into Magnolia Park, the homes look even better. Along certain blocks, like Indiana Avenue, homes share the same design, suggesting that larger-scale builders made their mark in this section. On block after block, tidy homes sit next to one another in uniform rows, the same, small lawns in front. Every now and again, a triplex appears, then a home that looks like it's been expanded, an extra room or two added on. Along Missouri Avenue, we pass by another even row of homes, then come upon an open front yard that breaks the steady rhythm. We peer down the yard, and notice a modest home sitting at the back of the lot, a vestige of prewar owner-building. It stands out among the others.

As we move into Home Gardens, the housing quality declines. These dwellings are a little smaller, a little shabbier than the ones we've passed. Some are older, some look like owner-built affairs that have been spruced up, expanded, and brought forward to the front of the lot. There is less uniformity, although here and there a cluster of homes sit in even rows and share the same shape. Yet we also see a mishmash of homes sitting helter-skelter on their lots, some in the middle, some in the back. For the most part, the chickens and goats are gone, replaced by housing add-ons, duplexes, or play space for children. On some residential blocks, the long narrow lots are crammed with multifamily dwellings. Duplexes and triplexes abound. A few half-acre lots have six or eight units on them, some sitting next to single-family homes. California Avenue is South Gate's "apartment row," with one multifamily structure after another, some big, some small, a few single-family homes nestled in between. In Home Gardens overall, the biggest visible change is infilling. Below Tweedy Boulevard, the same patterns are evident: density, uniform setbacks, but diverse shapes of dwellings.

Next, we go along Firestone Boulevard and notice how fully built up it has become. As we near the eastern end of South Gate, the industries along the north side of the road have completely filled in the open spaces. Along Otis Street, the buildings of General Veneer Manufacturing spread along the entire block. Homes abut the factory's backside, revealing the close co-existence of homes and factories in this part of town, and one area where the expectations of residential peace conflict with industrial need. Farther down Firestone, the Pabco Products factory sprawls out, followed by the Rheem steel products factory, then a foundry, and the huge American Pipe & Construction facility. And north of these factories, just beyond South Gate's border, sits a Douglas Aircraft plant that produces insulation materials. Along Atlantic Avenue, in the unincorporated area just above South Gate, perhaps the most symbolic change is evident. On the land where chicken coops and hen houses once stood, trailer parks now abound. The pressing need for housing, acquired with money, has overshadowed all others. Land once devoted to self-provisioning and animal husbandry is now thoroughly devoted to human shelter. The ruralism of the area has given way to suburbia.

Despite remnants of modest, sometimes even dilapidated homes, South Gate overall has a look of order and harmony, of tidy homes with lawns, and clean commercial strips. The factories on the western and northeastern edges of town remind us that this is still a working-class suburb, but the rest of the community looks like every other postwar suburb. South Gate has become a different kind of place.

6   The Suburban Good Life Arrives

In October 1946, a temporal cusp between the stresses of World War II and the flush years of postwar America, South Gate leaders announced a contest. The city was seeking a "typical family" to ride on its Rose Parade float on New Year's Day 1947. This family would act out a scene of domestic bliss, enjoying the suburban good life in South Gate. The float itself, covered in flowers, depicted a typical South Gate backyard, complete with barbecue, backyard lawn, and the back end of a suburban home. The lucky family chosen would play this scene: dad cooking juicy steaks on the barbecue, mom setting the table for an outdoor meal, teenage daughter playing records, and two younger kids romping on a swing set in the backyard. "[A] real family having real fun together," declared the local editor. The float's title would be "I am an American."

The float committee sought an actual South Gate family to play the part, preferably one that looked good and fit certain demographic criteria. The family would consist of a father, a mother, a daughter between sixteen and eighteen "or who looks that age—an attractive girl who'll look super in a play suit," a prepubescent boy, and a cute little girl. Despite the committee's contention that such a family was "typical," it presented a contingency plan just in case: "should no real family be found

which meets with the qualifications, a 'composite' family will be made up."
In other words, if the typical family did not really exist, the committee
would assemble its own.[1]

In choosing this image to represent the town, South Gate's float committee drew on powerful cultural symbols of postwar America—the nuclear family, suburbia, middle-class comfort. No chickens or vegetable
patches in this idealized backyard—this was a family that had made it. The
float depicted essential elements of a national suburban myth emerging in
the postwar era. In the idealized suburb, the "traditional" nuclear family—
breadwinning father, homemaker mother, well-groomed children—lived
in a ranch home with a neat lawn, two-car garage, and bicycles and tricycles
lining the sidewalk. These symbols embodied the spirit of the postwar
age—family togetherness, material comfort, simple pleasures.

The suburban myth, in fact, became a defining element of postwar
American history. To be sure, suburbanization itself was hardly fiction. The
period 1945 through 1970 was a pinnacle in the history of suburbanization. In the 1950s, suburbs grew ten times faster than central cities, while
the nationwide suburban population jumped from 35.1 to 75.6 million
from 1950 to 1970. Postwar suburbs differed from earlier ones in their
architectural similarity, affordability to a broad cross section of home buyers, thoroughness of racial homogeneity, and the critical role of federal
aid.[2] The suburban trend touched off impassioned cultural debates, out of
which the suburban myth emerged. The myth referred not to the existence of suburbia—the trend was clear enough—but rather to the new
way of life that suburbia seemed to be spawning. The suburban myth had
both sunny and noir versions. Constructing the bright version were suburban boosters, advertisers, and the television industry, who portrayed
suburbia as the ultimate embodiment of the middle-class American dream.
The suburbs signified the continued possibility of upward mobility, expanding opportunity, rising standards of living and income, and the latest tech-
nologies of the good life. In the suburbs, young clean-cut families lived in
neat homes, with well-maintained yards, good schools, and friendly neighbors. This image aimed both to sell and celebrate the suburbs. Cultural
critics of the decade took a dimmer view, insisting that suburban living promoted conformity, excessive sociability, and unhealthy family life. Social
life bordered on the hyperactive, with intensive neighboring, visiting, and
membership in local organizations. In the suburbs, homogeneity reigned,
religious activity was intense, and everyone was a Republican. Despite the
family-centeredness of life, many suburban families were dysfunctional,
child-centered matriarchies, where fathers were largely absent. As a 1956
magazine article summed it up, "Suburbs have few of the opportunities for

individuality found in the big city. One moves there, buys the right car, keeps his lawn like his neighbor's, eats crunchy breakfast cereal and votes Republican."[3]

In these mythic portrayals, dominant themes of the era coalesced. Postwar abundance and affluence created the middle class that moved to the 'burbs. The Cold War, McCarthyism, and corporate cultures encouraged conformity. The desire for postwar "normalcy" and comfort in the atomic age revived domesticity. And a general spirit of consensus and political centrism allowed for thriving communities of homogeneous neighbors. Such a picture, of course, was too simple to be true. The fiction started at the broadest level. Portrayals of the 1950s as "the era of affluence, the zenith of family values, 'the proud decades,' the age of consensus, happy days" ignored the many complexities and conflicts of the decade. The experiences of poor whites, migrant farmers, and unemployed industrial workers defied stereotypes about affluence. The civil rights movement was a piercing challenge to political consensus. And cultural dissenters—from highbrow to lowbrow—contradicted the image of conformity and a domineering corporate ethos.[4] Within suburbs too the myth crumbled. Sociologists of the early 1960s found that suburbs contained a range of peoples and lifestyles, from middle to working class, liberal to conservative, native born to immigrant. Collectively, these studies argued against simplistic environmental determinism—suburbia did not shape people into bland conformists. Rather, people were agents in creating their own lifestyles in their respective suburbs.[5]

In postwar South Gate, elements of the myth rang true, others completely missed the mark. Yet the myth was perhaps most important not as a depiction of reality but rather as a community aspiration among homeowners, blue- and white-collar alike. The story of the Rose Parade float reflected this. The float committee envisioned a middle-class future for the suburb, where the suffering and struggle of earlier years would be wiped from memory. Yet the committee's contingency plan—to invent a composite family if need be—suggested a tacit recognition that a different reality existed in South Gate. The tensions between myth and reality in late 1946, as the suburb struggled to define itself to the world, portended themes in South Gate's social history in the generation to come. South Gate found itself torn between competing community identities: middle-class suburb versus working-class suburb on one level, city versus suburb on another. Some sought to make the sunny suburban myth a reality in South Gate by promoting an insulated community of homes and homeowners, protected from odious physical encroachments like expanding factories and garbage dumps, and from social threats like renters, broken families, and minorities. Their aspiration for the community reflected middle-class sensibilities.

Yet South Gate's postwar prosperity rested on an industrial, working-class base. The postwar years brought tremendous prosperity to South Gate, based on vigorous industrial growth. Local workers were earning more than ever, new unions protected their interests, and burgeoning cultural outlets allowed them to enjoy the good life. In many respects, they had become an *embourgeoised* working class, measured by their earning and spending power, making them exemplary suburbanites. Their rising status even helped break down older social barriers that had divided the town in earlier years, creating new areas of consensus between working families and merchants. Yet neither was South Gate completely united, socially, economically, or culturally. It remained a diverse community; middle-class and working-class culture coexisted, as did homeowners and tenants, housewives and working mothers, autoworkers and professionals, factories and homes. Hardly a bland, homogeneous suburb of identical homes and people, South Gate emerged as a community serving a range of human experiences and needs.

The denouement of the Rose Parade float story was one sign of things to come. The float committee narrowed the field to three families out of twenty-five entrants. "By a strange coincidence," noted the *South Gate*

Figure 6-1   South Gate's float in the 1947 Rose Parade depicted a scene of domestic suburban bliss and underscored the theme of Americanism. Photo courtesy of the South Gate Museum.

Press, "the fathers of all three families are electricians." The family chosen as "most typical" was the Braatens—father, mother, daughters Betty (age sixteen) and Carol (twelve), and son Gary (ten). Not only did they get to ride on the float, but they also won $1,200 worth of prizes donated by local merchants, including a five-piece bedroom set, a free room redecoration, an electric razor, a tune-up and brake job on the family car, kitchen appliances, a record player with albums by Benny Goodman and Frank Sinatra, a fishing rod, a bicycle, clothing, and a gift certificate from a local liquor store. Postwar abundance had dropped right in the lap of this upwardly mobile, blue-collar family. As it would for many local families, economic prosperity transformed the meaning of suburbia in South Gate.[6]

The Good War in Suburbia

World War II helped catalyze new social patterns and class relations in South Gate, setting off changes that reverberated well into the postwar era. The war had the paradoxical effect of introducing new cracks into the social structure while healing older fissures. Ultimately, it drew the community together in unprecedented ways.

The war's impact on population growth and housing was jolting and unsettling. As an important site of both defense production and military mobilization, Southern California attracted tremendous numbers of migrants. The numbers were staggering. In L.A. County, fully 25 percent of residents in 1944 had arrived since 1940. The overall county population jumped from 2.78 to 4.15 million from 1940 to 1950. South Gate received a hefty share of these migrants—both war workers and servicemen. By October 1946, the local population nearly doubled from that of 1940, jumping from 26,945 to 45,192. In adjacent Watts and southern Los Angeles, this same demographic momentum attracted thousands of African-American newcomers.[7]

The social implications of this population explosion touched many areas. For one, it instantly introduced a second generation of residents to the community. To some, it seemed South Gate had become a town of strangers. A local editor noted this in 1942: "there are too many of us in South Gate who don't know each other. Our city has grown so rapidly in recent years that we have scarcely had a chance to keep acquainted with even our older friends." Many residents hardly recognized new streets and subdivisions in the community.[8]

The population boom also began complicating South Gate's community identity. As its size shot upward, many began referring to South Gate as a city in its own right, and no longer a suburb. Local leaders proudly noted in 1946 that South Gate ranked as the sixth-largest city in L.A. County. By the early 1950s, the masthead of the *South Gate Press* read, "A good city in which to live, work," while a publicity pamphlet in 1960 called South Gate "The City of Opportunity." It was a place to "live, work, play, shop." No longer an appendage of Los Angeles, it sold itself as a self-contained city where one's entire life could be lived. The sounding of this theme, in fact, raised fundamental questions about the nature of South Gate's postwar identity. Although leaders were quick to call it a city, they also boasted of South Gate's wholesome family and community life. In their minds, South Gate was a city functionally but a suburb socially. It would offer urban amenities such as factories and jobs, but it would soften this urbanism with suburban advantages like homeownership, parks, clubs, and good schools. The tension between an urban and suburban identity, in fact, reappeared intermittently as the town resisted the more odious social repercussions of local urbanization, broadly defined as increasing social diversity.[9]

One such repercussion was the increase in tenancy in South Gate. As the housing shortage reached epidemic proportions during the war, with servicemen and defense workers desperately seeking shelter, any and all solutions were pursued. By 1944, the housing need in South Gate was intense, with four times as many people seeking homes as there were rental listings. The Troxel family was typical. With the husband away serving in the Coast Guard, the wife, a defense worker, and their four-year-old daughter found themselves in desperate need of housing when the home they were renting was sold. "We have no relatives to take us in," Mrs. Troxel worried. "I don't know what I will do if we can't find a place. I have my own furniture and can pay good rent. Can anybody help us?" The "Defense Bulletin Board," a wartime column in the local newspaper, regularly ran notices asking residents to shelter homeless servicemen, defense workers, and their families. Locals were encouraged to add rental rooms onto existing homes, spruce up empty bedrooms or a garage to rent, or rent out empty property. It was the patriotic duty of all citizens to help solve this crisis, grown so acute that it was "holding back the war effort in this community." As the chair of the L.A. County War Housing Committee put it, "During the war an overall generalized view based on generosity and the patriotic desire for victory should be adopted by property owners." The overarching message here was to rent, rent, rent.[10]

Couched in these terms, tenancy and other alternatives to single-family homeownership became socially acceptable, at least temporarily. Not only was the letting of rooms welcomed, but alternative housing forms began appearing in South Gate—motels, hostels, apartments, and even emergency public housing. In the spring of 1946, the town eagerly awaited the arrival of eleven prefabricated dwellings—shipped from Washington State—to house fifty veteran families under jurisdiction of the federal public housing authority. The *South Gate Press* ran a compelling story about a young couple awaiting this shelter. For months, they had been living in a single room but had been evicted just hours before their baby was born. The couple and their five-day-old baby became the first to move into the new single-room apartments when they finally opened in October. As long as the dwellers were white families contributing to the war effort, local public housing was accepted as a temporary necessity. Under better circumstances, they would have been typical South Gate homeowners, but the housing crisis prevented them from achieving this status. In this way, the war opened the door to tenancy in South Gate. While local approval hinged on the temporary, emergency nature of conditions, tenancy ultimately had real staying power. Apartments and renters would become permanent local fixtures, representing a diversifying force and a cause for alarm among those seeking a traditional suburban identity for South Gate.[11]

Similarly, women's wartime entry into the paid workforce represented a phenomenon temporarily accepted in the name of patriotism, but met with ambivalence at war's end. During the war, South Gate women found work in nearly all sectors of the job market, from clerical to manufacturing, following on both metropolitan and national trends. A good number worked in factories converted for defense, such as Firestone in South Gate and Vultee Aircraft in nearby Downey. The community endorsed this trend in several ways. At South Gate High School, evening classes offered training for women in sheet metal, general shop, general mathematics, mechanical drafting, and blueprint reading. The local YWCA organized recreation classes and dinners for young women entering defense work, to help them forge social links and occupy their spare time. When women defense workers decried the lack of child-care facilities, the community responded by opening a new public nursery school and offering supervision at public playgrounds from 10 A.M. to 6 P.M. every day in the summers. These efforts, although they fell short of need, reflected public acceptance of working women as part of the defense emergency. Like the housing crisis, the labor crisis opened a door to change that did not readily close when the war ended. Many South Gate women remained in the paid workforce, their numbers climbing steadily in the postwar era. By 1960, fully 41 percent of local women worked outside the home, nearly twice the 1940 rate.[12]

Wartime growth and defense mobilization thus ushered in unprecedented social diversity, evident in the new presence of renters, working women, and, in neighboring towns, people of color. South Gate's earlier suburban identity—so clearly marked by homeownership and traditional family structures—was challenged by these changes. Yet during the war, few people objected. Instead, an overwhelming sense of sacrifice and patriotism prompted residents to accept and even encourage these changes as temporary necessities.[13]

At the same time the war seemed to be diversifying the texture of local life, it also provided new avenues for social solidarity. As it did in neighborhoods nationwide, World War II pulled South Gate together in unprecedented ways. Citizens of all classes and ages united behind the war effort, signing up for military duty, taking jobs in defense plants, rolling bandages for the Red Cross, collecting newspapers and kitchen grease for recycling, buying war bonds, aiding local civil defense, and willingly rationing supplies. Local newspapers ran poignant stories of South Gate boys serving in the military, listing their accomplishments and tragedies alike, putting the face of home on the war. The result was an outpouring of voluntarism. In the process, timeworn class barriers between workers and businessmen began to crumble, and a new sense of community emerged.

South Gate's home front effort was truly impressive. As individuals, some residents helped by renting out a spare bedroom to defense workers, donating blood, riding a bicycle to the grocery store to conserve gas, or volunteering as air-raid wardens or block mothers. Other residents served through organizations. Women's groups were especially active, often assuming leadership roles. Members of the South Gate Woman's Club performed numerous service activities, including rolling bandages for the Red Cross, knitting for Army and Navy garments, plane spotting, serving as block and air wardens, and helping to run blood drives. PTA and YWCA members formed Red Cross sewing units, organized social activities for defense workers, and served as USO hostesses. Several new women's groups coalesced during the war. The Junior Woman's Club was established in 1944 for the young wives of soldiers. The Mrs. G.I. Club formed a year later, also for the spouses of servicemen; they held dinner parties and organized outings to the Pike in Long Beach, restaurants, and shows. Other women took more direct action to help the war effort by joining the WAVES and WACS. "Tojo likes bridge!" proclaimed a local WACS recruitment ad in 1944. "American bridge—matinees, and afternoon naps. Tojo's fond of anything that keeps American women out of the war." In South Gate, the war brought women of all classes together in defense-oriented voluntarism, breaking down older social barriers and providing new means of public participation for working-class women. Among block mothers and PTA members aiding in defense, for example, there were twice as many from blue-collar households as from white-collar ones.[14]

Children's groups also organized for the war effort. Boy Scout troops held book and newspaper drives; Camp Fire Girls volunteered with the Red Cross, collected magazines for the USO, and filled defense stamp books; and local Jewish children participated in "Self Denial Month," donating one month's spending money to Jewish victims of Nazism in Europe. About 4,000 local youth volunteered for defense work through the Youth Defense Council. Adult organizations mobilized as well: the Kiwanis, Moose Lodge, businessmen's groups, and churches. Workers at Vultee aircraft in nearby Downey donated one Sunday of labor to the war effort. Newly formed defense-oriented organizations spearheaded many of these efforts, such as the Victory Committee, the South Gate Defense Council, and the merchant-dominated Community Chest.[15]

Perhaps the most famous and creative home front project was Hospitality House, a sort of suburban rendition of the USO. A group of local residents, spearheaded by Mrs. Margaret Cargill, converted a suburban home into an "open house" for servicemen who were welcome to drop in for a meal, friendly socializing, and even a place to sleep. The kitchen was always stocked with fresh homemade cookies, cakes, milk, and sodas, and hostesses on duty would prepare "warm, wholesome meals at the drop of a hint." Specially screened "junior hostesses," volunteers from the community, danced with servicemen on Saturday nights. The suburban homey feel of the place struck broadcaster Stu Wilson, who described it to his L.A. listeners in 1943:

> While the U.S.O. and other organizations were opening recreation centers, Mrs. Cargill realized that their efforts would be directed to the thickly populated areas in Los Angeles and Hollywood. So, she started out to do something for her community. . . . [H]ere's the part that I get a kick out of— instead of some imposing edifice of brick and steel, or, some abandoned store building, South Gate's Hospitality House is just exactly that . . . a five-room residence—and exact counterpart of the home left behind by 95 percent of the service men. Out in the kitchen is a 10-foot refrigerator, and the boys are encouraged to "raid" the icebox, just the way they did in their own homes.
>
> As for the rest of the house . . . the living room is furnished like the average American home . . . many boys coming in for the first time, say "Whose home is this—who lives here?" . . . The middle bedroom is a den where the boys can write, play cards, or stretch out on the day bed and sleep. The other bedroom is unusually large and contains a ping-pong table.

Free to all servicemen, Hospitality House quickly caught on, drawing an average 1,600 visitors per month and more than 3,000 during peak months. By the time it closed in 1946, 200,000 people had passed through its doors.[16]

Hospitality House attracted support from all sectors of South Gate—service clubs, labor unions, churches, businesses, and individuals—displaying an unprecedented level of class-transcending unity in South Gate. The house was wholly dependent on volunteers, who hailed from a range of occupations. The board of directors of the house included an escrow clerk, a doctor, a court clerk, and a journalist, as well as the wives of a railway employee, a supervisor, an autoworker, two oil workers, a machine shop foreman, a collector, a grocer, and a chemist. Financial donors were equally diverse. The city council paid rent on the house, local markets donated food and gave discounts on supplies, and monetary contributions came from a girls' club, the Kiwanis Club, a CIO union, the Odd Fellows, and several churches, businesses, and industries.[17]

At the war's end, veterans groups helped maintain the momentum of community solidarity forged during the war. In South Gate, veterans constituted fully 42.6 percent of the adult male population by 1960.[18] Many gravitated to veterans groups that proliferated in postwar South Gate, including two American Legion posts, a ladies' auxiliary of the Legion, a Veterans of Foreign Wars post and auxiliary, the Disabled American Veterans, and the American Veterans Committee. In 1957, the American Legion broke membership records both nationally and locally; one South Gate post alone boasted 334 members. Perhaps more than any other service organization, the veterans groups attracted a broad cross section of members. For example, VFW commanders in these years included a former CIO official and a grocer, while other officers included skilled factory workers, office workers, and businessmen. And the VFW Auxiliary president in the mid-1950s was the wife of a truck driver. Recalled one American Legionnaire of his group's membership, "Some were mechanics, some worked for General Motors, some of them worked for Firestone, and some of them worked downtown." Merchants certainly did not dominate these groups, as they did other service organizations in South Gate. Instead, they shared leadership posts with members of the working class.[19]

Veterans forged connections with traditional civic leaders in South Gate—the merchants—and soon began performing the type of service work earlier left to merchant organizations. In 1946, veterans groups and the Chamber of Commerce joined forces to organize the first annual Fourth of July celebration to honor local servicemen. Merchant-dominated civic groups, like the Kiwanis and Rotarians, frequently invited veterans as speakers. By the late 1940s, veterans groups moved into broader community affairs—some social, others political, a few economic. Their presence was ubiquitous and diverse. For example, the VFW began hosting weekly dances in 1946 and helped organize

community parades, while the American Veterans Committee sponsored a local beauty pageant. In the economic realm, veterans were a vocal presence on
the picket line during the GM strike in 1945–46. The same month that strike
ended, members of the South Gate VFW picketed Huntington Park city hall
when two vets were denied permits to operate cabs.[20]

By the 1950s, veterans groups had shifted their focus away from economic concerns to political ones, particularly the crusade against communism. Reviving the political moderation first expressed locally in the
cooperatives of the 1930s, which stressed self-help, hard work, and Americanism, veterans groups infused this position with a new urgency demanded by the Cold War. In doing so, they aligned locally with groups like
the Kiwanis and Rotarians, nationally with working-class citadels like the
Democratic Party and UAW leadership, and most broadly with federal definitions of patriotism. They helped define the contours of a postwar working-class political culture.[21]

Veterans and merchant groups—often in tandem—spearheaded local
anticommunist activity in the postwar era. The Kiwanis and Rotary clubs
frequently hosted speakers—sometimes veteran leaders—who attacked
communism and promoted the "American way of life." The Kiwanis brought
religion into the anticommunist crusade, running large ads in the 1950s
that urged residents to attend church as a way of reinforcing American
strength and freedom. An ad sponsored by forty local businesses asked,
"Are you shutting your child behind an IRON CURTAIN? It is every child's
right to share in the religious heritage of our nation." For its part, the VFW
launched a campaign urging residents to sign petitions asking Congress to
outlaw the Communist Party in the United States. And in perhaps the most
public effort to define local civic culture in the postwar years, the South
Gate VFW organized the first annual Loyalty Day Parade in 1955, held on
May 1 to counter the Communist-inspired May Day holiday. Fifty local
groups participated, including the Kiwanis and Lions clubs, National Guard
units, patriotic groups such as the Native Sons of the Golden West, service
organizations, fraternal lodges, drill teams, Cub Scouts, bands, and of course
veterans groups. Although labor unions were notably absent—perhaps too
closely associated in the public mind with May Day—working people
found avenues of participation through these other groups.[22] Even in a
blue-collar town like South Gate, the voice of organized labor was scarcely
audible in public life, drowned out as it was by fierce anticommunist sentiment. Instead, civic life in the 1950s was an amalgamation of patriotism,
Americanism, Christianity, and the memory of war as defined by the many
veterans who inhabited the homes of this postwar suburb.[23]

THE SHIFTING TERRAIN OF CLASS IN POSTWAR SUBURBIA

In the prewar to postwar transition, the meaning of class in South Gate began to change. The working-class desperation that so powerfully defined
prewar South Gate dissolved into a new sense of security. As blue-collar
families enjoyed the fruits of postwar prosperity, older conflicts between
wage earners and merchants subsided, the line between blue- and white-
collar blurred, and a social convergence of all property owners emerged.
These processes ultimately reconstructed the character of the suburb.

Both national and metropolitan developments undergirded this transformation. First and most importantly, the federal government impacted
the lives of working people in unprecedented ways, with sometimes paradoxical implications for class identities. Expanded in scope and power since
the New Deal, the federal government promised security not only interna-
tionally but also domestically. Franklin Roosevelt's programs promised
white Americans "'social security,' the security of private homeownership,
and the security of stable, unionized well-paid employment." Postwar defense spending sustained the promise, fortifying the federal government's
role as the primary safety net for working families. By the late 1940s and
1950s, most white Americans possessed a sense of entitlement to programs
that ensured old-age security, a home, a job, and a union. For white working-class, homeowning families, the Federal Housing Administration and
GI Bill were especially important. They provided new means toward home
acquisition and education, offering economic stability and potential upward
mobility to working-class families. The citizens of South Gate—white and
working class—were frequent beneficiaries of such programs. The same
programs also excluded significant groups—racial minorities, the chroni-
cally unemployed, and unmarried mothers, among others—reinforcing social schisms that widened in the postwar era.[24]

While the federal government began easing the pressing survival problems of many working families, it also gave workers a stronger voice in the
workplace by strengthening unionism. But because the state was also providing economic security outside the workplace, the nature of labor's goals
began to change. As Steve Fraser has written, "Somehow the political
chemistry of the New Deal worked a double transformation: the ascendancy of labor and the eclipse of the 'labor question.'" Thus, at the same
time that industrial unionism was "legalized and federalized" under the
Wagner Act (and the Fair Labor Standards Act of 1938), labor's objective
shifted from "workers' control" to "full employment" and concerns with
the "American Standard of Living." Labor's older struggle over power and
property was superceded by the demand for a bigger piece of the capitalist

pie, through issues like wages and benefits. Although this shift occurred most clearly at the national levels of union leadership, it reverberated down to the rank and file. This shift reflected a transformation not only of labor but also of liberalism more broadly, which was loosening its engagement with the labor question and turning increasingly to the problems of race.[25]

At the metropolitan level, Los Angeles's remarkable economic upsurge in the postwar era also set the stage for shifting class identities in two ways. First, Los Angeles was thriving as a center of new high-tech defense industries and as a destination of the plant relocations depleting older industrial cities like Detroit and Pittsburgh, where signs of deindustrialization were already evident. For Los Angeles, this was a flush period of expansion. Partly by virtue of this regional advantage, South Gaters could enjoy the full bounty of America's postwar prosperity. They resided in the heart of the expanding L.A. industrial belt, fattened by federal largesse. This insulated Los Angeles's white working-class somewhat from the kinds of pressures bearing down on factory workers in older industrial cities, where already by the 1950s unions mobilized to resist runaway plants and otherwise fought to protect their threatened economic status from the forces of nascent economic restructuring. It is true that in the 1950s and 1960s, some of the pressures afflicting industrial labor in the East, like automation, began to affect Los Angeles workers. Yet for the time being they were spared the worst threat of all: plant closures. There were plenty of jobs to go around as factories continued to proliferate both regionally and locally. This context of economic expansion allowed white working-class residents in South Gate and neighboring suburbs to experience the so-called embourgeoisement that propelled them toward the middle-class. The collective upward mobility of South Gate residents was a sign of this, as was the changing nature of the suburb itself.[26]

A second metropolitan factor was the demise of the open shop in Los Angeles, beginning in the mid-1930s. With the aid of federal policy and rise of the CIO, some union organizing took place in Los Angeles in the 1930s, especially in the garment trades, the railway, auto, steel, rubber, and aircraft industries, and among retail clerks. But major progress was yet to come. L.A. unions continued to battle the forces of antilabor well into the 1930s, as several powerful organizations launched new open-shop drives and offset the advantages labor was making through federal initiative. By the end of 1939, L.A. unions still lay on the cusp of full-fledged expansion. The massive industrial surge spurred by World War II was the key turning point, bringing unionism to Los Angeles once and for all. Immediately after the war, the largest strikes took place, mirroring national events.[27] South Gate workers asserted their fair share of labor militance in the 1940s and

1950s, in demands for wages and benefits commensurate with the postwar American standard of living.

As South Gate's working class began enjoying the benefits of the "security state," the character of working-class suburbia changed. The first sign of this was a shift from the "use value" to "commodity value" of property. Older practices like owner-building and self-provisioning declined, replaced by home purchasing and purely residential, nonproductive uses of property. Backyard gardens and small livestock gave way to manicured lawns and domestic pets. The change occurred throughout the 1940s, with the war representing a significant transition stage. On the one hand, food, material, and labor shortages during the war impelled citizens to rely on homegrown foods and homemade shelter. To aid the war effort, residents were encouraged to grow victory gardens for home consumption, and to renovate and expand their homes for rental.[28] On the other hand, this was a different kind of sweat equity at work, as a new suburban generation engaged in these practices for the first time. Residents now had to be taught skills that had once been timeworn strategies for survival. During the war, nurseries and the high school offered classes on growing victory gardens, canning, and raising small livestock—a first for the community. Another sign of change was a new assumption that sweat expended in wartime homebuilding was far from a survival tactic—it had become a patriotic means for profit. "It's the patriotic duty of every American who owns suitable old property to fix it up for rent," read a 1942 ad. "Repair! Redecorate! Remodel! Make your home provide good living quarters for some of Uncle Sam's defense workers—better living for your own family—and an income!" Some residents heeded the call and modified their properties— sometimes haphazardly and without permits. The signs were clear, however, that the underlying motivations had changed. Self-building and self-provisioning had become less about survival and class-based need and more about patriotism, conservation, and even revenue (see fig. 6-2). And they were temporary. Once the war ended, such public encouragement of "homemade" practices ceased, and residents were urged to show good citizenship by buying locally and behaving as good American consumers.[29]

By the late 1940s and 1950s, older vestiges of working-class suburbia began to fade. The role of animals in South Gate was an excellent symbol— they moved up in status from meat to pets. Instead of advice columns on poultry and rabbit raising, the newspapers now ran stories on pet shows, pigeon races, and a dog obedience club. The South Gate Dog Drill Team was a regular participant in parades, while dog training classes and cat shows had become local fixtures. Local retail establishments reflected the trend as well. By the 1950s, feed stores gave way to pet shops, veterinarians, and poultry

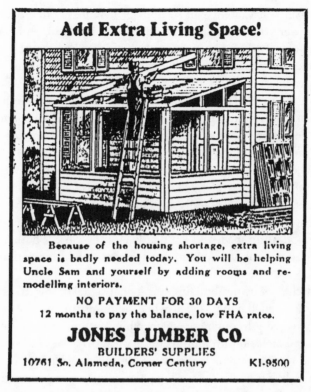

Figure 6-2   A 1942 lumber advertisement encouraged residents to build onto homes to ease the
wartime housing shortage. In this new context, self-building practices shifted from
representing a means of survival to becoming a means for profit. *South Gate Press,* June 11,
1942.

markets. The fate of the Magner business was telling: it transformed from a
coal and chicken feed store to a moving and storage company. The change in
the status of local animals was finally codified into law in 1962, when the
ordinance on backyard livestock reduced the allowable number of chickens
or rabbits from fifty to ten.[30]

Gardens likewise shifted from productive to decorative in character. In
the 1950s, local garden societies proliferated. They hosted annual garden
shows at the municipal auditorium, with horticulture classes and flower
and plant displays. The increase in lawnmower companies and nurseries
for lawn and garden care also attested to the change; the latter jumped from
two in 1930 to nine in 1951. Yards had become sites of rest and relaxation,
barbecues and lawns, calla lilies and hydrangeas. They took on the middle-
class suburban function of a decorative barrier to the outside world, denot-

ing suburban respectability. In sections of new mass-produced housing, backyards were often too small for much activity at all, eliminating the possibility of self-provisioning due to lack of space. A migrant from Oklahoma, looking over such identical homes in the nearby working-class suburb of Lawndale, noted this problem. "You'd have to be right sober to find your home if you lived on this here street. I'd like to buy one of them there houses, but they're too close together. Roosevelt ought to look into what they're a'doin'. We'uns from Oklahoma has got to have room for chickens, a garden, and a rabbit hutch or two after this war's over." Such spacious suburban homesteads would be harder and harder to find after the war. The tight housing market accelerated the trend, as backyards became places to expand housing into multifamily dwellings. The older productive use value of suburban backyards had given way to their commodity value as real estate. The local editor made this eminently clear in 1963: "South Gate's lots have become far too valuable to use for crops—with or without fertilizer!"[31]

The decline of owner-building was a final signal of the change. As detailed earlier, self-building faded while home purchases and apartment rentals increased. Although homeownership continued to represent a sign of status and inclusion in South Gate, it was now achieved through purchase. The relationship of homeownership to class identity is a complex one. Some scholars have suggested that the status of homeownership per se signified middle-class status in the postwar era. "[H]omeowning," writes Barbara Kelly, "took on a greater relative value in defining class [in the postwar era], outweighing the traditional standards of education and occupation, background and wealth as measures of social standing." As more working-class Americans joined the ranks of homeowners with the help of the FHA and GI Bill, they increasingly "self-identified with the needs and values of the prewar middle class."[32] Yet as the longer history of South Gate shows, homeownership in and of itself did not make residents middle class. Workers had been homeowners all along. What *did* change for working people in the postwar era were the means to achieving homeownership. With the help of federal programs, owner-building gave way to mortgages. South Gate families had broken free from a reliance on sweat equity, now buying homes rather than jerry-building them. Local housing had become commodified, a sign that working people were fully enmeshed in the wage-based economy, with less of a need to skimp and scrounge. The increased purchasing power of blue-collar suburbanites, albeit with federal underwriting, was a more important signifier of "middle-classness" than homeownership per se. The working-class suburb had transformed in meaning:

no longer was it a site of domestic production for the attainment of family security. Homes became purely residential in function.[33]

Housing in postwar South Gate served to blur distinctions between white- and blue-collar residents. As homes appreciated in value and new homes were increasingly standardized and uniform in appearance, housing began exerting a leveling effect among residents. D. J. Waldie observed as much during his childhood in nearby Lakewood. As he recalled, "There was no obvious way to tell a factory worker from a business owner or a professional man when I grew up. Every house on my block looked much the same." While South Gate was not a master-planned suburb like Lakewood, it did have its share of mass-produced housing after the war with similar effects.[34]

The decline of older working-class suburban practices marked an important change in South Gate, signaling an end to the period of working-class desperation and the emergence of working-class prosperity. Residents shed earlier habits of self-provisioning and resistance to wage dependence, and entered fully into America's postwar pecuniary culture, based on secure wages, purchasing power, and avid consumption. The postwar affluence so celebrated in the folklore of 1950s America was a reality in South Gate. These working-class families achieved a level of security that had so painfully eluded them in earlier years, allowing them to move beyond sheer survival to comfort and even affluence.

Signs of the change were everywhere. South Gate experienced a sort of collective upward mobility after the war, peaking around 1950. Relative home values rose, as did income and education levels. Data on median home values and income revealed that South Gate surpassed most other working-class suburbs by 1950, while approaching parity with middle-class communities like Glendale and South Pasadena. This was a reflection of higher wages, job stability, and strong unions to protect these gains. As local resident and union leader Virgil Collins put it, residents "made above the average because they were union. . . . They could buy their home, they could afford a car, and afford some of the niceties of life." The increase in white-collar workers and two-income households also helped push up these measures.[35]

Education was another marker of upward drift. By the 1950s, the level of interest in college among South Gate citizens had visibly increased. The principal of South Gate High School recognized the change, noting that the number of local graduates who went on to college jumped from 61 percent in 1941 to more than 85 percent in 1950. For the first time, the South Gate newspaper ran regular stories about local college alumni club meetings, col lege advisement at South Gate High, and local youth graduating from area universities like USC. The Firestone plant even joined in, offering college scholarships for the children of employees. But the biggest impetus to college enrollments was the GI Bill, instrumental in opening the door to higher learning to the broad cross section of veterans in the population.[36]

South Gate's retail sector also illustrated increasing affluence. A host of businesses opened in the 1950s, hawking luxury items and services aimed at customers with disposable incomes. Appearing for the first time by 1951 were interior decorators, jewelers, masseuses, party supply stores, photographic portrait studios, and an antiques dealer. Businesses multiplying faster than the rate of population included furniture stores, gift shops, music studios, painters and decorators, and sporting goods stores. In the early 1950s, South Gate also saw a tremendous proliferation of chiropractors and therapy salons aimed at women, offering massage, corrective diet counseling, "electro-therapy," and herbal healing. Sandra's Slenderizing Salon in Huntington Park, which advertised in South Gate, provided hair removal, cosmetics, and "Howard Cabinet baths."[37]

Ironically, although the retail sector was becoming more refined, many of South Gate's merchants remained stagnant. Ed Greenspan, owner of a men's apparel store in South Gate, noted the trend. After the war, he recollected, many of the merchants were farm kids with a high school education. While everyone else was going to college, especially on the GI Bill, the merchants were staying behind to tend their stores, especially the family-owned businesses. The same pattern appeared in nearby Lawndale. An observer there noted in 1944 that owners of "small business concerns . . . worked for less than the defense worker's wage." The static position of merchants, juxtaposed against the rising status of wage earners, suggests a social leveling occurred among these groups.[38]

As they became more prosperous, South Gate's workers began assuming a place in the suburb's civic and organizational life. For example, at the South Gate Silver Jubilee in 1948, a citywide celebration of the town's twenty-fifth anniversary, the master of ceremonies was George Roberts, a local CIO leader. Dale Lewis, a railway worker and union activist, served as head of the South Gate Civic Club in 1945, as leader of the popular South Gate Junior Athletic Association in the mid-1950s, and as a board member of the Welfare Federation of Los Angeles. Two men with working-class occupations—a tool and die maker and a postal clerk—were elected to the city council in the 1950s. And by the mid-1960s, Virgil Collins, an autoworker and president of UAW Local 216 at GM, served on the South Gate Civil Service and Planning Commission.[39]

Although the blue-collar residents of South Gate were becoming more affluent and active in civic life, evidence remained of the community's working-class character. The most obvious sign of this was the tremendous presence of factories in South Gate, numbering 245 in the mid-1950s and exceeding 300 by the early 1960s. Certain businesses also reflected a working-class orientation. South Gate had its fair share of liquor stores, with twenty of them by 1951.[40] It was also home to a bail bondsman, two pawnbrokers, and six secondhand stores. Some recreational outlets reflected working-class tastes as well, including three pool halls, an illicit pinball gambling operation, a wrestling arena, and a motor speedway. Certain bars, stores, and restaurants also catered to workers. In 1947, the new proprietor of the Back Door Café, located across the street from the GM factory, assured patrons that "the place will remain strictly union. . . . Lunches will still be 75 cents." And the Shopping Basket Market helped the local autoworkers union distribute food, through its welfare fund, to disabled workers. Pockets of poverty also persisted in South Gate. Organizations like the Rotary Club and YMCA held fund-raisers to aid needy children in the community, the clearest sign yet of economic diversity in the suburb.[41]

In the early 1960s Shirley Nauman, a USC master's student, studied the social complexity of South Gate. Characterizing South Gate as "a close-knit community with a small-town atmosphere," she observed, "The economic status of the citizens is considered to be middle class and upper-middle class." South Gate remained first and foremost a suburb of homeowners. These were the "conservative and stable citizens," spanning the occupational gamut from factory worker to professional but united by their common status as homeowners. Yet Nauman also noted the emerging presence of tenants, signifying a new level of social diversity: "a transient group has been increasing in size since multiple housing units began to appear a few years ago." The coexistence in South Gate of a middle-class suburban aura with blue-collar homeowners and renters defined the social identity of postwar South Gate—a sort of middle-ground community that defied suburban stereotypes. Working-class families were living out the middle-class suburban dream at home, while drawing paychecks from factories around the area. Their identity, in a sense, transcended traditional class boundaries, allowing for new social alliances with groups like the merchants. D. J. Waldie observed this in nearby Lakewood: "The houses never were middle class, nor were the people living in them. They became altogether something else."[42] In South Gate, this process of "becoming something else"— and the resulting tensions between middle-class images and working-class needs—shaped much of the postwar social history of the suburb.

STRIKE!

The community's first experience with a major labor protest—the GM strike of 1945–46—offers a good illustration of the rising aspirations among blue-collar families and of the postwar convergence between workers and merchants in South Gate. In a climate of emerging economic comfort and security, this strike illustrated the merchants' sober recognition of workers' rising strength both as workers and consumers. Although strike negotiations largely occurred at the national level, the local reactions to the strike exposed the shifting terrain of social and class relations in South Gate.

The story of the national strike against GM is well-known. With the lifting of the wartime no-strike pledge in 1945, the pent-up demands of labor unleashed a flurry of strikes nationwide. Walter Reuther, head of the United Automobile Workers, demanded a 30-percent wage increase from GM. The union not only believed that take-home pay would drop once the war ended and the company returned to the forty-hour week, but it felt GM possessed the corporate wealth to afford this wage increase without raising the price of cars. Reuther boldly demanded that GM open its books to prove this; the company refused, and nearly 200,000 workers walked off the job in November 1945, including 1,100 in South Gate.[43] The strike dragged on in the face of arbitration stalemates in Detroit and Washington, D.C. After 120 days of striking, both sides finally agreed in late March 1946 to a 18.5-cent per hour increase, a disappointment to most in the UAW. Not only did GM never have to open its books, but the company stubbornly refused to link wage increases to price stability. Workers in South Gate held out an extra 13 days to settle certain local issues, focused mainly on working conditions and union grievance procedures.[44]

In South Gate, perceptions of and responses to this strike revealed a new community dynamic. Bolstered by the newly powerful UAW-CIO, local autoworkers emerged in 1945 with an unprecedented degree of economic clout, a fact not lost on many merchants. As a result, a sense of interdependence between these groups developed during the strike. From the community's perspective, this strike was much more about purchasing power than corporate profiteering. In local discourse, labor emphasized the wage issue more than the union's desire to pull corporate pricing policy into the realm of collective bargaining. Purchasing power would directly impact the community, a perception reflecting the suburb's ongoing shift from a sweat-based to a cash-based orientation. To workers and merchants, this strike was about consumption more than production.

To local autoworkers, the strike's aim was to bolster their earning power.

With self-provisioning largely a thing of the past, the union had become another source—along with the federal government—of economic security for families. With their power to demand a good wage and their welfare fund for disabled workers, unions became a new safety net. During the strike, UAW Local 216 in South Gate explained how GM policy undercut this security: "Pay was cut $13.08 per week for the average G.M. worker when the work week was reduced to 40 hours. A pay reduction from $56.68 to $43.30—the average worker simply could not live on the reduced check after taxes, bonds and insurance were deducted. He had to have more money or use up his savings to support his family and himself at today's high prices. Thirteen dollars a week meant the difference between living and slow starvation. G.M. refused to budge so he struck."[45]

Yet autoworkers also expected more than a mere survival wage. They sought to participate fully in the booming postwar economy as active consumers. At the least, they believed, they were entitled to afford the products they produced, a view management did not necessarily share. One UAW leader relayed an exchange between South Gate GM plant manager H. L. Clark and union leaders over this very point: "The [union] committee stated they were interested in the wellfare [sic] of the men and also their purchasing power so as to enable them to buy the products they produced. Mr. Clark said that the new cars which were being built in this plant were not made for the men that were building them here as they were not in the upper class to buy these cars. That they were in the class of people who should buy these cars when they were three or four years old, in other words they were used car buyers only."[46] To South Gate autoworkers with their rising aspirations, the epithet "used car buyer" stung like a slap in the face. With class status increasingly divorced from workplace identities and rooted in the neighborhood, to question one's ability to buy represented the ultimate insult.[47]

The strikers especially emphasized the issue of consumption when appealing to the community for support. This was a logical approach since the buying power of the strikers had a direct impact on the local economy. In January 1946, Local 216 sent a letter to 2,000 "business and professional men in South Gate, Lynwood, Maywood, Huntington Park and Bell," which read, "the G.M. strikers are fighting the battle of the whole American people in their struggle to compel mass production employers to raise wages and build up purchasing power for full production, full employment, and full consumption. . . . This increased purchasing power will be spent in this area. We urge you to support our strike and to let General Motors know of your sympathy with our case, that you agree that $13.08 a week more in our pay envelopes is $13.08 more put into the business life of this area."[48] The union used the language of consumption and a promise of loyal patronage, which translated the conflicts of the workplace into terms that resonated communitywide, particularly with the merchants. This strike was about more than just the paychecks of individual autoworkers— it concerned the economic strength of the entire community.[49]

Most merchants recognized their interdependence with the strikers. As much as they might disagree with the politics and even concept of union- ism, they realized their own livelihoods depended on the purchasing power of these potential customers. Their responses to the strike, thus, aimed to avoid friction with the autoworkers. Merchant reaction ranged from im- partial to supportive. As union man Virgil Collins recalled, the real estate agents and proprietors who sat on the city council remained neutral on the strike, even though they were "very conservative." "They stayed out of it because most of them were real estate agents. They was looking down the road, they were no dummies. Hell these guys were thinking, 'I'll be selling them a home. I don't want to make any of them mad.'" This reflected broader community sentiment, as Collins recollected. "[The community] supported us to the extent that they didn't make any big to-do about it— 'gosh you should get this thing settled so you can get back to work, we need you people working.' They supported us to the extent that they stayed out of it." Under the influence of the merchant-led city council, the local police too refrained from interfering with the pickets or provoking violence.[50]

Some merchants were more than neutral—they actively supported the strikers. In an era before union-based strike benefits, Local 216 solicited do- nations of food, clothing, and cash from local merchants to help sustain the striking autoworkers. They met with respectable success. The list of donors reveals a web of support for the autoworkers among the working-class neighborhoods of southern Los Angeles. The first to contribute was the owner of Mays Café, located across the street from GM. She donated $100 and a 100-pound sack of sugar for the workers' commissary. The *People's Daily World* reported, "Other small businessmen who realize their pros- perity lies with good wages for the working man are responding liberally to strike committee requests for donations of cash and food and full strike support." This statement was not an exaggeration. A total of 300 area busi- nesses donated to the strikers, giving $473 in cash and an array of goods and services such as groceries, gasoline, and medical prescriptions. South Gate supplied the greatest number of donors with 107, most of them smaller mer- chants along the Tweedy corridor. This was followed by the adjacent com- munities of Florence and Lynwood, with 59 and 38 donors respectively, then Walnut Park, Huntington Park, Watts, and Compton. Even a few merchants on Central Avenue, the heart of the African-American community, donated to the strikers.[51] In South Gate, about one-quarter of all local merchants donated to the strikers, a respectable showing of local support.[52] While this assistance had little material bearing on the strike's outcome—negotiations were occurring in Detroit and Washington, D.C.—it did lift the morale of workers. Collins admitted that although actual donations were modest, they were important symbolically for showing that "yes, there are some people out there who are concerned about you. . . . Number one, the person giving it felt that he was involved, which is what we wanted. The person receiving it felt that there are some people that's concerned about us."[53] This spoke to the character of the community.

Other local institutions displayed a range of responses. Local newspapers showed the most hostility to the strikers, both by avoiding coverage and running occasional stories slanted toward management. This reflected the editor's conservative bent, as well as a probable fear of bad publicity this labor action cast upon the suburb's image.[54] Churches largely stayed out of the fray, with a few exceptions. The local Methodist church had a sympathetic liberal minister who attended several union meetings. An Evangelical Baptist preacher from a Compton church served as chaplain of Local 216, holding special services for the strikers and soliciting donations from his parish.[55]

The most enthusiastic support for the strikers came from the workers' families and from other unions around Los Angeles—the veritable family of labor. Wives and girlfriends served hot coffee, donuts, and sandwiches to the strikers at a union commissary, and they organized a Christmas party right on the picket line with Santa Claus himself holding a picket sign (see fig. 6-3).[56] Many were members of the UAW Auxiliary, which gave them an organizational base. In this way, families continued to play an integral role in their own economic well-being, even as the safety net began shifting out of the home. The biggest support, however, came from the newly invigorated labor movement in Los Angeles. The CIO led the effort. In early December, the L.A. CIO Council formed the "General Motors Strike Planning Committee," which mobilized CIO resources to aid the autoworkers for the long haul. Assistance poured in from many corners. Some unions offered direct support. Two busloads of steelworkers from Torrance joined the GM picket line before they punched in at work at 7:30 A.M., and Douglas Aircraft workers in Long Beach donated $100 per week from their own strike fund to help the GM strikers. Donations came from numerous other CIO unions as well, including cannery workers, the steelworkers at Bethlehem Steel in Vernon, and maritime workers in San Pedro. CIO unions in the region formed "flying squads" to be "ready for General Motors picket line duty on short notice." They recognized the importance of the GM strike to

Figure 6-3   The wives of the striking autoworkers at G.M. South Gate organized a Christmas
party on the picket line in December 1945, a month into the strike. The "family of labor"—
wives, children, and members of other L.A. unions—provided critical support for the
autoworkers during the 120-day strike. Photo courtesy of the Walter P. Reuther Library,
Archives of Labor and Urban Affairs, Wayne State University, Detroit, Michigan.

all industries. As the utility workers wrote to Local 216, "Recognizing that
the General Motors strike has a direct bearing on the living conditions of all
of us, we want to assure you that you have our full sympathy and support
in your struggle." Even Hollywood joined the effort. In late February, the
CIO staged a "Hollywood Show and Strike Rally" at Huntington Park
High School, with promised appearances by actors John Garfield and Olivia
de Havilland. By this time, the CIO Council was busy coordinating support
for strikers citywide, as the number of walkouts multiplied in Los Angeles,
reflecting the national surge of labor assertiveness after the war.[57]

The autoworkers strike at GM revealed certain critical changes in local
factory workers' lives. It demonstrated, particularly, organized labor's new
strength and the demise of the open shop in Los Angeles. With the backing
of federal policy, workers had gained a voice for asserting their interests in
the workplace and could turn now to collective strategies for survival, rather
than individual ones. The far-flung web of labor-based support for the strikers indicated the new power of this collective approach and a transformed

climate of labor relations in the metropolis. The strike also illustrated the shifting terrain of class relations in South Gate. Erstwhile antagonists, workers and merchants, began to recognize their shared interests, based especially around the notion of a democratized consumerism. Healthy paychecks for working-class residents had become a realistic possibility, lifting not only their standard of living but that of the entire community. Businesses, in turn, would prosper, as their customer base finally emerged from the world of sweat equity into the pecuniary culture of the postwar world.

THE TEXTURE OF SOCIAL LIFE

As for many Americans, World War II was a life-transforming event for Mary DeVries. A shy high school student and daughter of a construction foreman, she began volunteering at Hospitality House both to do her part and because she "loved to dance." "I was a good dancer," she recalled. "I would go there maybe twice a week." One warm June evening, she responded to a last-minute call for volunteers. She made her way to the house, said her hellos, then went out back to play pool with the servicemen. Before long, a girlfriend approached and introduced Mary to Bill North, a handsome young serviceman from Missouri. They began dating and were engaged the following year. During their three-year courtship prolonged by the war, Mary worked as a teletypist, earning $80 a month. She squirreled away her earnings along with the money Bill sent home, building a solid nest egg for their future. On the bus ride home from work one day, she noticed a "for sale" sign on an empty lot in South Gate; it was well located, near church and schools. She bought the lot for $1,400. When the war ended a few months later, the value had doubled. The couple married, and soon hired builders to construct their home, paid for with a GI loan.[58]

The Norths soon settled into married life. When Mary became pregnant in 1946, she quit her job to become a full-time homemaker. Bill went to "television school" on the GI Bill to improve his marketability as a skilled technician. He was hired by Pacific Bell in the switching department, a skilled blue-collar position that Bill considered a good job. He commuted to work in Los Angeles for several years, then to Compton when he was transferred to the toll department. Though he enjoyed his work, he rarely socialized with coworkers. Instead, Bill and Mary found their richest social interaction in South Gate during the 1950s. The Community Presbyterian Church was their focal point. They joined a club of young married couples at the church and socialized with them on a regular basis, going to shows, picnics, and barbecues. These couples spanned the occupational spectrum, from manager and engineer to fireman, accountant, and blue-collar work-ers. Mary became active in women's groups at the church and the PTA; the family also participated in a birthday club with ten neighbor families, where they came together to celebrate birthdays. Bill joined the YMCA with his son, and coached girls teams in a church league when his daughters were active in sports. Recreation was a central activity for the Norths, act-ing as a source of family cohesion as well as a link to the community. Yet the North family did not always stay close to home. They camped frequently in Yosemite and visited family back in Missouri. With Bill's good earnings, this family enjoyed the fruits of postwar prosperity and recreational abun-dance.[59]

The Norths' experience reflected certain key patterns in local social life during the postwar era—commuting to work, weak social ties at work, strong ties at home and in the neighborhood, mobility in leisure, and links with a diverse range of friends and neighbors, blue- and white-collar alike. The Norths, too, exemplified how important federal assistance was in se-curing the status of a family. The GI Bill launched them upward: it allowed them to build a home and it paid for the training Bill needed to earn a good income for his family. Although Bill North had a blue-collar job, the Norths, like many blue-collar families in the 1950s, enjoyed the rewards of the postwar suburban good life.

In South Gate after the war, the tenor of social life had changed notice-ably. The suburb became a richer source of social opportunity, and many residents were now secure enough economically to participate. While the Norths exemplified this important trend, other family types and experi-ences coexisted in South Gate. What all South Gate residents shared, how-ever, was a suburb offering more opportunity than ever to connect with neighbors, pursue one's interests, and enjoy the apotheosis of recreation in postwar Los Angeles.

Changing family life

The nuclear family remained a fundamental institution in postwar South Gate, both ideologically and concretely. The town shared in the post-war suburban exaltation of families as central to wholesome living and Americanism, a potent weapon against communism and a bastion of secu-rity in the atomic age. Indeed, the image of the intact nuclear family as an emblem of life in South Gate was ubiquitous. Families maintained a central place in local social life even as they endured dramatic change. The nuclear family began feeling new pressures both from within and without. Not only did the number of working mothers increase, but the number of single adults in South Gate also rose. This changing reality, a sign of new social diversity in the community, soon clashed with idealized expectations of the postwar suburban good life.

The ideology of the family in South Gate was stronger than ever in the postwar period, reflecting the national mood during the Cold War. As Elaine Tyler May has shown, America's return to a domestic ideal in the 1950s reflected a linking of the personal and political, as well as a bulwark against threats both international and national. In the context of the atomic age and the Cold War, the self-contained home and family promised security in an increasingly unstable world.[60] Images of domesticity were pervasive in South Gate, sometimes intermingling Cold War anxieties and Americanism with idealizations of family life. Recall the "typical family" from South Gate's 1947 Rose Parade float. This picture of domestic life was not only meant to represent South Gate to the world, but also to embody the theme "I Am An American." Churches and merchant groups ran ads imploring residents to nurture American democracy by bringing their families to church—Christian families were portrayed as the first defense against communism. The "Mrs. South Gate" pageant of the 1950s exalted the homemaker role for women. The winner, chosen based on her abilities as a housewife, would progress on to the "Mrs. California" and "Mrs. America" pageants. Marilyn Echols, Mrs. South Gate in 1956, epitomized the image. She was a mother of two youngsters, a member of the Tweedy PTA, and counted as hobbies crafts, sewing, crocheting, and reading. Domesticity was further encouraged by community groups like the YMCA and PTA, which offered courses on marriage, parenting, and "family living," and the newspaper ran occasional articles on parenting. While a housewife during the 1950s, Mary North, along with her mother, took a course in "consumer education" for twelve years, offered at a local elementary school. They learned homemaking skills, tested recipes, and were otherwise tutored in the ways of domesticity.[61]

Beyond the imagery, families continued to play a central role in the social lives of South Gate residents.[62] For children, families were at the center of life both at home and in the community. Pamela Lawton, a youngster in South Gate during the 1950s, recalled the home-centeredness of her spare hours. Her family struggled financially during the decade. They lived in a tiny triplex, her father held two jobs, and her mother stayed home to raise four children. Pamela, the oldest child, helped with the babies at home. Her daily routine included school during the day, then time at home caring for the infants, playing outside, and listening to rock and roll on the radio. "Mostly it was finding stuff to do outside." Weekends were similarly home centered. "Weekends were always for work. Once you were off work, you had to clean the house. My dad made bread from scratch and cooked." For this family, struggling financially, economic privation worked to reinforce family togetherness—as it had in South Gate's earlier years.[63]

For those doing better, family togetherness revolved around recreation. In the general climate of postwar economic prosperity, leisure and recreation became the primary context for family activity, superceding the prewar routines of domestic subsistence. As children participated in sports, scouts, the YMCA, and the like, they often drew their parents along. Truck driver Ray Markle coached baseball and basketball when his two sons were teenagers, activities that brought "the family together." He also recalled frequent family picnics at South Gate Park, where his children met other children and eventually brought entire families into friendship networks. Telephone worker Bill North coached girls sports when his daughters played on volleyball, softball, and basketball teams, and he became active in the YMCA along with his son. Even Pamela Lawton's mother, struggling to raise her four children on limited financial resources, found time to participate in Girl Scout activities when her daughter was active in that organization. Youth recreational activity reached epic proportions in postwar South Gate, representing a means for entire families to mix with the broader community.[64]

Families also took frequent excursions to leisure sites around Los Angeles—including the beach, drive-in movies, and Disneyland—continuing the pattern of far-flung recreation of the prewar years. Notable too was the rise in long-distance family trips during the 1950s. Ray Markle's experience was typical: "I'd tell my wife, 'Let's get the hell out of here.' . . . Sometimes we'd wind up having lunch in Oxnard. . . . We'd go to Big Bear for the day and I'd rent a cabin and we'd go to San Diego or we'd go to Mexico. . . . We were forever on the go." All of these destinations were at least a two-hour drive from South Gate. The North family was similarly mobile, making frequent visits to Yosemite and Missouri, among other places. And closer to home, families provided important social networks. When Mary North started her own family in the postwar years, she still maintained her closest social relations with her mother and sisters. "I'd see them easily once a week. . . . We'd just have lunch and the kids would play. . . . It was always my sisters that I was very close to." Similarly, Ray Markle and his wife socialized regularly with his brothers and their wives, going to dinner and dancing at nightspots around Los Angeles. Families, thus, maintained a central place in the social lives of residents.[65]

Yet the resurgence of the domestic ideal masked a more complex, diverse reality of family life and gender roles in South Gate and the nation more broadly.[66] By the end of the 1950s, working women were almost as common as homemakers in South Gate. The number of single-parent homes also increased, providing a counterpoint to the nuclear family. And although nuclear families remained the majority, there were also numerous cases of adult children, grandparents, or other relatives living with these families. The 1960 census indicates that the 20,139 households of South Gate contained 5,300 persons who were adult children or extended kin of the household head. In the 1950s and early 1960s, South Gate's families were becoming more diverse than ever, challenging the domestic ideology that dominated public discourse. South Gate's embrace of postwar domesticity, thus, reflected not only the localization of a national ideology but also a counteroffense to dramatic changes in local family structure.[67]

The most significant change in South Gate, however, was the entry of women into the paid workforce. Many gained their first work experience during the war, taking jobs in offices and factories. A good number found the experience lucrative, gratifying, and, especially for factory workers, worth keeping. A 1944 L.A. survey found that 42 percent of "war industry women" sought to remain in factory work, while 34 percent preferred returning to housewifery.[68] Although the factory door slammed shut for most women when the war ended, many remained in the workforce in secretarial jobs. For South Gate women, the paycheck bug had bitten for good. Their numbers rose rapidly: 22 percent of all adult women worked for wages in 1940, 32 percent in 1950, and 41 percent by 1960. Of the latter group, nearly 60 percent were married and many were middle-aged, suggesting their permanence in the labor force. A 1961 survey of female high school graduates with "business training" (including clerical and secretarial skills) confirmed that marriage did not dampen the desire to work. Among those who had married, 71 percent were either working or intended to find a job within two years. For some, the status of "homemaker" was merely temporary until they could land employment—a reversal of the image of women working temporarily for "pin money" until marriage.[69]

Working mothers became typical in South Gate by the 1960s. Compared to first-generation families in South Gate, these women exhibited a fundamental change in their thinking about family security strategies. Rather than pursue domestic subsistence, they sought jobs. Just as working-class families no longer relied on sweat equity to build homes, neither did they require female labor to stretch domestic resources through self-provisioning, sewing, and the like. As families achieved greater earning power, household necessities could now be purchased—and the mother's paycheck contributed to this ability. This shift was encouraged both by the cultural emphasis on consumerism in the postwar years, creating new demands for goods, and by the rise in available credit. As the pastor of the First

Baptist Church in nearby suburban Lakewood put it, "A lot of mothers have to work. They're buying everything at one time and some make payments running higher than their incomes."[70]

The 1950s represented a transitional decade in women's shift from sweat-based to cash-based contributions to the family. For a time, old and new habits coexisted. Among families with homemaker mothers, especially those struggling financially, women continued certain cost-cutting practices such as cooking from scratch and sewing their families' clothing. Until the Sheehy family in South Gate bought the family's second car in 1959, the mother was virtually confined to stores within walking distance. The sheer limitation of being carless in suburban Los Angeles may have contributed to women's inclination to make-at-home rather than shop.[71] Whether women worked for a paycheck or stayed at home to raise families, they continued to contribute to the family economy. The trend, however, was increasingly toward a wage-based contribution.

As the work experience instilled a new sense of autonomy and power in women, the local divorce rate rose. Indeed, South Gate had the highest rate in Los Angeles county. During an eleven-month period in the mid-1950s, 841 divorces and annulments were granted, yielding a divorce rate of 58 per 1,000 married females. This was nearly six times the national average.[72] Superior Court Judge Clyde Triplett, who presided over these cases, blamed the high rate on two factors: the prevalence of female industrial employment and excessive credit purchases. He argued that wives who worked the swing shift in factories were a major problem, because they developed social ties independent of the family. "A wife on the swing shift gets through work in the middle of the night," Triplett observed. "She goes bowling, automobile riding or to a beach party. Her social activities are carried on at night. . . . Husband and wife almost never work the same shift, so their social life can't be integrated." The second factor he noted was "the incautious manner in which industrial workers buy on credit. In trying to work out property settlements in these cases, I often found that the family auto, furniture, and appliances were not paid for. In many cases, monthly charges for articles bought on credit exceed the combined income of husband and wife. . . . This situation leads to attachments of wages and ensuing family quarrels, which end in divorce court." Triplett also noted that many of the divorcing couples were recent arrivals from the South and Southwest, "without settled traditions."[73]

Triplett's biases and discomforts aside, his observations were on target. For factory women, work opened up new avenues for independent socializing, apart from family and neighborhood. If she commuted to work as many did, she left the suburb.[74] Although these women did not travel far to work, most made their way outside of South Gate proper, suggesting a spatial broadening in their everyday lives. The friendships cultivated at work also contributed to a social life independent of the family, far beyond the domestic realm. The work-based friendships noted by Triplett were probably strongest for swing-shift workers, forged as they were by the odd hours of their work schedules. This made it impossible to participate in the more common range of daytime activities for women, such as clubs and school-based groups like the PTA. In contrast to most South Gate residents, swing-shift workers found their greatest social ties at work.

Limited child-care options may have impelled working mothers to take the swing shift, so a spouse might look after the children at night. The local child-care shortage first surfaced during the war. At the Firestone plant, women workers began quitting because they could not find affordable day care. Their only options were to pay baby-sitters or find family to help out—no public or company facilities were available. Fearing even more turnover, Firestone management appealed to the Family Welfare Association for assistance, which in turn presented the problem to the South Gate Coordinating Council. The community responded in limited fashion, opening a nursery school in Hollydale and supervised playgrounds during the summer. Even when adequate facilities were provided, working mothers did not always utilize them. In 1943, the director of a child-care facility in nearby Bellflower surveyed that community and found that 259 working women, mostly employed at Vultee Aircraft in Downey, did not have their children in day care. Of these women, 70 percent did not know about the facilities or want their kids there. Some respondents claimed the program was "impractical," while one said she didn't want her children "regimented." Five percent felt the fees were too high. So on both the supply and the demand sides, day care met a mixed reception.[75]

In the postwar years, day-care facilities remained in undersupply. In 1951, only one nursery school existed in South Gate. The number rose to three in 1953, and four by 1961; three of them were located in the small Hollydale section of the suburb. With 1,024 women with children under six years old earning a paycheck in 1960, four nursery schools could not meet local day-care needs. Most working mothers pursued individual solutions, like working the swing shift. Other women simply waited to return to the workforce until their children were older. Census data from 1960 suggest as much, showing fully 62 percent of working women were between thirty-five and sixty-four years old; only 11 percent of working women had children under six. Another strategy was to rely on extended family or neighbors for help, which appeared to be a common practice. Helen Henry, a divorced mother who worked at Hiram's market in nearby

Lynwood, was a good example. Helen left her two children with her own mother, who looked after them every day when they returned home from school. When the Lawton family had only one child, they worked out a system where the mother worked at a department store during the day and the father tended bar at night, so that each could care for the child during their time at home. Grace Sheehy, a secretary, relied on neighbors to look after her child after school, while Ray Markle's mother-in-law tended to their children when the parents were at work.[76]

In South Gate two domestic realities coexisted. In one, women stayed at home to raise their children. In the other, women left home to work. For South Gate's homemakers, life revolved around family and neighborhood. Often lacking the geographic mobility afforded by a second family car, they found themselves more closely tied to the local community. For these women, fulfilling the domestic ideal was a real possibility. For women who left home every day for an office or factory, social life could be severed from family and neighborhood, and experienced instead at work. In the routine of their lives, these women launched a frontal assault on the domestic ideal at the very moment this ideology crescendoed in the public imagination. Working women were a graphic symbol of social diversification and change, and a discomforting reminder to some that suburban myths and realities were growing ever more distant in South Gate.

Work life

As cash income became the lifeblood of South Gate residents after the war, the workplace took on new importance in the lives of workers. An invigorated labor movement allowed them to assert their power and interests in the workplace, which they did with an unprecedented display of labor militancy during the 1940s and 1950s. Yet even as the workplace became a focal point for ensuring family security, it still played a secondary role in defining workers' identities, loyalties, and social lives. For the most part, workplace militancy was a means for improving their lives as suburbanites, rather than challenging the economic system more broadly. Workers used their unions and jobs to achieve a better life at home, the more compelling locus of loyalty and identity to South Gate residents.

The labor militancy of the postwar years emerged in the context of South Gate's thriving industrial economy. From 1940 to 1970 local industry expanded tremendously, drawing from the area's fortuitous standing within the broader process of national economic restructuring. As big industry in the East grew wary of labor's growing power, corporations began using capital mobility as a strategy to regain control and profits. Corporations relocated factories away from older eastern industrial cities to sites in the Far and Middle West. And within cities, they preferred the sprawling suburbs to dense urban areas. Detroit epitomized the losing end of this equation. From 1948 to 1967, it lost nearly 130,000 manufacturing jobs— almost half of them during the 1950s.[77] In the same decades, Los Angeles generally and South Gate in particular had an opposite experience. They not only welcomed these migrating eastern plants, but they scored numerous federal defense contracts that fueled new high-tech industrial growth. South Gate seemed doubly lucky—a suburb in a thriving western city, the favored destination of mobile capital. From the mid-1930s to 1964, the number of factories in South Gate jumped from 35 to 455, employing more than 37,000 workers. The "blue chip" companies among them included GM (employing 4,000), Firestone (employing 2,500), Armstrong Cork, American Pipe, Anchor Hocking Glass, and Pittsburgh Steel. A minority of local plants were high-tech industries dependent on Cold War defense contracts, such as International Glass (which made optical instrument supplies). The bulk of South Gate's factories produced machinery, primary metals, and chemical products for use by high-tech firms located elsewhere, while the suburb's largest plants, GM and Firestone, continued to manufacture cars and tires. Postwar South Gate in some ways resembled a mini-Detroit in its heyday. And like the real Detroit, it would eventually suffer from deindustrialization—but this happened two decades later. Chronologically, South Gate was two steps behind the Motor City. In the postwar era, South Gate was a thriving industrial center that employed a prosperous, white working class.[78]

Scattered evidence suggests that although some residents took jobs in South Gate plants, many continued to commute to work.[79] The best journey-to-work data comes from the early 1960s. For 1960, the Census Bureau collected data on place of work and means of transportation. Although it lacked specificity, it did indicate several things. First, the vast majority of South Gate residents commuted by automobile or streetcar (89 percent); only 5 percent worked close enough to walk to their jobs. Second, nearly one-third of residents worked in L.A. city, 2 percent in Long Beach, and the remainder in various spots around Los Angeles County (including South Gate). Despite the data's limitations, it strongly suggests the prevalence of commuting to work. Another data set tracked female clerical workers who lived in South Gate in the early 1960s; for them too jobs were well beyond the range of a comfortable walk. Fully 96 percent worked within a ten-mile radius of South Gate, but that distance included Los Angeles, Huntington Park, Vernon, Downey, and other places that required driving out of South Gate. A 1965 report confirmed the presence of commuters, claiming "many of the city's residents work elsewhere in the region." The evidence suggests the scales tipped toward commuters among South Gate residents, although a good number also labored in local factories.[80]

The persistence of spatially dispersed work patterns meant that South Gate residents experienced some level of disconnection between workplace and home neighborhood. Hardly a "company town," South Gate was a suburb of many factories and many different types of workers. This diversity of work experiences meant that no unified work-based culture dominated in South Gate. Instead, work—and unions—represented one realm among several that competed for the attentions and loyalties of residents. Unions in South Gate did win the allegiance of many factory workers. The strongest unions were those at the largest plants, like GM and Firestone, and at companies with multiple plants such as Continental Can. In general, the construction, transportation, auto, and rubber industries were "predominantly unionized," as were plants like South Gate Aluminum and Magnesium. Virgil Collins recalled that the larger, better organized plants (like GM and Firestone) lay in western South Gate, while smaller, less-organized plants clustered in the eastern part of town.[81]

From 1940 through the 1960s, union activism ran high in South Gate. The most visible actions were taken by two CIO unions, United Auto Workers Local 216 at GM and United Rubber Workers Local 100 at Firestone. Postwar labor conflict in these plants reflected two levels of labor-management relations, national and local. When nationwide contracts were being hammered out, the locals followed the lead of their national leadership if strikes were called. In general, this leadership focused on wages, hours, and benefits, with less attention to working conditions. This was the period of "business unionism," marked by the bureaucratization of labor relations as big unions institutionalized their operations in order to gain bargaining power against large, powerful corporations. National union leaders also tended toward political moderation, in the climate of Cold War anticommunism. In this context, the rank and file lost autonomy and power in contract negotiations. One outcome of this was a wave of wildcat strikes across the country, often focused on humanizing working conditions that were deteriorating as management tried to maximize profits. South Gate's unions were part of this trend.[82]

In the 1950s and early 1960s, strikes became almost annual events at GM and Firestone. Most began as part of national stoppages during periods of contract negotiations. They invariably dragged on when local grievances remained unsettled, usually centered on working conditions like speedups and seniority policy. Each plant also had at least one major wildcat strike in the 1950s. At Firestone in 1955, for example, nearly 2,000 workers in the fuel tank division walked out in protest over low piecework pay rates, which fell below the hourly rate guaranteed by their contract. Many of those who led the stoppage were women in skilled and semiskilled positions. The strike was finally settled when Firestone agreed to pay the original contract rate, a modest victory at best. Two months later, autoworkers at GM staged their own wildcat strike, part of a national wave of such actions. This walkout focused on working conditions like speedups, break periods, and protective clothing, among other issues. Union officer Virgil Collins called working conditions at GM at the time "horrible." "In 1955, over 10,000 people were hired and they were just in and out. They wouldn't stay. The conditions were bad, like speed up . . . which simply means that they want you to get your head down and your fanny up, and don't you look up 'til you hear that bell. . . . No consideration whatsoever for you as a human being." The walkout ended after two days, the speedup issue still unresolved. Similar strikes occurred well into the 1960s, often focused on speedup policies. Unions were active at other plants as well, like the steelworkers at South Gate Aluminum and Magnesium and the teamsters at several local trucking firms.[83]

These actions signaled the presence of labor militancy and assertiveness among blue-collar workers in the community. At GM and Firestone, enthusiasm for unionism ran high; workers were generally willing to walk off the job to demand higher wages, protest poor job conditions, and insist on some control over the work process, with the backing of their strong unions. In these challenges to management, workers displayed elements of economic populism, demanding fairness and equity in the distribution of economic resources. Yet certain factors mitigated their militancy. Increased incomes and the local context of industrial expansion dampened the desperation of labor's demands. Unlike their counterparts in Detroit, they escaped the pernicious management strategy of plant migration that posed the threat of layoffs.[84] If work conditions got too unbearable, as at GM in 1955, or if a strike lasted too long, workers could simply quit and find a job elsewhere. This was the ultimate, individualized solution, contributing to a utilitarian attitude toward unions among many workers.

Another factor that softened local militancy was the coexistence of economic populism and political conservatism. The larger unions were often divided into left-leaning and conservative factions. At Firestone, the union election in 1955—a virtual referendum on the wildcat strike of that year—illustrated such a cleavage. The rank and file divided almost evenly; the prostrike candidate won by a slim 39-vote margin, out of 2,500 votes. The rest sided with the incumbent, who had supported management in urging the strikers to return to work. At GM the political divisions were pronounced. Several factions coexisted in UAW Local 216—Communists, Socialists, Trotskyites, a right-wing caucus, even a conservative Masonic bloc. Though the left-wing faction tended to dominate union leadership, the local still saw its share of internal conflict. Perhaps the biggest rift erupted when the union splintered over the Taft-Hartley Act of 1947, which required all union leaders to sign anticommunist affidavits. Several leaders resisted the measure, some on principle and others because they were Communists and feared the repercussions. A conservative group put these leaders on trial, setting off a heated battle that the radicals finally won. Yet the conservatives remained a strong presence in the union, voicing their anticommunist concerns throughout the 1950s. "Know the communists in your union," warned a union newsletter in 1950. "Bone up on the facts necessary to distinguish a Communist from a legitimate trade-unionist." Conservatives finally captured control of Local 216 in the early 1960s. During their term, the union called at least two strikes, one over the perennial problem of speedups. Here, labor militancy coexisted with a rabid suspicion of leftist politics, reflecting a political orientation that embraced both moderate politics—typifying the Democratic Party—and economic populism.[85]

For most South Gate workers, unions commanded loyalties inside the workplace, but not necessarily outside of it. Beyond a general inclination toward economic justice, there were few signs that the worker militancy in the factory permeated the broader community. This became evident in workers' utilitarian attitudes toward unions, the lack of a working-class public culture in South Gate, and the failure of union doctrine to guide local political life.

Despite the best efforts of union leaders to command broad worker loyalty, most workers maintained a utilitarian relationship with their unions. Ray Markle, a member of the Teamsters Union, exemplified this attitude. A loyal union man, Markle believed the union's primary purpose was to maintain good wages and benefits. The Teamsters had a picnic once a year, which he attended "a couple of times" in his thirty years as a truck driver. "I went to find out what they were going to do for us," he recalled. He expressed gratitude for what the union accomplished, especially for supplying a good pension when he retired. UAW leader Virgil Collins ruefully observed a similar attitude among the rank and file at GM. Attendance at union meetings remained dismal throughout the 1950s. "They get off work at 3:30, I said, 'Come over and spend one hour, find out what's going on. If you've got some problems, bring them up.' They'd say, 'Nah, that's what we elected you for, Virgil. I'm going home.'" A highly pragmatic conception of unions ran deep, Collins recalled. "They was only interested in it to the extent of 'What can the union get for me?' And after you got what you can get, 'why the hell can't you get more?' So it's not a very pretty picture."[86]

Following CIO tradition established in the 1930s, the UAW promoted social activities as a way of strengthening worker camaraderie and building ties outside the workplace that would translate into loyalty inside it. They held dances, showed free movies every other week, and sponsored baseball, basketball, and volleyball teams. While decent turnout sustained these activities in the late 1940s, by the 1950s only a few workers attended, usually the leaders who were totally involved in the union. For most, competition from other forms of leisure and entertainment overwhelmed union efforts. By contrast to the workers, some plant managers maintained strong social ties with their colleagues. Juanita Hammon's husband was a good example. Having worked his way up the ranks at Firestone, Ernie Hammon emerged as head of the instrument shop after the war. Juanita and Ernie soon entered the social world of Firestone management. "They had a lot of good parties for the supervisors. Firestone was very generous. . . . We'd go down to Long Beach for dinner dances, things like that. We'd socialize with the supervisors from Firestone more than anyone else." That Firestone subsidized these shindigs undoubtedly boosted participation, a perk not offered to the line workers. Although Firestone workers and managers generally avoided socializing together outside of work, this did not preclude neighborhood interaction among supervisors and workers from different plants, a pattern quite evident in South Gate.[87]

The absence of a working-class public culture was another sign of the labor movement's failure to capture broad worker loyalty, and of the stark separation between work and social life. Though dominated by blue-collar workers and strong unions, South Gate never organized public celebrations of Labor Day in the postwar years.[88] Given the frequency of public celebrations that *did* occur in South Gate, the absence is notable. Local public culture instead centered around patriotism and Americanism, led by veterans and divorced from any association with labor. Holidays like Memorial Day and Fourth of July were commemorated every year with speakers, picnics, and entertainment at the park. On the rare occasion when Labor Day was acknowledged, it was tinged with Christian Americanism. An ad commemorating the holiday in 1957, sponsored by the churches of South Gate, proclaimed, "Hats off to labor . . . the skilled and dedicated laborers that have graced our land," but it quickly reminded readers that all labor should be done in the name of "God who gives meaning to all labor done in His name." The intent of this tribute was to erase any association with un-Christian communism.[89] Even more telling was the overt message of South Gate's 1947 Rose Parade float. Not only did the float lionize the suburban good life, but it labeled this imagery as labor's true identity. The float depicted the contented suburban family celebrating Labor Day not in a parade or with union comrades but rather in the privacy of the family backyard. In this idyllic image, coming on the heels of a year of intensive labor activism, the working family was depoliticized, benign—in essence, domesticated (see fig. 6-1).

Finally, most working-class residents refused to apply union principles to community governance. Blue-collar residents rejected union-backed candidates in city council elections.[90] And more emphatically, they rejected the unions' progressive stance on racial equality when it came to neighborhood politics. Here loomed the greatest schism between workplace and community life.

In the 1940s and 1950s, CIO leadership vigorously championed the cause of racial equality in Los Angeles, South Gate's CIO unions included. The barriers began to fall during World War II, encouraged by FDR's 1941 executive order banning discrimination in defense industries with federal contracts. In the L.A. metropolitan area, progress came gradually. By early 1942, blacks were still locked out of most defense industries, including the Firestone plant in South Gate. This began to change under the combined pressures of expanding industries, acute labor shortages,[91] and sustained protests both by the black community and organized labor. The greatest advances occurred in the shipyards and aircraft plants. The L.A. CIO also helped pressure the aircraft and rubber industries to hire blacks by 1943, and such efforts continued after the war. While postwar reconversion put many African Americans out of work, those who labored in defense plants tended to retain their positions after the war.[92]

In South Gate, UAW Local 216 was especially active in fighting discrimination both inside and outside the factory. The union worked vigorously to open the factory gates to African-American and Latino workers, challenging the forces that had long excluded them from higher-paying and higher-skilled manufacturing jobs in the area. When the war ended and auto production resumed at GM, Local 216 pressured management to end its Jim Crow hiring policies, which lasted longer in California than elsewhere. In July 1946, GM responded by hiring the first blacks—ten in all, eight of them as janitors and warehousemen. The black community considered this a victory. "White union members at the plant have welcomed the Negro workers with open arms," proclaimed the *California Eagle*. Virgil Collins remembered that the company placed the first African American in a job alongside the union president: "In management's eye, that was a punishment." The union stepped up its fight against racial discrimination in the early 1950s. Shop committeeman Ed Gurske, an avowed leftist, went directly to nearby black and Latino neighborhoods to encourage journeymen electricians, carpenters, and plumbers to apply at GM. By 1955, significant numbers of African Americans and Latinos were hired, although they were relegated to the hardest, dirtiest jobs in the plant. Local 216 combated this internal discrimination by winning plantwide seniority, which allowed minorities to transfer to different departments.[93]

Local 216's commitment to racial equality originated with the leadership, then diffused among the members. The officers "took a firm position on this at all times," Collins recalled. "We said that everybody that worked in this plant had to belong to the union, and was a union brother. Black, white, yellow, red, green—we didn't give a damn what they were, they were union brothers." Although rank-and-file support was not unanimous, most autoworkers in South Gate tolerated the union's antidiscrimination policy. Significantly, there were no racial incidents at GM when minorities began entering the plants, something Collins called "a small miracle." He attributed this to the position of the officers "who was willing to stand up and say, 'This guy is a workingman, same as you are. He's got to earn a living, and he's got a right to a job here, same as you have.'" This stance typified L.A. industry, which largely avoided the "hate strikes" between white and black workers that plagued cities like Detroit, Youngstown, and Mobile (see fig. 6-4).[94]

Local 216 attempted to extend the antidiscrimination crusade into the community. For example, when a Jewish synagogue in Huntington Park was defaced in 1947, the union offered its concern and support. "It is the opinion of our organization," one union leader asserted, "that such practices as Anti-Semitism, Anti-Racial and other anti-Democratic trends have no place in American life, or indeed in human relations anywhere." In 1948, the union denounced the killing of a black AFL plasterer by an L.A. policeman: "Often the sadistic actions of police against minority members of our own community . . . are not given enough publicity. Terror with club and gun, whether against union men on the picket line or against peaceful members of the Negro and Mexican-American communities, will not be tolerated."[95] But when the union's push for racial equality began to encroach on residential life—by testing the boundaries of segregation—rank-and-file tolerance quickly dissipated. This resistance was clearest in the realm of local politics, both in the failure of labor-backed politicians and in the suburb's staunch resistance to the civil rights movement. Most autoworkers who accepted blacks as coworkers did not accept them as neighbors, nor did they accept the principle of racial equality in the community. Alameda Street remained the impermeable racial border it had long been. Struggling to explain this phenomenon, Collins said, "In the

Figure 6-4   By the mid-1950s, UAW Local 216 in South Gate reflected more racial and ethnic
diversity than ever. The union successfully fought for the hiring of African Americans and
Mexican Americans at the plant, although they were often relegated to the hardest, dirtiest
jobs. Photo courtesy of the Walter P. Reuther Library, Archives of Labor and Urban Affairs,
Wayne State University, Detroit, Michigan.

workplace, people take a little different attitude than they do in their
home. . . . They've got this feeling, permeating for years, that 'my home is
my castle and I can do what I want,' even though the law might say you
can't."[96]

Many of South Gate's blue-collar workers were good unionists on the
job, who could quickly shed those principles once they walked outside the
factory gate. The economic comfort they enjoyed in the postwar era explained part of this. Their militance, their willingness to go on strike and assert their collective voice, all paid off handsomely. These workers purchased
homes, owned cars and televisions, took family vacations, indulged in the
commercial culture of Los Angeles, and otherwise enjoyed the good life in
postwar South Gate. Unionized workers in particular enjoyed a standard of
living that looked middle class, often surpassing their white-collar neighbors. The payoffs of unionism allowed blue-collar workers to identify with
the middle class, once they left the factory. "They made the kind of money
that they could afford to buy a home," recalled Collins, "plus they had the
benefits." Among all South Gate residents, "Firestone and G.M. workers
were better off." John Sheehy, a postal worker, claimed that autoworkers

lived in the nicer homes in South Gate because "they were high paid guys
. . . hell, they made $30 a week." Another resident concurred, claiming, "If
you belonged to a union you got a pretty fair wage, and if you did not belong to a union . . . you had to struggle along the best way you could."[97]

For South Gate's blue-collar residents, social ties forged at work rarely
carried over into the neighborhood. For most, the schism between work life
and neighborhood left room for workers to find common ground with the
business class of South Gate. Economically, unions could foster a sense
of militancy and economic populism, which ultimately financed a new
lifestyle in the postwar era. Politically, union principles failed to translate
into community politics. The workers who walked the picket line and tolerated racial integration in the factory were the same people who mobilized
against civil rights in the neighborhood. At the border of community, an
impenetrable line protected workers' identity as white, suburban homeowners.

Leisure, social, and religious life

As in many American suburbs, the postwar era in South Gate saw the
apotheosis of the "recreational good life." This was a period when opportunities for recreation and leisure abounded, and an ethos of leisure dominated neighborhood life. For many suburbs, this was nothing new. Elite and
middle-class suburbs had incorporated recreation and outdoor living as integral elements of their design and community vision as early as the mid-
nineteenth century. But for the working-class suburb, the leisure element
was fully realized only in the postwar era, reflecting both the advancing status of American workers and a widespread public acceptance of recreation.
As a 1959 planning report for South Gate put it, "Recreation is no longer
considered to be a luxury. It is recognized as an essential to life." In suburbs
like South Gate, Lakewood, and even Levittown in the postwar era, working-class residents could finally afford the recreational good life.[98]

South Gate residents had a rich range of recreational choices in this period, from the local to the metropolitan. Within South Gate, opportunities
for recreation multiplied after the war. As a 1953 report on local recreational
resources explained, "Recreation is a vital and significant segment of living
and is essential in a democratic society. . . . Wholesome recreation opportunities . . . are a powerful force in prevention of delinquency; and support the
prosperity of the community."[99] Beginning in 1941, an explosion of public
works projects focused on leisure and recreation facilities, mostly built on
tax-delinquent land. South Gate Regional Park was the centerpiece of this
effort. This ninety-six-acre park was the largest of its kind west of the

Rocky Mountains and attracted tens of thousands of visitors each month from southern Los Angeles. Of the park's many offerings, the biggest draws were the swimming pool, the golf course, dance classes, arts and crafts classes, club meetings for twenty different organizations, musical programs, family movie nights, and numerous sporting activities. Most of the sports programs were aimed at youth, such as little league baseball, basketball, football, volleyball, archery, roller-skating, gymnastics, and track and field. But several offerings targeted adults, including bowling, volleyball, "slim gym" (an exercise class for women), church basketball leagues, softball, and horseshoes. Semipro baseball teams also played on park diamonds. In one year during the mid-1950s, sporting activities at the park drew 60,600 participants and 33,600 spectators; aquatics classes and recreational swimming drew 144,000; and the golf course drew 55,900. The same year, 99,200 engaged in "general play" at the park, and 397,000 came to picnic. The municipal auditorium, also on park grounds, was used an average of four times per day.[100]

The financing of the park was a clear sign of how far South Gate had come since its early penurious days. In fiscal year 1957–58, expenditures in the Parks and Recreation Department topped $377,000, amounting to 15 percent of the total city budget. With Parks Department revenues at $91,000 to offset some of this expense, it still left $286,000 in net expenditures. Citizens were generally willing and able to foot this bill.[101]

Certain sporting activities acted as bridges between the classes. The presence of a golf course in town, traditionally considered an upper-class sport, was one sign of this. The nine-hole course opened in 1954 as part of the regional park. Admission was about a dollar, an affordable rate for the occasional player. Public golf courses like this one stood in contrast to private country clubs in the suburbs, which historically had been the site for golf. Public courses symbolized the democratization of the sport and of suburbanization more broadly in the postwar era, as public daily fee courses— often situated in the suburbs—proliferated much faster than private club courses. Another activity that drew a range of participants was a "housewives' recreation class" at the park, with sports like tennis and volleyball. In the late 1940s, when union recreational activity was at its peak, local leagues mixed teams from labor unions and businessmen's clubs. In 1947, for example, groups like the Elks Club, Moose Club, and UAW Local 216 had teams in common volleyball, bowling, and basketball leagues. The South Gate Softball Association was organized into two leagues: one for service clubs, churches, and fraternal orders, and a second for commercial and industrial teams.[102]

By the late 1950s, churches had become a major supplier of teams for adult sports through an interdenominational league. Teams representing the Baptists, Presbyterians, Four Squares, Lutherans, Church of Christ, Mormons, and Methodists competed in common baseball, softball, and basketball leagues. Because congregants at these churches hailed from a range of occupational backgrounds, the church league represented a field of class inclusion. The enthusiastic participation of so many churches in this league, including the Evangelicals that had shunned such activity before the war, showed the ubiquity of the recreational ethos.[103]

New commercial amusements appeared in South Gate as well. In the late 1940s, supper clubs and nightclubs proliferated. At places like DiMaggio's Hula Inn, the Blue Note, and the Trianon Ballroom Café, patrons could indulge in cocktails and steak dinners, and then dance to live music. These clubs attracted well-known musicians popular in Southern California. The Trianon, a favored spot with its sprawling dance floor, two bars, live orchestras, and fried chicken dinners, accommodated 700 couples. In the early 1940s, live broadcasts from the Trianon went out over the Mutual Broadcasting System three nights a week. At Humphrey's Café, the popular Kelley Sisters performed "Spanish castanet," Hawaiian routines, and double-accordion numbers. Truck driver Ray Markle recalled frequenting spots like these with his wife and friends. They made a night of it, eating and dancing until about 1 A.M.[104]

Several other commercial outlets also opened. A new movie theater, seating 1,000 in its modern surroundings, and a roller-skating rink had appeared by the early 1950s. Even more popular were two sporting venues that catered to working-class tastes: Ascot Speedway and the South Gate Arena. Constructed in 1936 at the corner of Tweedy and Atlantic, Ascot Speedway helped establish South Gate's reputation as a car and racing center in Southern California (GM and Firestone first associated South Gate with cars; Ascot introduced a recreational element). Seating more than 5,000 in grandstands that encircled an oval track, Ascot was typical of small speedways in this period, which achieved immense popularity. Ascot hosted weekly races for motorcycles, stock roadsters, midget cars, and late model stock cars, as well as occasional thrill shows by Hollywood stuntmen and spectacles like staged plane crashes. Earning fame as the first venue to broadcast auto races on television, Ascot drew some of the top racers in America. Several settled in South Gate, including Hal "King" Cole, "Tex" Saunders, and Ed Barnett, all West Coast race champions.[105] The South Gate Arena, a multipurpose venue that opened in 1946, was best known for its professional wrestling matches, drawing names like Ed "Strangler" Lewis, Lou Thez, and Jimmy Londos. Even boxing great Joe Lewis fought an exhibition match at the hall. Nevertheless, the arena was not profitable, and after an unsuccessful struggle to compete against "big time wrestling promoters," the arena's owner in 1958 converted it into a $2 million, forty-eight-lane bowling center and restaurant. Both car racing and wrestling were emphatic expressions of working-class popular culture, illustrating how working-class sensibilities survived in the consumer culture of the postwar era.[106]

In the postwar era, South Gate's local scene also showed signs of southernization, reflecting both the backgrounds of recent migrants and a broader trend of southernized working-class culture in this period.[107] Several restaurants with southern motifs opened, including the Lone Star Café, Angel's Barbecue, and McDonnel's Plantation Restaurant. Opened in 1941, McDonnel's was designed as a "modified Southern mansion" with red brick patio floors, a low picket fence out front, a broad lawn, flowers, and a garden wall. The house specialty was chicken, raised on the restaurant's own farm. Other signs of southern culture were square dances at South Gate Park, country barn dances featuring "Stuart Hamblin and his Covered Wagon Jubilee," the founding of First Southern Baptist Church in the 1950s, and the continued proliferation of Evangelical churches. Residents also enjoyed southern culture (perhaps ersatz) in television shows such as the "Country Scene Talent Show," "Hollywood Hoe Down," "Ozark Jubilee," and "Country Music Jubilee." In South Gate as in other suburbs of southeast Los Angeles, southern influences permeated local cultural life, creating a familiar milieu for recent migrants and allowing southern sensibilities—political and otherwise—to flourish in the area.[108]

Besides these local offerings, South Gate residents continued to commute to play in Greater Los Angeles and beyond. While Hollywood represented the symbolic center of this leisured ethos, other commercial attractions grew extremely popular, welcoming huge numbers of visitors and giving residents of towns like South Gate new opportunities to engage in the postwar good life at an affordable admission price.[109] South Gate was well situated in this metropolitan environment. A 1961 map depicted the range of amenities nearby—Marineland to the south, horse racing at Hollywood Park, the Hollywood Bowl, Griffith Park, the Rose Bowl in Pasadena, Disneyland, Knott's Berry Farm, and the many beaches of the region—most of these less than twenty miles from the suburb. Farther out were the mountain resorts of Big Bear and Mount Waterman, and seaside spots like Catalina Island and Laguna Beach (see fig. 6-5). The suburb itself increasingly encouraged its citizens to venture out. In the 1950s, the South Gate Parks and Recreation Department organized group outings to places like Disneyland, the L.A. Zoo, Marineland, the Pomona Fair, and Long Beach Harbor, as well as to baseball games at Gilmore Stadium, Wrigley Field,

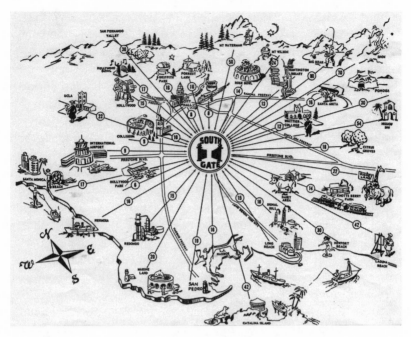

Figure 6-5 This 1961 map depicts South Gate in relation to key sites in postwar Los Angeles. *South Gate "Blue Book" Criss Cross City Directory, 1961* (Anaheim: Luskey Brothers & Co., September 1961).

and, by the late 1950s, Dodger Stadium. "South Gate Night" at Gilmore Stadium was the biggest draw. Located in the Fairfax district, this "workingman's stadium"—so named for its low ticket prices—was the home field of the Hollywood Stars ball club of the Pacific Coast League. South Gaters showed special interest in this league because several local boys went on to play for league teams. "South Gate Night" became an annual affair starting in 1953, with city-sponsored chartered buses carrying hundreds of residents to the ballgame each year. Other city-organized excursions catered to higher brow tastes. The Parks Department and school district organized evening outings to the Greek Theater and Hollywood Bowl for concerts by jazz and classical musicians. The YWCA sponsored annual nine-day "caravan tours" for local high school girls to the Grand Canyon, Bryce, and Zion national parks. Clearly, the suburb was now promoting cosmopolitanism.[110]

South Gate residents enjoyed far-flung leisure as well. Long-distance family trips became commonplace by the 1940s and 1950s. In 1955, a canvass of members of the State Street School PTA found that families took summer vacations to places like Balboa (in Orange County), Washington State, Idaho, New York, Las Vegas, and Minneapolis. Several other families camped in Northern California and at L.A. area mountain resorts. The Markle and North families, both blue-collar, took regular family trips to sites like Yosemite, Big Bear, San Diego, Mexico, and Missouri during the 1950s and early 1960s.[111] South Gate residents also took advantage of the many leisure opportunities in Greater Los Angeles. Truck driver Ray Markle, with his wife and friends, enjoyed frequent soirees at dance venues around Los Angeles. They danced to Spade Cooley's country-and-western band at the Santa Monica Pier, to big bands at the Hollywood Palladium, and to Latino musicians at a Culver City hall. John and Grace Sheehy, a postal worker and a secretary, square-danced regularly in Compton, Huntington Park, and Lynwood. Both the Markles and the Sheehys shunned South Gate's movie theaters—one local drive-in had a reputation as a "flea pit"—opting for theaters in Huntington Park and downtown Los Angeles. For South Gate residents of all classes, leisure occurred in an ever-broadening spatial universe.[112]

Beyond commercial pursuits, residents engaged actively in local community life. Neighbors knew one another, they joined clubs and churches, and they picnicked in the park. In the postwar era, "there was tremendous community spirit, there really was. . . . It was easy to get people to participate," Sheehy recalled, in contrast to the prewar era when economic pressures too often overwhelmed families and prevented them from community participation. Local institutional life flourished in South Gate, authenticating the image of postwar suburbanites as enthusiastic joiners. Fully seventy-one new organizations appeared in South Gate between 1940 and 1965.[113] It was not unusual for a group to have well over 100 members. For example, the YMCA had 721 members in 1945, the Chamber of Commerce 524 in 1947, and the South Gate Art Association 100 in 1961. The best figures come from clubs that met at South Gate Park, from 1956 to 1958 (see table 6-1). At least five clubs for adults met twice each month, with consistent attendance ranging from fifteen to thirty-nine people each time. As an observer noted in 1962, these groups exerted "a strong stabilizing influence" on South Gate.[114]

South Gate's organizations catered to an array of interests and social preferences. Some remained class exclusive, but many welcomed all classes. Service groups such as the Kiwanis, Rotary, Elks, and Optimist clubs continued to include only businessmen and professionals. Ladies auxiliaries to these clubs, like the Lawanis and Rotary Anns, consisted of the wives of members; they mostly supported the projects of the men's clubs. The South Gate Women's Club also continued to draw the wives of businessmen and

Table 6-1   Attendance Figures for Clubs That Met at South Gate Park, 1956–1958

| | 1956–57 | | 1957–58 | |
	Meetings per year	Participants per meeting (average)	Meetings per year	Participants per meeting (average)
Adventure (boys)	2	4	12	4
Art Club (adults)	9	34	12	32
Boys Club	26	34		
Foto Forum	28	24	33	26
Garden Club	13	25	8	14
Golf Club	2	12		
Green Thumb			12	36
Horseshoe Club	34	19		
Horticulture Society	10	58	12	71
Junior Athletic Association	4	40		
Mineral Society (adults)	21	39	18	47
Pebble Pups	1	31	27	18
Rock & Roll Club	8	7		
Rod & Gun Club	13	69		
Senior Citizens Club	17	18	70	34
Starlettes (girls)	11	10	40	14
Tennis Club (adults)	8	14		
T.O.P.S. (women)	28	15	41	15
Variety Club (teenage girls)	35	17	37	12
Welsh American Society	7	40	13	40

Sources: South Gate Parks and Recreation Department, *This Is the Story of the South Gate Parks and Recreation Department, 1956–57,* 19; City of South Gate Parks and Recreation Department, *Annual Report, 1957–58,* 23.

professionals, as it had before the war. By the 1950s, these service clubs, especially the Kiwanis, the Rotarians, and the Chamber of Commerce, often took the lead with veterans groups in coordinating public celebrations in South Gate. Their Independence Day galas, community fairs, and Halloween parties all drew thousands of residents.[115] Other community organizations attracted a broader cross section of members, particularly the PTAs, veterans groups, the South Gate Civic Club, the Junior Athletic Association, and clubs like the Eagles, Odd Fellows, and Masons. Groups serving children drew diverse members, illustrating how youth continued to act as a source of social cohesion. The Tweedy PTA was a good example. In 1949, 80 percent of parents at the school, representing a wide range of occupations, belonged to the PTA. They held frequent bake sales, spaghetti din-

ners, and paper drives to fund various youth activities. By 1963, the PTA
president was the wife of a mechanic, reflecting the group's class inclusiveness. The Junior Athletic Association, the important coordinating body for
all youth sports in South Gate, was headed by a railway worker active in his
union. The Masons—and their various offshoots and auxiliaries—also embraced an occupationally diverse range of members. And the Eagles reached
out to blue-collar men, evident in their sliding-scale dues rates.[116]

Finally, some groups began reflecting new areas of social diversity
in South Gate. Perhaps the most vivid example was Parents Without Part-
ners in the early 1960s, signaling the rise in single-parent households.
Women's changing economic status also revealed itself in club life. Groups
like the Soroptimist, Toastmistress, and Businessmen and Professional
Women's clubs represented counterparts to the male-dominated businessmen's groups. In contrast to ladies auxiliaries of male clubs, these groups
existed independently and required that members be working women, usually in white-collar positions. They focused on service projects for the community. For example, the Soroptimist Club, comprising executives and
professionals, raised money for college scholarships for local students, for
medical equipment at a nearby hospital, and for low-income senior-citizen
housing. Mindful of their class identity, these new women's groups maintained some exclusivity perhaps to protect their small but growing niche in
the local economy and to build networks; they largely followed the model
of male merchant clubs in the community. Comparable groups for working-class women were nonexistent, yet these women still found ample opportunity to join clubs without an occupational requirement.[117]

Churches too proliferated after 1940. Between 1940 and 1965, fifty-two
churches existed in South Gate, thirty-four of them founded after 1940.
They spanned the religious spectrum, from conservative to liberal, Pentecostal to Reform. Most shared a new outward, community-focused orientation, even the once-insular Evangelicals. Evangelical churches continued to
hold an important place in local ecumenical life; several new Pentecostal
and Nazarene churches appeared, as did two Southern Baptist churches. As
in the early years, these churches reflected the influx of southern migrants
to the area. Yet this second generation of Evangelical churches emerged
with a new willingness to unite with one another, embrace social activity,
and participate in broader community life.

A wave of revivals during and immediately after the war invigorated local religious life. Starting in 1944, summertime tent revivals drew thousands seeking "a better world to come." Typical was a ten-day revival by the
Seventh-Day Adventists, held on an open field between South Gate and
Lynwood in June 1944. The church set up 500 family tents for the 2,000

participants who attended. They camped out for the duration, attending six meetings each day starting at 6 A.M. and ending at night with an "evangelistic" service. In September, a revival billed as an "American Soul Clinic" raised hope among organizers that it would help develop South Gate "into a great interdenominational training school for Christian workers." A 1945 revival, organized by twenty-five Evangelical churches in South Gate and neighboring suburbs, lasted three weeks with services every night. Overflow crowds topping 2,000 turned out nightly to hear nationally known preachers, followed by gospel singers, youth rallies, and special children's programs. All churches in the area were invited to participate. Similar revivals followed over the next several years. Increasingly, these revivals became interchurch affairs showing new levels of cooperation among local denominations.[118]

Recognizing the power of the postwar recreational ethos, South Gate churches increasingly embraced social and recreational programs. At youth revivals in the 1950s, worship and fun intermingled. Church of Christ revivals included speakers as well as movies, sports in the church gym, talent shows, and parties. The South Gate First Four Square Church held regular family nights, with singing, films, and music interspersed with worship. Community Presbyterian organized parish picnics, youth sports, and a club for young married couples, which met monthly for movies, barbecues, and picnics. For members like Mary North, the couples club became a focal point of social life. The Methodist Church was very active in community affairs, sponsoring Gra-Y clubs for boys, film screenings, and sports teams. Perhaps the most vivid illustration of the new recreational emphasis was the formation of church sports leagues in the mid-1950s. A church youth league, conceived to teach good sportsmanship and cooperation to youngsters, included touch football and basketball teams for boys, and volleyball for girls. For adults, a baseball league included teams from fourteen area churches, including the Mormons, Four Square, First Baptist, Southern Baptist, and First Nazarene. This league spanned the spectrum from Evangelical to moderate Protestant, signaling a radical shift among the Evangelicals in their willingness to participate in secular activities. Religion thus became another common ground for residents of diverse backgrounds.[119]

As Evangelical churches made their way into public life, they gained a new voice in local politics and civic culture. Their conservative philosophy, tinged by the southern background of congregants, undergirded the powerful strains of working-class political conservatism that emerged in the postwar era. Yet Evangelicals were not completely dominant in South Gate. Churches expressing more liberal political views included First Methodist, First Baptist, and St. Margaret's Episcopal, whose ministers were variously involved in efforts to improve race relations, aid organized labor, and fight Red-baiting. But the voice of Evangelical conservatism ultimately rose above the others when the community faced its biggest political challenges in the postwar years.[120]

Social life in postwar South Gate showed both continuity and change from earlier years. Residents continued commuting to work and play in Los Angeles, revealing a mobile, metropolitan orientation in their everyday routines.[121] Yet despite these outward pulls, they also found compelling forces drawing them more firmly than ever to their suburb. Family, recreation, youth activities, clubs, and churches all acted as anchors securing residents to South Gate. Their economic status rising, working residents now had the resources and time to partake in flourishing social opportunities. Local organizational life became relevant. As they pursued various leisure interests, residents of diverse class backgrounds—particularly merchants and wage earners—healed old divisions and converged on new common ground.

Divisions, Diversity, Disneyland

The same postwar prosperity that united South Gate residents in certain respects undermined the social stability of the suburb in other ways. Merchants, professionals, and factory workers indeed found new common ground, particularly as their income levels reached parity and as social status was measured by factors other than occupation—ability to consume, club affiliations, veteran status, homeownership. Yet this very prosperity also led residents to expect more from their community. Now that they could afford it, residents wanted better homes, bigger yards, and cleaner environs—in short, a more purely middle-class suburb. By the postwar years then a middle-class suburban ideal had taken hold in South Gate. It became hegemonic to the extent that it was supported structurally by federal housing policy and culturally by the town's institutions and its upwardly mobile residents. The earlier working-class suburban ideal, where property served purely economic functions, had transformed.

South Gate was hard-pressed to meet these rising expectations. The community did improve in certain ways, offering new housing in certain sections of town, parks and recreational outlets, and more clubs and civic groups than ever. Yet it was never able to shed fully its blue-collar heritage. Factories remained, trucks and trains continued to rumble through town, and working-class culture persisted. The tension between suburban ideal and working-class reality reached a head in the 1950s, as the suburb's growing diversity of people, housing, and land use began driving away the most successful residents. The prosperous strata—white- and blue-collar alike—began moving to greener suburban pastures in Downey, Bellflower, and the new communities of Orange County. Those who stayed searched for ways to defend, reinvent, and when all else failed re-imagine an idealized suburban existence.

Grassroots activism in the 1950s often focused on efforts to defend the suburban ethos in South Gate against various threats. These efforts revealed a deeper truth about the newfound economic security of residents: it was a status rattled by anxiety, the fear that what came so quickly could be just as swiftly lost. The invasion of certain forces—especially those that symbolized the ills of city life—could bring an end to the suburban good life. For South Gate in the 1950s, the immediate threats were tenants, juvenile delinquents, and encroaching industry, which together portended the urbanization of their suburb. The tenor of their protest most closely mirrored the sort of defensive protectionism and NIMBYism[122] characteristic of postwar neighborhood associations, especially those that bordered on areas of class or racial instability.[123] But in South Gate, grassroots mobilization did not occur through neighborhood associations. Because South Gate was politically independent, residents lodged protests with city hall and, when the foe was outside the community, in the courts.

Housing was one critical issue. The postwar era saw the rise of rentals and multifamily dwellings, and a growing shortage of single-family homes on ample lots. With homeownership regarded as a cornerstone of suburbanism and good homes a prerequisite to this, South Gate's drift toward rentals raised alarm. In 1955, a panel of city leaders identified the "apartment house menace" as the cause of the suburb's most pressing social problems.[124] Echoing prewar platitudes about the civic virtues of homeownership, local leaders feared that the growing tenant population was transient, rootless, and without a stake in the community. "The tendency," they believed, "is toward congestion, deterioration of 'community' feeling, a decreasing sense of responsibility, and a greater drift toward delinquency and denial of opportunities for educational benefits and other services." In short, as Reverend Norman Taylor of the First Methodist Church perceived it, tenants were harder to integrate into the community.

For South Gate, the problem was compounded because not only were tenants uninvolved in the community, but the homeowners who did participate were moving out. As prospering residents sought upward mobility through housing—better homes on larger properties—South Gate found itself unable to meet this demand. The suburb reached its saturation point for single-family homes in the 1950s as available land dwindled. Future housing units came through increasing density, by building multifamily dwellings and zoning for smaller and smaller lots. For upwardly mobile families, this trend was unacceptable because it was not suburban. So they moved to suburbs like Downey, where ample open land enabled good-quality housing development. Their departure created a "brain drain," a shortage of "intelligent community leadership," and an increase in social problems among those left behind. One solution, community leaders believed, was to elevate the suburban ideal over the industrial ideal: more homes and fewer factories. Rev. Taylor offered a more drastic suggestion: merge South Gate with Downey. South Gate would contribute its strong municipal administration and Downey would provide its better housing stock. Ultimately, local leaders called for surveys on delinquency and planning to help identify solutions that would put South Gate on a better course. A coalition—ranging from the Chamber of Commerce to labor leaders—supported these surveys, representing the interests of homeowners seeking to preserve property values and the suburban ideal.[125]

A related issue was the role of industry. Manufacturing was a mixed blessing for South Gate. Although it ensured the economic vigor of the suburb, constituting the lifeblood of local prosperity, it also threatened South Gate's suburban identity. As the suburban ideal was articulated with greater clarity in the postwar years by the national media, South Gate's own character gradually stood in stark contrast to that image. Recognition of the disparity was gradual. In the late 1940s, city leaders clung to an older conception of South Gate as a well-balanced suburb, where clean industries coexisted successfully with homes. The community worked for all, they believed, providing a stable workforce for industry and a healthy place to raise a family for workers. In 1948, Merle Beckley, chair of the South Gate Planning Commission, asserted that the balance could persist over the next twenty-five years. He envisioned the even, harmonious growth of retail, industry, and residences. Yet by the early 1950s, citizens began objecting to the encroachment of industry on their suburban way of life. They launched efforts to prevent factories from threatening their peace, quiet, and property values. In early 1952, for example, residents lodged several complaints against "the terrific vibrations" emanating from A&M Casting, which were strong enough to "knock the pictures off the walls." Four years later, the same plant's attempt to secure a zoning variance to expand its facilities set off intense citizen protests. Homeowners claimed it would increase parking congestion, pose safety hazards, and increase odors that "will cause our property values to go down." After a protracted battle involving pollution impact reports and court rulings, the factory won the zoning variance. Residents raised similar objections to the expansion of Weiser Lock, while neighbors of Allied Engineering complained of the incessant noise and parking problems. Reports of hazardous gas leaks and pollution violations, like the escaping sulfur dioxide at an equipment storage yard on Tweedy, did not help matters.[126]

Complaints of industrial nuisances abounded in the South Gate City Council minutes of the 1950s. Above all, residents feared the threat to property values posed by such nuisances, a concern that surfaced repeatedly. At one meeting, a resident raised a lone voice in defense of industry. He claimed that industry was good for South Gate and that residents "should accustom themselves to the noise," as he had done. While this was local orthodoxy before the war, by now it had become anachronistic.[127]

Not only did factories bring noise, parking congestion, and grime too close to home, destroying the green aura of suburbia, but they also made South Gate a magnet for other nuisances. Beginning in the mid-1950s, regional authorities chose the South Gate area as the site for a juvenile hall facility and a garbage dump transfer station, both to be situated near factories in the eastern end of town. Horrified by this possibility, residents protested vigorously, arguing that property values would drop, undesirables would overrun the area, and the stench of garbage would be intolerable. The garbage proposal was especially objectionable, because it meant refuse from neighboring suburbs—including black communities—would end up in South Gate. As the local editor opined, residents "abhor the thought of a fleet of garbage trucks from Watts, Compton, Huntington Park, Bell, Maywood, and neighboring areas dripping refuse up and down our city streets." Residents lost both fights. The juvenile hall went forward after several court rulings against local protesters. And the garbage transfer site was approved, with the slim backing of the South Gate City Council. City Councilman Leland Weaver, who opposed both measures, noted that in the past, the council had guided "the city to a place where it was a nice, clean, and well regulated city. . . . [Now] the county has found us easy marks." The protesters against industrial expansion, the juvenile hall, and the garbage site were overwhelmingly homeowners, blue- and white-collar alike.[128]

Another threat to South Gate's suburban aura was the specter of juvenile delinquency. Echoing fears gripping communities nationwide, South Gate leaders began voicing their concerns in the mid-1950s. Up to this time, juvenile behavior was not problematized locally. In the late 1940s, South Gate leaders proudly boasted of its low juvenile delinquency rate, attributed to the suburb's stable, homeowning citizenry, its many youth organizations, good police work, lack of racial conflict, and the strong economic status of residents. By the mid-1950s, as baby-boom children began reaching adolescence, delinquency emerged as a crisis. Teens were drag racing at all hours, youth gangs harassed businessmen in the Hollydale district, and others made trouble here and there. When local leaders tried to explain this behavior, they invariably pointed to changing social patterns. More women were working, leaving teens without supervision at home. More cars per household meant family members were splitting off in all directions. More "hoodlums" from other towns were coming into South Gate, part of a burgeoning local car culture. And the exodus of good citizens moving out in search of better homes left a gap in leadership for youth.

The city responded in several ways. It began enforcing a 10 P.M. curfew law, penalizing the parents of teens who violated it. Trying the "carrot" approach, the Parks and Recreation Department formed the Rock 'n' Roll Club, hoping to attract kids into a supervised social milieu. But the response was dismal; only fifty-five teens attended eight meetings from 1956 to 1957. Some service and civic clubs stepped up their programs for youth. The most creative—and controversial—overture came from a group of police officers concerned about teenage dragsters racing on the L.A. River bed running through South Gate. Several sympathetic policemen urged the city to make it an official racing strip, with three officers supervising at all times. But a group of 300 residents strongly objected, fearing the noise, rowdiness, and threat to property values. They successfully blocked the proposal with a petition drive that convinced the city council and chief of police to kill the plan.[129]

The forces of change sweeping South Gate—the rise in tenants, youthful delinquents, working women, and offensive facilities—propelled a closing of ranks among South Gate property owners. Factory workers, clerks, businesspeople, and professionals united to defend their suburban turf and preserve the suburban ideal to the best of their ability. Their climactic moment came in the early 1960s, when the biggest threat of all—the civil rights movement—set off the most tightly organized, successful campaign of resistance yet. In the 1950s, local politics had not become fully racialized as it would in the 1960s. Indeed, concerns about race and class converged for a time, marking a key transition stage for South Gate. Up to 1948, maintaining racial barriers around South Gate was economically easy. The key mechanism was restrictive covenants, which cost nothing. For a working-class suburb like South Gate, this was an optimal, affordable strategy. When the U.S. Supreme Court struck down such covenants in *Shelley v. Kraemer* (1948), this tool of segregation became unworkable. White residents had to find new ways. One was to use class as a barrier. If South Gate residents could maintain a solid, middle-class suburban identity, they might successfully shut out the "undesirables." This meant keeping the town free of immediate threats to that identity, like renters, juvenile delinquents, and dump sites. So in the 1950s, they struggled willy-nilly to preserve South Gate as a place where a "typical family" might live out the postwar suburban dream. Their success was mixed. Threats remained.

For some, refuge was outside of South Gate. Some found it by moving away, to better homes in more stable neighborhoods. Others found it in new safe spaces in the postwar metropolis, at places like Disneyland. As perhaps *the* prototype of suburban popular culture in the postwar era, Disneyland epitomized America's quest for security, order, and homogeneity in a world grown increasingly diverse and threatening. It was a sanctuary from change. Located in Anaheim, about twenty-two miles southeast of South Gate, Disneyland opened in July 1955 to an incredibly enthusiastic public. Disneyland obviously touched a nerve, tapping into a public desire for a "privatized, controlled, even 'contained' experience." In the L.A. metropolis, Disneyland offered a sense of order in a context of unbridled growth, a reference point of familiarity, hospitality, and predictability for Los Angelenos, and ultimately a model for western cities seeking control and containment in their designs.[130]

As a new kind of amusement space, Disneyland sought to reassure and uplift its audience. It purposely distanced itself from earlier models of amusement parks like Coney Island, with its "tawdry rides and hostile employees," dirty grounds, and rude patrons. Coney Island was the sorry epitome of working-class leisure, a sign of eastern urban decay both physical and social. Disneyland would be different: a sanitized, spotless environment that reassured its patrons with a wholesome, "enriched version of the real world." As one designer put it, "we program out all the negative, unwanted elements and program in the positive elements." It especially sought to recapture an idealized past, "evoking the truer human nature" of times gone by. As Walt Disney put it, "This is very real. . . . The park is reality. The people are natural here; they're having a good time; they're communicating. This is what people really are." Such idealized nostalgia was expressed in Main Street U.S.A., with its turn-of-the-century shops and quaintness, and in Frontierland, which portrayed a hearty, well-meaning western spirit.[131] In the totality of its environment, Disneyland celebrated self-reliance, masculinity, westward movement, the importance of small property ownership and small business, while delineating racial separateness and inferiority. Patrons would be uplifted by their visit through a series of carefully orchestrated manipulations designed to "soothe and to sell." They would emerge happier, better behaved, more middle class.[132]

South Gate residents responded enthusiastically. The local press praised Disneyland not for its escapism but rather for "the authenticity of all exhibits and entertainment." Main Street, railroads, riverboats, and buildings all conveyed this enhanced reality. "[S]uper-commercialism appears to have been ruled out. Entertainment and education are keynoted, not salesmanship," the *Press* noted approvingly. The year the park opened, residents could buy Disneyland tickets at the local Vons supermarket for a special Christmas Festival featuring the Mickey Mouse Club. In subsequent years, the suburb organized group excursions to Disneyland. The 1957 trip drew 270 residents. The South Gate Youth Band performed several times at the theme park, while various individuals ventured to the "Magic Kingdom" on their own. Mary North recalled making annual trips to the theme park with her husband and children, from the time it opened. To her, it was "another world. The lights, the music, just like you left all your cares behind."[133]

For Pamela Lawton, verging on adolescence, Disneyland was a safe retreat. A shy child who spent most of her spare hours helping care for her infant siblings, Pamela remembered juvenile delinquency as a real threat in her universe in 1950s South Gate. She recalled "a lot of rough kids, especially at my age and going into junior high. . . . They beat people up, they smoked, they would hang out. . . . The area was rough for kids, and junior high got much worse." Fearing this environment, Pamela retreated to her home, where she read avidly and she loved listening to rock-and-roll music on the radio. One of Pamela's neighbors, Helen Henry, made a point of taking her own children and Pamela to special places around Los Angeles. They visited museums and the tar pits, they saw Elvis at the Pan Pacific Auditorium, and they went to Disneyland the week it opened.

At Disneyland, Pamela found a better reality, the images of her books brought to life. "That was so thrilling to see from Main Street on. Here were things you knew about from your grandmother's day on Main Street, old-fashioned things. Walking down Main Street, absolutely a fantasy world that was so thrilling for kids because it was real, it was right there. . . . What I knew from books I actually got to see. Things about history . . . I was drawn by the excitement of what was out there in the world. The shops sold old-fashioned candy, people wore dresses from the turn of the century. Other costumes in Frontierland, Fantasyland . . . I was really experiencing things that I'd only known about in books."

To Pamela, Disneyland offered the best of what was good in the world. "It was immaculate. Streets used to be clean in those days, for instance in South Gate they had street cleaners and things were kept pretty clean. But Disneyland was immaculate and shiny and big. And the people, and everyone who worked there was so friendly. It reminded me of the counselors at camp, who were so open, gregarious people. I was self-conscious and shy. I kind of thrived on that. . . . All the people on the rides were so theatrical, so warm. You felt really happy there, like life was really hopeful." When Pamela started baby-sitting and earning some extra money, she "wanted to go every weekend." Her family moved to Orange County when she was fourteen, into a bigger, better home, and to Pamela's delight, much closer to Anaheim. Disneyland soon became a regular part of her life. Realizing a person could buy admission to the park for $1.25 without the expense of the ticket book for rides, Pamela went as often as she could as a teen. Her dad drove her, dropped her off near the entrance, and she spent the entire day wandering the park alone. "I'd walk and look at everything, look in all the windows, walk around looking in the stores. Everything seemed so interesting. . . . Sometimes I would sit and just watch people. I just loved being out in the world like that, and it was a safe environment. . . . At the time, it seemed okay to do that. It felt very safe, probably because it was so familiar because of the television, too." For Pamela Lawton, Walt Disney's intention was realized. Disneyland succeeded in creating an "enriched version of the real world" for a working-class child, who found a sanctuary from the tougher realities of postwar life.[134]

By the early 1960s, the quest for security and insularity in South Gate took on a heightened sense of urgency. Those who remained faced the biggest threat yet to the postwar suburban ideal: racial encroachment. As the civil rights movement blossomed in Los Angeles, South Gate became an easy target for activists seeking to tear down that most highly color-conscious element of idealized suburbia—racial homogeneity. This conflict politicized South Gate residents in new ways, pushing racialized politics to the forefront of local concerns. The social bridges built during the 1950s helped residents wage this battle more effectively, as erstwhile adversaries —workers and merchants—closed ranks in defense of their suburb. When class divisions dissolved into postwar consensus, race moved to the fore. It ultimately stood at the heart of a nascent political culture that united Americanism, anticommunism, economic populism, and white identity. South Gate was giving birth to the silent majority.

7   The Racializing of Local Politics

At the close of 1963, the *South Gate Press* listed the "top ten stories" of the year in its annual retrospective. Ranked number one was an issue so "emotionally charged" it eclipsed all others —including the assassination of President John F. Kennedy. That event came in second. To residents of South Gate, the most significant story of 1963 was the local fight against integrated schools.[1]

Even Juanita (Smith) Hammon, then in her fifties, entered the fray. In September 1963, she wrote a letter to the editor of the *Press*, attacking a teacher at South Gate High who supported recent campaigns to desegregate the local schools. "This man, who does not live in the area," she railed, "has the gall to tell South Gate people what is necessary for them. He claims integration is necessary if we are to be truly educated. He goes further, and I quote, 'We cannot really learn about one another, unless we have been living with one another.' If you do not agree with this, please take the time to let him and his boss, Glenn Miller, know your feelings."[2] Hammon's assumption was crystal clear. The idea of "race mixing," of integrating neighborhoods and schools, was unthinkable, so wrong that it demanded forceful public statements against it. Juanita Hammon, whose forebears typified the early settlers of South Gate, was again an exemplar of the community, this time of a postwar suburb highly concerned about race, protectionism, and separation. Her life continued to embody the broader social changes transforming South Gate, namely the rise from working-class insecurity to middle-class prosperity. Juanita had married a man who became a manager at Firestone, and she herself entered the merchant ranks when she became a realtor in the early 1960s. In the process, her mentality shifted. No longer concerned with working-class survival, she now focused on the new community priority: keeping South Gate white.

If Juanita Hammon exemplified the first generation of South Gate settlers, Floyd Wakefield represented the second. Wakefield emerged as a local leader whose political career was born and sustained by racialized politics, and who became the unequivocal voice of South Gate's "silent majority." Born in Denver in 1919, he and his family moved to Southern California in 1923, settling in working-class Maywood. Wakefield's father abandoned the family when Floyd was seven, forcing them to rely on county aid when his mother became ill and could no longer work. Most of their relatives lived far away, in Texas and Oklahoma. As a teenager, Floyd worked in grocery stores, mowed lawns, and did odd jobs around the neighborhood. After graduating from Bell High School, he worked as a molder at Alcoa foundry in Vernon. Even at this age, Floyd prized the ideal of individualism. "I always did things myself, and I didn't have to worry about somebody else." He joined the union there because he "more or less had to." This same philosophy shaped his politics: already "very conservative," he believed FDR was a "great socialist." Wakefield married in 1940, bought a house in South Gate, then shipped out to Europe to serve in the war.[3]

Upon his return, Wakefield entered the ranks of the business class. His family—including wife and three children—made this happen at great sacrifice. They "sold everything, car, refrigerator, stove, house" to raise capital, and took out a $9,000 GI loan. The family lived in a tent in Floyd's mother's backyard for several months, then in a Quonset hut in South Gate Park for more than a year. Everything went into the business. Wakefield operated a Goodyear store for five years, then opened a sporting goods store in the early 1950s to serve the burgeoning demand for recreational goods. In the 1960s, he belonged to the Kiwanis Club, American Legion, Veterans of Foreign Wars, YMCA, United Republicans of California, and Constitutional Republican Educational Workers, and he served as president of the South Gate Rod & Gun Club.[4]

Wakefield first gained public attention as founder and chair of the South Gate Education Committee, devoted to fighting school integration. Local civic groups applauded his efforts, bestowing him with the Distinguished

Service Award in 1964. A week after the award ceremony, he announced his candidacy for the Fifty-second Assembly District of California. As a Republican, Wakefield's campaign centered on the issue of race. He criticized civil rights measures in general but especially denounced fair housing laws, which resonated with his white homeowner constituents. Articulating a discourse of white rights, he blasted fair housing laws for taking "away one of our most cherished rights . . . 'The right to choose.'" He won endorsements from Republicans and Democrats alike, revealing the makings of a major political realignment. Local Democrats, frantic over the possibility of forced integration, rallied behind the Republican. They mounted a write-in campaign and formed the Democrats for Wakefield Committee.

Although he lost the 1964 race, he achieved victory two years later on the heels of the Watts Rebellion. Combining his old platform with the new theme of "law and order," Wakefield won a seat in the state assembly, defeating his opponent despite an overwhelming preponderance of registered Democrats in the district. He especially valued the support of union members. As he recalled of the 1966 assembly campaign, "I'd have union guys drive down the street when we were putting up signs. . . . And truck drivers would stop on the other side of the road and run across and say, 'Hey Floyd, just because we're union, that doesn't mean we're listening to them. We're supporting you.' We had that kind of talk all the time." Wakefield considered himself the voice of the hardworking, taxpaying homeowner. "When government power increases, it is being taken from the people," he observed. "When the people become aware of this, they are more apt to vote for individuals with a reasonable philosophy rather than those who holler on the street corners." Thus characterizing his constituents as modest, quiet citizens—even as he ignored the clamor they generated in fighting civil rights—Wakefield painted a crystalline portrait of the emerging "silent majority." These were the working people, taxpayers, homeowners, and small businessmen, Democrats and Republicans alike, whose political sensibilities were reshaped by the politics of race.[5]

Wakefield served for seven years in the California State Assembly, where he gained notoriety as a tireless opponent of busing. He essentially took the values he formulated in South Gate and transplanted them to the canvass of state politics. Eventually Wakefield's ideas earned broad acceptance. "I have probably talked before 500 or 600 groups over the last years about this busing," he said in 1970. "Almost every time someone has gotten up and called me a 'racist' or a 'bigot.' But now, all of a sudden, I am no longer a 'bigot.' Now I am called 'the leader of the antibusing' effort. I'm just saying the same thing I always have." The widespread resistance to busing nationally, from small neighborhoods to the Nixon White House, confirmed Wakefield's claim.[6]

Wakefield's rise to power symbolized the political transformation of postwar South Gate. As earlier pressures of economic survival receded in the postwar era and residents found themselves enjoying middle-class lifestyles, the path was cleared for new political concerns to emerge. The new preoccupation became protecting their prosperity and status by guarding against the creeping effects of urbanization, namely the threats of social, industrial, and racial encroachment. By the early 1960s, the race issue was paramount. While racial concerns had simmered beneath the surface during the interwar years, by the postwar era prospering residents could act more decisively to draw racial boundaries and safeguard their identity as white, upwardly mobile, working Americans. Residents, finally, could afford to act on their fears about race.

Yet class concerns did not simply give way to racial concerns; indeed, the two were inextricably intertwined. As class identity continued to be defined in the neighborhood, the character of one's neighborhood became critical to that identity. For South Gate residents, grasping willfully for middle-class lives in a town with working-class roots, their progress was quick and precarious. Threats persisted. In the postwar years, racial purity became an increasingly important aspect of community identity—of the suburban ideal itself—during a historical moment when challenges to racial purity erupted. Not only were timeworn tools of segregation like race-restrictive covenants abolished by the courts, but activists aggressively campaigned for racial equality in many areas of life. Whites responded by assuming a defensive posture. This stance was not simply a product of racism or a desire for a socially comfortable community life, although these certainly played a role. It stemmed too from the class anxieties of factory and office workers, newly arrived in the pecuniary world of the middle class, who sought to protect their position in this universe. Racial encroachment, they were convinced, would destroy property values, obliterate their community-based status, and ultimately jettison them down the ladder back to an existence of struggle and want. Their own grave interests in this scenario ultimately compelled them to evoke the language of white rights.

Like many American neighborhoods on the front lines of civil rights pushes in the North and West—often white working-class towns that bordered on black ones—South Gate reacted defensively. The racialization of politics ultimately reconstituted local political mentalities, pushing erstwhile Democrats rightward while underscoring the values that guided residents before the war—individualism, hard work, private property, and antistatism. They surfaced now as the ideological bedrock of an emergent working-class conservative ethos.[7]

Postwar political identity fused the old and new in another respect. The arrival of a second generation of residents after the war meant that recent migrants brought with them distinct value systems. Those migrants from the South, part of the enormous white southern diaspora transforming postwar America, brought not only a continued affinity for southern culture, music, and Evangelical religion, but also a penchant for southern politics. In the 1950s and 1960s, this emerged as a new style of working-class populism, melding racism, economic populism, and anti-elitism. Politicians like George Wallace built careers around these values. In South Gate, recent southern migrants applied these principles to the new political challenges facing them. And people like Floyd Wakefield, with ancestral roots in Texas and Oklahoma, spearheaded such efforts. In this sense, South Gate experienced the "southernizing" of its working-class populace, as these ideals helped shape the suburb's position on the most important political events affecting the community. Yet this sensibility also dovetailed with South Gate's indigenous political heritage. The values forged in the distinctive context of working-class suburbia during the interwar years fused smoothly with these imported ideals. Self-help, individualism, Americanism, homeowner rights, and a distaste for activist government persisted as core values; in the new context of economic prosperity and racial encroachment, they blended easily with the southern political style.[8]

The political story of postwar South Gate starts, above all, as a local one. The political allegiances of residents were not shaped by national leaders, swaying them with rhetorical abstractions. Instead, their sensibility emerged in the context of immediate crisis and concrete threats. In the "crabgrass-roots" campaign for neighborhood preservation, South Gate residents—like their counterparts in Detroit, Chicago, Boston, Baltimore, Brooklyn, and elsewhere—began with a highly localized focus. For them, the crisis was imminent and visceral. Only later would their ideas translate into broader agendas, larger political visions, and party politics, spanning from Los Angeles to Sacramento and all the way to the White House.[9]

The Terrain of Local Politics

In terms of local political structure and governance, South Gate entered a period of stability after World War II. A coterie of businessmen and professionals continued to dominate city hall, although several men from working-class backgrounds also emerged as leaders. As shown in table 7-1, from

Table 7-1   South Gate City Council Members (Including Mayors), 1940–1964

Council Member	Council Term	Occupation(s)
Beckley, Merle	1942–50	Proprietor: real estate, insurance
Bunnett, Francis	1940–52	Attorney
Dellmann, Milo	1950–66	Tool and die maker
Fike, Earl	1934–42	Proprietor: barbershop
Grant, Floyd	1938–52	Superintendent, concrete and pipe company
Hardy, Russell L.	1952–68	Postal clerk and proprietor (real estate & investment)
Henville, Joe	1960–72	Proprietor: real estate
Hobart, Dewey	1938–42	Electrician
Huddleston, D.	1942[a]	Proprietor: escrow company
Hutchinson, R. Earl	1954–62	Firestone chemist, executive, building contractor (retired by 1961)
Nellar, Ernest[b]	1938–42	—
Olsen, John C.	1942–54	Market manager
Peckenpaugh, Chas.H.	1952–60	Salesman
Sawyer, Donald R.	1962–78	Proprietor: real estate and insurance
Taylor, John M.	1950–52	Proprietor: automobile dealership
Weaver, Leland	1944–66	Proprietor: insurance company, travel agency, credit and collection bureau

[a]Huddleston served only three days as mayor.
[b]Nellar's occupation was not available.

Sources: Bicentennial Heritage Committee, *South Gate 1776–1976* (South Gate: South Gate Press, 1976), 21; *South Gate Tribune,* June 27, 1938; South Gate files, FWP; South Gate City Council minutes and resolutions, SGCH; *South Gate and Walnut Park City Directory. June 1, 1940* (K.I. Strand, 1940); *South Gate City Directory. July 1951* (K.I. Strand & Dean S. Woodbury, 1951); *South Gate "Blue Book" Criss Cross City Directory. 1961* (Anaheim, Ca.: Luskey Brothers & Co., September 1961).

1940 to 1964 only sixteen men served on the city council. Half were proprietors, five were managers or professionals, and two were skilled blue-collar workers.[10] These councilmen had a tighter grip over city hall than their prewar predecessors. Their average tenure in office was 12.2 years, compared to 3.6 years for councilmen before the war.[11] As well, clusters of councilmen tended to dominate city hall over several years: one ruled from 1944 to 1950, another from 1952 to 1960, and a third coalesced in 1962. The slate that dominated during the 1950s—Milo Dellman, Russell Hardy, Earl Hutchinson, Charles Peckenpaugh, and Leland Weaver—included three men with working-class roots and a fourth who considered South Gate a "workingman's city." They helped solidify the bond between blue-collar residents and business interests. Councilman Hardy's own career trajectory embodied this unity: he rose from postal clerk to real estate proprietor

during his tenure on the council. The city council had become a stable, secure body, free from the volatility that had plagued it in earlier years.

South Gate stabilized in other ways as well. It coped with rapid growth
more effectively and economically than ever. No longer was unbridled
spending the rule. The watchword had become municipal economizing.
This new approach was shaped by the hard lessons of the Mattoon Act. In
1940, the city council legislated a guarantee that it would never repeat the
earlier mistakes of frenzied development and taxation. It passed a "pay-as-
you-go" ordinance, which prohibited the city from engaging in any municipal development that required long-term bonds. The measure still allowed
the council to establish special assessment districts, but only when a majority of property owners demanded improvements. For the most part, the city
would launch improvements only when sufficient funds were on hand. The
pay-as-you-go ordinance, approved by 80 percent of voters, earned glowing
praise in South Gate. One resident referred to it as "the great reformation
and experiment in civic Utopia in South Gate—progress and innovations
that have won the plaudits and respect of the state and nation." When the
new City Hall was erected in 1942, a publicity pamphlet noted, "South Gate
citizens will be particularly proud of this beautiful new building, which is
ENTIRELY FREE OF DEBT." In the 1950s and 1960s, city leaders boasted that
South Gate had the lowest bonded indebtedness of any city of comparable
or greater size in the nation.[12]

The most telling evidence of a local consensus on the tax issue was a
small agenda item at a city council meeting in 1954. The president of the revived South Gate Chamber of Commerce expressed his group's opposition
to "any raise in the present tax levy" and to any sales or recreation taxes.
This signaled a 180-degree turn. Now that merchants had converged with
working-class residents on taxation, it virtually died as a political issue.[13]

Such austerity initially became possible through a combination of federal assistance and local misfortune. In the late 1930s, the Works Progress
Administration aided the construction of several public buildings, lifting
the fiscal burden from the locality. Meanwhile, the city earned more than
$1 million from the sale of tax-delinquent land, fallout of the Mattoon Act,
which prompted one newspaper editor to quip that "South Gate quit the realty business" when these sales finally ended. City leaders used this money
to launch a $1 million civic building program, the kind of improvements
they had pined for all along. Throughout this period, the tax rate held
steady at $1 or less per $100 assessed valuation, significantly lower than
prewar levels and much lower than in neighboring communities. This rate
was maintained without extra levies for special services (typical in most

communities), sales taxes, or parking meters. By 1964, the tax rate had dropped to $0.59 per $100.[14]

South Gate's newfound fiscal conservatism reflected a milestone in the suburb's political history. The drastic legal restraint on spending symbolized the final, painfully reached fruition of a philosophy that working-class residents had embraced since the 1920s. In their opposition to excessive growth, taxation, and spending, they essentially sought to curb government's power and to manage growth at a pace they could live with. The irony was that once residents could actually afford to finance improvements in the postwar era, the door was shut. Moreover, as local development reached a saturation point in the 1950s, it diminished as a political issue. Taxing and spending—as applied to the infrastructure of their suburb—no longer dominated political discourse. Yet these issues did not simply go away. Instead, they reemerged in new terms, along with new political antagonists. No longer were *local* leaders—high spending and misguided—the enemy. Now, outside forces constituted the primary threat to South Gate's way of life.

Signs of this shift abounded. One was the city council's preoccupation with excluding interlopers from the community in the 1950s and 1960s. Non-residents—be they competing merchants, fund-raising Boy Scouts, or political activists—were not welcome in South Gate. While this followed on prewar policy that banned outside businesses, the postwar council accelerated the trend. It started out small. In December 1952, a man who lived three blocks beyond South Gate's border was denied a permit to sell Christmas trees in the suburb. He pleaded with the council, saying he had a wife and children to support and that he'd spent the last of his money on fixtures for the Christmas tree lot. The council apologized but held firm. Two years later, it denied a business permit to a disabled merchant, again because of his nonresident status. By the mid-1950s, the council had extended the exclusion policy to nonprofit groups, including the Disabled American Veterans on a fund-raising drive, the Compton Miracle Church seeking to hold a tent revival, and the John F. Kennedy Memorial Youth Fund selling tickets for a talent show. All were rejected because they were nonresidents.[15]

Hostility to outside threats emerged as a recurring theme in local politics. The forces of communism, civil rights "meddlers," and liberal bureaucrats who knew nothing about South Gate became the new enemies. The community, it seemed, was under siege. Political life became a defensive battle, a struggle to protect the suburb from the forces tampering with the very institutions that defined it.

Much to its chagrin, South Gate found itself swept into the maelstrom of a national political crisis centered on the turbulent issue of race. As this national crisis manifested locally, the traditional preoccupations of local politics—municipal development, financing, and maintenance—began to fade from view. In turn, the city council also diminished in importance. It was simply not equipped to fight these larger battles. As residents quickly learned, the broadened political arena that now encompassed South Gate required a different strategy, one capable of fighting off intrusive metropolitan, state, and even federal policymakers. And it required new leaders at higher levels of governance. In postwar South Gate, the political enemy was no longer internally contained. It loomed as threats from the outside, ranging from schoolchildren in Watts to politicians in Washington, D.C. Postwar politics became an exercise in reacting to these threats, in preserving the suburb's character, and ultimately in resisting the forces of progressive change.

The Diminution of Class Concerns: Labor's Political Failure in South Gate

Several national political impulses converged in South Gate after the war. The confluence of these tenets nurtured a conservative political outlook among residents, one that diminished class-based concerns as it foregrounded race. As this occurred, organized labor surrendered power and influence on the local scene, hampered by an agenda too progressive for the tastes of most residents. As labor unions embraced leftist politics and civil rights, South Gate's residents moved in an opposite political direction, defined by suspicions of minorities, communists, and even unions. Organized labor, as a result, became politically irrelevant in the suburb.

Anticommunism was one impulse emerging in South Gate that worked against labor-based politics. Led by merchant and veterans groups, South Gate became a bastion of anti-Red sentiment as early as the 1930s. The veterans who led the co-ops during the Depression, for example, underscored their aversion to communist and socialist doctrine, stressing instead the principles of democracy and Americanism. By the late 1930s, the local newspaper ran political ads that Red-baited the CIO, while civic groups hosted speakers decrying the evils of communism. In speeches to the Kiwanis and Rotary Clubs, for example, the president of the California Elks Association warned that communism posed a grave "peril to government" and fomented "agitation among Negroes in the South." As the Cold War set in by the late 1940s, these political sentiments intensified, often cloaked in the guise of patriotism. In 1948, 275 city employees in South Gate—

without being asked to do so—volunteered to take loyalty oaths. They presented their affidavits to the city council, explaining that South Gate taxpayers deserved an assurance that their city employees "believed in the American way of life." By the early 1950s, Floyd Wakefield formed an Americanism program in South Gate, organizing outside speakers to address students during school hours and adults in the evening. In 1952, South Gate hosted the House Un-American Activities Committee at a banquet in the civic auditorium. A prominent Democratic leader announced the event to the city council, which in turn praised all "the work being done to bring this outstanding organization to South Gate." Patriotism reached fever pitch in the mid-1950s. "Surprised and humiliated" that so few flags were displayed on patriotic holidays, the merchants along Tweedy Boulevard raised money in 1954 to buy ninety large American flags to line their street (see fig. 7-1). The following year, the suburb held its first annual

Figure 7-1   In 1954, South Gate merchants raised funds to purchase flags to line Tweedy
   Boulevard. Patriotism reached fever pitch in the 1950s, fueled by Cold War anticommunism.
   From the *Los Angeles Examiner*, Hearst Collection. Photo courtesy of University of Southern
   California, on behalf of the USC Library Department of Special Collections.

"Loyalty Day Parade," billed as the first such procession in the nation. South Gate's patriots, in fact, were not chasing shadows when it came to their own suburb. Some local labor organizations, particularly the CIO unions, had Communists, Socialists, and other radicals in their ranks. The association of organized labor with the "Red menace" boded ill for the po- litical aspirations of labor candidates.[16]

Another political impulse gaining momentum in South Gate was resis- tance to civil rights, which dovetailed with anticommunism. Many early civil rights campaigns in the late 1940s were spearheaded by the Commu- nist Party, a tireless advocate in the struggle for black equality in Los Ange- les. As efforts to desegregate housing and education began hitting close to home, South Gate residents responded with a fervent campaign of resis- tance. Organized labor's stand on this issue—in favor of civil rights—fur- ther alienated residents from labor-based politics. While workers might accept racial equality inside the factory, their tolerance broke down in the neighborhood. The breach between workplace and community politics be- came all too clear when organized labor entered the political arena.[17]

In the postwar period, labor unions made the first organized effort to bring their social vision to the suburb, marking a significant milestone in the history of South Gate. While merchants had been doing this from the start, it was uncharted territory for labor. The unions would have to face the entrenched leadership of merchants and professionals, who continued to dominate the city council. Labor's first effort came in 1946, when a rubber worker named Winston Dodge ran for city council. Endorsed by UAW Lo- cal 216, he promised to bring more "representative government" to South Gate. "Five councilmen whose private interests are closely associated," he asserted, "cannot adequately represent all of South Gate, however sincere and honest they may be." Despite Dodge's appeals, the three incumbents— all business owners—won the contest, with Dodge trailing in fifth place.[18]

Two years later, organized labor launched a more concerted political ef- fort. It was spearheaded by the South East Committee for Labor Candidates (SECLC), a political coalition formed in early 1948 by UAW Local 216. They targeted the city council elections of five suburbs in southern Los An- geles—South Gate, Huntington Park, Maywood, Bell, and Lynwood—all with substantial blue-collar populations. The coalition's goals were to run labor candidates and to mobilize the labor vote. Noting that this was "the first time that organized labor has ever considered participating in these sixth class city elections," the SECLC explained itself: "labor must begin its fight at the lowest rung on the political ladder if it is ever to achieve victo- ries at the top." And the coalition chair intoned, "Labor must take the lead in solving the problems of the community, since the community is made up primarily of working people." Appealing to the interests of merchants, he added that the prosperity of local businesses and professionals hinged on labor's standard of living.[19]

The coalition drew participants from several sources. Workers from a variety of trades, representing both AFL and CIO unions, served as leaders and supporters. The SECLC also welcomed any "liberal-minded citizens" not associated with the labor movement. Seeking to penetrate both the workplace and the neighborhood, the SECLC established a speakers' bureau and publicized its cause through press releases, leaflets, placards, radio broadcasts, and rallies. They handed out fliers at factories and solicited donations from unions.[20]

The SECLC endorsed candidates, all active union men, for each suburb's election. In South Gate, candidate George Fisher, a toolmaker, had been active in early CIO organizing in Los Angeles. He had served as chair of the South Gate Civic Club and as a PTA member. A second candidate, Dale Lewis, was a railway worker who hailed from Arkansas. He was secretary of his union, a member of the PTA, and had also served as chair of the South Gate Civic Club. All SECLC candidates consciously disassociated themselves from any political party and accepted endorsements only from nonpartisan groups. By doing so, they hoped to focus attention on policies advantageous to labor, regardless of party.[21]

The SECLC candidates for all five council races ran on the coalition's broader platform, which called for policies favorable to labor; a state program of low-cost housing; the continuation and extension of child-care centers; an increase in old age benefits; the abolition of local and state sales taxes "which fall heaviest on those least able to pay"; rent controls; and a civil rights policy that called for "equal rights for all citizens, and full civil rights for all government employees." The South Gate labor candidates also promised adequate supervised playground and recreational facilities, better and cheaper local services (such as garbage disposal, streetlights, and transportation), and "zoning practices designed to protect small home owners and other residents from encroachment by industries providing hazards, obnoxious odors or other nuisances." In 1948, the last issue had yet to become a pressing local concern.[22]

In South Gate, the labor candidates ran against several professed businessmen, who vowed to apply business principles to municipal management. "I only hope that our city can continue to be operated as a business and not as a political merry-go-round," proclaimed one office seeker, a retired factory manager. Another candidate, a realtor, promised that no public pool would be built in South Gate because of the "probable race problems involved." Another ran a vague campaign under the slogan "No Promises. Only Sincerity." For the most part, the business candidates ran indistinct, issueless campaigns, in stark contrast to the specificity of the labor campaign. As election day neared, the labor candidates highlighted the class differences between themselves and their opponents. The southern suburbs, charged a publicity flier, "have been controlled since they started by business men, real estate men and big corporations. From our past experience we've seen that candidates put up by these interests aren't really interested in the welfare of the worker's families. . . . You will want to vote for [the labor candidates] because they are all union members and working people like yourselves." This was the most explicit expression of class conflict ever made in a South Gate election.[23]

Despite their working-class appeals, the labor candidates lost badly in South Gate—each earned less than 10 percent of votes. In the other four suburbs, the results were equally dismal. None of the SECLC's candidates won, and most trailed in last place. The blue-collar citizens of these suburbs chose businessmen over fellow workers. One union man attributed labor's failure to poor organization and the race issue, particularly labor's advocacy of low-cost housing and civil rights. As he recalled, "Everybody looked on low-cost housing as being the ghetto. . . . [Supporting this position] would kill you in South Gate." While the SECLC made a small effort to continue its work, it soon disbanded, and labor candidates continued to fare poorly in subsequent years.[24] The unsuccessful labor-liberal alliance in South Gate, in fact, resembled national patterns in the immediate postwar period, when similar coalitions were thwarted in other cities. In South Gate, labor's political failure of the late 1940s signaled the demise of class-based politics and a rise in suspicions about progressive, civil rights politics.[25]

While organized labor could not make inroads into city councils, by the 1950s individual candidates from working-class backgrounds had better luck. Milo Dellmann and Russell Hardy, a tool and die maker and a former postal clerk, respectively, began long reigns on the council in the early 1950s. They represented working-class interests derived in the neighborhood—divorced from organized labor's agenda. Together with three other councilmen, including a salesman, a building contractor, and a businessman, they formed the slate that dominated the city council in the 1950s. Although their role diminished in the broader scheme of postwar politics, they did preside over a period when class distinctions faded from view. And they represented a united front against the biggest challenge of all: the civil rights movement.

Up Against Civil Rights

The growing importance of race in local politics and in the formation of working-class identity was revealed when the civil rights movement exploded in southern Los Angeles. As African Americans waged the struggle for equality in the realms of education, housing, employment, and other arenas, white Los Angelenos were forced to confront the fact that discrimination existed in their city and to contend with increasingly aggressive efforts to end that discrimination. Although white responses varied, in the southern suburbs most working-class whites opposed civil rights efforts, despite their allegiance to the Democratic Party. Race cracked the labor-liberal alliance that had sustained the New Deal, jettisoning those working-class Democrats into the ranks of the Republicans.

Racial politics became the key catalyst for this political realignment, in South Gate as in many "Middle America" neighborhoods nationwide. In the 1960s, traditional Democrats, such as southerners, ethnic Catholics, blue-collar workers, and union members, bolted from their party to become a "reborn right." The defections began in Democratic blue-collar neighborhoods, often squeezed directly by integration conflicts, then spread to middle-class areas. The Republicans successfully tapped into the resentments of this constituency, who longed to restore America to its former self before the social revolutions of the era. As Jonathan Rieder has noted, if there was one "single source of displeasure that shook the New Deal coalition to its core, it was the civil rights revolution."[26]

Race became a central preoccupation for working-class whites in southern Los Angeles because it started directly affecting their lives. This happened when the civil rights movement began using the area's stark social geography to illustrate their points about segregation and discrimination. Black and white were sharply divided here, with Alameda Street constituting a virtual "wall" between the races. Blacks lived to the west, whites to the east. In this area, segregation was a visible reality, especially in the realms of housing and education. Thus, it came as little surprise that white working-class suburbs like South Gate, Huntington Park, and Lynwood, which abutted Alameda, were targeted by civil rights protesters. These lily-white neighborhoods were clear symbols of the problem. When the civil rights movement burst forth in Los Angeles, it slammed hard against these communities.

And the white suburbs slammed back. In South Gate, residents vociferously resisted the demands of civil rights activists, demands that portended real change in their everyday lives. The politics of race was not a distant issue or abstraction for these suburbanites. It affected their lives directly. Local politics, thus, became the politics of reaction, and the civil rights movement became a localized phenomenon. While the same general issues prevailed as before the war—education, housing, and even taxes—they were now defined by the broader, national debate about race. In South Gate, postwar politics obsessively focused on protecting the racial purity of the suburb, particularly two key institutions of the community—schools and homes. Because these entities were the touchstones that defined residents and their town, they became the objects of fierce protectionism.

The Politics of Education

In the early 1960s, South Gate found itself at the center of a momentous school desegregation battle. Begun as a localized protest by African Americans to bring the essence of *Brown v. Board of Education of Topeka* to the southern suburbs of Los Angeles, it escalated into a legal and political battle of national significance. This episode represented not only a key chapter in the story of the civil rights movement in Los Angeles, but also a defining moment in the development of white working-class politics. As whites mobilized in opposition to educational civil rights, they began formulating the ideological and organizational bases of a conservative countermovement. The story of education politics presents a dramatic illustration of how radically working-class concerns had changed. Whereas families before World War II agreed to send their children to racially integrated schools for the sake of low taxes, by the 1960s their urgent goal became keeping their children out of such schools.

The struggle for civil rights in Los Angeles began in earnest during World War II. Wartime protests for racial equality—especially in the shipyards—lay the foundation for postwar civil rights activism. By the late 1940s, a nascent civil rights movement had emerged. Spearheaded by the Communist Party, the NAACP, the Urban League, the CIO, and individual blacks and whites, the early movement focused mainly on fighting police brutality and housing and job discrimination. While these efforts achieved several notable victories, particularly in court decisions striking down race-restrictive covenants, the movement had yet to achieve the far-reaching, high-profile results of the 1960s. It was partly hamstrung by the involvement of the Community Party, fiercely dedicated to the civil rights cause, an alliance that became a liability as the Cold War intensified.[27]

By the early 1960s, the civil rights campaign reemerged in Los Angeles, energized by events at the national level. The summer of 1963 was pivotal.

On the heels of the Birmingham campaign for integration, which pene-trated the national conscience with the brutality of white resistance and the eloquence of Martin Luther King Jr.'s impassioned letter from the Birming-ham jail, the movement finally began making political headway. In June, President John F. Kennedy sent his civil rights bill to Congress, calling for an end to discrimination in public places and for intensified pressure on school districts to desegregate. Two months later, 200,000 people joined the March on Washington to demand passage of the civil rights bill, and to hear King deliver his famous "I Have a Dream" speech. In early September, a bomb exploded at Birmingham's Sixteenth Street Baptist Church, killing four black girls and arousing anger and frustration within the movement. It was a time of intense activity and action, headway and resistance, a time when the movement reached a new level of momentum and sophistica-tion.[28]

Invigorated by these events and the appearance of Martin Luther King Jr. in their city, African Americans in Los Angeles stepped up their own civil rights efforts during that seminal summer. They drew on the southern movement's philosophy and tactics, particularly the integrationist approach of King and the Southern Christian Leadership Conference. In Los Angeles, the key leading groups were the Congress of Racial Equality (CORE), the National Association for the Advancement of Colored People (NAACP), and the United Civil Rights Council (UCRC), a coalition of seventy-six or-ganizations in the city. All three groups represented the moderate wing of the movement, striving for integration and equality within white society. To push their cause, they adopted the strategy of nonviolent protest, such as marches and sit-ins, as well as the favored NAACP tactic of legal re-course.

The newly formed UCRC had launched its first major push for civil rights in June 1963. They demanded of the city's power structure—busi-nessmen, manufacturers, and public officials—that Los Angeles end segre-gation immediately or face mass demonstrations such as those taking place in the South. They called for "full equality without delay" in employment, housing, education, and police relations, and gave the city's "captains of industry" ten days to respond affirmatively to these demands. In the mean-time, they organized committees and began anticipating the demonstra-tions likely to occur in the face of white intransigence. "We will use every legal non-violent means at our command to achieve our goal of total inte-gration into the Los Angeles community," announced Christopher Taylor, president of the NAACP and a leader of the UCRC. From the outset, they targeted the public school system, calling on the L.A. Board of Education to end de facto segregation.[29]

The schools, indeed, embodied racial inequality in the metropolis. As early as 1938, the L.A. Board of Education itself acknowledged the existence of racial segregation in the district. Educational segregation deepened during and after World War II, with the influx of African Americans and Mexicans into the city. It "climbed to mammoth proportions," according to one expert, following patterns of residential segregation. By 1967, 218 of the L.A. Unified School District's 544 regular schools were classified as segregated (defined as more than 50 percent minority). Of these segregated schools, 95 were predominantly black and 69 Mexican. By the early 1970s, school segregation was more intense in Los Angeles than in any southern city and in most states. Black students were the most segregated group of all. About 94 percent of black pupils in the L.A. district attended schools that were at least half minority. In Watts, the needs of black students were compounded by the influx of southern migrants, who were typically two to five years behind their peers in scholastic ability. At Jordan High in the early 1960s, half of the students entering tenth grade fit this description.[30]

In the early 1960s, activists began pressing the L.A. Board of Education to confront the problem. At a board meeting in June 1962, the ACLU, NAACP, and CORE lodged the first protests. They demanded that the board form a citizens committee to investigate de facto segregation, and they called for a racial census of schools in the district to disclose the extent of the problem. The board's initial response presaged its later ones: it denied that segregation existed, then formed an ad hoc committee of board members—not citizens—to make recommendations. At this stage, the board appeared to be "faintly puzzled by the whole affair," according to one observer. After a slow year of meetings, the ad hoc committee finally issued four recommendations articulating a commitment to equal educational opportunity, and it promised to issue more suggestions later. By the summer of 1963, however, the committee's work had been shelved.[31]

Civil rights activists did not sit still. Inspired by events in Birmingham, they launched a vigorous campaign to eradicate educational inequality in Los Angeles. They focused special attention on two schools that vividly exemplified the problem: Jordan High in Watts and South Gate High. Laying only a mile apart, separated by the proverbial railroad tracks that ran along Alameda Street, both schools were part of the L.A. Unified School District. Over the prior three decades, they had grown severely segregated: Jordan High was 99 percent black, South Gate High 97 percent white. South Gate High had five black students out of 1,800 total, and conditions there were far superior than at Jordan. This was a physically blatant case of "separate and unequal" conditions. In June 1963, the UCRC demanded that the L.A.

Board of Education redraw school boundaries along Alameda to promote integration; that minority students be transported from overcrowded, half-day session schools to under-enrolled white schools; and that black teachers be assigned throughout the district.[32]

These demands were the opening salvo in a protracted battle over racial equity in the public schools. It soon became a tripartite struggle among the civil rights groups, the L.A. Board of Education, and the white suburbs of southern Los Angeles. A recurring pattern soon emerged: civil rights groups engaged in nonviolent protests, the board responded slowly and ineffectively, and the white suburbs mobilized ideologically and organizationally against civil rights. As the conflict heightened in 1963 and 1964, working-class suburbanites began to redefine their political loyalties. Older values of independence and antistatism, private property and homeowner rights reemerged in newly racialized terms. And the imported political culture of southern migrants, particularly its strains of racism and localism, found expression in the context of this suburban crisis.

In waging the battle to integrate the L.A. schools, civil rights groups mounted an impressive campaign of nonviolent direct action. Most of these protests centered on the L.A. Board of Education building downtown, to heighten visibility and impact. In the first major action, 1,000 demonstrators marched through downtown to the board building in late June 1963 (fig. 7-2). Two hundred of them squeezed into the board meeting, cheering and booing as board members debated integration. When the board offered no concessions but only a promise to study the problem further, the protesters redoubled their efforts. More demonstrations at board meetings followed, as well as another march through downtown led by national civil rights leaders like James Farmer of CORE and James Forman of the Student Nonviolent Coordinating Committee (SNCC). Actors Rita Moreno and Tony Franciosa joined in, along with about 600 others. At the school board building where the march ended, they were greeted by counterprotesters, including seven members of the Committee Against Integration and Intermarriage waving signs that read "Civil Rights for Caucasians," and two white supremacists bearing placards proclaiming "We Can Prove the NAACP and CORE Are Backed by Communist Jews." In the board meeting, amid the protesters' heckling, both Farmer and Forman implored the school board to act immediately. "The money can be found," Forman asserted. "If we can find money to send rockets to the moon, we can find the money to educate the children in our schools. . . . We are determined that we are going to have some measure of freedom in our lifetime." Board member Charles Smoot responded, "The Negroes want special status and

Figure 7-2   Civil rights protesters marched through downtown Los Angeles (top, at the
intersection of Broadway and Ninth Streets), on their way to the L.A. Board of Education
building, 1963. Numerous demonstrations that year pressed for integration in the L.A.
Unified School District. Herald-Examiner Collection, Los Angeles Public Library.

privilege. They want us to gerrymander the school district on a racial basis." Other white citizens voicing opinions called African Americans a
"child race" and implored them to go "back to Africa."[33]

As the protests intensified, the school board's intransigence hardened.
Four of the five board members opposed integration outright, including
Charles Smoot, J. C. Chambers, Georgianna Hardy, and Arthur Gardner.
Smoot was the staunchest opponent. "I say no de facto segregation exists,"
he asserted. "I resent pressure put on the board. . . . We represent majorities too." He believed blacks "don't want equal educational opportunities,
they want advantages." The lone voice on the side of integration was Mary
Tinglof, board president during these years. In insisting that "integration is
long overdue," she drew high praise from movement leaders, who considered her the only board member "acting right and thinking right."[34]

As the movement perceived it, the board's inaction openly flouted the
Brown v. Board of Education decision. So they turned to the courts to force
compliance. In the summer of 1963, the NAACP, supported by the UCRC,
the ACLU, and the American Jewish Congress, began preparing a lawsuit
against the L.A. Board of Education. Elnora Crowder, an African-American
schoolteacher and civil rights activist, set the wheels in motion by volunteering to find a Watts family willing to be named as plaintiffs. When she
approached several teenagers in a park in Watts, she recalled, "They actually recoiled from me saying, 'Blacks go to a white school?' It was like I was
asking them to go to the moon." She persisted, ringing doorbells in the
neighborhood like "an Avon lady" until she found two willing participants,
Mary Ellen Crawford and Inita Watkins, both students at Jordan High. In
the original suit, *Crawford v. Los Angeles Board of Education*, the plaintiffs
sought to halt the expenditure of public funds to renovate Jordan High until the board desegregated the school. That meant redrawing the school
boundary between Watts and South Gate. "The Board proposes to spend a
million dollars [on Jordan High] in what will amount to making it the best
segregated high school in the city," read an editorial in the *California Eagle*.
"All else has failed; maybe the courts can prod the Board into some positive
action." Marnesba Tackett, head of the UCRC's education committee, recalled why her group targeted South Gate in the suit: "The education at
South Gate was so much better, there was no comparison. Alameda Street,
the boundary which separated them, was called 'the line.' . . . We noticed
that the school board kept expanding Jordan's boundary as more black children moved into it instead of sending them to South Gate. On that basis we
felt Jordan was the strategic school to target." The legal basis of the suit
rested not only on *Brown v. Board of Education* but also on the recent California Supreme Court decision *Jackson v. Pasadena*, which ordered school

boards to "take steps . . . to alleviate racial imbalance in schools regardless of its causes." Residential patterns as a cause was no exception.[35]

In South Gate, now at the center of this unwelcome storm, racial animosities flared. South Gate resident Andi Pointer was an early target. A white elementary-school teacher, Pointer had married then divorced a black mail carrier, who had since left the city. They had five children together, who drew attention in the suburb because of their color. Their neighbors refused to speak to them; the classmates of the fourteen-year-old daughter refused to touch her test papers. In mid-June, the hostility turned violent. Angry whites lobbed a Molotov cocktail and a two-foot burning wooden swastika at the Pointers' home, shattering a window and burning the grass and front steps. Deeply shaken, Pointer went outside to investigate and noticed her neighbors had also come out. None came to offer help—they just stared. Pointer called the police, who made a quick investigation then informed her they could provide no protection to her family; they dismissed the incident as a juvenile prank. In the face of police indifference, Pointer turned to CORE for help, which sent members to stand vigil over the house. A local television station picked up the story, portraying South Gate as a "bitterly prejudiced" community. After the broadcast, Pointer began receiving death threats. One caller, with a southern drawl, spoke of housing and how people like her were "asking for trouble" by moving into the neighborhood. She ultimately decided to leave South Gate because she could no longer take the hostility and hatred.[36]

A second racial episode involved the five black students attending South Gate High, who publicized their experiences in a local television news report. The students, who had obtained transfers to attend the school, told reporters about the constant harassment they suffered. In one instance, white students threw eggs at a car picking them up. Another described how male students constantly taunted her, calling her a bitch and throwing pennies at her. In the same broadcast, a white student, urged on by her friends, screamed into the camera, "We don't want 'em here! That's all. We just don't want 'em here!" While school officials labeled these incidents quirks, the city assigned extra police officers to the campus on the last day of school in June 1963. But the broadcast had sealed South Gate's reputation as an enemy of civil rights.[37]

In September 1963, the conflict intensified, sparked by the initiation of the *Crawford* case, the beginning of the school year, and ardent anticipation over the board's long-awaited ad hoc committee report. On the first day of school, Jordan High students picketed their campus, charging the school board with "Jim Crowism." A few days later, eight CORE members launched a weeklong hunger strike at the Board of Education building, demanding an end to discrimination and segregation in the schools. The strikers included novelist Martin Goldsmith and actress Juliana Francis, among others. And the marches and demonstrations continued. In one, 350 protesters marched from Wrigley Field in the Vernon-Central area to the school board headquarters downtown, singing songs of the civil rights movement along the way. In the board meeting where they ended up, Goldsmith, weak from the hunger strike, received a standing ovation after making an impassioned plea to the board. But later, the segregationists cheered when a speaker referred to blacks as "a child race."[38]

In mid-September, the board's ad hoc committee finally issued its long-awaited report. The forty-one-page document, which took fifteen months to produce, offered only mild suggestions to promote integration. Its moderation ended up angering both sides. It opposed busing then called for further study of the school boundary issue, for a race census of the schools, for record keeping of hires by race, and for better publicity of the voluntary transfer program. The report denied charges of racial gerrymandering of school boundaries, claiming instead that segregation was caused by the historical evolution of residential patterns. And it denied that black teachers seeking interschool transfers were met with administrative prejudice. The report finally presented a series of recommendations for the board to consider, one by one.[39]

On both sides of Alameda, the response was negative. Whites in South Gate acknowledged that the report provided a "momentary lessening of danger," as the local editor put it, yet they realized it also left the door open for school boundary changes down the line. A few days later, the newly formed South Gate Education Committee voiced forceful objections to sections in the report that accepted certain "false premises," in their eyes, such as the notion that integrated schools offered better educational opportunities. The South Gate City Council also weighed in, reading a lengthy resolution against integration into the school board's record. West of Alameda, African Americans expressed anger and frustration, claiming the report failed to make any positive recommendations on the fundamental issue at hand—de facto segregation. The most glaring defect, they believed, was the failure to recommend school boundary changes and student transfers from overcrowded "Jim Crow schools" to underpopulated white schools. As Marnesba Tackett charged, "the findings are absolutely nil . . . Nothing specific—just further study—and no urgency." CORE education chair Kenneth Fry called the report a "complete fiasco," merely a collection of "suggestions to survey already obvious facts." Civil rights advocates complained that promoting voluntary transfer permits was no solution at all, since it placed all responsibility for transportation on the students' families. The ad hoc committee report, in fact, is what spurred the hunger strike.[40]

At this juncture, whites began to fight back. From Santa Monica and Long Beach to the San Fernando Valley and Hollywood, whites mobilized an opposition movement. South Gate's citizens were at the center of this effort, and they typified broader white resistance—particularly working-class resistance—to racial integration in Los Angeles. September 1963 marked the starting point of South Gate's countermovement. As residents formulated ideological and organizational responses, they began expressing an antiliberal sensibility and a new discourse of white rights. In the face of aggressive civil rights activism, particularly the filing of the *Crawford* case, residents realized they could no longer stand by and watch events unfold. They would have to take a more dynamic role in shaping their future. A group of South Gate citizens thus launched a multipronged attack against the movement for black equality, now clamoring at their doorstep.

Both men and women participated in these efforts. In contrast to similar campaigns elsewhere where housewives took the lead, gender played a lesser role in South Gate's "crabgrass-roots" politics. In places like Detroit, Queens, and even Lakewood, women often "formed the vanguard of a neighborhood's defense." This not only stemmed from the domestic ideology that made it women's responsibility to create a safe, wholesome environment for their children, but it grew out of the networks housewives forged in kaffeeklatsches and the like. And it occurred especially in communities with a preponderance of women who stayed at home to raise children. While this domestic sensibility certainly existed in South Gate, the suburb had more than its share of women in the workforce, which mitigated against female leadership. South Gate women did participate as "foot soldiers" in the campaign, knocking on doors to gather signatures, attending board meetings, and writing letters. But leadership roles were left primarily to men.[41]

Floyd Wakefield was prominent among them. His efforts first became public in early September 1963, when he organized the South Gate Education Committee (SGEC). This group was more of a coordinating body than a true committee—at the outset, it consisted of Wakefield and his wife. As he admitted, "We never was much at forming an organization except for what we could do ourselves." Still, the SGEC solicited an impressive outpouring of support from the community, drawing in large numbers of volunteers. As Wakefield recalled, their cause attracted support from the vast majority of residents, Democrats and Republicans alike. Political identity in this regard hinged less on party and more on whether one was liberal or conservative, as Wakefield saw it. "They either believed in what the students [protesters] were doing or disapproved. They believed in integration and swapping kids around or didn't."[42]

The first act of the SGEC was a petition drive, demanding that the Board of Education reject busing and any changes to current school boundaries. If the board forced South Gate children to attend school in Watts, the petition warned, "we shall take legal action against the school board in violation of our children's rights under the 14th Amendment." The local press, an unflagging supporter of the campaign, urged citizens to sign the petitions to counteract the integrationists' "social experimentation" that was "unwise and dangerous." The drive achieved astounding results. The committee mustered 450 volunteers, who gathered 17,500 signatures in thirteen days. Wakefield and several South Gate residents triumphantly presented the petitions at a Board of Education meeting, urging that they be used as evidence in the *Crawford* case defense.[43]

Weeks later, the SGEC announced its broader agenda as safeguarding the "rights, privileges, and environment" of the suburb's children, serving "as a watchdog against aggressive acts by any organization or groups outside the local school area," resisting "special privileges sought by outside pressure groups" and pressing for secession from the L.A. Unified School District. Wakefield printed thousands of fliers and distributed them to his store's customers and door-to-door with the help of volunteers. His wife wrote press releases, which the South Gate and Huntington Park newspapers eagerly picked up. The SGEC also launched a series of counterprotests, calling on residents to attend school board meetings to let South Gate's voice be heard and uphold the "rights" of the suburb's children. They sponsored buses—departing from Wakefield's sporting goods store—to transport citizens to board headquarters downtown; the local newspaper printed their departure times and contact persons. Citizens responded immediately. At the next board meeting, fifty-five South Gate residents attended, including the mayor and several councilmen, and they continued attending over the next several weeks. During the heated meetings in late September, when the "ad hoc committee" report was about to come out, several South Gate residents spoke on the record against integration, articulating an ideological opposition to civil rights. Their statements, according to Tinglof, were often "rude" and "biting," in contrast to the more "dignified" remarks of the civil rights advocates.[44]

Other South Gate institutions soon joined the fight. One of the first was the city council, which threw municipal resources behind the effort. It drafted a resolution against boundary changes and busing, instructed the city attorney, mayor, and councilmen to attend school board meetings, and

authorized the city attorney to lend legal help if necessary. At a board meeting in mid-September, South Gate Mayor Donald Sawyer read the council's
resolution into the record. The city council also aided the campaign by controlling the outlets of public debate. It allowed Floyd Wakefield to lead a
"town hall" meeting in a public venue (South Gate Civic Auditorium), at
which the SGEC would openly recruit volunteers. Yet around the same
time, the council denied a request by the ACLU to hold a forum in a public
park on "de facto segregation," citing a city rule that prohibited the use of
public facilities by "any group agitating any political, labor or other controversial issue, or any group listed by the U.S. Government or attorney general as being subversive." The ACLU, claimed the council, was clearly
subversive, a charge Wakefield reiterated in several public statements. The
ACLU, never one to roll over on such issues, threatened to sue the city on
the grounds that the policy was discriminatory and unconstitutional. This
skirmish dragged on for about two years. In November 1963, the South
Gate Coordinating Council also joined the fight. This entity, a coalition of
all service groups for youth in South Gate, issued a statement opposing any
changes to school boundaries.[45]

In the public dialogue over integration, the contours of South Gate's
ideological position emerged. Because the civil rights movement promised
to impact their lives directly, residents formulated a defense that addressed
the specific conditions of their community. In this way, a national issue
was locally construed. As well, they appropriated the language and logic of
the civil rights movement in constructing an opposition argument, which
hinged partly on a defense of their status as working, taxpaying white citizens. As white homeowners, they were entitled to their own set of rights.
Certain themes emerged in how they explained the problem, how they proposed to solve it, and how they defended their solution.[46]

First and foremost, South Gate citizens devised an explanation for the
current state of school affairs. There was no denying that segregation existed. Yet it had evolved "naturally," they asserted, a result of developing
residential patterns. Residential segregation was to blame, not any conscious effort on their part to segregate the schools. Their argument rested
on the ingenuous assumption that these residential patterns were not of
their making. By assuming geographic determinism, residents could blame
segregation on forces beyond their control. This reasoning challenged the
Crawford suit, which demanded school desegregation even if it was caused
by residential segregation. South Gate residents argued that this "cause"
was not their fault. This defense, of course, ignored reality. For years, South
Gate residents had promoted race-restrictive covenants and exclusionary
real estate policies, which helped create the racial divide in southern Los

Angeles. Yet by maintaining a position that exonerated themselves, South Gate residents could speak of their desire for "equal educational opportunity" for all while opposing concrete steps toward integration.

Whites offered other explanations as well. One argument shifted the blame for current education problems away from segregation and onto teaching techniques. Mary Frisina, a Huntington Park resident and key figure in the white countermovement, claimed that the problems of black students stemmed from "progressive education." This misguided strategy, she asserted, caused the high drop-out rates and poor performance of black pupils. She asked the board, "If you haven't been able to educate these children and teach them the art of reading and enunciation, and the multiplications through progressive education, what makes you think that integration will?" Frisina's critique echoed a broader national attack on "progressive education" in the 1950s.[47] Finally, residents blamed the entire controversy on outsiders who sought to enter in and stir things up. These interlopers knew nothing of South Gate's community life, yet they presumed to dictate how residents should run their schools. This was particularly galling, prompting letters like the one Juanita Hammon wrote to the local paper.

As a solution, residents of South Gate and neighboring suburbs demanded that the board leave things alone: no changes to school boundaries and no busing. Most expressed a willingness to let a limited number of black students into the South Gate schools, but under no circumstances would their own children be bused out. And black students would be welcomed best, they cautioned, if their attendance had nothing to do with the agitation of the movement. "If these children from other areas come to South Gate as 'children' and not as members of some so-called minority group, we believe they will be accepted and treated as equals," intoned the local editor. Again, this position of purported acceptance freed them from culpability and charges of racism, even as it ignored the hostile racial climate in the schools.[48]

South Gaters also began agitating for more power in school affairs, asserting their right to community control. They demanded representation on the school board's citizens advisory groups, especially since South Gate was the second largest of twenty-two cities in the L.A. Unified School District. And they revived talk of separating from the L.A district all together, echoing sentiments first voiced more than thirty years earlier. Recall that in the late 1920s and early 1930s, local efforts to break away into a separate school district (or join more costly neighboring districts) were defeated by voters who feared a rise in taxes. Citizens opted to participate in a racially integrated district because it was the cheapest option. This time, however, the reasoning and responses were different. The revived school secession movement first surfaced around 1959, when several working-class suburbs proposed forming the San Antonio Unified School District. It would include about 17,000 students from Huntington Park, Maywood, Bell, Vernon, Cudahy, Walnut Park, and South Gate. The initial rationale for the district was to provide "home rule" in school decisions, to ensure better use of tax revenue, and to stave off racial integration.[49]

The plan soon met a series of rejections by the city and state boards of education. The LAUSD initially opposed it because of the substantial loss in tax revenue, particularly from wealthy, industrial Vernon. Plan organizers responded by dropping Vernon from the proposal. But the plan met its most serious rejection at the state level. The California Board of Education first turned it down in September 1962, claiming it would create a lily-white island of segregated education in L.A. County, in violation of the *Brown v. Board of Education* mandate. (This concern was heightened by an incident the prior week, in which five black students tried to register at South Gate High and were rejected. As principal Glenn Miller put it, "We're not in the integration business. We're in the education business.") South Gate complained that the state board's rejection of the secession plan stood "in conflict with a long standing historic school board policy requiring strong community identity within a school district—i.e., the neighborhood school concept." With civil rights pressures mounting in the winter of 1963–64, white citizens redoubled their effort to secede by revamping and resubmitting the San Antonio Plan. They amended the plan by adding to their proposed district the Lillian Street Elementary School, which lay west of Alameda. Of the 750 pupils at this school, half were Spanish speaking, one-third were black, and the remainder comprised Caucasian and "other races." This, they hoped, would satisfy the racial diversity requirement, even though it represented the only "minority" school in the entire proposed district. After several short-term delays, State Attorney General Stanley Mosk, an advocate of fair housing and equal access, squashed the proposal. Despite its failure, this secession campaign illustrated how working-class whites were countering civil rights demands. Their argument for community control, as a defense against school integration, was a tactic used in other white neighborhoods facing similar pressures.[50]

In formulating a defense of their position, South Gate citizens most clearly articulated the substance of their beliefs on the race issue. The integration campaign, they contended, was not only driven by questionable motives, but it was bad for blacks and whites alike. By avoiding the crass, overt racism of southern reaction, this defense presented an image of reason and logic, concern and equity. South Gate citizens appropriated the language of civil rights and turned it upside down, by defending both the best interests of blacks and the rights of whites. This position, which carefully dodged racist pronouncements and presented a face of tolerance, resembled the stance of white working-class liberals facing similar integration pressures in the North. Contending that racism was a moral problem of irrational individuals, not a systemic one, they could exonerate themselves from perpetuating the inequalities. This proved to be a cunning—and for the time being, more convincing—argument for resisting civil rights.[51]

At the broadest level, white South Gate attacked school integration for detracting from the educational process itself. It was, instead, a ploy to promote race mixing, social experimentation, and "special interests." The purpose of the current civil rights "agitation," charged the local editor, was "the mixing of races in schools for integrations [sic] sake rather than basic improvement of education of children." Schools should not be used as a "social or moral arbiter," resident Dorothy Lamkin asserted. "The role of the school is simply to provide education." Mayor Sawyer echoed this idea in a statement to the board: "Schools were set up to educate children . . . solely. You have now been handed the herculean task of not only educating children but of physically correcting economic and political problems. This is far afield from the purpose and intent of schools." Others attacked the integration cause for promoting special interests. As the city council resolution put it, civil rights agitators, representing "special interest groups," had exerted "unwarranted and unfounded pressure" on the board to force integration upon this area of Los Angeles. Mrs. F. C. Yetter took it further, demanding that three school board members affiliated with the NAACP disqualify themselves because they "represent a special interest group."[52]

Some went so far as to argue that South Gate had no segregation problem to begin with. In statements that ignored reality, a few citizens claimed that South Gate had plenty of diversity. Mayor Donald Sawyer noted, for example, that South Gate schools were "integrated at the present time and peacefully so." Floyd Wakefield concurred, recalling, "There were blacks in South Gate already . . . there weren't many. In fact, there was people that lived just several blocks from us in South Gate." The Hodges family of South Gate claimed, "Most Southeast children meet other races and creeds under ideal conditions through numerous youth activities." Mary Frisina of Huntington Park maintained that the southeastern suburbs were falling victim to the L.A. district's race problems. "We in the Southeast District have no such problems," she insisted. Finally, Virginia Glendon, active in school and civic affairs in Huntington Park, denied that the schools discriminated in hiring.[53]

White citizens also boldly argued that integration failed to serve the best interests of blacks. "There is not one shred of evidence . . . that an integrated school provides any educational advantages," declared the local editor, voicing a popular argument in South Gate. They took their cue from Robert E. Kelly, associate superintendent in charge of secondary schools for the L.A. district. At a deposition hearing for the *Crawford* case, Kelly testified that no systematic evidence existed to prove the educational benefits of integrated schools. Floyd Wakefield picked up on this argument and repeated it often, citing it as a reason to delay action until further studies were conducted to prove "scientifically" whether or not integration really helped. This rationale completely flouted the premise of the *Brown v. Board of Education* decision, a fact that CORE seized upon in demanding Kelly's resignation. Kelly's statement, they charged, reflected "a complete lack of understanding of the consequences of segregated schools, and a lack of understanding of the intent of the Supreme Court ruling in 1954 that separate but equal is not equal at all." The school board rejected CORE's demand and backed Kelly.[54]

To prove that black interests were not being served, South Gate residents cited the results of a poll taken in Watts in November 1963. The survey, commissioned by the SGEC, canvassed 60 percent of residents in the Jordan District and 22 percent of homes with schoolchildren. It found that 63 percent believed that moving their children to schools outside the neighborhood would *not* help them educationally. Most preferred improving their own local schools. To a question asking "which of the following six things . . . would most benefit your child educationally?" only 3.8 percent chose transferring pupils to another school. (The highest responses called for more library books, job training, and counseling.) These responses revealed a potential split between black leaders in the civil rights movement and the black community. Some black parents undoubtedly questioned the value of integration for its own sake, which rested on the assumption that education alongside whites was implicitly superior. They favored, instead, the right to community control and better schools in their own neighborhoods.[55] The SGEC, unsurprisingly, focused on this black opposition to busing. They presented the survey results to the L.A. Board of Education and publicized them in the press. "[P]arents of Jordan pupils . . . are more interested in a good education for their children than disruptive efforts by self-appointed 'rights groups' leaders artificially to speed integration," declared the local editor. The poll results merely confirmed what "South Gate residents have long suspected."[56]

They waged a similar argument when a pilot busing program, launched in January 1964, attracted few takers among black families. Only a handful of parents applied for transfers to schools in South Gate, although other schools drew much greater interest. While some whites cited this as further proof of black distaste for integrated schools, other factors were surely at work. The history of racial hostility at the South Gate schools, poor publicity on obtaining transfer permits, and a shortage of application forms at some of the schools discouraged black parents from seeking transfers. By August 1964, a "parade" of black parents who participated in the program appeared at a school board meeting, where they harshly criticized conditions in their own neighborhood schools and called for the continuation of the busing program. Popular support for student transfers, thus, was greater than the poll suggested.[57]

South Gate residents waged the most forceful arguments against integration by emphasizing the rights and well-being of whites. They translated the notion of their entitlement as homeowners into the more powerful language of rights, a discourse with great currency in the context of the 1960s. They spoke of the rights of their own children and community members. "The public is being misled to believe that the majority has no rights, and that freedom and liberty belong only to the minority," declared Floyd Wakefield. "As Americans we must realize that freedom and liberty belong to all, regardless of race, color or creed. . . . We must not tolerate those who would come into our cities and destroy the very things we believe in." Ray Bradford, an accountant and member of the SGEC, concurred. His concern was "with the civil rights of his own children and with the rights of parents, young people and citizens of my community. . . . We pray that the rights given us by God and our Nation shall not be taken away." As taxpaying homeowners, South Gate residents claimed the right to control their community and the integrity of their property. This was their entitlement as homeowners, promised in the New Deal and reinforced in the suburban ideal. The white rights theme was sounded repeatedly, summed up in the SGEC goal of safeguarding "our students' rights and environment."[58]

Another compelling argument invoking white rights rested on the practical issue of safety. Alameda Street, which divided South Gate and Watts, was "one of the most dangerous areas to cross within the entire unified district, whether on foot or on wheels," in the words of one South Gate resident. Another added, "I heard Alameda Street referred to as a 'wall.' Actually this is an excellent description of the area. It is a wall of industrial plant buildings, a wall of heavy truck traffic, and a wall of junk yards with giant piles of rusty, wrecked automobiles. . . . In rainy weather, children would be ankle deep in water and mud if they attempted to cross on foot." Yet others disputed this picture. Board member Georgianna Hardy noted that safe crossing points did exist, while Reverend John Killingsworth of the Emmanuel United Church of Christ in Watts pointed out that South

Gate schoolchildren crossed Firestone Boulevard, which was just as busy as Alameda, all the time. Furthermore, civil rights proponents pointed out that black students were forced to make equally treacherous crossings to attend all-black schools. Why shouldn't white students, they asked, be required to do the same?[59]

Another argument emphasized the economic costs of integration. This reasoning revived the central preoccupation of South Gate residents before 1940—taxes—and racialized it, adroitly intermingling a hostility to taxes with a hostility to integration. At the center of this was Mary Frisina, resident of Huntington Park and state chair of the newly formed Taxpayers' Rebellion of California. Formed in mid-1963, the Taxpayers Rebellion attracted 100 groups in twenty-two counties across the state within six months. Their purported goal, in Frisina's words, was "to vote out of office those governmental officials who ignore the wishes of the people to cut cost of government." In repeated appearances at L.A. Board of Education meetings, Frisina articulated a new anti-tax ideology—often in caustic terms—that racialized the nature of public spending: no public money should be spent on programs to promote integration, give special privilege to minorities, or otherwise drain the pockets of white taxpayers for programs that would not help them. They made a clear distinction between the taxpayer and tax recipient, demonizing and racializing the latter. Taking a stab at CORE demonstrators in late December, Frisina told the board that her group was "above such demonstrations you have been witnessing for the past year. We are all hard working people who do not have time, nor the money to leave our jobs week after week to come before you." Nor, she added, did they have welfare checks awaiting them. In so many words, she equated civil rights activism with civic irresponsibility and welfare dependency. Busing was a prime example of the kind of program her group opposed. "We saw this board vote 6-1 against bussing children from one school to another only to find out now that you are hell bent to ram it down our throats whether we like it or not and whether or not we can afford it," she scolded the board. "We intend to show our strength at the polls, I can assure you."[60]

By January 1964, the Taxpayers Rebellion organized a group of women, dubbed "Women on the War Path," in a downtown protest demanding that the county board of supervisors cut taxes in 1964. In numerous public statements, "taxes" became a coded reference to civil rights and programs for minorities, an excellent local example of the national trend that saw an overlapping of race and taxes as political issues. "While you work and sweat to protect your earnings and property, the politicians scheme with their minority supporters to put you in a hopeless position to protect yourself against raids of everything you work for. . . . Today CORE, NAACP, COPE and their like are the only participants who pressure our legislators for the kind of government we have now, while today's citizen is a drone, quite impotent in local affairs because he stays home, and our taxes continue to go up, up and up." The Taxpayers Rebellion thus drew on the long political heritage of suburban homeowners in southern Los Angeles. And it echoed campaigns for financial austerity in other regions of the nation that targeted the least-advantaged groups benefiting from social welfare programs.[61]

South Gate's final argument maintained that integration would destroy the suburb's "community identity," the very fabric of local social life. As the city council resolution phrased it, "historically, politically, and culturally, the City of South Gate developed and does now exist as a close-knit family community. . . . the South Gate High School has existed since its origin as part of the social and cultural life of the City. . . . the boundaries of said school were established in the interest of the health, safety and welfare of the children going to and from South Gate High." Boundary changes and busing threatened the community's identity as a wholesome postwar suburb. "What, local citizens ask, could be more disruptive to a small city such as South Gate, Huntington Park, Bell, Maywood or Cudahy, than the dilution of the school as a community center?" asked the local editor. "What move could more surely cool parents' interests in schools . . . than unnatural boundary shifts to move their children . . . into a strange environment?" To gird their argument, they cited the California Board of Education's prior use of the "neighborhood school" concept, in which students with common interests, concerns, and social experiences were grouped into distinct school districts. Now, it seemed, the state board was ignoring its own policy. Yet this argument likewise ignored the past, when first-generation residents violated the neighborhood school concept in the name of low taxes. That precedent was long forgotten.[62]

Throughout the fall of 1963, the UCRC and CORE continued demonstrating at the Board of Education building while the board debated its ad hoc committee's recommendations. The civil rights groups kept up an impressive show of force, routinely drawing a hundred or more protesters to each demonstration. They held sit-ins, sleep-ins, and study-ins. The climax was a series of study-ins that drew hundreds of student protesters, who lined the corridors of the Board of Education building and disrupted meetings with chants and singing. By contrast, attendance of South Gate residents at board meetings had dropped off, although the SGEC still monitored developments. Civil rights advocates also began countering the growingly sophisticated arguments of whites across the tracks. In a compelling statement, CORE member Daniel Gray told the board that all it took was a two-hour drive through the city to see what had to be done. "The studies have all been made. We are waiting for action," he said. A *California Eagle* editorial answered the "white rights" argument by stating: "South Gate is a good example of what happens to the thinking and attitudes of residents of a city which practices residential segregation. Long exclusion of Negroes from that city has bred the attitude that it has a 'right' to exclude Negroes from its boundaries and that it has a complementary 'right' to maintain segregation in its schools. . . . [T]he Board should not permit South Gate hostility to deter it from its plain legal duty to correct what our Supreme Court has called 'racial imbalance' in our schools."[63]

In late November 1963, the board issued several rulings that favored the white rights cause. It refused to redraw the school boundary between South Gate and Watts, and it ruled that no South Gate children would be bused out of the area. While black and Latino children were free to attend schools in South Gate and Huntington Park, only thirty-four transfers were made available at the high school level, with similarly small numbers at the middle schools. South Gate residents considered this a victory, while civil rights leaders expressed deep disappointment, branding the ruling as "tokenism at its worst." The *Eagle* called the report "fraud of the worst kind, designed to maintain the present segregation on the one hand and to allay criticism on the other." This "open enrollment" plan, in fact, became a favorite solution of conservative school board members. It put no pressure on white families to abide by integration, and it ultimately became an escape hatch for white flight to all-white schools.[64]

The civil rights groups immediately tried a new strategy. In early December, the UCRC proposed that minority children be bused from overcrowded elementary schools operating on a half-day schedule, to vacant slots in full-day white schools. Many of the receiving schools would be in South Gate. This proposal, like all the rest, generated more heated debate. CORE resumed nonviolent demonstrations. And South Gate leaders quickly articulated their opposition. Mayor Sawyer called it a ruse for integration: "This proposed . . . transporting [of] children from their own schools, their own people, their own friends is preposterous and should not be indulged in for the sole purpose of instituting a . . . pilot program of integration. South Gate is being used as a pawn." With uncharacteristic speed, the school board issued a decision within two weeks. Again, it paid lip service to civil rights demands. The board approved a "compromise" busing plan that applied to a much smaller number of students than the UCRC envisioned. And much to the delight of South Gate residents, the board's plan excluded the southeastern suburbs completely. The school board, it appeared, continued to ignore the *Brown* decision mandate. It supported measures like remedial programs in the segregated schools but refused to take a race census, to release data on minority enrollments and employment, and to take more than nominal steps to promote integration.[65]

In the heat of battle, an astonishing event took place that revealed the ingenuous self-perception of South Gate's residents. Since the early 1950s, South Gate High had hosted a Christmas party for Graham Elementary School, whose student body was 55 percent Mexican American, 30 percent black, and 10 percent white, with a scattering of Asians. With Christmas approaching, South Gate High extended its invitation as usual, seemingly oblivious to the local fight over integration. The Graham School balked, resenting the hypocrisy of South Gate for its "once-a-year integration" gesture. Reverend Killingsworth, whose Watts church was near the Graham School, chastised the suburb for interpreting the Christmas party as complete fulfillment of "brotherhood," while denying Graham children respect when they became adults by barring them from jobs and homes in South Gate. The annual party, he asserted, had failed to improve race relations, evident in the fact that students who'd been involved in it for ten years had now become the adults in South Gate resisting civil rights. "We hope," he concluded, "to create more communication on a basis of equality." The South Gate editor took offense to such charges. "Peace on Earth, Goodwill to Men, apparently ends when integration controversy begins," he wrote. The annual party had become "a casualty" of the civil rights battle. South Gate High found another school to entertain, while Graham held its own party for the children, complete with Santa Claus, treats, and an appearance by a TV personality. On the heels of this fracas, the *South Gate Press* published its list of top stories in 1963, with its stunning ranking of the "the high school boundary struggle" over the president's assassination. In the "emotionally charged" climate of southern Los Angeles, where the politics of race hit so close to home, a figure like Floyd Wakefield loomed larger than John F. Kennedy.[66]

In this first round, South Gate and its neighboring suburbs emerged victorious. The school board's actions at this stage—hesitant and ineffective—would be repeated throughout the decade. By the late 1960s, the board continued to advocate only the mildest of integration programs, such as transitory interracial contacts through one-day programs, a small-scale voluntary busing program, and open enrollments, while rejecting mandatory, large-scale busing. The fate of the *Crawford* case, languishing in the courts, was a final sign of slow progress. A series of postponements requested by the plaintiffs and judge alike had stalled the case for several years, stifling progress on the judicial front. In 1967, an ACLU spokesman observed the repercussions of this. An unconscionable number of students in Los Angeles's Class of 1967, he noted, had gone from kindergarten to twelfth grade in segregated schools, and were now graduating as if the landmark *Brown* case had never occurred. The hopes that the *Crawford* suit might bring the spirit of the *Brown* decision to Los Angeles would not materialize until the 1970s. Meanwhile, in 1960s Los Angeles, the white rights campaign was prevailing.[67]

On top of the board's intransigence and the stalled *Crawford* case, the struggle for civil rights in education was thwarted by the arrival of Proposition 14 on the political scene. This state ballot measure, designed to overturn the state's equal housing laws, soon diverted the energies of civil rights advocates, leaving the school fight to languish. Yet at the same time, Proposition 14 also brought a new twist to the public discourse over civil rights, one that linked education and housing. Part of the debate in Los Angeles over segregated schools had centered on the causes of segregation. Anti-integrationists argued that it wasn't their fault that the local schools were segregated. It was simply a result of evolving residential patterns, for which they claimed no responsibility. Civil rights advocates disagreed, asserting that citizens in suburbs like South Gate absolutely influenced residential patterns. Their insidious methods for maintaining residential apartheid were as bad as Jim Crow laws in the South and ultimately formed the basis for school segregation. The civil rights movement, thus, saw the issues of housing and education as inseparably intertwined.

South Gate steadfastly rejected this connection. This became clear when the L.A. Board of Education entered the debate over Proposition 14. In May 1964, when the Proposition 14 campaign was in full swing, board member Mary Tinglof moved that the board take a stand on the controversial referendum. "Until we can solve the housing problem," she intoned, "we cannot hope to solve the educational problems of our district." Conservatives on the board disagreed, insisting that the proposition had nothing to do with school issues. The board deadlocked, preventing it from taking a public stand on the initiative. Floyd Wakefield voiced his support for keeping housing and education politics separate. A school district is not "a redevelopment commission or a resettlement commission or an open occupancy administrator, but being a school system must take residential patterns as it finds them. . . . This is what we in the South Gate school area have been arguing for almost a year."[68]

Wakefield had effectively captured the sentiments of his suburb, a talent that was beginning to pay off politically. At the time he made this remark, he was running for state assembly, had garnered prestigious local civic recognition, and was emerging as an important leader. The higher his profile rose, the more strident his opposition to civil rights grew. Continually touting the victories won by his suburb in staving off integration, Wakefield had become the voice of reactionary South Gate. This fact was brought home in August 1964 when Wakefield, by now a fixture at L.A. Board of Education meetings, waged a bold attack on the most liberal member, Mary Tinglof. He charged Tinglof with "malfeasance in office" and demanded her resignation on the grounds that she was using her board position solely "to further integration." She should resign, he insisted, "so that she can use her own time to devote to her political views and social reforms." This included her vocal opposition to Proposition 14, a stance that pushed Wakefield to fever pitch in public statements.[69]

The fever, in fact, had risen on both sides. At this same board meeting in August 1964, during which the board voted down yet another small-scale busing program, one civil rights advocate offered a prescient observation. Dr. H. H. Brookins, chair of the UCRC, warned the board: "Take what I am saying anyway you wish, but these children must come out of the ghetto or the price that Southern California will pay will be more than the $117,000 for this bus program." Yet suburbs like South Gate failed to listen. In their minds, the school integration battle was not about black rights, but rather about white rights. By June 1965, when the controversy had simmered down for the moment, the local editor historicized the conflict in a very telling way. He portrayed the civil rights struggle as a campaign "against South Gate," meant "to harass South Gate and to stir up strife here." Two months later, the police and citizens of South Gate stood guard over their suburb clutching guns and rifles, watching as the communities across the tracks exploded in fire and anger.[70]

For South Gate residents, politics ultimately became the best weapon against civil rights. The battle over school desegregation pushed many local citizens rightward, galvanizing an antiliberal sensibility and severing their historic roots in the Democratic Party. For blue-collar suburbs like South Gate, thrust on the front lines of the conflict, racial politics was an issue not of vague abstraction but of concrete experience. It was not surprising, thus, that during the week between Christmas and New Year's 1965, a metropolitanwide citizens committee formed to influence the upcoming school board elections. Drawing members from all over Los Angeles—Westchester, Canoga Park, San Pedro, Reseda, and Monterey Park—the group met to plan a strategy for the next several months. It was no irony that their first meeting drew them to the very heart of the struggle—South Gate—and the specific site where resistance first coalesced: Floyd Wakefield's living room.[71]

THE POLITICS OF HOUSING

Just as the politics of education emerged with a racialized face in the post-war era, the politics of housing also became intertwined with race. While South Gate had long supported residential segregation, residents had the opportunity to politicize this commitment in the 1964 campaign for Proposition 14. This statewide initiative was one of several postwar measures in California that boldly challenged the ideals of the civil rights movement. Like Propositions 187 and 209 in the 1990s, the 1964 initiative pitted the interests of whites against those of minorities in an impassioned conflict over race and rights.

Proposition 14 was a backlash against the Rumford Fair Housing Act, enacted by the Democrat-controlled state legislature in 1963. The Rumford law provided for the enforcement of nondiscrimination in about 70 percent of the state's housing market. As the act read, "The practice of discrimination because of race, color, religion, national origin, or ancestry in housing accommodations is declared to be against public policy." It went on to identify the housing situations to which the law applied, and assigned the Fair Employment Practices Commission to enforce the measure. Rumford was designed to end housing discrimination once and for all, ensuring "the right of a Negro family to live in a home of its own choice," as Governor Edmund G. Brown put it.[72]

As soon as the Rumford Act passed in June 1963, a movement coalesced to dismantle it. It was headed by the California Real Estate Association (CREA), which formed the Committee for Home Protection (CHP) along with the California Apartment Owners' Association. Eschewing the strategy of a state referendum on the Rumford Act, which would merely overturn this specific law, the CHP opted instead to support a constitutional amendment—a proposition—with more permanent, far-reaching effects. Their initiative, designated Proposition 14, read: "Neither the State nor any subdivision or agency thereof shall . . . limit or abridge . . . the right of any person . . . to decline to sell, lease or rent [his real] property to such . . . persons as he, in his absolute discretion, chooses." Proposition 14 would not only overturn the Rumford Act; it would prohibit the enactment of similar fair housing measures at the state or local level. The CHP's initial justification in this campaign was that it opposed special privileges for minorities.[73]

As a virtual referendum on civil rights, Proposition 14 became the most controversial issue of the 1964 state election. It generated bitter debate and frequently acted as a litmus test for candidates running for state office. Numerous public figures weighed in on the issue, from politicians to Hollywood stars. It was rumored that cars bearing bumper stickers on the proposition—whether urging a "yes" or "no" vote—ran the risk of a tire-slashing. Both sides waged vigorous campaigns. The "Yes on 14" effort, loosely organized, was spearheaded by the CHP, neighborhood taxpayers' associations, and most importantly an enthusiastic army of local realty boards. The latter were instrumental in coordinating activity at the local level. The "No on 14" campaign garnered the support of the Democratic Party, the California Fair Practices Committee, the State Board of Education, the L.A. County Board of Supervisors, the L.A. City Council, numerous civil rights, religious, and human relations groups, as well as the California Labor Federation, representing the AFL-CIO. Even Casper Weinberger, Republican state chairman, came out against Proposition 14.[74]

The battle over Proposition 14 extended from the state house to the suburban house. Predictably, South Gate and its neighboring suburbs were caught up in the campaign. In South Gate especially, the timing could not have been more pointed. Proposition 14 burst on the scene just as the suburb was waging its own bitter struggle against educational civil rights, a time when race matters occupied the forefront of local political consciousness. With its massive groundswell of statewide support, the Proposition 14 campaign became a powerful validation for South Gate residents, undergirding a position they were struggling to define and defend.

As early as July 1963, a month after the Rumford Act passed and two months before it took effect, conservatives in South Gate began attacking the new law. The Young Republicans of South Gate vigorously chastised the measure, charging that it would "deprive property owners the right to operate property, according to his own dictates, which in effect, will take away the right of ownership. The right to own property is one of the basic freedoms as guaranteed in the Constitution of the United States." Looking back on the measure, Floyd Wakefield reiterated: "Just as simple as A-B-C. You have a right to your property. . . . The government has no right to come in and dictate policy to you, unless you've been abusing somebody or mistreating them." This reproach harkened back to fundamental ideas about the rights of local homeowners first advanced in the 1920s and sanctified by the New Deal in the 1930s. The right to own and control property, without government interference, had defined the essence of prewar politics. New government directives, now at the state instead of local level, threatened this right once again in new ways. And it demanded a response as vigorous as that of the first generation of South Gate homeowners.[75]

By November 1963, early support for Proposition 14 had coalesced in southern Los Angeles. The Southeast Board of Realtors, headquartered in Huntington Park, became the center of operations. Newspaper ads and articles called on residents to circulate petitions to get the measure on the ballot, generating an enthusiastic response. In the midst of the campaign, the Ku Klux Klan issued its own warning against fair housing by burning a nine-foot cross in the front yard of Dr. Ross Miller, who had moved into the white section of Compton. The forces of reaction simmered at many levels in southern Los Angeles. As the drive wore on, public discourse heated up. While the Southern California Council of Churches lodged its opposition to Proposition 14, a group of fifteen fundamentalist churches—some representing South Gate denominations—voiced their support. They contended that fair housing laws violated the rights of private property, represented a dangerous step toward "a police state," and breached the constitutional guarantee of "freedom of religion by forcing people of different religions to live in close proximity contrary to their personal preferences." By March 1964, the Proposition 14 campaign had gathered so many signatures, it represented the largest number ever certified for an initiative measure in California.[76]

Proposition 14 had become the critical political issue in South Gate, eclipsing even the school controversy. Because it impacted a significant aspect of blue-collar identity in South Gate—homeownership—Proposition 14 was of foremost concern. Most residents, anxious about defending the suburban ideal of racial homogeneity and the value of property, vigorously supported the initiative. Yet Proposition 14 also mobilized a smaller, respectable countermovement in support of Rumford and civil rights more generally. More than the school controversy did, this housing initiative spurred a battle of local organizations over these issues, exposing a degree of internal community conflict over racialized politics. It suggested too that working-class conservatism, while strong and widespread, was not a singular political orientation in South Gate. Liberalism survived in the suburb, although it was now overshadowed by forces on the right, a fact that became eminently clear when election day arrived.

In April 1964, two area groups formed to oppose Proposition 14. The Southeast Committee of Citizens United for Fair Housing, based in Compton, brought together several organizations, including the Compton Council on Human Relations, the Consolidated Realty Board, the ACLU, and the Catholic Human Relations Council. They held voter registration drives, workshops, educational forums, and communitywide meetings on the initiative. A second organization, the South Gate Committee for Better Human Relations, explained its purpose: "In keeping with the high standards of the community of South Gate, and in recognition of the changing climate of race relations throughout the nation, which will sooner or later affect our community, this committee is being formed to help promote the creation of a wholesome atmosphere in which these changes can take place in a mature and orderly manner." The group sponsored public forums and made "available basic information and diverse points of view" on race issues. It also made clear its opposition to Proposition 14. Committee Chair Russell Brown, a teacher, considered the measure both a "moral and political problem" that deserved utmost public attention. This committee was small, composed of four ministers (of the First Baptist, Community Presbyterian, and First Methodist Churches, and the president of the South Gate Ministerial Association), a labor activist, a teacher, and a member of the South Gate Planning Commission. As such, it commanded only modest clout in the suburb. For example, when it requested permission to hold a public forum on Proposition 14 at a local park, the city council denied it on the grounds that the city prohibited "controversial" meetings in public venues. The council's decision was clearly partisan, evident when conservative groups were given more favorable treatment. The city power structure, it appeared, was aligned against this liberal organization.[77]

By contrast, the forces supporting Proposition 14 in southern Los Angeles were strong and vocal. The South Gate newspaper ran stories showing the extent of support in the area, from local Republican clubs hosting speakers on the initiative, to South Gate realtors issuing statements, to the Mexican Chamber of Commerce of Los Angeles endorsing the "Yes on Prop. 14" campaign. The Association for the Protection of American Rights (APAR), a conservative group headquartered in Bell, ran fund-raising and voter registration drives. This group was convinced that "Communist infiltration" was behind the "No on Prop. 14" effort.[78]

Other indicators pointed to the depth of popular opposition to civil rights. In fall 1963, a poll of residents in the Twenty-third Congressional District found that 96 percent opposed allowing the government to regulate the sale of homes or personal property (the essence of Proposition 14).[79] Nearly 77 percent opposed granting the U.S. attorney general authority to file suit to desegregate schools; 74 percent opposed "compelling" businesses to serve customers of all races; and 84 percent opposed the formation of a Federal Fair Employment Practices Commission to enforce nondiscrimination in hiring. Residents elaborated these opinions, particularly their support of Proposition 14, in a flurry of letters to the editor in September and October 1964. These missives revealed the depth of conservative fears among residents, a confluence of political sensibilities that intermingled anticommunism, a fierce defensiveness of their homes, veiled racism, and a hostility to outsiders. Several letter writers Red-baited their opponents, linking the Rumford Act with communism. "I have lived in California all my life," wrote Beverly Simms, "and we have never had minority problems here until the red agitators, minority bosses, and self-interested politicians commenced to stir up ill will, dissension, and even 'hate' they are always talking about. It is strange that when people are incensed over having their property rights taken away, angry at being dictated to by the state and a few power hungry politicians . . . that any complaint on their part is labeled Fascist, hater or extremist by those who will take unlimited power." Another attacked the Hollywood establishment for opposing Proposition 14. Stars who spoke out, like Burt Lancaster, Gregory Peck, Nat King Cole, James Garner, and Polly Bergen, were "fellow travellers," the writer charged. And Richard Bray asserted, "Those who claim that anyone has a 'right' to acquire the property of another, without the other's absolute consent, are not talking about 'buying,' they are talking about collectivizing, confiscating, and stealing."[80]

South Gate's political leaders expressed similar sentiments. Vice-Mayor Donald Sawyer chastised the "Rumford 'forced' Housing Act" as "bad legislation. It is class legislation at its worst. . . . A 'yes' vote on Prop. No. 14 will restore the rights of all property owners both now and in the future to have a free choice in the disposition of their properties." More forceful was Leland Weaver. Signing his letter "Native Son of California, Third Generation, and Councilman of the City of South Gate. I am not a Realtor," he wrote to the editor: "I disagree that realtors as such have formed ghettos, nor have they used discrimination practices. . . . [O]pponents of Proposition 14 encourage racists and bigots and are trying to narrow the thinking of the masses . . . to lead us all to believe that Proposition 14 refers only to Negroes. . . . [T]he challenges [we face] are to defend the rights we inherited with our Constitution. These rights are for all our citizens, not just one race. . . . I recommend an end to the Rumford Act . . . to protect the freedom of everyone, not just a few." In 1964, residents took their heritage of fighting politically to protect their homes, and applied it to the new racialized politics of the suburb.[81]

In South Gate, the language of race was more defensive than offensive. It focused more on protecting white rights rather than attacking blacks. In contrast to white reactionary discourse in the South, riddled with epithets and unsubtle language, white South Gate attempted to shift the focus from their distaste for blacks to their entitlement as homeowners. This was a more justifiable posture in their eyes, and exonerated them from charges of racism. It represented a tempering of racism among southern migrants to Southern California, where the new suburban milieu would not countenance the kind of expression typical of the region they left. It also resembled a national shift in white attitudes about race after the war, which increasingly defined racism as an individual moral problem rather than a systemic one. This allowed individuals to claim innocence for a problem not of their making.[82]

The racial overtones of Proposition 14 not only redefined the politics of housing but also dislodged traditional partisan loyalties. The measure had a devastating effect on the local Democratic Party, aggravating a split between conservative and liberal factions. Perhaps more than any other issue, housing created powerful tensions in the political identity of local blue-collar Democrats because it tampered with a core element of their social identity: homeownership. Maintaining the value of one's home meant protecting one's status as a full-fledged member of suburban South Gate. And it meant protecting one's economic stability in a setting where threats to home values, like the Rumford Act, had to be beaten back. Proposition 14 aimed to do this. For registered Democrats, this meant rejecting their party and embracing a more conservative approach. As the 1964 election drew near, Proposition 14 began influencing a number of political races. In southern Los Angeles, a faction of conservative Democrats endorsed candidates only if they openly repudiated the Rumford Act and supported Proposition 14. Their influence helped several Republicans win key races in the area, revealing how powerful the conservative impulse in South Gate—a bastion of the Democratic Party—had become.[83]

Demands on the other side of the fence were equally exacting. Opponents of Proposition 14 predicted serious racial turmoil if the measure passed. Dr. Christopher Taylor, head of the NAACP in Los Angeles, explained, "When you give the Negro a promise after you haven't given him anything for a hundred years, and then you take that promise away, you leave him in great despair. He becomes more downhearted, more frustrated than he is now. And then, then anything can happen." An African-American pastor predicted, "If the initiative passes, God forbid, it will block the Negro's legal avenues of progress in fair housing. Then he doesn't have too many ways to go. He can hope the courts rule the initiative unconstitutional. . . . But for the moment, he will be forced to take his fight into the streets." And a black homeseeker put it in simplest terms: "People just forget how the Negro feels when doors keep slamming in his face. He has feelings like everybody else." Given the importance of homeownership in Los Angeles, representing a basis of civic participation, identity, and success, such exclusion was stinging.[84]

Despite the dire predictions, Proposition 14 passed resoundingly in California—65.4 percent in favor, 34.6 percent opposed. In South Gate, approval was more emphatic: 87.5 percent of residents voted "yes." L.A. blacks reacted with deep frustration and anger. One writer claimed the vote

Figure 7-3   This cartoon appeared in the African-American newspaper *California Eagle* in 1964.
Such images conveyed the frustration of L.A. African Americans over white resistance to
integration. *California Eagle,* November 19, 1964.

proved that California "exists in a state of intellectual, moral, and social
darkness." The majority of whites who voted "yes" proved "they were no
better than their Dixiecratic brothers and sisters in Mississippi. . . . The victory for Proposition 14 proves not only the deep-seated racial prejudices
of most California Caucasians . . . but also the reigning stupidity of white
people when it comes to Negroes." The *California Eagle* concurred: "The
single fact that emerges with crystal clarity is that, by and large, white
Americans—for a complex of reasons including that of race prejudices—do
not want to live next door to Negroes. No amount of rationalizing can sub-
merge this truth." Other editorials in the black press reiterated (see fig.
7-3). L.A. Police Chief William H. Parker offered perhaps the most misguided reaction to the vote. He reassured the public that no racial violence

would break out. "The Negro community is not prone to reckless or violent demonstration," he insisted. Like many in Los Angeles, Chief Parker severely misjudged the repercussions of insistent white opposition to civil rights. L.A. blacks would soon take the opportunity to remind their city just how bad things were getting.[85]

THE POLITICS OF CONSUMPTION

Along with education and housing, consumption also took on racial overtones in postwar South Gate. Before the war, conflicts over consumption reflected the divergent class interests of workers and merchants. After the war, consumption became politicized around race rather than class. White merchants used consumption as a tool of racial exclusion. Black activists then turned consumption into a political weapon through the use of boycotts, a key strategy of the national civil rights movement.

Throughout much of southern Los Angeles in the postwar years, merchants discouraged the patronage of minorities. In the flush economic climate of the times, racial homogeneity in retail became more desirable than a few more sales. In 1947, a sociologist of Los Angeles observed that merchants in the lily-white communities of southern L.A. tended "to discourage any Negro or Mexican trade. The police of these communities reputedly cooperate by harassing Negroes and Mexicans with trumped-up charges whenever the opportunity offers." Virgil Collins concurred: "If a black crossed over [Alameda Street] and came into South Gate, first thing is they'd be stopped by a policeman to check 'em out. You never saw a black shopping in South Gate. No way." Merchants also excluded minorities by controlling the retail base itself. John Sheehy, who became South Gate postmaster in 1966 and served as mayor in the 1970s, recalled several instances when local merchants resisted the arrival of department stores in South Gate. The reason, he stated bluntly, was "because they didn't want black people to come over here to shop." When the Whitefront department store, a large California chain, tried to establish an outlet in South Gate, the city council resisted because it would not only compete with local merchants but draw in "undesirable customers." Similar reasoning kept the May Company department store out of South Gate.[86]

The African-American community in Los Angeles seized on consumption as a tool to fight such discrimination. As early as the 1940s, black activists had picketed stores that refused to hire blacks, spanning from South Central to Santa Monica. In the early 1960s, energized by the national civil rights movement, they launched boycotts aimed at an array of businesses.

One target was the Southwest Realty Board, implicated for supporting Proposition 14 and for excluding black realtors from its membership. In December 1963, CORE initiated a Christmas boycott of stores that refused to hire blacks; by Easter, it was extended against national chains with outlets in Los Angeles. In February 1964, CORE targeted merchants in Huntington Park, a key southern L.A. retail center. They called a meeting, inviting Huntington Park businessmen, ministers, and civic leaders as a way of improving communication between the local black and white communities. When only a handful of Huntington Park residents showed up, CORE stepped up its campaign. They drew up a "Memorandum of Agreement," which outlined steps for merchants to take to increase minority hiring in all job categories and a plan for oversight that included monthly meetings with CORE representatives. CORE sent the memorandum to the Chamber of Commerce and individual business owners in Huntington Park. While these demands were exacting, they were not unrealistic; CORE had recently reached an agreement with the Safeway stores, a large supermarket chain, to abide by these standards. As long as merchants complied, CORE promised, "there will be no action, boycotting or picketing of the stores in the area." The Huntington Park situation was watched closely by other southern suburbs where, the South Gate editor noted, "it is felt that other areas may next be on CORE's list."[87]

The initial response of Huntington Park merchants was tentative. Most either refused public comment or insisted there was no need for such a program. Within a week, however, their caution hardened into aggressive resistance. Fomenting this response was the Association for the Protection of American Rights (APAR), a recently formed conservative organization based in nearby Bell. Its purpose was "to coordinate and promote activities designed to protect the rights of all Americans, and to organize groups dedicated to equality of opportunity, without forced integration," and it would accomplish this by adopting the tactics of the civil rights movement —marches, picketing, boycotts—to counteract civil rights activity. The group's founder, UCLA student Bob Walters, explained that APAR was "a completely new approach to the problem of protecting our American rights from the attacks of special interests, privilege-minded minority groups and so-called 'liberals.'" It would serve as a "coordinating council" for existing conservative groups, it promised to keep membership confidential, and it offered to "reinforce with massive anonymous assistance" activities that supported their cause. By March 1964, APAR claimed 50 individual members and 750 group members in Los Angeles and San Francisco.[88]

A few days after CORE made its demands on Huntington Park merchants, APAR leaders issued a resolution condemning this attempt to "forceably integrate business in Huntington Park" and calling for "swift" retaliatory action. They threatened a "massive white boycott against any firm which agrees to abide by CORE's demands." APAR soon made good on its threat. In late March 1964, they targeted the Safeway supermarket chain, chastising the store for abiding by CORE's "Memorandum of Agreement." They picketed Safeway stores in Huntington Park, South Gate, Westwood, Glendale, and Norwalk, handing out 15,000 pamphlets that called on customers to protest to Safeway managers and to patronize stores that "stand up to CORE attacks." APAR ordered Safeway to renounce its agreement with CORE or face even larger demonstrations. This show of force gave Huntington Park merchants the wherewithal to resist CORE's demands.[89]

These episodes revealed how consumption, too, became subsumed by the politics of civil rights. Whether fighting to include or exclude, protesters on both sides used their buying and selling power as a tool for controlling access for minorities. It was yet another example of how the critical political issues before the war—education, housing, and consumption—emerged as matters of race in the postwar era.

THE ELECTION OF 1964 AND THE EMERGENCE OF A NOT-SO-SILENT MAJORITY

In mid-October 1964, local and national politics converged when President Lyndon Johnson's campaign caravan alighted in South Gate. It marked the first time a U.S. president had ever stepped foot in the suburb. At a Democratic rally in South Gate park, Johnson called for unity, "one nation—one people," before a crowd of 15,000. Yet here in South Gate, the schisms dividing the nation surfaced in microcosm. In one section of the park, a group of conservative Barry Goldwater supporters chanted, "We want Barry!" Several fights broke out between Goldwater and Johnson backers, a few people suffering minor injuries.

LBJ's visit sparked off more factious discourse in South Gate, invariably bringing the issue back to race. Several angry residents complained that the Democrats "took over the City of South Gate," with the help of Councilman Milo Dellmann who had openly participated in the rally. "Now Mr. Dellmann," charged M. Siebert, "we can only assume by your endorsement of the candidates at the Democratic rally, that you also have taken your stand endorsing the 'Rumford Forced Housing Bill.' . . . Do you have any idea of the number of people in this area who have worked hard to get the Rumford Forced Housing Bill repealed?" Another resident chastised Dellmann for showing partisanship, a gaffe for any city councilman. The worst of it was the side Dellmann was on: "I can only surmise that Councilman Dellmann supports a no vote on Prop. 14." Finally, resident Ewen Carter blasted all participants in the rally, who represented a "sudden influx of integrationists, education race balancers, Rumford enthusiasts, reapportionists, and sundry other characters who have no more interests in the people of South Gate than the man in the moon." These characters, he charged, supported "civil rights, Prop. 14, and in fact everything that the majority of the people of South Gate are tired of having shoved down their throats. These people have sponsored legislation and advocated laws that take away property rights, integrate our schools, sell us out in the Senate, and grant the federal government unlimited power over our rights and our lives."[90]

Many of Carter's neighbors agreed. The election results of 1964 revealed the makings of a major political realignment: a predominantly Democratic electorate began voting Republican. In June 1964, voter registration in South Gate was nearly two-to-one Democratic. Local voting behavior, however, reflected a much tighter divide between liberals and conservatives. In a remarkable 88 percent voter turnout, South Gate residents offered only lukewarm support for Democratic candidates and causes. President Lyndon Johnson won a majority of votes in the suburb, but even this backing paled by national standards. While South Gaters voted 56.6 percent for Johnson and 43.4 percent for Barry Goldwater, the national vote was 61.1 to 38.5 percent, respectively. At the congressional level, South Gate residents mostly voted for Republicans by substantial margins (see table 7-2). At the state level, Democrats continued to dominate the South Gate vote, although a conservative impulse was beginning to surface. Republican Floyd Wakefield made a respectable showing in his run for the Fifty-second Assembly District seat. In South Gate, he won 44.8 percent of local votes to Democrat George Willson's 55.2 percent (in the whole district, Wakefield earned 40.4 percent of votes).[91]

One congressional race illustrated the rightward realignment particularly well: the House of Representatives, Twenty-third Congressional District. Encompassing a cluster of white working-class suburbs that included South Gate, this district was considered a traditional Democratic stronghold critical to the party's success in the state (see fig. 7-4). Since 1945, moderate Democrat Clyde Doyle represented the district. When he died suddenly in office in 1963, a special election to choose a replacement placed Del Clawson in office, the first Republican ever to represent the district. Clawson had a long history of public service, working with the Federal Public Housing Authority and the Mutual Housing Association of Compton and serving on the Compton city council and as director of three L.A.

Table 7-2   South Gate Voting Patterns, 1964 (Percentage of Total South Gate Votes)

Election	Democrat		Republican	
President	Johnson	56.6%	Goldwater	43.4 %
U.S. Congress: Senate	Salinger	42.2	Murphy	57.8
U.S. Congress: House				
23rd District (85 precincts)	Van Petten	41.5	Clawson	58.5
21st District (28 precincts)	Hawkins	61.2	Lundy	38.8
State Assembly				
52nd District (84 precincts)	Willson	55.2	Wakefield	44.8
55th District (28 precincts)	Ferrell	57.7	Greene	42.3
38th District (1 precinct)	Porter	57.7	Stevens	42.3
	No		Yes	
Proposition 14	12.5%		87.5%	

Note: "Precinct" refers to the number of precincts in South Gate, encompassed in the relevant district.

Sources: California Secretary of State, *Statement of Vote—General Election, and Supplement* (Sacramento: Secretary of State, 1964); Election Returns by Precinct, General Election, November 3, 1964, Los Angeles County, CSA.

County sanitation districts. He was mayor of Compton from 1957 to 1964.[92]

Clawson's victory threw the local Democratic Party into turmoil. Given the rising tide of conservatism in the area, the Democrats faced a tough decision. Should they join the right-leaning bandwagon and water down their principles, or should they stick to the agenda of the national party, which was finally beginning to back civil rights? Local Democrats quarreled fiercely over these questions. In January 1964, conservative and liberal factions faced off in a turbulent meeting to decide the leadership of the Twenty-third District Coordinating Council, which oversaw party efforts in the district. When the dust settled, the liberal faction had seized control. They were backed by the UAW, teamsters, and rubber workers, and Democratic leaders at the county and state levels. At its first meeting in February, the new coordinating council took a stand on *the* critical issue dividing local Democrats—the Rumford Act. Their endorsement of Rumford and opposition to Proposition 14 pushed the conservative wing even further away.[93]

But the conservative Democrats hardly retreated. They mobilized against the liberal faction in an effort to reclaim the party. Nate Benson of South Gate, a leader of this group, chastised the "ultra left" coordinating council for its "pro-Communist" inclinations, such as supporting China's entry to the United Nations, opposing loyalty oaths, and holding academic

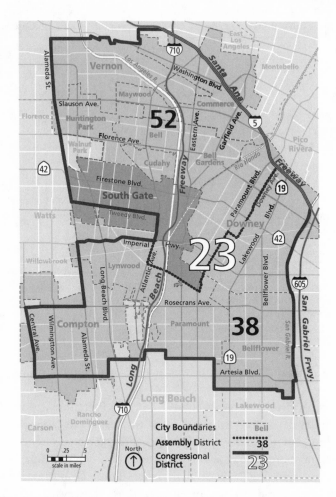

Figure 7-4   Boundary of the Twenty-third Congressional District (U.S. House of
Representatives) in Los Angeles, 1965. Map derived from County of Los Angeles,
Los Angeles County Almanac and Buyers Guide for 1965.

freedom above national security. In March, the conservatives organized the
Clyde Doyle Democratic Club, attracting 142 members in two months. But
when it applied for a charter, the Democratic Central Committee of the area
turned it down, partly on technical grounds but also because two members
of the club were real estate brokers who circulated petitions for Proposition
14. To the central committee, this action violated basic party principles.[94]

As the 1964 congressional campaign heated up, the schism widened
between conservatives and liberals. Almost immediately, race became the
major dividing point. With civil rights insinuating itself into local life, race

issues—particularly the integration of schools and neighborhoods—came to represent a litmus test for the candidates. Republican Del Clawson openly expressed his opposition to civil rights. Without mincing words, he criticized the pending 1964 civil rights bill as a grab for federal power. "I think we Californians have made great strides in handling racial problems. It is apparent that we want to continue to do the job ourselves and not have a government bureau telling us how to solve our problems," he explained. He surprised few by voting "no" on the bill. Clawson supported other orthodox Republican positions, such as anticommunism, strong defense industries—critical to the Twenty-third District's economy—and support for school prayer.[95]

On the Democratic side, internal dissention immediately surfaced. During the primaries, the frontrunners were H. O. Van Petten of Downey and Richard English of Lynwood, both attorneys. The conservative was Van Petten. He came out against the Rumford Act, the key issue that defined him politically. While he won support from the conservative Clyde Doyle Democratic Club, his opposition to Rumford put him on organized labor's blacklist. By contrast, English championed the Rumford Act, earning him an endorsement from the L.A. County Federation of Labor. While both candidates supported the civil rights bill pending in Congress, it was their stands on local race issues that set them apart. By the slimmest of margins, the conservative Van Petten won the primary. The depth of conservatism had grown to the point that some South Gate Democrats found even Van Petten too left wing. In the primary election, 504 of them wrote in Republican Del Clawson for the Democratic nomination.[96]

As the fall campaign progressed, Van Petten began waffling on the fair housing issue under pressure from both wings of his party. When the state Democratic platform included firm opposition to Proposition 14, Van Petten revised his own position, realizing it would be politically imprudent to contradict the state party's stance. This first became apparent when he stated publicly that he had *never* supported Proposition 14, but fully backed the state party platform. The conservative Democrats immediately jumped on him. The Bell-Cudahy Democratic Club, part of the conservative faction, pressed Van Petten on the issue. He ended up telling the club he would take *no* stand on the initiative. Quickly, he began losing key endorsements. Mrs. Clyde Doyle and Frank McEwan, former chairman of the Twenty-third District coordinating committee, both withdrew their support. McEwan charged that Van Petten "had turned his back on his primary friends and turned to his primary political enemies." Such reproach from members of his own party—just weeks before election day—debilitated Van Petten's campaign. Some disaffected Democrats, so occupied with race issues, gave up on their party altogether and defected to the Republicans. They formed the Democratic Committee to Re-Elect Congressman Del Clawson, running ads and lending enthusiastic support to the Republican incumbent.[97]

When election day arrived, the fissures among the Democrats surfaced where it counted most—the ballot box. Republican Del Clawson ended up winning the Twenty-third District by a 55 to 45 percent vote. In South Gate, Clawson's margin was even larger, 58.5 to 41.5 percent. At least 2,000 registered Democrats in South Gate had cast ballots for him. This fact was not lost on the victor, who expressed gratitude to his Democratic supporters. Nor was it lost on Democratic leaders, who blamed an array of culprits for their candidate's defeat. They first attacked disloyal Democratic clubs. Within weeks of the election, the County Democratic Committee began purging groups like the Bell-Cudahy Democratic Club for failing to support Van Petten and backing Proposition 14. One leader blamed the defeat on those labor unions that refused to rally behind Van Petten. Finally, some Democrats charged that ultra-right wingers, particularly the John Birch Society, helped orchestrate Clawson's victory. Van Petten himself accused several Republican city councilmen in his district of being Birchers and contributing to the political momentum against him.[98]

It wouldn't be long before many blue-collar conservatives in South Gate and nearby suburbs began questioning their party loyalty altogether. The Democratic Party, with its unrelenting support of civil rights, seemed increasingly out of touch with the pressing concerns of residents. As they gradually extricated themselves from the left wing of their own party, they found themselves perched on the edge of partisan identity, ready to take the leap toward a new party altogether. They just needed something to push them over that edge, something to confirm their beliefs and fears. That something exploded in August of 1965.

THE FALLOUT OF RACIALIZED POLITICS

On a hot Wednesday evening, August 11, 1965, about a mile from South Gate's westerly border, two white highway patrolmen arrested Marquette Frye, a twenty-one-year-old African American, on suspicion of drunk driving. Frye was in his car with his brother Ronald. They had been driving through a South Central neighborhood near Watts. Within minutes of the arrest their mother Rena, who lived nearby, approached the scene and began scolding her sons. Soon a scuffle broke out between the Fryes—including the mother—and the patrolmen. A crowd of black onlookers, sensing they were witnessing yet another case of police brutality in their neighborhood, began jeering the officers. The patrolmen responded by pulling out guns and calling for reinforcements. When 20 more officers arrived on the scene, the swelling crowd refused to be intimidated by this show of force. They began pelting the police with rocks and bottles. Within a couple of hours, the crowd had grown and their anger exploded into a full-fledged rebellion. They threw bricks and bottles, overturned passing cars driven by whites, and smashed store windows. The melee lasted five hours that night, and involved 1,000 persons and 100 officers. The next day, the L.A. County Human Relations Commission called a meeting of local community leaders and the media. Although the meeting's aim was to quell tempers and avert further violence, it backfired when black participants began voicing grievances and a black high school student predicted rioters would attack adjacent white suburbs that night. By nightfall, violence broke out again. This time, about 7,000 persons joined in, looting white-owned stores then torching them, flipping automobiles, smashing windows, and lobbing Molotov cocktails. Black anger was unleashed. After years of enduring police brutality, discrimination, exclusion, unemployment, and animosity—from their South Gate neighbors to the metropolitan power structure at large—the black community of southern Los Angeles exploded. This was a protest of last resort.[99]

In South Gate and other white suburbs bordering Alameda, a siege mentality set in. Being so close to the uproar, South Gate residents felt the riots viscerally. "That really scared the people of South Gate, believe you me," recalled John Sheehy. Several residents found themselves caught in the melee the first night as they drove through Watts without realizing what was happening. One South Gate man had his windshield smashed by a brick. In another car, a sixteen-year-old girl caught a sliver of glass in her arm as her family passed through Watts on their way home to South Gate. As her mother described it, "I heard someone yell, 'There's some more whites. Let's get them.' Then bricks and bottles started flying at us from both sides of the street. . . . By the time we got out of range, my daughter was screaming and crying." In another incident, four blacks threw rocks at a car driven by a Lynwood resident as she drove down Long Beach Boulevard. She was unhurt. On the third night, a South Gate man met the ultimate fate. Albert Flores, a resident of Dearborn Street, was found dead on a Watts street corner after a violent outbreak. In a separate incident, his brother Richard, a Huntington Park resident, was driving to his mother-in-law's house in Watts to take her away when he was shot in the chest by a National Guardsman. He was critically injured.[100]

As the rebellion wore on, residents watched the smoke billow upward, choking the air, laying a thick brown blanket above their heads. They breathed it in. The South Gate police chief stationed officers—armed with shotguns and tear gas—at every street crossing from Watts into South Gate and ordered them to stop any car containing a black person. Police in neighboring suburbs like Lynwood and Huntington Park did the same. Major intersections between white and black Los Angeles, like Imperial in Lynwood, became command posts for law enforcement officers. They stood guard, keeping people from driving into the riot area and defending the white suburbs from encroaching violence. To this end, they "chased cars with Negroes in them back across Alameda," according to one reporter. Rumors of "possible invasion" into South Gate, Huntington Park, and Lynwood had spread wildly by the third night. A number of residents took up arms to protect themselves and their property, standing vigil on rooftops, front porches, and street corners. Cars of white roaming vigilantes patrolled the streets of Lynwood. Assemblyman George Willson of the Fifty-second District called on the governor to "quarantine" the South Central area with tanks, armored cars, and National Guardsmen, to protect the white suburbs bordering the area. "Rioting, looting and killing in the Watts area must be quarantined in the same manner as a communicable disease is confined to prevent its spreading," he told the governor. False alarms were rampant in white working-class suburbia. At 3 A.M. on the fourth night, Lynwood resident John Tristany called the police, convinced the rioters had arrived on his doorstep. As a reporter described it, "Tristany was running around in his shorts, waving a gun and shouting, 'The niggers threw a Molotov cocktail on my roof. They set fire to my store on Central Avenue yesterday, and I fired a few shots at them. Now they're trying to get me good. I heard them fooling around out here.'" When police searched his property, they found the culprit—a smoldering barbecue had ignited a fire.[101]

When the Watts Rebellion of 1965 finally subsided after six days of violence, 34 people had been killed, 900 injured, 4,000 arrested, and $30 million worth of property destroyed. An estimated 50,000 African Americans had participated in the uprising, while 14,000 National Guardsmen and 1,500 police officers tried to quell it. Watts was the first of many racial eruptions in the United States during the 1960s. While it fit the pattern of riots elsewhere, a symptom of the country's chronic, unresolved problem with race, the Watts Rebellion also reflected the peculiarities of localized oppression. Dr. Alvin Pouissant, noted African-American psychiatrist and L.A. resident, spoke to the *Los Angeles Times* on the third day of rioting. He identified the root causes of the rebellion as police brutality, lack of broad citizen participation on police review boards, unemployment, and Proposition 14. The latter, he claimed, "had an enormous psychological effect on Negroes in ghetto areas. It made them feel trapped, as if there is no way of getting out of the low-income housing areas." Pouissant was neither the first nor the last to offer this explanation. Some had predicted such an outburst well before August 1965.

The white establishment, meanwhile, continued to misconstrue the big picture. LAPD Chief William Parker was foremost among them. "This was not a race riot in the true sense of the word," he explained. "There have been some outside agitators telling the Negroes they are treated unfairly, but I don't think that caused the riot. It's not like down South. What happened in Watts was a rebellion against authority—brought on partly by the hot, muggy weather." The McCone Commission, appointed by Governor Edmund Brown to investigate the riot's causes and to present solutions, was likewise misguided. Its interpretation of the school segregation controversy was the clearest evidence of this. The commission essentially blamed the problem on black students themselves. "It is our conclusion that the very low level of scholastic achievement we observe in the predominantly Negro schools contributes to de facto segregation in the schools. . . . We reason, therefore, that raising the scholastic achievement might reverse the entire trend of de facto segregation." To this end, the commission recommended remedial programs and better buildings, rather than enforcing the mandate of *Brown v. Board of Education*.[102]

In South Gate, many residents responded with an "I told you so" attitude. Integration with these people, they asked, not on your life. As resident Roger Lockwood put it, "Concerning the monstrous insurrection in Watts, I dread to think what surely would have happened to South Gate students if the dreamy utopians, brotherhood cult, assorted moralists, minority bosses, political leftists, extraneous influences, and dedicated Communists along with their sympathizers had as planned successfully enforced their preposterous demands to thereby force South Gate children into attending Jordan High School against their will and better judgment. What . . . would have been the outcome if these people had won out? . . . Needless to say white students coerced into such a hostile outburst of hate and discrimination would have been beaten, raped and killed. It cannot now be denied." He continued, "What if the whites in the surrounding areas had . . . seen fit to take matters into their own hands and descended upon Watts residents bent on revenge that would have surely resulted in bloody carnage and a massacre the likes of which we have not seen[?] . . . It is not only possible[,] it is in the cards as they say." Another resident, Edward Miller, echoed the refrain that South Gate had fallen victim to outsiders seeking to "impose their will on the residents of South Gate"—the minority bosses, communist opportunists, and West L.A. self-serving liberals who clamored for integration of the southeastern suburbs as a way of keeping it out of their

own neighborhoods. "The Watts riots of Aug. 11 were centered in the area
into which these organizations want and demand we send our children,"
Miller wrote. "Not their children but South Gate children. This is the area
into which teachers and ministers advocate we send our boys and girls . . .
like shock troops before real invasion begins."[103] The Watts Rebellion confirmed the righteousness of their stand against civil rights like nothing else
could have.

The history of politics in postwar South Gate—a story that localized
the national battle over civil rights—revealed a picture of deteriorating
race relations in Los Angeles. In contrast to the "golden age" for L.A. blacks
in the early twentieth century, the postwar years were times of heightened
racial anxiety, hostility, and defensiveness in a context of explosive population growth and pressures on residential space. The physical openness that
had earlier characterized the sprawling metropolis, allowing ample elbow
room, was filling up with successive waves of new migrants. In this pres-
surized spatial context, especially in places like southern Los Angeles, racial
borders became more material and significant. Whites responded by attempting to reassert control over this unstable environment. At the metropolitan level, they did this by reshaping the physical and cultural landscape
to foster white insulation.[104] At the local level in suburbs like South Gate,
they did this through defensive "crabgrass-roots" politics that drew on a
discourse of white rights. Either way, the 1950s and 1960s—the proverbial
age of white flight—was an era when race relations intensified and disinte-
grated.[105]

As these pressures politicized South Gate residents in new ways, their
political identity underwent a transformation. It first manifested in 1964
when registered Democrats in the area began voting Republican. Yet old
party allegiances persisted in national elections; a majority of South Gate
citizens voted for Democrat LBJ in 1964, a sign that local concerns had yet
to find a voice in a national leader. The New Deal coalition remained shak-
ily intact. By 1968, as the social revolutions of the decade intensified, the
coalition finally broke down. A majority of South Gate residents—still
mostly registered Democrats—voted for Richard Nixon or George Wallace.
Results were similar in neighboring suburbs (see table 7-3). Blue-collar
suburbia in southern Los Angeles had become a stronghold of Republicanism. In South Gate, historically a town of working-class Democrats, local
politics had incubated the "silent majority."[106]

In postwar South Gate, the articulation of white homeowner rights in
local political discourse represented the culmination of two generations of
social and political life. From the outset, homeownership had been central

Table 7-3 Presidential Voting Returns in Selected Blue-Collar Suburbs of Southern Los Angeles, 1968 and 1972

	1968			1972		
	Nixon	Humphrey	Wallace	Nixon	McGovern	Schmitz
Bell	44.2	42.9	12.5	57.9	37.0	4.6
Bell Gardens	32.5	46.5	20.7	52.9	41.8	4.8
El Segundo	59.3	31.2	9.4	70.2	25.6	3.5
Huntington Park	47.3	41.6	10.7	57.7	37.2	4.3
Inglewood	53.8	38.4	7.6	53.8	43.8	2.1
Lynwood	48.5	39.7	11.6	58.8	36.5	4.0
Maywood	39.5	46.7	13.4	56.0	39.4	4.0
Signal Hill	48.4	40.7	10.3	53.4	43.1	2.9
South Gate	48.0	40.7	11.0	61.6	33.9	4.0
Torrance	57.8	34.4	7.6	69.1	27.5	2.9

Sources: California Secretary of State, *Statement of Vote; General Election. Supplement*, November 5, 1968, compiled by Frank M. Jordan (Sacramento: Secretary of State, 1968), 82–83; idem, *Statement of Vote; General Election, Supplement*, November 7, 1972, compiled by Edmund G. Brown Jr. (Sacramento: Secretary of State, 1972), 61–62.

to this experience. It began as an economic strategy, evolved into a signifier of social and civic status, and ultimately emerged as the material basis of postwar conservatism. As residents perceived it, the movement to stave off African-American incursions into their neighborhood was merely the latest effort to control the integrity of their property and their capacity to benefit from its value. The perceived right to control property and residential space—from the 1920s through the 1960s—was constant throughout.

The grassroots activism of South Gate residents, along with similar efforts by whites in numerous neighborhoods across the United States, had the cumulative effect of reinforcing racial inequality in the postwar metropolis. As the suburban ideal became more emphatically racialized in the postwar years, politics likewise was construed in racial terms. To maintain their place in the postwar suburban world, South Gate residents felt the need to assert their whiteness all the more stridently. The pursuit of the American Dream had become a zero-sum game. And the victories, ultimately, bittersweet.

Epilogue

In the early twenty-first century, South Gate is once again a suburb of the working class, although now it is home to the working poor. In certain startling ways, the community has come full circle back to its original form, with residents living in garages, growing home gardens, and searching for ways to maximize the use of their domestic property. Yet in other ways, the labor and housing markets are so dramatically altered that family security is no more than an ethereal goal. Working-class suburbia has become vested with a much different meaning.

Profound demographic and economic change undergird this transformation. Perhaps the most important, visible turn is the ethnic transition that occurred after the Watts Rebellion of 1965. In a classic case of "white flight," frightened residents began leaving the area, making room for incoming waves of working-class Latinos. The demographic change was immense in southern Los Angeles. In South Gate, the Latino population leaped from 4 percent of the total in 1960, to 46 percent by 1980, and 83.1 percent in 1990.[1] Similar turnover occurred in Maywood, Huntington Park, Bell, Bell Gardens, and Lynwood, which are more than 90 percent Latino. While these towns remain working-class suburbs, their current demography aptly reflects the ethnic transformation of Los Angeles's working class and working poor.[2]

Economic erosion is the other critical element in the transformation of South Gate. Riding the swell of industrial expansion and capital mobility in the postwar era, South Gate was lucky to be on the receiving end of early economic restructuring. In the 1950s and 1960s, unions remained strong, wages high, and jobs plentiful. Beginning in the 1950s, blacks, Latinos, and women began entering the industrial workforce in greater numbers, benefiting from the strong industrial economy. Yet if Los Angeles escaped the ravages of deindustrialization already plaguing older industrial cities like Detroit in the 1950s, it was only a matter of time before the ax fell on the city of angels. By the 1970s and 1980s, deindustrialization hit Los Angeles, driven by the same forces of corporate profit seeking and global competition. Hit hardest were the southern industrial suburbs, where Fordist industry concentrated.

South Gate lay directly in the line of fire, losing more than 12,500 jobs by the mid-1980s. Weiser Lock shut down in 1979 and Firestone Tire and Rubber followed in 1980; the big blow came when GM permanently shut its doors in 1983. One of the first blacks hired at GM was Charlie Brown, one of more than 4,000 GM workers laid off. Recalling his last day of work, he said, "I felt like my whole life that I had worked for twenty-eight years was flushed down the drain. . . . I'm just beginning to see that I may never have the same standard of living anymore or be able to do what every American wants to do—keep his kids in college, put bread on the table, and keep a happy home." Woefully, many of these closures occurred soon after blacks, Latinos, and women made watershed breakthroughs in shop-floor seniority and local union leadership. As Mike Davis has noted, "While white workers for the most part were able to retire or follow their jobs to the suburban periphery, non-whites were stranded in an economy that was suddenly minus 40,000 high-wage manufacturing and trucking jobs [in the southern suburbs]."[3]

But this industrial core did not simply dry up. Rather, into the vacuum stepped local capitalists, many from Taiwan, eager to profit from the area's cheap tax rates and labor supply. They established a new sweatshop economy. Paying minimum wage (and sometimes less), these operations turned the clock backward about 100 years in terms of wages, work conditions, and the prevalence of the open shop. Symbolic of the change, the old Firestone plant now houses a nonunion furniture factory employing mainly immigrant labor. Jobs at these operations promise little hope of upward mobility, with their low wages, lack of security, and poor conditions. In the larger process of economic and urban restructuring starkly exemplified in Los Angeles, the high-tech, high-skilled jobs so celebrated in the region's unflappable economic growth took root in areas away from this "rust belt" of

L.A.—in far-flung places like Irvine, the airport area, and the San Fernando Valley. Southeast Los Angeles, meanwhile, became a center of the low-wage, immigrant labor market.[4]

In South Gate, the economic impact of restructuring has been enormous. The most visible effect has been the deterioration of local services. Plant closures resulted in the loss of millions of dollars in sales taxes, paid to the city not only by the once-thriving plants themselves but by customers buying locally. On top of this loss, the pay-as-you-go tax policy ended up hurting the aging suburb, as years passed without the building of new infrastructure or adequate maintenance of existing services. Property-tax rollbacks in the 1970s and 1980s exacerbated the problem. The result has been both quality of life and environmental decline. When overcrowded schools forced the L.A. Unified School District in 1999 to search for sites to build two new schools in South Gate, it unwisely chose an industrial tract of land contaminated by hazardous chemicals. The controversy sparked by this decision led to the downfall of the district superintendent—and left South Gate parents begging for its schools.[5]

Culturally, South Gate has experienced a full-scale metamorphosis. Mexicans predominate in the area, with a sprinkling of Peruvians who have formed tight-knit economic, social, and recreational networks. New businesses catering to the Latino population have revitalized major commercial strips like Tweedy and Long Beach Boulevard. Residents, meanwhile, have carved out their own social routines of family, religious, leisure, and organizational life. Signs of cultural amalgamation have appeared as well. The hip-hop group Cypress Hill, for example, came out of South Gate. This bilingual rap trio, whose music juxtaposes "the futility of gangbanging with the joys of pot smoking," has achieved national success, crossing over to white alternative rock fans. Amalgamation is also evident in intermarriage. Mary (DeVries) North, one of few longtime Anglo residents who continue to live in South Gate, has gained kin ties to the Latino community. Her grandson married a Latina, bringing together two families that exemplify successive generations of South Gate's working class.[6]

In the midst of these changes, most of South Gate's contemporary working class finds itself in similar straits as its predecessors of the 1920s. Both search for the ever-elusive good life, and they do so in the suburbs. But working-class suburbia of the early twenty-first century is a starkly different kind of place. In South Gate, the most poetic symbol of that change is captured in the fate of one simple structure: the garage. The edifice that once acted as temporary shelter to homebuilding families of the 1920s and 1930s has made a comeback as a dwelling unit.

Garages now house Mexican immigrants, who rent the meager spaces because they cannot afford apartments.[7] Typical rents for a garage in 1987 were $200 to $300 a month, compared to $300 and up for the worst of one-bedroom apartments. Representing the very bottom of the housing market, a mere rung above homelessness, the auto garage is no temporary shelter of yesteryear but rather a permanent dwelling. It magnifies the conditions of the local housing market—saturated, decaying, and overpriced. In the 1950s, the Whitnall report claimed South Gate had reached a comfortable saturation point at 55,000 persons, with nearly all lots developed. The suburb's population has since risen to more than 85,000. The excess 30,000 inhabitants, thus, have been absorbed into a housing market that is dense, illicit, and costly. The shadow market of garage dwellings is merely one part of it.

Immigrant families crowd into these cramped, windowless living spaces. The biggest problems with garage dwellings, say public health nurses, stem from the cold drafts, the absence of bathrooms, and the lack of kitchen facilities to allow for the proper cleaning, cooking, and storing of foods. Many dwellers use backyard ditches as toilets. Single extension cords strung across tree branches and through door jams supply electric power. With every lot occupied, intensive overcrowding results. Garbage cans overflow, residents cluster on the streets and sidewalks for fresh air, and the narrow streets are packed with cars that are displaced from the garages.

Like their 1920s predecessors, many of these garage inhabitants grow home gardens in backyards. As a disgruntled neighbor remarked, "They cut down trees to plant vegetables in the yard and they hang clothes on the fence. And people are always loitering." Such practices are latter-day efforts to maximize the use of domestic property, even though now it is rented, not owned, and the spaces have shrunk dramatically.[8]

Garage living is both illegal and widespread. The landlords who rent them violate sanitation, zoning, and safety laws, and they are subject to continual crackdowns by housing inspectors. But most evade arrest by concealing the dwellings, which are typically detached structures tucked away in backyards. Landlords take great pains to camouflage their operations through such strategies as phony walls that hide the living quarters when the garage door is open. Because the dwellings are unlawful, the tenants abrogate all legal rights.

The practice is alarmingly widespread in Southern California. In 1987, the *Los Angeles Times* conducted a survey based on a sample of 500 homes, and found that about 42,000 garages sheltered about 200,000 persons in L.A. County. Most were in Latino neighborhoods. The practice appears to be unique to Los Angeles, mainly because of the history of the region's housing landscape. In Tucson, Dallas, Houston, and Phoenix, which also have large Latino populations, the practice is nonexistent. Poor immigrants in those cities typically double and triple up in apartments, but they do not inhabit garages. The likely reason is that in these cities, homes have carports rather than detached garages. Thus, the history of Los Angeles housing and owner-building has contributed to the present-day practice. Working-class self-builders constructed detached garages as temporary shelter in the first step toward homeownership, and their handiwork continues to shelter the poor of the metropolis.

Local officials launched a crackdown on the dwellings in 1984, which received "incredibly widespread support throughout the city." When South Gate hired extra housing inspectors to evict the illegal dwellers, they ousted more than 1,000 families from 1985 to 1987. Still, South Gate officials estimated that 4,000 garage dwellings continued to house 20,000 persons, representing 25 percent of the suburb's population. For many, garage dwelling is a small step above homelessness. One public health nurse admitted she did not "report them all" because they could end up homeless. "You sometimes decide they're cleaner and safer in a garage."

The phenomenon of garage living in South Gate reveals the altered context of working-class suburbia in contemporary Los Angeles. The garage is no longer a waystation on the road to self-generated homeownership. It is simply a shelter, sometimes for years, on the road to apartment living at best. For this latter-day working class, homeownership is an elusive goal, choked by the limitations of the labor and housing markets. To these Latino suburbanites, the "good life" has taken on a very humble tone. But some things remain constant. Just as the goal of economic security propelled Juanita Smith and her struggling family from Tennessee to South Gate, families from Mexico make their way to the very same suburb for identical reasons. The goals may be alike, but the chances for success are indeed an epoch away.

South Gate Weave, 1997

Robbert Flick

Photographer Robbert Flick captures the built landscape of present-day South Gate in this photographic trajectory encompassing several blocks of the old Home Gardens section of the suburb.

Acronyms for Collections and Archives

ALUA:	Walter P. Reuther Library, Archives of Labor and Urban Affairs, Wayne State University, Detroit, Michigan.
CSA:	California State Archives, Sacramento, California.
FOH:	Oral History Project, California State University Fullerton.
FWP:	Federal Writers Project Collection, Department of Special Collections, Charles E. Young Research Library, University of California Los Angeles.
JAF:	John Anson Ford Papers, Huntington Library, San Marino, California.
LACBSA:	Los Angeles County Board of Education collection, Los Angeles County Board of Supervisors Archives.
LACFL:	Los Angeles County Federation of Labor (AFL-CIO) collection, Urban Archives Center, California State University Northridge.
LC, ALUA:	Louis Ciccone collection, Walter P. Reuther Library, Archives of Labor and Urban Affairs, Wayne State University, Detroit, Michigan.
RG 183, NA:	Record Group 183, Records of the Bureau of Employment Security, National Archives, Washington, D.C.
RG 195, NA:	Record Group 195, Records of the Federal Home Loan Bank Board, National Archives, Washington, D.C.

RG 212, NA: Record Group 212, Records of the Committee for Congested
                    Production Areas, National Archives, Washington, D.C.
SGCH: South Gate City Hall, South Gate, California.
SGHWL: South Gate History Archives, Weaver Library, South Gate,
                    California.
UAW216, ALUA: United Auto Workers Local 216 collection, Walter P. Reuther
                    Library, Archives of Labor and Urban Affairs, Wayne State
                    University, Detroit, Michigan.
YRL-UCLA: Department of Special Collections, Charles E. Young Research
                    Library, University of California Los Angeles.

Notes

Introduction

1. Mike Davis, "Sunshine and the Open Shop: Ford and Darwin in 1920s Los Angeles," *Antipode* 29 (1997): 358–361; Greg Hise, "'Nature's Workshop': Industry and Urban Expansion in Southern California, 1900–1950," *Journal of Historical Geography* 27 (2001): 74–92; Ed Soja, *Postmodern Geographies: The Reassertion of Space in Critical Social Theory* (London: Verso, 1989), chapter 8.

2. Examples of the vast literature focusing on elite and middle-class suburbs include Kenneth T. Jackson, *Crabgrass Frontier: The Suburbanization of the United States* (New York: Oxford University Press, 1985); Robert Fishman, *Bourgeois Utopias: The Rise and Fall of Suburbia* (New York: Basic Books, 1987); Zane Miller, *Suburb: Neighborhood and Community in Forest Park, Ohio, 1935–1976* (Knoxville: University of Tennessee Press, 1981); Carol A. O'Connor, *A Sort of Utopia: Scarsdale, 1891–1981* (Albany: SUNY Press, 1983); John Stilgoe, *Borderland: Origins of the American Suburb, 1820–1939* (New Haven: Yale University Press, 1988); Margaret Marsh, *Suburban Lives* (New Brunswick: Rutgers University Press, 1990). For historiography, see Margaret Marsh, "Reconsidering the Suburbs: An Exploration of Suburban Historiography," *Pennsylvania Magazine of History and Biography* 112 (1988): 579–605. While Kenneth Jackson's seminal study acknowledges the presence of service workers in elite suburbs of the late nineteenth century, he leaves the impression that they were not true suburbanites—they were in, but not of, suburbia. He argues that working-class families entered suburbia in earnest only after 1945, with the help of Federal Housing Administration loans and expanding postwar affluence.

3. Richard A. Walker, "A Theory of Suburbanization: Capitalism and the Construction of Urban Space in the United States," in Michael Dear and Allen J. Scott, eds., *Urbanization and Urban Planning in Capitalist Society* (New York:

Methuen, 1981), 383–429; Richard Walker, "The Transformation of Urban Structure in the Nineteenth Century and the Beginnings of Suburbanization," in Kevin Cox, ed., *Urbanization and Conflict in Market Societies* (Chicago: Maaroufa Press, 1978), 165–212.

4.   These early studies (sociological and otherwise) particularly focused on class variations. For example, see Margaret Byington, *Homestead: The Households of a Mill Town* (1910, reprint, Pittsburgh: University of Pittsburgh Press, 1974); Graham R. Taylor, *Satellite Cities: A Study of Industrial Suburbs* (New York: Appleton, 1915); Harlan Paul Douglas, *The Suburban Trend* (New York: Century, 1925); Robert Whitten and Thomas Adams, *Neighborhoods of Small Homes: Economic Density of Low-cost Housing in America and England* (Cambridge: Harvard University Press, 1931). In the 1960s, sociologists "rediscovered" working-class suburbia. See Bennett Berger, *Blue Collar Suburb: A Study of Auto Workers in Suburbia* (Berkeley and Los Angeles: University of California Press, 1960); William M. Dobriner, *Class in Suburbia* (Englewood Cliffs, N.J.: Prentice-Hall, 1963); Herbert J. Gans, "Urbanism and Suburbanism as Ways of Life: A Re-evaluation of Definitions," in Arnold M. Rose, ed., *Human Behavior and Social Processes: An Interactionist Approach* (Boston: Houghton Mifflin, 1962), 625–648.

5.   James Wunsch, "The Suburban Cliché," *Journal of Social History* 28 (spring 1995): 654.

6.   Richard Harris, *Unplanned Suburbs: Toronto's American Tragedy, 1900 to 1950* (Baltimore: Johns Hopkins University Press, 1996); Richard Harris, "Chicago's Other Suburbs," *Geographical Review* 84 (1994): 394–410; Richard Harris and Robert Lewis, "Constructing a Fault(y) Zone: Misrepresentations of American Cities and Suburbs, 1900–1950," *Annals of the Association of American Geographers* 88 (1998): 622–639; Andrew Wiese, "Places of Our Own: Suburban Black Towns Before 1960," *Journal of Urban History* 19 (1993): 30–54; Andrew Wiese, "The Other Suburbanites: African American Suburbanization in the North before 1950," *Journal of American History* 85 (1999): 1–26; Robert Bruegmann, "Schaumburg, Oak Brook, Rosemont, and the Recentering of the Chicago Metropolitan Area," in John Zukowsky, ed., *Chicago Architecture, 1923–1993* (Chicago: Art Institute of Chicago, 1993); James Borchert, "Residential City Suburbs: The Emergence of a New Suburban Type, 1880–1930," *Journal of Urban History* 22 (March 1996): 283–307. Other examples include Kevin David Kane and Thomas L. Bell, "Suburbs for a Labor Elite," *Geographical Review* 75 (1985): 319–334; Timothy J. Sehr, "Three Gilded Age Suburbs of Indianapolis: Irvington, Brightwood, and Woodruff Place," *Indiana Magazine of History* 77 (1981): 305–332; Fred Viehe, "Black Gold Suburbs: The Influence of the Extractive Industry on the Suburbanization of Los Angeles, 1890–1930," *Journal of Urban History* 8 (November 1981): 3–26; Ann Durkin Keating, *Building Chicago: Suburban Developers and the Creation of a Divided Metropolis* (Columbus: Ohio State University Press, 1988); Olivier Zunz, *The Changing Face of Inequality: Urbanization, Industrial Development, and Immigrants in Detroit, 1880–1920* (Chicago: University of Chicago Press, 1982).

Two important early studies that encompassed (but did not focus on) working-class suburbs are Sam Bass Warner Jr., *Streetcar Suburbs: The Process of Growth in Boston (1870–1900)* (Cambridge: Harvard University Press, 1962); and Jon Teaford, *City and Suburb: The Political Fragmentation of Metropolitan America, 1850–1970* (Baltimore: Johns Hopkins University Press, 1979).

7.   Becky M. Nicolaides, "'Where the Working Man Is Welcomed': Working-Class Suburbs in Los Angeles, 1900–1940," *Pacific Historical Review* 68 (November 1999): 517–559.

8.   Harris, *Unplanned Suburbs;* Anne Mosher and Deryck Holdsworth, "The Meaning of Alley Housing in Industrial Towns: Examples from Late-Nineteenth and Early-Twentieth Century Pennsylvania," *Journal of Historical Geography* 18 (1992): 174–189; Sam Bass Warner Jr., *The Private City: Philadelphia in Three Periods of Its Growth* (Philadelphia: University of Pennsylvania Press, 1968); David Ward, *Cities and Immigrants: A Geography of Change in*

Nineteenth Century America (New York: Oxford University Press, 1971); James Borchert, *Alley Life in Washington: Family, Community, Religion and Folklife in the City, 1850–1970* (Urbana: University of Illinois Press, 1982); Zunz, *The Changing Face of Inequality.*

9.   Louis Wirth, *On Cities and Social Life: Selected Papers,* edited by Albert J. Reiss Jr. (Chicago: University of Chicago Press, 1964), 62.

10.   This is a summary of E. P. Thompson's approach, as presented by Paul Faler in a discussion of trends in working-class historiography. Paul G. Faler, "E.P. Thompson and American History: A Retrospective View," *History Teacher* 28 (1994): 32–33. On the 1930s, see Lizabeth Cohen, *Making a New Deal: Industrial Workers in Chicago, 1919–1939* (Cambridge: Cambridge University Press, 1990).

11.   Faler, "E.P. Thompson," 35. Studies on the American working class that show class fragmentation by factors such as race, ethnicity, gender, and skill are too numerous to list here. A few notable examples include Cohen, *Making a New Deal;* David Roediger, *The Wages of Whiteness: Race and the Making of the American Working Class* (London: Verso, 1991); Richard J. Oestreicher, *Solidarity and Fragmentation: Working People and Class Consciousness in Detroit, 1875–1900* (Urbana: University of Illinois Press, 1986); Steven J. Ross, *Workers on the Edge: Work, Leisure, and Politics in Industrializing Cincinnati, 1788–1890* (New York: Columbia University Press, 1985); Daniel J. Walkowitz, *Worker City, Company Town: Iron- and Cotton-Worker Protest in Troy and Cohoes, New York, 1855–1884* (Urbana: University of Illinois Press, 1978); Susan Porter Benson, *Counter Cultures: Saleswomen, Managers, and Customers in American Department Stores, 1890–1940* (Urbana: University of Illinois Press, 1986); Roy Rosenzweig, *Eight Hours for What We Will: Workers and Leisure in an Industrial City, 1870–1920* (New York: Cambridge University Press, 1983); Francis G. Couvares, *The Remaking of Pittsburgh: Class and Culture in an Industrializing City, 1877–1919* (Albany: State University of New York Press, 1984); Patricia A. Cooper, *Once a Cigar Maker: Men, Women, and Work Culture in American Cigar Factories, 1900–1939* (Urbana: University of Illinois Press, 1987).

12.   Recent reviews of the labor historiography include David Brody, "Reconciling the Old Labor History and the New," *Pacific Historical Review* 62 (1993): 1–18; John Patrick Diggins, "Comrades and Citizens: New Mythologies in American Historiography," *American Historical Review* 90 (June 1985): 614–638, and comments, 639–649; Eric Arnesen, "Up From Exclusion: Black and White Workers, Race, and the State of Labor History," *Reviews in American History* 26 (March 1998): 146–174.

13.   For example, see Cohen, *Making a New Deal;* Ronald Edsforth, *Class Conflict and Cultural Consensus: The Making of a Mass Consumer Society in Flint, Michigan* (New Brunswick: Rutgers, 1987). A notable exception is Gary Gerstle, *Working-Class Americanism: The Politics of Labor in a Textile City, 1914–1960* (Cambridge: Cambridge University Press, 1991).

14.   In recent years, historians have emphasized the need for considering race in labor history. See Arnesen, "Up From Exclusion"; Herbert Hill, "The Problem of Race in American Labor History," *Reviews in American History* 24 (1996): 180–208; Alan Dawley and Joe William Trotter, "Race and Class," *Labor History* 35 (fall 1994): 486–494; David Roediger, "Race and the Working-Class Past in the United States: Multiple Identities and the Future of Labor History," *International Review of Social History* 38 (1993): supplement, 127–143; Noel Ignatiev, "The Paradox of the White Worker: Studies in Race Formation," *Labour/Le Travail* 30 (1992): 233–240; Nell Irvin Painter, "The New Labor History and the Historical Moment," *International Journal of Politics, Culture, and Society* 2 (spring 1989).

15.   This idea is elaborated further in Robert Self's forthcoming book (Princeton University Press) on urban space and American political culture in postwar Oakland.

16.   Thomas J. Sugrue, *Origins of the Urban Crisis: Race and Inequality in Postwar De-*

troit (Princeton: Princeton University Press, 1996); Thomas J. Sugrue, "Crabgrass-Roots Politics: Race, Rights, and the Reaction against Liberalism in the Urban North, 1940–1964," *Journal of American History* 82 (1995): 551–578; Arnold R. Hirsch, "Massive Resistance in the Urban North: Trumbull Park, Chicago, 1953–1966," *Journal of American History* 82 (1995): 522–550; Arnold R. Hirsch, *Making the Second Ghetto: Race and Housing in Chicago, 1940–1960* (Cambridge: Cambridge University Press, 1983); John T. McGreevy, *Parish Boundaries: The Catholic Encounter with Race in the Twentieth-Century Urban North* (Chicago: University of Chicago Press, 1996); Eileen M. McMahon, *What Parish Are You From? A Catholic Irish Community and Race Relations* (Lexington: University Press of Kentucky, 1995); Jonathan Rieder, *Canarsie: The Jews and Italians of Brooklyn Against Liberalism* (Cambridge: Harvard University Press, 1985); J. Anthony Lukas, *Common Ground: A Turbulent Decade in the Lives of Three American Families* (New York: Vintage, 1985); Ronald P. Formisano, *Boston Against Busing: Race, Class, and Ethnicity in the 1960s and 1970s* (Chapel Hill: University of North Carolina Press, 1991); Robert Self, "Writing Landscapes of Class, Power and Racial Division: The Problem of (Sub)Urban Space and Place in Postwar America," *Journal of Urban History* 23 (January 2001): 237–250.

Chapter 1

1. *Southgate Gardener*, August 1918.

2. Robert M. Fogelson, *The Fragmented Metropolis: Los Angeles 1850–1930* (Cambridge: Harvard University Press, 1967), 74–84.

3. The story of the Smith family is from Juanita (Smith) Hammon, interview by author, South Gate, California, July 5, 1990.

4. In the late nineteenth and early twentieth centuries, physicians commonly recommended clean, fresh air and a climate that allowed outdoor exercise as treatment for tuberculosis. Barbara Bates, *Bargaining for Life: A Social History of Tuberculosis, 1876–1938* (Philadelphia: University of Pennsylvania Press, 1992), 29. On Southern California as a destination for health seekers, see Fogelson, *Fragmented Metropolis*, 64; John E. Baur, *The Health Seekers of Southern California, 1870–1900* (San Marino: Huntington Library, 1959).

5. In 1927, Home Gardens was annexed to South Gate.

6. On the home's role in the transition from rural to urban life, Richard Bushman wrote, "The house was an urban surrogate for the self-sufficient family farm . . . protected against the fits and starts of the urban economy and vicissitudes of personal health." Bushman, "Family Security in the Transition from Farm to City, 1750–1850," *Journal of Family History* 6 (fall 1981): 248–249; Richard Harris, "Working-Class Home Ownership in the American Metropolis," *Journal of Urban History* 17 (November 1990): 46–69.

7. On the shift from a "small farm" to a "pastoral" aesthetic in suburbia, see Margaret Marsh, *Suburban Lives* (New Brunswick: Rutgers University Press, 1990), 6–7. On Los Angeles, see Becky M. Nicolaides, "'Where the Working Man Is Welcomed': Working-Class Suburbs in Los Angeles, 1900–1940," *Pacific Historical Review* 68 (November 1999): 517–559.

8. On suburbanization in general, see Kenneth T. Jackson, *Crabgrass Frontier: The Suburbanization of the United States* (New York: Oxford, 1985); on working-class suburbia, see Richard Harris, *Unplanned Suburbs: Toronto's American Tragedy, 1900–1950* (Baltimore: Johns Hopkins University Press, 1996).

9. South Gate was one of several working-class suburbs subdivided in the late 1910s and incorporated in the early 1920s. Others were Torrance (incorporated 1921), Lynwood (1921), Hawthorne (1922), Signal Hill (1924), and Maywood (1924). *Los Angeles County Almanac* (Los Angeles: Republican Central Committee of Los Angeles County, 1974), 158–159.

10.   Tom Thienes, "Contributions Toward the History of the City of South Gate, California" (unpublished manuscript for the Works Progress Administration, 1942, SGHWL), 40–51; Bicentennial Heritage Committee, *South Gate 1776–1976* (South Gate: South Gate Press, 1976), 5–7; Marc Weiss, *The Rise of the Community Builders* (New York: Columbia University Press, 1987), 88; "Tract No. 3254," 1918, pamphlet, Box 160, FWP.

11.   Ann Durkin Keating, *Building Chicago: Suburban Developers and the Creation of a Divided Metropolis* (Columbus: Ohio State University Press, 1988); Harris, *Unplanned Suburbs*.

12.   Thienes, "Contributions," 54; *Los Angeles Realtor,* January 1927; Glenn T. Seaborg, "Journal of Glenn T. Seaborg, January 1, 1927, to August 10, 1934," unpublished typewritten manuscript in author's possession, ii–iii; *Home Gardens Booster,* March 28, 1924; *Home Gardens Press,* August 21, 1925; *South Gate Press,* March 22, 1929, June 18, 1959.

13.   The connection between real estate and religion was sometimes direct. At the Full Gospel Church of Bell Gardens, neighbor to South Gate, the congregation sang a hymn celebrating the "boom in Canaan":

The price is paid and you may enter in,
It's the finest place that you have ever been.

Charles Spaulding, "The Development of Organization and Disorganization in the Social Life of a Rapidly Growing Working-Class Suburb within a Metropolitan District" (Ph.D. dissertation, University of Southern California, 1939), 198. Showmanship was virtually codified into the professional practices of L.A. realtors. The local trade magazine for realtors published detailed procedures for subdividing land and included "publicity stunts" as a critical step (*Los Angeles Realtor,* February 1926, 17).

14.   *South Gate Tribune,* February 14, 1924; *Hopper Tour Topics,* September–October 1920; *South Gate Gardener,* September–October 1919; John Quinn, interview by Elizabeth I. Dixon, 1963, 300/35, UCLA Oral History Project, YRL-UCLA. Zane Miller sees suburbs, from 1920 to 1950, contributing to a commonweal defined as the "metropolitan community." See *Neighborhood and Community in Forest Park, Ohio, 1935–1976* (Knoxville: University of Tennessee Press, 1981).

On radical activity in Los Angeles, see Hyman Weintraub, "The I.W.W. in California, 1905–1931" (M.A. thesis, UCLA, 1947); Carey McWilliams, *Southern California Country* (New York: Duell, Sloan & Pearce, 1946), 290–293; Upton Sinclair, *The Goslings: A Study of the American Schools* (Pasadena, 1924), chapter 1; Louis Adamic, *Laughing in the Jungle* (New York: Arno Press, 1969).

On the national discourse, see Ronald Tobey, Charles Wetherell, and Jay Brigham, "Moving Out and Settling In: Residential Mobility, Home Owning, and the Public Enframing of Citizenship, 1921–1950," *American Historical Review* 95 (December 1990): 1395–1422; Marsh, *Suburban Lives,* 5–7, 129–134; Greg Hise, *Magnetic Los Angeles: Planning the Twentieth-Century Metropolis* (Baltimore: Johns Hopkins University Press, 1997), 38–40. Marsh points out that the working class historically had higher rates of homeownership than the middle class, so the appeal for middle-class homeownership was that much more urgent.

Several strains of American political thought can be traced in realtors' ideas about the civic value of suburban life and homeownership, beginning with republican ideology of the Revolutionary and early national period, to more modern articulations of civic virtue expressed by the Progressives. For a small sample of this profuse literature, see Robert Shalhope, "Republicanism and Early American Historiography," *William and Mary Quarterly* (1982): 334–356; Sean Wilentz, "Of Class and Politics in Jacksonian America," *Reviews in American History* (December 1982): 45–63; *Yale Law Journal* 97 (1988), for essays on the modern "republican revival";

Richard Bushman, "'This New Man': Dependence and Independence, 1776," in *Uprooted Americans,* Richard Bushman et al., eds. (Boston: Little, Brown, 1979).

In fact, the "republican" potential of suburbanization was identified as early as 1859 by the architectural critic Andrew Jackson Downing. He wrote, "Whatever, therefore, leads men to assemble the comforts and elegancies of life around his habitations, tends to increase local attachments, and render domestic life more delightful; thus not only augmenting his own enjoyment but strengthening his patriotism, and making him a better citizen" (from *A Treatise on the Theory and Practice of Landscape Gardening* [New York, 1859], cited in Jackson, *Crabgrass Frontier,* 65). Also see Marsh, *Suburban Lives,* on this point.

The idea of civic fulfillment reflected the suburban counterpart to the "modern community housing" movement of the 1920s and 1930s. Centered in urban areas, this movement aimed to improve living standards, lower housing costs, and strengthen the sense of community among residents—all to improve the social conditions of urban life. The goal of revitalizing neighborhood ties and commitments was a high priority. See Gail E. Radford, *Modern Housing for America: Policy Struggles in the New Deal Era* (Chicago: University of Chicago Press, 1996).

15. Charles B. Hopper, *Thru My Window at Southgate,* 1918 pamphlet; *Southgate Gardener,* September–October 1919; Spaulding, "Development . . . Working-Class Suburb," 116; Thienes, "Contributions," 43. On Smythe, see Marsh, *Suburban Lives,* 131.

16. Los Angeles was boosted as an antidote to urban America. See especially Kevin Starr, *Inventing the Dream* (New York: Oxford, 1985); and Fogelson, *Fragmented Metropolis,* chapter 7.

17. *Southgate Gardener,* February 1919. See other issues of *Southgate Gardener* for similar statements.

18. In 1930, South Gate had only nine dwellings for three or more families. U.S. Bureau of the Census, *Fifteenth Census of United States, 1930: Population,* vol. 6, *Families* (Washington, D.C.: GPO, 1933), 183.

19. *Southgate Gardener,* September–October 1919, p. 3; Bicentennial Heritage Committee, *South Gate 1776–1976,* 29–31; Alberta Schermerhorn, "Historical Sketch of South Gate, California," unpublished manuscript, 1938, SGHWL; *South Gate Tribune,* October 30, 1928 (from Weber field notes, May 2, 1941, Box 160, FWP); "Race Restrictions in South Gate," Thienes book notes, March 7, 1941, Box 160, FWP. On residential deed restrictions, also see *South Gate Press,* June 28, 1929; *South Gate Police Annual, 1927* (South Gate, 1927), 11, SGHWL. Chapter 4 treats racial concerns of the era.

20. Spaulding, "Development . . . Working-Class Suburb," 111–112; *South Gate Press,* June 18, 1959; Harris, *Unplanned Suburbs,* passim.

21. Hopper, *Thru My Window; Los Angeles Times,* March 1, 1918; U.S. Bureau of the Census, *Historical Statistics of the United States, Colonial Times to 1970* (Washington D.C.: GPO, 1975), 166; Seaborg, "Journal," ii–iii; *Home Gardens Booster,* February 15, 1924; "Local History Questionnaire," December 1940, SGHWL; Thienes, "Contributions," 42; Bicentennial Heritage Committee, *South Gate 1776–1976,* 8, 31; *South Gate Tribune,* February 7, 1924; *Home Gardens Press,* 1924 (for classified ads); Hazal Liggett, "The Relation of Wages to the Cost of Living in Los Angeles 1915 to 1920," *Studies in Sociology* 5 (March 1921): 5–6.

22. *Home Gardens Booster,* March 7, 1924; *Home Gardens Press,* December 12, 1924, December 18, 1925.

While the cost of living for other life necessities soared in Los Angeles during World War I, housing costs had the lowest rate of increase among working-class families. See Liggett, "Relation of Wages," 2. The affordability of Los Angeles housing continued through 1940, as shown in Harris, "Working Class Homeownership," 58.

23. Bicentennial Heritage Committee, *South Gate 1776–1976,* 31; *Huntington Park*

Daily Signal, January 19, 1973; (Smith) Hammon interview; South Gate City Council minutes, November 3, 1926, SGCH.

24.   Robert Phelps, "The Search for a Modern Industrial City: Urban Planning, the Open Shop, and the Founding of Torrance, California," *Pacific Historical Review* 64 (November 1995): 528–529. Also see Margaret Crawford, *Building the Workingman's Paradise: The Design of American Company Towns* (London: Verso, 1995).

25.   Thienes, "Contributions," 45; (Smith) Hammon interview; South Gate City Council minutes, May 17, 1924, SGCH; *Home Gardens Press,* November 27, 1925 (Weber field notes, June 20, 1941, Box 160, FWP). Chapter 4 details the political story.

In other cities, working-class homeowners likewise resisted special assessments to keep taxes low. See Olivier Zunz, *The Changing Face of Inequality: Urbanization, Industrial Development and Immigrants in Detroit, 1880–1920* (Chicago: University of Chicago Press, 1982); Roger D. Simon, *The City-Building Process: Housing and Services in New Milwaukee Neighborhoods, 1880–1900,* Transactions of the American Philosophical Society, vol. 68, p. 5 (Philadelphia, 1978). Both Keating, *Building Chicago* and Robin Einhorn, *Property Rules: Political Economy in Chicago, 1833–1872* (Chicago: University of Chicago Press, 1991) describe varying public works priorities among different classes in nineteenth-century Chicago. Einhorn notes that workers in the 1870s supported the "segmented" system of municipal governance—radically localized control over public works—which allowed them to maintain homeownership cheaply because they could refuse infrastructure development (*Property Rules,* 238–239).

26.   Thienes, "Contributions," 46. While South Gate had zoning laws as early as 1924, they were poorly enforced and many exceptions were granted. See *South Gate Tribune,* February 7, November 28, 1924, November 27, 1925.

27.   *South Gate Tribune,* September 12, 1924; *Home Gardens Press,* June 10, 1927; Los Angeles Chamber of Commerce, "South Gate edition," from Weber field notes, June 13, 1941, Box 160, FWP.

28.   *South Gate Tribune,* January 31, July 11, 1924, October 17, 1930; *Tax Talk* 301 (July 11, 1938): 2–3 (from Gaddis field notes, Box 164, FWP); *Home Gardens Press,* July 22, 1927.

29.   Thienes, "Contributions," 116–117; Thienes and Weber field notes, October 1, 10, 1941, December 10, 1941, Box 164, FWP; *Home Gardens Press,* March 27, 1925, July 22, 1927; *South Gate Police Annual, 1927,* 111; *Huntington Park Daily Signal,* January 19, 1973. For examples of industrial boosterism, see *South Gate Tribune,* March 13, July 11, September 12, November 14, 28, December 25, 1924, November 27, 1925, November 30, 1928; *Home Gardens Booster,* July 11, 1924, March 27, 1925, October 29, 1926, June 10, 1927; *South Gate Press,* January 4, June 14, 1929.

General Motors and Firestone, the two largest local factories, lay just beyond South Gate's borders. In 1937 their tax rates were $41.75/acre and $84.64/acre, respectively, and they were exempt from harbor taxes. By contrast Goodyear Tire and Rubber—located in L.A. city—paid $348.34/acre (*South Gate Press,* August 4, 1938; Thienes, "Contributions," 117–118).

30.   Mike Davis, "Sunshine and the Open Shop: Ford and Darwin in 1920s Los Angeles," *Antipode* 29 (1997): 356–382; Greg Hise, "'Nature's Workshop': Industry and Urban Expansion in Southern California, 1900–1950," *Journal of Historical Geography* 27 (2001): 74–92.

31.   On zoning exceptions, see *South Gate Tribune,* November 28, 1924, July 2, 1935; South Gate Board of Trustee minutes, November 17, December 1, 1925, SGCH.

32.   South Gate Board of Trustee minutes, Ordinance No. 28, February 5, 1924 (from Weber field notes, April 18, June 6, 1941, Box 160, FWP); *South Gate Tribune,* January 24, 1924, November 27, 1925, September 24, 1929; *South Gate Press,* June 14, 1929; South Gate City

Council minutes, February 21, 1928, SGCH; Thienes field notes, Box 164, FWP; *Huntington Park Daily Signal*, January 19, 1973.

33.   *South Gate Press*, December 14, 1928; Weber field notes, May 11, June 6, 20, 1941, Box 160, and Weber and Thienes field notes, Boxes 160, 164, FWP; Robert Homiston, "A Creative Program for the First Methodist Episcopal Church of South Gate" (master's thesis, University of Southern California, 1938), 1.

34.   *Home Gardens Press*, October 9, August 7, 21, 1925, March 1927 (masthead). By contrast, the *South Gate Press*, June 8, 1928, boosted South Gate as offering affordable homes for the middle class.

35.   On the importance of homeownership to working-class families, see Harris, *Unplanned Suburbs*; John Bodnar, "Changing Risks, Changing Adaptations: American Families in the Nineteenth and Twentieth Centuries," in *Kin and Communities: Families in America*, Allan J. Lichtman and Joan R. Challinor, eds. (Washington, D.C.: Smithsonian Institution Press, 1979), 128–129; Zunz, *The Changing Face of Inequality*, chapter 6; James R. Barrett, *Work and Community in the Jungle: Chicago's Packinghouse Workers, 1894–1922* (Urbana: University of Illinois Press, 1987), 104–107.

36.   Ira Katznelson, *City Trenches: Urban Politics and the Patterning of Class in the United States* (Chicago: University of Chicago Press, 1981), 52. On the precarious condition of working-class life in the 1920s, see Frank Stricker, "Affluence for Whom? Another Look at Prosperity and the Working Classes in the 1920s," *Labor History* 24 (winter 1983): 5–33.

37.   John Sheehy, interview by author, South Gate, California, June 19, 1990.

38.   David Brody, *Workers in Industrial America* (New York: Oxford, 1980), 48–81; Cohen, *Making a New Deal*, chapter 4.

39.   Classic statements of the "lawns for pawns" thesis are in Matthew Edel, Elliott D. Sclar, and Daniel Luria, *Shaky Palaces: Homeownership and Social Mobility in Boston's Suburbanization* (New York: Columbia University Press, 1984); Davis, "Sunshine and the Open Shop." For other perspectives on homeownership, see Constance Perrin, *Everything in Its Place* (Princeton: Princeton University Press, 1977); Gwendolyn Wright, *Building the Dream* (Cambridge: MIT Press, 1983); Jackson, *Crabgrass Frontier*; Bushman, "Family Security"; Harris, "Working-Class Home Ownership."

40.   On working-class versus middle-class homeownership rates, see Marsh, *Suburban Lives*. On the open shop in Los Angeles, see Robert Gottlieb and Irene Wolt, *Thinking Big: The Story of the Los Angeles Times* (New York: Putnam, 1977); Louis Perry and Richard Perry, *A History of the Los Angeles Labor Movement* (Berkeley and Los Angeles: University of California Press, 1963).

41.   Einhorn, *Property Rules*; Keating, *Building Chicago*; Zunz, *The Changing Face of Inequality*; Simon, *The City-Building Process*; Harris, *Unplanned Suburbs*; Andrew Wiese, "Places of Our Own: Suburban Black Towns Before 1960," *Journal of Urban History* 19 (1993): 30–54; Andrew Wiese, "The Other Suburbanites: African American Suburbanization in the North before 1950," *Journal of American History* 85 (1999): 1–26; Jon Teaford, *City and Suburb: The Political Fragmentation of Metropolitan America, 1850–1970* (Baltimore: Johns Hopkins University Press, 1970).

42.   Damaris Rose, "Home Ownership, Subsistence and Historical Change: The Mining District of West Cornwall in the Late Nineteenth Century," in *Class and Space: The Making of Urban Society*, Nigel Thrift and Peter Williams, eds. (London: Routledge, 1987), 110.

43.   Homes historically have been an important locus of family subsistence practices, such as food production, outworking, and lodging boarders. For descriptions of these practices, see Bushman, "Family Security"; Carl Bridenbaugh, *Cities in Revolt: Urban Life in America*,

1743–1776 (New York: Oxford, 1971); Virginia Yans-McLaughlin, *Family and Community: Italian Immigrants in Buffalo, 1880–1930* (Urbana: University of Illinois Press, 1982), 164; Bettina Bradbury, "Pigs, Cows, and Boarders: Non-Wage Forms of Survival among Montreal Families, 1861–91," *Labour/Le Travail* 14 (1984): 9–46.

44.   Harris, *Unplanned Suburbs;* Michael R. Haines, "Poverty, Economic Stress, and the Family in a Late Nineteenth-Century American City: Whites in Philadelphia, 1880," and Claudia Goldin, "Family Strategies and the Family Economy in the Late Nineteenth Century: The Role of Secondary Workers," both in *Philadelphia: Work, Space, Family, and Group Experience in the Nineteenth Century,* Theodore Hershberg, ed. (New York: Oxford, 1981); Yans-McLaughlin, *Family and Community,* 164–177; Dana Frank, "Housewives, Socialists, and the Politics of Food: The 1917 New York Cost-of-Living Protests," *Feminist Studies* 11 (summer 1985): 255–285.

45.   Davis contends that working-class self-provisioning was a boon to capital because it reduced the cost of living and wages. "Sunshine and the Open Shop," 374.

46.   On the use versus commodity values of self-built housing, see Dennis Conway, "Self-Help Housing, the Commodity Nature of Housing and Amelioration of the Housing Deficit: Continuing the Turner-Burgess Debate," *Antipode* 14 (1982): 40–46. Harris contends that owner-built homes represent a "process in which production and consumption were one." Richard Harris, "Self-Building in the Urban Housing Market," *Economic Geography* 67 (January 1991): 20.

On recent tensions between use and exchange value of property, see John R. Logan and Harvey L. Molotch, *Urban Fortunes: The Political Economy of Place* (Berkeley and Los Angeles: University of California Press, 1987).

47.   John Sheehy, interview by author, South Gate, California, May 1, 1990; Sheehy interview, June 19, 1990; (Smith) Hammon interview; Wallace McFadden, interview by Sandy McFadden, June 12, 1971, Oral History 1029, FOH; Ruth (Barrett) Lampmann, interview by author, South Gate, California, February 13, 1991; Spaulding, "Development . . . Working-Class Suburb," quote at 127–128. On tenancy in the South, see Steven Hahn, *The Roots of Southern Populism* (New York: Oxford, 1983); on "plain-folk Americanism," see James Gregory, *American Exodus: The Dust Bowl Migration and Okie Culture in California* (New York: Oxford, 1989).

48.   See chapter 2.

49.   *Hopper Tour Topics,* November 1920, p. 2; South Gate City Council minutes, November 3, 1926, SGCH; *Home Gardens Booster,* February 15, 1924; Spaulding, "Development . . . Working-Class Suburb," 46–48, 129.

50.   (Smith) Hammon interview; Spaulding, "Development . . . Working-Class Suburb," 48, 128; Arthur Newton, *City Directory of Greater South Gate, 1930* (South Gate: Tribune-News Publishing, 1930). Lumber was one of the largest imports to Los Angeles in the early twentieth century, suggesting its affordability. See Henry Riddiford, "Could Build a Walk Around the World," *Southern California Business* (April 1922): 19; "Enough Lumber to Build a Big City," *Southern California Business* (June 1925): 20; Fogelson, *Fragmented Metropolis,* chapter 6. On Toronto, see Harris, "Self-Building," 9–10.

51.   This method was borrowed from Harris, "Self-Building."

52.   Sheehy interviews, May 1, June 19, 1990; (Smith) Hammon interview; McFadden interview; (Barrett) Lampmann interview; Spaulding, "Development . . . Working-Class Suburb," 127–128; Sanborn Map Company, "Insurance Maps of Los Angeles, California: Map of South Gate," vols. 28, 30–31 (New York: Sanborn Map Company of New York, 1929–1930). On building permits, see chapter 5, note 52. An analysis of building permits along several

blocks of San Miguel Avenue in northwest South Gate found that permits issued to owners peaked in the 1920s, then fell off by the 1930s. The drop likely resulted from a problem with local property taxes, outlined in chapter 4.

53.   Spaulding, "Development . . . Working-Class Suburb," quotes at 47–48, 96–97, 130; (Smith) Hammon interview.

54.   (Smith) Hammon interview.

55.   Sheehy interview, June 19, 1990; John Sheehy, interview by author, South Gate, California, June 21, 1990; (Smith) Hammon interview.

56.   Spaulding, "Development . . . Working-Class Suburb," 74–75 (emphasis in original); Sheehy interview, May 1, 1990; Quinn interview; *City Directory of South Gate, 1930*, 42.

57.   (Smith) Hammon interview; (Barrett) Lampmann interview; *Home Gardens Booster*, April 18, 1924.

58.   "Ordinance No. 4" (1923) and "Ordinance No. 86" (1926), SGCH; *Home Gardens Booster*, March 28, 1924; *South Gate Press*, December 28, 1928, April 9, 1929; *Southgate Gardener*, August 1919, p. 3, June 1918, p. 1, July–August 1918. The *Southgate Gardener* and *Hopper Tour Topics* (1918–1922) ran regular articles on raising vegetables, rabbits, and poultry. The South Gate newspapers continued such articles into the 1930s, testifying to the persistence of this practice.

59.   U.S. Bureau of the Census, *Historical Statistics of the United States*, 166, 327; Sheehy interview, June 19, 1990. The consumer spending figures are averaged from figures given for people with incomes $1,000–1,500 and $1,500–2,000, since $1,543 (the average annual income of a wage earner in construction or manufacturing) falls so closely between them.

60.   "The March of the Cities," *World's Work* 27 (November 1913): 114; quote from *Hopper Tour Topics*, September–October 1920, p. 2; Arthur Newton, *City Directory of South Gate, 1926* (South Gate: Tribune News Publishing Co., 1926); Sanborn Map Company, "Insurance Maps of Los Angeles, California: Map of South Gate," vols. 28, 30–31.

61.   (Smith) Hammon interview.

62.   *South Gate Tribune*, May 23, 1924.

63.   I am indebted to photographer Robbert Flick for his inspired approaches to visualizing Los Angeles. In this section, I borrow loosely from Flick's technique of taking "photographic trajectories" of the city, where the camera captures continuous, steady images of life along urban thoroughfares. Although it is virtually impossible for a historian to re-create this process photographically, it is possible to take an imaginary journey along the streets of a bygone era through the use of historical maps and city directories.

The existence of certain extraordinary maps make such an imagined journey possible. The maps consulted here are Sanborn Fire Insurance Atlases, 1929 and 1939; County of Los Angeles Regional Planning Commission, "Land Use Survey—County of Los Angeles," prepared with the assistance of Works Progress Administration, project # 65-3-3734 (Jan. 21, 1936 to Nov. 14, 1936) and project # 165-03-6999 (November 15, 1936 to 1937), Huntington Library, San Marino, California. I also drew upon the city directories for these years.

64.   Spaulding, "Development . . . Working-Class Suburb," 45–46.

Chapter 2

1.   Occupational information comes from Arthur Newton, *City Directory of South Gate, 1926* (South Gate: Tribune-News Publishing Co., 1926).

2.   Becky M. Nicolaides, "'Where the Working Man Is Welcomed': Working-Class Suburbs in Los Angeles, 1900–1940," *Pacific Historical Review* 68 (November 1999): 524–531.

3.   U.S. Bureau of the Census, *Fifteenth Census of United States, 1930: Population,* vol. 3, *Composition and Characteristics, Part 1* (Washington, D.C.: GPO, 1932), 262; U.S. Bureau of the Census, *Sixteenth Census of the United States, 1940: Population,* vol. 2, *Characteristics of the Population, Part 1* (Washington, D.C.: GPO, 1943), 602.

4.   I make this inference because there is close similarity between Los Angeles and South Gate in terms of ethnic composition by 1930. Immigrants in Los Angeles were predominantly from Northern and Western Europe, especially England and Germany. The big exception was Mexican immigrants, but because they were largely segregated into their own neighborhoods, they were a minor presence in most Anglo suburbs. See Robert M. Fogelson, *The Fragmented Metropolis: Los Angeles 1850–1930* (Cambridge: Harvard University Press, 1967), 74–84.

5.   James Gregory, *American Exodus: The Dust Bowl Migration and Okie Culture in California* (New York: Oxford University Press, 1989), 39–45. Urban and rural data was based on an analysis of marriage licenses, in Gregory Singleton, *Religion in the City of Angels: American Protestant Culture and Urbanization, Los Angeles, 1850–1930* (Ann Arbor: UMI Research Press, 1979), 122.

6.   Gregory, *American Exodus,* 40–42, 52; Fogelson, *Fragmented Metropolis,* chapter 4; Charles Spaulding, "The Development of Organization and Disorganization in the Social Life of a Rapidly Growing Working-Class Suburb within a Metropolitan District" (Ph.D. dissertation, University of Southern California, 1939), 55, 58; John Sheehy, interviews by author, South Gate, California, May 1, June 19, June 21, June 26, 1990; Virgil Collins, interview by author, Artesia, California, August 20, 1991; Virgil Collins, interviews by author, Laguna Hills, California, August 25 and September 15, 1991. Records of the First Baptist Church in South Gate show letters of referral of newcomers from places like Memphis, Texas, Shawnee, Oklahoma, Abilene, Texas, and Springfield, Missouri.

7.   Gregory, *American Exodus,* chapter 5, quote at 142.

8.   Ruth (Barrett) Lampmann, interview by author, South Gate, California, February 13, 1991; Juanita (Smith) Hammon, interview by author, South Gate, California, July 5, 1990; Collins interviews, August 20, 25, and September 15, 1991; Wallace McFadden, interview by Sandy McFadden, June 12, 1971, Oral History 1029, FOH, p. 5. And see Sheehy interviews, May 1, June 19, June 21, June 26, 1990; Glenn T. Seaborg, "Journal of Glenn T. Seaborg, January 1, 1927–August 10, 1934," unpublished typewritten manuscript in author's possession.

9.   U.S. Bureau of the Census, *Fifteenth Census of United States, 1930: Population,* vol. 3, *Composition and Characteristics, Part 1,* 269, 272; U.S. Bureau of the Census, *Sixteenth Census of United States, 1940: Population,* vol. 2, *Characteristics of the Population, Part 1,* 566, 568. Census tract data from 1940 and later also suggests a dispersal of immigrants in South Gate. "Mexicans" (and note the historical problem of census definitions of Mexican) represented about 7.7 percent of the Los Angeles area population in 1930 (figures are quite similar for L.A. city and county).

10.   U.S. Bureau of the Census, *Fifteenth Census of United States, 1930: Population,* vol. 3, *Composition and Characteristics, Part 1,* 262; U.S. Bureau of the Census, *Fifteenth Census of United States, 1930: Population,* vol. 6, *Families* (Washington, D.C.: GPO, 1933), 183; Arthur Newton, *City Directory of Greater South Gate, 1930* (South Gate: Tribune-News Publishing Co., 1930); U.S. Bureau of the Census, *Sixteenth Census of the United States, 1940: Population,* vol. 2, *Characteristics of the Population,* 612. The rate of young adults living at home was determined from the city directory. The U.S. Census did not collect comparable data on family status for South Gate in 1940.

11.   Figure taken from a 50 percent sample of the *City Directory of South Gate, 1926.*

12.   *City Directory of South Gate, 1926;* (Smith) Hammon interview; Collins interview,

August 20, 1991; Virgil Collins, telephone interview by author, November 25, 1991. Similar financial support from adult family members occurred in the Seaborg, Smith, and Sheehy families; see respective interviews.

Richard White found that the pressures of working-class life could have an opposite effect, creating tensions and the impetus among family members to leave. See Richard White, *Remembering Ahanagran: Storytelling in a Family's Past* (New York: Hill and Wang, 1998).

13.   U.S. Bureau of the Census, *Fifteenth Census of the United States, 1930: Population,* vol. 3, *Composition and Characteristics, Part 1,* 262; U.S. Bureau of the Census, *Sixteenth Census of the United States, 1940: Population,* vol. 2, *Characteristics of the Population,* 602.

14.   The second-largest western city was San Francisco, with 634,000 people in 1930.

15.   U.S. Home Owners Loan Corporation, "Survey of Economic, Real Estate and Mortgage Finance Conditions in Metropolitan Los Angeles" (field report, October 10, 1939), 2, and U.S. Home Owners Loan Corporation, City Survey Files for Los Angeles, RG 195, NA.

16.   Fogelson, *Fragmented Metropolis,* 78–79, 148, 131; Frank L. Kidner and Philip Neff, *An Economic Survey of the Los Angeles Area* (Los Angeles: Haynes Foundation, 1945), 13–14; John Parke Young, "Industrial Background," in *Los Angeles: Preface to a Master Plan,* George W. Robbins and L. Deming Tilton, eds. (Los Angeles: Pacific Southwest Academy, 1941), 61–73; Greg Hise, *Magnetic Los Angeles: Planning the Twentieth-Century Metropolis* (Baltimore: Johns Hopkins University Press, 1997).

17.   Fogelson, *Fragmented Metropolis,* 78–79, 129; Mike Davis, "Sunshine and the Open Shop: Ford and Darwin in 1920s Los Angeles," *Antipode* 29 (1997): 356–382; Louis Perry and Richard Perry, *A History of the Los Angeles Labor Movement* (Berkeley and Los Angeles: University of California Press, 1963); Carey McWilliams, *Southern California Country: An Island on the Land* (New York: Duell, Sloan & Pearce, 1946), 277.

18.   Young, "Industrial Background," 69; and see Fogelson, *Fragmented Metropolis,* 129.

19.   Los Angeles's seeming insulation from the Depression resulted from several factors. First, the film industry survived the economic downturn relatively well, catering to a poor but escape-hungry population willing to pay for this "product." After a relatively short-lived crisis that lasted from 1931 to 1933, the movie business rebounded and climbed steadily for the duration of the decade. Second, Los Angeles's population continued to grow—577,000 added to the metropolitan area in the 1930s—even in the midst of economic depression, defying typical migration patterns. The influx created new demands for manufactured goods. Third, after 1936 American and foreign governments stepped up their demands for aircraft in response to the international crisis, stimulating the expansion of the regional aircraft industry. See Robert Sklar, *Movie-Made America: A Cultural History of American Movies* (New York: Vintage, 1975), 162–163; Tino Balio, *Grand Design: Hollywood as a Modern Business Enterprise, 1930–1939* (Berkeley and Los Angeles: University of California Press, 1993), 13–18, 30–32; HOLC, "Survey of Economic . . . Conditions," 5; Federal Housing Administration, "Housing Market Analysis, Los Angeles, California, as of May 1, 1939" (Federal Housing Administration, Division of Economics and Statistics, July 28, 1939), 27; Hise, *Magnetic Los Angeles.*

20.   More specifically, during the 1930s in Los Angeles, 1,363 new plants were established employing 31,599 people, while 1,987 industries expanded, creating 44,480 new jobs.

21.   James T. Lemon, *Liberal Dreams and Nature's Limits: Great Cities of North America Since 1600* (Toronto: Oxford University Press, 1996), 197; James F. Bone and A. Slater, "The Facts About Industrial Employment in Los Angeles County," in Los Angeles (County) Chamber of Commerce, *Collection of Eight Studies on the Industrial Development of Los Angeles County* (Los Angeles: Los Angeles [County] Chamber of Commerce, Industrial Department, 1944), 6–7; Myrna Cherkoss Donahoe, "Workers' Response to Plant Closures: The Cases of

Steel and Auto in Southeast Los Angeles, 1935–1986" (Ph.D. dissertation, University of California Irvine, 1987), 95; FHA, "Housing Market Analysis . . . 1939," 17–18, 21.

22. Davis, "Sunshine and the Open Shop," 358–361; Greg Hise, "'Nature's Workshop': Industry and Urban Expansion in Southern California, 1900–1950," *Journal of Historical Geography* 27 (2001): 74–92; Donahoe, "Workers' Response," 95.

23. Richard Harris, *Unplanned Suburbs: Toronto's American Tragedy, 1900–1950* (Baltimore: Johns Hopkins University Press, 1996), 51–55; Allan R. Pred, "The Intrametropolitan Location of American Manufacturing," *Annals of the Association of American Geographers* 54 (June 1964): 178–179; David Gordon, "Capitalist Development and the History of American Cities," in William K. Tabb and Larry Sawers, eds., *Marxism and the Metropolis* (New York: Oxford, 1978), 25–63. A good number of L.A. industrialists shared the belief that suburban dispersal would thwart the labor movement. See Edward Soja, Rebecca Morales, and Goetz Wolff, "Urban Restructuring: An Analysis of Social and Spatial Change in Los Angeles," *Economic Geography* 59 (1983): 197–198, 207; William B. Friedricks, "Capital and Labor in Los Angeles: Henry E. Huntington vs. Organized Labor, 1900–1920," *Pacific Historical Review* 59 (1990): 375–395; Davis, "Sunshine and the Open Shop," 364–368 and passim.

24. George Eastman, "Industrial Development in Southern California," *Southern California Business* 7 (July 1928): 10; Fogelson, *Fragmented Metropolis*, 115–119, 144–154; Kidner and Neff, *Economic Survey*, 3; *Home Gardens Press*, July 10, 1925; George W. Robbins, "Transport: The Movement of Commodities," in *Los Angeles: Preface to a Master Plan*, George W. Robbins and L. Deming Tilton, eds. (Los Angeles: Pacific Southwest Academy, 1941), 121; Fred Viehe, "Black Gold Suburbs: The Influence of the Extractive Industry on the Suburbanization of Los Angeles, 1890–1930," *Journal of Urban History* 8 (November 1981): 3–26; Marc Weiss, *The Rise of the Community Builders* (New York: Columbia University Press, 1987), 83–85; G. Gordon Whitnall, "Industrial Analysis of Los Angeles," *Los Angeles Realtor* (February 1922): 4–5.

25. *City Directory of South Gate, 1926; City Directory of South Gate, 1930;* U.S. Bureau of the Census, *Sixteenth Census of the United States, 1940: Population,* vol. 2, *Characteristics of the Population,* 620.

26. *City Directory of South Gate, 1926; City Directory of South Gate, 1930;* U.S. Bureau of the Census, *Sixteenth Census of the United States, 1940: Population,* vol. 2, *Characteristics of the Population,* 620.

27. Figures computed from analysis of *City Directory of South Gate, 1930;* U.S. Bureau of the Census, *Fifteenth Census of the United States, 1930: Distribution.* Vol. 1, *Retail Distribution, U.S. Summary, 1929* (Washington, D.C.: GPO, 1933), 260–261; and *Retail Distribution in California,* 99.

28. Sanborn Map Company, "Insurance Maps of Los Angeles, California: Map of South Gate," vols. 28, 30–31 (Sanborn Map Company of New York, 1927–41). Also see *City Directory of South Gate, 1926;* and *City Directory of South Gate, 1930.*

29. Spaulding, "Development . . . Working-Class Suburb," 147–150.

30. *City Directory of South Gate, 1930; South Gate and Walnut Park City Directory, June 1, 1940* (South Gate: K.I. Strand, 1940).

31. Lizabeth Cohen, *Making a New Deal: Industrial Workers in Chicago, 1919–1939* (Cambridge: Cambridge University Press, 1990), 116. On the recovery of department stores in Los Angeles, see FHA, "Housing Market Analysis . . . 1939," 13. The FHA claimed "the volume of department store sales in Los Angeles reached a recovery high in March 1937."

32. U.S. Bureau of the Census, *Fifteenth Census of the United States, 1930: Distribution,* vol. 1, *Retail Distribution, U.S. Summary, 1929,* 260–261. South Gate's per capita sales rate

($176) contrasted even more sharply with larger, older cities with more developed retail centers, such as Pasadena, Glendale, and Long Beach, where rates were $789, $587, and $551, respectively.

33.　Sheehy interview, May 1, 1990; U.S. Bureau of the Census, *Fifteenth Census of the United States, 1930: Distribution*. vol. 1, *Retail Distribution, U.S. Summary, 1929*, 99, 260–261.

On the rise of the consumer culture, advertising, and department stores, see Stuart Ewen, *Captains of Consciousness* (New York: McGraw-Hill, 1976); Richard Wightman Fox and T. J. Jackson Lears, eds., *Culture of Consumption* (New York: Pantheon Books, 1983); Roland Marchand, *Advertising the American Dream: Making Way for Modernity, 1920–1940* (Berkeley and Los Angeles: University of California Press, 1985); Gunther Barth, *City People: The Rise of Modern City Culture in Nineteenth-Century America* (New York: Oxford, 1980); Susan Porter Benson, *Counter Cultures: Saleswomen, Managers, and Customers in American Department Stores, 1890–1940* (Urbana: University of Illinois Press, 1986); William Leach, *Land of Desire: Merchants, Power, and the Rise of a New American Culture* (New York: Vintage, 1994); Cohen, *Making a New Deal*.

34.　U.S. Bureau of the Census, *Fifteenth Census of United States, 1930: Population*, vol. 6, *Families*, 183; Federal Housing Administration, "Housing Market Analysis, Los Angeles, California. Vol. 1, Part II" (Federal Housing Administration, Division of Economics and Statistics, December 1, 1937), 452; U.S. Bureau of the Census, *Sixteenth Census of the United States, 1940: Housing*, vol. 2, *General Characteristics, Part 2* (Washington, D.C.: GPO, 1943), 312.

35.　Building permit data from W. D. Bretz, South Gate City Coordinator, WPA Field Notes, Box 160, FWP; and FHA, "Housing Market Analysis, Los Angeles, California, as of December 1, 1937," vol. 1, Statistical Appendix (Federal Housing Administration, Division of Economics and Statistics, 1938), 455. Census data from U.S. Bureau of the Census, *Fifteenth Census of United States, 1930: Population*, vol. 6, *Families*, 181–188; U.S. Bureau of the Census, *Sixteenth Census of the United States, Census of Population, 1940: Housing*, vol. 2, *General Characteristics, Part 2*, 291–293.

36.　"Adults" excludes spouses, but includes relatives or boarders. The *Los Angeles Times*, February 13, 1927, reported that 96 percent of South Gate residents owned their own homes, probably erroneously high. Homeownership rates for 1926 and 1929 were calculated from the city directories.

37.　U.S. Bureau of the Census, *Historical Statistics of the United States, Colonial Times to 1970* (Washington D.C.: GPO, 1975), 646; U.S. Bureau of the Census, *Fifteenth Census of the United States, Census of Population, 1930: Population*, vol. 6, *Families*, 174, 183; U.S. Bureau of the Census, *Sixteenth Census of the U.S., 1940: Population*, vol. 2, *Characteristics of the Population*, 142.

On high rates of immigrant homeownership, see Carolyn Kirk and Gordon W. Kirk, "The Impact of the City on Homeownership: A Comparison of Immigrants and Native Whites at the Turn of the Century," *Journal of Urban History* 7 (1981): 471–487; John Bodnar, Roger Simon, and Michael Weber, *Lives of their Own: Blacks, Italians, and Poles in Pittsburgh, 1900–1960* (Urbana: University of Illinois Press, 1982); Olivier Zunz, *The Changing Face of Inequality* (Chicago: University of Chicago Press, 1982), 153–158.

38.　Sheehy interview, May 1, 1990; (Smith) Hammon interview; *Home Gardens Booster*, passim; U.S. Bureau of the Census, *Sixteenth Census of the United States, 1940: Population and Housing, Statistics for Census Tracts. Los Angeles-Long Beach, California* (Washington, D.C.:GPO, 1942), 243; *City Directory of South Gate, 1926; City Directory of South Gate, 1930; South Gate City Directory, 1940* (South Gate: K.I. Strand, 1940).

39.　Spaulding, "Development . . . Working-Class Suburb," 70–76.

40. (Barrett) Lampmann interview; Collins interview, September 15, 1991.

41. Unemployment figures calculated from data in *South Gate Tribune*, May 5, 1932; for Los Angeles, see Gregory, *American Exodus*, 42. For 1938 figures, see *South Gate Press*, January 27, 1938.

42. *South Gate Tribune*, May 5, June 2, 1932; *Los Angeles Times*, January 8, June 7, 15, 1932; *South Gate Press*, January 27, 1938; Bureau of the Census, *Sixteenth Census of the United States, 1940: Population*, vol. 2, *Characteristics of the Population*, 620. The 1938 figure counted part-time and public works employees as employed.

43. Tom Thienes, "Contributions Toward the History of the City of South Gate, California" (unpublished manuscript for the Works Progress Administration, 1942, SGHWL), 92; FHA, "Housing Market Analysis . . . 1939," 82, 95. For sources of homeownership rates, see table 2–5; and rate of 1935 from *South Gate Press*, March 1, 1935. Mobility rates were computed from an analysis of the 1926 and 1930 city directories.

44. *South Gate Press*, January 20, 27, February 20, 1938; *South Gate Tribune*, December 22, 1933, February 7, 28, 1938. The Graham "Hoover Town" was documented in a series of photographs taken by the L.A. Health Department. L.A. County Department of Health Services Collection, Huntington Library, San Marino, California. Thanks to William Deverell for pointing out these photos.

45. *South Gate Press*, March 17, 1933 (clip from Field Notes, Box 160, FWP); *South Gate Tribune*, February 1, 1935; John L. Chapman, *Incredible Los Angeles* (New York: Harper & Row, 1965), 189; McWilliams, *Southern California*, 201.

46. Robert Fogelson has waged this argument most strongly in *Fragmented Metropolis*.

47. Kenneth T. Jackson, *Crabgrass Frontier* (New York: Oxford, 1985), 99–100; Andrew Wiese, "Struggle for the Suburban Dream: African American Suburbanization since 1916" (Ph.D. dissertation, Columbia University, 1993), chapter 3; Harris, *Unplanned Suburbs*, 50.

48. Ira Katznelson, *City Trenches: Urban Politics and the Patterning of Class in the United States* (Chicago: University of Chicago Press, 1981), 52.

49. See Clark Davis, *Company Men: White-Collar Life and Corporate Cultures in Los Angeles, 1892–1941* (Baltimore: Johns Hopkins University Press, 2000), chapter 3. While Stuart Blumin argues that the division between blue- and white-collar workers became key in the nineteenth century, Ileen DeVault sees much more fluidity between white- and blue-collar by the turn of the century. The reorganization of office work, according to scientific management principles, was one important sign that the "collar line" was waning, as was the increasing feminization of clerical work. See Stuart Blumin, *The Emergence of the Middle Class: Social Experience in the American City, 1760–1900* (Cambridge: Cambridge University Press, 1989); Ileen DeVault, *Sons and Daughters of Labor: Class and Clerical Work in Turn-of-the-Century Pittsburgh* (Ithaca: Cornell University Press, 1990).

50. The material from Chicago comes from Cohen, *Making a New Deal*. On Los Angeles, see Fogelson, *Fragmented Metropolis*, 79–83.

The literature on working-class immigrant life in America is immense and well-known. Although it is too voluminous to list here, a few notable examples of the literature are Zunz, *The Changing Face of Inequality;* John Bodnar, *Immigrants and Industrialization* (Pittsburgh: University of Pittsburgh Press, 1977); Bodnar et al., *Lives of Their Own;* Donna Gabaccia, *From Sicily to Elizabeth Street* (Albany: SUNY Press, 1984); Thomas Kessner, *The Golden Door: Italian and Jewish Mobility in New York City, 1880–1915* (New York: Oxford University Press, 1977); Stephen Thernstrom, *The Other Bostonians: Poverty and Progress in the American Metropolis, 1880–1970* (Cambridge: Harvard University Press, 1973); Virginia Yans-McLaughlin, *Family and Community: Italian Immigrants in Buffalo, 1880–1930* (Urbana: University of Illinois Press, 1977); Mary Murphy, *Mining Cultures: Men, Women, and Leisure in Butte, 1914–41* (Urbana: University of Illinois Press, 1997); Sarah Deutsch, *No Separate Refuge: Culture, Class, and Gender on an Anglo-Hispanic Frontier in the American Southwest, 1880–1940* (New York: Oxford University Press, 1987); Vicki L. Ruiz, *Cannery Women, Cannery Lives: Mexican Women, Unionization, and the California Food Processing Industry, 1930–1950* (Albuquerque: University of New Mexico Press, 1987); George J. Sanchez, *Becoming Mexican American: Ethnicity, Culture, and Identity in Chicano Los Angeles, 1900–1945* (New York: Oxford University Press, 1993). For an interesting study of ethnically and racially mixed neighborhoods of Los Angeles, see H. Mark Wild, "A Rumored Congregation: Cross-Cultural Interaction in the Immigrant Neighborhoods of Early Twentieth Century Los Angeles" (Ph.D. dissertation, U.C. San Diego, 2000).

51.   Cohen, *Making a New Deal*, 54–97, 101–115.

52.   Ronald Edsforth, *Class Conflict and Cultural Consensus: The Making of a Mass Consumer Society in Flint, Michigan* (New Brunswick: Rutgers University Press, 1987), 79–96.

53.   Tyler Stovall, *The Rise of the Paris Red Belt* (Berkeley and Los Angeles: University of California Press, 1990), chapter 3, quotes at 40, 81. For an equally provocative comparative perspective, see James Holston, "Autoconstruction in Working-Class Brazil," *Cultural Anthropology* 6 (1991): 447–465.

54.   Louis Adamic, *Laughing in the Jungle* (New York: Arno, 1969), 216.

Chapter 3

1.   Juanita (Smith) Hammon, interview by author, South Gate, California, July 5, 1990; Juanita (Smith) Hammon, telephone interview by author, August 31, 1992.

2.   Virgil Collins, interviews by author, Laguna Hills, California, August 25, September 15, 1991.

3.   James L. Stamps, *The Historical Volume and Reference Works*, vol. 4 (Arlington, Calif.: Historical Publishers, 1965), 264; Dorothea Weaver, telephone interview by author, November 18, 1991.

4.   On the earlier period, see Alexander Von Hoffman, *Local Attachments: The Making of an Urban Neighborhood, 1850–1920* (Baltimore: Johns Hopkins University Press, 1994).

5.   Lummis quotes from *Land of Sunshine* 3 (June 1895): 137, and *Land of Sunshine* 6 (1897): 261.

6.   On boosterism in Los Angeles, see Clark Davis, "From Oasis to Metropolis: Southern California and the Changing Context of American Leisure," *Pacific Historical Review* 61 (August 1992): 357–386; Norman Klein, *History of Forgetting* (London: Verso, 1997), chapter 1.

7.   Thomas Bender, *Community and Social Change in America* (Baltimore: Johns Hopkins University Press, 1978), 71, and passim; Thomas Bender, "Community," in *A Companion to American Thought*, Richard Wightman Fox and James T. Kloppenberg, eds. (Cambridge: Blackwell, 1995), 137–140. For a good discussion of community in L.A. history, see Denise Spooner, "Neighbors or Strangers: The Character of Southern California Community" (unpublished paper presented at the 89th Annual Meeting of the American Historical Association, Pacific Coast Branch, San Francisco, 1996). On changes in American cities generally, see Jon Teaford, *The Twentieth-Century American City*, 2nd edition (Baltimore: Johns Hopkins University Press, 1993).

8.   Robert K. Merton, "Local and Cosmopolitan Influentials," in *Perspective on the American Community: A Book of Readings*, Roland L. Warren, ed., 2nd edition (Chicago: Rand McNally & Co., 1973), 188–202.

9. (Smith) Hammon interview, July 5, 1990; Charles B. Spaulding, "The Development of Organization and Disorganization in the Social Life of a Rapidly Growing Working-Class Suburb within a Metropolitan District" (Ph.D. dissertation, University of Southern California, 1938), 166.

10. Because there was a tendency for a wife to join before her husband, the true percentage of "family joiners" is probably higher than early church membership lists suggest.

11. Membership rosters, 1931 and 1932, First Baptist Church of South Gate; "Church Register of the Community Presbyterian Church of South Gate, California," chronological roll, South Gate Community Presbyterian Church; Spaulding, "Development . . . Working-Class Suburb," 167; (Smith) Hammon interview, July 5, 1990; Mary (DeVries) North, interview by author, South Gate, California, July 12, 1999; Collins interview, August 25, 1991.

12. Seaborg was an exceptional individual, casting some doubt on how representative his experience was. In his adult life, he went on to study chemistry at U.C. Berkeley and became a Nobel Prize–winning chemist. He served as chancellor of U.C. Berkeley, chair of the Atomic Energy Commission under three presidents (1961–1971), and head of the Lawrence Berkeley Laboratory. Although he was exceptional, his youthfulness in the period of this study—he lived in South Gate from age fifteen to twenty-two—may place him more close to his peers. Glenn T. Seaborg, "Journal of Glenn T. Seaborg, January 1, 1927–August 10, 1934," unpublished manuscript in author's possession. Also see Robert Parry et al., *Chemistry: Experimental Foundations* (Englewood Cliffs, N.J.: Prentice-Hall, 1982), 379; Thomas H. Maugh, "Chemistry Nobelist Glenn Seaborg Dies," *Los Angeles Times,* February 27, 1999.

13. Seaborg, "Journal," 42–55; John Sheehy, interview by author, South Gate, California, May 1, 1990.

14. Scott Bottles, *Los Angeles and the Automobile: The Making of the Modern City* (Berkeley and Los Angeles: University of California Press, 1987), 31, 33, 49.

15. Spencer Crump, *Ride the Big Red Cars* (Corona del Mar: Trans-Anglo Books, 1970), 181.

16. Crump, *Ride the Big Red Cars,* 181, 201, 225–226; Kelker, De Leuw & Company, *Report and Recommendations on a Comprehensive Rapid Transit Plan for the City and County of Los Angeles* (Chicago: Kelker, DeLeuw & Co., 1925); *Home Gardens Booster,* April 18, 1924.

17. The rise of autos and demise of public transportation have been the subject of debate: see Bottles, *Los Angeles,* 1–5 for a review of this. Also see Mark S. Foster, "The Model-T, the Hard Sell, and Los Angeles's Urban Growth: The Decentralization of Los Angeles during the 1920s," *Pacific Historical Review* (1975): 459–484; Ashleigh E. Brilliant, *The Great Car Craze: How Southern California Collided with the Automobile in the 1920s* (Santa Barbara: Woodbridge Press, 1989), 17–18.

18. Bottles, *Los Angeles,* 92–93, 107. Similar data on comparatively high auto ownership in Los Angeles is in Faith M. Williams and Alice C. Hanson, *Money Disbursements of Wage Earners and Clerical Workers in Five Cities in the Pacific Region, 1934–36* (Washington, D.C.: GPO, 1939), 25.

19. Williams and Hanson, *Money Disbursements,* 25; Works Projects Administration, *Report of Traffic and Transportation Survey* (Los Angeles: Citizens Transportation Survey Committee, Haynes Foundation, 1940), 64–67, 85, 99, from Seaver Library, Museum of Natural History, Los Angeles; Brilliant, *Great Car Craze,* 121–127.

20. Emory S. Bogardus, *The City Boy and His Problems: A Study of Boy Life in Los Angeles* (Los Angeles, 1926), 71–72, quoted in Marlou Belyea, "The Joy Ride and the Silver Screen: Commercial Leisure, Delinquency and Play Reform in Los Angeles, 1900–1980" (Ph.D. dissertation, Boston University, 1983), 174; Sheehy interview, May 1, 1990; (Smith) Hammon

interview, July 5, 1990; Julia M. Sloane, *The Smiling Hill-Top and Other California Sketches* (New York: Scribner, 1919), 83 and Syl McDowell, "Highway Hikers vs. Asphalt Turtles," *Touring Topics* 15 (February 1923): 22, both quoted in Brilliant, *Great Car Craze*, 53, 55.

21. *South Gate City Directory, 1940* (South Gate: K.I. Strand, 1940), preface; "South Gate: The Complete City," pamphlet, South Gate Chamber of Commerce, January 1931, SGHWL. For a discussion of similar "complete" suburbs, see Greg Hise, *Magnetic Los Angeles: Planning the Twentieth-Century Metropolis* (Baltimore: Johns Hopkins University Press, 1997).

22. The number of blue-collar workers was computed from Arthur Newton, *City Directory of South Gate, 1926* (South Gate: Tribune News Publishing Co., 1926), using a 50 percent sample. The data on industrial employment was extrapolated from the sources for table 3–1.

23. Kelker, De Leuw & Co., *Report and Recommendations*. This report divided L.A. County into nineteen districts. District R combined northwest South Gate with Huntington Park, which was occupationally similar. District S included southern South Gate, Home Gardens, Watts, and Lynwood, also similar in terms of occupations.

24. Key exclusions of that survey were the Pacific Electric Watts line and District S, which included southern South Gate and Home Gardens. The survey results were reported in Kelker, De Leuw & Co., *Report and Recommendations*, 71–74.

25. For tracing journey-to-work patterns, the study was problematical because it excluded people employed in their hometown who drove or walked to work. At the same time, it included people on shopping and other nonwork excursions. For suggesting the general flow of people, it was instructive.

26. Kelker, De Leuw & Co., *Report and Recommendations*, 72–73 and plate 13.

27. This very rough estimate is based on employment figures reported in 1940, and on an estimate of 750 employed each at Firestone and the National Paper Co. (from newspaper accounts). The true employment figures were probably lower than the 2,000 estimate, especially as the Depression took hold.

28. Tom Thienes, "Contributions Toward the History of the City of South Gate, California," (unpublished manuscript for the Works Progress Administration, 1942, SGHWL), 123–140; South Gate Book field notes, FWP; *South Gate Press*, January 24, 1924; address list of members 1940, UAW216, ALUA.

29. WPA, *Report of Traffic*, 67.

30. *South Gate Press*, July 27, August 3, 1928. The indifference of branch plants to the plight of local residents occasionally manifested during the 1920s and 1930s. For example, Firestone in 1928 announced that it would import 400 skilled workers and their families from the company's headquarters in Akron. After receiving complaints from residents hungering for jobs, the company reversed its decision, assuring its desire "to make this local plant serve the community in which it is located."

31. On Chicago, see Lizabeth Cohen, *Making a New Deal: Industrial Workers in Chicago, 1919–1939* (Cambridge: Cambridge University Press, 1990), 17–33. Also see James R. Barrett, *Work and Community in the Jungle: Chicago's Packinghouse Workers, 1894–1922* (Urbana: University of Illinois Press, 1987); Francis Couvares, *The Remaking of Pittsburgh: Class and Culture in an Industrializing City, 1877–1919* (Albany: State University of New York Press, 1984); William Hartford, *Working People of Holyoke: Class and Ethnicity in a Massachusetts Mill Town, 1850–1960* (New Brunswick: Rutgers University Press, 1990); Daniel Walkowitz, *Worker City, Company Town: Iron and Cotton-Worker Protest in Troy and Cohoes, New York, 1855–84* (Urbana: University of Illinois Press, 1978). One study that deals with working-class commuting is John Cumbler, *Working-Class Community in Industrial*

America: Work, Leisure, and Struggle in Two Industrial Cities, 1880–1930 (Westport, Conn.: Greenwood Press, 1979).

32.   There is some disagreement in the literature about the extent to which dispersal/ commutes defined the working-class experience in Los Angeles. On the metropolitan level, we still lack sufficient evidence on journey-to-work patterns to clarify which model best captures the working-class experience: the "commuting" or "walking city" model.

The case for dispersal is supported by the argument that capital *purposefully* dispersed operations to thwart the organizing potentials of labor. Likewise, recent work on the industrial geography of Los Angeles has identified distinct patterns of industrial deconcentration. Mike Davis identified three distinct "industrial zones" in Los Angeles, marked both by clustering at the urban core and dispersal to the suburbs. Those that dispersed included branch plants (especially auto, rubber, and steel) and industries producing for national markets (especially motion pictures, oil, and, after 1940, aircraft). But other scholars have emphasized cases where work and residence coalesced, obviating the need for commutes. In some parts of Los Angeles—especially around the CMD—working-class neighborhoods were close enough to factories that a "walking city" framework emerged. Oil refining areas often had working-class neighborhoods nearby as well. And by the late 1930s, as Greg Hise has shown, dispersed aircraft factories were developed in conjunction with working-class suburbs, to maintain a tight link between work and residence.

On the efforts of L.A. capital to disperse an increasingly militant labor movement, see sources in chapter 2, note 23.

Studies emphasizing the proximity of workplace to neighborhood include Fred Viehe, "Black Gold Suburbs: The Influence of the Extractive Industry on the Suburbanization of Los Angeles, 1890–1930," *Journal of Urban History* 8 (1981): 3–26; Greg Hise, "'Nature's Workshop': Industry and Urban Expansion in Southern California, 1900–1950," *Journal of Historical Geography* 27 (2001): 74–92; Hise, *Magnetic Los Angeles*.

33.   Quoted in Myrna Cherkoss Donahoe, "Workers' Response to Plant Closures: The Cases of Steel and Auto in Southeast Los Angeles, 1935–1986" (Ph.D. dissertation, University of California, Irvine, 1987), 156.

34.   The implications of dispersal on working-class community are explored in Cumbler, *Working-Class Community.*

35.   Virgil Collins, interview by author, Artesia, California, August 20, 1991.

36.   Seaborg, "Journal," 183, 185, 350; Glenn T. Seaborg, telephone interview by author, August 17, 1990.

37.   For an excellent description of working-class bonding in the 1930s, see Cohen, *Making a New Deal.*

38.   James H. Collins, "Let's Take Stock of Motors," *Southern California Business* 15 (June 1936): 8–9.

39.   Donahoe, "Workers' Response," 128–129; Thienes, "Contributions," 129–130.

40.   *South Gate Tribune*, October 24, 1938; Collins interview, August 20, 1991; John Sheehy, interview by author, South Gate, California, June 21, 1990; Donahoe, "Workers' Response," 154. Donahoe places the workforce at 3,000 in 1937, which seems inordinately high (see "Workers' Response," 137).

41.   James Gregory, *American Exodus: The Dust Bowl Migration and Okie Culture in California* (New York: Oxford, 1989), 160–161; Collins interview, August 20, 1991.

42.   Donahoe, "Workers' Response," 137; handbill, June 1937, and finding guide, UAW216, ALUA. To buttress their precarious, newly won status, the union early on ordered members to wear their union button or face a fine of 25 cents each time they did not.

For descriptions of organization efforts of autoworkers in other cities, see Ronald Edsforth, *Class Conflict and Cultural Consensus: The Making of a Mass Consumer Society in Flint, Michigan* (New Brunswick: Rutgers University Press, 1987), 157–189; Peter Friedlander, *The Emergence of a UAW Local, 1936–1939: A Study in Class and Culture* (Pittsburgh: University of Pittsburgh Press, 1975).

43.　Wage proposal, November 23, 1937, Box 7, UAW216, ALUA; Collins interview, September 15, 1991; Peter Noteboom Oral History, quoted in Donahoe, "Workers' Response," 153. Also see Richard Harris, "'Canada's All Right': The Lives and Loyalties of Immigrant Families in a Toronto Suburb, 1900–1945," *Canadian Geographer* 36 (1992): 25–28.

Collins and Noteboom both recalled the dismal working conditions at GM South Gate, including foremen who would not let workers take a toilet break, one-hour waits (on the workers' own time) to punch out at the day's end, and three-hour waits to receive a paycheck.

A parallel heritage of southerners, one that embraced collective radicalism, peaked with the Populist movement. See Bruce Palmer, *Man Over Money: The Southern Populist Critique of American Capitalism* (Chapel Hill: University of North Carolina Press, 1980); Lawrence Goodwyn, *The Populist Moment* (New York: Oxford, 1978). John C. Leggett found that among Detroit blue-collar workers in 1960, those from rural backgrounds were the most militant. See "Uprootedness and Working-Class Consciousness," *American Journal of Sociology* 68 (1962–1963): 682–692.

44.　Cohen, *Making a New Deal*, passim.

45.　Handbills, UAW Local 216, 1937–1941; UAW 216 minutes, June 12, 1937, January 23, 1941; UAW 215 Women's Auxiliary file, all in UAW216, ALUA; Collins interviews, August 20, 25, September 15, 1991; quote of Bethlehem steelworker from Donahoe, "Workers' Response," 156; Wyndham Mortimer, "Reflections of a Labor Organizer," UCLA Oral History Program, p. 142, YRL-UCLA. In Bell Gardens, nearly 20 percent of working residents belonged to unions outside of Bell Gardens. See Spaulding, "Development . . . Working-Class Suburb," 276.

The difficulty unions had in forging a "culture of unity" among commuting workers is also treated in William Kornblum, *Blue Collar Community* (Chicago: University of Chicago Press, 1974). Similarly, James Grossman found that the exclusion of black stockyard workers from union-centered working-class neighborhoods made it difficult to organize them. *Land of Hope: Chicago, Black Southerners and the Great Migration* (Chicago: University of Chicago Press, 1989).

46.　The Lynds found a similar function of unions in their study of Middletown. Robert S. Lynd and Helen Merrell Lynd, *Middletown: A Study in Modern American Culture* (New York: Harcourt, Brace & World, 1929), 77–80.

47.　Collins interview, September 15, 1991.

48.　Among the voluminous literature on working-class leisure, the most helpful to this study were Cohen, *Making a New Deal;* Roy Rosenzweig, *Eight Hours for What We Will* (Cambridge: Cambridge University Press, 1983); Kathy Peiss, *Cheap Amusements* (Philadelphia: Temple University Press, 1986); Michael Denning, *The Cultural Front* (New York: Verso, 1996); Steven J. Ross, *Working-Class Hollywood: Silent Film and the Shaping of Class in America* (Princeton: Princeton University Press, 1998); Lary May, *Screening Out the Past* (Chicago: University of Chicago Press, 1980); Mary Murphy, *Mining Cultures: Men, Women, and Leisure in Butte, 1914–41* (Urbana: University of Illinois Press, 1997).

49.　In 1910, Los Angeles had only 5 percent of the state's saloons (compared to 41 percent in San Francisco), 4 percent of the dance halls (50 percent in San Francisco), and 15 percent of the boxing rings (42 percent in San Francisco).

50.　Belyea, "Joy Ride," 28, 33–38; historian's quote from Patricia Rae Adler, "Watts:

From Suburb to Black Ghetto" (Ph.D. dissertation, University of Southern California, 1977), 188. For a general treatment of the dispersal of vice into the suburban fringe in the early twentieth century, see Perry Duis, *The Saloon: Public Drinking in Chicago and Boston, 1880–1920* (Urbana: University of Illinois Press, 1983), 276.

51.   Developer Sam Dudlext ran Dudlext Auditorium in Home Gardens, while fire chief Ed Dahlgren operated Dahlgren Hall in northwest South Gate.

52.   *Home Gardens Booster,* May 16, 1924; *Home Gardens Press,* July 24, 1925; (Smith) Hammon interview, July 5, 1990; Ruth (Barrett) Lampmann, interview by author, South Gate, California, February 13, 1991; *South Gate Press,* January 19, 1983.

53.   *Home Gardens Weekly,* February 1, 15, 1924; *Home Gardens Booster,* October 17, 1924. The rejection of local movie houses by South Gate residents contrasted with the practices of immigrant workers in Chicago during the 1920s, who continued to patronize neighborhood theaters enthusiastically in this period. For the latter, moviegoing represented a means for reinforcing ethnic identity. See Cohen, *Making a New Deal,* 120–129.

54.   *South Gate Tribune,* November 27, 1925, August 1, 1929; South Gate City Council minutes, August 25, 1927, SGCH; *South Gate Press,* September 27, 1929, June 19, July 17, 1931; Seaborg, "Journal," 58, 112, and passim; Seaborg interview.

55.   Belyea, "Joy Ride," 42–44; Arthur Newton, *City Directory of South Gate, 1930* (South Gate: Tribune-News Publishing Co., 1930); *South Gate Press,* June 22, July (various issues) 1928; Bicentennial Heritage Committee, *South Gate, 1776–1976* (South Gate: South Gate Press, 1976), 42; Seaborg, "Journal," 64. On boxing in Los Angeles, see Gregory Rodriguez, "Palaces of Pain–Arenas of Mexican American Dreams: Boxing and the Formation of Ethnic Mexican Identities in Twentieth-Century Los Angeles" (Ph.D. dissertation, U.C. San Diego, 1999).

56.   *South Gate Tribune,* September 25, December 4, 18, 1925, February 26, April 23, 1932; *South Gate Press,* March 1, 1929; *Home Gardens Press,* May 29, 1925; John Sheehy, interview by author, South Gate, California, June 19, 1990.

57.   Typically, a single merchant sponsored one baseball player, usually just out of high school. Encouraged by the publicity the ball club was generating for South Gate, the city council in 1926 appropriated $175 to help pay for the team's uniforms and equipment, and donated $25 on another occasion.

58.   Sheehy interview, June 19, 1990; Seaborg, "Journal," 2; South Gate City Council minutes, March 16 and November 3, 1926, SGCH; *South Gate Tribune,* February 26, April 16, July 2, 1935; *South Gate Press,* June 19, 26, 1931.

59.   On the arrests of local bootleggers, see *South Gate Tribune,* December 25, 1924, February 1, 1929, July 25, August 1, 1930; *South Gate Press,* June 22, July 27, 1928, November 29, 1929; Seaborg interview. On kitchen barrooms in other working-class neighborhoods, see Peiss, *Cheap Amusements,* 27–29; Rosenzweig, *Eight Hours,* 42–44; Madelon Powers, *Faces along the Bar: Lore and Order in the Workingman's Saloon* (Chicago: University of Chicago Press, 1998).

60.   Clarence E. Miller, "A Study of Certain Community Forces of South Gate, California, in Their Relation to Character Education" (M. Theology thesis, University of Southern California, 1935), 26–29, 33, 35–35a; "South Gate City Ordinance No. 240," May 17, 1932, "South Gate City Ordinance No. 320," August 17, 1936, "South Gate City Ordinance No. 264," March 7, 1933, "South Gate City Ordinance No. 263," March 7, 1933, "South Gate City Ordinance No. 266," April 4, 1933, SGCH; Weber field notes, July 18, 1941, Box 160, FWP; *South Gate Tribune,* July 16, 30, 1935. See *South Gate Tribune,* December 19, 1933, on a failed effort to legalize gambling in South Gate.

61. Spaulding, "Development . . . Working-Class Suburb," 166–167.

62. Spaulding, "Development . . . Working-Class Suburb," 166, 171–172.

63. For a brief description of middle-class "gentleman farming" in early Los Angeles, see *Land of Sunshine* 3 (February 1895): 134–137. Mary Corbin Sies argues that middle- and working-class suburbanites resembled each other more in this regard than might be expected. See Sies, "North American Suburbs, 1880–1950: Cultural and Social Reconsiderations," *Journal of Urban History* 27 (March 2001): 313–346.

64. During radio's early years, it was common for consumers to assemble their own sets. See Susan Douglas, *Inventing American Broadcasting, 1899–1922* (Baltimore: Johns Hopkins University Press, 1987).

65. *Home Gardens Press,* October 9, 1925; *Broadcasting* (November 1, 1932): 13; U.S. Bureau of the Census, *Fifteenth Census of United States, 1930: Population,* vol. 6, *Families* (Washington, D.C.: GPO, 1933), 183.

66. Seaborg, "Journal," 30, 43, 48–51, 224; Cohen, *Making a New Deal,* 129–143; Douglas, *Inventing American Broadcasting,* passim.

67. *Home Gardens Press,* November 6, 1925; *South Gate Tribune,* March 23, 1932, June 17, 1930, June 14, 1935; Miller, "Community Forces," 154; *Huntington Park Daily Signal,* January 19, 1973; South Gate City Council minutes, May 31, December 6, 1927, SGCH. On the upper-class suburb, see especially Margaret Marsh, *Suburban Lives* (New Brunswick: Rutgers University Press, 1990).

68. Davis, "From Oasis to Metropolis"; Kevin Starr, *Inventing the Dream: California through the Progressive Era* (New York: Oxford, 1985); Kevin Allen Leonard, "Years of Hope, Days of Fear: The Impact of World War II on Race Relations in Los Angeles" (Ph.D. dissertation, U.C. Davis, 1992), 45; Arthur Verge, telephone interview by author, August 26, 1997.

69. Charles E. Funnell, *By the Beautiful Sea: The Rise and High Times of That Great American Resort, Atlantic City* (New Brunswick: Rutgers University Press, 1983); Jeffrey Stanton, *Venice of America: "Coney Island of the Pacific"* (Los Angeles: Donahue Publishing, 1987); John F. Kasson, *Amusing the Millions: Coney Island at the Turn of the Century* (New York: Hill and Wang, 1978).

70. Sheehy interview, May 1, 1990; Seaborg, "Journal," passim; Seaborg interview; (DeVries) North interview; (Smith) Hammon interview, July 5, 1990.

71. Wallace McFadden, interview by Sandy McFadden, June 12, 1971, Oral History 1029, p. 2, FOH; Walter Fiss, "Take Your Nerves to the Mountains," *Southern California Business* 9 (April 1928): 20; Los Angeles City Playground and Recreation Commission, *A Brief Report of Recreation Department City of Los Angeles* (n.p., 1921); George Hjelte, "Mountain Parks and Summer Vacations," in Los Angeles Junior Chamber of Commerce, *Los Angeles County Sportland* (n.p., 1929), Haynes Collection, YRL-UCLA.

Located in the San Bernardino Mountains around Big Bear and Lake Arrowhead, the municipal camps included large community lodges, cabins, toilet facilities, and swimming pools. In the 1920s, a two-week stay at the camp, which included transportation, food, and housing, ranged from $6.50–12.50 for children to $14.25 for adults.

72. Florence Nesbitt, "Study of a Minimum Standard of Living for Dependent Families in Los Angeles," report for Research Division, Los Angeles Community Welfare Federation, November 1927, Haynes Collection, YRL-UCLA; Spaulding, "Development . . . Working-Class Suburb," 177.

On movies as a form of working-class leisure, see Ross, *Working-Class Hollywood;* May, *Screening Out the Past,* passim; Cohen, *Making a New Deal,* 120–129; Rosenzweig, *Eight Hours,* 192–204; Elizabeth Ewen, "City Lights: Immigrant Women and the Rise of the Movies," *Signs* 5 (1980): S45–S65.

73.   Seaborg interview; (Smith) Hammon interview, July 5, 1990; (DeVries) North interview; Sheehy interview, May 1, 1990; Collins interview, September 15, 1991.

74.   Seaborg, "Journal," passim; Seaborg interview.

75.   Sheehy interview, June 19, 1990; see the local newspapers for coverage of university games.

76.   Seaborg, "Journal," 26, 236–237, 343.

77.   Miller, "Community Forces," 30–31. While smaller stores downtown were in decline from 1900 to 1930, the number of department stores had risen. See Robert M. Fogelson, *The Fragmented Metropolis, Los Angeles 1850–1930* (Cambridge: Harvard University Press, 1967), 148–150, 250, 261–262; Hale H. Huggins, "Decentralization of Shopping," *Los Angeles Realtor* 3 (April 1934): 5; Richard W. Longstreth, *City Center to Regional Mall: Architecture, the Automobile, and Retailing in Los Angeles, 1920–1950* (Cambridge: MIT, 1997).

78.   Sheehy interviews, May 1, June 21, 1990; (Smith) Hammon interview, July 5, 1990; *South Gate Press*, June 14, 1929.

79.   Seaborg, "Journal," passim, quotes at 60, 214, 130.

80.   Spaulding, "Development . . . Working-Class Suburb," 150–152.

81.   On consumption as a tool of working-class assertion, see Dana Frank, *Purchasing Power: Consumer Organizing, Gender, and the Seattle Labor Movement, 1919–1929* (Cambridge: Cambridge University Press, 1994).

82.   Computed from *City Directory of South Gate, 1926; City Directory of South Gate, 1930; South Gate City Directory, 1940.*

83.   Persistence rates and subsequent occupations were determined from *City Directory of South Gate, 1926; City Directory of South Gate, 1930; South Gate City Directory, 1940.*

84.   Lucia Mason, "Early Days," unpublished manuscript, quoted in Thienes, "Contributions," 51; *Hopper Tour Topics*, November 1920; *Huntington Park Daily Signal*, January 19, 1973; *South Gate Police Annual, 1927* (South Gate, 1927), SGHWL; *Southgate Gardener*, July 1919 (from Weber field notes, Box 160, FWP); Church Register, Community Presbyterian Church of South Gate, California; *Home Gardens Booster*, February 15, 1924.

85.   Weber field notes, Box 164, FWP; Sheehy interview, May 1, 1990. Sheehy referred to the Elks Club of Huntington Park as "the center of power. . . . They were the power structure of the community."

86.   Homer Cotton, telephone interview by author, July 21, 1997; Rotary Club of South Gate–Walnut Park, "Charter Presentation," April 27, 1938, pamphlet, in author's possession; Weber field notes, August 8, 1941, Box 164, FWP.

87.   Weber field notes, Box 164, FWP.

88.   Marsh, *Suburban Lives;* Warren Leon, "High School: A Study of Youth and Community in Quincy, Massachusetts" (Ph.D. dissertation, Harvard University, 1979); Allison Baker, "The Lakewood Story: Defending the Recreational Good Life in Postwar Southern California Suburbia, 1950–1999" (Ph.D. dissertation, University of Pennsylvania, 1999).

89.   *Hopper Tour Topics*, November 1920, p. 2; *Huntington Park Daily Signal*, January 19, 1973; Bicentennial Heritage Committee, *South Gate, 1776–1976*, 11, 17, 49–51; Weber field notes, June 20, 1941, Box 164, FWP; Miller, "Community Forces," 39–60, 65–66.

90.   *Home Gardens Booster*, February 1, 1924 (from Weber field notes, April 11, 1941, Box 160, FWP); Miller, "Community Forces," 64–68, 77, 83–92, 147; Spaulding, "Development . . . Working-Class Suburb," 171–176.

91.   (Barrett) Lampmann interview; McFadden interview, p. 17.

92.   (Smith) Hammon interview, July 5, 1990; (Barrett) Lampmann interview; Seaborg, "Journal," passim.

93.   Jeanne Boydston, *Home and Work: Housework, Wages, and the Ideology of Labor in the Early Republic* (New York: Oxford, 1990), especially chapter 4, quote at 91; Deborah Fink, *Open Country Iowa: Rural Women, Tradition, and Change* (Albany: SUNY Press, 1986); Spaulding, "Development . . . Working-Class Suburb," 166. On women's work in a working-class suburb of Toronto, see Harris, "'Canada's All Right,'" 20–22.

94.   The identifiable occupations of husbands of South Gate Woman's Club members included chiropractor, postal superintendent, plaster contractor, accountant, druggist, mechanical and electrical engineer, salesman, and doctor. Husbands of the South Side Woman's Club members included two carpenters, a butcher, a railway worker, and a "tool keeper."

95.   Eleanor Cottrell, "South Gate History," typewritten manuscript, p. 2, SGHWL; Weber field notes, August 1, 1941, Box 164, FWP; *Huntington Park Daily Signal*, January 19, 1973; *City Directory of South Gate, 1930; South Gate City Directory, 1940*; Bicentennial Heritage Committee, *South Gate 1776–1976*, 51. The South Gate WCTU had remarkable staying power, lasting to the 1960s.

96.   *Southgate Gardener*, September–October 1919, p. 3.

97.   T. Scott Miyakawa shows how churches could allow "complete strangers" to "establish close personal relations quickly." *Protestants and Pioneers: Individualism and Conformity on the American Frontier* (Chicago: University of Chicago Press, 1964).

98.   Miller, "Community Forces," passim. My estimate is based on averaging out a church to membership ratio based on Miller's survey, then applying that ratio to the churches he did not count. The total percentage was probably substantially lower, for two reasons: first, the St. Helens membership skewed the average upward, and second, many of the churches Miller overlooked were small, which would have pushed the average downward.

99.   Miller, "Community Forces," 148, and passim; (Smith) Hammon interview, July 5, 1990; Spaulding, "Development . . . Working-Class Suburb," 200.

100.   Miller, "Community Forces," passim.

101.   Timothy Smith, "Religion and Ethnicity in America," *American Historical Review* (1978): 1178. For an interpretation that rests on modernization theory, see John Holt, "Holiness Religion: Cultural Shock and Social Reorganization," *American Sociological Review* (October 1940): 740–747.

102.   Gregory, *American Exodus*, 196–199. Also see Floyd Looney, *History of California Southern Baptists* (Fresno: Board of Directors of the Southern Baptist General Convention of California, 1954); William Edmondson, "Fundamentalist Sects of Los Angeles, 1900–1930" (Ph.D. dissertation, Claremont Graduate School, 1969).

103.   Miller, "Community Forces," 138, 150–151, passim. Gregory identifies the Churches of Christ as "the conservative Cambellite congregations." *American Exodus*, 199.

104.   Shahan said her wardrobe of longer skirts and white cotton stockings immediately tagged her as "Okie"; other girls wore shorter skirts and anklets. Wanda Audrey Shahan Wall, interview by Jackie Malone, October 6, 1976, Oral History 1555, p. 17, FOH.

105.   Anton T. Boisen, "Economic Distress and Religious Experience: A Study of the Holy Rollers," *Psychiatry* (May 1939): 186–187, 192–194; Gertrude Keene, "Distinctive Social Values of the Pentecostal Churches: A Sociological Field Study," (M.A. thesis, University of Southern California, 1938), 81. In the 1930s statewide, non-Evangelical churches tended to reject dust bowl migrants, and vice versa, based on class and theological differences. See Gregory, *American Exodus*, chapter 7.

106.   The churches with records that clearly indicated self-building by volunteers were

two Churches of Christ, the Mormon Church, South Gate Community Presbyterian, the Redeemer Lutheran Church, Grace Bible Church, and the First Baptist Church. *Huntington Park Daily Signal,* January 19, 1973; (Smith) Hammon interview, July 5, 1990; *Los Angeles Times,* May 30, 1926, pt. 5, p. 10; First Baptist Church minutes.

It is highly likely that the many small Evangelical churches of Home Gardens were similarly self-built, however scanty records make it difficult to confirm this.

107. Gregory, *American Exodus,* 201; Boisen, "Economic Distress," 186.

108. McFadden interview, p. 18; Weaver interview; Bicentennial Heritage Committee, *South Gate, 1776–1976,* 47–49; First Baptist Church minutes, January 5, 26, February 28, March 23, 1930.

W. Clark Roof makes a useful, cautionary conceptual distinction between substantive commitment and mere organizational affiliation in "The Local-Cosmopolitan Orientation and Traditional Religious Commitment," *Sociological Analysis* 33 (1973): 1–3.

109. *Home Gardens Press,* July 10, 1925; Miller, "Community Forces," 93, 148; Shahan Wall interview, p. 14. See Gregory, *American Exodus,* 204 and 211 for descriptions of the splintering and tight-knit character of Evangelical churches in other parts of California.

110. Boisen, "Economic Distress," 186–187, 193; Keene, "Pentecostal Churches," 28; Gregory, *American Exodus,* 212; Spaulding, "Development . . . Working-Class Suburb," 200; McFadden interview, p. 18; Miller, "Community Forces," 101–103, 136. Good descriptions of Pentecostal worship services are in Keene, "Pentecostal Churches," 76–80; Holt, "Holiness Religion," 740–741; Boisen, "Economic Distress," 185–194; Gregory, *American Exodus,* 199–201.

111. Melvin Gerald Shahan, interview by Jackie Malone, October 29 and December 7, 1976, Oral History 1556, p. 48, FOH.

Aimee Semple McPherson's Angelus Four Square Temple epitomized the mix of entertainment and religion. The flamboyant fundamentalist drew on all that Hollywood had to offer— her services were adorned with garish backdrops, props, costumes, and sermons ("The Lone Ranger Unmasked" likened Christ to the masked man). David Clark, "Miracles for a Dime: From Chautauqua Tent to Radio Station with Sister Aimee," *California Historical Quarterly* 57 (winter 1978–79): 354–363.

112. South Gate City Council minutes, August 2, September 6, 1927, May 2, June 5, 1928, SGCH; *Home Gardens Booster,* June 6, July 25, 1924; *South Gate Tribune,* December 25, 1924, January 2, 16, 1925.

113. Keene, "Pentecostal Churches," 32; *Home Gardens Press,* August 21, 1925; *South Gate Press,* June 1, 1928; First Baptist Church minutes, 1930–1933; Smith, "Religion and Ethnicity," 1179.

114. Lucia Mason, "Early Days," unpublished manuscript, quoted in Thienes, "Contributions," 52. Ralph DeVries chose to attend Community Presbyterian because it was close to home. (DeVries) North interview.

115. Miller, "Community Forces," 115–118; *Huntington Park Daily Signal,* January 19, 1973; (DeVries) North interview.

116. My analysis counted each family member (such as wives) separately, as part of a "white-collar" or "blue-collar" family. It classified each family member under the head of household's occupation, unless that family member's occupation was listed separately.

117. Miller, "Community Forces," 118; Sheehy interviews, May 1, June 19, 1990. The church membership analysis drew from records of the South Gate Community Presbyterian Church, South Gate, cross-referenced with the 1930 city directory to determine occupations.

118. Miller, "Community Forces," 119–121, 138; Sheehy interview, June 19, 1990; *Home Gardens Booster,* February 29, 1924.

119.   Miller, "Community Forces," 120, 127, 133.

120.   (Smith) Hammon interview, July 5, 1990; Collins interview, August 25, 1991. Spooner, "Neighbors or Strangers," describes several factors discouraging local community experience in Los Angeles during the twentieth century.

121.   (Smith) Hammon interview, July 5, 1990; Spaulding, "Development . . . Working-Class Suburb," 167–168, 97, 229.

122.   (Smith) Hammon interview, July 5, 1990; Seaborg, "Journal," especially 1928 entries; Sheehy interviews, May 1, June 19, 1990; (DeVries) North interview; (Barrett) Lampmann interview.

123.   Miller, "Community Forces," 4–5.

124.   With few exceptions (notably Cohen, *Making a New Deal*, and Ross, *Working-Class Hollywood*), the assumption that working-class consciousness declined with the advent of mass culture, automobiles, and suburbia is reiterated in a number of studies. For example, see Cumbler, *Working-Class Community*; and Edsforth, *Class Conflict and Cultural Consensus*. Even Cohen suggests that post–World War II mass culture contributed to this declension.

Chapter 4

1.   Tom Thienes, "Contributions Toward the History of the City of South Gate, California" (unpublished manuscript for the Works Progress Administration, 1942, SGHWL), 54–55; John Sheehy, interview by author, South Gate, California, May 1, 1990.

2.   *Home Gardens Press*, February 20, May 16, 1924.

3.   A classic statement of the democratizing effects of community building is in Stanley Elkins and Eric McKitrick, "A Meaning for Turner's Frontier," *Political Science Quarterly* 69 (September 1954): 321–353.

4.   *Home Gardens Press*, February 16, 1924; South Gate Board of Trustees minutes, November 20, 1923, and 1923 generally (from Weber field notes, July 4, 1941, Box 160, FWP), and SGCH; *Huntington Park Daily Signal*, January 19, 1973; Arthur Newton, *City Directory of South Gate, 1926* (South Gate: Tribune News Publishing Co., 1926); George Weber field notes, July 11, 1941, Box 160, FWP.

5.   See especially Dana Frank, *Purchasing Power: Consumer Organizing, Gender, and the Seattle Labor Movement, 1919–1929* (New York: Cambridge University Press, 1994); Lizabeth Cohen, *Making a New Deal: Industrial Workers in Chicago, 1919–1939* (Cambridge: Cambridge University Press, 1990); Ronald Edsforth, *Class Conflict and Cultural Consensus: The Making of a Mass Consumer Society in Flint, Michigan* (New Brunswick: Rutgers University Press, 1987); Roy Rosenzweig, *Eight Hours for What We Will* (Cambridge: Cambridge University Press, 1983).

6.   An excellent discussion of community in American history is in Thomas Bender, *Community and Social Change in America* (Baltimore: Johns Hopkins University Press, 1978).

7.   Lizabeth Cohen, "Encountering Mass Culture at the Grassroots: The Experience of Chicago Workers in the 1920s," *American Quarterly* 41 (March 1989): quote at 10. Also see Cohen, *Making a New Deal*, passim; Allan H. Spear, *Black Chicago: The Making of a Negro Ghetto, 1890–1920* (Chicago: University of Chicago Press, 1967); Kenneth L. Kusmer, *A Ghetto Takes Shape: Black Cleveland, 1870–1930* (Urbana: University of Illinois Press, 1978), 140–154, 228–234; James R. Grossman, *Land of Hope: Chicago, Black Southerners and the Great Migration* (Chicago: University of Chicago Press, 1989), 130–135, 143–145, 154–155.

8.   *South Gate Tribune*, April 19, August 13, 1935; *South Gate Press*, April 16, 1935.

9.   Carey McWilliams, *Southern California: An Island on the Land* (Salt Lake City: Peregrine Smith, 1995 [1946]), 302. Cohen describes how immigrant workers similarly turned away

from ethnic merchants during the Depression, in *Making a New Deal*, 234–238. On coopera-
tives in general, see Frank, *Purchasing Power*, chapter 2; National Consumers Committee for
Research and Education, *Consumer Activists: They Make a Difference: A History of Consumer
Action Related by Leaders in the Consumer Movement* (Mt. Vernon, N.Y.: Consumers Union
Foundation, 1982), chapters 1–4.

10.   *South Gate Tribune*, March 1, 1935, November 7, 1938; "Self-Help Activities of Unemployed in Los Angeles," *Monthly Labor Review* (April 1933): 717–740; Elizabeth Virginia
Watson, "The Consumers' Cooperative Movement in Los Angeles County" (M.A. thesis, University of Southern California, 1935), 14, 20.

11.   George Knox Roth, "The Compton Unemployed Co-operative Relief Association: A
Sociological Study, 1932–1933" (M.A. thesis, University of Southern California, 1934), 154–
155, 164.

12.   See chapter 3; Glenn T. Seaborg, telephone interview by author, August 17, 1990;
Ruth (Barrett) Lampmann, interview by author, South Gate, California, February 13, 1991.

13.   Cohen, *Making a New Deal*, 110–113. In her study of Chicago workers, Cohen emphasized "class harmony" between worker-residents and local merchants, based primarily on
shared ethnicity. But even this harmony eroded during the Depression, as "workers became
more aware of class differences within their own ethnic groups" (238).

14.   *Home Gardens Press*, January 6, 1928, November 6, 1925, February 26, 1926; Ronald
Tobey, Charles Wetherell, and Jay Brigham, "Moving Out and Settling In: Residential Mobility,
Home Owning, and the Public Enframing of Citizenship, 1921–1950," *American Historical
Review* 95 (December 1990): 1395–1422.

15.   *South Gate Press*, September 14, December 21, 1928, emphasis in original. For similar expressions, see *Home Gardens Booster*, February 1, 1924; *South Gate Tribune*, March 6,
1924, December 17, 1926; *South Gate Press*, November 30, 1928.

Roland Marchand describes, similarly, how advertising tactics in the 1920s attempted to
equate consumption with democracy. See Marchand, *Advertising the American Dream: Making Way for Modernity, 1920–1940* (Berkeley and Los Angeles: University of California Press,
1985).

16.   *Home Gardens Press*, December 10, 1926; *South Gate Press*, November 16, 1928, November 15, 1929 (reprinted from *Maywood Journal*).

17.   *Home Gardens Press*, December 21, 1926 (reprinted from the *Downey Champion*);
South Gate Press, November 16, 1928.

18.   *South Gate Press*, November 16, 23, 1928.

19.   *South Gate Tribune*, March 27, April 3, 1924, June 14, 1935; *South Gate Press*, August 10, 1928, February 6, 1931.

20.   *Home Gardens Press*, October 29, November 5, December 10, 1926.

21.   *Home Gardens Press*, May 7, 1926. The article did not identify which merchants
withheld support.

22.   *South Gate Tribune*, March 14, 1931.

23.   *South Gate Tribune*, August 8, 1924.

24.   *South Gate Tribune*, July 23, August 23, 1929, March 4, September 5, 9, 19, October
28, 1930, March 7, 20, 1931, quote from March 16, 1931.

25.   Cohen, *Making a New Deal*, 107, 116–120; Richard S. Tedlow, *New and Improved:
The Story of Mass Marketing in America* (New York: Basic Books, 1990); Richard W.
Longstreth, *City Center to Regional Mall: Architecture, the Automobile, and Retailing in Los
Angeles, 1920–1950* (Cambridge: MIT, 1997).

26.   *City Directory of South Gate, 1926; City Directory of South Gate, 1929* (South Gate:

Tribune News Publishing Co., 1929); *South Gate Tribune*, December 4, 1925; *South Gate Press*, January 30, 1931. Meat and produce stalls were commonplace in L.A. area grocery chains, as detailed in Richard W. Longstreth, *The Drive-in, the Supermarket, and the Transformation of Commercial Space in Los Angeles, 1914–1941* (Cambridge: MIT, 1999), 11–14.

27.   Persistence rates of local businesses were calculated using Arthur Newton, *City Directory of South Gate, 1930* (South Gate: Tribune-News Publishing Co., 1930); *South Gate City Directory, 1940* (K.I. Strand, 1940).

28.   *South Gate Press*, October 23, 1931, March 31, 1938; *South Gate Tribune*, February 22, 1935; Legislature of the State of California, *Journal of the Assembly: 51st Session, 1935* (Sacramento: California State Printing Office, 1935), 503.

29.   *South Gate Tribune*, January 31, August 15, 1924. See *South Gate Tribune*, March 14, 1932, for a story announcing that it would advertise for the new Montgomery Wards department store in Huntington Park.

30.   *South Gate City Directory, 1940*. The Ben Franklin Store was the only chain.

31.   Thanks to James Gregory for clarifying these ideas for me. Studies that discuss similar merchant-booster groups include Blaine Brownell, *The Urban Ethos in the South, 1920–1930* (Baton Rouge: Louisiana State University Press, 1975); Carl Abbott, *Boosters and Businessmen: Popular Economic Thought and Urban Growth in the Antebellum Middle West* (Westport, Conn.: Greenwood Press, 1981). Also see Daniel Boorstin, "The Businessman as City Booster," and Harry Scheiber, "Urban Rivalry and Internal Improvements in the Old Northwest, 1820–1860," in *American Urban History*, Alexander B. Callow Jr., ed. (New York: Oxford, 1973), 135–153; Christopher Cocoltchos, "The Invisible Government and the Viable Community: The Ku Klux Klan in Orange County, California during the 1920s" (Ph.D. dissertation, University of California Los Angeles, 1979), especially 1–23, for a discussion of similar "merchant elite" groups in Orange County.

32.   On similar conflicts in more recent times—pitting progrowth interests against small property owners—see John R. Logan and Harvey L. Molotch, *Urban Fortunes: The Political Economy of Place* (Berkeley and Los Angeles: University of California Press, 1987).

33.   Harry V. Law, "The South Gate Chamber of Commerce" in *South Gate Police Annual, 1927* (South Gate, 1927), SGHWL.

34.   *Home Gardens Press*, December 21, 1926; *South Gate Tribune*, February 14, 1924.

35.   *South Gate Tribune*, September 19, 1924; *Home Gardens Booster*, June 6, 1924; Richard Harris, *Unplanned Suburbs: Toronto's American Tragedy, 1900–1950* (Baltimore: Johns Hopkins, 1996), 236.

36.   *Home Gardens Press*, March 27, 1925; Abbott, *Boosters*, 207. On working-class homeowners in other cities, see Jon C. Teaford, *City and Suburb: The Political Fragmentation of Metropolitan America, 1850–1970* (Baltimore: Johns Hopkins University Press, 1979), 167–170; Olivier Zunz, *The Changing Face of Inequality: Urbanization, Industrial Development, and Immigrants in Detroit, 1880–1920* (Chicago: University of Chicago Press, 1982); Roger D. Simon, *The City-Building Process: Housing and Services in New Milwaukee Neighborhoods, 1880–1900*, Transactions of the American Philosophical Society, vol. 68, p. 5 (Philadelphia, 1978); Ann Durkin Keating, *Building Chicago: Suburban Developers and the Creation of a Divided Metropolis* (Columbus: Ohio State University Press, 1988).

The working-class residents of South Gate and Home Gardens may, in fact, represent the descendents in outlook (if not biology) of the southern yeoman farmer and Populist. See Harry Watson, *Jacksonian Politics and Community Conflict: The Emergence of the Second American Party System in Cumberland County, North Carolina* (Baton Rouge: Louisiana State University Press, 1981); Steven Hahn, *The Roots of Southern Populism: Yeoman Farmers and the*

Transformation of the Georgia Upcountry, 1850–1890 (New York: Oxford, 1983); Bruce Palmer, *"Man Over Money": The Southern Populist Critique of American Capitalism* (Chapel Hill: University of North Carolina Press, 1980).

37. McWilliams, *Southern California,* 277; *South Gate Tribune,* September 11, 18, 1925. Also see "Big Labor Drive in Los Angeles," *Business Week* (April 10, 1937): 39.

An example of a citywide incident that highlighted this problem occurred in 1907, when labor leaders opposed an impending booster campaign to attract construction workers for the Owens Valley Aqueduct project. "[I]t is evidently the purpose of the men who now have the project in hand," they warned, "to not only secure a surplus of water for this city but a surplus of labor likewise—such a surplus will guarantee the cheapest going price that the market affords." Quote from *The Los Angeles Citizen,* May 31, 1907. Also see Perry and Perry, *History of the Los Angeles Labor Movement,* 10–11, 15; Robert M. Fogelson, *The Fragmented Metropolis: Los Angeles, 1850–1930* (Cambridge: Harvard University Press, 1967), 98.

38. In a fascinating study, Quam-Wickham finds similar evidence of working-class resistance to unbridled oil development, in this case on environmental grounds. See Nancy Quam-Wickham, "Cities Sacrificed on the Altar of Oil: Popular Opposition to Oil Development in 1920s Los Angeles," *Environmental History* 3 (1998): 189–209.

39. *City Directory of South Gate, 1926; City Directory of South Gate, 1930;* and for National Paper Products Co., see *Home Gardens Press,* September 17, 1926 (Weber field notes June 20, 1941, FWP); Sanborn Map Company, "Insurance Maps of Los Angeles, California: Map of South Gate," vols. 28, 30–31 (Sanborn Map Company of New York, 1927–29); South Gate City Council minutes, May 3, 1927, April 17, 1928, SGCH.

40. Juanita (Smith) Hammon, interview by author, July 5, 1990; (Barrett) Lampmann interview. Also see Virgil Collins, interview by author, Laguna Hills, California, August 25, 1991; John Sheehy, interview by author, South Gate, California, June 21, 1990.

41. In 1932, the city was losing an average of $2,000 per month to operate the buses, and by 1933 they were abandoned. Thienes, "Contributions," 62, 67–68; *South Gate Press,* September 14, 1928; *South Gate Tribune,* August 22, 1930; South Gate City Council minutes, miscellaneous entries from 1925–1930, SGCH.

42. *South Gate Tribune,* August 22, 1930, November 6, 1925. In fact, the South Gate property tax rate still compared favorably against other L.A. suburbs of roughly the same class and stage in their development: Eagle Rock was $1.92, Highland Park was $1.63, San Pedro was $1.53 (*South Gate Tribune,* September 5, 1924).

43. Stephen Diamond, "The Death and Transfiguration of Benefit Taxation: Special Assessments in Nineteenth-Century America," *Journal of Legal Studies* 12 (1983): 201.

44. *South Gate City Directories* for 1926, 1929, 1930, 1940; *South Gate Tribune,* April 17, May 23, 1924; *Huntington Park Daily Signal,* January 19, 1973.

45. Dana Leventhal, "Public Art and Urban Identity in 1920s Los Angeles" (unpublished seminar paper UCLA, 1991, in author's possession), 9; William H. Wilson, *The City Beautiful Movement* (Baltimore: Johns Hopkins University Press, 1989); *South Gate Tribune,* May 8, 15, 1925.

Illustrating the popularity of ornamental street lights, the Los Angeles Municipal Art Commission approved more money for ornamental lights in 1924–25 and 1927–28 than for any other project (Leventhal, 12).

46. *South Gate Tribune,* July 3, 1925.

47. *South Gate Tribune,* July 17, 31, 1925; *City Directory of South Gate, 1926.* The recall petitioners attested in affidavits that they believed from 60 to 80 percent of local residents opposed the lights.

In an editorial on July 17, 1925, the *South Gate Tribune*, which had supported the lights all along, blamed the conflict on outside influences. The editor claimed that one of the companies that lost out in bidding for the job spread propaganda to discourage any lighting at all. This explanation seemed an easy way to avoid the specter of real internal conflict in South Gate, which was anathema to boosterism.

48.   The nominative plaintiffs in these suits were a building contractor, a carpenter, and a fruit wholesaler. The technicality was that the recall petitions should have stated that the circulator "saw written the signatures appended to the petition"; however, the word "written" was omitted. Because of this, the judge declared the petitions invalid.

49.   *South Gate Tribune*, July 31, September 25, October 16, November 6, 13, December 4, 18, 1925.

50.   In 1929, this would have brought approximately $10,500 to the Chamber of Commerce.

51.   Law, "South Gate Chamber of Commerce," 55; *South Gate Tribune*, December 4, 1925, February 26, August 27, 1929; *South Gate Press*, August 10, November 30, 1928, March 1, August 30, 1929.

52.   Robin Einhorn, *Property Rules: Political Economy in Chicago, 1833–1872* (Chicago: University of Chicago Press, 1991); Elizabeth Blackmar, *Manhattan for Rent, 1785–1850* (Ithaca: Cornell University Press, 1989); Jon C. Teaford, *The Unheralded Triumph: City Government in America, 1870–1900* (Baltimore: Johns Hopkins University Press, 1984); Terrence J. McDonald, *The Parameters of Urban Fiscal Policy: Socioeconomic Change and Political Culture in San Francisco, 1860–1906* (Berkeley and Los Angeles: University of California Press, 1986).

53.   An excellent historical treatment of special assessments is in Einhorn, *Property Rules*, and see pp. 17–18, 83–84 for definitions. Also see Diamond, "Death and Transfiguration," 201–240; and for the 1930s, Robert Phillip Hackett, "The Problem of Special Assessments," *National Municipal Review* 23 (1934): 466–470.

54.   The issue of consent is brought out in Thienes, "Contributions," 80, and Lange and Miller, *Study and Analysis of the Economic Status and Condition of Ad Valorem Assessment Districts in the County of Los Angeles, California* (Los Angeles, 1933), 19–21.

55.   *Los Angeles Reporter*, December 11, 18, 1925, January 1, November 13, 1926 (*Reporter* is from "California Scrapbook," vol. 1, Los Angeles Public Library); John Sheehy, interview by author, South Gate, California, June 19, 1990; Thienes, "Contributions," 65–66, 77–80; *Los Angeles Times*, June 25, 1925.

56.   On Progressivism in California, see George Mowry, *The California Progressives* (Berkeley and Los Angeles: University of California Press, 1951); William Deverell and Tom Sitton, eds., *California Progressivism Revisited* (Berkeley and Los Angeles: University of California Press, 1994); and Kevin Starr, *Inventing the Dream: California through the Progressive Era* (New York: Oxford University Press, 1985), chapter 8.

57.   Frederick Law Olmsted Jr., Harland Bartholemew, and Charles Henry Cheney, *A Major Traffic Street Plan for Los Angeles* (Los Angeles Traffic Commission, 1924); Scott Bottles, *Los Angeles and the Automobile: The Making of the Modern City* (Berkeley and Los Angeles: University of California Press, 1987), 111–113; Fogelson, *Fragmented Metropolis*, 250–251; *Los Angeles Times*, June 25, 1925; Thienes, "Contributions," 66; Robert Fishman, *Bourgeois Utopias: The Rise and Fall of Suburbia* (New York: Basic Books, 1987), 161–166. Neither Bottles nor Fogelson mentioned the Mattoon Act as the mechanism through which the plan was financed.

Once the Mattoon Act became law, a $5 million bond issue to finance the Traffic Plan was put to a vote. It was aggressively promoted by Los Angeles's civic elite, dominated by real estate interests, who favored automobile transportation since it ensured continued decentralization and development. Voters passed both the bonds and Traffic Plan by large majorities.

Matt Roth notes that the Mattoon Act seemed to occupy a midpoint between the traditional special assessment and the general property tax. According to the act's provisions, special assessment taxes funded the land acquisition, while general city taxes (presumably of all cities that fell in an assessment area) funded the construction work of an improvement. Thanks to Matt Roth for explaining this distinction. Also see Los Angeles City Engineer, *Annual Report, 1924–1925,* 81; Matt Roth, "Mulholland Highway and the Engineering Culture of Los Angeles in the 1920s," *Technology and Culture* 40 (July 1999): 545–575.

58.   *Los Angeles Times,* June 25, 1925; *Los Angeles Reporter,* December 11, 1925; *Home Gardens Press,* October 2, December 4, 1925, July 2, 1926, April 29, 1927, September 14, 1928.

59.   *South Gate Press,* December 7, 14, 21, 1928, April 19, 1929; *South Gate Tribune,* February 8, 1929; Thienes, "Contributions," 68, 79.

Also see South Gate City Council minutes, July 6, 1926, for an early reference to two Mattoon Act street improvements launched in 1926. The *Los Angeles Times* (January 2, 1929) reported that two South Gate projects completed in 1928 cost $625,000, and in early 1929 there were several projects underway costing $2 million.

60.   All subsequent figures refer to the tax rate per $100 valuation.

61.   The figure $5.18 is a very conservative estimate. It includes only about 33 percent of the *total* possible tax levy in these districts ($1.28 for the sewers and $3.90 for the street improvements). The sewer bond's tax levy ranged from $.01 to $3.89 per $100 valuation; the street bond tax ranged from $.01 to $11.82. Presumably, the rates could have gone much higher than my estimate; the *Tribune* was vague on exactly how these rates were calculated (*South Gate Tribune,* August 30, 1929).

62.   This is an estimated figure. The median home value in South Gate in 1930 was $4,264, according to the U.S. Census (*Fifteenth Census of United States, 1930: Population,* vol. 6, *Families* [Washington, D.C.: GPO, 1933], 183). And since "real estate taxes are assessed at about 50% of the 'true value' of the property," according to the HOLC in 1939, I used this guideline to estimate the "taxable" value of the typical South Gate home at $2,200. See Home Owners Loan Corporation, "Survey of Economic, Real Estate and Mortgage Finance Conditions in Metropolitan Los Angeles," HOLC Field Report, October 10, 1939, 22, Los Angeles City Survey files, RG 195, NA.

63.   National statistics show that the average earnings of a worker in manufacturing in 1929 was $1,543. See U.S. Bureau of the Census, *Historical Statistics of the United States from Colonial Times to 1970* (Washington, D.C.: GPO, 1975), 166. In 1927, the minimum annual income required to support a family of four in Los Angeles was $1,470. See Florence Nesbitt, "Study of a Minimum Standard of Living for Dependent Families in Los Angeles" (Los Angeles, November 1927), Haynes Collection, YRL-UCLA.

64.   Lange and Miller, *Analysis of the Economic Status,* 13, 23–25 (quote at 25); *Financial Statistics of State and Local Governments, California, 1932,* 16–17, 30–31, YRL-UCLA; HOLC, "Survey of Economic, Real Estate," 22, RG 195, NA; George M. Adams to John Anson Ford, September 9, 1939, John Anson Ford "Radio Address, KMTR," February 19, 1937, and John Anson Ford "Radio Address, KFVD," May 28, 1938, JAF.

Matt Roth points out that other cases of road development in Los Angeles, such as Olympic Blvd., used Mattoon Act funding but avoided these problems.

65.   *South Gate Press,* March 29, April 26, 1929; *South Gate Tribune,* April 26, 30, May 7, 10, June 16, 1929.

66. The minimum number of signatures required to call an election was 673; by late December 1929, they had collected slightly over this amount. When the council tried to delay the recall through legal action, Moffatt successfully counteracted.

67. *South Gate Tribune*, December 10, 1929, January 21, February 14, 28, July 1, 1930; *South Gate Press*, December 13, 31, 1929; *Huntington Park Signal*, January 11, 1946.

68. *South Gate Tribune*, April 11, 15, July 1, 1930. Also see April 1930 issues of the *South Gate Tribune*.

69. Moffatt went on to become a judge, sympathetic to labor and hostile to large property owners.

70. *South Gate Press*, August 2, 1929.

71. A similar interpretation of "tax fights" is made in Clarence Y. H. Lo, *Small Property versus Big Government: Social Origins of the Property Tax Revolt* (Berkeley and Los Angeles: University of California Press, 1990); and Mike Davis, *City of Quartz* (London: Verso Press, 1991). Davis, however, characterizes the class and motives of homeowners differently.

72. See Christopher Lasch, *The True and Only Heaven: Progress and Its Critics* (New York: W.W. Norton, 1991).

73. *South Gate Tribune*, March 19, 1929; *Los Angeles Times*, November 18, 1928. Rental figures were determined from an analysis of the *City Directory of South Gate, 1926*, and *City Directory of South Gate, 1929*.

The 9 percent figure includes only tenants who were *not* related to the homeowner.

74. *South Gate Press*, June 14, 21, 1929. On the public perception of renters' marginality in civic life, see Constance Perin, *Everything in Its Place: Social Order and Land Use in America* (Princeton, N.J.: Princeton University Press, 1977), chapter 2. Adame Krooke was not listed in the city directories of this period.

75. *South Gate Tribune*, May 2, June 3, 17, 20, July 1, 25, August 22, September 19, October 17, 1930, June 8, April 2, May 5, 1932; *South Gate Press*, January 23, September 18, March 20, August 21, 1931; George Baumgardner, "How South Gate Is Re-Lighting City Streets on Assessment Basis," *Western City* 15 (July 1939): 36.

76. South Gate appeared to have invoked the Mattoon Act especially often. One sign of this was that, of all cities in California with populations between 8,000 to 30,000, South Gate collected the largest proportion of its tax revenue from special assessments (59.4 percent) during the early 1930s.

77. *Financial Statistics of State and Local Governments, California, 1932*, 16–17, 30–31; Lange and Miller, *Analysis of the Economic Status*, 13, 23.

78. Thienes, "Contributions," 79, 92; *South Gate Press*, February 10, July 14, 1938, February 5, 1942 (contains statistics on delinquency rates); HOLC, "Survey of Economic, Real Estate," 22, RG 195, NA; Federal Housing Administration, "Housing Market Analysis, Los Angeles, California. Vol. 1, Part II" (Federal Housing Administration, Division of Economics and Statistics, December 1, 1937), 420, 431, 494.

In L.A. County in 1938, 280,000 parcels of land carried liens for delinquent taxes, and approximately 100,000 of these had reverted to the state. See "Report 1937/38 of County Assessor to County Board of Supervisors," October 1, 1938, YRL-UCLA.

No readily available data exists on the number of South Gate properties that reverted to the state.

79. The 1935 figure is from a building survey of South Gate and Walnut Park, reported in *South Gate Press*, March 1, 1935.

80. The local vacancy rate was 9.5 percent in 1926, 9.1 percent in 1930, and 4.8 percent in

1932. The 1926 and 1929 rates were computed from city directories; the 1932 rate from *South Gate Tribune*, April 1, 1932.

81.   *South Gate Tribune*, March 27, 1931; *South Gate Press*, November 6, 1931.

82.   *Los Angeles Times*, May 29, 1931, June 30, July 15, August 28, 1932, January 4, 1933; Thienes, "Contributions," 83. On the California Tax Reduction Club, see "Tax Reduction Club" booklet No. 11 (1932) (JK8 795), YRL-UCLA.

83.   The more important of these was the Debt Limitation Law, which the state legislature passed in 1931. See Thienes, "Contributions," 82–83.

84.   *The Property Owner* 2 (March 1934): 4, 10.

85.   David T. Beito, *Taxpayers in Revolt: Tax Resistance During the Great Depression* (Chapel Hill: University of North Carolina Press, 1989), 6; Harris, *Unplanned Suburbs*, 236–237.

86.   The Municipal Debt Adjustment Act was originally proposed as a conservative solution to the boom-and-bust problem in many small Florida cities during the 1920s and 1930s. The Florida situation resembled Los Angeles, which was in a similar developmental stage. Mark Gelfand, *A Nation of Cities: The Federal Government and Urban America, 1933–1965* (New York: Oxford, 1975), 50.

87.   Gelfand, *Nation of Cities*, 49–51; Thienes, "Contributions," 83–84. Also see *South Gate Tribune*, February 8, 22, April 12, 19, 1935; *South Gate Press*, January 29, April 23, 1935.

88.   Beito, *Taxpayers in Revolt*, xii, 6.

89.   "Annual Report of the Los Angeles City Engineer," 1931–32, Los Angeles City Archives, chapter 6, p. 4; Thienes, "Contributions," 82–84, 86; *South Gate Tribune*, February 8, 22, April 12, 19, 1935; *South Gate Press*, January 29, April 23, 1935. The California State Assembly gutted the Mattoon Act in the Special Assessment Investigation, Limitation and Majority Protest Act of 1931. Thanks to Matt Roth for pointing this out. Apparently, a California district court declared the 1935 state law unconstitutional, before the more important Florida decision (see South Gate field notes, Box 160, FWP).

90.   *South Gate Press*, January 19, 1983; Sheehy interview, June 19, 1990.

91.   Pomeroy accused the sitting administration of "well organized lawlessness," and of running a police department that promoted "gangster activity," bootlegging, and the "protection of vice." While the charges of municipal corruption had some basis in fact, Pomeroy misidentified its sources. The previous administration (1930–32) had actually commenced efforts to *clean up* local graft, suggesting the illegalities had begun during the 1920s boom. In 1929 the police chief was indicted for grand theft and embezzlement of city funds, while in early 1930, just as the Cooperative League administration took office, another police chief was charged with two counts of grand theft.

92.   *South Gate Tribune*, August 6, December 6, 13, 1929, June 20, 1930, June 28, 29, July 6, 11, 18, 28, 30, 1932; Clarence E. Miller, "A Study of Certain Community Forces of South Gate, California, in Their Relation to Character Education" (M. Theology thesis, University of Southern California, 1935), 26–27. See city ordinance nos. 221, 222, 223, 240, 263, and 264, SGCH.

93.   Thienes, "Contributions," 86. Thienes is unclear on the actual provisions and fate of their state bills. Also see *South Gate Press*, April 30, May 7, 14, June 11, 1935; *South Gate Tribune*, April 4, 1938, July 9, 1935.

94.   Thienes, "Contributions," 87.

95.   *South Gate Press*, March 31, April 7, 14, 1938; *South Gate Tribune*, April 4, 11, 1938; Miller, "Community Forces," 134.

96.   *South Gate Press*, April 28, May 5, 12, 19, 1938; *South Gate Tribune*, May 9, 16, June 27, July 4, August 25, September 12, 1938; Thienes, "Contributions," 88–93. See *South Gate Press*, April 28, 1938, and May 1938 for extensive coverage of the "Kill the Mattoon Act" campaign.

97.   *Los Angeles Times*, August 15, 1950; Bicentennial Heritage Committee, *South Gate, 1776–1976* (South Gate: South Gate Press, 1976), 23; "Post-War Building Program for City of South Gate," *Architect and Engineer* (May 1944): 33–36.

98.   Lawrence B. DeGraaf, "The City of Black Angels: Emergence of the Los Angeles Ghetto, 1890–1930," *Pacific Historical Review* 39 (1970): 323–352, quote at 329; Lonnie G. Bunch, "A Past Not Necessarily Prologue: The Afro-American in Los Angeles," in *20th Century Los Angeles: Power, Promotion, and Social Conflict*, Norman M. Klein and Martin J. Schiesl, eds. (Claremont: Regina Books, 1993); Raphael J. Sonenshein, *Politics in Black and White: Race and Power in Los Angeles* (Princeton: Princeton University Press, 1993), 21–28. Bunch refers to the "Golden Era."

99.   See especially Davis, *City of Quartz*, chapter 3; Norman M. Klein, *The History of Forgetting: Los Angeles and the Erasure of Memory* (London: Verso, 1997); Phoebe Kropp, "All Our Yesterdays: The Spanish Fantasy Past and the Politics of Public Memory in Southern California, 1884–1939" (Ph.D. dissertation, U.C. San Diego, 1999); Clark Davis, *Company Men: White-Collar Life and Corporate Cultures in Los Angeles, 1892–1941* (Baltimore: Johns Hopkins University Press, 2000).

100.   Patricia Rae Adler, "Watts: From Suburb to Black Ghetto" (Ph.D. dissertation, University of Southern California, 1977); MaryEllen Bell Ray, *The City of Watts, California, 1907 to 1926* (Los Angeles: Rising Publishing, 1985); Clara G. Smith, "Development of the Mexican People in the Community of Watts, California" (M.A. thesis, University of Southern California, 1933); Becky M. Nicolaides, "'Where the Working Man Is Welcomed': Working-Class Suburbs in Los Angeles, 1900–1940," *Pacific Historical Review* 68 (November 1999): 517–559. In 1920 in Watts, native-born whites constituted 63.4 percent of the population, immigrants 21.3 percent, and blacks 14.4 percent.

101.   Bicentennial Heritage Committee, *South Gate, 1776–1976*, 29–31; "Race Restrictions in South Gate," Thienes book notes, March 7, 1941, Box 160, FWP; *South Gate Press*, June 28, 1929, March 3, 1938; *South Gate Police Annual, 1927*, 11. For reports on black residential exclusion, see *Home Gardens Press*, January 6, 1928; *South Gate Press*, September 28, 1928, June 28, 1929, February 6, 1931.

102.   Mike Davis, "Sunshine and the Open Shop: Ford and Darwin in 1920s Los Angeles," *Antipode* 29 (1997): 377; Charlotta A. Bass, *Forty Years: Memoirs from the Pages of a Newspaper* (Los Angeles: Charlotta A. Bass, 1960), 95–113.

103.   Bunch, "Past Not Necessarily Prologue," 105–106, 113–114; James M. Ervin, "The Participation of the Negro in the Community Life of Los Angeles" (M.A. thesis, University of Southern California, 1931), 44; *South Gate Tribune*, October 31, 1930 (from Thienes field notes, Box 160, FWP); Douglas Flamming, "African-Americans and the Politics of Race in Progressive-Era Los Angeles," in *California Progressivism Revisited*, Deverell and Sitton, eds., 214–215; "First Baptist Church" program, approx. 1936, scrapbook, First Baptist Church of South Gate; *South Gate Tribune*, December 4, 18, 1925, April 23, February 26, 1932; *South Gate Press*, March 1, 1929; *Home Gardens Press*, May 29, 1925; "The Race Problem at Swimming Pools," *American City* 47 (August 1932): 76–77.

104.   Douglas Flamming, "African Americans and the Making of Los Angeles, 1890–1940" (unpublished paper presented at the Scholars & Seminars Program, Getty Research Institute, April 30, 1997). For more evidence on the permeability of racial lines in interwar Los

Angeles, see Josh Sides, "Working Away: African American Migration and Community in Los Angeles from the Great Depression to 1954" (Ph.D. dissertation, UCLA, 1999).

One piece of local evidence also points to positive relations between whites and Japanese during the 1930s, bolstered by Japanese support of white cooperatives. As a sociologist studying a Compton cooperative observed, "Not only have the unemployed helped themselves; they have been generously helped by Japanese. The [co-op] unit members are so heartily in favor of the Japanese that they have done much to destroy the racial antipathies formerly existing." Roth, "Compton Unemployed," 171.

105.   Irving G. Hendrick, *The Education of Non-Whites in California, 1849–1970* (San Francisco: R & E Research Associates, 1977), 90–94. Hendrick noted that while the board's position was to reject overt demands of segregation, it ultimately supported segregation in "a relatively subtle and less flamboyant manner" (91).

106.   Huntington Park was wealthier than South Gate, evident in median home values for 1930: $6,302 in Huntington Park compared to $4,264 in South Gate. U.S. Bureau of the Census, *Fifteenth Census of United States, 1930: Population,* vol. 6, *Families,* 182–183.

107.   *Home Gardens Booster,* July 25, 1924.

108.   Ibid.; *South Gate Tribune,* August 29, October 10, 1924; *Home Gardens Weekly,* October 3, 10, 17, 1924.

109.   Mark Keppel devoted much of his career to fighting economic inequality in the California schools. For example, he pushed through a state constitutional amendment that more equitably distributed state and county funds among school districts. See Raymond S. Luttrell, "Mark Keppel: His Life and Educational Career" (Ed.D. dissertation, UCLA, 1951), 79, 257–258; "Mark Keppel's Masterpiece," *Journal of Education* 103 (February 11, 1926): 147–148.

Keppel's overall policies obliquely suggest he favored racial integration. One tribute referred to him as a "man of the people" and "Lincolnesque" (*Overland Monthly,* August 1928, p. 289). More research is needed on Keppel's role in the racial integration of L.A. schools during the 1920s.

110.   *Home Gardens Press,* January 23, 30, February 6, August 7, 1925.

111.   *Home Gardens Press,* August 7, October 2, December 11, 1925, January 29, February 5, 1926.

112.   George Byington to Board of Supervisors, January 25, 1926, Earl Fike to Board of Supervisors, n.d., Home Gardens Community Church resolution to Board of Supervisors, January 24, 1926, all in Huntington Park City School District file, LACBSA.

113.   *Home Gardens Press,* January 29, 30, 1926.

114.   *Los Angeles Evening Express,* February 2, 1926; *Home Gardens Press,* February 5, 1926; Judith Rosenberg Raftery, "The Invention of Modern Urban Schooling: Los Angeles, 1885–1941" (Ph.D. dissertation, UCLA, 1984); Hendrick, *Education of Non-Whites,* 87–90. The *Evening Express* article referred to the petitioners as residents of Watts, which most likely was an error. The supervisors' hearing on this date was clearly on the Home Gardens petition. See L.A. County Board of Supervisors minutes, February 1, 1926, 198, LACBSA.

115.   Thomas Carter to Board of Supervisors, March 13, 1926, Eva Carter Buckner to Board of Supervisors of Los Angeles County, February 7, 1926, Mrs. A. Whyte to Board of Supervisors, February 2, 1926, all in Huntington Park School District file, LACBSA.

116.   *Huntington Park Signal,* March 2, 13, 20, 22, 27, 1926; *Home Gardens Press,* March 19, 1926.

117.   *Home Gardens Press,* March 26, 1926. There is some disagreement among historians about the reasons Watts consolidated with Los Angeles, although none of them mention the

school issue. Adler cited water rights as the key issue, and Ray cited lower costs for improvements and municipal services. DeGraaf, citing Robert Conot, claims that the local KKK instigated the consolidation to avoid the specter of black rule in Watts, since the black population was increasing at that time. Adler argues that the local KKK was *against* consolidation, however, fearing higher taxes. See Adler, "Watts," 199; Ray, *City of Watts*, 69–71; DeGraaf, "City of Black Angels," 347.

The land under Jordan School was officially annexed to Watts (i.e., L.A. city) in December 1944. See Bureau of Engineers, City of Los Angeles, "Annexation and Detachment Map" (Sept. 1979), Los Angeles City Archives.

118.   *Home Gardens Press*, April 2, 6, 1926; *Huntington Park Signal*, March 22, 30, 1926.

119.   *Huntington Park Signal*, April 3, 1926; *Home Gardens Press*, April 23, 1926; *City Directory of South Gate, 1930; South Gate City Directory, 1940*.

120.   *Home Gardens Press*, April 30, 1926.

121.   Glenn T. Seaborg, "Journal of Glenn T. Seaborg, January 1, 1927 to August 10, 1934," unpublished typewritten manuscript in author's possession; Glenn T. Seaborg, telephone interview by author, July 25, 1990; Melvin Gerald Shahan, interview by Jackie Malone, October 29 and December 7, 1976, Oral History 1556, p. 34, FOH; *"The Johi" Yearbook* (Los Angeles: Students of David Starr Jordan High School, 1932), Jordan High School, Watts.

122.   *Home Gardens Press*, April 30, June 11, 1926; on KKK activity, see *Home Gardens Booster*, May 16, 23, July 25, 1924; *South Gate Tribune*, March 6, May 1, 16, 23, 1924; Sheehy interview, June 19, 1990; Seaborg interview, August 17, 1990; Bass, *Forty Years*, 56–57. On the urban foundations of the KKK in the 1920s, see Kenneth T. Jackson, *The Ku Klux Klan in the City, 1915–1930* (New York: Oxford, 1967).

123.   Bicentennial Heritage Committee, *South Gate, 1776–1976*, 18.

124.   Members of the chamber school committee were businessmen and professionals, with the exception of one auto mechanic. People attending meetings on the school issue were described as city officials, educators, business leaders, and PTA leaders (*South Gate Tribune*, July 15, 1930).

125.   *South Gate Tribune*, July 1, 7, May 30, June 10, August 15, 1930.

126.   *South Gate Tribune*, May 30, June 10, August 15, 1930.

127.   A similar consolidation plan, patterned on the borough system of New York City, was proposed by South Gate realtor Sam Dudlext in 1925. However, it failed to gain support. See *South Gate Tribune*, December 19, 1924; *Home Gardens Press*, March 13, 27, June 12, 19, 26, 1925.

128.   *South Gate Tribune*, July 22, August 1, 5, 15, 1930, March 23, April 6, 7, 1931; *South Gate Press*, January 2, April 10, 1931.

129.   John Sheehy claimed that the impetus for Huntington Park to annex to the LAUSD was that Vernon had recently pulled out of the Huntington Park district, yanking away a substantial tax base in the process and leading to its near collapse. Sheehy interview, May 1, 1990; John Sheehy, interview by author, South Gate, California, June 26, 1990.

130.   *South Gate Tribune*, January 18, 1932; *Los Angeles Times*, January 19, 1932.

131.   Hendrick notes that the L.A. Board of Education ultimately promoted racial segregation in the area, in more subtle fashion than bowing to the racist demands of South Gate residents. As he notes, "[t]he segregation of Jordan was accomplished in stages," through the more quiet manipulation of school attendance areas. The results of this would become apparent by the postwar era (Hendrick, *Education of Non-Whites*, 92–94). Yet this tactic was never made public, nor was it perceived by residents as a solution to the school problem in the early 1930s; instead, the public discourse focused squarely on the tax issue.

132.   Lo, *Small Property versus Big Government*, 124.

133.   A good description of this ethos is in James Gregory, *American Exodus: The Dust Bowl Migration and Okie Culture in California* (New York: Oxford, 1989). This outlook set South Gate residents in direct contrast with their counterparts in Bobigny, France, who came to perceive of access to good infrastructure as a "right." Up to 1920, Bobigny residents faced similar conditions of underdeveloped public services, such as schools, street paving, sewers, electricity, and garbage collection. Yet their political response to these conditions was the stark opposite. They defined good public services as a *right* of all metropolitan citizens, to be enjoyed by everyone regardless of economic station. And these services, they believed, should be financed by the entire metropolitan populace. As a result, they agitated in favor of development and turned politically leftward in the process. They embraced the Communist Party as the best vehicle for bringing about the kind of redistributive metropolitan system that they envisioned. So while the working-class suburbanites of both Bobigny and South Gate politicized the neighborhood issue of development, they advocated very different solutions to the very same problems.
      The tenant status of Bobigny's residents undoubtedly shaped their political response. Property ownership was traditionally associated with wealth and capital, while tenancy was a symbol of proletarianization. The tenants of Bobigny, thus, could wage an argument for equitable distribution of municipal resources that logically employed a Communist critique of property, wealth, and capital. On these terms, they could support infrastructure development because its cost would fall on the backs of the propertied classes. See Tyler Stovall, *The Rise of the Paris Red Belt* (Berkeley and Los Angeles: University of California Press, 1990), part 2. And for another perspective, see James Holston, "Autoconstruction in Working-Class Brazil," *Cultural Anthropology* 6 (1991): 447–465.

134.   James Wunsch makes the perceptive point that while suburbs were differentiating into distinct communities of people sharing interests, and economic and social standing (as Harlan Paul Douglass had observed in the mid-1920s), this sorting out process had "unfortunate fiscal consequences." While the urban poor at least gained access to services through the city's broad tax base, "the poor suburb was obliged to provide service to its own needy population from the meager resources of a limited tax base." This balkanization tended to exacerbate economic injustice and inequity. James Wunsch, "The Suburban Cliché," *Journal of Social History* 28 (spring 1995): 655.

135.   James Gregory, "California's EPIC Turn: Upton Sinclair's 1934 Campaign and the Reorganization of California Politics" (unpublished paper delivered at the Los Angeles History Research Group, May 1995, Huntington Library, San Marino); Greg Mitchell, *The Campaign of the Century: Upton Sinclair's Race for Governor of California and the Birth of Media Politics* (New York: Random House, 1992).

136.   *South Gate Tribune*, November 28, December 19, 1924, March 8, 1929.

137.   U.S. Bureau of the Census, *Fifteenth Census of United States, 1930: Population*, vol. 6, *Families*, 183; *South Gate Tribune*, December 9, 1931; *South Gate Press*, February 13, 1931.

138.   *South Gate Tribune*, December 3, 5, 1931, January 24, February 24, March 9, 26, 28, 1932, August 15, 1938; *South Gate Press*, October 23, 1931; Cottrell, "South Gate History"; Miller, "Community Forces," 46, 60; Roth, "Compton Unemployed," 22; William H. Mullins, *The Depression and the Urban West Coast, 1929–1933: Los Angeles, San Francisco, Seattle and Portland* (Bloomington: Indiana University Press, 1991), 100. The difficulty of homeowners in securing county aid was confirmed in interviews Roth conducted with Compton co-op members (pp. 137–138).

139.   *South Gate Tribune*, February 6, 1932.

140.   *South Gate Tribune*, June 14, July 6, 1932, March 1, April 25, 1935, November 7, 1938; *South Gate Press*, April 2, 1935; Roth, "Compton Unemployed," 28.

141. Roth, "Compton Unemployed," 20, 26–27, 34.

142. Some homeowners allowed co-op members to move in for a few months, in exchange for repairing damage to their homes from the 1933 earthquake.

143. Roth, "Compton Unemployed," passim, quote at p. 157.

144. Ibid., 137–139, 141–142, 146–147.

145. Gregory, "California's EPIC Turn," 1–3; Upton Sinclair, *Immediate Epic* (Los Angeles: End Poverty League, 1934), 12–14.

146. Sinclair, *Immediate Epic,* 10, 12, 20–25; Alan Brinkley, *Voices of Protest* (New York: Vintage, 1982), 72.

147. McWilliams, *Southern California,* 293.

148. *South Gate Press,* April 30, 1935. On local EPIC activity, see *South Gate Tribune,* April 5, May 3, 10, June 7, August 23, 1935; *South Gate Press,* April 16, May 14, 1935.

149. At the state level, radical candidates for state assembly did slightly better in South Gate: in 1932, the Socialist candidate scored 6.1 percent of votes, while Communist candidates scored 2.7 and 3.6 percent in 1936 and 1940. This was miniscule compared to local support for Sinclair, which topped 61 percent.

150. Roth, "Compton Unemployed," 171–172.

151. General Election Voting Returns for Los Angeles, by precinct, California State Archives, Sacramento. On Shuler, see Bass, *Forty Years,* 55.

152. Thomas J. Sugrue, *The Origins of the Urban Crisis: Race and Inequality in Postwar Detroit* (Princeton: Princeton University Press, 1996), 58–59; Cohen, *Making a New Deal,* chapter 6. Cohen asserts that for workers in Chicago, welfare capitalism also fostered a sense of entitlement to certain rights. On the utilitarian support by the working class for the New Deal, see Jonathan Rieder, "The Rise of the 'Silent Majority,'" in *The Rise and Fall of the New Deal Order,* Steve Fraser and Gary Gerstle, eds. (Princeton: Princeton University Press, 1989), 245.

153. Donald F. Howard, *The WPA and Federal Relief Policy* (New York: Russell Sage Foundation, 1943), 397; *South Gate Press,* February 1, 1935, January 27, 1938; *South Gate Tribune,* May 5, 1932; U.S. Bureau of the Census, *Sixteenth Census of the United States, 1940: Population,* vol. 2, *Characteristics of the Population* (Washington, D.C.: GPO: 1943), 620. Thanks to Richard Lester for clarifying the relief situation in L.A. County.

154. Bicentennial Heritage Committee, *South Gate, 1776–1976,* 23.

155. Kenneth T. Jackson, "Race, Ethnicity, and Real Estate Appraisal," *Journal of Urban History* 6 (1980): 419–452; Tobey et al, "Moving Out," 1417.

156. FHA, "Housing Market Analysis," 420, 431, 494.

157. Home Owners Loan Corporation, "Special Comments and Explanation. Security Map and Area Descriptions. Metropolitan Los Angeles, California," p. 1, and City Survey Files for Los Angeles, both in RG 195, NA; C.W. Sirch, President West Eight Street Association, to Governor Culbert Olson, December 10, 1939, and John Anson Ford to C.W. Sirch, April 18, 1940, JAF.

158. John Anson Ford, "Radio Speech," December 15, 1939, JAF; City Survey Files for South Gate, RG 195, NA.

159. City Survey Files for South Gate, RG 195, NA; *South Gate Press,* March 21, 1938.

160. Sugrue, *The Origins of the Urban Crisis,* chapters 3 and 8; Cohen, *Making a New Deal,* chapter 6. Cohen argues that working-class people felt more justified in taking government relief than middle-class people, because the latter had "a greater orientation toward independence." In South Gate, however, the working class shared this orientation yet still felt justified.

161. To clarify how a community like South Gate, which was incubating blue-collar conservatism before the war, could support a program as radical as Upton Sinclair's EPIC, it helps to revisit the scholarly debate over the political meaning of EPIC. In simplest terms, the debate divides scholars who consider EPIC a fluke and those who see it as part of a longer political tradition in California. Carey McWilliams, one of the earliest scholars to weigh in, characterized support for EPIC as aberrant. He assumed that Sinclair's supporters were mainly "lower middle-class white-collar elements." Michael Rogin and John Shover reiterated this assumption more than twenty years later, writing, "In times of severe, tangible distress, when reality difficulties in the environment cannot be avoided, traditional right-wing constituencies have supported 'left-wing' movements. . . . This explains EPIC and the pension schemes in depression-ridden southern California. EPIC bordered on the panacea. . . . Moreover, southern California political leaders, left-wing under atypical depression conditions, moved right rather quickly." Sheridan Downey, Jack Tenney, Sam Yorty, and of course, Ronald Reagan were examples. Rogin and Shover, thus, did not characterize support for Sinclair as part of a genuine, long-lived liberal impulse, but rather as a right-wing impulse cloaked in leftist garments during the national emergency. By contrast, James Gregory considered EPIC's success to be "neither exotic nor inscrutable." He argued that EPIC's supporters were part of a "continuous pattern of urban liberalism" that had been evident "well before 1924" and would continue through the 1930s. "EPIC was supported by the same working-class base that had always underwritten urban liberalism." The main change wrought by the 1934 election was a shift in the regional base of liberalism in the state to L.A. County, whose dominance would continue to 1948. According to Gregory, Sinclair's success signified continuity more than fluke. McWilliams, *Southern California,* 297–299; Michael P. Rogin and John L. Shover, *Political Change in California: Critical Elections and Social Movements, 1890–1966* (Westport, Conn.: Greenwood Publishing, 1970), 211–212, n. 107; Gregory, "California's EPIC Turn," passim.

Chapter 5

1. Juanita (Smith) Hammon, interview by author, South Gate, California, July 5, 1990.

2. For an overview of American workers in the postwar years, see Robert Zeiger, *American Workers, American Unions,* 2nd ed. (Baltimore: Johns Hopkins University Press, 1994), chapters 5–6.

3. Kenneth T. Jackson, "Introduction: The Shape of Things to Come: Urban Growth in the South and West," in *Essays on Sunbelt Cities and Recent Urban America,* Raymond Mohl et al., eds. (College Station: Texas A & M University Press, 1990), 4.

4. "The Facts About Industrial Employment in Los Angeles County" in Los Angeles (County) Chamber of Commerce, Industrial Department, "Collection of Eight Studies on the Industrial Development of Los Angeles County" (Los Angeles: Los Angeles Chamber of Commerce, 1944), 3; James T. Lemon, *Liberal Dreams and Nature's Limits: Great Cities of North America Since 1600* (Toronto: Oxford, 1996), 197, 201; Greg Hise, "Home Building and Industrial Decentralization in Los Angeles: The Roots of the Postwar Urban Region," *Journal of Urban History* 19 (February 1993): 98–100.

5. Edward W. Soja, *Postmodern Geographies: The Reassertion of Space in Critical Social Theory* (London: Verso, 1989), 196.

6. Arthur C. Verge, "The Impact of the Second World War on Los Angeles, 1939–1945" (Ph.D. dissertation, University of Southern California, 1988), 209–211, 216–218; Los Angeles County Chamber of Commerce, Industrial Department, "Facts about Los Angeles County Industry" (Los Angeles County Board of Supervisors, 1947); Lemon, *Liberal Dreams,* 197–198. On Detroit, see Thomas J. Sugrue, *The Origins of the Urban Crisis: Race and Inequality in Postwar Detroit* (Princeton: Princeton University Press, 1996), chapter 5.

7.   Roger Lotchin, "California Cities and the Hurricane of Change: World War II in the San Francisco, Los Angeles, and San Diego Metropolitan Areas," *Pacific Historical Review* 63 (August 1994): 393–420. Also see Gerald Nash, *The American West Transformed: The Impact of the Second World War* (Bloomington: Indiana University Press, 1985); Gerald Nash, *World War II and the West: Reshaping the Economy* (Lincoln: University of Nebraska Press, 1990); Carl Abbott, *The New Urban America: Growth and Politics in Sunbelt Cities* (Chapel Hill: University of North Carolina Press, 1987), 17–19; Raymond A. Mohl, *The Making of Urban America* (Wilmington: Scholarly Resources, 1988), 189–198; Andrew Rolle, *California, A History,* fifth edition (Wheeling, Ill.: Harlan Davidson 1998), 269–270; David R. Goldfield and Blaine A. Brownell, *Urban America: A History,* 2nd ed. (Boston: Houghton Mifflin), 323; Jackson, "Introduction," 5.

8.   Arthur Verge makes a strong argument for World War II as a watershed for Los Angeles in *Paradise Transformed: Los Angeles During the Second World War* (Dubuque: Kendall/ Hunt Publishing, 1993).

9.   Ronald Tobey, Charles Wetherell, and Jay Brigham, "Moving Out and Settling In: Residential Mobility, Home Owning, and the Public Enframing of Citizenship, 1921–1950," *American Historical Review* 95 (December 1990): 1414; Gwendolyn Wright, *Building the Dream* (Cambridge: MIT Press, 1981), 242–243.

10.   HOLC refinancing was also widespread in Los Angeles. By 1939, the HOLC had refinanced 21 percent more homes in Los Angeles compared to the national average. See Home Owners Loan Corporation, "Survey of Economic, Real Estate and Mortgage Finance Conditions in Metropolitan Los Angeles," HOLC Field Report, October 10, 1939, p. 18, Los Angeles City Survey files, RG 195, NA.

11.   HOLC, "Survey of Economic . . . Conditions," 26; Glenn Beyer, *Housing and Society* (New York: Macmillan), 180, as quoted in Richard Harris, "It Flopped in Peoria: Lenders and Borrowers Resist the Federal Housing Administration, 1934–1950" (unpublished manuscript, 1995, in author's possession), 2; census data from James Gillies and Jay S. Berger, *Financing Homeownership: The Borrowers, the Lenders, and the Homes* (Los Angeles: Real Estate Research Program, Graduate School of Business Administration, UCLA, 1965), 14.

Harris notes that from 1945 to 1960 *nationally,* no more that 25 percent of new mortgages carried FHA insurance, which contradicts the census figures on *all* first mortgage loans. Gwendolyn Wright maintains that by 1957, the FHA had financed 4.5 million suburban homes, representing "about 30 percent of the new homes built in any one year." Wright, *Building the Dream,* 248.

12.   Kenneth T. Jackson, *Crabgrass Frontier: The Suburbanization of the United States* (New York: Oxford, 1985), 206–207; Greg Hise, *Magnetic Los Angeles: Planning the Twentieth-Century Metropolis* (Baltimore: Johns Hopkins University Press, 1997), 40–41, 133; Hise, "Home Building," 102–103.

13.   Richard Harris, "Pioneering the Jungle Suburbs: Owner-Building in North American Cities, 1900–1950" (unpublished manuscript, September 1991), 29–31; Los Angeles City Survey files, RG 195, NA; HOLC, "Survey of Economic . . . Conditions," 21; *South Gate Tribune,* March 21, 1938; Kenneth T. Jackson, "Race, Ethnicity, and Real Estate Appraisal: The Home Owners Loan Corporation and the Federal Housing Administration," *Journal of Urban History* 6 (1980): 447.

14.   HOLC, "Survey of Economic . . . Conditions," 21.

15.   In a fascinating study of Peoria, Illinois, Richard Harris found the persistence of owner-building at least through the early 1950s. This occurred in the context of intensive resistance to the FHA, spearheaded especially by savings and loan institutions that perceived FHA programs as favoring their competition: commercial banks. Harris identifies an important story

of resistance to the FHA, manifested in a spate of owner-building that was supported by the savings and loan associations, building supply dealers, a County Housing Authority, and most importantly individual owner-builders themselves. In Los Angeles, where federally insured mortgages were much more widespread, a different pattern was apparently in force, although more research is needed to confirm this. Harris, "It Flopped in Peoria," passim.

16.   Verge, *Paradise Transformed,* 109; Hise, *Magnetic Los Angeles,* 119–120, 132; *South Gate Press,* January 8, 1942, November 22, 1945.

17.   Hise, *Magnetic Los Angeles,* 132–149; Verge, *Paradise Transformed,* 110.

18.   One could argue that much of the black community resided in suburbanlike communities within L.A. city, dominated by detached single-family dwellings. So the urban-suburban dichotomy does not adequately describe the L.A. situation. Only a handful of outlying areas contained more than 1,000 blacks by 1950: Pasadena, Long Beach, Santa Monica, Compton, and Monrovia.

19.   Josh A. Sides, "Working Away: African American Migration and Community in Los Angeles from the Great Depression to 1954" (Ph.D. dissertation, UCLA, 1999), chapter 2; Lawrence B. De Graaf, "Negro Migration to Los Angeles, 1930 to 1950" (Ph.D. dissertation, UCLA, 1962), 186–187; Alonzo Smith and Quintard Taylor, "Racial Discrimination in the Workplace: A Study of Two West Coast Cities During the 1940s," *Journal of Ethnic Studies* 8 (spring 1980): 42; Aubrey B. Haines, "Words—And Deeds," *Frontier* 7 (August 1956): 11; Eshref Shevky and Marilyn Williams, *The Social Areas of Los Angeles: Analysis and Typology* (Berkeley and Los Angeles: University of California Press, 1949), 55; Charles B. Spaulding, "Housing Problems of Minority Groups in Los Angeles County," *Annals of the Academy of Political and Social Science* 248 (November 1946): 220–225; U.S. Bureau of the Census, *Seventeenth Census of the United States, Census of Population, 1950,* vol. 2, *Characteristics of the Population, Part 5* (Washington, D.C.: GPO, 1952), 5-163, 5-205; U.S. Bureau of the Census, *Eighteenth Census of the United States, Census of Population, 1960,* vol. 1, *Characteristics of the Population, Part 6* (Washington, D.C.: GPO, 1963), 6-136.

20.   Paul Bullock, "Watts: Before the Riot" in *Racism in California: A Reader in the History of Oppression,* Roger Daniels and Spencer C. Olin, Jr., eds. (New York: Macmillan, 1972), 284–286; Patricia Rae Adler, "Watts: From Suburb to Black Ghetto" (Ph.D. dissertation, University of Southern California, 1977), chapters 10–11; Lloyd H. Fisher, *The Problem of Violence: Observations on Race Conflict in Los Angeles* (American Council of Race Relations, Haynes Foundation, April 1947); 7, 10–11; Davis, *City of Quartz,* 164; Virgil Collins, interview by author, Laguna Hills, California, September 15, 1991; John Sheehy, interview by author, South Gate, California, June 21, 1990; *Los Angeles Examiner,* June 1, 1958.

21.   Jackson, "Race, Ethnicity, and Real Estate Appraisal," 422–436; Jackson, *Crabgrass Frontier,* chapters 11–12; Arnold Hirsch, "With or Without Jim Crow: Black Residential Segregation in the United States," in *Urban Policy in Twentieth-Century America,* Arnold R. Hirsch and Raymond A. Mohl, eds. (New Brunswick: Rutgers, 1993), 84–87.

22.   Residential Security Map of Metropolitan Los Angeles, California, 1939, U.S. Home Owners Loan Corporation, RG 195, NA. Also see Becky M. Nicolaides, "'Where the Working Man Is Welcomed': Working-Class Suburbs in Los Angeles, 1900–1940," *Pacific Historical Review* 68 (November 1999): 553–557.

23.   Los Angeles City Survey Files, 352, 354–5, 361, 383, 398, 405, RG 195, NA.

24.   *Los Angeles Herald Express,* June 9, 1961; U.S. Bureau of the Census, *Seventeenth Census of the United States, Census of Population, 1950,* vol. 2, *Characteristics of the Population, Part 5,* 5-107; U.S. Bureau of the Census, *Eighteenth Census of the United States, Census of Population, 1960,* vol. 1, *Characteristics of the Population, Part 6,* 6-282.

25.   By 1990, Latinos constituted 83.1 percent of South Gate's population. See the epilogue.

26.   U.S. Bureau of the Census, *Sixteenth Census of the United States, 1940: Population and Housing. Statistics for Census Tracts. Los Angeles-Long Beach, Calif.* (Washington, D.C.: GPO, 1942), 180–181; U.S. Bureau of the Census, *Seventeenth Census of the United States, Census of Population, 1950,* vol. 2, *Characteristics of the Population, Part 5,* 5-107 and *Census of Housing: 1950,* vol. 1, *General Characteristics, Part 2,* 5-48, 5-64; U.S. Bureau of the Census, *Eighteenth Census of the United States, Census of Population, 1960,* vol. 1, *Characteristics of the Population, Part 6,* 6-143.

27.   U.S. Bureau of the Census, *Eighteenth Census of the United States, Census of Population, 1960,* vol. 1, *Characteristics of the Population, Part 6,* 6-484, 6-485; U.S. Bureau of the Census, *Census of Population, 1970. General Social and Economic Characteristics, Part 6. California,* 6-372; D.J. Waldie, *Holy Land: A Suburban Memoir* (New York: St. Martin's Press, 1996), 162.

28.   U.S. Bureau of the Census, *Sixteenth Census of the United States, 1940: Population,* vol. 2, *Characteristics of the Population, Part 1* (Washington, D.C.: GPO, 1943), 612; U.S. Bureau of the Census, *Seventeenth Census of the United States, Census of Population, 1950,* vol. 2, *Characteristics of the Population, Part 5,* 5-94; U.S. Bureau of the Census, *Eighteenth Census of the United States, Census of Population, 1960,* vol. 1, *Characteristics of the Population, Part 6,* 6-59, 6-69, 6-120.

29.   U.S. Bureau of the Census, *Seventeenth Census of the United States, Census of Population, 1950,* vol. 2, *Characteristics of the Population, Part 5,* 5-104; U.S. Bureau of the Census, *Eighteenth Census of the United States, Census of Population, 1960,* vol. 1, *Characteristics of the Population, Part 6,* 6-143. The census did not collect data on family composition for South Gate in 1940.

30.   U.S. Bureau of the Census, *Seventeenth Census of the United States, Census of Population, 1950,* vol. 2, *Characteristics of the Population, Part 5,* 5-100, 5-104; U.S. Bureau of the Census, *Eighteenth Census of the United States, Census of Population, 1960,* vol. 1, *Characteristics of the Population, Part 6,* 6-297, 6-302. The L.A. rate was obtained by averaging the 1950 and 1960 rates, for the L.A. Standard Metropolitan Statistical Area.

31.   The rate was 26.5 percent in Los Angeles; 34.3 percent in San Diego; and 25.4 percent in San Francisco. U.S. Bureau of the Census, *Seventeenth Census of the United States, Census of Population, 1950,* vol. 2, *Characteristics of the Population, Part 5,* 5-96, 5-104.

32.   U.S. Bureau of the Census, *Eighteenth Census of the United States, Census of Population, 1960,* vol. 1, *Characteristics of the Population, Part 6,* 6-282.

33.   Hise, "Home Building," 112, 117; Waldie, *Holy Land,* 112.

34.   U.S. Bureau of the Census, *Sixteenth Census of the United States, 1940: Population,* vol. 2, *Characteristics of the Population,* 620; U.S. Bureau of the Census, *Seventeenth Census of the United States, Census of Population, 1950,* vol. 2, *Characteristics of Population, Part 5, California,* 5-124; U.S. Bureau of the Census, *Eighteenth Census of the United States, Census of Population, 1960,* vol. 1, *Characteristics of the Population, Part 6,* 6-342.

35.   *South Gate Press,* June 20, 1963; "Labor Market Developments Report for Los Angeles County, December 1942," and United States Employment Service, "Resurvey of Labor Market, Los Angeles, California, September 1942," p. 14, Los Angeles files, RG 183, NA; *South Gate Press,* February 12, 1942; Tom Thienes, "Contributions Toward the History of the City of South Gate, California" (unpublished manuscript for the Works Progress Administration, 1942, SGHWL), 123–140; South Gate Book field notes, FWP; U.S. Bureau of the Census, *County and City Data Book. 1949: A Statistical Abstract Supplement* (Washington, D.C.: GPO, 1952), 341;

South Gate City Directory, July 1951 (K.I. Strand & Dean S. Woodbury, 1951); U.S. Bureau of the Census, *United States Census of Manufactures 1954,* vol. 3, *Area Statistics* (Washington D.C.: GPO, 1956), 104-5 to 104-6; *South Gate "Blue Book" Criss Cross City Directory. 1961* (Anaheim, Calif.: Luskey Brothers & Co., 1961); South Gate Chamber of Commerce, "Standard Industrial Survey Report," (typewritten report, October 1970), SGHWL.

36.   On national trends, see Susan M. Hartmann, *The Home Front and Beyond: American Women in the 1940s* (Boston: Twayne Publishers, 1982); Sherna Berger Gluck, *Rosie the Riveter Revisited: Women, the War, and Social Change* (Boston: Twayne Publishers, 1987); William Chafe, *The American Woman: Her Changing Social, Economic, and Political Roles, 1920–1970* (New York: Oxford, 1972), 135–198; Elaine Tyler May, *Homeward Bound: American Families in the Cold War Era* (New York: Basic Books, 1988), 58–91.

37.   U.S. Bureau of the Census, *Historical Statistics of the United States, Colonial Times to 1970* (Washington D.C.: GPO, 1975), 139; U.S. Bureau of the Census, *Sixteenth Census of the United States, Census of Population, 1940: Characteristics of the Population, Part 1,* 620; U.S. Bureau of the Census, *Seventeenth Census of the United States, Census of Population, 1950,* vol. 2, *Characteristics of the Population, Part 5,* 5-124; U.S. Bureau of the Census, *Eighteenth Census of the United States, Census of Population, 1960,* vol. 1, *Characteristics of the Population, Part 6,* 6-302.

38.   U.S. Bureau of the Census, *Seventeenth Census of the United States, Census of Population, 1950,* vol. 2, *Characteristics of the Population, Part 5,* 5-466; U.S. Bureau of the Census, *Eighteenth Census of the United States, Census of Population, 1960,* vol. 1, *Characteristics of the Population, Part 6,* 6-293, 6-362.

39.   U.S. Bureau of the Census, *Seventeenth Census of the United States, Census of Population, 1950,* vol. 2, *Characteristics of Population, Part 5. California,* 5-466; U.S. Bureau of the Census, *Historical Statistics of U.S.,* 140; May, *Homeward Bound,* 76–77; Wright, *Building the Dream,* 256.

40.   Income rates for individuals had also risen in South Gate by 1950: in 1949, median income in South Gate was $2,632, higher than the averages for California ($2,184), Los Angeles ($2,243), and even San Francisco ($2,470). By 1960, these gains had leveled off; South Gate's mean income level reached parity with Los Angeles, at around $4,400. See U.S. Bureau of the Census, *Seventeenth Census of the United States, Census of Population, 1950,* vol. 2, *Characteristics of Population, Part 5, California,* 5-463 to 5-466; U.S. Bureau of the Census, *Eighteenth Census of the United States, Census of Population, 1960,* vol. 1, *Characteristics of the Population, Part 6,* 6-302, 6-362.

41.   Sheehy interview, June 21, 1990; U.S. Bureau of the Census, *Seventeenth Census of the United States, Census of the Population: 1950: Census Tract Statistics, Los Angeles, California and Adjacent Areas* (Washington, D.C.: GPO, 1952), 49; South Gate City Council minutes, June 2, 1965, SGCH.

42.   U.S. Bureau of the Census, *Fifteenth Census of the United States, 1930: Distribution,* vol. 1, *Retail Distribution, U.S. Summary* (Washington, D.C.: GPO, 1933), 90; U.S. Bureau of the Census, *United States Census of Business, 1948,* vol. 3, *Retail Trade—Area Statistics* (Washington D.C.: GPO, 1951), 4.13, 4.50; U.S. Bureau of the Census, *United States Census of Business: 1954,* vol. 2, *Retail Trade—Area Statistics* (Washington D.C.: GPO, 1956), 5-8, 5-68 to 5-69; U.S. Bureau of the Census, *United States Census of Business, 1954,* vol. 6, *Selected Service Trades—Area Statistics* (Washington D.C.: GPO, 1956), 5-8, 5-73; U.S. Bureau of the Census, *Census of Population, 1950,* vol. 2, *Characteristics of the Population, Part 5,* 5-18 to 5-20; South Gate City Council minutes, June 2, 1965, SGCH.

43.   Bicentennial Heritage Committee, *South Gate, 1776–1976* (South Gate: South Gate Press, 1976), 15; *South Gate City Directory, July 1951; Los Angeles Herald-Examiner,* June 5,

1947, January 15, 1948; John Sheehy, interview by author, South Gate, California, June 26, 1990.

44. U.S. Bureau of the Census, *United States Census of Business, 1954*, vol. 6, *Selected Service Trades—Area Statistics, Part 1*, 5-8, 5-73; *South Gate City Directory, July 1951*.

45. U.S. Bureau of the Census, *Census of Population, 1950*, vol. 2, *Characteristics of the Population, Part 5*, 5-18 to 5-20; U.S. Bureau of the Census, *United States Census of Business, 1954*, vol. 2, *Retail Trade—Area Statistics, Part 1*, 5-8.

46. "Housing Conditions Among Recipients of Old Age Security Living in Los Angeles County," Exhibit C-b, A Report . . . by Mrs. Hazel Olson, April 1950, Box 65, JAF.

47. *South Gate Press*, August 1, 1940 (from G. Weber field notes, Box 160, FWP); *South Gate Press*, March 18, 1943; Bicentennial Heritage Committee, *South Gate 1776–1976*, 23, 32; *South Gate Tribune*, February 21, 1938; "South Gate Guide—A City Evolves," FWP; U.S. Bureau of the Census, *Census of Housing, 1950*, vol. 1, *General Characteristics, Part 2*, 5-48; Los Angeles City Survey files, RG 195, NA; Division of Research and Statistics, Home Owners Loan Corporation, "Report of a Survey in Metropolitan Los Angeles, California," October 10, 1939, p. 56, RG 195, NA.

The first FHA housing units in South Gate sold for $3,900. The tight connection between the federal government and the suburb was symbolized in the appointment of Mayor George Baumgardner as chair of the FHA committee for South Gate.

48. Hise, *Magnetic Los Angeles*, passim; Los Angeles City Survey files, RG 195, NA; Sheehy interview, June 21, 1990; Marc Weiss, *The Rise of the Community Builders* (New York: Columbia University Press, 1987). On Meadow Park and South Gate Manor, see *South Gate Press*, May 8, 15, 1947. On other local large-scale developments, see *South Gate Press*, September 24, October 15, 1942, February 21, 28, March 28, 1946, February 6, 1947. But also see Harris, "It Flopped in Peoria."

49. U.S. Bureau of the Census, *Sixteenth Census of the United States, 1940: Housing*, vol. 2, *General Characteristics, Part 2* (Washington, D.C.: GPO, 1943), 312; U.S. Bureau of the Census, *Seventeenth Census of the United States, Census of Housing, 1950*, vol. 1, *General Characteristics, Part 2* (Washington, D.C.: GPO, 1953), 5-4; *South Gate Press*, January 8, 1942, January 6, 27, May 18, 1944.

The federal government contributed to this transition in a small way as well. Seeking to alleviate the massive housing shortage after the war, it converted eleven surplus buildings into fifty apartments, and moved them to a corner of the suburb's park. Fully 340 families applied for these fifty units. Bicentennial Heritage Committee, *South Gate 1776–1976*, 32; *South Gate Press*, April 4, May 2, 16, October 3, 1946.

50. U.S. Bureau of the Census, *Fifteenth Census of United States, 1930: Population*, vol. 6, *Families* (Washington, D.C.: GPO, 1933), 183; U.S. Bureau of the Census, *Sixteenth Census of the United States, 1940: Housing*, vol. 2, *General Characteristics, Part 2*, 293; U.S. Bureau of the Census, *Seventeenth Census of the United States, Census of Housing, 1950*, vol. 1, *General Characteristics, Part 2*, 5-4; Los Angeles City Survey files, RG 195, NA.

51. U.S. Bureau of the Census, *Seventeenth Census of the United States, Census of Population, 1950*, vol. 2, *Characteristics of the Population, Part 5*, 5-3.

In 1940, the mortgage rates were equally high in South Gate: 69 percent of owner-occupied units were mortgaged, suggesting the demise of owner-building even by this time. This figure probably represented the fallout of Mattoon Act defaults. U.S. Bureau of the Census, *Sixteenth Census of the United States, 1940: Housing*. vol. 1, *Data for Small Areas, Part 1* (Washington, D.C.: GPO, 1943), 142.

52. Taken from an analysis of 479 building permits along the same blocks (8100–8400,

9800–10400) of San Miguel Avenue in South Gate, from 1920 to 1965, SGCH (shown in table as a percentage of total for each decade).

Receiver of permit	1920s ($n = 84$)	1930s ($n = 113$)	1940s ($n = 87$)	1950s ($n = 113$)	1960s ($n = 82$)
Owner	26.2	6.2	24.1	14.2	14.6
Contractor	14.3	31.0	44.8	28.3	24.4
Specialized contractor	21.4	52.2	26.4	51.3	58.5
Not specified	38.1	10.6	4.6	6.2	2.4
Total	100	100	100	100	100

53.   *South Gate City Directory, July 1951;* Fred E. Case, *Cash Outlays and Economic Costs of Homeownership* (UCLA, Real Estate Research Program, Bureau of Business and Economic Research, 1957), 15, 17. On the importance of home improvements in Levittown, see Barbara Kelly, *Expanding the American Dream: Building and Rebuilding Levittown* (Albany: SUNY, 1993).

54.   Robert Marley Jordan, "A Comparative Study of the Organization, Function and Social Contributions of Selected Adult Secular Groups as Found in Bell Gardens in 1937–1938 and in 1946–1947" (M.A. thesis, University of Southern California, 1948), 72–75.

55.   Los Angeles City Survey files, RG 195, NA; Sheehy interview, June 21, 1990; *South Gate Press,* April 2, 1942.

56.   The *South Gate Press* reported in 1964 that the homeownership rate was about 80 percent in South Gate, but this does not correspond with U.S. Census statistics. *South Gate Press,* January 5, 1964.

57.   *Los Angeles Herald Express,* June 9, 1961; Gordon Whitnall and Associates, *Report on Proposed Comprehensive General Plan for South Gate, California* (unpublished report, 1959), 6, SGCH. An excellent treatment of the recent history of land economics, detailing increasing population density in suburbia and its consequences, is in Evan McKenzie, *Privatopia: Homeowner Associations and the Rise of Residential Private Government* (New Haven: Yale University Press, 1994), especially chapter 4.

58.   Fisher, *Problem of Violence,* 11–12.

59.   On race-restrictive covenants in Los Angeles, see de Graaf, "Negro Migration," 199–203; Haines, "Words—And Deeds," 12; Loren Miller, "Scotching Restrictive Covenants," in *Los Angeles: Biography of a City,* John and LaRee Caughey, eds. (Berkeley and Los Angeles: University of California Press, 1976), 388–391; Davis, *City of Quartz,* 160–164. Davis emphasizes the role of homeowners associations in enforcing exclusionary policies.

60.   This phrase was a veiled restatement of policy before *Shelley v. Kraemer.* Previously, Article 35 was unchanged except for this clause: " . . . use of property for occupancy by members of any race or nationality or any individual whose presence will be detrimental to the neighborhood."

61.   The description of this incident is in Ralph Guzman, "The Hand of Esau: Words Change, Practices Remain in Racial Covenants," *Frontier* 7 (June 1956): 13, 16. On similar practices nationally, see George Lipsitz, "The Possessive Investment in Whiteness: Racialized Social Democracy and the 'White' Problem in American Studies," *American Quarterly* 47 (September 1995): 369–387.

62.   *South Gate "Blue Book" Criss Cross City Directory, 1961.*

63.   Sanborn Map Company, "Insurance Maps of Los Angeles, California: Map of South Gate," vols. 28, 30–31 (Sanborn Map Company of New York, 1955).

64.   On the tenants of local motels, see Jim Crisp et al., "Evaluation and Summary of Planning Study, City of South Gate" (unpublished seminar paper, University of Southern California, May 1965), 27, Box 3, SGHWL.

Chapter 6

1.   *South Gate Press,* October 24, 1946.

2.   Kenneth T. Jackson, *Crabgrass Frontier: The Suburbanization of the United States* (New York: Oxford University Press, 1985), 238–245.

3.   Good overviews of the suburban myth are in J. John Palen, *The Suburbs* (New York: McGraw-Hill, 1995), chapter 6; Bennett M. Berger, "The Myth of Suburbia," *Journal of Social Issues* 17 (1961): 38–49; Scott Donaldson, *The Suburban Myth* (New York: Columbia University Press, 1969).

4.   Thomas Sugrue, "Reassessing the History of Postwar America," *Prospects* 20 (1995): 493–495; George Lipsitz, *Class and Culture in Cold War America: A Rainbow at Midnight,* 2nd ed. (Urbana: University of Illinois Press, 1994); Lary May, ed., *Recasting America: Culture and Politics in the Age of Cold War* (Chicago: University of Chicago Press, 1989), especially the essay by Warren Susman, with Edward Griffin, "Did Success Spoil the United States? Dual Representations in Postwar America."

5.   Bennett Berger, *Working Class Suburbs* (Berkeley and Los Angeles: University of California Press, 1960); William M. Dobriner, *Class in Suburbia* (Englewood Cliffs, N.J.: Prentice-Hall, 1963); Herbert Gans, *The Levittowners* (New York: Random House, 1967). Historians have been slower to produce detailed, systematic social histories of postwar suburbs, but see Rosalyn Baxandall and Elizabeth Ewen, *Picture Windows: How the Suburbs Happened* (New York: Basic Books, 2000), chapters 11–12; Barbara Kelly, *Expanding the American Dream: Building and Rebuilding Levittown* (Albany: SUNY Press, 1993); Zane Miller, *Suburb: Neighborhood and Community in Forest Park, Ohio, 1936–1976* (Knoxville: University of Tennessee Press, 1981); Allison Baker, "The Lakewood Story: Defending the Recreational Good Life in Postwar Southern California Suburbia, 1950–1999" (Ph.D. dissertation, University of Pennsylvania, 1999).

6.   *South Gate Press,* December 5, 19, 1946.

7.   Greg Hise, "Home Building and Industrial Decentralization in Los Angeles: The Roots of the Postwar Urban Region," *Journal of Urban History* 19 (February 1993): 98–100; Leonard Pitt and Dale Pitt, *Los Angeles A–Z* (Berkeley and Los Angeles: University of California Press, 1997), 403; *South Gate Press,* June 13, October 3, 1946; on "congested production area" designation, see Los Angeles Area Production Files, RG 212, NA; Josh A. Sides, "Working Away: African American Migration and Community in Los Angeles from the Great Depression to 1954" (Ph.D. dissertation, UCLA, 1999), chapter 2.

8.   *South Gate Press,* June 11, 1942, May 15, 1947.

9.   *South Gate Press,* October 3, 1946; "Live, Work, Play, Shop," pamphlet, City Planning file, SGHWL.

10.   *South Gate Press,* January 8, 1942, January 6, 27, May 18, 1944, November 22, 29, December 6, 1945.

11.   *South Gate Press,* March 5, 1942, March 18, 1943, September 13, 1945. On the local public housing project, see *South Gate Press,* March 28, April 4, May 2, 16, October 3, 1946.

Public housing has evolved through many stages, in its perceived purpose, its target "market," and in the philosophies of both supporters and detractors. By the war period, a key strain of thinking (among national leaders) continued to hold that public housing represented a waystation for the temporarily impoverished, who would ultimately end up as homeowners.

The wartime housing emergency bolstered this attitude. See Gwendolyn Wright, *Building the Dream: A Social History of Housing in America* (Cambridge: MIT Press, 1981), 220–233; J. Paul Mitchell, "Historical Overview of Direct Federal Housing Assistance," in *Federal Housing Policy and Programs: Past and Present,* J. Paul Mitchell, ed. (New Brunswick, N.J.: Center for Urban Policy Research, 1985), 187–206; Jon Teaford, *The Rough Road to Renaissance: Urban Revitalization in America* (Baltimore: Johns Hopkins University Press, 1990).

12.   *South Gate Press,* June 11, August 20, September 17, December 3, 1942, July 15, 1943, January 27, September 21, 1944; U.S. Bureau of the Census, *Sixteenth Census of the United States, 1940: Population,* vol. 2, *Characteristics of the Population* (Washington, D.C.: GPO, 1943), 617; U.S. Bureau of the Census, *Seventeenth Census of the United States, Census of Population, 1950,* vol. 2, *Characteristics of the Population, Part 5, California* (Washington, D.C.: GPO, 1952), 5-124; U.S. Bureau of the Census, *Eighteenth Census of the United States, Census of Population and Housing, 1960: Census Tracts, Los Angeles–Long Beach, Calif.* (Washington, D.C.: GPO, 1961), 520; South Gate City Council minutes, September 19, 1940, from George Weber, South Gate Book field notes, FWP.

13.   Roger Lotchin argues that the "renaissance of community" during the war was ephemeral at best, as part of his overall argument that World War II had a more "ambiguous" impact on California cities than previously assumed. Roger W. Lotchin, "California Cities and the Hurricane of Change: World War II in the San Francisco, Los Angeles, and San Diego Metropolitan Areas," *Pacific Historical Review* 63 (August 1994), 393–420.

14.   Bicentennial Heritage Committee, *South Gate 1776–1976* (South Gate: South Gate Press, 1976), 28; *Huntington Park Daily Signal,* January, 19, 1973; *South Gate Press,* July 23, 30, 1942, July 15, 1943, January 27, February 24, June 29, August 17, September 21, 1944, March 1, May 10, June 28, July 12, 1945, June 20, 1963; *South Gate City Directory, 1940* (K.I. Strand, 1940).

15.   *South Gate Press,* January 8, February 5, 26, March 5, 19, July 30, 1942, March 18, June 3, 10, November 11, 1943, April 13, 1944.

16.   Bicentennial Heritage Committee, *South Gate 1776–1976,* 34–36; *South Gate Press,* March 19, April 16, May 7, September 3, October 26, 1942, July 6, September 13, October 29, 1944, January 17, 1946.

17.   *South Gate Press,* September 3, 1942, June 29, 1944; Mary (DeVries) North, interview by author, South Gate, California, July 12, 1999; *South Gate City Directory, 1940.*

18.   For Los Angeles, the number was 43.6 percent; for the United States, it was approximately 35 percent. U.S. Bureau of the Census, *Eighteenth Census of the United States, Census of Population, 1960,* vol. 1, *Characteristics of the Population, Part 6, California* (Washington, D.C., GPO, 1963), 6-282; U.S. Bureau of the Census, *Statistical Abstract of the United States, 1965,* 86th ed. (Washington, D.C.: GPO, 1965), 24, 270.

19.   *South Gate Press,* December 17, 1942, May 10, 1945, January 17, 1946, February 7, 1957; Ray Markle, interview by Cecily Feltham, South Gate, California, August 24, 1998. Names of members culled from *South Gate Press,* February 24, 1944, December 6, 1945, March 21, April 4, June 13, July 11, 1946, October 7, 1954, May 24, 1956; occupations were culled from *South Gate City Directory, 1940,* and *South Gate City Directory, July 1951* (K.I. Strand & Dean S. Woodbury, 1951).

A 1998 South Gate American Legion membership list yielded a small sample of members who had lived in South Gate in the 1950s. The largest occupational category of this group was blue-collar, with proprietors second.

20.   *South Gate Press,* August 23, November 22, 1945, January 17, 24, February 7, 14, June 13, August 1, 1946, July 10, 1947; *People's World,* November 24, 1945.

21. Gary Gerstle, *Working-Class Americanism: The Politics of Labor in a Textile City, 1914–1960* (Cambridge: Cambridge University Press, 1989), chapters 9–10.

22. The Loyalty Day parade took place from 1955 to 1957. By 1959, the May 1 parade in South Gate had become the "Clean Up, Paint Up" parade, featuring the merchants' civic groups (*South Gate Press,* May 3, 1959).

23. *Los Angeles Herald Express,* April 29, 1957; *Los Angeles Examiner,* May 2, 1955; *South Gate Press,* March 14, 25, August 29, December 30, 1954, April 24, 28, 1955, April 29, October 14, 1956, March 24, April 25, May 2, September 1, 1957.

24. Sugrue, "Reassessing," summarizes this well.

25. Ibid.; Steve Fraser, "The 'Labor Question,'" and Nelson Lichtenstein, "From Corporatism to Collective Bargaining: Organized Labor and the Eclipse of Social Democracy in the Postwar Era," both in *The Rise and Fall of the New Deal Order, 1930–1980,* Steve Fraser and Gary Gerstle, eds. (Princeton: Princeton University Press, 1989); Michael Kazin, "Struggling with Class Struggle: Marxism and the Search for a Synthesis of U.S. Labor History," *Labor History* 28 (1987): 497–514; David Brody, *Workers in Industrial America: Essays on the 20th Century Struggle* (New York: Oxford University Press, 1980), 173–211; David Montgomery, *Workers' Control in America* (Cambridge: Cambridge University Press, 1979), 161–175.

In fact, this is a much more complex development than described here. Lichtenstein shows, for example, that in the *immediate* postwar era, American trade unions not only displayed an "extraordinary" union consciousness but also broadened their focus from the workplace to the political arena, where they would seek to shape "the overall political economy and expansion of the welfare state." Yet by the end of the 1945–46 GM strike, Lichtenstein notes, even this changed, reflecting the shift away from workers' control to workers' benefits: "social unionism gradually tied its fate more closely to that of industry and moved away from a strategy that sought to use union power to demand structural changes in the political economy. Instead the UAW worked toward negotiation of an increasingly privatized welfare program that eventually succeeded in providing economic security for employed autoworkers." Ultimately, the UAW moved away from workplace/industry control issues to a concern with economic growth and the expansion of the welfare state. See Lichtenstein, "From Corporatism," 125–133.

26. On industrial decline in the east during the 1950s, see Thomas J. Sugrue, *The Origins of the Urban Crisis: Race and Inequality in Postwar Detroit* (Princeton: Princeton University Press, 1996), chapter 5; Sugrue, "Reassessing"; James Green, *The World of the Worker: Labor in Twentieth Century America* (New York: Hill and Wang, 1980), 210–214. Sugrue makes the good point that Detroit's workers escaped the process of embourgeoisement, assumed by many contemporaries to have affected all workers of the period.

27. Louis Perry and Richard Perry, *A History of the Los Angeles Labor Movement* (Berkeley and Los Angeles: University of California Press, 1963), especially chapters 12 and 15.

28. In 1942 the city council allowed the planting of victory gardens on vacant lots. South Gate City Council minutes, April 6, 1942, SGCH; Bicentennial Heritage Committee, *South Gate 1776–1976,* 37.

29. *South Gate Press,* January 8, 22, March 12, April 23, June 11, 1942, March 18, April 1, 1943, May 4, June 29, 1944; John Sheehy, interview by author, South Gate, California, June 19, 1990.

30. Bicentennial Heritage Committee, *South Gate 1776–1976,* 26; *South Gate Press,* August 17, 1944, May 9, 1946, December 20, 27, 1951, April 11, June 20, August 15, 1954; South Gate City Ordinances Nos. 4, 86, 863, 1048, SGCH. Pet stores and veterinarians appeared for the first time in the 1951 city directory listing of businesses. D. J. Waldie confirmed the decline of backyard chicken coops in Lakewood after World War II. See Waldie, *Holy Land,* 103.

31.   Arthur Newton, *City Directory of South Gate, 1930* (South Gate: Tribune-News Publishing Co., 1930); *South Gate City Directory, July 1951*; Grace Elizabeth Dahle, "A Personnel Study of High School Pupils in an Industrial Community" (M.S. thesis, University of Southern California, 1945), 27–28; *South Gate Press*, June 10, 1954, June 20, 1963; Pamela (Lawton) James, interview by author, San Diego, California, June 16, 1999; Jackson, *Crabgrass Frontier*, 60. Dahle did not identify the community by name in her study but did so in a telephone conversation with the author.

32.   Kelly, *Expanding the American Dream*, 16–17.

33.   Regarding homeownership, the dichotomy between working- and middle-class suburb has been complicated in recent work by Margaret Marsh and Mary Corbin Sies. Both authors note lower percentages of suburban homeownership among the middle class, compared to the working class in the early twentieth century. Margaret Marsh, *Suburban Lives* (New Brunswick: Rutgers, 1990); Mary Corbin Sies, "North American Suburbs, 1880–1950: Cultural and Social Reconsiderations," *Journal of Urban History* 27 (March 2001): 313–346.

34.   Waldie, *Holy Land*, 112.

35.   See chapter 5; Virgil Collins, interview by author, Laguna Hills, California, September 15, 1991. Some of the upward drift in home values might have resulted from home renovations and improvements. Kelly sees ample evidence of this in Levittown by the 1960s, which she argues pulled up the collective status of that famous suburb. Kelly, *Expanding the American Dream*.

36.   *South Gate Press*, November 6, 1947, February 25, June 17, 1954, June 12, October 16, November 3, 1955, April 5, June 10, 1956, March 2, 1958.

37.   *South Gate City Directory, July 1951.*
Historically, chiropractic had strong connections to the working class in America, especially in terms of entry into the profession. This began to change by the 1910s, with the onset of professionalization. See Steven C. Martin, "Chiropractic and the Social Context of Medical Technology, 1895–1925," *Technology and Culture* 34 (1993): 808–834; J. Stuart Moore, *Chiropractic in America: The History of a Medical Alternative* (Baltimore: Johns Hopkins University Press, 1993), 42.

38.   Edward Greenspan, interview by author, South Gate, California, October 25, 1998; Dahle, "Personnel Study," 69; *South Gate Press*, June 20, 1963.

39.   *South Gate Press*, May 10, 1945, January 15, 1948, April 4, 7, 28, 1954; Collins interview, September 15, 1991.

40.   *South Gate City Directory, July 1951*. South Gate's share of liquor stores (per capita) fell in a mid-range among other suburbs around Los Angeles. The rate was comparable to Compton, Gardena, and Glendale, but less than Burbank, Culver City, Huntington Park, Inglewood, and Long Beach. U.S. Bureau of the Census, *United States Census of Business, 1948*, vol. 3, *Retail Trade—Area Statistics* (Washington, D.C.: GPO, 1951), 4.34–4.50.

41.   *South Gate City Directory, July 1951; South Gate Press*, February 5, March 5, 1942, June 3, 1943, December 27, 1953, December 30, 1954, June 1, 1958; *Los Angeles Herald Express*, December 30, 1960; *The Assembler*, December 2, 1947, ALUA; Virgil Collins, interview by author, Laguna Hills, California, August 25, 1991.

42.   Shirley Nauman, "A Follow-Up Study of the Business Education Graduates of South Gate High School, 1958–1960" (M.S. thesis, University of Southern California, 1962), 21–22; Waldie, *Holy Land*, 104.

43.   Handbill dated October 24, 1945, UAW216, ALUA.

44.   Nelson Lichtenstein, *Labor's War at Home: The C.I.O. in World War II* (Cambridge:

Cambridge University Press, 1982), 224–232; Brody, *Workers in Industrial America*, 173–211; Gene B. Tipton, "The Labor Movement in the Los Angeles Area During the 1940s" (Ph.D. dissertation, UCLA, 1953), 153–155; *Huntington Park Signal*, March 25, 1946; "Demands for Local Negotiations, Local 216 South Gate," November 1945, LC, ALUA; Collins interview, August 25, 1991.

45. Cleao Jones and Eugene Judd to local businessmen, January 11, 1946, LACFL.

46. "Clark Statement," no date, LC, ALUA. This document was identified by Virgil Collins during an oral history session. Clark was the man who threw the coins out to the children at the company picnic, in chapter 3.

47. For an expanded discussion of the consumer identity of autoworkers, see Ronald Edsforth, *Class Conflict and Cultural Consensus: The Making of a Mass Consumer Society in Flint, Michigan* (New Brunswick: Rutgers University Press, 1987).

48. Cleao Jones and Eugene Judd to local businessmen, January 11, 1946, LACFL.

49. Such appeals emphasizing the community welfare were hardly new. At least since the nineteenth century, striking workers often based appeals for public support on the idea that raising the standard of living for workers—through wage increases or simply the right to organize—would benefit the entire community. In Chicago during the 1904 meatpackers strike, for example, strikers argued that a decent wage for workers would eliminate many of the social problems of the city, such as overcrowding, poverty, and high mortality. The difference between these appeals and those of the postwar period was one of degree: earlier strikers sought to avoid poverty, while strikers in the mid-twentieth century sought a degree of affluence. On Chicago, see James R. Barrett, *Work and Community in the Jungle: Chicago's Packinghouse Workers, 1894–1922* (Urbana: University of Illinois Press, 1987), 168–171; Cohen, *Making a New Deal*. Also see Herbert Gutman, *Work, Culture, and Society in Industrializing America: Essays in Working Class and Social History* (New York: Random House, 1978).

50. Collins interview, August 25, 1991.

51. "Donations for Strike Fund," Correspondence files, 1945–1946, UAW Local 216 File 3–2, all in UAW216, ALUA; *People's Daily World*, November 29, 1945.

52. It is difficult to compare this figure to rates of business support for strikers in other cities, because historians of postwar labor generally ignore this issue. They concentrate more on strike negotiations at the national level, or on the workplace exclusively. For example, see Edsforth, *Class Conflict*, chapter 8; Gerstle, *Working-Class Americanism*; Nelson Lichtenstein, "Conflict over Workers' Control: The Automobile Industry in World War II," in *Working-Class America: Essays on Labor, Community, and American Society*, Michael Frisch and Daniel Walkowitz, eds. (Urbana: University of Illinois Press, 1983), 284–311.

53. Collins interview, August 25, 1991.

54. For example, see *South Gate Press*, November 29, 1945, February 14, March 7, 1946. In contrast, the more liberal editors of the *Huntington Park Signal* ran daily articles about the strike at the outset, then maintained regular coverage thereafter (*Huntington Park Signal*, November 1945 to March 1946).

55. "Credentials" letter, November 29, 1945, and "Donations, 1945–1946" receipt list, both in UAW216, ALUA; *People's Daily World*, November 27, 1945.

56. Local 216 was bold enough to ask for donations for the Christmas party from salaried employees and even management at GM.

57. "City Wide Strike Strategy Committee" minutes, February 18, 1946, File 10–23, "G.M. Strike Planning Committee, Los Angeles CIO" minutes, December 14, 1945, File 16–21, and "Citywide Strike Strategy Committee, 1946," File 10–11, all from LACFL; "Record of Donations, 1945" Box 3, and K. D. Brown to UAW Local 216, November 28, 1945, and Cleao Jones

and Eugene Judd to All Salaried Employees, GM South Gate, December 15, 1945, Correspondence file, all from UAW216, ALUA; *People's Daily World,* November 23, 24, 29, December 1, 1945.

By early 1946, the CIO's revamped Citywide Strike Strategy Committee served as a clearinghouse for donations for all CIO strikers in Los Angeles. In early 1946 they collected 7,000 cans of food, which were divided among strikers in different industries: 50 percent went to steelworkers, 25 percent to electrical workers, and 25 percent to GM workers.

58.   Evidently, a number of local volunteer women met their future husbands at Hospitality House. Many of these couples ended up settling in South Gate, the hometown of these women, after the war. *South Gate Press,* January 17, 1946.

59.   (DeVries) North interview.

60.   Elaine Tyler May, *Homeward Bound: American Families in the Cold War Era* (New York: Basic Books, 1988).

61.   *South Gate Press,* January 17, 1946, September 4, 1947, October 13, 1955, April 5, October 14, 1956, June 1, 1958; (DeVries) North interview. See Baker, "Lakewood Story," 137, for a description of the similar "Mrs. Lakewood" contest.

62.   Sociologist Scott Greer confirmed this for Los Angeles more broadly. In the 1950s, he studied a range of community types in L.A.—from urban to suburban, working-class to middle-class—and concluded that "the conjugal family is extremely powerful among all types of population. This small, primary group structure is the basic area of involvement." Not only did families spend the most time together at home in informal interaction, but they visited kin at least once a month. Although all social groups showed this proclivity, it was particularly strong in communities that were suburban and blue-collar. Scott Greer, *The Urbane View: Life and Politics in Metropolitan America* (New York: Oxford University Press, 1972), 41, 73.

63.   (Lawton) James interview.

64.   Markle interview, August 24, 1998; (DeVries) North interview; (Lawton) James interview. In her study of Lakewood, Allison Baker identified "recreational culture"—often linked with family togetherness—as key to community activity and identity in postwar suburbia. Baker, "Lakewood Story," passim.

65.   Markle interview, August 24, 1998; Ray Markle, telephone interview by author, October 8, 1999; (DeVries) North interview; (Lawton) James interview.

66.   On national trends, see Joanne Meyerowitz, ed., *Not June Cleaver: Women and Gender in Postwar America, 1945–1960* (Philadelphia: Temple University Press, 1994); Stephanie Coontz, *The Way We Never Were: American Families and the Nostalgia Trap* (New York: Basic Books, 1992); Susan J. Douglas, *Where the Girls Are: Growing Up Female with the Mass Media* (New York: Times Books, 1995).

67.   U.S. Bureau of the Census, *Eighteenth Census of the United States, Census of Population, 1960,* vol. 1, *Characteristics of the Population, Part 6,* 6-143; (Lawton) James interview. Barbara Kelly also found cases of three-generation households in postwar Levittown (Kelly, *Expanding the American Dream,* chapter 6).

68.   L.A. (County) Chamber of Commerce, "Facts about Industrial Employment in L.A. County," 8. Significantly, only 3 percent of "all war industry women" had done factory work before the war; most had worked previously as domestics, waitresses, clerks, and housewives.

69.   U.S. Bureau of the Census, *Eighteenth Census of the United States, Census of Population, 1960,* vol. 1, *Characteristics of the Population, Part 6, California,* 6-293, 6-302, 6-362; Nauman, "Follow-Up Study," 39, 41.

70.   Quoted in Baker, "Lakewood Story," 133. On postwar consumer culture, see May, ed., *Recasting America;* May, *Homeward Bound,* chapter 7; Roland Marchand, "Visions of Class-

lessness, Quests for Dominion: American Popular Culture, 1945–1960," in *Reshaping America: Society and Institutions, 1945–1960*, Robert H. Bremner and Gary W. Reichard, eds. (Columbus: Ohio State University Press, 1982); Karal Ann Marling, *As Seen on TV: The Visual Culture of Everyday Life in the 1950s* (Cambridge: Harvard University Press, 1994); Stuart Ewen and Elizabeth Ewen, *Channels of Desire: Mass Images and the Shaping of American Consciousness* (Minneapolis: University of Minnesota Press, 1992).

71.   John Sheehy, interview by author, South Gate, California, June 26, 1990; (Lawton) James interview. For similar evidence on Lakewood, see Baker, "Lakewood Story," 79–80, 148; Waldie, *Holy Land*, 102.

72.   *Los Angeles Herald Examiner*, March 10, 1955; U.S. Bureau of the Census, *Seventeenth Census of the United States, Census of Population, 1950*, vol. 2, *Characteristics of Population, Part 5, California*, 5-104; May, *Homeward Bound*, 8. The rate for South Gate was determined by using 850 divorces (for a twelve-month period) against the number of married females in South Gate in 1950 (14,655).

The pattern of rising divorces contradicted the findings of one sociological study conducted in 1954, which concluded that working-class families valued family cohesion over occupational mobility to a greater extent than middle-class families. Leonard Reissman, "Class, Leisure, and Social Participation," *American Sociological Review* (February 1954): 76–84.

73.   *Los Angeles Examiner*, March 10, 1955; *Los Angeles Herald Express*, March 11, 1955; *South Gate Press*, March 10, 1955.

74.   The best journey-to-work data for South Gate women was from a 1961 study that tracked graduates of the high school's "business program." Although 96 percent worked within a ten-mile radius of South Gate, only 18 percent worked in South Gate. The rest worked in Los Angeles or other suburbs around the area. Female factory workers likely shared similar commuting patterns, finding jobs in the industrial suburbs around South Gate. Nauman, "Follow-Up Study," 50.

75.   Untitled study of Los Angeles, Bureau of Employment Security, Labor Market Survey Reports, 1943 (?), Los Angeles files, RG 183, NA; Federal Regional Advisory Council, "Monthly Report on Region XII," October 1, 1943, Region XII files, RG 183, NA; *South Gate Press*, June 11, August 20, 1942.

76.   *South Gate City Directory, July 1951; South Gate City Directory, July 1953* (South Gate: K.I. Strand and Dean S. Woodbury, 1953); *South Gate "Blue Book" Criss Cross City Directory. 1961* (Anaheim, Calif.: Luskey Brothers & Co., 1961); (Lawton) James interview; Grace Sheehy, telephone interview by author, October 8, 1999; Markle interview, October 8, 1999; U.S. Bureau of the Census, *Eighteenth Census of the United States, Census of Population, 1960*, vol. 1, *Characteristics of the Population, Part 6*, 6-302.

77.   Sugrue, *Origins*, 143.

78.   For industrial statistics, see *South Gate Press*, January 22, 1948, June 20, 1963; *Los Angeles Herald Express*, January 24, 1964; *Huntington Park Daily Signal*, January 19, 1973; Industrial Department, Los Angeles Chamber of Commerce, *Industrial Establishments in Los Angeles County Employing 25 or More Persons* (Los Angeles: Chamber of Commerce, 1952); and see sources in chapter 5, note 35. Despite the general climate of expansion, there were cases of capital out-migration even by the early 1960s. Rheem Manufacturing, for example, announced it would transfer the production of water heaters to its Chicago plant, because of rising labor costs in South Gate (*South Gate Press*, September 3, 1961).

79.   A 1942 survey found 80 percent of workers in southeast L.A. commuted by car. Census and union data for one job sector—auto assembly—suggest only a small proportion of residents found jobs in South Gate's largest factory, General Motors. From 1940 to 1960, GM employed only 1.9 to 3.4 percent of South Gate's labor force, again suggesting that others were

forced to commute. U.S. Employment Service, "Resurvey of Labor Market, Los Angeles, California, September 1942," 36, Los Angeles files, RG 183, NA; UAW Local 216 Membership List 1940, UAW216, ALUA; U.S. Bureau of the Census, *Seventeenth Census of the United States, Census of Population, 1950,* vol. 2, *Characteristics of Population, Part 5, California,* 5-124; U.S. Bureau of the Census, *Eighteenth Census of the United States, Census of Population, 1960,* vol. 1, *Characteristics of the Population, Part 6, California,* 6-342.

The *South Gate Press* (June 20, 1963) reported that of GM's 3,600 workers in 1962, "most of the employees live in the South Gate area" but that others commuted from ninety-two different southern California communities. However, this did not correspond with census data.

80.   U.S. Bureau of the Census, *Eighteenth Census of the United States, Census of Population and Housing, 1960: Census Tracts, Los Angeles—Long Beach, Calif.,* 520; U.S. Bureau of the Census, *Eighteenth Census of the United States. Census of Housing, 1960,* vol. 1, *States and Small Areas, Part 2* (Washington, D.C.: GPO, 1961), 6-64; Nauman, "Follow-Up Study," 50; Jim Crisp et al., "Evaluation and Summary of Planning Study, City of South Gate" (unpublished seminar paper, University of Southern California, May 1965), Box 3, p. 4, SGHWL; John Sheehy, interview by author, June 21, 1990; Collins interview, August 25, 1991.

81.   South Gate Chamber of Commerce, "Standard Industrial Survey Report," October 1970, Box 3, SGHWL; Collins interview, September 15, 1991. For a sampling of articles on these unions, see *South Gate Press,* April 24, May 19, 1955, October 4, 1956, December 1, 1957, August 14, 1958.

82.   Green, *World of the Worker,* chapter 7; Sugrue, *Origins,* 125–152.

83.   Collins interview, September 15, 1991. On strikes at Firestone, see *South Gate Press,* September 3, 1953, August 15, 22, 1954, January 20, April 24, 28, May 15, 1955, November 15, 1956, May 3, 7, June 12, 1959. On strikes (and strike threats) at GM, see *South Gate Press,* May 19, June 9, 12, 16, 26, 1955, September 16, 20, 1956, September 28, October 2, 1958, March 10, 17, 1960, September 21, 1961, November 14, 1963, September 27, October 29, 1964; *The Assembler,* May 8, 1959, ALUA. On various teamster strikes and protests, see *South Gate Press,* August 15, 19, 22, 1954, May 22, 1955, September 18, 1958; on steelworker strikes, see *South Gate Press,* December 1, 1957. Also see Myrna Cherkoss Donahoe, "Workers' Response to Plant Closures: The Cases of Steel and Auto in Southeast Los Angeles, 1935–1986" (Ph.D. dissertation, University of California Irvine, 1987), chapters 5 and 6.

84.   Sugrue, *Origins,* chapter 5.

85.   *South Gate Press,* May 15, 1955, November 14, 1963, September 27, October 29, 1964; *The Assembler,* July 21, 1950, ALUA; Virgil Collins, interview by author, Artesia, California, August 20, 1991; Collins interview, September 15, 1991; Donahoe, "Workers' Response," 177–180, 201–203.

86.   Markle interview, August 24, 1998; Markle interview, October 8, 1999; Collins interviews, August 25, September 15, 1991.

87.   Cohen, *Making a New Deal,* chapter 8; *The Assembler,* December 1947 issues, and December 17, 1959, ALUA; Collins interview, August 25, 1991; Juanita (Smith) Hammon, interview by author, South Gate, California, July 5, 1990. Sociologist Scott Greer found similar patterns in greater Los Angeles. He concluded that "work associates are a minor proportion of the individual's primary relations when he is away from the job," especially for people in the working class. Greer, *Urbane View,* 72–73.

88.   This is based on a scan of the *South Gate Press* in 1945, 1950, 1954–1961, 1963.

89.   *Los Angeles Herald Express,* April 29, 1957; *Los Angeles Examiner,* May 2, 1955; *South Gate Press,* March 14, 25, August 29, December 30, 1954, April 24, 28, 1955, April 29, October 14, 1956, March 24, April 25, May 2, September 1, 1957. See Gerstle, *Working-Class*

Americanism, on the importance and changing nuances of Americanism in the postwar era. An excellent treatment of the history of Labor Day is Michael Kazin and Steven J. Ross, "America's Labor Day: The Dilemma of a Workers' Celebration," *Journal of American History* 78 (March 1992): 1294–1323, especially 1320–1322 on the postwar period.

90.   See chapter 7.

91.   In 1944, the manpower shortage in "must" (or top priority) plants was 18,000 in Los Angeles, compared to 7,000 in Cleveland and 3,000 in Detroit.

92.   John Morton Blum, *V Was for Victory* (New York: Harcourt, Brace, Jovanovich, 1976), 182–220; T. Bowen to C. E. Wilson, May 22, 1944, Los Angeles Area Production Urgency Committee, RG 212, NA; United States Employment Service, "Resurvey of Labor Market, Los Angeles, California, September 1942," and "War Housing Program No. 21—Los Angeles, California (Los Angeles Harbor Sublocality)," June 7, 1944, Los Angeles files, RG 183, NA; Lawrence Brooks de Graaf, "Negro Migration to Los Angeles, 1930 to 1950" (Ph.D. dissertation, University of California Los Angeles, 1962), 189, 192, 195; Alonzo Smith and Quintard Taylor, "Racial Discrimination in the Workplace: A Study of Two West Coast Cities during the 1940s," *Journal of Ethnic Studies* 8 (spring 1980): 35–54.

Josh Sides correctly notes that while CIO leadership in Los Angeles favored racial equality, there was often resistance on the shop floor. He characterizes the CIO's overall wartime record on race as "ambiguous." See Sides, "Working Away," 136–147. For a compelling portrayal of the black experience in the L.A. shipyards during World War II, see Chester B. Himes, *If He Hollers Let Him Go* (New York: Thunder's Mouth Press, 1986).

93.   *California Eagle,* July 11, 1946; Collins interview, August 25, 1991; Donahoe, "Workers' Response," 183. Nationally, the UAW's commitment to racial equality was strongest at the leadership level but dissipated in the locals, where informal agreements and seniority practices often discriminated against blacks. See August Meier and Elliott Rudwick, *Black Detroit and the Rise of the UAW* (New York: Oxford, 1979), 180–174; Lichtenstein, *Labor's War at Home,* 124–126. Sides contends that in California into the 1950s, the UAW had a poor record on race (Sides, "Working Away," 172).

94.   Collins interview, August 25, September 15, 1991; Sides, "Working Away," 162–163; Lichtenstein, *Labor's War at Home,* 124–126.

95.   Louis Ciccone to L.A. Industrial Union Council, February 25, 1947, LACFL; *The Assembler,* October 27, 1948, ALUA.

96.   Collins interview, September 15, 1991.

97.   Ibid.; Sheehy interviews, June 21, 26, 1990; Wallace McFadden, interview by Sandy McFadden, June 12, 1971, Oral History 1029, p. 21, FOH.

98.   Quote from Gordon Whitnall and Associates, *Report on Proposed Comprehensive General Plan for South Gate, California* (unpublished report, 1959), 51, Community Development Department, SGCH. An excellent discussion of the historical roots and evolution of the "recreational good life" is in Baker, "Lakewood Story." Also see Waldie, *Holy Land;* Kelly, *Expanding the American Dream.*

99.   Untitled report, 1952–53, South Gate Commission, Box 3, SGHWL.

100.   *Los Angeles Examiner,* July 11, 1954; *South Gate Press,* May 2, 1946, January 14, 1954, January 19, 1983; South Gate Parks and Recreation Department, *This Is the Story of the South Gate Parks and Recreation Department, Report for 1956–57* (South Gate, 1957), 19–22; *Huntington Park Daily Signal,* January 19, 1973; Ralph D. Cornell and George Hjelte, "Planning a Modern City Park," *Western City* 22 (September 1946): 42–43.

101.   City of South Gate, Parks and Recreation Department, *Annual Report, 1957–1958* (South Gate, n.p.), 11, 14.

102.   Steven A. Riess, *City Games: The Evolution of American Urban Society and the Rise of Sports* (Urbana: University of Illinois Press, 1989), 59, 62; Herbert Warren Wind, *The Story of American Golf: Its Champions and Championships*, 3rd ed. (New York: Alfred A. Knopf, 1975), 491–492; Editors of Golf Magazine, *Golf Magazine's Encyclopedia of Golf: The Complete Reference*, 2nd ed. (New York: Harper Collins, 1993), 25–26; *South Gate Press*, May 2, 1946, March 6, 27, 1947; South Gate Parks, *This Is the Story*, 22; City of South Gate, *Annual Report, 1957–1958*, 20–25; Jackson, *Crabgrass*, 98–99; on golf courses in Lakewood as a symbol of suburban democratization, see Baker, "Lakewood Story," 65–66.

103.   City of South Gate, *Annual Report, 1957–1958*, 27–28; *South Gate Press*, July 2, 1964.

104.   *South Gate Press*, November 21, 1946, February 6, April 17, 1947; *South Gate City Directory, July 1951;* South Gate field notes, October 10, 1941, FWP; Markle interview, October 8, 1999.

105.   Tom Thienes, South Gate field notes, October 10, 1941, FWP; *South Gate Press*, February 5, March 5, 1942; Harold L. Osmer, *Where They Raced: Auto Racing Venues in Los Angeles, 1900–1990* (Los Angeles: Harold Osmer Publishing, 1996), 51, 61.

South Gate's reputation as a car center was reinforced by the tremendous level of automobile sales in the suburb. By 1965, automobile lots were everywhere; auto sales represented 35 percent of all retail sales in South Gate. Crisp et al., "Evaluation," 25.

106.   *South Gate Press*, May 2, 1946, December 30, 1954, December 12, 1957; *South Gate City Directory, July 1951.* An insightful discussion of car racing as a working-class "symbolic inversion" of postwar consumer culture is in George Lipsitz, *Rainbow at Midnight: Labor and Culture in the 1940s* (Urbana: University of Illinois Press, 1994), 266–276.

107.   James Gregory, "Southernizing the American Working Class: Post-war Episodes of Regional and Class Transformation," *Labor History* 39 (1998): 135–154, plus commentary and responses, 155–168.

108.   *South Gate City Directory, 1940;* Weber field notes, October 30, 1941, FWP; City of South Gate, *Annual Report, 1957–1958; South Gate Press*, June 3, 1943, May 23, 1954; (Lawton) James interview; *Los Angeles Times*, September 4, 1955, September 1, 1957.

109.   On the importance of Los Angeles to the postwar leisured ethos and its far-ranging influence on western cityscapes, see John Findlay, *Magic Lands: Western Cityscapes and American Culture After 1940* (Berkeley and Los Angeles: University of California Press, 1992). Also see Eric Avila, "Reinventing Los Angeles: Popular Culture in the Age of White Flight, 1940–1965" (Ph.D. dissertation, U.C. Berkeley, 1997).

110.   *South Gate Press*, April 15, May 20, June 6, August 15, September 2, 1954, June 23, 1955, July 7, 1957, June 1, July 13, August 14, 1958, July 26, 1964; South Gate Parks, *This Is the Story*, 21; City of South Gate, *Annual Report, 1957–1958*, 24. On Gilmore Stadium, see Pitt and Pitt, *Los Angeles A–Z*, 174; Osmer, *Where They Raced*, 44.

111.   *South Gate Press*, January 8, 1942, July 21, 1955; Markle interview, August 24, 1998; Markle interview, October 8, 1999; (DeVries) North interview.

112.   Markle interview, October 8, 1999; Markle interview, August 24, 1998; Sheehy interview, June 26, 1990.

113.   The PTA was counted once for the entire suburb—and not separately for each school. The number includes all clubs that appeared at some point, including those that eventually merged or disappeared.

114.   Sheehy interview, June 26, 1990; *South Gate City Directory, 1940; South Gate City Directory, 1945; South Gate City Directory, July 1, 1947* (K.I. Strand, 1947); *South Gate City Directory, July 1949* (K.I. Strand & Dean S. Woodbury, 1949); *South Gate City Directory, July*

1951; South Gate "Blue Book" Criss Cross City Directory, 1961; South Gate Press, January 24, 1946, January 3, 1960; Bicentennial Heritage Committee, *South Gate 1776–1976,* 47–55; South Gate Parks, *This Is the Story,* 19; City of South Gate, *Annual Report, 1957–1958,* 23; Nauman, "Follow-Up Study," 23.

115.   Sheehy interview, June 26, 1990; Markle interview, October 8, 1999; *South Gate Press,* June 9, October 16, November 3, 1955, August 21, November 11, 1956, June 20, 1963; *Huntington Park Daily Signal,* January 19, 1973; *South Gate City Directory, 1940; South Gate City Directory, July 1951;* Bicentennial Heritage Committee, *South Gate 1776–1976,* 47–55.

116.   *South Gate Press,* December 13, 1953, September 13, 1956, June 20, 1963; Bicentennial Heritage Committee, *South Gate 1776–1976,* 47–55; Markle interview, October 8, 1999.

117.   *South Gate Press,* September 29, 1963; Bicentennial Heritage Committee, *South Gate 1776–1976,* 52–53.

118.   *South Gate Press,* June 1, September 21, 1944, August 30, September 13, 1945, July 4, 25, 1946, May 22, July 10, 1947, June 21, 1956.

119.   *South Gate Press,* June 17, 1954, August 7, 11, October 13, 1955, August 21, 1956, March 17, July 28, September 8, 1957, February 4, 1960; (DeVries) North interview.

Available evidence does not indicate the proportion of residents who attended church in South Gate versus in other communities. The only statement on this—a vague one at best—came from a local minister who claimed that "many" residents attended church outside of South Gate. *South Gate Press,* October 7, 1954.

120.   *South Gate Press,* April 14, 1957, June 27, July 11, 1963; *People's World,* November 27, 1945.

121.   Some historians have identified a temporal divide in the evolution of urban culture: the years 1890 to 1950 represented the era of democratized urban leisure and civic sociability, as people participated in urban leisure outlets that brought together broad cross sections of the population. This changed in the 1950s, with the rise of more segmented leisure forms like shopping malls, theme parks, and suburban sports stadiums, all accessed by automobile. See Tim Gilfoyle, "White Cities, Linguistic Turns, and Disneylands: The New Paradigms of Urban History," *Reviews in American History* 26 (1998): 178–179.

122.   NIMBY is an acronym for "not in my backyard."

123.   Robert Fisher, *Let the People Decide: Neighborhood Organizing in America* (New York: Twayne, 1994), chapter 3; Evan McKenzie, *Privatopia: Homeowner Associations and the Rise of Residential Private Government* (New Haven: Yale University Press, 1994), chapter 3; Sugrue, *Origins,* chapter 8; Baker, "Lakewood Story," chapter 3. Mike Davis sees postwar efforts to defend the suburban dream "against unwanted development (industry, apartments and offices) as well as against unwanted persons" as mainly upper-class efforts, often cloaked in the guise of environmentalism. Mike Davis, *City of Quartz: Excavating the Future in Los Angeles* (London: Verso, 1990), 169–173. For an interesting contrast to this interpretation, see George Ramos, "Creating Parkland Along the River," *Los Angeles Times,* April 2, 2000.

Both Sugrue and Baker note that women were often leaders in postwar homeowner activism, especially in efforts to preserve the "suburban ideal." Such was not the case in South Gate, however. While they certainly participated, women did not assume a notable place as leaders. This might be explained by the higher rates of working women in South Gate, compared to a suburb like Lakewood.

The social changes affecting South Gate in the 1950s predated those of graying suburbs in the 1970s and 1980s. See Mark Baldassare, *Trouble in Paradise: The Suburban Transformation in America* (New York: Columbia University Press, 1986); Hugh A. Wilson, "The Family in Suburbia: From Tradition to Pluralism," in *Suburbia Re-examined,* Barbara M. Kelly, ed. (New

York: Greenwood Press, 1989), 85–93; Mark Baldassare and Georjeanna Wilson, "More Trouble in Paradise: Urbanization and the Decline in Suburban Quality-of-Life Ratings," *Urban Affairs Review* 30 (May 1995): 690–708.

124.   The South Gate Coordinating Council issued the initial report on this problem. As part of the L.A. County Federation of Community Coordinating Councils, the South Gate group was "a local clearinghouse for community problems and needs." It was a nonpartisan, nonsectarian group of community leaders, concerned especially with the welfare of local youth. Members of the panel that issued the "apartment menace" report included Rev. Norman Taylor of the First Methodist Church, Pastor F. L. Bennetts of the Community Presbyterian Church, Rotary Club president Homer Cotton, police officer Ed Haley, and junior high vice principal Paul Chance. "Constitution and By-Laws of the South Gate Coordinating Council," February 11, 1963, SGHWL; *South Gate Press,* December 8, 1955, December 29, 1960.

125.   *South Gate Press,* November 3, December 8, 1955, April 5, 1956, August 1, 1957.

126.   *South Gate Press,* January 22, 1948, July 28, 1955, November 15, 1956, January 13, 17, 31, February 17, March 17, 21, 24, May 12, June 20, 30, July 14, 28, 1957, September 22, December 1, 1963. Firestone and A&M Casting were also cited for pollution violations: *South Gate Press,* February 3, 1957.

127.   For complaints about industrial nuisances, see South Gate City Council minutes, February 25, March 3, 10, 24, April 7, 14, June 9, 16, September 22, 29, October 6, 20, December 8, 15, 1952; March 9, May 11, 25, October 26, 1953; February 23, March 1, 8, 15, June 21, 28, October 4, 18, November 1, 15, December 6, 1954; January 10, 24, April 25, 1955; on GM, see March 28, April 11, July 11, 1955, SGCH.

128.   *South Gate Press,* June 17, 24, 27, December 16, 1954, January 6, July 28, August 4, 1955, February 3, 10, 14, 21, September 1, 1957; *South Gate City Directory, July 1951.*

129.   *South Gate Press,* January 3, 17, 1946, January 22, 1948, May 20, 23, 27, June 10, 1954, December 8, 1955, April 15, May 3, July 26, 1956, January 10, February 7, October 13, 1957; South Gate Parks, *This Is the Story,* 19.

130.   Quote from Avila, "Reinventing Los Angeles," 230. Excellent treatments of Disneyland's urban and cultural implications are in Avila, "Reinventing Los Angeles"; Findlay, *Magic Lands;* and Michael Sorkin, ed., *Variations on a Theme Park: The New American City and the End of Public Space* (New York: Hill and Wang, 1992). Many thanks to Susan Davis for her insights on Disneyland and its potential connections to towns like South Gate.

131.   The futuristic Tomorrowland gave Disneyland management its biggest problem because it grew obsolete so quickly. By the late 1990s, Disneyland abandoned efforts to predict the future and instituted a "retro-themed" Tomorrowland, evoking 1950s-era images of the future. Findlay, *Magic Lands,* 71; *Los Angeles Times,* January 4, 1998.

132.   Findlay, *Magic Lands,* 64–88.

133.   City of South Gate, *Annual Report, 1957–1958,* 24; *South Gate Press,* July 17, November 24, December 1, 1955, December 6, 1956, December 15, 1957, August 3, 1961; (DeVries) North interview; (Lawton) James interview.

134.   (Lawton) James interview.

Chapter 7

1.   *South Gate Press,* January 2, 1964.

2.   Ibid., September 29, 1963.

3.   Floyd Wakefield, telephone interview by author, April 6, 2000.

4. Ibid.; *California Blue Book* (Sacramento: Office of State Printing, 1967), 138; Assemblyman Information Card, Floyd Wakefield, California State Library, Sacramento; *South Gate Press,* June 20, 1963, February 23, 1964; *Sacramento Bee,* March 8, 1967.

5. *South Gate Press,* January 30, February 6, 13, 20, 23, 27, May 24, 31, October 1, 11, 15, 29, November 1, 26, 1964; *Report of Registration,* compiled by Frank M. Jordan, secretary of state, January 1962 and June 1964; Election Returns by Precinct, General Election, November 3, 1964, L.A. County, CSA; *Sacramento Bee,* March 8, 1967; Wakefield interview.

6. *Sacramento Bee,* March 8, 1967, April 14, 1970. Key works on resistance to busing include J. Anthony Lukas, *Common Ground: A Turbulent Decade in the Lives of Three American Families* (New York: Vintage, 1985); and Ronald P. Formisano, *Boston against Busing: Race, Class, and Ethnicity in the 1960s and 1970s* (Chapel Hill: University of North Carolina Press, 1991). On California, see Lillian B. Rubin, *Busing and Backlash: White against White in a California School District* (Berkeley and Los Angeles: University of California Press, 1972); and on national policy, see Harvard Sitkoff, *The Struggle for Black Equality, 1954–1992* (New York: Hill & Wang, 1993), 212. Three important recent studies of the rise of conservatism in Southern California emphasize the postwar era. See Kurt Schuparra, *Triumph of the Right: The Rise of the California Conservative Movement, 1945–1966* (Armonk, N.Y.: M.E. Sharpe, 1998); Lisa McGirr, *Suburban Warriors: The Origins of the New American Right* (Princeton: Princeton University Press, 2001); Denise S. Spooner, "The Political Consequences of Experiences of Community: Iowa Migrants and Republican Conservatism in Southern California, 1946–1964" (Ph.D. dissertation, University of Pennsylvania, 1992).

7. Key studies that focus on civil rights struggles in northern neighborhoods include Thomas J. Sugrue, *Origins of the Urban Crisis: Race and Inequality in Postwar Detroit* (Princeton: Princeton University Press, 1996); Lukas, *Common Ground;* Formisano, *Boston against Busing;* Arnold R. Hirsch, *Making the Second Ghetto: Race and Housing in Chicago, 1940–1960* (Cambridge: Cambridge University Press, 1983); John T. McGreevy, *Parish Boundaries: The Catholic Encounter with Race in the Twentieth-Century Urban North* (Chicago: University of Chicago Press, 1996); Eileen M. McMahon, *What Parish Are You From? A Chicago Irish Community and Race Relations* (Lexington: University Press of Kentucky, 1995); Jonathan Rieder, *Canarsie: The Jews and Italians of Brooklyn against Liberalism* (Cambridge: Harvard University Press, 1985). Finally, see Robert Self, "Writing Landscapes of Class, Power and Racial Division: The Problem of (Sub)Urban Space and Place in Postwar America," *Journal of Urban History* 27 (January 2001): 237–250; Michael Kazin, "The Grass-Roots Right: New Histories of U.S. Conservatism in the Twentieth Century," *American Historical Review* 97 (February 1992): 136–155.

Two important recent studies of the rise of conservatism in Southern California (namely Orange County) locate the roots in the 1950s. See Kurt Schuparra, *Triumph of the Right: The Rise of the California Conservative Movement, 1945–1966* (Armonk, N.Y.: M.E. Sharpe, 1998); Lisa McGirr, *Suburban Warriors: The Origins of the New American Right* (Princeton: Princeton University Press, 2001).

8. James Gregory, "Southernizing the American Working Class: Post-war Episodes of Regional and Class Transformation," *Labor History* 39 (1998): 135–154, plus commentary and responses, pp. 155–168; Kenneth Durr, "When Southern Politics Came North: The Roots of White Working-Class Conservatism in Baltimore, 1940–1964," *Labor History* 37 (1996): 309–331; Dan T. Carter, *The Politics of Rage: George Wallace, the Origins of the New Conservatism, and the Transformation of America Politics* (New York: Simon and Schuster, 1995). In discussing George Wallace's popularity in the North and West, Gregory notes that relocated southerners in those regions made their critical contribution to his campaigns as "start-up audience and campaign cadre."

9. See note 7, and Thomas J. Sugrue, "Crabgrass-Roots Politics: Race, Rights, and the Re-

action against Liberalism in the Urban North, 1940–1964," *Journal of American History* 82 (1995): 551–578; Arnold R. Hirsch, "Massive Resistance in the Urban North: Trumbull Park, Chicago, 1953–1966," *Journal of American History* 82 (1995): 522–550; Gregory, "Southernizing," 146; Carter, *Politics of Rage.*

10. The occupation of one councilman was unidentified.

11. The 12.2 average excluded Earl Fike, Dewey Hobart, and Ernest Nellar, who all served either half or most of their term before 1940. D. Huddelston was excluded because he served only three days.

12. Tom Thienes, "Contributions Toward the History of the City of South Gate, California" (unpublished manuscript for the Works Progress Administration, 1942, SGHWL), 93–94; *South Gate Press*, April 2, 1942, January 5, 1964; "New City Hall," March 1, 1942, pamphlet, FWP; *Los Angeles Herald-Examiner*, September 25, 1954; *South Gate Tribune*, August 28, 1948.

13. South Gate City Council minutes, March 29, 1954, SGCH.

14. Bicentennial Heritage Committee, *South Gate 1776–1976* (South Gate, Calif.: South Gate Press, 1976), 23; *Los Angeles Times*, August 15, 1950; "New City Hall," March 1, 1942, pamphlet, FWP; *Los Angeles Herald Express*, September 25, 1954; *South Gate Tribune*, August 28, 1948; *South Gate Press*, January 5, 1964; *Los Angeles Examiner*, March 8, 1953.

15. South Gate City Council minutes, December 8, 1952, December 6, 1954, October 22, 1956, August 10, 1959, December 12, 1960, August 10, 1961, May 28, 1962, April 26, 1965, SGCH.

16. *South Gate Tribune*, November 7, 14, 21, 28, 1938; *South Gate Press*, November 3, 1938; Royce D. Delmatier et al., eds., *The Rumble of California Politics, 1848–1970* (New York: John Wiley & Sons, 1970), 287; *Los Angeles Examiner*, July 5, 1945, December 20, 21, 1948, May 30, 31, 1954, May 2, 1955, April 30, 1956, April 5, 1957; South Gate City Council minutes, September 15, 1952, SGCH; Wakefield interview.

17. On the CP's involvement, see Josh Sides, "Working Away: African American Migration and Community in Los Angeles from the Great Depression to 1954" (Ph.D. dissertation, UCLA, 1999), chapter 4. On the split between workplace and neighborhood politics, see Ira Katznelson, *City Trenches: Urban Politics and the Patterning of Class in the United States* (Chicago: University of Chicago Press, 1981).

18. General Meeting minutes, February 18, 1946, General Membership Meeting file, UAW216, ALUA; South Gate City Council minutes, April 16, 1946, SGCH; *South Gate Press*, April 4, 1946.

19. Jack A. Shepard to "Brother," February 2, 1948, and South East Committee for Labor Candidates (hereafter SECLC) "Press Release," February 2, 1948, all from LC, ALUA.

20. SECLC minutes, January 3, 18, March 7, 14, 1948, Jack A. Shepard to "Sirs and Brothers," February 23, 1948, and SECLC "Press Release," February 2, 1948, all from LC, ALUA. See subsequent minutes for the range of workers present at meetings.

21. "For South Gate City Council" pamphlet, April 1947, and SECLC minutes, March 21, 27, 1948, LC, ALUA.

22. "Proposed General Program for all Candidates of the Southeast Committee for Labor Candidates" (n.d.), "For South Gate City Council" pamphlet, April 1948, and "Let's Get Into the Political Arena" flier of SECLC, February 1948, all in LC, ALUA; *South Gate Press*, April 8, 1948; *Assembler*, October 13, 1948, ALUA.

23. *South Gate Press*, April 8, 15, 1948; "You Must Register Now" SECLC flier, 1948, LC, ALUA.

24. *South Gate Tribune*, April 17, 1948; *South Gate Press*, April 15, 1948; South Gate

City Council minutes, April 20, 1948, SGCH; Virgil Collins, interview by author, Laguna Hills, September 15, 1991; SECLC minutes, April 18, 1948, LC, ALUA. The election returns for the other four suburbs were from Bell City Council Resolution, April 20, 1948, Bell City Clerk's Office; election results for April 13, 1948, Huntington Park City Council Minute Book, no. 19, p. 399, Huntington Park City Clerk's Office; Maywood City Council Resolution to Canvass the Election Ballot, April 20, 1948, Maywood City Clerk's Office; Lynwood City Council minutes, April 20, 1948, Lynwood City Clerk's Office.

25.   For example, on Oakland see Marilynn S. Johnson, *The Second Gold Rush: Oakland and the East Bay in World War II* (Berkeley and Los Angeles: University of California Press, 1993). For a broader view, see Nelson Lichtenstein, "From Corporatism to Collective Bargaining: Organized Labor and the Eclipse of Social Democracy in the Postwar Era," in *The Rise and Fall of the New Deal Order, 1930–1980,* Steve Fraser and Gary Gerstle, eds. (Princeton: Princeton University Press, 1989).

26.   Jonathan Rieder, "The Rise of the 'Silent Majority,'" in *The Rise and Fall of the New Deal,* Fraser and Gerstle, eds., 243–268, quote at 244; Walter Dean Burnham, *Critical Elections and the Mainspring of American Politics* (New York: W.W. Norton, 1970), 91–193.

27.   On early civil rights activism in Los Angeles, see Sides, "Working Away," chapter 4; Kevin A. Leonard, "Years of Hope, Days of Fear: the Impact of World War II on Race Relations in Los Angeles" (Ph.D. dissertation, U.C. Davis, 1992).

28.   A good overview of the these events is in Sitkoff, *Struggle for Black Equality,* chapter 5.

29.   *California Eagle,* June 13, 1963; *South Gate Press,* June 27, 1963; John Caughey and LaRee Caughey, *To Kill A Child's Spirit: The Tragedy of School Segregation in Los Angeles* (Itasca, Ill.: F.E. Peacock Publishers, 1973), 20.

30.   Caughey and Caughey, *To Kill,* 2, 7, 11, 31–32; Elizabeth Poe, "Segregation in Los Angeles Schools," *Frontier* 13 (October 1962): 13. For overviews of school segregation in Los Angeles and California, see Caughey and Caughey, *To Kill;* Charles Wollenberg, *All Deliberate Speed: Segregation and Exclusion in California Schools, 1855–1975* (Berkeley and Los Angeles: University of California Press, 1976); Irving G. Hendrick, *The Education of Non-Whites in California, 1849–1970* (San Francisco: R & E Research Associates, 1977).

31.   Caughey and Caughey, *To Kill,* 15–20; Poe, "Segregation," 12–13.

32.   *California Eagle,* June 13, August 8, 1963; *South Gate Press,* June 27, 1963; Hendrick, *The Education of Non-Whites,* 104–105.

33.   *South Gate Press,* June 27, July 18, 28, August 11, 1963; *California Eagle,* August 8, 15, 1963; *Los Angeles Times,* August 9, 1963.

Earlier in the day at a press conference, James Farmer contended that civil rights were as necessary in Los Angeles as in the South: "There is no such thing as a little bit of discrimination being acceptable." He was "appalled and disappointed" in the school board's foot-dragging and reiterated the need to redraw school boundaries "which now conform to the ghettos" (*Los Angeles Times,* August 9, 1963).

34.   *South Gate Press,* June 27, July 28, August 11, 1963; Caughey and Caughey, *To Kill,* 17; *Los Angeles Times,* August 9, 1963.

35.   *Los Angeles Times,* April 6, 1989; *California Eagle,* August 8, 1963; *South Gate Press,* September 8, 1963; Wollenberg, *All Deliberate Speed,* 136–142.

36.   *California Eagle,* June 20, 1963; *South Gate Press,* June 13, 16, 1963.

37.   *California Eagle,* June 20, 1963; *South Gate Press,* June 16, 23, 27, 1963.

38.   *Los Angeles Herald,* September 4, 5, 10, 14, 16, 20, October 5, 1963; *California Eagle,* September 19, 1963; Caughey and Caughey, *To Kill,* 23; *South Gate Press,* October 6, 1963.

39. *South Gate Press,* September 15, 1963; *California Eagle,* August 14, September 19, 1963. The citizen members of the ad hoc committee issued a separate statement, calling for the board to take more forceful action to end segregation than the report recommended.

40. *South Gate Press,* September 15, 19, 1963; *California Eagle,* September 19, 1963.

41. *South Gate Press,* September 12, 1963. On white resistance to civil rights in Los Angeles, see Caughey and Caughey, *To Kill,* 40–41, and passim; Mike Davis, *City of Quartz: Excavating the Future in Los Angeles* (London: Verso, 1990); Dana Stall, "'Bus Me Not': The Move to the Right and the Racialization of Politics in Los Angeles, 1963–1981" (unpublished senior thesis, U.C. San Diego, 1998). On the role of women in suburban grassroots politics, see Sugrue, *Origins of the Urban Crisis,* 250–251; Allison Baker, "The Lakewood Story: Defending the Recreational Good Life in Postwar Southern California Suburbia, 1950–1999" (Ph.D. dissertation, University of Pennsylvania, 1999), chapter 3; Sylvie Murray, "Suburban Citizens: Domesticity and Community Politics in Queens, New York, 1945–1960" (Ph.D. dissertation, Yale University, December 1994).

42. Wakefield interview.

43. *South Gate Press,* September 12, 15, 19, 22, 26, 1963.

44. *South Gate Press,* September 12, 15, 19, 22, 26, October 27, 1963.

45. *South Gate Press,* September 12, 19, 26, October 17, 24, November 7, 14, 17, 21, 24, 1963, July 1, 4, 11, 18, August 12, 1965.

46. For an excellent study that explores the contrasting, complex perspectives among blacks and whites involved in a controversy over the public schools, see Jerald E. Podair, "Like Strangers: Blacks, Whites, and New York City's Ocean Hill–Brownsville Crisis, 1945–1980" (Ph.D. dissertation, Princeton University, 1997).

47. *South Gate Press,* July 28, 1963; *Sacramento Bee,* April 14, 1970; on the national situation, see Lawrence Cremin, *The Transformation of the School: Progressivism in American Education, 1876–1957* (New York: Knopf, 1964).

48. *South Gate Press,* September 12, October 3, 1963.

49. *South Gate Press,* April 1, 5, 8, 12, 19, 1962. When the school secession issue was raised in the spring of 1962, the integration issue was not mentioned. Proponents emphasized that tax money would be directed at local students more effectively, and that residents would have a greater say in school affairs.

50. *South Gate Press,* September 16, 20, 1962, September 12, 29, December 29, 1963, January 2, 5, 9, February 2, 27, March 1, 5, April 26, May 3, 7, 24, 28, 1964; *Los Angeles Examiner,* October 5, 1961. On Mosk, see Caughey and Caughey, *To Kill,* 7. On the "community control" argument as employed in the Ocean Hill–Brownsville controversy, see Podair, "Like Strangers," 39–87.

51. Thomas J. Sugrue, "The Tangled Roots of Affirmative Action," *American Behavioral Scientist* 41 (April 1998): 886–897.

52. *South Gate Press,* September 12, 15, 22, 29, October 3, 1963.

53. *South Gate Press,* September 29, October 3, 10, 1963; Wakefield interview.

54. *South Gate Press,* September 12, 19, 22, 26, 1963.

55. Similar black skepticism is described in Podair, "Like Strangers," 46; Stall, "'Bus Me Not,'" 35–36.

56. *South Gate Press,* November 24, 28, 1963, January 9, 1964.

57. *South Gate Press,* December 26, 1963, January 9, 30, February 23, August 5, 1964.

58. *South Gate Press,* June 24, 1965.

59. *South Gate Press,* September 12, 19, 22, October 3, 1963; Poe, "Segregation," 13.

60. *South Gate Press,* September 20, 26, October 13, December 22, 29, 1963.

61. *South Gate Press,* January 16, February 2, 1964. On anti-tax, fiscal austerity campaigns in other areas, see Podair, "Like Strangers," 325–342; Thomas B. Edsall with Mary D. Edsall, *Chain Reaction: The Impact of Race, Rights and Taxes on American Politics* (New York: W.W. Norton, 1992).

62. *South Gate Press,* September 15, October 3, 1963.

63. *South Gate Press,* October 27, November 3, 7, 21, 1963; *California Eagle,* October 3, 10, 1963.

64. Caughey and Caughey, *To Kill,* 43; *California Eagle,* December 5, 1963.

65. *South Gate Press,* November 28, December 1, 12, 19, 22, 26, 29, 1963; Caughey and Caughey, *To Kill,* 20–23.

66. *California Eagle,* December 12, 19, 1963; *South Gate Press,* December 26, 1963, January 2, 1964.

67. *South Gate Press,* January 16, May 10, July 5, 1964; *California Eagle,* October 10, 1963; Caughey and Caughey, *To Kill,* 33–34, 42–45, 52–53.

The denouement of the *Crawford* case had significant repercussions for civil rights in Los Angeles and nationwide. In 1968, civil rights leaders revived the suit and amended it significantly by demanding desegregation throughout the entire school district. As historian John Caughey, a witness in the case, later wrote, "The hope was that this action, *Crawford v. Los Angeles Board of Education,* would have the effect of bringing *Brown* north and west. . . ." The revived case also aimed to erase the distinction between de facto and de jure segregation, contending that school districts had a legal obligation to integrate regardless of cause. This element gave the case national significance. After a sixteen-month trial, Judge Alfred Gitelson ruled in favor of the plaintiffs—the first decisive victory for civil rights in Los Angeles. Gitelson ordered the L.A. School Board to institute districtwide integration by June 1972. This ruling was the first in the nation to order a school board to integrate regardless of the cause of segregation. And it provided the legal basis for busing.

Gitelson's ruling had profound reverberations in Los Angeles. Beyond impacting the schools, it shaped political careers, political discourse, and partisan loyalties. Gitelson, labeled the "busing judge" by critics, went down in defeat in 1970 after an acrimonious election that became a referendum on integration. New figures soon emerged. Superior Court Judge Paul Egly, who took over the case, ordered mandatory busing in 1978, which made him the target of recall attempts, hate mail, and death threats. In Encino in 1975, housewife Bobbi Fiedler and a group of angry residents formed a grassroots organization called BUSTOP to counteract the busing mandate. Fiedler went on to serve on the L.A. Board of Education and in the U.S. Congress. Roberta Weintraub spearheaded a recall campaign against Howard Miller, a school board member who supported integration. She was subsequently elected to the school board and served as board president for several years. And Floyd Wakefield won a seat in the California State Assembly on a rabidly antibusing campaign. The list goes on. Gitelson's ruling also set off a long series of court appeals and counterappeals in the *Crawford* case that extended over nineteen years. It reached an anticlimactic conclusion in March 1989, when a federal judge dismissed the last remaining defendant, the California Department of Education. By that time, neither side in the battle could claim true victory. Despite the busing order, the L.A. Unified School District remained racially segregated by the late 1980s. Antibusing advocates, meanwhile, considered the *Crawford* case a waste of public money and the cause of overcrowded schools in Anglo neighborhoods. When the federal court dismissed the lawsuit in 1989, the NAACP declined to continue pressing the case because of lack of funds. As UCRC education head Marnesba Tackett lamented, "It's the same kind of thing. People who have the money outlasted the people with limited funds. They won by default. The schools are more segregated than they have ever been." And Judge Egly remarked, "I thought about all of those well-meaning people who wanted good results, the tremendous amount of energy expended. The case could have done a lot of good, yet it whimpered out like a wet firecracker."

Caughey and Caughey, *To Kill,* 56–62, 134–140; *Los Angeles Times,* April 6, 1989; Patt Morrison, "Bitter Memories of the Busing Years," *Los Angeles Times Magazine,* September 28, 1997.

68. *South Gate Press,* May 7, 10, 1964.

69. *South Gate Press,* August 9, 1964.

70. *South Gate Press,* August 9, 1964, June 20, 24, 1965.

71. *South Gate Press,* December 31, 1964. The thrust and timing of white South Gate's resistance to school integration was mirrored in the Ocean Hill–Brownsville part of Brooklyn, New York. See Podair, "Like Strangers," 39–56.

72. Thomas W. Casstevens, *Politics, Housing and Race Relations: California's Rumford Act and Proposition 14* (U.C. Berkeley, Institute of Governmental Studies, 1967), 1–2, 18, 32, 40–41; *California Eagle,* October 3, 1963.

73. Casstevens, *Politics, Housing and Race Relations,* 40–41, 48–49, 96; *California Eagle,* October 3, 1963.

74. *California Eagle,* November 7, December 5, 19, 1963, January 16, May 7, 1964; Casstevens, *Politics, Housing and Race Relations,* 57–63.

75. *South Gate Press,* July 4, 1963; Wakefield interview.

76. *South Gate Press,* November 10, 14, December 1, 5, 1963, January 9, March 8, 15, 1964; *California Eagle,* November 21, 1963; Casstevens, *Politics, Housing and Race Relations,* 48–50.

77. *South Gate Press,* March 22, April 16, 26, 30, May 14, 21, 28, 1964; *California Eagle,* December 5, 1963.

78. *South Gate Press,* June 11, August 2, 20, 27, September 6, 1964; *California Eagle,* August 20, 1964.

79. The district encompassed the white working-class suburbs of southeast Los Angeles, including South Gate, Huntington Park, Bell, Maywood, Vernon, Bell Gardens, Cudahy, Lynwood, Compton, Paramount, Bellflower, and Downey. The poll was a self-selected sample: it included 25,000 residents who responded to a questionnaire from Congressman Del Clawson. On the poll, see *South Gate Press,* September 29, October 17, 1963.

80. *South Gate Press,* September 6, 24, November 1, 1964.

81. *South Gate Press,* September 6, 24, November 1, 1964.

82. Carter, *Politics of Rage;* Sugrue, "Tangled Roots."

83. *South Gate Press,* September 6, 1964.

84. Joe and Barbara Saltzman, "Proposition 14: Appeal to Prejudice," *Frontier* 15 (October 1964): 5–8.

85. *California Eagle,* November 12, 19, 1964.

86. Lloyd H. Fisher, *The Problem of Violence: Observations on Race Conflict in Los Angeles* (American Council of Race Relations, Haynes Foundation, April 1947), 14; Virgil Collins, interview by author, Artesia, California, August 20, 1991; John Sheehy, interviews by author, South Gate, California, May 1, June 21, 1990. Sheehy claimed that such racially motivated views were openly expressed at Chamber of Commerce and Rotary Club meetings.

87. *California Eagle,* October 31, November 14, 1963; *South Gate Press,* February 27, 1964. On early picketing efforts, see Sides, "Working Away," 230–237.

88. *Huntington Park Signal,* March 6, 1964.

89. *South Gate Press,* March 1, April 9, 1964.

90. *South Gate Press,* October 15, 29, November 1, 1964.

91. Casstevens, *Politics, Housing and Race Relations,* 68 (on California vote of Prop 14); *South Gate Press,* May 28, 1964; Election Returns by Precinct, General Election, November 3, 1964, L.A. County, CSA; California Secretary of State, *Statement of Vote, General Election, November 3, 1964* (Sacramento, 1964).

In June 1964, voter registration in South Gate was 16,778 Democrat, 8,547 Republican, and about 600 unidentified.

92. *South Gate Press,* January 26, June 7, October 8, 1964; *Biographical Directory of the American Congress, 1774–1996* (Alexandria: CQ Staff Directories, 1997).

93. *South Gate Press,* January 26, February 20, 1964.

94. *South Gate Press,* January 26, March 22, May 24, 1964.

95. *South Gate Press,* October 17, 1963, May 14, October 15, 1964.

96. *South Gate Press,* February 20, March 22, May 28, June 4, 7, July 12, 1964. Van Petten beat English by only 137 votes, out of nearly 48,000 total votes cast in the district (*South Gate Press,* July 12, 1964).

97. *South Gate Press,* September 6, October 1, 15, November 1, 1964.

98. *South Gate Press,* November 8, 15, 22, 26, 29, December 3, 1964; Election Returns by Precinct, General Election, November 3, 1964, L.A. County, CSA.

99. Robert Conot, *Rivers of Blood, Years of Darkness* (New York: Bantam Books, 1967); *Los Angeles Times,* August 12, 13, 1965; Sitkoff, *Struggle for Black Equality,*186–187; California Governor's Commission on the Los Angeles Riots, *Violence in the City—an End or a Beginning?* (Los Angeles, December 2, 1965), 13.

100. *Huntington Park Signal,* August 12, 14, 1965.

101. *Huntington Park Signal,* August 13, 14, 16, 1965; *South Gate Press,* September 5, 1965; John Sheehy, interview by author, South Gate, California, June 26, 1990. In perhaps the most bizarre local twist to this momentous incident, the *South Gate Press* gave *no* coverage to the riot until it was well over. Even then, the topic arose mainly in letters to the editor.

102. *Los Angeles Times,* August 14, 1965; *Huntington Park Signal,* August 12, 1965; Caughey and Caughey, *To Kill,* 27–28. Pouissant had served as chief resident of Los Angeles's Neuropsychiatric Institute, then accepted a job as southern field director for the Medical Committee on Human Rights in Jackson, Mississippi, a month before the Watts violence broke out.

103. *South Gate Press,* August 19, September 5, 1965.

104. Eric Avila, *Chocolate Cities and Vanilla Suburbs: Popular Culture in the Age of White Flight* (Berkeley and Los Angeles: University of California Press, forthcoming); John Findlay, *Magic Lands: Western Cityscapes and American Culture after 1940* (Berkeley and Los Angeles: University of California Press, 1992).

105. Other works that present a picture of deteriorating race relations in L.A. are Avila, *Chocolate Cities;* Sides, "Working Away," especially chapters 4–5; Edward J. Escobar, *Race, Police, and the Making of a Political Identity: Mexican Americans and the Los Angeles Police Department, 1900–1945* (Berkeley and Los Angeles: University of California Press, 1999). And see Davis, *City of Quartz,* 153–219. Doug Flamming argues in "A World to Gain: African Americans and the Making of Los Angeles, 1890–1940" (unpublished manuscript) that up to 1940, in some ways conditions for African Americans deteriorated (especially in housing) but in other ways they improved (in business prosperity and politics).

106. California Secretary of State, *Statement of Vote, General Election, Supplement,* No-

vember 5, 1968, compiled by Frank M. Jordan (Sacramento: Secretary of State, 1968), 82–83; California Secretary of State, *Statement of Vote, General Election, Supplement,* November 7, 1972, compiled by Edmund G. Brown Jr. (Sacramento: Secretary of State, 1972), 61–62.

Epilogue

1. Blacks, meanwhile, remained a small minority, only 1.7 percent of the total in 1990.

2. Raymond A. Rocco, "Latino Los Angeles: Reframing Boundaries/Borders," in *The City: Los Angeles and Urban Theory at the End of the Twentieth Century,* Allen J. Scott and Edward W. Soja, eds. (Berkeley and Los Angeles: University of California Press, 1996), 368–369.

3. Jonathan Tasini, "The Down-and-Out South Gate General Motors Blues," *Los Angeles Reader* 5 (April 29, 1983), 8–9, 11; Mike Davis, "The New Industrial Peonage," *Heritage* (summer 1991): 8; Ed Soja, *Postmodern Geographies: The Reassertion of Space in Critical Social Theory* (London: Verso, 1989), chapter 8.

4. Ibid.

5. Rocco, "Latino Los Angeles," 375; John Sheehy, interview by author, South Gate, California, June 19, 1990; *Los Angeles Times,* October 15, 22, 23, 1999.

6. *Los Angeles Times,* February 10, March 22, 1992, August 25, 1993; Mary (DeVries) North, interview by author, South Gate, California, July 12, 1999.

7. The information on garage dwellings comes from Stephanie Chavez and James Quinn, "Garages: Immigrants In, Cars Out," *Los Angeles Times,* May 24, 1987. And see John Sheehy, interview by author, South Gate, California, June 21, 1990.

8. A similar story is told in the urban garden established in South Central, after the 1992 riots. Developed by L.A. city to help the poor and homeless become more self-sufficient, the garden was organized into a co-op of 320 community members. A family of four earning under $11,000 annually qualified for access to a twelve-foot square plot of land, for growing food. Retired factory worker Elias Rodriguez said the vegetables he grew helped his family make ends meet. *Los Angeles Times,* September 29, 1998.

Index